Terrorism and Counterterrorism

D0221991

Focusing on the continued terrorist threat by jihadist groups, such as Al Qaeda and ISIS, and homegrown violent Far-Right and Far-Left extremists in the West, *Terrorism and Counterterrorism* investigates this form of political violence in a historical and contemporary context. In this comprehensive and highly readable text, renowned expert Brigitte Nacos clearly defines terrorism's diverse causes, actors, and strategies; outlines anti- and counterterrorist responses; and highlights terrorism's relationship with the public and media. *Terrorism and Counterterrorism* introduces students to the field's main debates and helps them critically assess our understanding of, and our strategies for, addressing this complex and enduring issue.

New to the Seventh Edition:

- The new Chapter 3 reviews the history of terrorism—both domestic and international, whereas the new Chapter 4 analyses the terrorist landscape in the third decade of the twenty-first century—including the transnational links between violent Far-Right and Far-Left violent extremists.
- The discussion of religious terrorism in Chapter 5 ends with an added section about QAnon as religiopolitical cult.
- An extended section in Chapter 7 is devoted to the increasingly militant roles of females in violent Far-Right extremism.
- The revised Chapter 10 starts with the withdrawal of U.S.-led troops from Afghanistan and an account of total costs spent on the post-9/11 war against terrorism before discussing the counterterrorism strategies of presidents G.W. Bush, Obama, Trump, and Biden.
- The failures and successes of the U.S. intelligence community in efforts to prevent terrorism at home with relevant data and case studies are new features in Chapter 12.

Brigitte L. Nacos, a political scientist and journalist, was a long-time U.S. correspondent for newspapers in Germany and has taught political science courses at Columbia University for close to three decades.

Praise for *Terrorism and Counterterrorism*

The book is well written and informative. I find it is written so the new student or second year students can easily understand its contents and the vocabulary being used. New vocabulary is part of the teaching process.

Dennis W. McLean, *Keiser University*

The main strength is that the book is comprehensive and updated. The academic study of terrorism has been rapidly developing and new ideas and insights occur rapidly and constantly. I would argue that the pace of change in terrorism studies is generally greater than other subfields of political science. Moreover, the nature of the threat of terrorism evolves constantly and rapidly, which further complicates being able to develop a coherent and cohesive textbook. Nacos' efforts in this regard are laudable—she does an excellent job of incorporating and summarizing new findings and new events.

Jeffrey Bosworth, *Mansfield University*

The students are generally very positive about the text. It is well written, well-paced and accessible, which is important for first year students. It is general enough to be used as a comprehensive introduction, but has enough depth to give the students some of the subtleties and complexities of the topic... The advantages are that the book is updated and timely and that it provides a very good focus on both hard and soft approaches, including communications theory and terrorist / counterterrorist messaging and the internet.

Julian Droogany, *Macquarie University, Australia*

Terrorism and Counterterrorism

Seventh Edition

Brigitte L. Nacos

Routledge
Taylor & Francis Group

NEW YORK AND LONDON

Designed cover image: Tasos Katopodis/Stringer via Getty (top);
Paula Bronstein/Getty (bottom)

Seventh edition published 2023
by Routledge
605 Third Avenue, New York, NY 10158

and by Routledge
4 Park Square, Milton Park, Abingdon, Oxon, OX14 4RN

Routledge is an imprint of the Taylor & Francis Group, an informa business

© 2023 Taylor & Francis

First edition published by Pearson Education, Inc. 2005
Sixth edition published by Routledge 2019

Library of Congress Cataloging-in-Publication Data
Names: Nacos, Brigitte Lebens, author.
Title: Terrorism and counterterrorism / Bridgette L. Nacos.
Description: Seventh Edition. | New York, NY: Routledge, 2023. |
Revised edition of the author's Terrorism and counterterrorism, 2019. |
Includes bibliographical references and index.
Identifiers: LCCN 2022049590 (print) | LCCN 2022049591 (ebook) |
ISBN 9781032264622 (paperback) | ISBN 9781032266527 (hardback) |
ISBN 9781003289265 (ebook)
Subjects: LCSH: Terrorism. | Terrorism—Prevention.
Classification: LCC HV6431 .N34 2023 (print) |
LCC HV6431 (ebook) | DDC 363.325—dc23/eng/20221014
LC record available at https://lccn.loc.gov/2022049590
LC ebook record available at https://lccn.loc.gov/2022049591

ISBN: 978-1-032-26652-7 (hbk)
ISBN: 978-1-032-26462-2 (pbk)
ISBN: 978-1-003-28926-5 (ebk)

DOI: 10.4324/9781003289265

Typeset in Sabon
by codeMantra

Brief Contents

Extended Contents

Illustrations

Figures

Tables

Preface

More than two decades ago, when I put together the syllabus for the very first terrorism course I taught, it was difficult to find good articles and chapters—forget textbooks—that covered the whole range of what I considered important aspects of transnational and domestic terrorism and counterterrorism. After September 11, 2001, there was a flood of new publications that dealt mostly or exclusively with: 9/11; the perpetrators of that horrific event; the motives of bin Laden, Al Qaeda, and like-minded individuals and groups; the implications for American domestic and foreign policy; and the impact on U.S. foreign policy and/or international relations, and so on.

Fine textbooks by single authors are often written for readers with special interests, for example, students in criminal justice courses or members of the emergency response community; others cover all conceivable topics in too short sections; and still others are exclusively devoted to transnational terrorism. Even the best among edited volumes seem less suited to serve as basic texts than as valuable supplements to a basic textbook written by one author.

So, I decided to write a textbook about terrorism and counterterrorism to serve as the core reading in pertinent lecture courses and seminars. The students in my terrorism/counterterrorism classes have been predominantly political science majors, mostly concentrating on the study of international relations, American government, and comparative politics. I have also had students who majored in sociology, history, urban studies, and psychology. I wrote this textbook with these undergraduate students in mind, but even graduate students who have a good basic knowledge of the topic will find here the background and tools with which to study terrorism and counterterrorism at an advanced level. While teaching graduate courses on media and politics, for example, I learned that many students did not study this area as undergraduates but could be brought up to speed for more advanced studies by working their way through a good textbook.

New to This Edition

- The new Chapter 3 reviews the history of terrorism—both domestic and international, whereas the new Chapter 4 analyses the terrorist landscape in the third decade of the twenty-first century—including the transnational links between violent Far-Right and Far-Left violent extremists.
- The discussion of religious terrorism in Chapter 5 ends with an added section about QAnon as a new religiopolitical cult.
- An extended section in Chapter 7 is devoted to the increasingly militant roles of females in violent Far-Right extremism.
- The revised Chapter 10 starts with the withdrawal of U.S.-led troops from Afghanistan and an account of total costs spent on the post-9/11 war against terrorism, before discussing the counterterrorism strategies of presidents G.W. Bush, Obama, Trump, and Biden.
- The failures and successes of the U.S. intelligence community in efforts to prevent terrorism at home and relevant data and case studies are new features in Chapter 12.

A successful textbook is a work in progress. While the first editions of *Terrorism and Counterterrorism* were well received, comments and suggestions by instructors and students who used those volumes were instrumental in extended revisions, additions, and changes in the following editions. For this volume, the seventh edition, I did not simply update and revise the material but rewrote whole chapters, in particular Chapters 3 and 4, and extended sections in most of the other chapters.

Acknowledgments

The topics introduced and discussed in my seminars on terrorism and the notes prepared for lecture courses on terrorism and on the media in American politics informed the organization and the content of this volume, as did the thoughtful input by my students at Columbia University and Barnard College during our lively but always civil class discussions.

I am very grateful to the following reviewers for their detailed comments, suggestions, and constructive criticism:

- Sean K. Anderson, Idaho State University
- Victor Asal, SUNY Albany
- Vincent Auger, Western Illinois University
- Shaheen Ayubi, Rutgers University, Camden
- Peter A. Barone, University of Bridgeport
- Jeffrey Bosworth, Mansfield University
- Tom Brister, Wake Forest University
- Sabina Burton, University of Wisconsin, Platteville
- Rachel Bzostek, California State University, Bakersfield
- Timothy A. Capron, California State University, Sacramento
- Lamont Colucci, Ripon College
- Michael V. Deaver, Sierra College
- Julian Droogan, Macquarie University, Australia
- Larry Elowitz, Georgia College and State University
- William Eppright, Columbia College, Orlando
- John Fielding, Mount Wachusett Community College
- James L. Freed, University of Maryland University College
- Hasan Kosebalaban, University of Utah
- Tobias J. Lanz, University of South Carolina
- Jecek Lubecki, University of Arkansas, Little Rock
- C. Augustus Martin, California State University, Dominguez Hills
- Dennis W. McLean, Keiser University
- Dean A. Minix, Northern Kentucky University
- Tricia Mulligan, Iona College
- Thomas R. O'Connor, North Carolina Wesleyan College

- William Rose, Connecticut College
- Gabriel Rubin, Montclair State University
- Stanley E. Spangler, Bentley College
- George C. Thomas, Marquette University
- Ronald Vardy, University of Houston
- Michael Joel Voss, University of Toledo
- Carlos Yordan, Drew University
- Jeffrey Bosworth, Mansfield University
- Julian Droogan, Macquarie University, Australia
- Dennis W. McLean, Keiser University
- Gabriel Rubin, Montclair State University
- Michael Joel Voss, University of Toledo

For this edition, the thoughtful reviews by Michael Deaver, Professor at Sierra College, and Alex Schmid, Professor Emeritus at Leiden University, were tremendously helpful when I decided what topics and chapters would benefit from significant revisions.

The author posts her observations and comments about terrorism, counterterrorism, the mass media, and current events on her blog, *reflectivepundit* (www.reflectivepundit.com). Readers are invited to visit her blog, comment on posts, or email questions and comments.

About the Author

Brigitte L. Nacos, a long-time U.S. correspondent for newspapers in Germany, received a Ph.D. in political science from Columbia University, where for more than 25 years she has taught courses in American politics and government. Her research concentrates on the links between the media, public opinion, and decision-making; domestic and international terrorism and counterterrorism; and, more recently, on social movements. Besides publishing many articles and several book chapters, she is author of *The Press, Presidents, and Crises* (Columbia University Press, 1990); *Terrorism and the Media: From the Iran Hostage Crisis to the World Trade Center Bombing* (Columbia University Press, 1994 and 1996); *Mass-Mediated Terrorism: The Central Role of the Media in Terrorism and Counterterrorism* (Rowman & Littlefield, 2002, 2007, 2016); (with Oscar Torres-Reyna) *Fueling Our Fears: Stereotyping, Media Coverage, and Public Opinion of Muslim Americans* (Rowman & Littlefield, 2006). She is also coauthor of *From Bonn to Berlin: German Politics in Transition* (Columbia University Press, 1998) with Lewis J. Edinger, and coeditor of *Decisionmaking in a Glass House* (Rowman & Littlefield, 2000) with Robert Y. Shapiro and Pierangelo Isernia. Finally, she is coauthor with Yaeli Bloch-Elkon and Robert Y. Shapiro of *Selling Fear: Counterterrorism, the Media, and Public Opinion* (University of Chicago Press, 2011). Apart from teaching, researching, and writing, she loves playing golf, cooking, and barbecuing for her family and friends, as well as tending to her indoor and outdoor flowers.

Image used with permission of the Nacos family.

1 Introduction

Terrorist Threats at Home and Abroad

How serious is the threat of terrorism in the third decade of the twenty-first century—more than 20 years after the 9/11 attack—existential, serious, not serious? This was the question I asked the students in my seminar on terrorism and counterterrorism in our first meeting and shortly before I began to revise the previous edition of this volume. Even those students who were babies or toddlers on that fateful day had heard about the horrific terrorist attacks on the World Trade Center in New York, the Pentagon in Washington, DC, and onboard United Airlines Flight 93 that crashed in Shanksville, Pennsylvania. "I grew up in the years after 9/11 and often heard people talk about the attack," said a 22-year-old student. A number of his classmates nodded their agreement. They all were familiar with the persistent legacy of the most lethal attack on the U.S. mainland by foreign, nonstate belligerents. All were aware of the lasting memories attached to that day. And all thought that terrorism was a serious but not an existential threat to the United States and other Western countries.

One student compared the close to 3,000 people killed on 9/11 to about one million Americans killed by the Covid virus. Some brought up the number of Americans killed by gun-violence and in car accidents each year—every single year many, many more than those killed on 9/11. But they also recognized that acts of terrorism are perceived as particularly frightening and shocking events because they are planned and deliberately designed to kill and maim human beings. "People being killed by terrorists is different than people dying in car accidents or pandemics," one student said. Someone mentioned the many incidents of mass shootings by perpetrators without ideological motives and found them just as horrible and frightening as terrorist attacks. This led to a longer discussion of the differences and similarities between a criminal and a terrorist, between organized crime syndicates and terrorist organizations. Some students knew about the controversies surrounding the USA PATRIOT Act that, as several noted, had curbed Americans' civil liberties. One member of the class was critical of security agencies' eavesdropping on American citizens' private communications. Another thought that governments

DOI: 10.4324/9781003289265-1

tend to overreact to terrorist strikes mentioning the war in Afghanistan and the invasion of Iraq. Several students in my seminar were veterans of those wars. They spoke about the number of American military men and women killed and injured during the so-called war on terrorism—and the far larger numbers of civilian victims of the military conflicts and terrorist attacks in Afghanistan, Pakistan, Iraq, Syria, and other places. In our discussions during the semester, it became clear that their experiences in Afghanistan, Iraq, or deployments elsewhere shaped their views about terrorism and counterterrorism—and most of all about the effects of violence on victims of both terrorism and responses to terrorist attacks. 9/11 and its aftermath were very personal for them.

Never before had one terrorist attack reshaped the priorities and the actual policy agenda of a victimized state as drastically, and impacted international relations as severely, as the assault on targets in New York and Washington. This was possible, according to one scholar, because "the myths of American Exceptionalism and Barbarism vs. Civilization" shaped the post-9/11 narrative of the terrorist threat and led to a "shared, mythologized understanding of the significance of 9/11."[1]

In response to 9/11, U.S. President George W. Bush, backed by most members of the U.S. Congress and a vast majority of the American people, declared war, not against a conventional enemy, a foreign country, but rather against a violent activity—a war against terrorism. Less than four weeks after 9/11, military actions by an American-led, international coalition commenced in Afghanistan against the assumed masterminds of the terror on American soil, Osama bin Laden and his close associates in the Al Qaeda (meaning "the base") terror organization, and against the ruling Taliban that had harbored Al Qaeda terrorists and their Afghan training camps for many years. According to President Bush, Afghanistan was merely the first battleground in a long and difficult campaign against a web of terrorist cells and organizations scattered around the globe and against states actively supporting terrorist activities. Furthermore, the president, in a speech at West Point on June 1, 2002, and the White House in a comprehensive follow-up "National Strategy to Combat Weapons of Mass Destruction," formulated a new doctrine of preventive wars that justified preemptive military actions against "emerging threats before they are fully formed."[2] By citing evidence of existing weapons of mass destruction (WMDs) in Iraq and the threat that the country's ruler, Saddam Hussein, might place such weapons into the hands of terrorists, the Bush administration followed the new doctrine when it decided to invade the country and force a regime change.[3]

Even before the dust had settled around the totally destroyed World Trade Center and the partially demolished Pentagon, people in the United States and abroad began to recognize that this terrorist assault pushed the United States and much of the world into a crisis that seemed just as dangerous as, or perhaps more explosive than, the Cold War conflict between the Soviet Union and the United States and their respective allies in the decades following the end of World War II. In some quarters, the end of the Cold War had led to expectations of an era of greater international understanding and cooperation and a "peace dividend" that would better the economic conditions in the underdeveloped world and bring improvements in the industrialized nations. But during the 1990s, such dreams did not come true. Instead, there was a troubling wave of conflicts in many parts of the world.

The Fear of Super-Terrorism

The mainstream media had an important role in Washington's reactions to 9/11. Instant commentary in the hours and days after the attacks compared the events of 9/11 again and again with the Japanese attack on Pearl Harbor 60 years earlier, claiming that both incidents had been as unexpected as bolts of lightning from a blue sky.[4] That was not correct. Experts had warned for some years of more catastrophic terrorism to come. A case in point was the renown historian Walter Laqueur. Up to the late 1990s, he considered terrorism a nuisance, not a serious threat to the security of Western countries and their people. But before the turn of the century, he revised his threat assessment and warned,

> Terrorism has been with us for centuries, and it has always attracted inordinate attention because of its dramatic character and its sudden, often wholly unexpected occurrence. It has been a tragedy for the victims, but seen in historical perspective it seldom has been more than a nuisance... This is no longer true today, and may be even less so in the future. Yesterday's nuisance has become one of the gravest dangers facing mankind.[5]

He was not the only expert in the field alarmed by several horrific incidents in the 1990s. One could argue that the age of catastrophic terrorism began in December 1988 with the downing of Pan Am Flight 103 over Lockerbie, Scotland, caused by a terrorist bomb that killed a total of 270 civilians on board (most of them Americans) and on the ground (all of them Scots). This was, at the time, the single most devastating act of terrorism in terms of the number of victims. Actually, nearly as many Americans were killed when extremists of the Lebanese Hezbollah drove an explosive-laden truck into the United States Marine barracks near Beirut Airport in 1983. While the victims of that massacre were peace-keepers and thus not combatants in the sense of fighting a war, they nevertheless were not civilians like the passengers and crew aboard Pan Am Flight 103 and the people who died on the ground in Lockerbie. As I will explain in the next chapter, whether civilians or members of the military are targets and victims figures prominently in the discussions of what kinds of violent acts constitute terrorism.

The fate of Pan Am Flight 103 in 1988 along with the Oklahoma City bombing in 1995 that caused the deaths of 168 persons represented turning points in the lethality of terrorism. Until these events, the widely held supposition was that "terrorists want a lot of people watching and a lot of people listening and not a lot of people dead."[6] But after Pan Am Flight 103 and the high number of fatalities in Oklahoma City, this assumption was no longer valid. Another terrorist incident inflamed the growing fears of changed intentions on the part of terrorists and even more deadly terrorist strikes to come: In 1995, members of a Japanese doomsday cult named Aum Shinrikyo (meaning "supreme truth") released poison gas in the Tokyo subway system, killing 12 persons and sickening thousands of commuters. As devastating as the consequences were, experts concluded that the release of the nerve gas sarin could have killed far more people had members of the Aum cult handled the poison differently. Pointing to the Japanese group's ability to develop nerve gas and to acquire toxic materials and know-how from sources in Australia, the United States, Russia, and elsewhere, U.S. Senator Sam Nunn concluded that the Japanese case meant the beginning of "a new era" in terrorism. He warned that WMDs could spread indiscriminately and fall into the hands of terrorists.[7]

For Americans, the threat of a major bioterrorist catastrophe hit close to home three weeks after the terror of 9/11, when letters containing anthrax spores were delivered to several media organizations and members of the U.S. Congress. Although in this case "only" five persons died and a dozen or so fell sick as a result of inhaling the finely powdered biological agent, an anthrax attack designed to kill as many people as possible could have easily caused a much more lethal catastrophe. Even before the anthrax case frightened the American public, *New York Times* reporters Judith Miller, Stephen Engelberg, and William Broad published a book in which they called germ weapons "the poor man's atom bomb" and warned that

> the threat of germ weapons is real and rising, driven by scientific discoveries and political upheavals around the world. As Aum Shinrikyo's failed efforts [to inflict far more harm than planned] suggest, the crucial ingredient in a successful biological attack is not advanced laboratory equipment or virulent microbes alone, but knowledge. Such expertise is increasingly available.[8]

And then came the attacks of 9/11. Never before had a terrorist coup inflicted so much devastation, so much grief, and so much fear of further, and more lethal, attacks. It was a most painful conclusion to the first World Trade Center bombing in 1993 that had failed to tumble the towers as planned by the perpetrators. At this point, the terrorism of the past had turned into something much more catastrophic, much more threatening—what experts came to call super-terrorism, postmodern terrorism, or new terrorism.

Several months after 9/11, high officials in the U.S. administration warned that terrorists would inevitably acquire WMD. Testifying before a Senate committee, U.S. Defense Secretary Donald H. Rumsfeld said terrorists "would seek to obtain nuclear, chemical, and biological weapons, and ultimately would succeed despite U.S. efforts to prevent them [from doing so]."[9] Worse yet, in June 2002 the U.S. government announced the arrest of Abdullah Al Mujahir, an American citizen who years earlier had been a Chicago street gang member named Jose Padilla. The Brooklyn-born Muslim convert, who had allegedly trained in Al Qaeda camps in Afghanistan, was accused of conspiring with fellow terrorists to acquire and detonate a so-called dirty bomb in Washington, DC, or elsewhere in the United States. Although this would not trigger a nuclear explosion and would not be as lethal as sophisticated nuclear weapons, a dirty bomb would nevertheless release enough radioactive material over several city blocks to harm many people and contaminate the affected area. As it turned out, there was no evidence that Padilla had planned to get his hands on a dirty bomb but the news of such a threat contributed to American officials and the American people's worries.

Nearly two decades later, violent political extremists were still obsessed with small-scale "germ weapons" and with most destructive WMDs. That was the case for international and domestic terrorists. In February 2020, for example, when the Covid-19 outbreak had not yet grown into a health crisis in the United States, an Intelligence Brief by the U.S. Federal Protective Service warned other security agencies that "White Racially Motivated Violent Extremists" had told their followers it was "an obligation to spread [Covid-19] should any of them contract the virus... via saliva, a spray bottle, or laced items."[10] The brief seemed to be based on conversations in an encrypted channel on the app. Telegram that propagates the neo-Nazi theory of "accelerationism" and the need of attacking non-Whites and their White enabler in order to hasten the breakdown of society and the triumph of White Supremacy. Ironically, the idea of accelerationism was the core mission of one of the most extreme White Supremacy groups of the twenty-first century: Atomwaffen Division. The German term Atomwaffen (meaning nuclear weapons) was presumably chosen by this group as signal of its true intentions.

The Rise of Non-Jihadist Domestic Terrorism

Returning to the discussions in my terrorism/counterterrorism seminar in 2022, my students seemed well aware that several Far-Right groups with records of violence had participated in the breach of the U.S. Capitol on

January 6, 2021. A few also remembered the 2017 "Unite the Right" march of White Supremacists and neo-Nazis in Charlottesville, Virginia, that ended tragically, when a neo-Nazi drove his car intentionally into a group of counter-protesters killing a young woman. But most seemed surprised when I cited data showing that after the 9/11 attacks, more persons were killed in the United States by non-Muslims domestic terrorists than by jihadists connected to or influenced by international terrorist groups.

In this volume, international and domestic terrorism will receive the attention both types of political violence demand as will the interconnections between them. But even-handedness will not alter the fact that 9/11 like no other terrorist event was in the past two decades and remained in the early 2020s the supreme attention-getter, when experts and lay people talked about terrorism. At times, 9/11 was exploited for political reasons. Thus, in November 2017, more than 16 years after 9/11, then Acting Secretary of Homeland Security, Elaine Duke, warned during a congressional hearing with the title World Wide Threats: Keeping America Secure in the New Age of Terror,

> I want to begin by noting that right now the terror threat to our country equals, and in many ways exceeds, the period around 9/11. We are seeing a surge in terrorist activity because the fundamentals of terrorism have changed. Our enemies are crowd-sourcing their violence online and promoting a 'do it yourself' approach that involves using any weapons their followers can get their hands on.[11]

A year later, in October 2018, President Donald Trump warned: "Radical Islamic terrorists are determined to strike our homeland, as they did on 9/11, as they did from Boston to Orlando to San Bernardino and all across Europe."[12] Such risk assessments were clearly gross overstatements of the international terrorist threat that the United States faced at that time and, just as important, such evaluations excluded cases of lethal domestic terrorism during the same time period, such as the mentioned shooting of nine Black worshippers in Charleston and 11 Jewish celebrants in Pittsburgh, by White home-grown terrorists. As one expert noted,

> The 9/11 attacks have become what psychologists call an "anchoring event" which, owing to its vivid and dramatic nature, is long remembered because human memory and perceptions filter out less dramatic or contradictory information. Moreover, the anchoring event shapes subsequent analysis and the degree of probability that are attributed to future events, in this case, the extent and nature of the terrorist threat.[13]

The U.S. government does not keep comprehensive records of domestic terrorist incidents. The FBI releases annual lists of hate crimes in the United States that in many cases overlap with terrorist offenses. But even hate crime statistics are never complete because a significant number of police jurisdictions fail to report these types of wrongdoings. A number of non-government organizations compile lists of violent extremism, especially cases involving fatalities. However, because the distinctions between acts of terrorism and hate crimes are fuzzy, different organizations end up with different counts. But there is agreement on one point: After 9/11 and particularly in the second and early third decade of the twenty-first century, there were more attacks and fatalities caused by domestic extremists in the United States than by jihadists.[14] This trend grew stronger in the last ten years. The Anti-Defamation League (ADL) includes and categorizes for many years politically, socially, and ideologically influenced violence in its comprehensive quantitative and qualitative analyses, regardless of whether the incidents are characterized as terrorism or hate crimes by the authorities or news organization. As Figure 1.1 shows, according to ADL, 443 persons were killed by violent extremists in the ten years from 2012 through 2021. 332 individuals or 75 percent were the victims of Far-Right extremists, 89 percent or 20 percent by jihadists, and 17 percent or 4 percent by Far-Left extremists, among them anarchists and Black nationalists. The cruel mass murder of 11 African Americans in Buffalo by a White Supremacist/neo-Nazi in 2022 added further to the high percentage of persons killed by Far-Right extremists.

Again: Between 2012 and 2021, 443 people were killed in domestic terrorism incidents in the United States. Of these, 332 people (or 75 percent) were killed in attacks conducted by Far-Right extremists.

A Gallup poll conducted in February 2022 revealed that 94 percent of Americans considered domestic terrorism a critical (68 percent) or important but not critical (26 percent) threat to the vital interests of the United States with only 6 percent without an opinion or refusing to answer.[15] Since the survey took place around the first anniversary of the violent breach of the U.S. Capitol on January 6, 2021, this unprecedented incident may have played a role in the public's perception of domestic terrorism as a serious threat. Ninety-six percent of the same poll respondents believed that international terrorism was a critical (71 percent) or important but not critical (25 percent) threat to America's vital interests the with only 4 percent without an opinion or refusing to answer. Given the margin of error, the poll showed that more than two decades after 9/11, the American public considered domestic and international terrorism equally critical or serious threats to the United States.

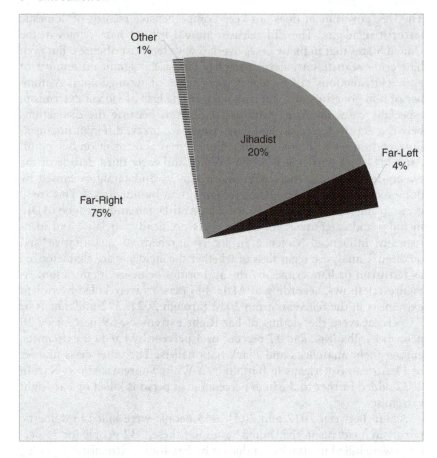

Figure 1.1 Killings by Domestic Violent Extremists 2012–21
Source: Anti-Defamation League

Terrorist Trends during the Last Decades

Acts of terrorism caused more deaths and injuries in the last several years of the twentieth century and the first decades of the twenty-first century than in several of the preceding decades combined. Whereas the number of incidents with respect to both international and domestic terrorism decreased markedly, the total number of casualties increased significantly.

As Figure 1.2 shows, the increase in casualties started in the mid-1990s. In the five-year period from 1988 through 1992, a total of 2,345 international terrorist incidents were recorded that caused 4,325 casualties (persons killed and injured). The number of incidents decreased by 552 during the following five years (1993 through 1997) to 1,793, but there were 8,767 more casualties, or a total of 13,092 killed or

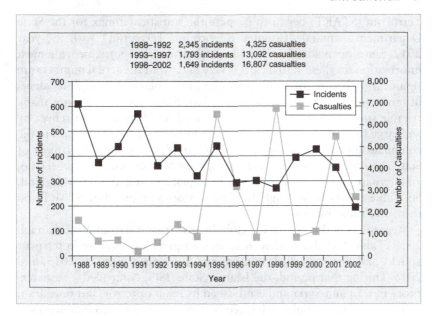

1988–1992	2,345 incidents	4,325 casualties
1993–1997	1,793 incidents	13,092 casualties
1998–2002	1,649 incidents	16,807 casualties

Figure 1.2 Trends in International Terrorist Incidents and Casualties (1988–2002)

Source: U.S. State Department, "Patterns of Global Terrorism"

injured victims. Finally, the next five years (1998 through 2002) witnessed a further decline in terrorist deeds to a total of 1,649 and yet another jump in casualties to a total of 16,807.[16] These trend statistics end with the year 2002 because of a controversy that arose after the initial release of the numbers for 2003 by the U.S. Department of State. The 2003 numbers reflected a rather sharp decline in international terrorist incidents and casualties, encouraging a State Department official to tell the press, "You will find in these pages clear evidence that we are prevailing in the fight [against terrorism]."[17] But it turned out that not all relevant international incidents were counted and that the true numbers in the revised report represented increases in both casualties and incidents. These and other problems led to the suspicion that the numbers had been massaged to support the claim that progress was made in the war against terrorism. Whereas the State Department had prepared the "Patterns of Global Terrorism" report for years, the newly established Terrorist Threat Integration Center, a creature of the Department of Homeland Security, FBI, and Department of Defense, was in charge of the 2003 issue.

Following the controversy concerning the 2003 statistics, the National Counterterrorism Center gathered and analyzed relevant statistics before the National Consortium for the Study of Terrorism and Responses to

Terrorism (START) began to prepare the statistical annex for the State Department's annual "Country Reports on Terrorism" with the year 2012. Since open sources, first of all news media reports, provide most information for these statistics, it is very likely that the actual numbers are significantly higher. In a number of countries plagued by high incidents of terrorism (i.e., Syria, Yemen, Somalia), there were and are not many reliable sources. Nevertheless, the reported numbers seem to reflect by and large the actual trends. There was another change with respect to the compilation of global terrorism data in 2018, when the Department of State awarded the contract to Development Services Group, Inc. (DSG), an international research firm with headquarters in Bethesda, Maryland. So, Table 1.1 shows through 2017 the statistics prepared by START and thereafter those by DSG.

Regardless of the switch, the global terrorism trend from 2012 through 2019 (Table 1.1) shows that there was a significant increase in terrorist attacks and persons killed, injured, and kidnapped in 2014, 2015, and 2016. During that period, the Islamic State (ISIS) controlled a large territory in Iraq and Syria and established its reign of terror. But once Iraqi and Syrian Kurdish fighters backed by U.S. forces defeated ISIS jihadists, there was a measurable decrease in terrorist strikes and victims. Perhaps, one of the more striking revelations in this table is the large number of persons kidnapped during terrorist incidents—from a "low" of more than one thousand in 2012 to a record high in 2016 of more than 15,000

Table 1.1 Global Trends in Terrorist Incidents and Victims

Year	Total Attacks	Persons Killed	Persons Injured	Persons Kidnapped
2012	6, 771	11,098	21,652	1,283
2013	9,707	17,891	32,577	2,990
2014	13,463	32,727	34,791	9,428
2015	11,774	28,328	35,320	12,189
2016	11,072	25,621	33,814	15,543
2017	8,584	18,753	19,461	8,937
2018	8,117	32,952	22,651	3,534
2019	8,872	26,273	19,924	2,895
2020	10,172	29,389	19,413	4,471

Source: U.S. Department of State.

In the table above, the space between 2017 and 2018 signifies that, described in text, another organization prepared the State Department's statistical analyses starting in 2018.

Table 1.2 Countries with Most Persons Killed 2002–19

Country	Number of Deaths	Major Terrorist Group
Iraq	67,153	Islamic State
Afghanistan	45,083	Taliban
Nigeria	23,686	Boko Haram
Pakistan	17,510	Tehrik-i-Taliban (TTP)
Syria	10,831	ISIS
India	8,748	Maoists/Communist Party
Somalia	7,180	Al-Shabaab
Yemen	6,045	Ansar Allah
Democratic Rep. Congo	4,335	Allied Democratic Forces
Philippines	3,448	New People's Army

Source: Institute for Economics & Peace.

hostage-takings. There was another uptick in the number of attacks and fatalities with the latter coming close or reaching the high numbers of the 2014–16 era.

As Table 1.2 shows, in the nearly two decades from 2001 through 2019, four countries with overwhelming Muslim majorities (Iraq, Pakistan, Afghanistan, and Syria) and one nation with a population evenly divided between Muslims and Christians (Nigeria) recorded by far the largest number of victims killed as a result of terrorist attacks. More than 67,000 persons died in Iraq and more than 45,000 in Afghanistan such incidents

In sharp contrast, during the 2002–19 period, 456 persons were killed in terrorist attacks in the United States and an additional 539 Americans died in terrorist incidents abroad according to START statistics (Table 1.3). There is no doubt that the numbers of attacks and persons killed in the United States were in fact significantly higher than listed, if only because politically motivated hate-crimes were not included. But, as noted earlier, the actual numbers for the listed countries in the Middle East, South Asia, and Africa were likely higher as well. Important here are the stark differences between the numbers in the two tables. Because most American and other Western mainstream media tend to cover terrorism in the United States and other Western countries far more extensively and prominently than this sort of political violence in non-Western parts of the world, many news consumers are not aware that parts of the Middle East, South Asia, and Africa suffer far more from the persistence of terrorism than do Western countries.

Table 1.3 Terrorist Attacks against U.S. and American Victims 2002–19

Year	No. of Attacks in U.S.	Number of Deaths in U.S.	Number of U.S. Victims Abroad
2002	33	4	30
2003	33	0	17
2004	9	0	5
2005	21	0	3
2006	6	1	4
2007	8	0	1
2008	18	2	14
2009	12	22	23
2010	17	4	6
2011	10	0	3
2012	20	7	12
2013	20	23	29
2014	29	26	41
2015	39	54	68
2016	68	68	79
2017	66	98	102
2018	73	45	50
2019	64	51	52
Total	**546**	**405**	**539**

Source: START.

When Non-Lethal Attacks Become Major Crises

As one would expect, acts of international and domestic terrorism have significant impact on target societies when they are particularly lethal. But in the past, there were also many incidents that did not result in large numbers of casualties, or that resulted in none at all, but that still achieved the status of terrorist spectacular because political leaders perceived such incidents as acute crises and reacted accordingly. In early 1975, for example, members of the Baader-Meinhof group kidnapped Peter Lorenz, a Christian Democratic candidate for mayor of West Berlin. Four days later and after the West German government released five jailed terrorists and paid $50,000 in ransom, Lorenz was released unharmed. This was not the first time the authorities in the Federal Republic of Germany had given in to terrorists' demands. But, according to Peter Katzenstein

> two months later the government stood firm when West German terrorists seized eleven hostages in the West German embassy

in Stockholm. It refused to make any concessions in 1977 when terrorists kidnapped and eventually murdered Martin Schleyer, one of the most prominent business leaders of the Federal Republic.[18]

The boldness of Lorenz's kidnapping and the fact that, for the first time, a politician had been targeted elevated the Lorenz case in the minds of the West German public and government to the level of a major crisis—even though no one had been killed or injured. As a result, the West German authorities altered their response to terrorism, decided to make no more concessions to terrorists, and stuck to their new policy of toughness.

The murder of former Italian Prime Minister Aldo Moro in 1978 by the Red Brigade had a similar effect on the Italian government and public. In this case, the terrorists killed their immediate victim (the well-liked Moro) and, during the kidnapping, five of his bodyguards; the incident was quickly perceived as a major crisis. This was not simply because of the number of casualties—after all, Europe had witnessed far more lethal terrorism before the Moro case—but because the Red Brigade had laid bare the vulnerability and impotence of the Italian authorities to protect even a former head of government. As Jeffrey Simon observed, "the subsequent crackdown on the Red Brigade by the Italian police and security forces was not seen as repressive by the public, but as a welcome response."[19] In the summer of 2006, when members of the Lebanese Hezbollah crossed into Israel and abducted two Israeli soldiers, this kidnapping triggered massive retaliation by Israel and a major military conflict between it and Hezbollah.

Conversely, although none of the Americans held as hostages died during the 444 days of the Iran hostage crisis (1979–81), this incident was criticized by President Jimmy Carter's opponents as sign of a weak crisis management and eventually seen by the U.S. public as failure of the commander-in-chief to flex the American superpower's muscle against a bunch of young Iranian hostage-takers—backed by their government.

Content and Organization of This Volume

We enhance our understanding of many aspects of terrorism in general if we know the most pertinent details of those terrorist incidents with outstanding characteristics and effects. But younger generations do not know about many incidents of anti-American terrorism abroad that older Americans remember very well. Younger Americans certainly have no personal recollection of the Iran hostage crisis or the long ordeal of American hostages in Lebanon in the 1980s. For this reason, this book's appendix ("Major Terrorist Incidents since the Late 1970s") provides readers with a number of both extensive and brief summaries of terrorist events in two categories: (1) major incidents that targeted Americans and/or American interests, and (2) major international incidents without American targets and victims.

Following this introduction, the rest of the book is divided into three distinct sections: Part I: Terrorism, Part II: Counterterrorism, and Part III: Terrorism in the News Media and on the Internet. Chapter 2, the first of Part I, addresses fundamental definitions and disagreements surrounding the terms *terrorism* and *terrorist*. This includes views in the oftentimes heated debate about the question: Is terrorism never or sometimes justified? Although in the past it was rarely as serious a threat as it is today, terrorism in one form or another has existed at every time and was typically committed by groups who were too weak to fight for their causes in open conflicts.

Drawing on the past forms of and experiences with terrorism will often illuminate recent and present developments, events, and issues and can help us to make comparisons and find similarities and differences. Given the important development in the last several years, I rewrote Chapters 3 and 4 because the differentiations between international or transnational terrorism on the one hand and domestic terrorism on the other hand are today less useful than they were in the past. Thus, the new Chapter 3 provides a historical review of various types and waves of terrorism through the last 2,000 or so years, whereas the new Chapter 4 is devoted to the terrorism landscape in the 2020s with attention to the contemporary threats by Far-Right and Far-Left violent extremists and their international alliances; the state of violent jihadist groups and their international networks; single-issue political violence, such as anti- and pro-abortion terrorism, and the threat of eco- and environmental terrorism. Chapter 5 remains devoted to terrorism committed in the name of God and religious beliefs and ends with the violent QAnon conspiracy theorists with features resembling those of religious cults. In Chapter 6 that describes various explanations of how and why persons become terrorists, I added a section on "cult thinking in terrorist groups" that explains in particular the psychological aspects of leader-follower relationships. Chapter 7 is devoted to the roles of females and children in terrorist groups. I added a section on the growing militancy of women in Far-Right extremism using data on female participants in the violence on January 6, 2021. I updated Chapter 8 that addresses the goals, targets, and tactics of terrorists, and Chapter 9 that deals with the organization of terrorist groups, their sponsors, and their finances.

Part II of the book, devoted to counterterrorism, begins with Chapter 10 with a new review of the costs of the war on terrorism from 9/11 through the chaotic withdrawal of the U.S.-led NATO coalition from Afghanistan in 2021. This is followed by a discussion of the counterterrorism strategies against jihadist terrorism that were in large part shared by international partners. This new edition takes note of an important change early on in the Biden administration, when the White House released the first-ever National Strategy for Countering Domestic Terrorism. In the heavily devised Chapter 11, I discuss the utility of hard and soft power in the fight against terrorism. While the chapter's focus was in previous editions on dealing with foreign entities, I added a section on how to counter domestic violent extremism. Chapter 12 discusses terrorism prevention and the importance of intelligence in foiling plots; Chapter 13 presents the difficulties in achieving a balance between the need for security and the respect for civil liberties and human rights in the face of serious terrorist threats.

The two chapters in Part III of the book address the centrality of media and communication in the terrorist calculus. Chapter 14 explains first the comprehensive propaganda/publicity scheme of terrorists before turning to the symbiotic relationship between mainstream media and the perpetrator of terrorist violence. The revised Chapter 15 assesses the threat of cyber terrorism before dealing with terrorists' utilization of the world wide web, in particular social media.

Finally, the concluding last Chapter 16 evaluates some of the book's major arguments and suggests ways to cope with the perennial terrorist threat without overreacting to the real but oftentimes overblown danger of this sort of violence.

Notes

1 Joanne Esch, "Legitimizing the War on Terror: Political Myth in Official-Level Rhetoric," *Political Psychology* 31 (3) (2010), p. 365.
2 Stated in a letter that accompanied the *National Strategy to Combat Weapons of Mass Destruction* (Washington, DC: 2002), ii. For an analysis of the doctrine of pre-emptive wars, see Robert Jervis, "Understanding the Bush Doctrine," in Demetrios James Caraley, ed., *American Hegemony: Preventing War, Iraq, and Imposing Democracy* (New York: Academy of Political Science, 2004), 3–26.
3 In January 2005, the White House announced that the United States had ended the search for WMD in Iraq without finding any evidence of banned weapons. The 1,200 specialists of the Iraq Survey Group had spent nearly two years searching many sites, such as laboratories, factories, and military installations.
4 Brigitte L. Nacos, Yaeli Bloch Elkon, and Robert Y. Shapiro, *Selling Fear: Counterterrorism, the Media, and Public Opinion* (Chicago, IL: University of Chicago Press, 2011), chapter 1.
5 The quote is from Walter Laqueur, *The New Terrorism: Fanaticism and the Arms of Mass Destruction* (New York: Oxford University Press, 1999), 3–4. In an earlier book, Laqueur had called terrorism "a sideshow" in comparison to far greater problems. See Walter Laqueur, *The Age of Terrorism* (Boston, MA: Little, Brown, 1987).
6 Brian Jenkins is quoted in Bruce Hoffman, *Inside Terrorism* (New York: Columbia University Press, 1998), 198.
7 Christopher Drew, "Japanese Sect Tried to Buy U.S. Arms Technology, Senator Says," *New York Times*, October 31, 1995.

8 Judith Miller, Stephen Engelberg, and William Broad, *Germs: Biological Weapons and America's Secret War* (New York: Simon & Schuster, 2001), 315–16.

9 According to the *Washington Post*. See Bill Miller and Christine Haughney, "Nation Left Jittery by Latest Series of Terror Warnings," *Washington Post*, May 22, 2002, A1.

10 This is the link to a homeland security website reporting on the brief, https://www.mcac.maryland.gov/newsroom/HomelandSecurityNews/20200323-federal-law-enforcement-document-reveals-white-supremacists-discussed-using-coronavirus-as-a-bioweapon-yahoonews, accessed May 22, 2022. Yahoo News elaborated on the brief, see https://news.yahoo.com/federal-law-enforcement-document-reveals-white-supremacists-discussed-using-coronavirus-as-a-bioweapon-212031308.html, accessed Mary 22, 2022.

11 The transcript of her testimony is available at https://www.dhs.gov/news/2017/11/30/oral-testimony-dhs-acting-secretary-elaine-duke-house-committee-homeland-security, accessed May 17, 2022.

12 The citation was published in "The National Strategy for Counterterrorism of the United States of America," October 2018; https://trumpwhitehouse.archives.gov/wp-content/uploads/2018/10/NSCT.pdf, accessed April 25, 2022.

13 George C. Fidas, "The Terrorist Threat: Existential or Exaggerated? A 'Red Cell' Perspective," *International Journal of Intelligence and Counter Intelligence* 21 (2008), p. 521.

14 See, for example, the statistics by the New America Foundation that show more persons killed in the post-9/11 years by Far-Right political violence than jihadist terrorism, https://www.newamerica.org/international-security/reports/terrorism-in-america/what-is-the-threat-to-the-united-states-today, accessed May 17, 2022.

15 The Gallup poll was conducted February 1–17, 2022.

16 The incident/casualty numbers were compiled from statistical data published by the Department of State in its yearly editions of "Patterns of Global Terrorism."

17 Deputy Secretary of State Richard Armitage was cited by Paul Krugman, "Errors in Terror," *New York Times*, June 25, 2004, A23.

18 Peter Katzenstein, "West Germany's Internal Security Policy: State and Violence in the 1970s and 1980s," Western Societies Program, Occasional Paper no. 28, Center for International Studies (Ithaca, NY: Cornell University, 1990), 31.

19 Jeffrey D. Simon, *The Terrorist Trap: America's Experience with Terrorism* (Bloomington: Indiana University Press, 1994), 322.

Part I

Terrorism

2 The Perennial Debate
What Is Terrorism?

In post-9/11 America, it has been common for public officials, the media, and rank-and-file Americans to perceive violence in public places carried out by Muslim attackers as acts of terrorism but the same types of violence by non-Muslims as crimes or hate crimes. Thus, in December 2019, after a Saudi aviation student at the Naval Air Base in Pensacola, Florida, shot three Americans to death, this was called an act of terrorism by law enforcement officials and news organizations. U.S. Attorney General William Barr, FBI Director Christopher Wray, members of Congress along with pundits called the incident terrorism and the perpetrator a terrorist. Rightly so. Investigators discovered that the 21-year-old second lieutenant in the Saudi Royal Air Force had ties to Al Qaeda in the Arabian Peninsula (AQAP) and was radicalized by the video-taped recruitment sermons of the American-Yemeni preacher Anwar al-Awlaki. Earlier that same year, when a 19-year-old Californian man entered the Chabad of Poway synagogue near San Diego, shot a woman to death and injured three other worshippers before his AR-15 semi-automatic rifle malfunctioned, he was characterized as "synagogue shooter" and his violence called a "hate crime." In the manifesto that the young man posted online, he described himself as a defender of Christianity who hated Jews and Muslims and who had earlier set fire to a mosque in the area. Like the Pensacola shooter, he was a religiously motivated violent extremist; in other words, he was as much a terrorist as the Pensacola shooter.

There were, however, notable signs that the linguistic double standards were weakening. Slowly. In 2017, after a deadly car attack by a White Supremacist in Charlottesville, Virginia, that killed a young woman, Attorney-General Jeff Sessions declared that the "unequivocally unacceptable and evil attack" did indeed meet "the definition of domestic terrorism."[1] While the headline "Was the Charlottesville Car Attack Domestic Terrorism, a Hate Crime or Both?" in the *Washington Post* asked the right questions and the article underneath reported the Attorney-General's conclusion in this particular case, legal experts cited in the same article did not even try to clarify what distinguishes terrorism from ordinary crime. Nearly five years later, following the mass shooting

DOI: 10.4324/9781003289265-3

of African Americans in Buffalo, President Biden rejected terms like hate crime and Far Right violent extremism, when he said during his visit to the targeted community: "What happened here is simple and straightforward terrorism. Terrorism. Domestic terrorism. Violence inflicted in the service of hate and the vicious thirst for power that defines one group of people being inherently inferior to any other group."[2]

The uneven usage of the term terrorism pre-dates the post-9/11 era. In 2001, before the attacks on the World Trade Center and the Pentagon, the Federal Bureau of Investigation's (FBI) list of the "Ten Most Wanted Fugitives" included three men sought for their involvement in acts of political violence: Osama bin Laden, the mastermind of lethal attacks on the American battleship USS *Cole* in the fall of 2000 and on the American embassies in Kenya and Tanzania two years earlier; Eric Robert Rudolph, who was sought for the deadly bombing of an abortion clinic in Alabama, the fatal explosion in Atlanta during the 1996 Olympic Games, and similar attacks on other facilities; and James Charles Kopp, who was charged with the assassination of Dr. Barnett Slepian, a provider of legal abortions. At the time, bin Laden was called a "terrorist" in the United States—by U.S. government officials, the media, and the public. However, with the exception of activists in the pro-choice movement, hardly anyone characterized Rudolph and Kopp publicly as "terrorists"; each was described as a "criminal," "murderer," or "extremist." After Slepian's violent death, President Bill Clinton said, "I am outraged by the murder of Dr. Barnett Slepian in his home last night in Amherst, NY."[3] Yet, neither Kopp nor Rudolph was an ordinary murderer. Both were antiabortion extremists who killed in the name of an elusive "Army of God" and single-issue politics as pursued by the most violent wing in the pro-life movement. Just like bin Laden, they acted to publicize, dramatize, and further their political and religiously motivated and justified political and social agenda. Why, then, did public officials, the media, and Americans in general choose different terms to explain the same types of deeds and the same types of perpetrators?

At first sight, one might guess that the severity of an act of violence, the damage inflicted, and especially the number of victims influence the language that describes the deeds and their perpetrators. After all, even before the attacks of 9/11, bin Laden and his associates had caused the deaths of hundreds of innocent victims, whereas Kopp had shot "just" one person and Rudolph had killed two people while injuring more than 100 others. But the number of killed and injured victims does not determine whether an act of political violence is labeled "terrorism" or "crime." To this day, for example, the Iran hostage crisis (1979–81) is widely perceived as a major terrorist incident, although none of the 49 Americans who were held for 444 days in the U.S. embassy in Tehran was physically harmed, nor were the three U.S. embassy officials who were stuck in Iran's foreign ministry. The Lebanese men who in 1985 hijacked a TWA airliner en route from Athens to Rome, brutally killed a young U.S. Navy diver, and held other passengers hostage were also considered "terrorists" in the United States.

One plausible explanation is the likelihood that government officials and reporters are more inclined to call political violence "terrorism" when it is committed abroad and "crime" when perpetrated at home. But this speculation does not solve the definitional puzzle either, as a review of pertinent domestic cases reveals. Timothy McVeigh, the man responsible for the 1995 Oklahoma City bombing and the death of 168 innocent people, was considered a terrorist and still is.[4] In the past, the FBI and news organizations described homegrown arsonists from the radical environmental groups Earth Liberation Front and Animal Liberation Front as "terrorists" and their deeds as "terrorism," although the perpetrators did not kill or injure people but were content to damage buildings and research projects. Similarly, Europeans have been more inclined to characterize political violence as terrorism when it is committed in their own country or their neighborhood. In the past, the German government and media, for example, tended to call politically motivated violence *Terrorismus* (terrorism) when it was committed by indigenous groups, such as the Red Army Faction and its successor groups and cells, or by organizations in other Western European countries, such as the Basque separatist organization Euskadi Ta Askatasuna (ETA) in Spain. But the same officials and media organizations characterized the Abu Sayyaf separatists in the distant Philippines as *militante Moslemrebellen* (militant Muslim rebels), *Rebellengruppe* (a rebel group), or *Separatisten* (separatists)—even at a time when the Filipino group held three Germans hostage. Public officials, the news media, and the public in England called acts of violence by the Irish Republican Army and by splinter groups thereof terrorism but avoided the controversial "T"-word when reporting on politically motivated violence abroad. However, the attacks on the World Trade Center and the Pentagon, although occurring on another continent, were condemned as terrorism in these and other European countries in the days and weeks after 9/11.

All of this begs one conclusion: When public officials, the news media, and experts in the growing field of terrorism studies (what one observer has called "terrorology") make definitional choices, the severity and the venues of violent deeds are not unequivocal guides.[5] Nor is the nationality of the victims. While research has shown that the U.S. media have been more inclined to characterize political violence as terrorism when it is committed against Americans rather than against other nationals, this has not been a consistent determinant either.[6] The ambiguity about what constitutes terrorism—and what does not—deserves attention because the choice of language determines, or at least influences, how politically motivated violence is perceived inside and outside a targeted society: If violent acts for political ends are described as criminal activity, the perpetrators are readily seen as social misfits and compared to other dangerous criminals that every society must deal with; if, however, political violence is labeled "terrorism," the perpetrators are easily perceived as threats to the political, social, and/or economic fabric of the societies they terrorize. In the first case, the problem is simply seen as one of the criminal justice system; in the second case, it is more likely to be seen in the larger context of national security. As one leading terrorism scholar observed,

> It is clear from surveying the literature of terrorism, as well as the public debate, that what one calls things matters. There are few neutral terms in politics, because political language affects the perceptions of protagonists and audiences, and such effect acquires a greater urgency in the drama of terrorism. Similarly, the meanings of the terms change to fit a changing context.[7]

Even when there is agreement that the perpetrators of violence are not ordinary criminals but are politically motivated, the definitional ambiguities remain. The greatest difficulty is rooted in the tendency of different people to perceive one and the same act as either a despicable or a justifiable means to political ends, as either an evil deed carried out by terrorists or a courageous act committed by warriors or revolutionaries in pursuit of just causes. The slogan that "one person's terrorist is another person's freedom fighter" captures these contrasting value judgments. There is no doubt that the terms *terrorism* and *terrorist(s)* have negative connotations. As one terrorism expert recognized, "to call an act of political violence terrorist is not merely to describe it but to judge it," because "nobody wants to be called a terrorist; terrorism is what the *other* side is up to."[8] There were exceptions along the way. After the Russian revolutionary Vera Zasulich shot and wounded the dictatorial governor of St. Petersburg Fydor Trepov in 1878 she dropped her gun instead of using it to avoid her arrest. "I am a terrorist not a murderer," is how she explained her actions. However, as James Forest concluded, the Zasulich case "represents one of relatively few examples in which the term 'terrorist' was embraced by the perpetrators of the violence."[9]

Before he was sentenced to 240 years in prison, Ramzi Yousef, the mastermind of the first World Trade Center bombing in 1993, stood in a New York courtroom and declared defiantly, "Yes, I am a terrorist, and I'm proud of it."[10] Anarchists in the second half of the nineteenth century did not reject the "T"-word either. On the contrary, some of them called themselves terrorists and their violence terrorism. However, a Jewish terrorist group that was active in the 1940s and known as the Stern Gang is believed to be among the last of such groups to describe themselves as a terrorist organization.[11] Most contemporary perpetrators of political violence reject the "T"-word. In the mid-1990s, when members of the Peruvian Tupac Amaru group occupied the Japanese embassy in Lima and held scores of people hostage, the then Peruvian president Alberto Fujimori repeatedly called the hostage-holders terrorists and their actions terrorism, while the captors inside the embassy insisted that they were commandos of a revolutionary movement and that their violent takeover was a military occupation. Like the Tupac Amaru leaders, most contemporary perpetrators of political violence understand well that the choice of words and the invocation of metaphors affect how friends and foes perceive them and their actions.

The Meaning of *Terrorism* over Time

The usage of the term *terrorism* has changed a great deal over time. In its original definition in the eighteenth century, it described violent actions by those in control of a state or, in other words, political violence "from above," as exercised during the Reign of Terror in the wake of the French Revolution, when *terrorism* meant the mass guillotining of the aristocracy and other real or perceived enemies of the state. During the nineteenth century, the meaning of *terrorism* expanded to include violence against those in power from those not in control of a state or government, and thus stood also for violence "from below," such as the assassinations of leaders and other politicians.[12] By the end of the century, mostly because of bombings and assassinations by anarchists, *terrorism* was predominantly associated with antistate, antigovernment violence. In the twentieth century, *terrorism* even more so came to mean political violence "from below" both in domestic and international settings. This latest shift in the definitional evolvement worked in favor of governments in that officials were quite successful in rejecting the terrorist label for their government's or friendly countries' violent actions.

Even when applied to political violence committed by groups, not all nonstate actors are treated equally in this respect either; rather, small groups are more often called terrorists than large groups, and the latter are more frequently identified as guerrillas or revolutionaries. According to Richard E. Rubenstein,

> Descriptively "terrorism" suggests violent action by individuals or small groups. Judgmentally, it implies illegitimacy. These meanings are closely related, since there are very few situations in which assassinations, bombings, kidnappings, or bank robberies seem justified. By contrast, wars and revolutions are frequently considered not only justified but holy.[13]

Similarly, Martha Crenshaw has argued,

> Terrorism is not mass or collective violence but rather the direct
> activity of small groups, however authentically popular these groups
> may be: even if supported by a larger organization or political party,
> the number of active militants who engage in terrorism is small.[14]

Precisely because an act of political violence is more likely to be seen as
illegitimate, as an act of terrorism, when carried out by individuals or
small factions, most groups, regardless of their true size, describe themselves as large organizations with significant popular support; they also
invoke metaphors of war, revolution, and liberation. These linguistic
tactics are reflected in the names they choose for themselves, as the following examples demonstrate: Tupac Amaru Revolutionary Movement,
Irish Republican Army, Red Army Brigade, Red Army Faction, Armed
Islamic Group, Popular Front for the Liberation of Palestine, and
Revolutionary Armed Forces of Colombia. Members of such organizations call themselves and want to be perceived as commandos, fighters,
soldiers, warriors, guerrillas, or revolutionaries.

   The case of Richard C. Reid, a self-proclaimed disciple of Osama bin
Laden and member of the Al Qaeda organization, was a case in point.
Sentenced to life for his attempt to blow up an American airliner with
explosives hidden in his shoes, the would-be shoe bomber told Judge
William G. Young of the Federal District Court in Boston, "I am at war
with your country." But the judge rejected vehemently the assertion that
Reid was a soldier, telling him, "You are not an enemy combatant, you
are a terrorist. You are not a soldier in any army, you are a terrorist."[15]

The Definitional Potpourri

Government officials are in a more advantageous position than other
political actors to confer the "T"-word on groups or withhold it and
thereby affect public perceptions because most of the time the mass
media cover officialdom far more frequently than other sources. Indeed,
this is true not simply in authoritarian systems where the government controls the media but also in liberal democracies.[16] It has been
argued that during the Cold War era, government officials, terrorism
experts, and the news media in the West, especially in the United States,
denounced violent left-wing groups and movements inside and outside
the United States as terrorists because these organizations were hostile
to the economic and political arrangement in Western liberal democracies, and that the same Western establishment supported equally or more
violent right-wing perpetrators of political violence as freedom fighters
because of their anticommunist pedigree.[17] But to whatever degree this
criticism was valid, these lines of demarcation faded away once the Cold
War was over. In a 2002 review of domestic terrorism, for example, the
FBI stated,

During the past decade we have witnessed dramatic changes in the nature of the terrorist threat. In the 1990s, right-wing extremism overtook left-wing terrorism as the most dangerous domestic threat to the country.[18]

Contrary to the suggestion that "individual governments have been swift to ratify their own definitions" of terrorism and that the continuing "definitional haze" remains simply a dilemma for the international community, individual governments have not solved this definitional problem either; if they managed to streamline their terminology, they did not apply their own definitions in consistent ways.[19] The United States was, for a long time, a case in point in that the executive departments and agencies of the federal government did not adopt a standard definition. The Federal Emergency Management Agency (FEMA), for example, defined terrorism as violence "for purposes of intimidation, coercion, or ransom" without including the provision that it must be politically motivated; this definition covered many ordinary crimes.[20] It was only in the aftermath of 9/11, when the press reported and a congressional committee complained about the lack of a uniform definition within the government, that FEMA adopted the general definition of terrorism that was used by the FBI, namely, that terrorism is the "unlawful use of force or violence against persons and property to intimidate or coerce a government, the civilian population, or any segment thereof, in furtherance of political or social objectives."[21]

As the law enforcement agency that is charged with preventing terrorism and with investigating terrorist incidents once they occur, the FBI developed the following working definitions that distinguish between domestic and international terrorism and, not surprisingly, focus heavily on the unlawful nature of terrorism and the violation of criminal laws by the perpetrators of political violence:

- Domestic terrorism is the unlawful use, or threatened use, of violence by a group or individual based and operating entirely within the United States or its territories, without foreign direction, committed against persons or property, to intimidate or coerce a government, the civilian population, or any segment thereof, in furtherance of political or social objectives.
- International terrorism involves violent acts dangerous to human life that are a violation of the criminal laws of the United States or any state, or that would be a criminal violation if committed within the jurisdiction of the United States or any state. Acts of international terrorism are intended to intimidate or coerce a civilian population, influence the policy of the government, or affect the conduct of a government. These acts transcend national boundaries in terms of the means by which they are accomplished, the persons they are intended to intimidate, or the locale in which perpetrators operate.[22]

The Department of State, with jurisdictions in the area of international terrorism but not in the domestic realm, adopted a terminology that was closest to an official U.S. government definition because it was contained in Title 22 of the *United States Code*, Section 2656f(d), a federal statute, which requires the State Department to provide Congress with annual reports on terrorist groups and countries that sponsor terrorism. According to this statute's and the Department of State's definitions:

- "Terrorism" means premeditated, politically motivated violence perpetrated against noncombatant targets by subnational groups or clandestine agents, and is usually intended to influence an audience.
- "International terrorism" means terrorism involving citizens or the territory of more than one country.
- "Terrorist group" means any group practicing, or that has significant subgroups that practice, international terrorism.

This definition and particularly its first part delineate not only the most important, but also the most contested, attributes assigned to terrorism.

First, the motives are political. Unlike the term crime, which implies that perpetrators act for personal gain and satisfaction, material and otherwise, terrorism is understood as politically motivated. There is no disagreement on this characteristic regardless of whether the perpetrators are guided by secular or religious beliefs. However, while it is not difficult to differentiate between criminal and political motivations most of the time, sometimes the lines are blurred—especially during ongoing incidents. In the fall of 2002, for example, when a pair of snipers terrorized millions of people in Washington, DC, and the surrounding areas of Virginia and Maryland for 21 long days, killing ten and seriously injuring three persons, law enforcement specialists had no clue about the nature of these attacks, that is, whether they were criminal or terrorist acts. Even in the face of threats that the random killings would continue unless a large sum of money was paid, nobody was sure whether the crime-or-terrorism mystery was completely solved. In the past, politically motivated groups frequently committed violent crimes, such as attacks on armored cars, bank robberies, and kidnappings for ransom, in order to support themselves and their terror operations. As for the Washington snipers, even after their arrest, it was not clear whether their motives were purely criminal or were influenced by political grievances as well. After all, as terrorism expert Jessica Stern pointed out, one of the pair, John Allen Muhammad, "reportedly told a friend that he endorsed the September 11 attacks and disapproved of U.S. policy toward Muslim states."[23]

Second, the targets are civilians or noncombatants. In declared or undeclared wars and other military conflicts, the warring sides target members of each other's armed forces; terrorists intentionally and randomly target civilians and what one might call innocent bystanders.

However, terrorists are also known to single out the citizens of one or more countries or the members of particular religious, racial, or ethnic groups. In the 1970s and 1980s, for example, some Palestinian groups and the Lebanese-based Hezbollah (or Party of God) targeted U.S. citizens and especially Jewish Americans. Terrorists would typically force the passengers of a hijacked plane to surrender their passports to identify Americans and, based on their names, single out those who they believed to be Jews. Domestic terrorists as well have targeted innocent bystanders randomly but sought out members of particular groups. Over the July Fourth weekend of 1999, for example, a young adherent of the White Supremacy hate group World Church of the Creator went on a killing spree in Illinois and Indiana that left an African American basketball coach and a Korean graduate student dead and six orthodox Jews injured. There was no doubt Benjamin Nathaniel Smith, the perpetrator, encountered the victims by chance but shot them because he could identify them as black, Asian, and Jewish.

For Jihadis All Americans and/or All Westerners Are Combatants

In May 2010, after a series of foiled and a few successful terrorist incidents inside the United States that involved homegrown or immigrated Muslim plotters, the Yemeni-American cleric Anwar al-Awlaki rejected the distinction between combatants and civilians. In an interview with Al Jazeera, he justified the targeting of civilians along the lines of Osama bin Laden's often expressed position. While Awlaki, who was killed in a U.S. drone strike, spoke in the following excerpts about American targets, the Islamic State expanded his justification of "legitimate" targets to both military and civilian infidels throughout the West.

INTERVIEWER: Do you support such operations [like the foiled Christmas Day bombing] even though they target what the media calls "innocent civilians"?

ANWAR AL-AWLAKI: Yes. With regard to the issue of "civilians," this term has become prevalent these days, but I prefer to use the terms employed by our jurisprudents. They classify people as either combatants or noncombatants. A combatant is someone who bears arms—even if this is a woman. Noncombatants are people who do not take part in the war.

(Continued)

(Continued)

The American people in its entirety takes part in the war because they elected this administration, and they finance this war. In the recent elections, and in the previous ones, the American people had other options, and could have elected people who did not want war. Nevertheless, these candidates got nothing but a handful of votes. We should examine this issue from the perspective of Islamic law, and this settles the issue—is it permitted or forbidden? If the heroic mujahid brother Umar Farouk could have targeted hundreds of soldiers, that would have been wonderful. But we are talking about the realities of war.

For 50 years, an entire section of people—the Muslims in Palestine—has been strangled, with American aid, support, and weapons. Twenty years of siege and then occupation of Iraq, and now, the occupation of Afghanistan. After all this, no one should even ask us about targeting a bunch of Americans who would have been killed in an airplane. Our unsettled account with America includes, at the very least, one million women and children. I'm not even talking about the men. Our unsettled account with America, in women and children alone, has exceeded one million. Those who would have been killed in the plane are a drop in the ocean.[24]

ISIS: Kill Any Disbeliever

If you can kill a disbelieving American or European—especially the spiteful and filthy French—or an Australian, or a Canadian, or any other disbeliever from the disbelievers waging war, including the citizens of the countries that entered into a coalition against the Islamic State, then rely upon Allah, and kill him in any manner or way however it may be. Do not ask for anyone's advice and do not seek anyone's verdict. Kill the disbeliever whether he is civilian or military, for they have the same ruling.

Will you leave the disbeliever to sleep safely at home while the Muslim women and children shiver with fear of the roars of the crusader airplanes above their heads day and night? How can you enjoy life and sleep while not aiding your brothers, not casting fear into the hearts of the cross worshippers, and not responding to their strikes with multitudes more?

So O muwahhid wherever you may be, hinder *those who want to harm your brothers and state* as much as you can. The best thing you can do is to strive to your best and kill any disbeliever, whether he be French, American, or from any of their allies.[25]

White Supremacists: No innocents among Non-White "Invaders."

It is not unusual for public officials, law enforcement officers, reporters, and eyewitnesses to characterize the targets of terrorist attacks as *innocent* victims. But many perpetrators of political violence believe that the enemies they fight are collectively guilty; that not even children are innocent.

For Brenton Tarrant, the Christchurch mass killer of 51 peaceful Muslim worshippers, his killer mission was to remove non-White, non-Christian "invaders" violently from Western countries. For him, not even the children of the "invaders," whether "Roma, African, Indian, Turkish, Semitic or other" were innocent and therefore not to be spared. As he wrote in his manifesto "The Great Replacement,"[26]

> When you discover a nest of vipers in your yard, do you spare the adolescents? Do you allow them to grow freely, openly, to one day bite your child as they play in their own yard? No. You burn the nest and kill the vipers, no matter their age.
>
> The enemies of our children are being born in our lands right now, even as you read this. These same children will one day become teens, then adults, voting against the wishes of our people, practicing the cultural and religious practices of the invaders, taking our peoples lands, work, houses and even attacking and killing our children.

Similarly, for Peyton Gendron, the Buffalo mass killer of 10 African Americans who copied much of his so-called manifesto from his idol Tarrant, the mission was "to deport those invaders already living on our soil." This was a totally non-sensical statement to make about African Americans who were in America long before many European immigrant groups. Yet, Gendron judged all of them and all Jews living in a Western country to be guilty, none of them innocent. "There is no non-white living in White lands who is innocent," he wrote.[27]

It is noteworthy that the most authoritative definition used by the U.S. government does not characterize the deliberate targets of terrorism as "civilian" but as "noncombatant" and thus puts civilians, government officials, and military personnel into the same category of targets and victims as long as public officials and members of the armed forces are not engaged in combat. If one embraces the "noncombatant" definition, the Iranian hostage crisis (1979–81) was a terrorist incident because the American captives, although members of the U.S. embassy staff, were not involved in an armed conflict. The U.S. Marines in the embassy compound were there to protect the embassy. Similarly, the 2001 attack on the USS *Cole* in the Yemeni port of Aden during a refueling stop that resulted in the death of 17 crew members would qualify as an act of terrorism, as was a truck bombing of the U.S. Marine barracks outside Beirut in 1983 that killed 241 Americans. If one subscribes to the "civilian" definition, these three incidents do not qualify as terrorism. In the Beirut case, the supporters of the lethal truck bombing and some Muslim clerics justified the so-called suicide bombing by rejecting the "noncombatant" definition; instead, they explicitly called the targets and victims of the attack members of a hostile military. The U.S. Marines had been dispatched to Lebanon as peacekeepers, but they did get involved in the country's civil strife.[28] In the case of the strike against the USS *Cole* and other Al Qaeda-related incidents, bin Laden and his associates did not even bother to justify these terrorist acts as directed against U.S. military personnel. After all, several years earlier, bin Laden had called on all Muslims to kill Americans everywhere—civilians and members of the armed forces.

Third, the perpetrators are nonstate actors. Neither the Department of State's nor the FBI's definitions leave to doubt that, in their understanding, political violence is terrorism only when carried out by groups, subgroups (State Department definition), or individuals (FBI definition) who intentionally target noncombatants. Unlike some scholars, among them Crenshaw and Rubenstein, U.S. government agencies and departments do not distinguish between small and large groups, but the FBI's definition does include political violence by individuals without the requirement that they be members of or directed by a group. Conversely, Bruce Hoffman seems to exclude politically motivated violence by lone wolves when he states that "terrorism is conducted by an organization with an identifiable chain of command or conspiratorial cell structure."[29] Following this definitional element, one would not categorize individuals such as the Oklahoma City bomber Timothy McVeigh or Benjamin Smith, the White Supremacist mentioned earlier, as terrorists. This book reflects the view that one individual or several persons can commit terrorist acts if they have political motives and goals—regardless of whether they are members of a group. McVeigh, for example, was not a formal member of one of the organizations in the right-wing, antigovernment movement, but he moved in these circles and was familiar with and embraced the extremist ideas and grievances common in this milieu.

More importantly, because they do not include governments or states and their agents as possible perpetrators of terrorism, the United States and other parties have been accused of applying a double standard. Thus, Edward Herman and Gerry O'Sullivan explained these definitional choices with the ideological Cold War biases of Western governments, Western terrorism experts, and the Western media, accusing them of looking upon the West as the sole victim of terrorist activities. They argued in particular that "the Western establishment has defined terrorism so as to exclude governments, which allows it to attend closely to the Baader-Meinhof gang and the Red Brigades and to play down the more severely intimidating actions of governments that they support."[30] Actually, the long-standing definition of the U.S. Department of Defense was in this respect more useful to critics, who insisted all along on the inclusion of states or governments in any explanation of terrorism. The Defense Department's terminology was broader than the definitions embraced by the FBI and the U.S. Department of State, and not explicit as to the characteristics of the perpetrators of terrorism. For the Defense Department, terrorism meant

> the unlawful use of—or threatened use of—force or violence against individuals or property to coerce or intimidate governments or societies, often to achieve political, ideological, or religious objectives.[31]

However, the FBI's and the U.S. Department of State's more specific versions that single out nonstate actors as the perpetrators of terrorism, not the Department of Defense's less specific definition, have been the preferred models for other executive agencies in the U.S. administration. There is no disagreement on one important point: Terrorism is committed in order to intimidate and terrorize a target audience. Therefore, the target society is far more important in the terrorist calculus than the immediate victims, in that terrorists are after a targeted public's and government's psychological mindsets in order "to make them act in a way which the attackers desire."[32] Michael Stohl has explained terrorism as a three-step process that consists of the "act or threat of violence, the emotional reaction to such an act or threat, and the social effects resultant from the acts and reaction."[33] With this process model in mind, Stohl concluded that "terrorists are primarily interested in the audience and not the victims" and that the "act or threat of violence is but the first step [in the three-part process]."[34]

Obviously aware of the definitional difficulties, the European Convention to Combat Terrorism that was adopted in 1977 by the member states of the European Union did not contain a definition of terrorism and listed instead a number of crimes that made perpetrators of such criminal acts liable to be extradited from one European country to another. Agreement on the definition of terrorism was never achieved in the larger setting of the United Nations (UN), although there were many efforts to embrace a single definition as the precondition for a truly international convention to have all member states agree to condemn and fight terrorism. The efforts to agree on one understanding of terrorism began between World War I and World War II, and continued throughout the rest of the twentieth and into the twenty-first centuries. In 1937, the League of Nations Convention made the first attempt to embrace an internationally accepted definition of terrorism that would allow the unconditional condemnation of terrorism. This first effort was identified as terrorism

> all criminal acts directed against a state and intended or calculated to create a state of terror in the minds of particular persons or a group of persons or the general public.[35]

Sixty-two years later, in 1999, a resolution of the UN General Assembly suggested that

> criminal acts intended or calculated to provoke a state of terror in the general public, a group of persons, or particular persons for political purposes are in any circumstance unjustifiable, whatever the considerations of a political, philosophical, racial, ethnic, religious or other nature that may be invoked to justify them.[36]

But the member states of the UN have not agreed to this or any other proposal and have adopted instead a dozen conventions and protocols over the last several decades that prohibit specific acts of terrorism, such as hijacking, hostage-taking, attacks on diplomats, and nuclear terror. Even after the events of September 11, 2001, renewed efforts to agree on a definition of terrorism and adopt a comprehensive agreement to combat this kind of violence failed. While the United States, the European Union, and many other countries agreed to focus on the victims of terrorism and condemn the targeting of civilians, a bloc of nations led by the Organization of the Islamic Conference insisted on the exclusion of national liberation movements and resistance to foreign occupation.[37] In 2002, Islamic nations adopted an agreement that obliged them to support a definition of terrorism that made a distinction between terrorism and legitimate struggle against foreign occupation. The delegates declared specifically, "We reject any attempt to link terrorism to the struggle of the Palestinian people in their exercise of their inalienable right to establish their independent state."[38]

Given these difficulties, one prominent terrorism expert, Walter Laqueur, has suggested that it is even less likely now than it was in the past to formulate and agree upon one definition, and that therefore new approaches are needed to solve the increasingly more complex problem. According to Laqueur,

> Today there are more varieties [of political violence] than existed thirty years ago, and many are so different from those of the past and from each other that the term terrorism no longer fits some of them. In the future, new terms will probably be found for the new varieties of terrorism.[39]

In the search for a value-free definition of the term *terrorism*, it has been suggested that the focus must be on the acts of political violence and not on the motives and justifications of those who commit them. Terrorism expert Brian Jenkins, for example, has proposed that political violence needs to be defined "by the nature of the act, not by the identity of the perpetrators or the nature of their cause."[40] Many news organizations have made this choice in that they use the term *terrorism* sparingly or forget about it altogether. Instead, they describe the methods of violence as bombing, hijacking, kidnapping, and so on, and the perpetrators as bombers, hijackers, hostage-takers, and the like. The news media are particularly influential in shaping the public's perception of what political violence qualifies as terrorism. A content analysis of leading American newspapers found that stories about political violence contained the terms *hijacker(s)*, *gunman(men)*, and *guerrilla(s)* far more often than *terrorist(s)* and refrained from characterizing the acts as terrorism but described them rather as hijackings, killings, bombings, explosions, attacks, blasts, shootings, seizures, and so on.[41] Just as revealing was the study's finding that more than 94 percent of these characterizations were chosen by the media in headlines and journalistic descriptions, compared to less than 6 percent that were attributed to the way that government officials, witnesses, and other sources defined acts of political violence.

Following the events of 9/11, some news organizations came under attack for avoiding the term *terrorism* in reporting about the strikes against the World Trade Center and the Pentagon. The news agency Reuters in particular prohibited its reporters and editors from using the "T"-word even in the context of 9/11 because, as members of the management explained in memos to the staff and in interviews,

> We all know that one man's terrorist is another man's freedom fighter and that Reuters upholds the principle that we do not use the word terrorist.
>
> We're trying to treat everyone on a level playing field, however tragic it's been and however awful and cataclysmic for the American people.[42]

As it turned out, the news agency's decision was not simply motivated by the determination to appear even-handed but by practical considerations as well. One of the organization's news executives explained, "We don't want to jeopardize the safety of our staff... in Gaza, the West Bank, and Afghanistan."[43]

Other news organizations were accused of applying a double standard in deciding when to use and not to use the "T"-word. The *Star Tribune* in Minneapolis, for example, defended its practice of avoiding the term *terrorism* in reports about the Israeli–Palestinian conflict and explained that this was decided "because of the emotional and heated nature of the dispute." The newspaper stated furthermore, "In the case of the term 'terrorist,' other words—'gunman,' 'separatist,' and 'rebel,' for example—may be more precise and less likely to be viewed as judgmental. Because of that we often prefer these more specific words." However, after 9/11 the *Star Tribune* did describe Al Qaeda as a terrorist network, explaining that the term is permitted in some circumstances. In the case of Al Qaeda, the exception was made because, as the newspaper's assistant managing editor explained, the network had been identified by the U.S. government and other countries as a terrorist organization; furthermore, the argument was that some of its members had been convicted as terrorists.[44]

More than two years after 9/11, *Washington Post* ombudsman Michael Getler defended the newspaper's choices with respect to the language of terrorism in response to readers' complaints about bias in the *Post*'s coverage of the Israeli–Palestinian conflict. Getler argued, "Terrorism and terrorist can be useful words, but they are labels. Like all labels, they do not convey much hard information. We should rely first on specific facts, not characterization."[45] He also explained what the *Post* considered differences between different organizations according to their activities and goals as he rejected attempts to equate the "U.S. battle against Al Qaeda with the Israeli battle against Hamas."[46] As Getler put it,

> Hamas conducts terrorism but also has territorial ambitions, is a nationalist movement and conducts some social work. As far as we know, Al Qaeda exists only as a terrorist network. It is composed of radicals from several Islamic countries. The Palestinian resistance is indigenous. Al Qaeda launched a devastating surprise attack on the United States. Israelis and Palestinians have been at war for a long time. Palestinians have been resisting a substantial and, to Palestinians, humiliating, Israeli occupation of the West Bank and Gaza since they were seized in the 1967 war. That resistance has now bred suicide bombers.[47]

Of the four letters to the editor that the *Post* published in response to Getler's op-ed piece, three were critical and one was supportive of

Getler's position, a fact that underlined the vast disagreements in this debate. Most Western news organizations avoided the "T"-word and called nonstate actors that deliberately commit violence against civilians "militants" or "militant groups" or the like and characterized their actions according to the methods used—bombing, rocket attack, kidnapping. But even this did not satisfy all critics who wanted a distinction between organizations that besides perpetrating terrorist acts have other, even legitimate, roles and those exclusively involved in violence. In the midst of the Israeli–Hamas confrontation of late 2008 and early 2009, one critic wrote:

> At present, American papers' reflexive use of the words "militant organization," or some variation thereof, closely mirrors the U.S. government's political stance on Hamas, which is that it's a "terrorist organization." But the phraseology is simply too stark, given the complexity of forces at play in this decades-old conflict.[48]

Downplaying and Emphasizing the "T"-Word

In an interview with the German newsweekly *Der Spiegel*, U.S. Secretary of Homeland Security Janet Napolitano said that avoiding the term *terrorism* in her first appearance before Congress did not mean the absence of a terrorist threat. Rather, she explained,

> although I did not use the word 'terrorism,' I referred to 'man-caused' disasters. That is perhaps only a nuance, but it demonstrates that we want to move away from the politics of fear toward a policy of being prepared for all risks that can occur.[49]

The term *man-made disaster* did not sit well with critics of the administration who noted that President Barack Obama and other administration officials, too, avoided the term *terrorism* and rather spoke of *violent extremism* and instead of *terrorists* about *violent extremists*. Contrary to the Bush administration, they also spoke rarely about the "war on terrorism" or the "global war against terrorism." Former Vice President Richard Cheney and other critics pointed to these linguistic changes to question President Obama's commitment to fighting terrorism. Obviously, language matters in the politics of counterterrorism policies. In early January 2010, when asked by George Stephanopoulos of ABC News for recommendations to tighten aviation security, U.S. Representative Peter King (R-N.Y.) said up front, "I think one main thing would be to—just himself [President Obama] to use the word terrorism more often."[50] Shortly thereafter, in his State of the Union address, the president said pointedly, "Since the day I took office, we've renewed our focus on the terrorists who threaten our nation." In the previous year, he had used the "T"-word sparingly but, contrary to his critics' claims, not avoided it altogether. However, as time went by, the White House and others in the Obama administration as well as European Union agencies preferred to call nonstate political violence against civilians and non-combatants "violent extremism." During his campaign and presidency, Donald Trump spoke often and forcefully of "radical Islamic terrorism" and thus suggested that terrorism and Islam are closely linked. He denied the existence of domestic terrorism carried out by White Supremacists and handcuffed intelligence and counterterrorism communities' efforts to respond to this threat.

In the first-ever "National Strategy for Countering Domestic Terrorism" released by the White House in 2021, political violence by home-grown non-state actors was called consistently "domestic terrorism."[51] However, the document contained also an assessment by the intelligence community that was titled "Assessment of the Domestic Violent Extremism Threat" and throughout used the terms racially and ethnically motivated violent extremism (RMVE). The 2021 intelligent assessment of domestic terrorism by the FBI and Department of Homeland Security refers to two major types of domestic terrorists: Racially or Ethnically Motivated Violent Extremists (RMVEs) and Anti-Government or Anti-Authority Violent Extremists (AGAAVEs) plus sub-groupings.[52] If anything, these alternative terms specifically tailored to domestic terrorism sharpened the different perceptions and treatments of domestic terrorists on the one hand and international terrorists on the other hand.

What Is Violence

While there is no consensus among scholars on the definition of terrorism, it is agreed that terrorism involves acts of violence. When it comes to defining violence, however, we find different explanations as well.

The English Dictionary (online) defines violence as "behavior involving physical force intended to hurt, damage, or kill someone or something." Other definitions transcend the notion that violence is limited to physical force and physical consequences. Philosopher Robert L. Holmes, an expert on nonviolence, put forth the following definition:

Physical violence, which is what we most often have in mind when we speak about violence, is the use of physical force to cause harm, death, or destruction, as in rape, murder, or warfare. But some forms of mental or psychological harm are so severe as to warrant being called violence as well. People can be harmed mentally and emotionally in ways that are as bad as physical violence.[53]

Sociologist Mary R. Jackman defines violence as "actions that inflict, threaten, or cause injury. Actions may be corporal, written, or verbal. Injuries may be corporal, psychological, material, or social."[54] Addressing harmful spoken and written words, Jackman concludes,

> Verbal and written actions that derogate, defame, or humiliate an individual or group may inflict substantial psychological, social, or material injuries without being as conspicuous or flagrant as physical violence.[55]

There are indeed indications that words of hate and threat can cause physical harm besides psychological, social, and material injuries. This is precisely what the legal scholar Mari Matsuda argues, namely, that "violence of the word" can inflict physical injury in that "victims of vicious hate propaganda have experienced physiological symptoms and emotional distress ranging from fear in the gut, rapid pulse rate and difficulty in breathing, nightmares, post-traumatic stress disorder, hypertension, psychosis, and suicide."[56]

Add to this the fact that hate speech can encourage individuals and groups to resort to violent actions against the targets of violent words. Take the example of Dylann Roof who in 2015 shot to death nine African Americans at the end of a Bible study meeting in a Charleston, S.C., church. In his online "manifesto" he described how posted words on White Supremacy websites had awoken his racial awareness and convinced him to move from mere words of violence to actual deeds. He singled out the website of the Council of Conservative Citizens, a White Supremacy organization, as the first and deepest influence on his hatred of African Americans.

Violence can also be carried out by acoustical devices. Long Range Acoustic Devices are utilized by police and military units. In the United States, these devices have been used for crowd control—for example, in Ferguson, Missouri, following the 2014 shooting of Michael Brown, and during protests at the G20 Summit in Pittsburgh, Pennsylvania, in 2009. Targets of acoustic blasts feel sharp pain with the potential for long-term hearing impairment. The military siege of Fallujah in 2004 began by "bombarding the city with music—supposedly, with

(Continued)

(Continued)

Metallica's 'Hells' Bells' and 'Shoot to Thrill' among other things."[57] It does not matter whether music or other sound bombs are deployed. Rather, as Suzanne Cusick notes, "the use of music as a weapon is perceived to be incidental to the use of sound's ability to affect a person's spatial orientation, sense of balance, and physical coordination."[58] Similarly, "no touch torture" that was carried out in U.S.-run prison facilities during the interrogation of terrorists or suspected terrorists included the non-stop playing of super-loud music.

Last but not least, there is visual violence with harmful consequences. Research pioneered by George Gerbner links the prevalence of violence in television news and entertainment to the heightened fear on the part of heavy TV watchers (more than three hours a day) of becoming victims of violence themselves.[59] Pointing to what she calls "media violence" and "entertainment violence" Sissela Bok, too, recognizes a direct relationship between the preponderance of violent visuals in television and motion pictures and "emotional disturbances such as persistent nightmares, depression, irritability, inability to concentrate, and hypervigilance at sounds or motions that might constitute a threat."[60] Research shows also that the multitude of violent screen images can affect heavy TV watchers to respond with heightened aggressiveness or desensitization which can cause some of them to commit violence or consider violence to be the normal state of affairs.

On the day of Halloween 2017, Sayfullo Saipoy drove a truck into pedestrians and cyclists in New York City killing eight persons. When questioned by investigators he claimed that he was inspired to carry out the attack after watching ISIS videos on his cellphone. Indeed, the FBI found 90 videos on one of his phones, among them images of ISIS fighters running over a prisoner with a tank, of beheading scenes, and of Abu Bakr al-Baghdadi, the group's leader. Whether displayed on TV, computer, or smartphone screens violent images seem to have similar effects.

After working for three months as content moderator for Facebook in Berlin, Burcu Gueltekin Punsmann left his job. As he explained,

> I had to quit as I was particularly disturbed by what I saw as signs of professional deformation in me: a kind of hyper vigilance (especially about the risks for my family). I was dreaming about

the job and my own perception of reality shifted in a most concerning way. The terrible Las Vegas Shooting suddenly seemed entirely normal to me.[61]

In conclusion, then, violence can be corporal, written, verbal, acoustical, and visual.

State Terror(ism)

By suggesting a focus on terrorism by nonstate actors, this book does not minimize or excuse the violence perpetrated by governments and their agents against civilians and noncombatants—more often than not in covert ways. Acknowledging that "governments and their agents can practice terrorism" inside their countries or abroad, Crenshaw points out that such "use is usually carefully concealed in order to avoid public attribution of responsibility."[62] Moreover, when committed by governments, violence against civilians and noncombatants can be and has been in many instances equally as brutal and lethal as the actions of nonstate actors and, in fact, far more cruel and deadly. But when governments commit this type of violence, there are a number of appropriate pejorative terms, such as *war crimes, crimes against humanity, human rights violations, genocide, atrocities*—and *terror*. As the linguist Geoffrey Nunberg has noted, "Unlike 'terrorism,' 'terror' can be applied to states as well as to insurgent groups."[63] Bruce Hoffman, too, points to the distinction between *terror* to characterize state violence "mostly against domestic populations" and *terrorism* to describe violence by "nonstate entities."[64]

Post-World War I Germany can serve as an example here. Beginning in the 1920s, well-organized, violent groups of Adolf Hitler's followers attacked political opponents and stirred the political instability that brought him to power in 1933. Clearly, the terrorist tactic (i.e., political violence against civilians by nonstate actors) was successful in this case, as it was in the coming to power of another fascist ruler, Hitler's contemporary Benito Mussolini in Italy. The state of violence during the Hitler years was primarily directed against Jews, who were the victims of genocide, and also against other "undesirable elements," such as communists, socialists, and gypsies. During Hitler's reign of terror, more than 10 million innocent civilians were brutally tortured and killed according to government policies. This was unspeakable state terror, as were the imprisonment and killing of many millions of people in the Soviet Union during Joseph Stalin's rule. More recently, totalitarian regimes in various parts of the world oppressed, persecuted, tortured, and killed thousands, hundreds of thousands, and millions of people within their borders—in Argentina, Cambodia, Uganda, Iraq, Sudan, and many other places. No case of nonstate political violence comes even close to the enormity of these atrocities. To characterize this kind of political violence committed by the power-holders in states as "terrorism" would actually minimize the enormity of systematic political violence and mass killings of civilians by those in control of states.

In his extensive documentation, explanation, and discussion of "death by government," R. J. Rummel, too, does not include state terrorism or government terrorism as definitional concepts, but distinguishes between genocide (the killing of people because of their ethnic, racial, religious, and/or linguistic group membership), "politicide" (the killing of persons because of their "politics or for political purposes"), mass murder or massacre (the indiscriminate killing of persons), and terror (defined as "extrajudicial execution, slaying, assassination, abduction, or disappearance forever of targeted individuals").[65] More important, Rummel comes up with a useful definition of illegitimate state violence ("democide") that includes genocide, politicide, mass murder, terror, and, in addition, what each of these four categories excludes. Thus, the author explains democide as

> the intentional killing of an unarmed or disarmed person by government agents acting in their authoritative capacity and pursuant to government policy or high command (as in the Nazi gassing of Jews)... It is democide if governments promoted or turned a blind eye to these deaths even though they were murders carried out "unofficially" or by private groups (as by death squads in Guatemala or El Salvador). And these deaths also may be democide if high government officials purposely allowed conditions to continue that were causing mass deaths and issued no public warning (as in the Ethiopian famines of the 1970s). All extra-judicial executions or summary executions comprise democide. Even judicial executions may be democide, as in the Soviet show trials of the late 1930s.[66]

So, choosing different definitions is a way to mark the distinction between different perpetrators of deliberate political violence against civilians and noncombatants—one when governments commit this sort of violence (democide, terror), and another when groups or individuals are the perpetrators (terrorism). The decision to use the same word or different terms in itself does not make value judgments and minimize or maximize the seriousness and scope of either state or nonstate political violence. Conceptual differentiation in this particular case offers the opportunity of dealing separately with terrorism (the topic of this book) and state terror or democide (not the topic of this book).

The Meaning of *Terrorism* in This Volume

I agree with Walter Laqueur's suggestion that new and multiple definitions are needed to get a better handle on the distinctive features of different kinds of political violence committed by different types of actors. For the time being, I prefer the distinction between *terror* and *terrorism*. This, then, is my definition of terrorism in the context of this volume:

> *Terrorism is political violence or the threat of violence by groups or individuals who deliberately target civilians or noncombatants in order to influence the behavior and actions of targeted publics and governments.*

Is Terrorism Ever Justified?

Some of the leading political theorists of our time have lined up on sharply opposite sides in arguing against and for the notion of just terrorism. Drawing on his comprehensive work on just and unjust wars Michael Walzer rejects any suggestions that in certain cases terrorism in the sense of political violence against civilians can be justified. Instead, he states categorically, "every act of terrorism is a wrongful act."[67] In order to strengthen his position, Walzer refutes the four most commonly made arguments to justify or excuse nonstate actors' political violence against civilians: (1) that terrorism is a last resort which is only perpetrated when all other options fail; (2) that terrorism is justifiable in case of national liberation movements fighting against mighty states; (3) that unlike other options terrorism does work, does achieve the ends of the perpetrators; and (4) that all politics comes down to terrorism.[68] Similarly, Jürgen Habermas stated shortly after the 9/11 attacks,

> From a moral point of view, there is no excuse for terrorist acts, regardless of the motives or situation under which they are carried out. Nothing justifies our "making allowance for" the murder or suffering of others for one's own purposes. Each murder is one too many.[69]

Habermas pointed to the difference between violence as crime and political tool, and recognized the possibility of terrorists drawing "at least retrospectively, a certain legitimation for their criminal actions, undertaken to overcome a manifestly unjust situation." But he seemed to exclude catastrophic terrorism from the possibility of any such future legitimation when he said, "Today, I cannot imagine a context that would some day, in some manner, make the monstrous crime of September 11 an understandable or comprehensible political act."[70]

Other philosophers in Europe and the United States, such as Jacques Derrida, Ted Honderich, and Noam Chomsky, have rejected definitions and arguments that differentiate between political violence against civilians by nonstate and state actors and between terrorism and war. After her long conversation with Jacques Derrida, Giovanna Borradori revealed, "In Derrida's mind, it is impossible to draw any distinctions regarding terrorism—between war and terrorism, state and nonstate terrorism, terrorism and national liberation movements, national and international terrorism."[71]

Along these lines, Honderich, Chomsky, and other philosophers point to past and present wrongs by the United States and other Western countries that killed and otherwise harmed many civilians in many parts of the world. To rise up in efforts to correct such wrongdoing, they justify certain types of nonstate political violence.

Honderich in particular considers liberation terrorism justified when it is the only means to win freedom from domestic or foreign oppressors. While his major focus is on violence in the Israeli and Palestinian conflict, he extends his arguments in favor of justified terrorism to other groups and settings. With respect to the 9/11 attacks, Honderich made the following statement:

> The wrong done on September 11 is untouched by the weak idea, having to do with our wrongful omissions, that two wrongs make a right or that two wrongs go somewhere towards making a right. Two wrongs do not make a right because the second victim was the first perpetrator—or because the second victim invited that second wrong. The attack of September 11 was wrong, rather, because there could be no certainty or significant probability, no reasonable hope, that it would work to secure a justifying end, but only a certainty that it would destroy lives horribly.[72]

In other words, had there been a chance that the just ends of 9/11 terrorism were achieved or furthered, the catastrophic strikes would be justified. Moving terrorism into the realm of "moral legitimacy" is strongly rejected by Walzer who argues, "Even if American policies in the Middle East and East Asia have been wrong in many ways, they don't excuse the terrorist attack; they don't even make it morally comprehensible. The murder of innocent people is not excusable."[73] But in an afterthought Walzer asks the question whether terrorism could be justified in a "supreme emergency," a concept he discussed earlier with respect to war and deliberate attacks on civilian populations. "It might be [justified terrorism], but only if the oppression to which the terrorists claimed to be responding was genocidal in character," he answers.[74] He adds that "this kind of threat has not been present in any of the recent cases of terrorist activity."[75]

Terrorism Studies, a Field in Search of Theory and Methodology

Terrorism and political violence studies have been criticized for their lack of theory and methodology suited for generalizations and comparative inquiries. The post-9/11 proliferation of terrorism experts, grants, studies, and publications "has not been accompanied by scientific quality and has experienced limited empirical investigation."[76] However, social movement theory, including its attention to contentious politics, could and should be utilized and adapted to study and explain what I define as "terrorism" and Donatella della Porta, a leading scholar in the field, calls "clandestine political violence"—probably a less controversial term than the "T"-word.[77]

Foremost social movement scholars, such as Sidney G. Tarrow, Doug McAdam, and Charles Tilly, have in fact argued "for an integration of social movement studies with the analysis of more violent forms of contention [including terrorism]."[78] To be sure, not all terrorist groups amount to or are part of a larger social movement but at a minimum, they all are staging violent acts of contentious politics. Tilly and Tarrow point out that "contentious politics involves many different forms and combinations of collective action."[79] While studies of both social movements and contentious politics deal overwhelmingly with peaceful collective actions, they include increasingly various forms of violence. That is a welcome opportunity to adapt contentious politics/social movement theory and develop theoretical frameworks for studying and explaining terrorism. While this is not the place to write in great detail about contentious politics and social movement theory, an explanation is needed of those theoretical components that seem most helpful in the context of terrorism studies.

For Tarrow, "contentious politics occurs when ordinary people... join forces in confrontation with elites, authorities, and opponents."[80] Typically, contentious politics are protests against governments and their policies. For contentious collective actions to grow into social movements, such protests must be frequent and backed by organized support groups and cultural symbols that arrive from ideology, grievances, and objectives. Tilly and Wood list the following combination of characteristics that elevate contentious politics to the level of social movements:

- Sustained, organized public efforts making claims on target authorities;
- Combinations of political actions or performances, what they call a repertoire;
- Public representations of WUNC (worthiness, unity, numbers, and commitment).[81]

Political actions here are compared to performances that are drawn from repertoires and staged in theaters or arenas for the benefit of those who are watching—in our times via various media of communication. Interestingly, terrorism scholars, too, have invoked the theater metaphor. According to Brian Jenkins, "terrorism is aimed at the people watching, not the actual victims. Terrorism is theater."[82] And Gabriel Weimann and Conrad Winn wrote perceptively that "modern terrorism can be understood in terms of the productions requirements of theatrical engagements."[83] No wonder, then, that Donatella della Porta suggests that "some explanation of violence [including clandestine political violence or terrorism] can be derived from their [social movement scholars'] research on repertoires of protest."[84] Applied to terrorism, the repertoire perspective strengthens with the inclusion of the suggested WUNC representations since all four types figure prominently in the explanation of terrorism as communicative act. Social movements, whether nonviolent or violent, require publicity and most try to stage mass-mediated events to propagate the worthiness of their motives and strength through unity, numbers, and commitment to their causes. The terrorist repertoire of performances and related publicity efforts are discussed in some detail in Chapters 14 and 15. While these repertoires of performances are central to the framing and self-framing of social movements, including those of the terrorist variety, two other perspectives in social movement theory—political opportunities and mobilizing resources—are utilized to examine expressions of political contention. In their efforts to bring theoretical frameworks into terrorism studies, several scholars have suggested borrowing from those social movement foci and linking macro-, mesa-, and micro-levels. As della Porta explains,

> They [macro-, mesa-, and micro-levels] address one of three questions: In what type of society is political violence most likely to develop—that is, what environmental conditions foster political violence? Which groups are most likely to use violent repertoires— that is, which characteristics of political organizations eventually lead them to adopt the most extreme forms of political violence? Which individuals are most likely to resort to political violence?[85]

To put it differently, there are three distinct levels in terrorism studies: (1) the larger environmental conditions, whether local, national, or transnational; (2) the dynamics within groups and movements, including organizational forms, resources, and ideology; and (3) membership, leadership, gender, roles, and cohesion.

Whenever possible I will pay attention to these levels of inquiry throughout the book.

Notes

1 Mark Berman, "Was the Charlottesville Car Attack Domestic Terrorism, a Hate Crime or Both?" *Washington Post*, August 14, 2017, https://search.yahoo.com/search?p=stabbing+attack+New+York+city&fr=yfp-t&fp=1&t oggle=1&cop=mss&ei=UTF-8, accessed January 15, 2018.
2 "Biden calls Buffalo mass shooting act of 'domestic terrorism'," *Yahoo News*, May 17, 2022, https://news.yahoo.com/biden-calls-buffalo-mass-shooting-171232967.html?fr=sycsrp_catchall, accessed May 27, 2022.
3 From "The Public Papers of the President, Administration of William J. Clinton," 1998, 2124.
4 For the most authoritative book on McVeigh, see Lou Michel and Dan Herbeck, *American Terrorist: Timothy McVeigh and the Oklahoma City Bombing* (New York: Regan Books, 2001).
5 Alex Houen, *Terrorism and Modern Literature: From Joseph Conrad to Ciaran Carson* (New York: Oxford University Press, 2002), 9.
6 A. Odasuo Alali and Kenoye Kelvin Eke, eds., *Media Coverage of Terrorism: Methods of Diffusion* (Newbury Park, CA: Sage, 1991), 30.
7 Martha Crenshaw, ed., *Terrorism in Context* (University Park: Pennsylvania State University Press, 1995), 7.
8 Richard E. Rubenstein, *Alchemists of Revolution* (New York: Basic Books, 1987), 17, 18.
9 James J. F. Forest, "Criminals and Terrorists: An Introduction to the Special Issue," *Terrorism and Political Violence* 24 (2) (2012), p. 173.
10 The words were part of Yousef's statement before he was sentenced by Judge Kevin Thomas Duffy of the Federal District Court in Manhattan on January 8, 1998. See, "Excerpts from Statements in Court," *New York Times*, January 8, 1998, B4.
11 Bruce Hoffman, *Inside Terrorism* (New York: Columbia University Press, 1998), 28–29.
12 The distinction between terrorism "from above" and "from below" is made in Walter Laqueur, *A History of Terrorism* (New Brunswick, NJ: Transaction Publishers, 2002), ch. 1; and Walter Laqueur, *The Age of Terrorism* (Boston, MA: Little, Brown, 1987), ch. 1.
13 Rubenstein, 17.
14 Crenshaw, 4.
15 Shoe bomber Reid and Judge Young were quoted in Pam Belluck, "Threats and Responses: The Shoe Plot: Unrepentant Shoe Bomber Sentenced to Life," *New York Times*, January 31, 2003, A13; and Thanassis Cambanis, "Sentenced to Life, Reid Denounces US," *Boston Globe*, January 31, 2003, A1.
16 See, for example, W. Lance Bennett, *News: The Politics of Illusion* (New York: Longman, 2001); and Brigitte L. Nacos, *Mass-Mediated Terrorism: The Centrality of the Media in Terrorism and Counterterrorism* (Lanham, MD: Rowman & Littlefield, 2002), especially ch. 5.
17 Edward Herman and Gerry O'Sullivan, *The Terrorism Industry: The Experts and Institutions That Shape Our View of Terror* (New York: Pantheon Books, 1989).
18 "Statement for the Record of Dale L. Watson Executive Assistant Director Counterterrorism and Counterintelligence Federal Bureau of Investigation on the Terrorist Threat Confronting the United States before the Senate Select Committee on Intelligence Washington DC," February 6, 2002.
19 Houen, 7–8. Houen writes that individual governments have been "swift to ratify their own definitions" but that the international dimensions of 9/11

kept the definitional problem alive. But disagreements over the definition of political violence continue to exist with respect to both domestic and international terrorism.

20 This definition was mentioned in Oliver Libaw, "Defining Terrorism: Little Agreement on Where to Draw the Line," abcnews.go.com/sections/world/dailynews/stratfor001117.html, October 11, 2001.

21 This new definition of terrorism in general and FEMA's definitions of domestic and international terrorism were available on FEMA's website, www.fema.gov/hazards/terrorism/terror.shtm, accessed January 12, 2003.

22 The definitions are contained in many FBI documents and statements; see, for example, "Statement for the Record of Dale L. Watson."

23 Jessica Stern, "The Protean Enemy," *Foreign Affairs* (July–August 2003), p. 34.

24 For more extensive excerpts from the interview, see www.memri.org/report/en/0/0/0/0/0/0/4202.htm, accessed May 25, 2010.

25 From ISIS's online magazine Dabiq, issue 4, page 9.

26 The text of "The Great Replacement" is available at https://www.leftyliars.com/wp-content/uploads/2019/08/the-great-replacement.pdf, accessed September 14, 2022.

27 Peyton Gendron's manifesto is available at https://www.debarelli.com/post/payton-gendron-manifesto, accessed September 14, 2022.

28 For details on the U.S. military's involvement in Lebanon, see David C. Martin and John Walcott, *Best Laid Plans* (New York: Harper & Row, 1988), chs. 5 and 6.

29 Hoffman, 43.

30 Herman and O'Sullivan, 214.

31 The definition is quoted by Hoffman, 38.

32 C. J. M. Drake, "The Role of Ideology in Terrorists' Target Selection," *Terrorism and Political Violence* 10 (2) (Summer 1998), p. 53.

33 Michael Stohl, "Characteristics of Contemporary International Terrorism," in Charles W. Kegley Jr., ed., *International Terrorism: Characteristics, Causes, Controls* (New York: St. Martin's, 1990), 83.

34 Ibid.

35 The definition was quoted by the UN Office on Drugs and Crime on its website, www.unodc.org, accessed January 7, 2003.

36 Contained in GA Res. 51/210, "Measures to Eliminate International Terrorism," as excerpted by www.unodc.org.

37 For more on the failure to reach an agreement at the UN after 9/11, see Michael Jordan, "Terrorism's Slippery Definition Eludes UN Diplomats," *Christian Science Monitor* (February 4, 2002), p. 7.

38 Associated Press, "Muslim Meeting Won't Define Terror," *New York Times*, April 3, 2002.

39 Walter Laqueur, *The New Terrorism* (New York: Oxford University Press, 1999), 6.

40 The definition is quoted by Hoffman, 33.

41 Robert G. Picard and Paul D. Adams, "Characterizations of Acts and Perpetrators of Political Violence in Three Elite U.S. Daily Newspapers," in Alali and Eke, 12–21. The content analysis covered pertinent news coverage from 1980 through 1985.

42 Cited by John O'Sullivan, "Retracting Required," *National Review*, September 25, 2001, www.nationalreview.com/jos/jos092501.shtml, accessed January 12, 2002; and Norman Solomon, "Media Spin Revolved around the Word 'Terrorist'," *Media Beat*, October 4, 2001, www.fair.org/media-beat/o11004.html, accessed January 9, 2003.

43 Cited by O'Sullivan.
44 Lou Gelfand, "Newspaper Careful in Use of Label 'Terrorist'," *Star Tribune*, February 3, 2002, 27A. See also "'Terrorism' Is a Term that Requires Consistency: Newspaper and Its Critics Both Show a Double Standard on 'Terror,'" *Fairness and Accuracy in Reporting*, April 8, 2002, www.fair.org/press-release/terrorism.html, accessed January 4, 2003.
45 Michael Getler, "The Language of Terrorism," *Washington Post*, September 21, 2003, B6.
46 Ibid.
47 Ibid.
48 Katia Bachko, "War of Words," *Columbia Journalism Review* (Online), January 8, 2009. See www.cjr.org/campaign_desk/war_of_the_words.php, accessed January 11, 2009.
49 "Away from the Politics of Fear," *Der Spiegel*, March 16, 2010, www.spiegel.de/international/world/0,1518,613330,00.html, accessed May 25, 2010.
50 Ben Smith, "King: Use Word 'Terrorism' More," www.politico.com/blogs/bensmith/0110/King_Use_word_terrorism_more.html?showall, accessed May 12, 2010.
51 The document is available at https://www.whitehouse.gov/wp-content/uploads/2021/06/National-Strategy-for-Countering-Domestic-Terrorism.pdf, accessed May 22, 2022.
52 The text of the document is available at https://www.lawfareblog.com/fbi-and-dhs-release-strategic-intelligence-assessment-and-data-domestic-terrorism#:~:text=On%20May%2014%2C%20the%20FBI%20and%20the%20Department,You%20can%20read%20the%20report%20here%20and%20below%3A, accessed May 27, 2022.
53 Robert L. Holmes, *Nonviolence in Theory and Practice* (Belmont, CA: Wadsworth, 1990), 1–2.
54 Mary R. Jackson, "Violence in Social Life," *Annual Review of Sociology* 28 (2002), p. 405.
55 Ibid., 396.
56 Mari J. Matsuda, "Public Response to Racist Speech: Considering the Victim's Story," *Michigan Law Review* 87 (24) (1989), pp. 2320, 2336.
57 Suzanne G. Cusick, "Music as Torture/Music as Weapon," available at http://www.sibetrans.com/trans/articulo/152/music-as-torture-, accessed January 18, 2018.
58 Ibid.
59 George Gerbner et al., "The 'Mainstreaming' of America: Violence Profile No. 11, *Journal of Communication* 30 (3) (Summer 1980).
60 Sissela Bok, *Mayhem: Violence as Public Entertainment* (Reading, MA: Perseus Books, 1998), 65.
61 Burco Gueltekin Punsmann, "Three Months in Hell," *Sueddeutsche Zeitung*, January 6, 2018, https://sz-magazin.sueddeutsche.de/internet/three-months-in-hell-84381, accessed March 5, 2018.
62 Crenshaw, 4.
63 Geoffrey Nunberg, "How Much Wallop Can a Simple Word Pack?" *New York Times*, July 11, 2004, sec. 4, 7.
64 Hoffman, 25.
65 R. J. Rummel, *Death by Government*, ch. 2, www.hawaii.edu/powerkills/welcome.html. Rummel's website offers a great deal of information about cases in which governments systematically and intentionally killed large numbers of people inside and outside their own borders.
66 Ibid.

67 Michael Walzer, *Arguing About War* (New Haven, CT: Yale University Press, 2004), 52.
68 Walzer, 53–60.
69 Citation taken from Giovanna Borradori, *Philosophy in a Time of Terror: Dialogues with Jürgen Habermas and Jacques Derrida* (Chicago, IL: University Press of Chicago, 2003), 34.
70 Ibid.
71 Borradori, 153.
72 Ted Honderich, "After the Terror: A Book and Further Thoughts," *Journal of Ethics* 7 (2003): 175.
73 Walzer, 135.
74 Walzer, 54.
75 Ibid.
76 Donatella della Porta, *Clandestine Political Violence* (New York: Cambridge University Press, 2013), 11.
77 As the above note shows, "clandestine political violence" is the title of her book.
78 Sidney G. Tarrow, *Power in Movement: Social Movements and Contentious Politics* (New York: Cambridge University Press, 2011), xvii.
79 Charles Tilly and Sidney Tarrow, *Contentious Politics* (New York: Oxford University Press, 2007), 27.
80 Tarrow, 6.
81 Charles Tilly and Lesley J. Wood, *Social Movements*, 2nd ed. (Boulder, CO: Paradigm, 2009), 3–4.
82 Brian M. Jenkins, "International Terrorism: A New Kind of Warfare" (Santa Monica, CA: Rand Corporation, 1974), 6.
83 Gabriel Weimann and Conrad Winn, *The Theater of Terror: Mass Media and International Terrorism* (New York: Longman, 1994), 52.
84 Della Porta, 15.
85 Della Porta, 21. In her excellent book *Clandestine Political Violence* Donatella della Porta developed her three-pronged model of "mechanisms in the evolution of clandestine political violence" that distinguish between "Onset," "Persistence," and "Exit" phases in the life of terrorist networks and movements. Interestingly, she is able to utilize the same model for her study of left-wing and right-wing terrorism in Italy and Germany during the 1970s and 1980s; Basque ethno-nationalist terrorism in Spain during the same time period; and religious terrorism (Al Qaeda).

3 A Historical Review of Terrorism

On June 3, 2017, around 10:00 p.m., a van was driven in high speed into pedestrians on London Bridge before crashing into a pub at the end of the iconic London Bridge. The van's occupants jumped out of the vehicle. With pink steak knives taped to their wrists they stabbed people in and around restaurants in this crowded area. "This is for Allah," they screamed repeatedly. Within eight minutes, the attackers killed eight persons and injured 48 others. Home Secretary Amber Rudd called the killers "radical Islamic terrorists." The Islamic State of Iraq and Syria claimed that all three were ISIS fighters. As always in the aftermath of such deadly attacks breaking news around the world reported the incident extensively including the perpetrators' most important message: "This is for Allah." They wanted the world to know that they had killed in the name of their God. Five years after the attack, a Google search for "London Bridge and this is for Allah" resulted in more than 3.7 million results.

Almost two millennia earlier, members of the Sicarii sect attacked fellow-Jews who collaborated or tolerated Roman rule in Palestine. They acted mostly in crowded places, stabbed their targets with short daggers, and disappeared in the terrified crowds. One terrorism expert noted that the Sicarii wanted "to demonstrate that not even the most sacred occasions could provide immunity" to their enemies.[1] The religious extremists rejected "human leadership" because their credo was that "God is the only ruler."[2] The Jewish utopia they sought in the first century AD was very similar to ISIS's quest for their only authentic Islamic community ruled by their interpretation of the Koran in the twenty-first century.

I wrote the opening paragraphs of this chapter in order to emphasize the similarities of terrorists' motivations and tactics in the long history of terrorism. What changed over time were the environments in which terrorists operated—most of all brought about by technological advances that improved the connectivity of terrorist organizations, the reach of their propaganda, and the lethality of their weapons. The London Bridge ISIS-adherents had smartphones to plot their attack and used an automobile as deadly weapon—both not available to the Sicarii and other early terrorist groups.

DOI: 10.4324/9781003289265-4

In some historical accounts of terrorism, the Sicarii and Zealots are described as contemporaries fighting to liberate Palestine from Roman occupation. They did join forces with other anti-Roman factions to fight the occupiers. But they also had distinctly different motives, targets, and goals. Whereas the Sicarii often attacked Jewish establishment leaders and aimed for a purely religious community, the Zealots targeted Romans and "sought democratic rule, were opposed the priestly aristocracy, and did not maintain any 'philosophic' approach, as did the Sicarii."[3] After their short-lived success against the Roman military, the leader of the Sicarii was assassinated by rival Jewish factions and hundreds of Zealots committed mass-suicide rather than surrender to the victorious Romans.

Far more enduring than the Sicariis and Zealots were the Assassins (eleventh to thirteenth centuries), an extremist offshoot of the Ismaili branch of Shi'ite Islam, who were active in Persia (now Iran) and Syria. Hassan-i-Sabbah, the founder of this fiercely anti-Sunni sect, was poised to spread his brand of Ismaili Islam throughout the Middle East and defeat the Sunni rulers. He convinced his fanatically devoted followers that actively fighting for their cause would assure them a place in paradise. Recognizing that their membership was too small to fight their enemies openly, the Assassins operated clandestinely until the assigned member or members attacked a prominent leader—typically in front of large crowds. They assaulted their targets with daggers and made no attempt to escape but seemed content, even eager, to be caught and killed after they had accomplished their lethal missions. Thus, in today's parlance, the Assassins practiced a form of "suicide terrorism."

Rumor had it that the Assassins were under the influence of hashish when they envisioned paradise, when they attacked their targets, and when they went eagerly to their death. Indeed, because of the myth of their wide use of hashish, the members of the sect were called *hashishin* in Arabic; this name turned into "assassin" in the vocabulary of the Christian Crusaders and eventually came to mean political murder in many Western languages. The Assassins did not realize their religious and political goals but were wiped out when the Mongols conquered Iran and Syria in the middle of the thirteenth century. Nevertheless, as one terrorism expert pointed out, the Assassins "demonstrated a basic principle of contemporary terrorism: the ability of small groups to wage effective campaigns of terror against much stronger opponents."[4]

The Thugs, who organized in the eleventh century, terrorized India for hundreds of years before the British destroyed them in the nineteenth century. They targeted travelers and strangled their victims with a silk tie before robbing them. It was rumored that the Thugs worshiped the goddess Kali and nourished her with the blood of their victims. To this day, there is no answer to the question of whether the Thugs committed religiously motivated terrorism or were bandits out for material gains.

One way or the other, today the term *thug* characterizes a hoodlum, crook, thief—in other words, a criminal.

Beginning in the Middle Ages, Christian sects also resorted to violence. Typically following a charismatic leader or prophet, they claimed to fight for the purification of the Christian religion and Christian life. Their targets were Jews and whoever they considered Christians in name only. Following the Reformation, for example, the Anabaptists, a millennial sect, emerged in Germany. Members of the group considered the city of Muenster as the true Jerusalem and themselves as God's chosen instruments in the violent campaign against the anti-Christ—sinful Catholics and Protestants who stood in the way of the millennium.

No doubt, then, that terrorism originated with religious and pseudo-religious sects whose adherents, among them the Christians, Jews, and Muslims, justified their violence with their religious beliefs and perceived obligations. As the above examples of early political violence by groups show, terrorism has been used as weapon of the weak against militarily, politically, religiously, and economically stronger power-holders for a long time and in different parts of the world.

Interestingly, most terrorism scholars agree with Walter Laqueur's suggestion that "systematic terrorism begins in the second half of the nineteenth century..."[5] David C. Rapoport placed the beginning of the first of four waves of terrorism into the 1880s.[6] And for Tom Parker and Nick Sitter "[modern] terrorism has its origins...in the mid-nineteenth century"—some decades earlier than Rapoport's first wave.[7] There are multiple reasons for pointing to the second half of the nineteenth century as the advent of modern political violence from below. Rapoport, Parker and Sitter, and other experts in the field agree that not only the revolutionary ferment in Europe during this time but also significant technological advances in communication and transportation contributed to the quite rapid spread of challenging ideas far beyond limited areas into the international arena.

But the widely accepted starting time omits some interesting cases from historical review and categorization in Rapoport's Four Waves theory or Parker and Sitter's Four Strains concept. The political violence carried out by the Sons of Liberty in the run-up to the American War of Independence against the British in the second half of the eighteenth century was a case in point as were the attacks on immigrant newcomers by nativist extremists starting in the 1840s and reaching into the 1850s. Both of these movements were involved in political violence.

The Sons of Liberty: Historians tend to characterize frequent attacks by colonialists against British soldiers, administrators, and colonial loyalists to the crown as mob violence. The terms terrorism and terrorist did not yet exist at the time. While a good number of these attacks were indeed spontaneous actions of outrage, many others were meticulously planned and staged for the best possible propaganda effects. In sharp opposition to the Stamp Act of 1765 that laid taxes on all printed material, a group of influential men in Boston formed a secret group, the Sons of Liberty (1765–76) which was led by Samuel ("Sam") Adams. Similar groups were organized in towns and counties in all colonies. It is telling that two centuries after the Sons of Liberty functioned as a covert cell system, the White Supremacist Louis Beam praised this early organizational design as model for "leaderless resistance" that he considered superior to a hierarchical form.

A network of Committees of Correspondence that circulated subversive propaganda in form of speeches and printed pamphlets was the glue that held the autonomous cells together in their effort to stir the anti-British sentiments in the colonies. The inner circle of the movement staged events to showcase colonists' fearless resistance to the British with the Boston Tea Party of 1773 the most iconic of all. In response to the Tea Act that laid taxes on imported tea, a well-organized group of men boarded vessels of the East Indian Company in Boston Harbor casting 342 chests of tea into the water. Ashore, a huge crowd had gathered to witness the spectacle that they expected thanks to underground propaganda pushed by the Sons of Liberty. About 200 years later, Sam Adams, who orchestrated this event, was celebrated as originator of modern-day public relations.[8]

But aside from staging publicity stunts and spreading propaganda, the Sons of Liberty and the mobs they inspired and carried out many violent acts against civilians and non-combatants for political objectives.

Nativists against Immigrants: Beginning in the 1830s, in reaction to a large influx of Catholic immigrants from Europe, leading American nativists publicized metaphorical calls to arms. As depicted in Martin Scorsese's 2002 motion picture "Gangs of New York," anti-immigration nativist gangs in New York took those calls literally and engaged in a bloody street war against Irish Catholic immigrants. The movie's nativist gangster-in-chief Butcher Bill Cutting was modeled after Bill Poole, known as "Bill the Butcher," the leader of the Bowery Boys gang. In his review of the film, William J. Stern (2003) wrote that the nativists of that era "included among their number some of America's elite leaders and thinkers."[9] Samuel F. B. Morse, the inventor of the telegraph and the Morse code, was a well-known and influential member of those elite leaders and thinkers. In his columns in the *New York Observer* that he wrote under the pseudonym Brutus, he warned fellow-Americans that the wave of Catholic immigrants was the first step in a conspiracy of leading Europeans to prepare for the Pope's eventual dominance of America. "Popery is the antagonist to our free system," he wrote. "No one can doubt that the unusual efforts of despotic foreign governments to spread Popery in the United States has for its principal design the subversion of our republican institutions."[10] Morse, "laid the foundation for decades of American nativism that would follow."[11] He influenced the birth of two nativist groups, The Order of Native Americans and The Order of the Star-spangled Banner, the pillars of the later Know Nothing Party.

Extremists in the nativist movement attacked Catholic immigrants, most of them of Irish and German descent, in the North and South and often in efforts to prevent the newcomers from voting in local, state, and federal elections. For example, when the so-called Native American Party, the forerunner of the Know Nothing Party, staged in 1844 marches and parades in Philadelphia, this resulted in violent riots that lasted several months. Catholic churches and the homes of Catholic immigrants were burned down and an unknown number of people were killed and injured. On August 6, 1855, nativists associated with the Know Nothings prevented voters in German Catholic neighborhoods of Louisville, Kentucky, from casting their votes. In the following street clashes the well-armed natives attacked immigrants relentlessly. Around 20 persons were killed, many more injured, and a multitude of buildings were burned to the ground. The day is remembered as "Bloody Monday."

Both the ideas and deeds of the eighteenth century's Sons of Liberty and the nineteenth century's Nativists became ingrained in the fabric of America's tradition resurfacing at some times and diminishing at other times. Para-military groups in the United States have long identified with the patriotism and glorified the violent tactics of the Sons of Liberty and racially, ethnically, and religiously motivated violent extremists have long displayed the same resentments of immigrants as the eighteenth-century nativist movements. Both types of violent extremism had strong revivals in the twenty-first century (see next chapter).

The Dominant Types of Modern Terrorism

Following 9/11 that resulted in an increased expert and public interest in terrorism, David C. Rapoport's Four Waves concept became an influential framework for exploring and explaining nonstate political violence in the modern era. Rapoport distinguished between the Anarchist (1880s–1920s), Anti-Colonial (1920s–1960s), New Left (late 1960s–1990s), and Religious Wave (1979 and ongoing at the time, when he published his theory after 9/11). With the exception of a decade-long overlap of the New Left and Religious Waves, Rapoport put these four types into distinct time periods lasting 40–45 years with the New Left a bit shorter.[12]

While the Four Waves theory captured major terrorist movements and groups during the pinpointed time periods, it failed to accommodate groups that preceded waves or lasted through or even emerged during subsequent waves. For this reason, Tom Parker and Nick Sitter put forth an alternative concept distinguishing between Four Strains of terrorism starting in the nineteenth century: Nationalist, Socialist, Religious, and Social Exclusion terrorism, the latter category including groups such as the Ku Klux Klan and twentieth-century fascist movements' violent wings before coming to power.[13]

While Parker and Sitter include "lone wolf" terrorism in the Social Exclusion category, lone or solo terrorist actors were and continue to be radicalized by socialist, nationalist, religious, and social exclusion types of groups and ideologies. And while there were in the past individuals acting on the extreme ideas of groups and movements, the number of solo actors perpetrating major acts of terrorism has significantly increased in the last decades and will be addressed in the next chapter.

Utilizing both waves and strains theories I will discuss in the next sections the history of socialist/revolutionary/anarchist; nationalist/anti-colonial/separatist; religious; and social exclusion terrorism with the awareness that a number of movements/organizations of the past fit into more than one category. Chapter 4 on the contemporary landscape of terrorism will include a discussion of the state of twenty-first-century social exclusion terrorism and a number of outliers that do not fit the waves and strains theories.

Revolutionary, Anarchist, Socialist Terrorism

The Early Revolutionary and Anarchist Phase: Radical socialists and anarchists contributed to the theoretical underpinnings of a philosophy of violence as a means to fight and destroy oppressive leaders and governments. In 1849, a journal in Switzerland that was edited by political refugees from Germany published a radical tract under the headline "Der Mord" (Murder), in which its author, Karl Heinzen, laid out the rationale for terrorist action against "reactionaries" and "the mass party of the barbarians." Accusing the people in power of "mass murder, organized murder, or war, as it is called," he concluded,

> Even if we have to blow up half a continent or spill a sea of blood, in order to finish off the barbarian party, we should have no scruples about doing it. The man who would not joyfully give up his own life for the satisfaction of putting a million barbarians into their coffins carries no Republican heart within his breast.[14]

Heinzen advocated murder for political ends, or what soon thereafter was defined as terrorism, even if that meant death for members of what he called "the party of freedom." He anticipated the development of weapons that would make political violence "from below" far more lethal and effective when he wrote, "The greatest benefactor of mankind will be he who makes it possible for a few men to wipe out thousands."[15] One hundred and fifty years later, Osama bin Laden and the Al Qaeda organization embraced the same idea when they searched for weapons of mass destruction.

In Russia, Sergey Nechaev, Nikolai Morozov, Peter Kropotkin, and Michael Bakunin were among the most influential leaders who justified terrorist means in their writings and prescribed rules of conduct for the true revolutionary to follow. The terms *revolutionary* and *terrorist* were used interchangeably. The anarchist movement was truly international; the tracts of its leaders were read by radicals in Western Europe and North America but also in Latin America and Asia. Leading figures traveled widely, if only because they had to flee their homelands and secondary homes in order to prevent arrests. For example, Bakunin, after being imprisoned for six years in St. Petersburg and exiled to Siberia, fled to London, lived for a time in San Francisco and New York before returning to Europe propagating his revolutionary ideas from places in Switzerland and Italy. In France, Pierre-Joseph Proudhon was a radical propagandist and the first who called himself "anarchist." In a strange contradiction that he defended Proudhon stated that "property is theft" but also "property is freedom."[16]

During this era, the most feared and most admired terrorist-revolutionary organization in Russia was the Narodnaya Volga (The People's Will) because it made the step from radical rhetoric to actual terrorist acts, which included the assassination of Czar Alexander II in 1881. During the following decades, anarchists were responsible for a wave of political assassinations in several countries, among them Russia, France, Spain, and Italy. The anarchists of this era did not strike randomly but targeted high-ranking political figures, among them French President Sadi Carnot, Spanish Prime Minister Antonio Canovas, King Umberto of Italy, Empress Elisabeth of Austria, and U.S. Presidents James Garfield and William McKinley. Sometimes, anarchists aborted their assassination plans because they did not want to harm innocent bystanders. Attempts on the lives of other prominent figures, among them the German Chancellor Otto von Bismarck and the German Emperor William II, failed. But, as Laqueur has pointed out, "Inasmuch as the assassins were anarchists…they all acted on their own initiative without the knowledge and support of the groups to which they belonged."[17]

On September 6, 1901, while visiting the Pan-American Exposition in Buffalo, New York, President William McKinley was shot by an assassin and so severely wounded that he died soon thereafter. The perpetrator was caught at the scene of the attack and identified as Leon Czolgosz of Cleveland, a self-described anarchist and disciple of Emma Goldman, whose writings and speeches were well known in anarchist circles and who Czolgosz had met once. Although Goldman was arrested in Chicago as a suspected accomplice, she was soon released and never charged. However, John Most, the founder of the anarchist newspaper *Freiheit*, was charged and convicted for publishing an anarchist article and thereby committing "an act endangering the peace and outraging public decency."[18] The article was a reprint of Karl Heinzen's 50-year-old essay

"Murder," which justified terrorism and had appeared in the September 7 issue of the *Freiheit*—just one day after Czolgosz shot the president. Although the defense claimed that no copy had been sold, the judge ruled against Most and stated in his opinion,

> It is in the power of words that is the potent force to commit crimes and offenses in certain cases. No more striking illustration of the criminal power of words could be given, if we are to believe the murderer of our President, than that event presents. The assassin declares that he was instigated and stimulated to consummate his foul deed by the teachings of Emma Goldman.
>
> It is impossible to read the whole article [authored by Heinzen] without assuming that his doctrine claims that all rulers are enemies of mankind, and are to be hunted and destroyed through "blood and iron, poison and dynamite."
>
> It [the article] shows a deliberate intent to inculcate and promulgate the doctrine of the article. This we hold to be a criminal act.[19]

This was a remarkable ruling in that it made a direct connection between inflammatory words and illegal actions. Years before McKinley's violent death, Most and Goldman had coauthored an article that gave a nod of approval to violence; they wrote, "It cannot and it shall not be denied that most Anarchists feel convinced that 'violence' is not anymore reprehensible toward carrying out their designs than it is when used by an oppressed people to obtain freedom."[20] However, after McKinley's death, Goldman insisted that "Anarchy did not teach men to do the act for which Czolgosz is under arrest."[21]

In the decades preceding McKinley's assassination, labor union members were involved in violent clashes with plant managers over wages and working conditions. In many of these bitter conflicts, mine operators and foremen were killed by workers, and workers were murdered by company-hired guards and soldiers. The Molly Maguires, allegedly an Irish terrorist group, fought employers during bitter disputes in the coal mines of Pennsylvania. At times, anarchists got involved in this kind of violence. In 1892, for example, Alexander Berkman, a young anarchist, attempted to kill Henry C. Frick of the Carnegie Company because of Frick's position on striking workers. Berkman's deed divided the anarchist movement in that "[John] Most, in *Freiheit*, denounced him, while Emma Goldman in the *Anarchist* came to his defense."[22]

Although anarchists were far from popular before President McKinley's death, they became the targets of public outrage, threats, and violence afterward. In this climate, "Mobs forced dozens of anarchists to flee their homes and tried to wreck, in one case successfully, the offices of anarchist publications. Without warrants the police arrested scores, perhaps hundreds."[23] The "war on anarchists" continued for years. During this period, President Theodore Roosevelt ordered the establishment of a federal detective agency that became the forerunner of the FBI. Roosevelt pressed for increasingly tough measures in the fight against the anarchist danger. Addressing both chambers of Congress in 1908, he said,

> When compared with the suppression of anarchy, every other question sinks into insignificance. The anarchist is the enemy of humanity, the enemy of all mankind, and his is a deeper degree of criminality than any other. No immigrant is allowed to our shores if he is an anarchist, and no paper published here or abroad should be permitted circulation in this country if it propagates anarchist propaganda.[24]

Given these strong sentiments, anarchists were suspected and accused of violent deeds they had not committed but perhaps influenced by their radical propaganda. In 1910, when dynamite exploded in the building of the *Los Angeles Times*, killing 21 unorganized workers, newspaper owner Harrison Otis published an editorial that blamed "anarchist scum" for the act of terrorism.[25] Eventually, John McNamara, a union official, and his brother James were indicted, tried, and sentenced for the bombing of the *Times*.

In spite of the anti-anarchist climate, in the second half of the twentieth century, the Italian immigrant and anarchist Luigi Galleani organized the most cohesive and most violent anarchist group in the United States. Galleani was a gifted orator and writer. His newspaper *Cronica Sovversiva* (Subversive Chronicle) had merely a circulation of a few thousand exemplars but was according to one student of anarchism "one of the most important ...in the history of the anarchist movement" reaching Italian radicals not only throughout the United States but also in Europe, South America, North Africa, and Australia.[26] According to Paul Avrich, a foremost expert of anarchism, Galleani was "a zealot" who "preached a militant form of anarchism which advocated the overthrow of capitalism and government by violent means, dynamite and assassination not excluded."[27] He had thousands of devoted supporters in the United States, most of them manual laborers. Like their idol Luigi Galleani, they believed in the "propaganda of deed," meaning committing violence in order to get publicity for their cause.

From 1914 to 1920 Galleanistis unleashed an unprecedented bombing campaign that began with a failed attempt to harm John D. Rockefeller on his estate in Tarrytown, NY, and ended with a bombing of Wall Street in 1920 that killed 38 persons and injured many more. In between, members of the groups send many dozens of letters and package bombs to public officials who had interfered with the publication of *Cronica Sovversiva* or were involved in arresting and prosecuting Galleanistis. The fear of communism and subversive elements within the country was high toward the end of the decade. Thus, when one of another series of simultaneous bombings hit the house of U.S. Attorney General Mitchell Palmer, the Department of Justice responded with several raids, the so-called Palmer Raids, that led to the arrests of thousands of suspected communists and socialists, foremost among them alleged Italian anarchists. Among the more than 500 non-citizens, who were deported was Luigi Galleani. Strangely, whereas John Most and Emma Goldman became household words in the American history of the radical Left, Galleani's forced departure from American shores remained "virtually unknown in the United States outside a small circle of scholars and a number of personal associates and disciples."[28]

The New Left Phase: It was not until the latter part of the 1960s that leftists in the United States once again embraced terrorist methods to further their political ends. Just like similar groups in Latin America, Europe, and Asia, young Americans, most of them students, organized to bring about revolution and the defeat of capitalism and imperialism. In the late nineteenth and early twentieth centuries, the original anarchists and social reformers in the United States were long on terrorist theory and short on actual violence, and to the extent that terrorism was traced to anarchism, the perpetrators were typically individuals not directly associated with organized groups—except for the Galleanistis. In contrast, the self-declared revolutionary groups of the 1960s and 1970s practiced what they preached. The Weathermen, later renamed as Weather Underground to signify the prominent roles of women in the organization, was the best known among the white terrorist groups of this era. An offshoot of the Students for a Democratic Society, the founders took their name and the title of their first manifesto, "You don't need a weatherman to tell you which way the wind blows," from the lyrics of a Bob Dylan song. Their radicalism was driven by their opposition to the Vietnam War and to racial inequality in the United States. Shortly after organizing themselves in early 1969, the Weathermen began a campaign of agitation in Chicago during what they called "Days of Rage," causing riots and clashes with the police. By 1970, disappointed that they had been unsuccessful in winning over the working class to their cause, the core of the group went underground as a revolutionary vanguard and began a terrorist campaign against public and private institutional cornerstones of the existing political and economic order. The Weather Underground learned from the strategies and tactics of other guerrilla groups, According to Parker and Sitter, Bernardine Dohrn, a prominent member of the Weather Underground, wrote in one of the group's declarations, "Now we are adapting the classic guerrilla strategy of the Viet Cong and the urban guerrilla strategy of the Tupamaros to our own situation here in the most technically advanced country in the world."[29]

The Pentagon and other military symbols, police facilities, banks, and multinational corporations were the particular targets of violence. According to one account,

In a single eighteen-month period during 1971 and 1972 the FBI counted an amazing 2,500 bombings on American soil, almost five a day. Because they were typically detonated late at night, few caused serious injury, leading to a kind of grudging public acceptance. The deadliest underground attack of the decade, in fact, killed all of four people, in the January 1975 bombing of a Wall Street restaurant. News accounts rarely carried any expression or indication of public outrage.[30]

But many of those bombings were not carried out by the Weather Underground but like-minded groups and lone wolves. In the 1974 manifesto "Prairie Fire," the last communication by the group, the Weather Underground claimed responsibility for 19 major acts of terrorism and warned of more violence. Missing from the detailed list was an explosion in a Greenwich Village townhouse in March 1970 in which three members of the group blew themselves up, unwittingly, as they were constructing a bomb. Soon thereafter, the Weather Underground broke apart; some members joined or established new groups, and others surrendered after a time to the authorities and were tried and sentenced. Unlike their European soul mates, the Weather Underground never managed to terrorize the whole country by spreading massive fear and anxiety. Concluding that the Weather Underground was a failure, Ehud Sprinzak noted that the group had "never more than four hundred members and followers, and most of the time its inexperienced leaders and recruits worried not about the revolution but about their hideouts, survival logistics, and internal group relations."[31]

In "Prairie Fire," the Weather Underground expressed its admiration for black revolutionary groups, noting that the

> Black Liberation Army—fighting for three years under ruthless attack by the state—the fighters in prison, and recently the Symbionese Liberation Army are leading forces in the development of the armed struggle and political consciousness, respected by ourselves and other revolutionaries.[32]

Eventually, some members of the Weather Underground plotted joint terrorism ventures with the Black Liberation Army and similar organizations. In the fall of 1981, a group of heavily armed men and women in dark ski masks ambushed a Brink's armored vehicle in a shopping mall in Rockland County, NY, killing one of the guards and injuring two others. Two police officers were killed when state troopers and detectives stopped the perpetrators' cars at a hastily established roadblock. The perpetrators were identified as members of the Weather Underground, the Black Panther Party, the Black Liberation Front, and the Republic of New Africa, a separatist group with the goal of establishing an independent black state in the American South. Contrary to the fears of observers at the time, this incident was not a sign of renewed strength in leftist terrorist circles but an act of desperation.

The Black Panther Party for Self Defense was founded in the fall of 1966 by Bobby Seale and Huey P. Newton in Oakland, California, as an organization that was to protect the black community from police brutality. But the party's platform contained more ambitious goals and left-wing ideological fervor. In a speech in Oakland, Bobby Seale revealed the ten points of the Black Panther Party's platform, which demanded above all the freedom to determine the destiny of the black community, full employment, housing fit for human beings, education "which teaches us our true history and our role in the present day American society," exemption from military service for all black men, and the release of all black men from federal, state, county, and city jails and penitentiaries.[33] The Black cooperated with the Weather Underground for a short period. For white radicals, the "Black Panthers, who armed themselves heavily and fought the police fiercely, provided an attractive model to follow."[34] According to one observer, white radicals felt guilty because they were not treated as brutally as their black counterparts by the police.[35]

The Panthers' tough rhetoric and perhaps their uniforms of black leather jackets and black berets, attracted young black men to their ranks. Their membership was never higher than a few thousand, but the organization had chapters in inner cities across the country and published its own newspaper. But the group's militancy also attracted criminal elements that made it easier for law enforcement to justify the brutal treatment of the Panthers in general. In 1969 alone, 27 members of the organization were killed in clashes with the police and more than 700 members were arrested. On December 4, 1969, when the organization was no longer a factor because most of its leaders were either in prison or in exile, Fred Hampton, the 21-year-old chairman of the Panthers in Illinois, and Mark Clark, a 22-year-old member, were killed during a police raid on their apartment in Chicago. Five months later, a federal grand jury in Chicago decided that "the police had grossly exaggerated Black Panthers' resistance" and that "the police had riddled the Panthers' apartment with at least 82 shots, while only one shot was apparently fired from inside."[36] In reaction to and in memory of Hampton and Clark's violent deaths, surviving Panthers formed the December 4 Movement, but it disappeared nearly as quickly as it had emerged. Although involved in violent actions but often the target of unprovoked police violence, the Black Panther Party did not understand itself as a terrorist organization. As the full name indicated, the Panthers perceived themselves as black communities' defense against an overly aggressive police force, a rationale vindicated by incidents like the deadly raid on Hampton and Clark's apartment.

In Western Europe, too, breakaway groups from the New Left's student movements decided to fight the symbols of American imperialism and the ruling establishments in their respective countries. Like the Weather Underground in the United States, the Red Army Faction (RAF), better known as the Baader-Meinhof group, in Germany; the Red Brigades in Italy; and similar groups in other Western European countries considered themselves Marxist urban guerrillas fighting a class war against the existing capitalist arrangement and U.S.-led imperialism in the Third World. Although providing the theoretical context for their violent deeds in frequent communications, groups like the RAF insisted that it was time for terrorist action, not just terrorist doctrine. In "Stadtguerrilla und Klassenkampf" ("Urban Guerrilla and Class Struggle"), the RAF stated, "In this stage of history nobody can deny that an armed group, however small it may be, has a better chance to grow into a people's army than a group that limits itself to proclaim revolutionary principles."[37] The authors of the RAF's "Das Konzept Stadtguerrilla" ("The Concept of Urban Guerrilla") acknowledged that the idea of the urban guerrilla warfare originated in Latin America and that Carlos Marighella's "Minimanual of the Urban Guerrilla" was central to their own strategies and tactic.

Originally, the RAF committed violence inside West Germany, but eventually, the group became part of a "terrorist international" that was responsible for major terrorist acts abroad beginning in the mid-1970s. However, not Ulrike Meinhof, Andreas Baader, and their German comrades, but the PLO under Yassir Arafat pioneered international cooperation among terrorists. For that purpose, the PLO invited radicals from abroad to partake in their instructions in training camps in Jordan. Among the earliest trainees were Baader and Meinhof, who, upon their return to Germany, established the RAF. The Germans and Palestinians parted on a sour note at the end of the 1960s, but the rift was temporary. German leftists and Palestinian nationalists seemed strange bedfellows at first sight. But there was a meeting of the minds in that the Palestinians shared the RAF's anti-American sentiments because of the United States' strong support for Israel. By the time the Palestinian "Black September" group attacked and brutally killed members of the Israeli Olympic team during the 1972 Olympic Games in Munich, the links between the RAF and their Palestinian comrades were fully fixed. It was therefore long assumed that the RAF provided logistical support for the terror attack. But in 2012, a declassified police report about the Munich massacre revealed that not the RAF but rather a Neo-Nazi cell assisted "Black September" by providing weapons and logistics for the assault.[38] In the following years, the RAF and Palestinians planned and carried out numerous joint ventures, such as the terrorist attack during the 1975 OPEC (Organization of the Petroleum Exporting Countries) meeting in Vienna; the 1976 hijacking of an El Al plane to Entebbe, Uganda; and the 1977 hijacking of a Lufthansa plane to Mogadishu, Somalia. Another Marxist group that had close ties to Palestinian terrorists was the Japanese Red

Army that committed multiple terrorist attacks. Members of the group were responsible for the 1972 gun and grenade attack at Israel's Lod Airport, in which 26 persons, most of them Christian pilgrims, were killed and many more injured. Like the Weather Underground in the United States, some leftist groups in Europe were more inwardly oriented and less interested in and dependent on international cooperation. One commander of the Italian Red Brigades, for example, revealed in the early 1990s,

> Put simply and clearly, at the time [when the Red Brigades were still a factor] our approach excluded any contacts with foreign groups except contacts for materiel or those related to solidarity among revolutionary movements. We had one contact with a Palestinian faction for an arms shipment which we transported to our country and shared with three other Italian armed groups. Besides this, we adhered to the Maoist theory of "counting on one's own strength," both for weapons and for money.[39]

As the same Red Brigades commander pointed out, the RAF considered itself and acted as "the European fifth column of an 'anti-imperialist Front'" that reached into the Eastern Bloc and revolutionary movements in the Third World.[40] Not surprisingly, in the 1980s, German terrorists tried to forge a Euro-terrorist alliance, an attempt that was inspired by the example of their Palestinian friends. According to Bruce Hoffman,

> The profound influence exercised by the Palestinians over the Germans was perhaps never clearer than in 1985, when the RAF joined forces with the French left-wing terrorist organization, Direct Action (AD), in hopes of creating a PLO-like umbrella "anti-imperialist front of Western European guerrillas" that would include Italy's Red Brigades (RB) and the Belgium Communist Combatant Cells (CCC) as well.[41]

The ambitious plan did not succeed because many terrorists in various Western European countries were arrested or forced to flee to safe havens in the waning years of the Cold War. It has been argued that the RAF and related organizations could not have survived as long as they did without Palestinian support.[42] But this argument ignores or minimizes the significant support that these groups and individuals received from the Eastern side of the Iron Curtain. In fact, much of the terrorism that plagued the West during the 1970s and 1980s related in one respect or another to the Cold War confrontation between the two superpowers and their respective spheres of influence. And the Israeli–Palestinian conflict, too, was fought in this context. While communist countries were supportive of leftist groups in Europe, Latin America, and elsewhere, some governments with friendly ties to Moscow supported religiously motivated groups as well. For example, the Lebanese Hezbollah, which was created in 1982 and financially sustained by the Islamic Republic of Iran, was tolerated and at times backed by Syria, which shared Hezbollah's anti-Israeli stance.

Nationalist, Anticolonial, Separatist Terrorism

While Rapoport pinpointed the post-World War I years as the start of the anti-colonial wave of terrorism, violent nationalist and separatist movements existed already in the nineteenth century. Among the examples that Parker and Sitter mention in support of their Four Strains theory is that of American-based Irish nationalists who joined forces with like-minded leaders in Ireland.[43] In the 1880s, during the so-called "Dynamite Campaign," there were multiple bombings in London and other English cities. However, nationalist fervor became more intensive and spread more widely after the Versailles Peace Treaty, when "the empires of the defeated states (which were mostly in Europe) were broken up by applying the principle of self-determination."[44] Yet, it was the post-World War II era that experienced the most powerful outburst of political violence "from below" in many parts of the world, as people struggled for decolonization and national liberation as well as for revolutionary social change.

Developments like the retreats of the British, French, Dutch, and Americans from Aden, Cyprus, Palestine, Algeria, Indonesia, the Philippines, and other places were often preceded and accompanied by terrorist violence. In Latin America, the revolutionary ferment was directed against American interference on behalf of the ruling class and aimed at a new social order that challenged the capitalist model. In Africa and Asia, European powers were the targets. Frantz Fanon and Regis Debray provided the theoretical justifications for violent actions for the sake of national liberation and fundamental social change. Using the case of Algeria to indict the inhumanity of the Western model in general and colonialism in particular, Fanon endorsed all-out violence not only as a means to an end—national liberation—but also as an end in itself that would free the liberated individuals from their marks of oppression and empower them. In *The Wretched of the Earth*, he wrote,

> At the level of the individuals, violence is a cleansing force. It frees the native from his inferiority complex and from his despair and inaction; it makes him fearless and restores his self-respect.[45]

He also called for a new, just, and humane social and political model that was applicable beyond the special cases of Algeria and Africa to the Third World in general and the struggle of minorities for self-determination in the First World as well. As Fanon put it in the conclusion of his treatise,

Let us decide not to imitate Europe; let us combine our muscles and our brains in a new direction. Let us create the whole man, whom Europe has been incapable of bringing to triumphant birth.

Two centuries ago, a former European colony decided to catch up with Europe. It succeeded so well that the United States of America became a monster, in which the taints, the sickness, and the inhumanity of Europe have grown to appalling dimensions.

Comrades, have we not other work to do than to create a third Europe?[46]

In *Revolution in the Revolution*, Debray provided the rationale for the anti-imperialist, anticapitalist revolutionary uprisings in Latin America in particular. Unlike Fanon, who recognized the usefulness of terrorist action, Debray did not subscribe to the efficacy of terrorism but recommended larger-scale guerrilla warfare. anon (a native of Martinique) and Debray (a Frenchman) were outsider theorists focusing on Africa and Latin America; the Brazilian Communist Carlos Marighella was a homegrown Latin American revolutionary whose "Handbook of Urban Guerrilla Warfare" provided hands-on instructions for violent struggle "from below." Besides physical fitness and absolute dedication to the cause, Marighella recommended technical expertise, especially with respect to arms, such as machine guns, revolvers, shotguns, mortars, and bazookas. In one passage of his manual, he gave the following advice:

A knowledge of various types of ammunition and explosives is another aspect to consider. Among the explosives, dynamite must be well understood. The use of incendiary bombs, of smoke bombs, and other types is indispensable knowledge.

To know how to make and repair arms, prepare Molotov cocktails, grenades, mines, homemade destructive devices, how to blow up bridges, tear up and put out of service rails and sleepers, these are the requisites in the technical preparation of the urban guerrilla that can never be considered unimportant.[47]

In the 1960s and 1970s, Fanon, Debray, and Marighella, for their theoretical contributions, and Ernesto "Che" Guevara, for his influence on and participation in Fidel Castro's Cuban Revolution, affected terrorist passions, strategies, and tactics far beyond the Third World, including the New Left in North America and Europe.

Contrary to Rapoport who placed the end of the anti-colonial wave into the 1960s, the nationalist/separate strain continued throughout the twentieth century and beyond. A good example is the IRA, whose roots go back to the end of the eighteenth century. The organization was founded in 1919 to fight for Ireland's independence from the United Kingdom. In 1921, when moderate nationalists agreed to the establishment of an independent Irish state in the predominantly Catholic south and to continued British control over six counties in the north, radical nationalists opposed this solution. They wanted all of Ireland to be independent. The result was a civil war in which the extreme nationalists were defeated by the newly independent Irish state. Although the majority of the IRA denounced violence in the late 1920s, remnants of the group continued to fight for Northern Ireland's independence. This was not the end of divisions within the IRA. In 1969, after paramilitary Protestants brutally interfered with a peaceful demonstration by Catholics in Northern Ireland, a militant IRA faction broke away and took the name "Provisional IRA." In the decades since then, the Provisional IRA (also simply called the "IRA") was most instrumental and most violent in pushing the nationalist cause in Northern Ireland. At the same time, terrorism was also the weapon of choice of Protestant Loyalist groups, such as the Ulster Defense Association and the Ulster Vanguard Movement. In protest against a peace process that resulted in the Belfast Agreement or Good Friday Agreement of 1998 and in the hope of ending the violent conflict over the status of Northern Ireland once and for all, some IRA members formed the Real IRA. In the following years, members of this group carried out dozens of bombings and other terror attacks in Northern Ireland, Dublin, London, Birmingham, and elsewhere. In July 2005, the Provisional IRA declared an end to its armed struggle and announced that the organization would work within the democratic political process to achieve its goal. In the following three months, the group decommissioned its arms under the supervision of an Independent International Commission on Decommissioning. In May 2007, local government was restored to Northern Ireland when Ian Paisley, the leader of the Democratic Unionists, and Martin McGuinness, the representative of Sinn Fein, the IRA's political arm, were sworn in as leader and deputy leader of the Northern Ireland government in a power-sharing arrangement. And in February 2010, Prime Minister Gordon Brown of Britain and Prime Minister Brian Cowen of Ireland signed the Hillsborough Castle Agreement for handing over control of the six counties' police and justice system to Northern Ireland's government. Splinter groups, such as the Real IRA, the 32 County Sovereignty Movement, and the Continuity Army Council did not accept the peace agreement.[48] In the years since them, there was occasional violence in Northern Ireland—particularly in the face of problems with the governmental power sharing of unionists and loyalists in Belfast and the United Kingdom's withdrawal from the European Union.

Another example of an enduring nationalist/separatist organization is Euskadi Ta Askatasuna or ETA ("Basque Homeland and Liberty" or "Basque Country and Freedom") that was founded in 1959. Although Basques received a great deal of autonomy in the decades following the end of the oppressive Franco regime and the emergence of a democratic system, the organization continued to demand a separate Basque state. While its commandos always operated underground, the political party Batasuna pursued the organization's separatist goal in the legitimate political process until banned as undemocratic by Spain's Supreme Court. While not close to a majority party, Batasuna managed to win around 10 and 15 percent of the Basque vote. More recently, though, a solid majority of Basques rejects ETA outright. According to a November 2009 survey carried out by Euskobarometro of the Universidad del Pais Vasco, 63 percent of the Basque public rejected ETA totally while merely 1 percent supported the organization totally with a range of mixed views in between. In spite of this lack in public support and the decimation of its leadership during a wave of arrests both in Spain and in neighboring France—especially in 2009 and 2010—the organization continued its lethal violence throughout the first decade of the twenty-first century. Since resorting to terrorism in the late 1960s, ETA attacks killed more than 800 persons and injured many more. In the past, several cease-fire agreements between ETA and the Madrid government did not last long nor did unilateral truce announcements on the part of the group. Thus, following ETA's cease-fire message in March 2006, group members detonated a powerful bomb in a parking garage at the Madrid airport, killing two persons and causing the collapse of the building. In the summer of 2009, ETA celebrated its fiftieth birthday by detonating several bombs on the popular resort island of Mallorca that is visited each summer by tens of thousands of tourists from abroad. ETA bombs exploded in restaurants, in bars, and on streets killing two policemen and injuring dozens of civilians. The obvious target was Spain's all-important tourism sector at a time of economic hardship.

Traditionally, Spanish ETA members sought and found safe haven across the border in France in an area that Basque separatists consider part of their homeland. But after French authorities suspected ETA operatives to have had their hands in the killing of a French policeman in March 2010, French President Nicolas Sarkozy promised to do away with all ETA hideouts in France and hunt down ETA terrorists on French soil. The killing of the policeman was in reaction to the arrest of ETA's military leader Ibon Gogeascoechea in February by French police. By May 2010, his successor Mikel Kabikoitz Karrera Sarobe was in French custody as well. The Spanish–French cooperation resulted in a crippling blow against the resilient organization. After announcing a unilateral and permanent cease-fire in 2012, ETA claimed two years later that it had stored part of its weaponry beyond its membership's reach. But what was supposed a disarmament process was too slow for the authorities. In mid-2015, Spanish and French police raided an ETA weapons depot and seized firearms and explosive material. By 2017, ETA had completely disarmed and abandoned violence although some longtime ETA hardliners did not accept peace.

Religious Terrorism

From John Brown to Christian Identity: In attacking the federal armory of Harper's Ferry, Virginia, in October 1859 with twenty of fellow-abolitionists, the militant anti-slavery leader John Brown hoped to inspire other Blacks to join his fight for freedom. But there had not been previous contacts with the Black population of the area. Although Brown and his comrades had taken several locals hostage and got hold of an arsenal of weapons, they were soon defeated by federal troops. But in the clash, four residents of the town and ten of Brown's fighters, including two of his sons, were killed. Brown, a devout Christian, was swiftly tried, found guilty, and executed. Parker and Sitter consider Brown's violence at Harper's Ferry and earlier in Kansas as the first case of religious terrorism in the annals of modern terrorism.

While John Brown assembled just a few men to support his short-lived fight against slavery and slaveholders, American Christian Identity extremists formed far stronger and durable movement in the second half of the 1900s. Actually, Christian Identity originated in the nineteenth century in England as "British Israelism" and over the years developed the most elaborate theory of White Supremacy. At the heart of Christian Identity's original gospel is the claim that white Christians are the true Israelites of the Old Testament and therefore God's chosen people. When Christian Identity made its way to the United States in the 1940s, it developed an even more divisive and hateful pseudoreligious twist. British Identity teachings were clearly anti-Semitic and American adherents added a distinct racist element.

For many years, the Church of Jesus Christ/Aryan Nations and its founder and head, Richard Butler—Pastor Butler to his followers—were at the center of Christian Identity activity in the United States. Every year, adherents of Butler's gospel of hate as well as leaders and members of like-minded groups descended on the Aryan Nations' compound at Hayden Lake, Idaho, to participate in survivalist training and indoctrination reinforcement. "Church" was also instrumental in the establishment of the Aryan Brotherhood movement among white prisoners. Writing about the Aryan Nations, the Anti-Defamation League characterized the hate organization as the "once most infamous Neo-Nazi group in the United States."[49] As he advanced in age, Butler's influence declined, especially after he lost the Idaho compound in 2001 following legal action by the victims of an assault by Butler's guards. After his death in 2004, some of his followers tried to revitalize the Aryan Nations, others established their own groups, such as the new Church of the Sons of Yahweh. In 2009, former Butler associates tried to enlist support for the reestablishment of a Butler-like group in Idaho and promised to revive their idol's annual national conventions.[50] Although fragmenting further without Butler and his "Church" as rallying mechanisms, Christian Identity ideas remained alive in some of the most extreme right-wing hate movements with violent tendencies.

For many years, a number of right-extremists switched from one organization to another or founded their own group. Take, for example, Tom Metzger, who was active in the KKK, ordained as a minister in the Christian Identity milieu, and in 1983 founded his own organization, White Aryan Resistance (WAR). Even after a jury returned a $12.5 million judgment against him and his son for inciting the murder of an African immigrant by skinheads in 1990, Metzger continued to preach hate of non-Whites in ways that were especially tailored to appeal to skinheads and prison inmates. Robert Mathews, who founded The Order in the early 1980s as an offshoot of Richard Butler's Aryan Nations. Matthew's group was the most violent of the right-wing variety in the 1980s. In 1984, members of the group killed Denver talk show host Alan Berg, who had been very critical of White Supremacists on the air. Later that year, Mathews was killed in a shoot-out with police in the state of Washington. Even when it was assumed that The Order was defunct, the group remained attractive as a right-wing model. In 1998, law enforcement authorities discovered a plot to bomb the offices of the Anti-Defamation League by a group that called itself The New Order and modeled itself after Mathews's original group.

Hezbollah, Al Qaeda, and ISIS: For Rapoport, the wave of religious terrorism got its most important impulses from the Islamic revolution of 1979 in Iran and, a decade later, from the defeat of the Soviet Union in Afghanistan. The developments in both countries seemed to convince many Muslims "that religion now provided more hope than the prevailing revolutionary ethos did."[51] In both cases, formidable terror organizations emerged that had ties to the fundamentalist Muslim regimes in Iran and Afghanistan: Hezbollah and Al Qaeda.

In 1982, shortly after the Iranian revolution, the new regime of Ayatollah Khomeini was instrumental in the establishment of Hezbollah in Lebanon. Financed by the Iranian government and trained by Iranian Revolutionary Guards, "Hezbollah provided a means" for Iran of "spread[ing] the Islamic revolution to the Arab world" and "gaining a foothold in Middle East politics."[52] But besides fighting Israel and the foreign military presence and influence in Lebanon, Hezbollah did not have a grander anti-Western design. Hezbollah's focus was on Lebanon and the Israeli–Palestinian problem—not on a united Muslim front against the West. But Iran's proxy fighters in Lebanon carried out many violent and deadly terrorist attacks against Americans, Israelis, and other Westerners.

Osama bin Laden had much more ambitious plans for Al Qaeda. He and his associates were not just opposed to Western and U.S.-led influence in the Middle East and beyond; they also despised the regimes in the region that cooperated with the United States and the West. Indeed, bin Laden expressed as much contempt for Saudi Arabia's rulers as for the U.S. government. When he returned from Afghanistan to Saudi Arabia in 1990, he was offended by the presence and influence of Westerners in his homeland. After the Saudi rulers and other governments in the region supported the U.S.-led military coalition against Iraq in the early 1990s, he turned so vehemently against Saudi Arabia's government because of this issue that he lost his Saudi citizenship. He found a new base of operation in Sudan, also an Islamic republic. Here the group established businesses and plotted violent actions against the United States and the Saudi rulers. Under pressure from the United States, the Saudis, and other countries in the region, the Sudanese government asked Al Qaeda to leave the country. In the spring of 1996, accompanied by family members and supporters, bin Laden flew to Afghanistan, where he found agreeable surroundings. According to Simon Reeve,

> He had chosen Afghanistan, where he knew he could rely on the support of his old comrades [with whom he had fought against the Soviet invaders of Afghanistan in the 1980s]. Many of them had now reorganized into the fundamentalist Islamic militia known to the West as the Taliban, which was imposing harsh Sharia law in the country: forcing men into mosques at gunpoint five times a day, banning music and alcohol, and preventing women from working.[53]

Years before 9/11, political scientist Samuel Huntington predicted that the greatest dangers in the post-Cold War era would arise from conflicts between nations and groups of different civilizations, of different cultural backgrounds.[54] Several weeks after the events of 9/11, while rejecting the notion that these attacks signaled such a collision, Huntington was sure that "bin Laden wants it to be a clash of civilizations between Islam and the [Judea-Christian] West."[55] Bin Laden's statements validated this conclusion all along. In his 1998 declaration of war against "Jews and Crusaders," he listed the wrongdoings of the "Crusader–Zionist alliance" and reminded all Muslims that the "jihad is an individual duty if the enemy destroys the Muslim countries" and that "nothing is more sacred than belief except repulsing an enemy who is attacking religion and life." He then called on all Muslims "to kill the Americans and their allies—civilians and military... in any country in which it is possible to do." In October 2001, when the U.S. military commenced strikes against Al Qaeda camps and Taliban strongholds in Afghanistan, bin Laden declared,

> The events have divided the whole world into two sides. The side of believers and the side of infidels, may God keep you away from them. Every Muslim has to rush to make his religion victorious. The winds

of faith have come. The winds of change have come to eradicate oppression from the island of Muhammad, peace be upon him.[56]

Since Muslims did not rise in a massive united front to fight the Christian and Jewish infidels in the holy war that bin Laden had declared, the Al Qaeda leader and his supporters did not realize their most ambitious objective. On the contrary, they lost their safe haven, headquarters, training facilities, and weapon arsenals in Afghanistan. In this respect, bin Laden and his comrades in arms underestimated the resolve of the United States and the willingness of other governments to cooperate with Washington. But one must also doubt that the Al Qaeda leadership expected to provoke the existential clash of civilizations simply as a result of the 9/11 operation. Bin Laden and his lieutenants also wanted to harm the U.S. economically. They were aware of the resources needed to respond to 9/11 and the threat of further strikes in terms of military responses, protection of the homeland, and preparedness measures.

After bin Laden's death and the further decline of Al Qaeda Central, the Islamic State that had its start as an Al Qaeda affiliate in Iraq became the dominant jihadist organization. Upon declaring himself the Caliph of the Islamic State, Abu Bakr al Baghdadi, also called Amirul-Mu'minin (Leader of the Faithful), said,

> O Ummah of Islam, indeed the world today has been divided into two camps and two trenches, with no third camp present: The camp of Islam and faith, and the camp of kufr (disbelief) and hypocrisy – the camp of the Muslims and the mujahidin everywhere, and the camp of the Jews, the crusaders, their allies, and with them the rest of the nations and religions of kufr, all being led by America and Russia, and being mobilized by the Jews.[57]

ISIS had the plan to expand its caliphate significantly claiming in its online publications that the next conquered places would be first Constantinople and then Rome. But the period in which ISIS controlled significant parts of Iraq and Syria was short-lived. The territory was lost when ISIS soldiers were defeated decisively by Iraqi and Syrian fighters with the assistance of U.S. forces. Yet, the Islamic State recovered as described in the following chapter.

Social Exclusion Terrorism

The Ku Klux Klan: In the history of indigenous political violence in the United States, the KKK has the distinction of being the most enduring organization—albeit with periods of dormancy. Founded in 1865 to resist the consequences of the Civil War and in particular the adoption of the Thirteenth Amendment to the U.S. Constitution, which abolished slavery and thus slave labor, the KKK targeted black freedmen and whites supportive of African Americans' rights. Wearing white robes and masks, members of the KKK terrorized by beating and lynching their targets under the cover of night with the goal of upholding White Supremacy in the defeated South. Within a few years, the Klan perpetrated thousands of violent acts. In reaction, the federal government adopted laws that made "nightriding" a crime and allowed the president to deploy troops to end civil disturbances and even suspend habeas corpus for a time. As a result, President Ulysses S. Grant moved troops into the South, and many Klansmen were arrested. But by 1872, when the first KKK dissolved voluntarily, southern states began legislating measures that assured white dominance and racial segregation. Even though segregation was achieved and maintained by official policies in the South, white lynch mobs continued to kill many blacks.

The second KKK emerged after the release of D. W. Griffith's motion picture *Birth of a Nation*, which glorified the first Klan and the southern power structure and racial discrimination it stood for. At the peak of the second Klan period in the mid-1920s, the organization had a total membership of 3–4 million. This forceful revival came about for other reasons as well: (1) The perennial fear of southern whites that blacks could finally achieve equality and challenge White Supremacy once again— sentiments that were fueled by *Birth of a Nation*; (2) the uneasiness of northern whites over black migration from the South to the North; and (3) Protestant objections to immigration because many of the newcomers were Catholics and Jews—groups that were hated by the Klan as well. Moreover, newcomers were typically willing to work for lower wages than the existing workforce and thus threatened the economic status quo of the latter. All of these factors drove people in all parts of the country into the arms of the Klan. By casting themselves as the protectors of patriotism and moral values, the Klan recruited a large number of fundamentalist preachers—often by promising that the Klan would boost attendance in their churches.

In the 1920s, the KKK foreshadowed the organizational structure of more recent and contemporary terrorist organizations in that it worked both within the legitimate political process and at the same time had members who engaged in illegal political violence. As a powerful interest group, the Klan influenced politics and policies on the local, state, and federal levels and was especially successful in affecting election outcomes. A day after the 1924 election, the *New York Times* reported under the headline "Victories by Klan Feature Election: Order Elects Senators in Oklahoma and Colorado, Governors in Kansas, Indiana, Colorado" that "the candidates endorsed by the masked organization have apparently scored sweeping victories in Indiana, Kansas, Colorado, and Oklahoma, and later returns may add Montana to the list."[58]

While the KKK made strides in working within the political system, the organization did nothing to stop the violence committed by its members in the southern states, where "Klansmen tarred and feathered, tortured, and lynched blacks suspected of being involved with white women. Prosperous African Americans and immigrants who jeopardized white economic power found their businesses burned and their possessions stolen."[59] But as the press reported extensively on the Klan's terrorism and states adopted "antimasking" laws, the opposition to the KKK strengthened. By the end of the 1920s, the organization was only a shadow of its peak in 1924–25 in that its membership declined from a record high of 3–4 million to about 40,000.

The U.S. Supreme Court's milestone rulings in favor of desegregation in the 1950s (especially *Brown v. Board of Education*, 1954) and the activism of a strong civil rights movement in the early 1960s were met by yet another revival of the KKK in the 1960s and a wave of political violence against African Americans and whites who insisted on desegregation, the free exercise of voting rights by blacks, and the end of all discrimination. As James Ridgeway observed, the election of John F. Kennedy, the first Catholic president, "revived the Klan's old papist hatred, but that soon gave way to a new sense of desperation and dread as Greyhound buses filled with white and black kamikaze college students calling themselves Freedom Riders descended upon the South."[60] The result was a reign of terror by Klansmen against Freedom Riders and against southern blacks and Jews. Following the brutal murder of civil rights advocates in the South, the FBI began to crack down on the Klan. Klan leaders split into factions, some insisting on violent tactics and others favoring a "mediagenic call to nonviolence."[61] But those who presented themselves and their organization as nonviolent did not shed the tradition of hate. One of the leaders who typified the merely cosmetic change was David Duke. While recognizing the value of the soft sell as Grand Wizard and as a member of the Louisiana state legislature, Duke's core message remained. In 2003, the website of his latest organizational vehicle, the European–American Unity and Rights Organization (EURO), carried the following message: "Unless European-Americans organize and act soon, America will become a 'Third World' country—that is, European-Americans will become outnumbered and totally vulnerable to the political control of Blacks and other non-Whites."[62]

This was certainly the same "Great Replacement" message that White Supremacists/neo-Nazis propagated openly in the North America, Europe, and other western countries in the second and early third decade of the twenty-first century that will be discussed in the next chapter.

Fascist Militants in the Early 1900s: During their post-World War I rise to power, the fascist movements in Italy and Germany relied both on divisive politics supported by relentless propaganda and political violence carried out by their paramilitary wings. Benito Mussolini's Voluntary

Militia for National Security or Black Shirts, intimidated their leader's opponents by attacking some dissidents brutally. Hitler's Sturmabteilung (Sturmabteilung SA) or Brown Shirts, too, acted as paramilitary force against anti-fascist politicians and deployed a special commando, the Schutzstaffel, for especially brutal attacks on supporters of oppositional parties. While Hitler's ascent to power took many more years than Mussolini's take-over, the brutality of the Brown Shirts increased over time.

Before Mussolini and Hitler came to power in their respective countries, their parties' paramilitary units were nonstate actors committing political violence against civilians—in other words, terrorism. Once leaders and parties came to power, their governments' violence against members of certain groups became state terror.

*

This chapter's historical review of the four strains of modern terrorism does not cover all important movements, groups, and individuals involved in nonstate political violence but rather examples that characterize the grievances, demands, and tactics in the particular strains. The following chapter is devoted to contemporary terrorism including the social exclusion variety practiced by contemporary violent Far-Right and Far-Left extremists and outliers, such as anti-abortion and pro-abortion terrorism, eco- and environmental terrorism.

Notes

1 David C. Rapoport, "Fear and Trembling: Terrorism in Three Religious Traditions," *American Political Science Report* 78 (3) (September 1984), p. 670.
2 Sidney B. Honig, "The Sicarii in Masada: Glory or Infamy?," *Tradition: A Journal of Orthodox Jewish Thought* 11 (1) (Spring 1972), pp. 6, 7.
3 Ibid.
4 Jeffrey D. Simon, *The Terrorist Trap: America's Experience with Terrorism* (Bloomington: Indiana University Press, 1994), 27.
5 Walter Laqueur, *A History of Terrorism* (New Brunswick, N.J.: Transaction Publishers, 2002), 11.
6 David C. Rapoport, "The Four Waves of Rebel Terror and September 11," *Anthropoetics* 8 (1) (Spring/Summer 2002), p. 2.
7 Tom Parker and Nick Sitter, "The Four Horsemen of Terrorism: It's Not Waves, It's Strains," *Terrorism and Political Violence* 28 (2) (2016), p. 202.
8 Scott M. Cutlip, "Public Relations and the American Revolution," *Public Relations Review* 2 (4) (Winter 1976), p. 11.
9 William J. Stern, "What Gangs of New York Misses," *City Journal*, January 14, 2003, https://www.city-journal.org/html/what-gangs-new-york-misses-9983.html, accessed June 2, 2022.
10 Brutus, *Foreign Conspiracy against the Liberties of the United States* (New York: H.A. Chapin & Co, 1841), 19. The book is a collection of Morse's newspaper columns published in the 1830s.

11 Candace A. Czernicki, "The Catholic Press Response to Nativism in the 1850s and 1920s." M.A. thesis, Marquette University, 1999, 20–21.
12 David C. Rapoport, "The Four Waves of Rebel Terror and September 11."
13 Tom Parker and Nick Sitter, "The Four Horsemen of Terrorism: It's not Waves, It's Strains."
14 Heinzen's treatise is reprinted in Walter Laqueur and Yonah Alexander, *The Terrorism Reader: The Essential Source Book on Political Violence Both Past and Present* (New York: Penguin Books, 1987), 59.
15 Ibid.
16 Colin Ward, *Anarchism: A Very Short Introduction* (New York: Oxford University Press, 2004), 4.
17 Walter Laqueur, *A History of Terrorism* (New Brunswick, NJ: Transaction Publishers, 2002), 14.
18 Quote is taken from "Anarchy at the Turn of the Century," University Libraries, Pan-American Exposition Exhibit Group, University of Buffalo; http://ublib.buffalo.edu/libraries/exhibits/panam/copyright.html, accessed March 27, 2003.
19 Ibid.
20 John Most and Emma Goldman, "Anarchy Defended by Anarchists," *Metropolitan Magazine* 4 (3) (October 1896).
21 "Emma Goldman Is Arrested in Chicago," *New York Times*, September 11, 1901 (retrieved from ProQuest Historical News).
22 Walter Laqueur, *A History of Terrorism* (New Brunswick, NJ: Transaction Publishers, 2002).
23 Richard Bach Jensen, "The United States, International Policing and the War against Anarchist Terrorism, 1900–1914," *Terrorism and Political Violence* 13 (1) (Spring 2001), pp. 15–46.
24 Ibid., 32.
25 The quote is from Jeffrey D. Simon, *The Terrorist Trap: America's Experience with Terrorism* (Bloomington: Indiana University Press, 1994), 41.
26 Paul Avrich, *Sacco and Vanzetti: The Anarchist Background* (Princeton, NJ: Princeton University Press, 1991), 50.
27 Ibid., 51.
28 Ibid., 48.
29 Parker and Sitter, 200.
30 Bryan Burrough, "The Bombings of America that we Forgot," *Time*, September 20, 2016.
31 Ehud Sprinzak, "Extreme Left Terrorism in a Democracy," in Walter Reich, ed., *Origins of Terrorism: Psychologies, Ideologies, Theologies, States of Mind* (New York: Cambridge University Press, 1990), 77.
32 "Prairie Fire—Political Statement of the Weather Underground," in Walter Laqueur and Yonah Alexander, eds., *The Terrorism Reader* (New York: Penguin, 1987), 173.
33 The quote is from the "Ten-Point Party Platform of the Black Panther Party," www.pbs.org/hueynewton, accessed May 12, 2003.
34 Sprinzak, 77.
35 Ibid.
36 Fred P. Graham, "U.S. Jury Assails Police in Chicago on Panther Raid," *New York Times*, May 15, 1970, 1, 14.
37 For "Stadtguerrilla und Klassenkampf" and other RAF documents, see www.baadermeinhof.com.
38 Gunter Latsch and Klaus Wiegrefe, "Files Reveal Neo-Nazis Helped Palestinian Terrorists," *Der Spiegel*, June 18, 2012; www.spiegel.de/international/germany/files-show-neo-nazis-helped-palestinian-terrorists-in-munich-1972-massacre- a-839467.html, accessed April 12, 2018.

39 Xavier Raufer, "The Red Brigades: Farewell to Arms," *Studies in Conflict and Terrorism* 16 (4) (1993), pp. 315–25.
40 Ibid., 323.
41 Bruce Hoffman, *Inside Terrorism* (New York: Columbia University Press, 1998), 83.
42 Ibid., cites David Schiller, a German-Israeli counterterrorism analyst, who argued that "without assistance provided by the Palestinians to their German counterparts the latter could not have survived."
43 Parker and Sitter, 204–05.
44 Rapoport, "The Four Waves of Rebel Terror and September 11," 4.
45 Frantz Fanon, *The Wretched of the Earth* (New York: Grove Weidenfeld, 1963), 94.
46 Ibid., 313.
47 From excerpts of Carlos Marighella, "Handbook of Urban Guerrilla Warfare," in Laqueur and Alexander, 163.
48 Although denied by these groups, there seems some evidence that the 32 County Sovereignty Movement is the political arm of the Real IRA just as Sinn Fein is the political arm of the IRA.
49 "Breakup of Aryan Nations Leads to the Formation of Successor Groups," www.adl.org, accessed March 17, 2003.
50 "Aryan Nations Reappears in North Idaho," www.ktvb.com/news/localnews/stories/ktvbnapr2509-aryan_nations.10ea62923.html, accessed May 4, 2009.
51 Rapoport, 421.
52 Adam Shatz, "In Search of Hezbollah," *New York Review of Books*, April 29, 2004, 41.
53 Simon Reeve, *The New Jackals* (Boston, MA: Northeastern University Press, 1999), 186.
54 Samuel P. Huntington, *The Clash of Civilizations and the Remaking of World Order* (New York: Simon & Schuster, 1996).
55 "Q&A: A Head-On Collision of Alien Cultures," *New York Times*, October 20, 2001, A13.
56 "Text: bin Laden Statement," www.guardian.co.uk/waronterror/story/0,1361,565069,00html, accessed April 7, 2002.
57 According to the first issue of ISIS's online magazine *Dabiq*, http://media.clarionproject.org/files/09–2014/isis-isil-islamic-state-magazine-Issue-1-the-return-of-khilafah.pdf, accessed July 22, 2015.
58 "Victory by Klan Feature Election," *New York Times*, November 5, 1924 (retrieved from ProQuest Historical News).
59 Gough, 527.
60 James Ridgeway, *Blood in the Face: The Ku Klux Klan, Aryan Nation, Nazi Skin Heads, and the Rise of a New White Culture* (New York: Thunder Mouth Press, 1995), 68.
61 Jeffrey Kaplan, "Right Wing Violence in North America," *Terrorism and Political Violence* 7 (1) (1995), pp. 44–95.
62 From the website of the EURO, www.whitecivilrights.com, accessed March 10, 2003.

4 The Terrorism Landscape in the Third Decade of the Twenty-First Century

January 6, 2021: A huge crowd of President Donald Trump's supporters listen to and applaud his speech at the Ellipse of the National Park near the White House. He repeats his claim that he, not Joe Biden, won the 2020 election. This very day, the U.S. Congress is scheduled to certify the election results. Trump urges Vice-President Mike Pence and Republican members of the Congress not to validate Biden's victory. He tells the crowd, "If you do not fight like hell, you're not going to have a country anymore." Seconds later, he says, "We're going to the Capitol [the seat of Congress]." "Fight for Trump!" "Storm the Capitol!" "Hang Mike Pence!" "Take the Capitol!" the crowd chants moving towards the Capitol buildings. There, several hundred members of the violent Proud Boys group and its newly formed national planning committee called MOSD (Ministry of Self Defense) are strategically positioned to lead the enraged crowd in fighting outnumbered U.S. Capitol Police officer. They smash windows and doors to get inside the halls of Congress. At another side of the Capitol, several stacks of the paramilitary Oath Keepers lead or push other rioters forward in the breach of congressional buildings. Once one stack reaches the iconic Capitol Rotunda, the only female Oath Keeper in the group, an army veteran, screams, "We're in the fucking Capitol." It takes hours before National Guard troops arrive to help Capitol and Metropolitan police to remove the intruders. Four persons are dead and 138 police officers injured.[1] Late that day, a congressional majority votes to certify Biden's victory.

Pictures of the well-documented event showed that many of the 1/6 insurrectionists waved a multitude of historical banners and flags—from the Star-Spangled Banner to Confederate flags. But nothing expressed the rebellious spirit of organized militants within crowd better than the replicas of a historical yellow flag, designed in 1776, depicting a coiled rattlesnake with 13 rattles for each of the American states at the time, and carrying a warning in uppercase letters: DONT TREAD ON ME. Like other organized violent extremists—terrorists—the Proud Boys

DOI: 10.4324/9781003289265-5

and Oath Keepers considered themselves the heirs of America's original revolutionaries fighting British tyranny and winning independence and freedom for what became the United States of America. Shortly before 1/6, the Proud Boys' national chairman, Enrique Tarrio, had a nine-page plan in hand that was titled "1776 Returns." The document detailed how to breach and occupy buildings in Washington, DC, including "House and Senate office buildings around the Capitol with as many people as possible to show our politicians we the People are in charge."[2] Sometime earlier, a regional leader of the group posted on social media, "The spirit of 1776 has resurfaced and has created groups like the Proud Boys...We will grow like the flame that fuels us...We are unstoppable, unrelenting and now...unforgiving." Another leader replied, "Hopefully, the firing squads are for the traitors that are trying to steal the election from the American people."[3]

Similarly, the Oath Keepers' founder and leader, Stewart Rhodes, invoked 1776 and the patriotic fight for freedom led by George Washington and his men in an Open Letter to President Trump in December 2020. "The very survival of our nation as a free Constitutional Republic hangs in the balance," he wrote. "We have but one last chance to save it." Although the organization's mission statement describes the Oath Keepers as patriotic Americans who defend the U.S. Constitution against domestic and foreign enemies, Rhodes urged the president to take unconstitutional measures and use the U.S. military and militias like the Oath Keepers to stay in office. Earlier he had warned his membership, "We aren't getting through this without a civil war."[4] Thus, besides identifying his group with the patriots of the 1776 revolution, he also summoned the Civil War and the cause of slaveholders to rouse Oath Keepers' spirits. A number of 1/6 rioters carried the confederate flags, symbols of White Supremacy and racial hate. And even after the attack on America's democratic electoral system failed, the Oath Keepers bought additional firearms and ammunition in preparation for what their leader Rhodes called "civil war 2.0."[5]

Other paramilitary groups throughout the country, too, justified their missions with the examples set by patriotic, colonial revolutionaries and the Founding Fathers' grants of individual civil liberties as a bulwark against governmental power overreach. One of these militias, the Three Percenters, also violently involved on 1/6, claimed falsely that only 3 percent of Americans fought in the eighteenth century in the Revolutionary War against the British. Thus, their name and the claim of being a modern-day version of the original 3 percent colonialists and like their predecessors prepared to fight a revolution against tyrannical domestic state and federal governments.

If observers thought that the devotion of Far-Right extremists to their interpretation of historical figures, events, and symbols was another example of American exceptionalism, they were mistaken. Their ideological

Violent Far-Right Extremists and January 6, 2021

16.8 percent of those accused of criminal offenses for their roles in the breach of the U.S. Capitol on January 6, 2021, were members of extreme rightwing groups with histories of political violence. Of the 111 persons in this cohort, 32 percent were Proud Boys, 21 percent Oath Keepers, 21 percent QAnon conspiracy theorists, 10 percent Three Percenters, 8 percent were not members but loosely associated with one of the above organizations, and the remaining 8 percent belonged to some other Far-Right group, such as the Boogaloo Boys.

Twelve percent of the criminally charged persons had at the time of the insurrection or in the past jobs in the public sector, most of them serving in the military or as police officers and firefighters. Since the available information was often not complete, it is very likely that the number of those who served in a uniformed service, was higher than the 12 percent reflected in the data this research is based on.[6]

Like in the United States, violent Far-Right groups in other Western democracies have succeeded in recruiting members of the military. Thus, in 2020 one of the four companies in the German special forces Kommando Spezialkraefte (KSK) had become so infested with far-right extremism that it was dissolved. The other units were ordered to overhaul their recruitment, training, and leadership practices before being allowed to rejoin any international military exercises or missions.

brethren abroad showed shown the same obsession with insignia they linked to their respective countries' former greatness. Thus, several months before 1/6, Far-Right extremists in Germany's capital Berlin broke away from the path of a huge anti-waxer, anti-government demonstration and rushed toward the Reichstag, seat of the Bundestag near the iconic Brandenburg Gate. Reacting angrily to a police cordon, protesters hurled stones and bottles at the officers. Some in the crowd waved flags of the Greater German Reich; others displayed Nazi emblems as they tried to invade the seat of the federal legislature. Or take the Russian Imperial Movement (RIM) that was established in the early 2000s in order to fight for the reestablishment of the pre-revolutionary Russian empire with the political power in the hands of a tsar-like monarch and the Russian Orthodox Church as a spiritual authority. RIM, a White Supremacist organization, and its military arm, the Russian Imperial Legion, adopted the badges of the imperial Russian army.

More than reminding terrorism experts of violent Far-Right reactionaries' perennial embrace of racist and nationalist emblems and slogans, the events of January 6, 2021, called for a careful reassessment of the domestic and international terrorist landscapes in the third decade of the twenty-first century. In the following, I will discuss the growing domestic and transnational dimensions of Far-Right violent extremism and its influence on solo terrorists not directly affiliated with groups; the growing but rarely lethal violent activities of contemporary Far-Left extremist groups; the reconfiguration of Jihadist groups and networks; the persistence of old and the appearance of new radical outliers, such as longtime antiabortion and new proabortion terrorism; and the opportunities for terrorist groups to exploit human suffering in major crises, such as devastating droughts and wildfires caused by climate change.

Far-Right Violent Extremism

The post-Cold War prospect of a "new world order" that President George H. W. Bush and others lauded as the beginning of a peaceful era of international cooperation was seen by "true patriots" as proof of Americans losing control of their own affairs. Newly formed paramilitary groups were motivated by conspiracy theories that reported the sighting of UN or Russian tanks and helicopters and of UN stormtroopers or American GIs under UN command. In response, so-called citizen militias prepared themselves to defend the U.S. Constitution against what they perceived to be no longer a sovereign federal government. The movement grew in response to the apparent liberal policies of President Bill Clinton that allegedly threatened the Second Amendment's right to bear arms guarantee and other civil liberties. Violent clashes between federal agents with a White Supremacist family at Ruby Ridge, Idaho, and with the Branch Davidian cult at Waco, Texas, strengthened the movement further. After the Oklahoma City bombing in 1995, militia and patriot groups gained national attention because the perpetrator, Timothy McVeigh, had moved into the militia/patriot and Christian Identity milieu as he conceived of and planned the catastrophic bombing. But after gaining a great deal of publicity and blame in the wake of the Oklahoma City bombing, the movement weakened in the late 1990s and during the presidency of George W. Bush.

The election of Barack Obama, a Democrat and the first African American president in U.S. history, triggered a revival of patriot and militia groups as well as other types of right-extremists—all on the same page in their insistence on the original content and intent of the Constitution and their right and obligation to protect the constitutional rights of their communities from the evils of the federal government and those of "inferior" race, ethnicity, and non-Christian religious backgrounds. Add to this a strong discontent and anger over the impact of a major economic crisis, the changing demographics of the nation, and a perceived do-nothing attitude of the ruling political elite. A gathering of extreme right-wing representatives on Jekyll Island in Georgia a few months after Obama's inauguration "warned of 'increasing national instability,' worried about a coming 'New World Order,' denounced secret schemes to merge Canada, Mexico and the United States, and furiously attacked the new president's 'socialized' policies and failure to end illegal immigration."[7] According to one observer of the extreme-right scene, "this remarkable gathering appears to have played a key role in launching the current resurgence of militias and the larger antigovernment 'Patriot' movement."[8] Other conspiracy theories claimed that the federal government had established an elaborate surveillance network to spy on citizens and a multitude of concentration camps inside U.S. borders for the coming imprisonment of dissidents—especially leading members within the Patriot Movement.

As described at the beginning of this chapter, the Proud Boys and Oath Keepers were by far the best-trained and best-organized groups in the riotous storm on the U.S. Congress in January 2021. They both had a history of supporting extreme anti-government groups; both provided security details for Trump rallies and Far-Right politicians and public figures. As the Oath Keepers' leader Rhodes wrote on his organization's website two days before 6/1,

> Over the years, Oath Keepers has conducted hundreds of highly successful volunteer security operations all over the nation, protecting patriots from communist terrorist assault... including providing volunteer security escorts outside twelve Trump campaign rallies, and many PSD details for high profile VIPs, such as Roger Stone, as well as many elected officials and election fraud whistle-blowers and patriot office holders.[9]

Because Oath Keepers and Proud Boys shared similar ideologies and unconditional allegiance to President Trump, their immediate goals converged in the wake of the November 2020 presidential election and caused their leaders to actually meet the night before the assault on the Capitol. Eleven Oath Keepers, among them Stewart Rhodes, and five Proud Boys, among them Enrique Tarrio, were indicted for seditious conspiracy, the most serious criminal charge made against participants in the 1/6 insurgency. According to 18 U.S. Code § 2384, seditious conspiracy means,

> If two or more persons in any State or Territory, or in any place subject to the jurisdiction of the United States, conspire to overthrow, put down, or to destroy by force the Government of the United States, or to levy war against them, or to oppose by force the authority thereof,

or by force to prevent, hinder, or delay the execution of any law of the United States, or by force to seize, take, or possess any property of the United States contrary to the authority thereof, they shall each be fined under this title or imprisoned not more than twenty years, or both.

In one respect Oath Keepers and Proud Boys differed in that the former pursued their objective strictly in the domestic setting, while the latter had from the outset both domestic and transnational designs and established affiliates not only across the United States but also in Europe. Like the Oath Keepers, the Three Percenters were comprised of a multitude of local affiliates across the United States. The group's national leaders established a few cells across the border in Canada but they had no ambitions to spread across the Atlantic Ocean to Europe. In contrast, like the Proud Boys, the other Far-Right extremist entities (Table 4.1), established after Donald Trump entered electoral politics in 2015, were conceived as transnational organizations.

Besides revitalizing militia and patriot groups, the Far-Right opposition to President Obama led also to the establishment of new para-military organizations, most of all, the Three Percenters founded immediately after Obama's election victory in the fall of 2008 and the Oath Keepers initiated merely weeks after the Obama's inauguration in early 2009. Both groups appealed to and recruited present and former members of the military, police, fire departments, and the like. Both groups established chapters in literally all parts of the United States. The Oath Keepers' leadership collected yearly dues from individuals and entire militia groups who joined the organization formally. There were also informal relationships between the Oath Keepers, by far the largest paramilitary organization in the United States, and other domestic anti-government, racist, fascist groups, including the Three Percenters.

Table 4.1 Violent Far-Right U.S. Groups Established in the Twenty-First Century

Name of Group	Year of Founding	Geographical Reach
Three Percenters	2008	Domestic (+Canada)
The Oath Keepers	2009	Domestic
Atomwaffen Division	2015	Domestic + Transnational
Proud Boys	2016	Domestic + Transnational
Rise Above Movement	2017	Domestic + Transnational
The Base	2018	Domestic + Transnational

Source: Author.

The Proud Boys were founded in 2016 as a reactionary male-only, fascist, anti-immigrant, and anti-Semitic group that sought out and engaged in a multitude of violent street fights with real and alleged Antifa (anti-fascists) and Black Lives Matter activists across the country. Although rejecting the White supremacist label and pointing to non-Whites among their members and leaders, the group's propaganda fit extreme White Supremacist and anti-Semitic prejudices. Although the youngest violent Far-Right "kid on the bloc," the Proud Boys did not only participate in the violent 2017 "Unite the Right" march in Charlottesville, Virginia; they actually played a major role in organizing the event. They outnumbered all organized Far-Right violent extremists during the 1/6 attack on the Congress. During a hearing of the congressional Select Committee on January 6, Representative Peter Aguilar mentioned an informant telling the FBI that the Proud Boys wanted to kill Vice-President Mike Pence during the violent insurrection.[10] During pre-trial procedures, several Proud Boys produced a videotape that allegedly proved the leadership's directions to members, not to engage in violence. This was contrary to the bulk of other communications within the Proud Boys community. According to the group's website that closed down in the aftermath of 1/6, the Proud Boys had some 40 chapters abroad, among them affiliates in the United Kingdom and Canada. The Canadian government designated the group a terrorist entity adhering to a White Supremacy/neo-Nazi/male chauvinist ideology along with like-minded organizations, such as the Three Percenters and the Aryan Strikeforce in England.

Atomwaffen Division or AWD (the German term Atomwaffen means nuclear weapons), founded in 2015, was from the outset one of the most extreme and most violent neo-Nazi entities. Its European affiliate Feuerkrieg established cells across Northern Europe and eventually in Ukraine and Russia. In the United Kingdom, the AWD's branch became home to former neo-Nazi groups, such as National Action, and its German affiliate Atomwaffen Division Deutschland a factor in the violent German neo-Nazi scene. According to intelligence reports, members of the AWD trained with the Imperial Russian Movement in a camp outside of St. Petersburg. The American neo-Nazi James Mason became early on a close advisor to the group's leadership and his book "Siege" a required reading for all members. The book, a compilation of radical newsletters published over many years, is a blueprint for accelerating the collapse of existing Western societies and the rise of White fascism. This so-called acceleration theory is another version of "The Turner Diaries" that William Pierce, the founder of the neo-Nazi National Alliance published some 45 years earlier under the pseudonym Andrew Macdonald. According to terrorism experts at the Soufan Center, the AWD learned from and adapted the best of jihadist propaganda:

AWD has created several recruitment and propaganda videos that, apart from being notably well-produced, harken on symbolism and language used by Salafi-jihadist organizations, including ISIS. In October 2019, AWD posted a video titled "Fission" on an encrypted chat forum depicting a masked man who is wielding a knife and burning the U.S., EU, and Israeli flags – bearing a striking resemblance to ISIS videos featuring 'Jihadi John.' The masked man uses phrases like: 'We will vanquish the modern world in totality...' and '...join us, or perish with the rest!' and proclaims that there will be no negotiations and no compromises...[11]

The Base (Al Qaeda in Arabic), a violent group established in 2018, resembled the AWD in many ways. The two entities embraced the same hard-core White Supremacist, neo-Nazi mission and the same emphasis on recruiting well-trained military veterans. The Base grew into a domestic and transnational network of leaderless cells that reached from the United States to Canada, Australia, South Africa, and Europe. After several members of The Base were arrested for plotting violent strikes, the founder of the group, Rinaldo Nazzarom moved to Russia. Claiming to have worked for the FBI and U.S. Department of Defense before creating The Base, Nazzaro continued to direct the group from St. Petersburg—most likely with the blessing of the Russian government. The membership of The Base and Atomwaffen Division overlapped and shared Telegram channels as both groups allowed their members multi-group associations.

The Rise Above Movement (RAM), established 2017 in Southern California, looked like a street gang with a violent neo-Nazi, alt-right agenda. Emphasizing physical fitness among its members, the group sought out confrontations at rallies organized by political "enemies." Unlike other self-described alt-right entities, RAM did not hide its fascist convictions. Group members attended multiple martial arts (MMA) events within the United States but also overseas. According to the Soufan Center, its "members have traveled overseas to Germany, Ukraine, and Italy to celebrate Adolf Hitler's birthday and forge stronger organizational links with white supremacy extremists based in Europe."[12] The group attracted old skinheads of earlier White Power groups, such as the Hammerskins, and tried to recruit veterans of the Iraq and Afghanistan wars.

Taken together, several of the Far-Right extremist groups established between 2015 and 2018, large and small, linked up with similar groupings abroad, mostly in Canada and Europe. According to one report, by 2021 White supremacist, neo-Nazi groups were "building international networks to spread their violent ideology."[13] In some instances, these affiliates incorporated existing violent extremist cells or attracted members of banned or former Far-Right entities. While some groups allowed memberships in multiple organizations and cooperated on the leadership level with similar groups, there were no signs of domestic or transnational united fronts of Far-Right violent groups. The one major effort to unite Far-Right violent extremist groups under one domestic alt-right umbrella, failed with the infamous 2017 rally at Charlottesville, Virginia. However, as noted above, there were contacts between Oath Keepers and Proud Boys hours before the 1/6 violence and a number of criminally charged participants had overlapping membership in Proud Boys, Oath Keepers, Three Percenters, and other violent extremist entities.

In the aftermath of the 1/6 criminal indictments of a significant number of White Supremacy national leaders, the focus of these groups shifted more than before to local and regional activities, especially confrontations with non-reactionary individuals and groups in legitimate public settings. Here, Far-Right violent extremists took a page from the playbook of foreign terrorist organizations that established political arms and members who got involved in the legitimate political process of their respective countries and eventually ran for and won elected offices. Groups like the Proud Boys and Three Percenters were particularly active in disrupting meetings of small town, village, and school boards claiming to fight for the rights and best interest of these communities. In reality, they hoped to recruit new members and win new supporters for their radical ideas and actions. As one of the Proud Boys in North Carolina put it, "The plan of attack if you want to make change is to get involved at the local level."[14] The Proud Boys also sought and won leadership roles in local and regional Republican entities. A case in point was South Florida, where several persons associated with the group won seats on the Miami-Dade Republican Executive Committee, among them persons who were criminally charged for their activities during the 1/6 breach of the U.S. Congress. Last but not least, dozens of Proud Boys, Oath Keepers, and QAnon conspiracy theorists ran for state-wide and local offices in a number of states in the 2022 mid-term elections.

No other bizarre, extreme, and violent political ideas spread more quickly and more widely than the QAnon conspiracy theory and its claim that a cabal of "deep state" globalists and pedophiles, among them Hillary Clinton, Barack Obama, and George Soros, plotted to establish a world government at the expense of nation-states like the United States. For the virtual community of QAnon followers, Donald Trump was divinely selected to bring evil-doers to justice and make America great again. Although deeply seated in American political culture and current affairs, QAnon was embraced by disillusioned and angry anti-government crowds in many countries, especially in the West, where the number of Trump fans grew and QAnon-inspired country-specific adaptions were embraced. In Germany, for example, Far-Right, anti-Semitic groups claimed that the governments of Germany and Austria were illegitimate because the German Reich with the pre-World War II borders of 1939 still existed. Reaching out to QAnon's glorification of Donald

Trump, they argued that a reinstated President Trump, would install a legitimate government of the traditional German Reich. Among those pushing that crazy claim were members of the violent *Reichsbuerger* group, the German version of the Sovereign Citizens movement in the United States.

Solo or Lone Actors under White Supremacy Banners

May 14, 2022, was a warm spring day in Buffalo, New York. In the early afternoon, shoppers in Tops Friendly Market on Jefferson Avenue, the only grocery store in the predominantly Black neighborhood, were buying foodstuffs for the weekend. At 2:30 p.m., a man holding an AR-15 semi-automatic rifle, moved quickly from his car in the parking lot toward the store entrance shooting three persons along the way. Inside the store, he sprayed bullets in the direction of shoppers. The shots from the gun of a security guard, a former police officer, do not the shooter. He wore plated body armor. Instead, he continued to shoot killing the guard in cold blood. When the gunman left the store, he had shot 13 innocent persons—11 Blacks and 2 Whites. Ten persons, all of them Blacks, were dead; the other three injured. Outside, he removed his tactical gear and surrendered to police. After the massacre, local, state, and federal officials characterize the incident as "murder," "hate crime," and "racially motivated extremism." Visiting Buffalo three days later to comfort mourning families, friends, and neighbors of the victims, President Joe Biden called the mass shooting "domestic terrorism." That's what it was. A meticulously planned act of terrorism carried out by 18-year-old Payton Gendron in a reenactment of similar attacks in the past by a transnational line-up of lone terrorists acting in the name of White supremacy.

Following the 2019 deadly terrorist attack on Latinos in El Paso by one perpetrator, Juliette Kayyem wrote in the *Washington Post*, that "there are no lone wolves," because these horrific actions by single actors are not the result of "a poisonous belief held by isolated individuals."[15] She was right. The term "lone wolf" to characterize a single terrorist is a misnomer. Even without belonging formally to violent extremist groups, solo terrorists share the hateful views of groups, movements, and communities. It is not unusual that the most brutal and best-known solo terrorists become admired heroes and martyrs in the very communities that infected them with their hateful ideas (see text in the box on the next page). They are no heroes, no martyrs but solo terrorists with divisive and violent ideologies.

As described above, the nexus between White supremacy/neo-Nazi domestic and transnational communities grew stronger in the recent past. The lone actor terrorists from four different countries listed in Table 4.2 shared the same ideas that were spread by globally accessible White

White Supremacist Terrorists and Their Idols

On June 17, 2015, 21-year-old Dylann Storm Roof killed nine African Americans at the Emanuel African Methodist Episcopalian Church in Charleston, South Carolina. The young white man had entered the church, was welcomed by parishioners, and sat quietly next to his eventual victims during their regular Bible study. Once the meeting concluded, Roof got up, drew his revolver, and shot his victims cold-blooded one by one. According to a survivor, he said, "You rape our women and you're taking over our country. And you have to go." The manifesto left behind by Roof revealed that he was guided by racial hate as expressed by White Supremacy organizations and Neo-Nazi groups on social media and on websites.

Two years later, in August 2017, well-armed White Supremacy, neo-Nazi, Ku Klux Klan, and paramilitary groups assembled in Charlottesville, Virginia, for a "United the Right" rally conceived by Far-Right leaders in search to bring these groups under one, effective umbrella. During a shouting match between rally participants and coun-ter-demonstrators one White supremacist screamed in the direction of African Americans, "Dylann Roof was a hero…Go home to Africa!"

Similarly, more than two decades after Timothy McVeigh carried out the 1995 Oklahoma City Bombing that killed 168 children and adults, the perpetrator of the most lethal act of terrorism before 9/11 became a hero in the right-extreme milieu. One well-known contributor to the neo-Nazi website "Daily Stormer" suggest in 2017, crowdfunding for the purpose of building a monument for McVeigh.[16] This sort of admi-ration inspired several McVeigh fans to commit violence themselves. Thus, in May 2017, Jeremy Christian slashed the throats and killed two men after they tried to protect two Muslim women from Christian's harassment on a commuter train in Oregon. "May all the Gods bless Timothy McVeigh—a true patriot," Christian wrote in a Facebook post before the attack.[17] Plots by several other fans of the Oklahoma City mass killer were foiled.

In May 22, 2022, Payton Gendron posted a lengthy manifesto online before he carried out his lethal attack on African American tar-gets in Buffalo. He was obviously an admirer of well-known White Supremacists men who had committed heinous terrorist killings and inspired his own atrocious deed. Large parts of this mass-killer's writ-ings were simply lifted from the manifestos of his idols who had killed in Christchurch, El Paso, and Poway.

Table 4.2 Solo Terrorists under White Supremacy Banner

Date	Name	Place	Target	Victims Killed
July 22, 2011	A. Breivik	Oslo, Utoya, Norway	Government/ youth camp	77
June 17, 2015	D. Roof	Charleston, USA	Black Church	9
Oct. 27, 2018	R. Bowers	Pittsburgh, USA	Synagogue	11
March 15, 2019	B. Tarrant	Christchurch, New Zealand	Two Mosques	51
April 27, 2019	J. Earnest	Poway, USA	Synagogue	1[a]
August 3, 2019	P. Crusius	El Paso, USA	Walmart Market	23
Oct. 9, 2019	S. Balliet	Halle, Germany	Synagogue	2[b]
Feb. 19, 2020	T. Rathjen	Hanau, Germany	Two Bars	10
May 14, 2022	P. Gendron	Buffalo, USA	Supermarket	10

Source: Public Records.

[a]Perpetrator's AK-15 jammed.

[b]Perpetrator failed to open Synagogue's.

social exclusion propaganda; they admired, copy-catted each other, and claimed that they were inspired by their idols' earlier killing sprees.

Seven of the nine cases were horrific mass-killings, in the other two instances, one perpetrator's shotgun jammed and the other terrorist could not open the targeted synagogue's reinforced door. Eight of the nine terrorists posted extensive manifestos on social media platforms before they attacked their targets. And each one of those statements referred to easily available extremist propaganda. Thus, Anders Breivik who in 2011 killed 77 people in and near Oslo, Norway, drew in his lengthy manifesto extensively from the writings of American and British White supremacists; he cited Robert Spencer, who became years later one of the promoters of the alt-right movement, many times. Brenton Tarrant, who in 2019 went on a shooting spree in two mosques in Christchurch, New Zealand, killing 51 worshippers, titled his manifesto "The Great Replacement" without mentioning that the term "the great replacement" was coined by the French author Renaud Camus, when he described the alleged coming replacement of the native French majority by non-Western immigrants, many of them Muslims. Like others before him, the Buffalo terrorist referred to the manifestos of earlier prominent terrorists. Only Robert Bowers, who killed 11 worshippers in the Tree of Life synagogue in Pittsburgh, Pennsylvania, did not write and publicize a manifesto: the 46-year-old was older than the other eight perpetrators at the time of their terrorist assaults and perhaps the least internet-savvy among them. But he, too, posted hateful messages on social media in advance of his deadly attack. Finally, after Tarrant live streamed his unspeakably brutal mass shooting on a social media platform, S Balliet, the attacker of a synagogue in Halle, Germany, Stephan Balliet, and the Buffalo mass-shooter followed his example.

Far-Left Violent Extremism

As of this writing, there were no horrific attacks by lone Far-Left terrorists or by Far-Left groups in the second and third decade of the twenty-first century that were comparable to the Far-Right terrorism. While Antifa (antifascist) activists interrupted Far-Right events and facilities in the United States and Europe regularly, attacked and injured police, and caused property damage, they did not aim to kill their targets. That changed on August 29, 2020, when Michael Reinoehl, an Antifa activist, shot Aaron Danielson to death during a protest in downtown Portland, Oregon. Danielson was a member of the Far-Right group Patriot Prayer. Reinoehl was charged with second-degree murder and unlawful use of a weapon. He refused to turn himself in after the fatal shooting and became a fugitive. Federal and local law enforcement officers located him near Olympia, Washington, a few days later, killing him while attempting to apprehend him.

The absence of frequent lethal attacks by Antifa extremists does not mean that the movement is not a threat. A case in point was the G-20 summit in Hamburg, Germany, in July 2017. The event itself was overshadowed by tens of thousands of Far-Left extremists from across Germany and Europe. While not all of the protesters in the streets resorted to violence, thousands of masked and black-clothed Antifa activists and Black Bloc anarchists used Molotov cocktails and iron rods to torch cars, smash store windows, and attack police in the streets as well as police helicopters in the air by signal flares and laser beams. More than 200 officers were injured and more than 100 protesters arrested. Many thousands of protesters marched under the banner of the antiglobalization network ATTAC (Association for the Taxation of Financial Transactions and Aid to Citizens) and underlined the transnational character of this Far-Left movement. Whether they embraced the anarchist, Antifa, or ATTAC label, left-extremists were increasingly active in Europe and Australia.

As for the United States, just weeks after the violence-plagued G-20 summit in Germany, Americans became aware of the Far-Left movement in their country. In August 2017, when White Supremacists and Neo-Nazis marched in Charlottesville, Virginia, to demonstrate unity in the extreme alt-right movement; they shouted provoking slogans. However, even the most offensive racist ("Go back to Africa") and anti-Semitic ("Jews will not replace us!") shouts were overshadowed by violent clashes between White nationalists carrying firearms and a cadre of Antifa leftists who used sticks, chemical sprays, and balloons filled with paint or ink as weapons. After the police declared the rally "an unlawful assembly" and both sides dispersed, 20-year-old right-extremist James Alex Fields Jr. from Ohio drove his Dodge Challenger at high speed into a crowd of counter-protesters in an obvious case of car-ramming. As he reversed his car, more pedestrians were hit. Thirty-two-year-old Heather Heyer, who was among Charlottesville residents expressing their opposition to the rally, was killed; 19 persons suffered injuries.

Few Americans who watched TV reports about the violent scenes in Charlottesville knew about the Antifa movement's American roots. Like small, autonomous, antifascist groups around the world, contemporary American adherents believe that fascism must be fought before it defeats democracy. They are convinced that small, determined groups of activists could have easily prevented the growth of the Mussolini and Hitler movements and parties early on. From the late 1980s through the early 2000s, local antifascist groups fought White Supremacist and Neo-Nazis under the banner of Anti-Racist Action (ARA). Typically, group members would interrupt White Power Rock or other events staged by racist/White Supremacist organizations.

But, as Mark Bray, a student of the Antifa movement noted, the death of William Pierce, founder and leader of the National Alliance organization, and the imprisonment of Matt Hale, the leader of the World Church of the Creator, contributed to the ARA's passing "through a relative lull from the middle of the 2000s up until perhaps the start of the Trump campaign."[18] During the campaign, ARA and AFA (antifascist action) activists interrupted Trump's campaign rallies. A Trump speech planned at the University of Illinois in Chicago had to be canceled because antifascists successfully promoted the infiltration of the audience with the result of fist fights and shouting matches between the pro- and anti-Trump sides. Violent black blocs, typical for anarchist activists, caused injuries and property damages during the celebrations surrounding President Trump's inauguration. However, according to a 2020 assessment by Seth Jones,

> The threat from Antifa and other far-left networks is relatively small in the United States. The far-left includes a decentralized mix of actors. Anarchists, for example, are fundamentally opposed to the government and capitalism, and they have organized plots and attacks against government, capitalist, and globalization targets. . . . Antifa followers have committed a tiny number of plots and attacks.[19]

Far-Right extremists and influential voices in right-wing political discourse blamed Antifa for any political street violence—even the events of 1/6, when part of the Proud Boys contingent wore all-black outfits to fake the presence of Antifa extremists. Similarly, they blamed any violence committed during Black Lives Matter (BLM) protests on either BLM or Antifa and sometimes both.

Antifa activists were far more active in European cities than in the United States. Some of them were communists or anarchists, while others were radical leftists advocating for local justice, often on the side of what they perceived as disadvantaged minorities. Most of them were nonviolent but others sought violent encounters with the authorities, particularly, when police tried to remove illegal occupiers of buildings from the premises.

Since 2015 Europol reported sharp increases in left-wing violence in Europe. Individual European countries seconded that assessment. By 2016, for example, Germany's police agencies were aware of 28,500 left-wing extremists, of whom 8,500 were considered risks to become violent. Italy, Sweden, and Greece, along with Germany, seemed to harbor most of Far-Left extremist. While there were many different left-extreme individuals, cells, and groups, the greatest threat of violence came according to police and intelligence agencies from Antifa and autonomous militants with mostly local concerns. All of these groups shared hate and rejection of capitalism and globalism. Their targets were most often police and other public officials. Germany's Finance Minister Wolfgang Schaeuble, for example, was the recipient of a letter bomb in 2017 for which the left-extremist "Conspiracy of Fire Cell" claimed responsibility. The rise of populist, authoritarian leaders in Europe, the United States, Latin America contributed to the growth and the activities of the Antifa movement.

As noted in Chapter 1, terrorism statistics can differ greatly depending on what types of politically motivated violence by nonstate actors are counted as terrorist deeds and how reliable sources are. Some statistics reflect only incidents that caused deaths, others include injuries, property damage, and other criminal offenses. Some statistics include only premeditated political violence and other count all clashes during political events. Most importantly, when the authorities characterize racially, ethnically, and religiously motivated violence as "hate crimes," these cases will not be included in terrorism statistics. Thus, while the Global Terrorism Index reported for 2021 merely 42 politically motivated cases of terrorist violence in the West, that number did not come close to the total number of political violence all in Western countries. Just one example: According to the German government, in there were 987 cases of Far-Left and 686 cases of Far-Right politically motivated violence in 2021. Left-Extremists carried out significantly more violent attacks but they did not kill any of their targets. Far-Right extremists killed one person and attempted but failed to kill two other persons.[20] Overall, experts in the field agreed that in the last decades, Far-Right extremists tended to commit fewer attacks than their Far-Left counterparts but killed and injured more people.

The State of Violent Jihadism

"Although al Qaeda and ISIS are far weaker than they were at their peak," terrorism expert Daniel Byman wrote in 2021, 20 years after 9/11, "they have persisted in the face of tremendous pressure, and their reach, although at times more ambitious than their grasp, has only grown since 2001."[21] This was a welcomed assessment of the real state of organized jihadist terrorism early in the third decade of the twenty-first century, when spectacular jihadist attacks in the West had subsided after a wave of horrific attacks at the heights of the Islamic State's territorial and recruitment gains. At the same time, countries in the Middle East, North and Sub-Sahara Africa, South and East Asia were hit very hard. ISIS and Al Qaeda and their affiliates remained active even though they faced effective international counterterrorism alliances, most of them assisted by the U.S. troops, especially Special Operations Forces. European countries were more often targets than was the American homeland. Thus, in the three years from January 1, 2019, through December 2021, there were 19 jihadist attacks in Europe in which 25 victims were killed. In that same three-year period, there was one such attack in the United States in which 3 victims were killed. The sole U.S. strike was particularly troubling because the perpetrator Mohammed Al-Shamrani, a Saudi citizen, had been in direct contact with Al Qaeda in the Arabian Peninsula (AQAP) when he planned his deadly attack on servicemen at the Naval Air Station Pensacola, Florida, in December 2019.

Al Qaeda Central, the core jihadist groups that Osama bin Laden established, was at the height of its reign of terror in the years before and after the 9/11 attacks. A relatively small group of Mujahideen, some of whom had fought against Soviet occupiers of Afghanistan with CIA support, had plotted, financed, and trained young jihadists for an unprecedented attack on symbolic targets in the homeland of the most powerful country in the world. But while bin Laden and his crew were initially celebrated by extremists in certain Muslim quarters, their greatest achievement was also the beginning of the decline of bin Laden's and fellow leaders' power although they continued to issue threats. When forced to flee their Afghanistan headquarters and hide in Pakistan or the rugged region between the two countries, they lost their instant personal and remote connections to rank-and-file Al Qaeda members and leaders of Al Qaeda Central's affiliates. Most devastatingly, from their hiding places, they were not able to disseminate their propaganda stream frequently and immediately. As a result of Western counterterrorism efforts, the inner circle of the organization shrank.

Still, the U.S. invasion of Iraq and the political powershift from Sunnis to Shias drove many Sunni dissidents into a group established by the ambitious Jordanian jihadist Abu Musab al-Zarqawi in 1999 that became Al Qaeda in Iraq in 2004. After al-Zarqawi's death in 2006, the group seemed in decline but that changed when Abu Baka al-Baghdadi became its leader and eventually renamed the once again vital organization Islamic State of Iraq. The name change signaled the group's autonomy which was formalized in 2014, when al-Baghdadi declared himself the caliph of the Islamic State Caliphate and formalized the separation from Al Qaeda.

Ayman al-Zawahiri who became Al Qaeda's leader after bin Laden was killed by U.S. Navy Seals in his hide-out in Pakistan in 2011, was ill-regarded by ISIS and repeatedly criticized in its online magazines. Thus, the tenth issue of *Dabiq*, one of those online publications, published a photograph in a critical article on al-Zawahiri with the caption, "A leader with no real authority."

In the absence of any communications by al-Zawahiri in 2019 and 2020 there were rumors that he had died or was incapacitated. But in mid-2022 bin Laden's successor released several videotaped messages commenting on more recent events, such as the hostilities in Ukraine. He celebrated the Taliban's take-over in Afghanistan. His aggressive posture and tone matched the extreme nature of his call to arms against Islam's enemies and the unification of all Muslims in one *umnah* or Islamic community. Obviously, the triumph of the Taliban, Al Qaeda's onetime host and ally, energized al-Zawahiri and what was left of Al Qaeda Central. He confirmed bin Laden's often repeated threats against America and the West. This fighting posture of Al Qaeda's leader came shortly after the self-described "Al Qaeda Malahem Cyber Army" urged followers in its "Wolves of Manhattan" online magazine "to travel to Ukraine to acquire training and weapons to use in attacks against the West."[22] The appeal was deemed serious enough by the U.S. intelligence community that the Department of Homeland Security mentioned it in its "National Terrorism Advisory Bulletin."[23] According to one terrorism expert, even a diminished post-9/11 Al Qaeda had 20 years after their greatest accomplishment "a presence in, among other countries, Afghanistan, Algeria, Bangladesh, Egypt, India, Iran, Libya, Mali, Pakistan, Saudi Arabia, Somalia, Syria, Tunisia, Turkey, and Yemen."[24] This did not change after Zawahiri was killed by a U.S. drone strike on July 31, 2022, in Kabul.

ISIS, according to the same source, was "present in most of those countries plus Cameroon, Chad, Iraq, Mozambique, Nigeria, and Russia."[25] Although the territorial Islamic State ended in defeat in 2019, several of its leaders and thousands of its fighters went into hiding in Syria, Iraq, and a host of other countries. At that point, the organization that one might call the Islamic State Central was severely weakened but not paralyzed. ISIS survived the loss of its leaders, first al-Baghdadi in

October 2019, then his successor Abu Ibrahim al-Hashimi al-Qurayshi in February 2022. Although losing control of the huge pieces of real estate in Iraq and Syria that it had conquered with force, the group continued to terrorize the areas of its former triumphs. According to one astute analysis, in the early 2020s,

> ISIS is slowly regrouping in both Iraq and Syria, forming sleeper cells to launch attacks, while maintaining an effective command-and-control to wage a low-level guerrilla insurgency and mobilize new support. The Islamic State is able to conduct asymmetric attacks on civilians and security forces, but can also marshal the resources to launch spectacular attacks intended to destabilize the Iraqi government.[26]

ISIS made great efforts to free the thousands of their jihadists as well as the group's women and children captured and imprisoned in the region. In early 2022, an estimated 200 ISIS soldiers launched an attack on the Hasaka detention facility in Syria, detonating a series of IEDs. During the bloody fight, many of the attackers, prisoners, and members of the Syrian Defense Front (SDF) were killed, while a substantial but unknown number of detainees escaped. It took American and British Special Forces to retake the prison. The most militant among the detained ISIS men and women dominated their fellow prisoners in the region's detention centers using threats and violence to prevent defections. No doubt, by the early 2020s, ISIS, not Al Qaeda, was the most potent jihadist entity with transnational ambitions and a continued anti-American and anti-Western agenda. Thus, in June 2022, the U.S. Department of Homeland Security's informed law enforcement agencies about a threatening audio message, released by ISIS, that warned of "a new global campaign of attacks to avenge the deaths of the group's deceased leader. . . and urged ISIS supporters to carry out knife and vehicle ramming attacks in the United States and Europe."[27]

ISIS had vast financial resources amassed during its multi-year reign over parts of Syria and Iraq and was well positioned to support the Islamic State Central's leadership role within an expansive net of affiliates and franchises in a multitude of countries on different continents. As one observer put it, "A significant amount of its bandwidth has been dedicated to promoting its branches throughout sub-Saharan Africa and now, following the Taliban's takeover of Afghanistan, in various parts of South Asia."[28]

The ISIS-affiliated group that grew most rapidly in the early 2020s was Islamic State Khorasan Province (ISKP) that was established in 2015 by a Taliban faction in Afghanistan. The group drew its membership not only from militant Afghans and Pakistani but also from India and Bangladesh and was joined by the Islamic Movement of Uzbekistan and jihadist from

Tajikistan. Taliban and ISKP fighters clashed regularly. When die Taliban gained control over one after the other Afghan regions and released prisoners from detention facilities, many freed ISKP fighters returned to their group (just as many freed Al Qaeda militants rejoined their organization). The contemporary ISKP has ambitious designs in Afghanistan, where the group carried out numerous deadly attacks before and after the Taliban took over the Kabul government. Disillusioned members of the Afghan National Defense Forces which could not prevent the Taliban from coming to power have reportedly joined and strengthened the ranks of the ISKP—just as many officers of Saddam Hussein's defeated and dismantled military joined years earlier Al Qaeda in Iraq/ISIS in Iraq. Already affiliated with groups in several of the former Soviet republics, ISKP recruited and brought into its ranks Chechens and Uighurs risking countermeasures by the Russian and Chinese governments. The group was also on a potential collision course with the Iranian government because it attacked increasingly Shia churches, schools, and other facilities in Afghanistan killing and injuring large numbers of the targeted minority—a growing problem for neighboring Iran's Shia majority. The unanswered question remained, how the Taliban government would deal with the terrorist entities within Afghanistan, one of which—Islamic State Khorasan Province—was even more extreme in its religious rules than the Afghanistan, and another one—Al Qaeda—less dogmatic than the ruling Taliban.

The regional ambitions of the Islamic State grew step by step from centering merely on Iraq, then including Syria and eventually the Levant adding Lebanon, Cyprus, Israel, Jordan, Palestine, and Turkey's Hatay Province to the organization's interest. More than a decade after separating from Al Qaeda, the Islamic State had not only affiliates in South Asia but also in a growing number of African countries, particularly in the sub-Sahara region. The number of groups grew so rapidly that in 2019, when ISIS Central in Syria was close to its total defeat, its leadership nevertheless announced the establishment of the Islamic State Central Africa Province (ISCAP) "to promote the presence of ISIS associated elements within Central, East, and Southern Africa."[29] Although groups under the ISCAP umbrella, such as ISIS Mozambique and ISIS Democratic Republic of the Congo (ISIS-DRC) remained independent groups, the idea was to have them benefit from the regional organization's communication and propaganda skills and activities and perhaps promote mutual cooperation between individual entities.

Some ISIS groups were active in more than one country. A good example was Boko Haram, one of the most violent terrorist groups, that was founded in the early 2000s in Northern Nigeria to use violence in order to force the population to embrace "pure Islam" with the ultimate goal to overthrow the Nigerian government. Boko Haram opposed Western secular education and often targeted schools killing and maiming and kidnapping students and teachers. The group also terrorized several neighboring states, including Cameroon, Chad, and Niger. For years, Boko Haram was the most lethal terrorist group in the world terrorizing and killing members of the Nigerian military, police, and civilians. When the group's association with ISIS soured, a number of Boko Haram members formed a rival group naming it the Islamic State's West African Province (ISWAP). This opened a chapter of violent conflicts between the two groups. Boko Haram's leader Abu Bakar Shekau killed himself in May 2021 before the rival group could capture him during a fight between the two sides. Many members of his group deserted to ISWAP or surrendered to the Nigerian army. But it was far from clear that Boko Haram's reign of terror was finally over. In spite of Boko Haram's diminished manpower, a core of its fighters did not desert or surrender but continued to attack targets, preferably in neighboring Cameroon and Chad.

Taken together, the two dominant jihadist organizations and their widely spread networks of branches and franchises remained threats to be dealt with by counterterrorist communities around the globe.

Single-Issue and Crisis-Related Political Violence

The movements and groups examined above were and are motivated by ideologies and agendas resorting to political violence to further their particular goals. Single-issue or special-interest groups, on the other hand, are narrowly focused on one particular political issue or a package of closely related issues. And here, too, groups and individuals tend to fit either the conservative/right or the liberal/left side of the political spectrum, as exemplified by conservative antiabortion and liberal proabortion violent extremists or so-called ecoterrorists whose grievances and actions changed as progressing global climate caused emergencies in many regions around the world that terrorists could—and did—exploit.

Antiabortion and Proabortion Terrorism

Antiabortion Terrorism: In 1973, the U.S. Supreme Court ruled in *Roe v. Wade* that the U.S. Constitution grants women the right to abortion. In the wake of the controversial decision, antiabortion or pro-life organizations emerged with the explicit goal of overturning the *Roe v. Wade* decision and legalized abortion. The overwhelming number of pro-life activists and the groups they joined were and are distinctly nonviolent and willing to work within the legitimate political process. However, some individuals and factions were not content with bringing legal actions to the courts, lobbying members of Congress, organizing demonstrations, harassing abortion providers and seekers, and staging acts of civil disobedience; instead, they called for and/or committed violence—against abortion clinics and their personnel. Although pro-life or proabortion groups and particularly medical doctors and their staffs in abortion clinics were the targets of violent attacks, the pro-abortion movement did not have a violent appendix through the nearly five decades following the *Roe v. Wade* decision. However, as soon as there was evidence that the Supreme Court's majority would overturn the pro-abortion ruling, proabortion extremists carried out violence against the facilities of anti-abortion centers.

In the early 1990s, two physicians who worked in abortion clinics in Pensacola, Florida, were shot by followers of extremist antiabortion groups, namely, Rescue America and Defense Action. Clinics and personnel in other parts of the United States were before and after that event the targets of bombings and other violence. Such actions intimidated many physicians so that stopped working in abortion clinics. Those who carried on were not even safe away from their workplaces. Thus, in 1998, Dr. Barnett A. Slepian was shot and killed in the kitchen of his private residence in Amherst in western New York State by James C. Kopp, a longtime antiabortion radical. After his arrest, Kopp claimed that he targeted Dr. Slepian in his home in order not to harm innocent bystanders. Sentenced to 25 years to life in prison, Kopp allegedly told fellow-antiabortion extremists that he would do the same upon his release if abortions were still performed at the time.[30] The last physician killed for his services in a Wichita, Kansas, abortion clinic was Doctor George Tiller who was gunned down in April 2019 while he attended his local church. He had been injured in a previous attack. Ironically, shortly before Tiller was killed, the following statistical summary was published:

> Since 1993, eight clinic workers—including four doctors, two clinic employees, a clinic escort, and a security guard—have been murdered in the United States. Seventeen attempted murders have also occurred since 1991. In fact, opponents of choice have directed more than 6,100 reported acts of violence against abortion providers since 1977, including bombings, arsons, death threats, kidnappings, and assaults, as well as more than 156,000 reported acts of disruption, including bomb threats and harassing calls.[31]

Neither Doctor Tiller now other abortion providers received special police protection that might have prevented the assassination. Since 1977, the National Abortion Federation (NAF) has gathered data about anti-abortion terrorism that includes actual and threatened violence against persons and facilities. Among the violent cases the NAF listed for the 44 years from 1977 through 2020 were the following:

- 11 Murders of Personnel Providing Abortion Services;
- 26 Attempted Murders of Abortion Providers and Staff;

- 956 Death Threats/Threats of Harm;
- 42 Bombings of Anti-Abortion Facilities;
- 194 Cases of Arson;
- 104 Cases of Attempted Bombings/Arson;
- 100 cases of Butyric Acid Attacks;
- 368 Instances of Assault and Battery;
- 456 Cases of Invasion;
- 4 Kidnappings.

Mere threats to attack abortion clinics and kill abortion doctors can have devastating effects on the psyche of clinic personnel. Perhaps this was best understood after September 11, 2001, when the attacks on New York and Washington were followed up with a serious anthrax scare after news organizations and members of Congress received letters containing anthrax powder. Well before this scare, abortion clinics had received hundreds of anthrax threats and letters claiming to contain the lethal material. Although no anthrax was found in any of the mailings, the mere threat frightened the recipients. The self-proclaimed Army of God, the most extreme antiabortion groups, did not hide its violent agenda on its website as the following excerpt from its *Manual* revealed:

> Beginning officially with the passage of the Freedom of Choice Act— we, the remnant of God-fearing men and women of the United States of Amerika [*sic*], do officially declare war on the entire child-killing industry. After praying, fasting, and making continual supplication to God for your pagan, heathen, infidel souls, we then peacefully, passively presented our bodies in front of your death camps, begging you to stop the mass murder of infants. Yet you hardened your already blackened, jaded hearts. We quietly accepted the resulting imprisonment and suffering of our passive resistance. Yet you mocked God and continued the holocaust. No longer! All of the options have expired. Our Most Dread Sovereign Lord God requires that whoever sheds man's blood, by man shall his blood be shed. Not out of hatred for you, but out of love for the persons you exterminate, we are forced to take arms against you.[32]

Traditionally, a number of White Supremacy and antigovernment groups condemned abortion, at least as far as the procedure concerned Aryan women. And some individuals from this milieu committed antiabortion terrorism. According to law enforcement officials, Eric Robert Rudolph, a White Supremacist and survivalist, is such an individual. After detonating a bomb at the Olympic Games in Atlanta in 1996 and a gay nightclub in the region, he bombed two abortion clinics. When he was finally arrested in the spring of 2003, many people in and around Murphy, North Carolina, where he had hidden for years, expressed strong support for the man whose terrorist blasts had killed 2 and injured 111 persons. A mother of four said, "Rudolph's a Christian and I am Christian and he dedicated his life to fighting abortion. Those are our values. These are our woods. I don't see what he did as a terrorist act."[33]

The extremist agendas of anti-abortion activists and Far-Right violent extremists converged even more during the Obama and Trump presidencies. During the 1/6 breach of U.S. Capitol Buildings prominent anti-abortion extremists and antiabortion terrorists were in the crowd among White Supremacists and anti-government extremists. According to one source,

> Anti-abortion extremists have also expanded the targets of their violence beyond abortion providers. A number of prominent anti-abortion extremists were among those who participated in the siege of the U.S. Capitol that day cited their anti-abortion views as the reason they traveled to Washington, D.C., with one person explaining that her decision to come to the Capitol was, in part, "to fight for the unborn." Another extremist who filmed himself at the Capitol that day was previously convicted of planning to bomb an abortion clinic in 1988, and later admitted to setting fire to that clinic and another.[34]

For many decades, antiabortion violence increased in reaction to court decisions or legislation expanding or confirming pro-choice rights and decreased in reaction to court rulings or statutes favoring the prolife positions. However, even after the Supreme Court agreed to review a Mississippi law that challenged *Roe v. Wade* and after its decision to overturn the 1973 ruling, antiabortion extremists carried out numerous attacks on planned parenthood facilities that remained open. For these extremists, the overruling of the 1973 decision was just the first step. The demanded congressional legislation to totally ban abortions in all 50 states and signaled with intensified peaceful picketing of abortion clinics and some incidents of violence that they were poised to fight on.

While the antiabortion movement in the United States was in the past and remains today the best organized, best financed, and most violent in the world, there were and are antiabortion movements and activists and cases of antiabortion violence in several other countries, most of all in Canada, New Zealand, and Australia. Well-financed American anti-abortion interest groups have promoted their cause around the world, particularly in the European Union. While they do not encourage anti-abortion forces abroad to resort to violence, this could be the consequence given the transnational nature of the White Supremacy movement described earlier in this chapter.

Proabortion Terrorism: In the previous editions of this textbook, I did not include proabortion terrorism because it did not exist in

Western democracies. While the non-violent pro-life movement fought in the legitimate political process to change the Supreme Court's *Roe v. Wade* ruling, for example, by increasing the number of conservative justices, violent extremist antiabortion activists violated the law. The pro-choice movement and abortion providers had no reason to resort to violence against violent extremists those who were violating the law, were guilty of criminal offenses, and were often brought to justice. Indeed, in the 44 years between 1977 and 2020, there were a total of 33,867 arrests for anti-abortion violence and disruptions (such as picketing, bomb threats). However, this changed in 2021, when a leaked draft of the forthcoming Supreme Court decision on *Roe v. Wade* signaled the overturn of the 1973 rule and individuals or groups of prochoice extremists attacked and threatened pro-life centers and churches that advised pregnant girls and women. While nobody was killed or injured during the first wave of several attacks on pro-life facilities, there were planted explosives, incidents of arson, and smashed in windows and other property damage. And there was a failed attempt to kill Supreme Court Justice Brett Kavanaugh after the content of a leak draft of the upcoming *Roe v. Wade* decision was reported in the news. On June 8, a man dressed in black clothing carrying a backpack and suitcase was arrested after he appeared in front of Justice Kavanaugh's home but retreated when he saw a police officer. The would-be assassin was Nickolas Roske (26) of California who was in possession of a pistol, ammunition, a tactical knife, and other items. He told detectives that he planned to kill Kavanaugh and himself because of the expected overrule of *Roe v. Wade*.

Just like peaceful pro-life advocates condemned antiabortion terrorism, pro-choice groups and their leaders were opposed to any violence against pro-life groups and their facilities—and certainly against attacks on pro-abortion public officials. And just as the anti-abortion fanatics of the "Army of God" were an elusive underground initiative that carried out and glorified violence, an equally mysterious and new "Jane's Revenge" online group called on pro-choice supporters to attack the opponents after its establishment in May 2022. The initiative's slogan was, "If abortion isn't safe, you aren't either. We are everywhere." In its first so-called communique, Jane's Revenge stated:

> This is not a declaration of war. War has been upon us for decades. A war which we did not want, and did not provoke. Too long have we been attacked for asking for basic medical care. Too long have we been shot, bombed, and forced into childbirth without consent. . .
>
> We demand the disbanding of all anti-choice establishments, fake clinics, and violent anti-choice groups within the next thirty days. . .
>
> We are forced to adopt the minimum military requirement for a political struggle. . .

And we will not stop, we will not back down, nor will we hesitate to strike until the inalienable right to manage our own health is returned to us.

We are not one group, but many. We are in your city. We are in every city. Your repression only strengthens our accomplice-ship and resolve.[35]

Although the identity of those behind "Jane's Revenge" was not revealed, the name seemed to refer to the "Jane Collective" of leftist activists in Chicago who in the 1960s provided abortion to thousands of women. Announcing that "The night of June 24 was the Night of Rage," the online site seemed to invoke the violence in Chicago carried out by the Weathermen in the late 1960s. The photograph of a suspect inflicting damage on a pro-life advisory facility depicted a masked man in all-black clothing—the trademark of Far-Left extremists, such as anarchists and Antifa members.

Eco- and Environmental Terrorism

The destruction of the natural environment and habitat of animals led in the 1970s to the establishment of the leaderless resistance movement Animal Liberation Front (ALF) in the United Kingdom and in the 1990s of the Earth Liberation Front (ELF) which was a more extremist offshoot of the Earth First movement. Like Earth First, ALF and ELF found followers in Europe, North America, and elsewhere. Because ALF and ELF actions were often indistinguishable, the two were lumped together by students of violent groups such as Animal and Earth Liberation Front (AELF). Both advocated to use violence to draw attention to their causes—the preservation of all animal life and the protection of the environment against exploitation by "the capitalist society [that] is destroying all life on this planet."[36] The pro-animal rights and pro-environment groups espoused Far-Left ideologies often corresponding to anarchist views. By the early 2000s, activists in those groups were characterized by some law enforcement agencies as eco-terrorists.

The term environmental terrorism has been defined in various ways. I suggest that it is the appropriate term for actions taken by terrorist groups intended to exploit the dire consequences of climate change by causing or worsening environmental crises, for example, by committing arson to start destructive wildfires or by disrupting the water supply in drought-stricken areas. Climate change crises offer terrorist groups and individuals opportunities to exploit the suffering of affected populations for their own causes.

Eco-Terrorism: In the past, the FBI used the term terrorism rarely to characterize a domestic group. But ELF and ALF in North America received the terrorist label from the agency. In 2004, John E. Lewis, Deputy Assistant FBI Director, told the Senate Judiciary Committee that

ALF and ELF had "emerged as serious domestic terrorist threat."[37] In the same testimony, Lewis described new trends in the eco-terrorism movement as follows:

> These trends include a greater frequency of attacks in more populated areas, as seen in Southern California, Michigan and elsewhere, and the increased targeting of Sport Utility Vehicles (SUVs) and new construction of homes or commercial properties in previously undeveloped areas by extremists combating what they describe as "urban sprawl." Eco-terrorists have adopted these new targets due to their perceived negative environmental impact. Recent examples of this targeting include the August 1, 2003 arson of a large condominium complex under construction near La Jolla, California, which resulted in an estimated $50 million in property damages; the August 22, 2003 arson and vandalism of over 120 SUVs in West Covina, California; and the arson of two new homes under construction near Ann Arbor, Michigan in March 2003.[38]

The followers of ALF and ELF did not formally become members of these organizations and did not pay dues; they organized in small, autonomous, underground cells that planned and executed violent acts to achieve social and political change. The two groups worked closely together and may have had overlapping followers. In 2004 estimate the FBI stated, "ALF/ELF and related groups have committed more than 1,100 criminal acts in the United States since 1976, resulting in damages conservatively estimated at approximately $110 million." Those numbers did not reflect the consequences of threats against individuals and groups of people working in particular areas of the private sector. During a *Washington Post* online forum on ecoterrorism with FBI Special Agent James F. Jarboe, one participant described the tactics of ecoterrorists this way:

> I work for an industry that has been targeted by ecoterrorism—and in the past have been personally threatened by an animal rights activist who said he knew my address and was planning to come into my home one evening and slash my face to ribbons with a razor blade. Perhaps some of the people viewing this discussion don't feel that ecoterrorism is very real—but I can assure them that I was terrified and was very grateful that the FBI took the threat seriously. The group targeting me (they got my name off of a website) have been known to blow up boats, break into homes and offices and shut down computer systems. To me, that's terrorism.[39]

Eco-terrorists claiming responsibility in the name of ALF or ELF did not kill human beings during the several decades of their activity. However, in the late 1990s and early 2000s, their rhetoric was militant and threatening. The ELF website proclaimed in early 2003 that "the only way, at this point in time, to stop that continued destruction of life [on this planet] is to by any means necessary take the profit motive out of killing."[40] Placed above this text was an advertisement for ELF's free "Guide to Setting Fires with Electric Timers," which contained do-it-yourself material about "devices, fuel requirements, timers, security, and more." Visitors to the site were invited to print or download the manual. A similar ALF do-it-yourself guide ("Arson-Around with Auntie ALF: Your Guide for Putting the Heat on Animal Abusers Everywhere") was available on both the ELF and the ALF websites. "Auntie ALF, Uncle ELF and the Anti-Copyright gang" advised readers explicitly not to injure or kill "animals, human or otherwise" when resorting to arson, but by describing in detail the preparation of incendiary devices, these guidelines read like invitations to join ALF's and ELF's arson activists. In view of the FBI, the online instructions were followed by underground cells of the two groups. "By far the most destructive practice of the ALF/ELF to date is arson," FBI Deputy Assistant Director Lewis said at the time, "The ALF/ELF extremists consistently use improvised incendiary devices equipped with crude but effective timing mechanisms. These incendiary devices are often constructed based upon instructions found on the ALF/ELF websites."[41] Abroad, extremists among the animal rights/environmental movements went further than their American counterparts. Thus, Volker van der Graaf, an activist on behalf of animal rights and environmental protection, assassinated the Dutch right-wing politician Pim Fortuyn in May 2002 during the national election campaign in Holland. During his trial, van der Graaf said that he had targeted Fortuyn because of the politician's dangerous ideas, especially with respect to animals, the environment, immigrants, Muslims, and asylum seekers.

Following the increased militancy of ALF and ELF and the concurrent rise of eco-terrorist actions in the early 2000s, the FBI increased its investigations and arrested more persons involved in ALF and ELF violence. The Animal Enterprise Terrorism Act (AETA) passed by Congress in 2006 made damaging or interfering with the operations of an animal enterprise a federal crime punishable with prison terms up to 20 years. In reaction, the websites of the two groups removed bomb-making guidelines and other aggressive material. It was left to the group's press offices to report actions in support of animals and protection of the environment.

The actions listed in mid-2022 on the ALF's press office website were not breaking news items. Here are a few sample headlines of articles detailing the latest actions:

- AFL Shatters Windows at Butcher (Clifton, Bristol, UK);
- ALF Smashes Butcher Shop Windows (St. Werbergs, Bristol, UK);
- ALF Liberates 13 Hens (Luxemburg);

- 12 Rabbits Liberated from T&S Rabbits Fur Farm (East Bridgford, UK);
- ALF Sabotages 10 Hunting Towers, Smash Cameras in Solidarity with MBR Beagles (Sweden).[42]

After researching the state of eco-terrorism and environmental terrorism, Paolo Andrea Spadaro wrote in 2020,

> As these groups [ALF and ELF] do not generally seek harming human life, but only property, which they consider as ecologically destructive, their actions align more with those of ecotage that is violence against inanimate objects and not directly with terrorism.[43]

In other words, she called the actions sabotage, not terrorism. That may have been a sound assessment in the 2020s but less so more than a decade earlier. However, there were far more extremist eco-terrorist groups, some of which had splintered off from ALF and ELF. Justice Department, Animal Rights Extremists, Animal Rights Brigade, Deep Green Resistance, and Animal Liberation Brigade and Revolutionary Cells differed in one respect fundamentally from the Big Two organizations in that they did not rule out violence against persons. But according to some observers of the eco-terrorism movement, the most dangerous threat was and remained in the early 2020s the transnational group Individualities Towards the Savagery (ITS) that was founded in 2011 in Mexico with an ideology and mission reminiscent of Theodore Kaczynski's ideas expressed in a manifesto that was to explain why he, the so-called Unabomber, killed three persons and injured 23 more via letter bombs during a 17-year period. Reportedly active in Mexico and Chile members of the group killed according to one expert 37 persons and "claimed responsibility for attacks in Greece" as well.[44]

Still, as climate changes became more severe in the 2020s, environmental terrorism was likely to become a far greater threat than eco-terrorism ever was.

Environmental Terrorism: As I noted above, environmental terrorism means the exploitation of the extreme consequences of climate change by terrorists, either organized groups or individuals buying into the ideologies and actions of terrorist organizations. Among the most devastating effects of climate change have been for years be the lack of water and the resulting drought conditions and the susceptibility of areas plagued by drought condition to the spread of accidentally or intentionally set fire. Environmental terrorists exploit these conditions in two ways, (1) by contributing to environmental damages and increasing the suffering of people, and (2) by using crises caused by climate change to radicalize and recruit individuals or groups that are hard hit by such emergencies. The following examples show that it is not unusual for terrorists to pursue both goals at the same time:

- When Al Shabab's influence in Somalia waned in the second decade of the twenty-first century under effective international counterterrorism measures, the terrorist group retained an important source of power, its control over the most precious scarce resource—water supply for the cities. For years, the group was hoarding water sources, poisoning wells in small towns, and destroying a key part of water infrastructure—weirs, levees, pipes. Al Shabaab decided where water was available and where not and recruited youth from communities suffering water emergencies.
- Because the water in Lake Chad in Nigeria diminished as a result of the ever-longer drought conditions in the region, the competition for water became fierce. Terrorist groups like Boko Haram and IISIS's West African Province focused on winning control over local water resources and using the claim that they provided better community services than local and regional governments as recruitment tools.
- In 2014, when ISIS was increasing its control over Iraqi and Syrian territories, the group used control over water resources as an effective weapon in drought-stricken areas. In Iraq and Syria ISIS closed dams from releasing water into surrounding communities or released it selectively to some and withheld it from other areas. At one point, the Sunni group threatened Iraq's Shia community to withhold their complete water supply from the Mosul dam.

The three cases occurred in areas of Africa and the Middle East which were much harder hit by environmental crises than were Western regions and countries. However, in the more recent past climate change came to inflict damage on Western regions and countries as well. Thus, in mid-July 2022, reports about dangerous water shortages in the American Southwest described how severe the crisis war was. According to one report, as a consequence of climate change, [water] "supplies at Lake Mead and Lake Powell are dangerously low, holding just more than a quarter of their total capacities – and threatening the dams' ability to generate electricity and provide water to its nearly 40 million users."[45] This shocking reality meant that California and six other Western states had to

> shift away from a water source upon which it has relied for centuries, and, in some cases, make tough choices that are sure to ripple nationwide — such as whether to continue alfalfa farming for cattle feed or switch to more drought-hardy crops.[46]

Since global warming caused more and more severe droughts, the water shortage was expected to get worse in the future providing terrorists with ample opportunities to exploit these environmental crises.

Similarly, drought conditions increased the danger of rapidly spreading wildfires able to destroy whole communities. Al Qaeda and ISIS told their followers about the destructive impact of out-of-control fire on hard-hit areas and the stricken populations. They described the damages of huge fires in rural areas and inner-city buildings. In a 2012 issue of Al Qaeda's online magazine "Inspire," the question was posed, "Is it possible for us to cause a similar destructive impact using a similar weapon? The answer is: Yes, it is possible. Even in a shorter time and with much bigger destructive impact." This was followed by a detailed instruction on building an "ember bomb" and the advice that it was most important to spread terror in the affected communities. ISIS, too, asked supporters to participate in an "arson jihad" by setting on fire all kinds of buildings and wooded spaces adjacent to residential areas.[47] In the 2020s, more and more rapidly spreading wildfires devasted huge areas of the American west and, increasingly, drought-stricken regions of Spain, Portugal, Italy, Greece, Turkey, and other countries around the Mediterranean—all opportunities for environmental terrorism.

While there were some incidents of arson in the West, there were no known cases of political motives behind the setting of wildfires and no known involvement of environmental terrorists in the exploitation of severe water shortages in the United States or elsewhere in the West. Yet, it was certainly possible, if not likely, for a nexus between climate change and terrorism to become stronger as environmental damages would become more severe. In the West, antigovernment Far-Left and Far-Right violent extremists were most likely to copy-cat the jihadist exploitation of environmental disasters. According to one researcher,

> While eco-movements were traditionally linked to the left, in times of an increased threat from right wing activism, these actors can notice the rhetoric of antiimmigration and militarization of resources in response to the climate crisis, and potentially engage in environmental linked-extremism.[48]

The contemporary map of terrorism is shaped by a multitude of different types of political violence by nonstate groups and individuals, but relevant data show consistently that jihadist groups commit by far the most and the most lethal terrorist attacks. For this reason, the following Chapter Five is devoted to religious terrorism, most of all of the jihadist variety.

Notes

1 One female protester was shot dead by police as she used violence to enter the House chamber full of lawmakers, four died of heart attacks or other causes.

2 According to the indictment document of the five Proud Boys. Text is available at https://www.justice.gov/usao-dc/press-release/file/1510791/download, accessed June 10, 2022.

3 Ibid.

4 I copied the posts before they were deleted on the Oath Keepers' website https://www.oathkeepers.org/. The page was still operated in mid-2022 enlisting donations for "Steward Rhodes Legal Defense Fund."

5 Ibid.

6 While eventually more than 800 persons were charged, some of them more than a year after 1/6, I examined the cases of the first 659 people charged according to the FBI documents that are available at https://www.justice.gov/usao-dc/capitol-breach-cases, accessed March 22, 2022.

7 Heidi Beirich, "Midwifing the Militias," *Southern Poverty Law Center's Intelligence Report* (Spring 2010), www.splcenter.org/get-informed/intelligence-report/browse-all-issues/2010/spring/midwifing-the-militias, accessed June 1, 2010.

8 Ibid.

9 https://oathkeepers.org/2021/01/oath-keepers-deploying-to-dc-to-protect-events-speakers-attendees-on-jan-5-6-time-to-stand/, accessed January 8, 2021. The post was removed from the site a few days after being accessed and copied by the author.

10 This revelation is contained in a YouTube clip, https://www.youtube.com/watch?v=Bu01ypSzwDk, accessed June 22, 2022.

11 Soufan Center, "The Atomwaffen Division: The Evolution of the White Supremacy Threat." August 2020; https://thesoufancenter.org/wp-content/uploads/2020/08/The-Atomwaffen-Division-The-Evolution-of-the-White-Supremacy-Threat-August-2020-.pdf, accessed June 20, 2022.

12 Soufan Center, "IntelBrief: White Supremacy Extends Reach from Ukraine to US Military," September 30, 2019, https://thesoufancenter.org/intelbrief-white-supremacy-extremists-extend-reach-from-ukraine-to-u-s-military/, accessed June 22, 2022.

13 Sebastian Rotella, "Global Right-Wing Extremism Networks Are Growing." *ProPublica*, January 22, 2021, https://www.propublica.org/article/global-right-wing-extremism-networks-are-growing-the-u-s-is-just-now-catching-up, accessed June 23, 2022.

14 Sheera Frenkel, "Proud Boys Regroup, Focusing on School Boards and Town Councils." *New York Times*, December 14, 2021, https://www.nytimes.com/2021/12/14/us/proud-boys-local-issues.html, accessed July 4, 2022.

15 Juliett Kayyem, "There Are No Lone Wolves." *Washington Post*, August 4, 2019, https://www.washingtonpost.com/opinions/2019/08/04/there-are-no-lone-wolves/#:~:text=There%20are%20no%20lone%20wolves.%20A%20mass%20shooting,need%20to%20fight%20the%20%E2%80%9CHispanic%20invasion%20of%20Texas.%E2%80%9D, accessed June 24, 2022.

16 Bill Morlin, "McVeigh Worship: The New Extremist Trend," Southern Poverty Law Center "Hate Watch," June 27, 2017, www.splcenter.org/hatewatch/2017/06/27/mcveigh-worship-new-extremist-trend, accessed April 24, 2018.

17 Ibid.

18 Mark Bray, *ANTIFA: The Anti-Fascist Handbook* (Brooklyn, NY: Melville House, 2017), 104.

19 Seth Jones, "Who Are Antifa, and Are they a Threat?" Center for Strategic & International Studies, June 4, 2020, https://www.csis.org/analysis/who-are-antifa-and-are-they-threat, accessed June 23, 2022.

20 The German government's report is available at https://www.verfassungsschutz. de/SharedDocs/publikationen/DE/verfassungsschutzberichte/2022–06–07-verfassungsschutzbericht-2021.pdf?__blob=publicationFile&v=2, accessed June 28, 2022.

21 Daniel Byman, "The Good Enough Doctrine: Learning to Live with Terrorism." *Foreign Affairs*, September/October 2021, 32.

22 Department of Homeland Security Bulletin of June 7, 2022, is available at https://www.dhs.gov/ntas/advisory/national-terrorism-advisory-system-bulletin-june-7–2022, accessed June 27, 2022.

23 Ibid.

24 Byman, 34.

25 Ibid.

26 Soufan Center, "IntelBrief: The Islamic State Is Not Finished in Iraq and Syria." November 1, 2021, https://thesoufancenter.org/intelbrief-2021-november-1/, accessed June 28, 2022.

27 Department of Homeland Security Bulletin.

28 Ibid.

29 The U.S. Department of State announced the creation of the regional ISIS organization and designated at the same time ISIS Mozambique and ISIS Democratic Republic of Congo foreign terrorist organizations, https://www.state.gov/state-department-terrorist-designations-of-isis-affiliates-and-leaders-in-the-democratic-republic-of-the-congo-and-mozambique/, accessed June 28, 2022.

30 www.armyofgod.com/JamesKopp2.html, accessed September 30, 2015.

31 The statistics were assembled by NARAL Pro-Choice America Foundation and are available at www.prochoiceamerica.org/assets/files/Abortion-Access-to-Abortion-Violence.pdf, accessed July 10, 2010.

32 From "The Army of God Manual, Classic Third Edition," www.armyofgod. com/AOGsel6.html, accessed April 3, 2003.

33 The woman, Crystal Davis, was quoted in Jeffrey Gettleman with David M. Halbfinger, "Suspect in '96 Olympic Bombing and 3 Other Attacks Is Caught," *New York Times*, June 1, 2003, 1.

34 Kathy Spillar, "The Anti-Abortion Movement Has a Long History of Terrorism." *MS Magazine*, May 6, 2022, https://msmagazine.com/2022/05/06/anti-abortion-violence-terrorism-roe-v-wade/, accessed July 3, 2022.

35 The full text of the communique and other declarations are available on Jane's Revenge website, https://search.yahoo.com/search?p=jane%27s+revenge+we bsite&fr=yfp-t-s&fr2=p%3Afp%2Cm%3Asa%2Cct%3Asa%2Ckt%3Anon e&ei=UTF-8&fp=1, accessed July 4, 2022.

36 According to the ELF website, www.earthliberationfront.com, accessed June 5, 2003.

37 John Lewis's opening statement is available at https://archives.fbi.gov/archives/news/testimony/animal-rights-extremism-and-ecoterrorism, accessed July 5, 2022.

38 Ibid.

39 Washingtonpost.com: Live Online, www.washingtonpost.com, accessed April 5, 2003.

40 www.earthliberationfront.com, accessed April 5, 2003.

41 John Lewis's opening statement. . .

42 See, the ALF's website at https://animalliberationpressoffice.org/NAALPO/, accessed August 30, 2022.

43 Paola Andrea Spadaro, "Climate Change and Global Security," *Journal of Strategic Security* 13 (4) (2020), p. 58.

44 Ibid., 65.

45 Lara Korte, "The Southwest Is Bone Dry. Now, a Key Water Source Is at Risk,"
   Politico, July 6, 2022, https://www.politico.com/news/2022/07/06/colorado-
   river-drought-california-arizona-00044121, accessed July 6, 2022.
46 Ibid.
47 Bridget Johnson, "ISIS Claims Escalating Use of Wildfire Arson as Terror
   Tactic," *Homeland Security TODAY*, May 28, 2019, https://www.hstoday.us/
   subject-matter-areas/counterterrorism/isis-claims-escalating-use-of-wildfire-
   arson-as-terror-tactic/, accessed July 6, 2022.
48 Spadaro, 68.

5 Political Violence in the Name of God

October 31, 2017, was a warm, sunny Halloween day along the American East coast. In Lower Manhattan tourists and natives enjoyed the picturesque Hudson River Park. In nearby Stuyvesant High School, one of the city's best public schools, students got ready to be dismissed for the day. Outside, some parents waited for their children to drive them home. Suddenly, shortly after 3:00 p.m., a pick-up truck drove at high speed onto the park's bike path mowing down several cyclists and pedestrians in a horrific truck-ramming attack. Eight persons were killed, and 11 others were injured. After a one-mile killing spree, the truck collided with a school bus. Sayfullo Saipov (age 29) left the truck shouting "Allahu Akbar!" (God is great!) and brandishing what turned out to be pellet and paintball guns. Inside the truck, police found an ISIS flag and nearby a note in Arabic with the slogans, "No God but God and Muhammad is his Prophet" and "Islamic Supplication. It will endure."

After being shot by a New York Police Department (NYPD) officer Saipov, a native of Uzbekistan with permanent residency in the United States, said from his hospital bed that he was proud of what he had done and asked whether he could display the ISIS flag in his hospital room.

Who was this young man determined to kill in the name of Allah and ISIS—and obviously willing to die? His acquaintances and neighbors described him as aggressive, short-tempered, angry, and unfriendly. Working as a truck driver and later on as an Uber driver he had a multitude of traffic violations. Yet, as one acquaintance noted following the truck ramming, "He did not seem like a terrorist, but I did not know him from the inside."[1] He seemed not overly religious when he lived first in Ohio and then in Florida. But after moving to Paterson, New Jersey, he prayed regularly at a mosque near his residence—especially in the months preceding the attack. An Uzbek acquaintance remembered that they argued about religion and that Saipov's views were radical.

Obviously, ISIS's e-propaganda was instrumental in Saipov's transformation into a religious zealot. The investigator concluded that he "self-radicalized" by consuming ISIS propaganda. Saipov himself told

DOI: 10.4324/9781003289265-6

police and FBI agents that his deadly attack was inspired by ISIS videos that he had watched. On his cellphones, investigators found some 90 videos with several thousand mostly gruesome images—ISIS fighters decapitating, burning, or car-crashing infidels. There were also video downloads of ISIS leader Abu Bakr al-Baghdadi's speeches and instructions on how to build bombs. John Miller, Deputy NYPD Commissioner, noted that Saipov's lethal attack followed "almost exactly to a T" the Islamic State's calls on social media for followers in the West to kill infidels by "simple" means, for example, car ramming.

As the title of this chapter suggests, religious terrorism, just like secular terrorism, has political ends. Secular terrorists are motivated by political ideologies (e.g., Neo-Nazi groups by Hitler's racist White Supremacist views; left-wing groups like the Red Army Faction and Red Brigades of the past by Marxist ideas) or widely accepted principles, such as the right to self-determination or to equality. Religious terrorists are motivated by their strong desire to live according to their religion's teachings and follow what they have been taught is God's will, but they also have political grievances and goals. Thus, whether they are Christians, Jews, Muslims, Buddhists, Hindus, members of other religions, or devoted to religious sects (e.g., the Japanese Aum Shinrikyo), extremists commit violence for both religious and political ends. Mark Sedgwick has pointed out,

> Just as religious terrorism turns out to have important political elements, "secular" terrorism also has important religious elements. Many nationalists have spoken of their cause as "sacred," and it is not hard to conceive of a leftist speaking of the "cause of the opposed masses." A Russian terrorist of the first wave [of terrorism] wrote of terrorism as "uniting the two sublimities of human nature, the martyr and the hero."[2]

But although secular terrorists may invoke religious rhetoric and imagery, they are solidly grounded in worldly justifications. Religious or pseudoreligious terrorists share the belief that their deeds are not only what God wants them to do, but what God commands them to do. According to Magnus Ranstorp, "Despite having vastly different origins, doctrines, institutions, and practices, these religious extremists are united in their justification for employing sacred violence either in efforts to defend, extend or revenge their own communities or for millenarian or messianic reasons."[3]

The following three case studies demonstrate how strongly many religious terrorists believe that divine guidance gives them the strength to commit violence for what they consider to be just causes on earth and in heaven.

Case Study

Christians and Sacred Terrorism

On July 29, 1994, Paul Hill, an antiabortion activist, waited in front of an abortion clinic in Pensacola, Florida, for Dr. John Bayard Britton and his bodyguard James Herman Barrett, a retired Air Force Lieutenant Colonel, to arrive. As their car entered the parking lot, Hill first shot Barrett and, after reloading his shotgun, aimed at Britton. He killed both men. When he was arrested by police officers a few minutes later, he proclaimed loudly, "I know one thing, no innocent babies are going to be killed in this clinic today."[4] Well known in radical antiabortion circles, Hill did not act impulsively, but planned his lethal attack carefully and, so he felt, under the guidance and as an instrument of God. From his prison cell, he later described his preparation and justification:

> I was not standing for my own ideas, but God's truths—the same truths that have stopped blood baths and similar atrocities throughout history. Who was I to stand in God's way? He now held the door open and promised great blessing for obedience. Was I not to step through it?
>
> When Monday arrived, I knew I had to decide. When I went from mentally debating whether to act, in general, to planning a particular act, I felt some relief. Romans 14:23b says "and whatever is not from faith is sin." If I had not acted when I did, it would have been a direct and unconscionable sin of disobedience. One of the first things I told my wife, after the shooting was, "I didn't have any choice!" That cry came from the depths of my soul. I was certain, and still am, that God called me to obey His revealed will at that particular time.

This conviction did not weaken during his time in prison. In Hill's own words,

> The inner joy and peace that have flooded my soul since I have cast off the state's tyranny makes my 6 × 9 cell a triumphant and newly liberated kingdom. I shudder at the thought of ever returning to the bondage currently enforced by the state.

(Continued)

(Continued)

But Hill also hoped for worldly rewards, namely, that his deed would radicalize the pro-life movement. As he put it, "using the force necessary to defend the unborn gives credibility, urgency, and direction to the pro-life movement which it has lacked, and which it needs in order to prevail." He thought that his deed "would also help people to decide whether to join the battle on the side of those defending abortionists, or the side of those defending the unborn."[5] Before he was executed by injection in September 2003, Hill said with a smile on his face, "I expect a great reward in heaven. I am looking forward to the glory." But again, he also thought of immediate goals right here on earth, when he said, "I think it [killing the man he called 'the abortionist' and his bodyguard] was a good thing and instead of people being shocked at what I did, I think more people should act as I acted."[6] For Hill, a former minister in the Presbyterian Church in America and the Orthodox Presbyterian Church, his had been a "defensive action" on behalf of the unborn in that he prevented his victim from ever killing defenseless babies again.

His supporters shared his conviction. The day Hill was executed, one antiabortion extremist declared, "Paul Hill should be honored today. The abortionists should be executed and the judges that rule it's okay to kill children should be run out of Dodge."[7] On its website, the extreme antiabortion "Army of God" continues to praise Paul Hill as an "American hero."

Case Study

Muslims and Sacred Terrorism

On January 7, 2015, two heavily armed brothers, Said and Chérif Kouachi, stormed into the Paris headquarters of the satirical magazine *Charlie Hebdo* and shot to death one by one 11 staffers, calling out several of their victims' names and shouting again and again, "Alluhu Akbar!" (Allah is the greatest). As they fled the scene, they screamed, "We have avenged the Prophet Mohammad! We have killed *Charlie Hebdo*." They claimed to have acted in the name of Al Qaeda in the Arabian Peninsula whose leaders had put *Charlie*

Hebdo's editor-in-chief Stephane Charbonnier on their "most wanted" hit list calling jihadists to punish the evil-doer and his collaborators who had published caricatures of the Prophet repeatedly.

While hiding from the police in an old print plant, Chérif Kouachi talked to a French radio reporter. Here is the transcript of the conversation:

CHERIF KOUACHI: I just want to tell you that we are defenders of the Prophet. I, Chérif Kouachi, was sent by al-Qaeda in Yemen. I was over there. I was financed by Imam Anwar al-Awlaki.

JOURNALIST: OK. How long ago, roughly?

KOUACHI: A long time ago. Before he was killed.

JOURNALIST: OK, so you came back to France recently.

KOUACHI: No, a long time ago. I had to know how I could do things properly.

JOURNALIST: Are you just there with your brother?

KOUACHI: That's not your problem.

JOURNALIST: Do you have other people there with you?

KOUACHI: That's not your problem.

JOURNALIST: Do you intend to kill again in the name of Allah? Or not?

KOUACHI: Have we killed other people in the last few days when you were looking for us? Go on. Tell me.

JOURNALIST: You killed journalists.

KOUACHI: Wait. Did we kill civilians when you were looking for us in the last two days?

JOURNALIST: Have you killed anyone this morning?

KOUACHI: We are not killers. We are defenders of the Prophet. We are not like you. We defend the Prophet. There, there is no problem. We can kill. But we don't kill women. It is you that kill the children of Muslims in Iraq, in Afghanistan, in Syria. That's not us. We have a code of honour, us, in Islam

JOURNALIST: But you took vengeance...

KOUACHI: That's right. We took vengeance. That's it. You said it all. We took vengeance.[8]

Soon thereafter, the brothers were killed by police bullets as they tried to leave their hideout. Obviously, they considered themselves martyrs for the glory of Allah and the Prophet Mohammad.

Case Study

Jews and Sacred Terrorism

In the early morning of February 25, 1994, Dr. Baruch Goldstein, a well-known resident of the Jewish settlement Kiryat Arba near the West Bank town of Hebron and an active member of the religious right-wing organization Kach, went to the shrine at the Tomb of the Patriarchs in Hebron/al Khali. Built over the site where Abraham, Sara, and other revered religious figures are buried, the shrine provided Jews and Muslims separate worship halls. This morning, Goldstein went right to the Muslim side, pulled an assault rifle from under his coat, and fired 111 shots, killing 29 Muslim worshipers and injuring many more before he himself was beaten to death.

Although Goldstein did not leave an explanatory note, the political realities in the mid-1990s and the teachings of his late spiritual mentor Rabbi Meir Kahane explained his immediate political and higher religious motives. Like others of the so-called messianic right in Israel, Goldstein was upset about political developments: the Oslo Peace Agreement negotiated by Israel's Prime Minister Yitzhak Rabin and PLO leader Yassir Arafat, the freeze on further Jewish settlements in the occupied territories, and the growing attacks by Palestinian extremists on Jewish settlements. As Ehud Sprinzak explained,

> Goldstein suffered a severe crisis in the months before the Hebron massacre. Not only was the future of Judea and Samaria put in great doubt, but the neighboring Palestinians became increasingly aggressive and violent. As the community's emergency physician and the doctor responsible for first aid to Jewish victims of terrorism, Goldstein was exposed to the consequences of these circumstances more, perhaps, than anybody else. Several victims of the intensifying Palestinian terrorism died in his hands.[9]

These, then, were the immediate political grievances. But how did Goldstein's religious convictions figure in the Hebron massacre? For many years a disciple of Rabbi Meir Kahane, Baruch Goldstein ultimately became what Sprinzak called "the new Kahane Jew"[10] who acted in accordance with the glorification of violence that the rabbi preached. Kahane and his followers "not only responded to violence but also produced it in new acts of death and destruction, a spiral of violence that continued long after the zealous rabbi's death."[11]

In Kahane's "catastrophic messianism," the central point is that "the Messiah will come in a great conflict in which Jews triumph and praise God through their successes... Anything that humiliated the Jews was not only an embarrassment but a retrograde motion in the world's progress toward salvation."[12]

For Kahane, both Arabs and secular Jews prevented the Israeli people's redemption that would come only after all Arabs were removed from the sacred land of Israel. According to Sprinzak, Goldstein believed in Kahane's tenet:

> There are numerous indications that following the 1990 assassination of the rabbi, whom Goldstein loved dearly, the consecutive disasters after the 1992 elections, especially the Oslo agreement, Goldstein started to slowly move into a desperate messianic defiance. He felt that only a catastrophic act of supreme Kiddush Hashem (sanctification of the name of God) could change, perhaps, the course of history and put it back on the messianic track [Kahane's prescription for redemption]. A responsible person who never was trigger happy, he had to carry out this exemplary mission.[13]

In other words, Goldstein unloaded his shotgun on worshiping Muslim Arabs in the conviction that this was the will of God.

While many Israelis condemned Baruch Goldstein for his lethal act of terrorism, he was an instant hero for members of the religious right. At his burial, one fellow settler said, "There's no question about it, he was a great man. There's no question about it."[14] Another settler added, "This was desperation for a man who was a moral man for every instant of his life."[15]

Defending the Faith in "Cosmic Wars"

The similarities among the three cases are striking in that terrorist violence was sanctioned by Christian, Muslim, and Jewish leaders of extreme movements and carried out by their followers in the conviction that they acted on behalf of God and in defense of their faith, tradition, right, and interest. The men who committed the lethal acts of terrorism lived seemingly normal and moral lives before they resorted to violence against what they perceived as forces of evil. Such conversions can occur when persons slip into what Albert Bandura has described as "moral disengagement" that "is accomplished by cognitively restructuring the moral value of killing, so that the killing can be done free from self-censoring restraints."[16] And since religious terrorists believe they follow God's orders, they can displace responsibility for their deeds. According to Bandura, when it comes to displacement of responsibility, "the higher the authorities, the more legitimacy, respect, and coercive power they command, and the more amenable are people to defer to them."[17] Once terrorists reach this psychological stage, they are convinced they must fight "satanic" enemies in a "cosmic war."[18] According to Mark Juergensmeyer,

> The process of creating satanic enemies is part of the construction of an image of cosmic war... When the opponent rejects one's moral or spiritual position; when the enemy appears to hold the power to completely annihilate one's community, one's culture, and oneself; when the opponent's victory would be unthinkable; and when there seems no way to defeat the enemy in human terms—all of these conditions increase the likelihood that one will envision one's opponent as a superhuman foe, a cosmic enemy. The process of satanization is aimed at reducing the power of one's opponents and discrediting them. By belittling and humiliating them—by making them subhuman—one is asserting one's own superior moral powers.[19]

Religious terrorists draw strength from their conviction that they are totally right, good, and moral and that their enemy is totally wrong, evil, and immoral. As Jessica Stern has pointed out, "religious terrorism attempts to destroy moral ambiguities." The idea of defeating the evil and Satan in an existential battle for God was central to Paul Hill's, Baruch Goldstein's, and the Kouachi brothers' convictions. When he decided to kill Dr. Britton and his guard, Paul Hill considered the "abortionist's knife as [the] 'cutting edge of Satan's current attack' on the world."[20] When he decided to kill worshiping Muslim Arabs, Baruch Goldstein had come "to the conclusion that unless stopped by a most dramatic act that would shake the foundations of Earth and please God, the peace process would disconfirm the dream of redemption."[21] When the Kouachis shot their way into the *Charlie Hebdo* offices and killed staffers, they considered themselves defenders of the Prophet Muhammad willing to die as avengers.

Audrey Kurth Cronin lists the following five reasons that make religious terrorists more dangerous than right-wing, left-wing, and nationalist/ separatist extremists:

- Religious terrorists believe that they are involved in a "Manichaean struggle of good against evil." All nonbelievers are legitimate targets.
- Religious terrorists desire "to please the perceived commands [to commit violence] of a deity."

- Religious terrorists have a complete disregard for "secular values and laws."
- Religious terrorists are alienated from the existing social system. "They are not trying to correct the system... they are trying to replace it."
- Religious terrorists have "dispersed popular support in civil society." For example, "groups such as al-Qaeda are able to find support from some Muslim nongovernmental foundations throughout the world, making it a truly global network."[22]

Are some practitioners of sacred terrorism "evil" and others perhaps not? After interviewing many religious extremists and their supporters, Stern made a distinction: "Few of the terrorists described in these pages are single-mindedly thoughtful villains like those who masterminded the September 11 attacks. In some cases the ethical basis of their actions is complicated."[23] More specifically, she made the following observation:

> Although none of the terrorism described in this book can be described as morally acceptable, at least in my view, the pro-life doc- tor killers probably come closest and are worth examining in detail for that reason. Unlike the September 11 hijackers, the doctor killers are discriminating: they target individuals who, in their view, are in the business of murder.[24]

But considering that for bin Laden and Al Qaeda or al-Baghdadi and ISIS, as well as like-minded individuals and groups, Americans collec- tively are guilty of killing innocent Muslims, the difference between the killer of one doctor, several worshipers, and those responsible for the mass killings of 9/11 is in the number of victims, not in the moral distinc- tion between justifiable and nonjustifiable murder.

The Proliferation of Religious Violence

For David Rapoport, the 9/11 attacks and similar violence by Al Qaeda and like-minded groups and cells are part of a wave of religious terrorism that began at the end of the 1970s and overlapped the "New Left Wave," which, apart from a few exceptions, disappeared after the end of the Cold War. Since the "Anarchist Wave" (beginning in the 1880s) and the "Anti-Colonial Wave" (beginning in the 1920s) preceded the "New Left Wave" (beginning in the late 1960s), he considers the "Religious Wave" as the fourth in the history of modern terrorism, and Islam the most important religion in this latest period—but not the only one.[25] Unlike Rapoport, who names three near-simultaneous events (the "Iranian Islamic Revolution in 1979, the start of the Islamic *hijri* calendar, and the Soviet invasion of Afghanistan") as starting points of the "Fourth Wave," Mark Sedgwick considers 1967 as the crucial date:

> It was the shockingly sudden and complete defeat of the Arab armies by Israel in that year that began the shattering of the Arab nationalist dream incarnated by Egypt's President Nasser, a process completed by President Sadat's concessions at Camp David in 1979... It was after 1967 that the re-Islamization of Egyptian society started. The Arabs who went to fight for Islam in Afghanistan were in the middle of the wave, not at the start of it. The fourth wave, then, started not in Iran or Afghanistan, but in Palestine and Israel, in almost the same year that the third wave started in Europe and—to a lesser extent—in America.[26]

Like Rapoport, this writer considers the Iranian Islamic revolution and the Soviet invasion of Afghanistan (not the start of the fifteenth *hijri* century) as triggers of the "Fourth Wave," not the Arab–Israeli war of 1967. While the "re-Islamization of Egyptian society started"[27] after that war, the more immediate result was the establishment of secular Palestinian terrorist organizations that fit into the third or "New Left Wave" and actually cooperated with European Marxist terrorist groups. But whatever the exact date of the jihadist movement's birth, there is no denying that religiously motivated and justified political violence of this sort has increased dramatically in the last several decades.

The Most-Deadly Terrorist Groups in the early 2020

For most of the first two decades of the twenty-first century, jihadist groups caused by far the largest number of deaths and committed the largest number of terrorist attacks. This trend continued in the early 2020s. Thus, in 2021, ISIS, Al Shabaab, the Taliban, and Jamaat Nusrat Al-Islam wal Muslimeen (JNIM) were the most lethal terrorist groups among the global line-up of terrorist entities. Together, these four groups were responsible for 3,364 deaths, 47% of the total number of persons killed in terrorist incidents that year. ISIS was also the group that carried out the largest number of terrorist attacks, 794 according to the Global Terrorism Index. Three of these groups, ISIS, Taliban, and Al Shabaab were also among the four most deadly groups in 2020 but JNIM moved in 2021 into fourth place held previously by Boko Haram.

Alienation, Humiliation, and Fear

Although Sedgwick argues that Al Qaeda's short-term or immediate goals are more political than religious and "owe more to European radicalism than to Islam," he also recognizes that the organization is "clearly marked by Islam, and not only in its ultimate [religiously defined] aims. Al Qaeda's potential constituency is the world's Muslims, and the means it uses to mobilize support in this constituency are derived from Islam."[28] The connection between shared Islamic concepts and images and terms on the one hand and the need to recruit members and sympathizers on the other is important in that it provides the movement with a large pool of potential supporters. Al Qaeda is not unique in this respect as al-Shabaab, Boko Haram, ISIS, and like-minded groups demonstrate. Juergensmeyer notes with respect to all kinds of religious movements,

> The groups that have made a long-term impact, such as Hamas, the Khalistan movement [in India], Christian Identity, and the Jewish right wing, have used violence not only to draw attention to themselves but also to articulate the concerns of those within their wider cultures.
>
> Radical though they may be, they have represented widely held feelings of alienation and oppression, and for this reason their strident language and violent acts have been considered by their cohorts as perhaps intemperate but understandable.[29]

Those who have studied religious terrorists seem to agree that underneath their tough words and deeds, there is a great deal of alienation, humiliation, and even fear. Stern concluded that the grievances expressed by religious terrorists "often mask a deeper kind of angst and a deeper kind of fear. Fear of a godless universe, of chaos, of loose rules, and of loneliness."[30] It is not unusual that religious extremists are frustrated by the loss or pending loss of their privileged station in society. Thus, radical elements in the Christian Identity movement do not hide that they hate African Americans and Jews, whom they blame for all the ills in American society and in particular "for pornography, for the lack of morality, for the economic situation in America, for minority rights over white rights, and for kicking god out of schools."[31] Since many of the rank-and-file members of such groups have at best finished high school, work in low-wage jobs, or are unemployed, they blame nonwhite, non-Christian groups for their predicament. In other societies, for example in the Middle East, the frustration of university-educated males stems often from their inability to find high-level jobs that require the skills they have.

After her conversations with Kerry Noble, a leader in the Covenant, the Sword, and the Arm of the Lord, a Christian Identity group, and many religious extremists abroad, Stern concluded,

> The grievances Noble described were similar to those of religious extremists around the world. Al Qaeda's complaints about the new world order sound remarkably similar to Kerry Noble's for example. Ayman Zawahiri, Osama bin Laden's second in command, accuses Western forces of employing international institutions such as the United Nations, multinational corporations, and international news agencies as weapons in their "new crusade" to dominate the Islamic world. They often reject feminism in favor of "family values," whether their families are in Oklahoma or Peshawar.[32]

Real or perceived humiliation, too, seems to drive males into violent groups. Thus, extremists like Al Qaeda's Ayman al-Zawahiri believe that "violence is a way to cure Muslim youth of the pernicious effects of centuries of humiliation at the hands of the West." Similarly, Christian Identity extremists join violent groups to regain their masculinity and forget that they were humiliated by gender and racial equality. Thus, Kerry Noble told Stern that "he felt strong for the first time in his life when he joined a violent, racist cult." He said he had been humiliated from elementary school on when he was forced to play on the girls' side in physical education classes.[33] And violent Jewish individuals and groups as well "see the peace process and giving up the occupied territories as humiliating to Jews."[34]

Whether Christian, Jewish, Muslim, Buddhist, Sikh, or devoted to idiosyncratic sects, religious extremists and fanatics resort to violence in opposition to the overbearing, permissive, change-oriented, postmodern world that spreads secular values and in the process threatens and even destroys their way of life. This explains why the immediate objectives of these groups and individuals are political. They choose the path of violence in efforts to regain control of their environment and remake the world around them according to their vision in order to achieve their ultimate religious ideal—eventually. In the process, though, they distance themselves from the mainstream tenets of their respective religions. Even when aware that they are out of step with the mainstream of their faiths, religious extremists in various parts of the world tend to insist that "their groups are in fact revivals of the original forms of their traditions."[35] Unfortunately, the targets of religious terrorism are often unable or unwilling to distinguish between nonviolent mainstream religions and their teachings on the one hand and the "new religions" of extremist leaders that justify terrorism in the name of God on the other. As a result, a whole religion may be stereotyped by the image of its most extreme fringe groups.

Well before the 9/11 attacks, terrorism scholar Magnus Ranstorp recognized the causes and dangers of the "virtual explosion of religious terrorism in recent times" when he stated:

> The uncertainty and unpredictability in the present environment as the world searches for a new world order, amidst an increasingly complex global environment with ethnic and nationalist conflicts, provides many religious terrorist groups with the opportunity and ammunition to shape history according to their divine duty, cause, and mandate while it indicates to others that the end of the time itself is near.[36]

This assessment sums up the setting that is conducive to the proliferation of international religious terrorism and the domestic variety as well. Indeed, many seemingly domestic religious terrorists—for example, adherents of Christian Identity in the United States or Al Qaeda-like groups in Arab countries (e.g., Hezbollah)—are driven by grievances that transcend the domestic context. Ironically, in many instances, the same religious extremists, who resent what they perceive as the negative effects of globalization, exploit vehicles of globalization, most of all global communication and transnational arms and drug trafficking, to finance their organizations and terrorist operations.

However, in spite of the long history of terrorism in all religious settings, among the adherents of the same and different religions, and in spite of the numerous similarities between these violent fanatics, the self-proclaimed warriors in the name of Islam pose at the present time the greatest threat because of the large number of individuals, cells, organizations, and even networks devoted to the so-called jihadi cause. The following section therefore deals exclusively with the theoretical underpinnings of the jihadi movement, its justification of violence, and the impact of jihadi ideology on contemporary terrorists' holy war against infidels in their own and other religions.

The Jihadi Movement and Political Violence

Shortly before the 2008 presidential election, during an appearance on NBC TV's *Meet the Press* program, former Secretary of State Colin Powell criticized opponents of Senator Barack Obama who claimed that he was a Muslim. The retired general added,

> What if he was? Is there something wrong with being a Muslim in this country? The answer is no, that's not America. Is there something wrong with some 7-year-old Muslim American kid believing that he or she could be president?[37]

This was a much-needed civics lesson on tolerance and on the fundamental value of equality in a nation of immigrants. As Mark Juergensmeyer noted, "Most Muslims regard Islam as a religion of peace, and Christians and Jews regard their own religion in the same way."[38]

Yet, it is indisputable that since the mid-1990s, and even more so since the attacks of September 11, 2001, the most serious terrorist threat has been closely tied to the most extreme strain of Muslim revivalism. After 9/11, there was a sudden surge of interest in Islam in the United States and elsewhere in the West. University courses on Islam were oversubscribed and books on the subject were written and bought in unprecedented numbers. But most Americans were not interested and remained clueless.

In 2006, Jeff Stein, the national security editor at *Congressional Quarterly*, concluded his series of interviews with Washington's counterterrorism officials in Congress, the FBI, and other agencies with the question, "Do you know the difference between a Sunni and a Shiite?" He was not looking for theological explanations, but rather some basic knowledge about the rivalries between the two groupings and their political strengths and differences in Iraq and other settings. As he reported,

> Most American officials I've interviewed don't have a clue. That includes not just intelligence and law enforcement officials, but also members of Congress who have important roles overseeing our spy agencies. How can they do their jobs without knowing the basics?[39]

One would assume that none of these clueless counterterrorism experts knew any details about the ideology of those they fought in the "war against terror." The following section explains the various constituent groups within the overall Muslim population and, in particular, the religiopolitical underpinnings of the ideas that fuel the violent mission of Al Qaeda Central's leaders as well as like-minded groups and individuals.

Muslims

Of the about 1.3 billion Muslims around the world, 85 percent are Sunnis and the rest are Shias (or Shi'ites). They all follow the teachings of the Prophet Muhammad and the Qu'ran. The two branches of Islam split after Muhammad's death, and to this day Sunnis believe that the most competent among his companions were right in succeeding him, whereas Shias believe that Muhammad's descendants were his spiritual heirs, with his son-in-law Ali first in line. Vali Nasr has explained that the Sunni–Shia division "somewhat parallels the Protestant–Catholic difference in Western Christianity."[40] In the post-9/11 era, there is particularly in the West a notion that Islam is the problem, that Islam encourages violence. But John Esposito cautioned that "in discussing political Islam, it is important to distinguish between mainstream and extremist movements. The former participate within the political system, whereas the latter engage in terrorism in the name of Islam."[41] The vast majority of Muslims do not agree with their extremist and violent brethren, especially not when the religious fanatics harm women, children, and old people or attack fellow Muslims and harm Muslim interests.

Islamists

Within the Muslim population at large, Islamists, who strive for the establishment or strengthening of the Islamic state on the basis of Islamic law, constitute the next largest component on both the Sunni and the Shia sides. Fueled by a strong religious revival since the 1960s and growing dissatisfaction with their authoritarian, pro-Western governments, religion, mosques, and mullahs became a rallying point when there was no space allowed for any other. The use of the mosque–mullah network was critical in the Iranian revolution, as have been private (nongovernmental) mosques and their imams in Egypt and many other countries.[42]

Most Islamists support peaceful change, but a growing minority believes that violence will advance their cause. The oldest and most influential Islamist movement is the transnational Muslim Brotherhood that was founded in Egypt in 1928 by Hassan al-Banna in opposition to the British-backed monarchy. In the mid-twentieth century, it spread throughout the Arab world and took root in countries such as Algeria, Libya, the Palestinian territories, Sudan, Syria, and Tunis. Officially, the Brotherhood has claimed to oppose violence but it makes an exception for Palestinians in their fight against Israelis. In reality, however, the Muslim Brotherhood in Egypt and affiliates elsewhere have resorted to terrorist means in various settings and situations. As the 9/11 Commission Report noted, "In some countries, its [the Brotherhood's] oppositional role is nonviolent; in others, especially Egypt, it has alternated between violent and nonviolent struggle with the regime."[43] In some instances, the most violent elements formed their own units within the Brotherhood; in other cases, they established separate and more extremist groups.

Salafis and Wahhabis

The Salafi movement within the larger Muslim population comprises the most puritanical form of Sunni Islam and promotes the return to the original teachings of the Prophet Muhammad and his companions. Some observers have compared this school of thought to the seventeenth-century Puritan movements in England and America. Salafis believe that the Qu'ran and the Prophet Muhammad's practices (Hadith), not the later interpretations of these sources by Islamic scholars, are the most authentic guidelines for the devout Muslim. Like other puritanical movements, Salafis believe that the end of Islam's golden age, when Muslim rule extended into Europe, was caused by their own "rulers and people who turned away from the true path of their religion, thereby leaving Islam vulnerable to encroaching foreign powers eager to steal their land, wealth, and even souls."[44] Afghanistan under the rule of the Taliban movement reflected best what the Salafi school of thought envisions as the societal ideal.

The most influential Salafis are Saudi clerics who preach an old version of Salafism called Wahhabism, an eighteenth-century movement named after its founder, Muhammad bin Abd al Wahhab. Since the modern kingdom of Saudi Arabia was established in 1932, Wahhabi clerics have enjoyed a great deal of influence on all aspects of their country's religious, political, social, and cultural realities. The symbiotic relationship between Saudi rulers and Wahhabi leaders spread religious puritanism and intolerance throughout the kingdom, and it also bought the ruling House of Saud protection from violent upheaval arising from Salafi opposition to Westernized members of the royal family and to the influence of the West on the Saudi Arabian Peninsula. This arrangement came with a price tag: The Saudi government and wealthy Saudis financed the spread of Wahhabi militancy throughout the Middle East as well as in other parts of the world, including Europe and the United States. In more recent times, moreover, Saudi Arabia has produced growing numbers of terrorists. Fifteen of the nineteen 9/11 terrorists were citizens of Saudi Arabia. And records of foreign nationals who entered Iraq between August 2006 and August 2007 to fight within the Islamic State of Iraq, an Al Qaeda-affiliated group, revealed that of the 595 entries that listed the nationality of these jihadis, 41 percent were of Saudi Arabian origin.[45]

Jihadis

Although most Salafis do not engage in violence and do not support the terrorist acts of fellow Salafis, today's most dangerous and by far most numerous terrorist groups and cells are part of the Salafi movement. Marc Sageman speaks of the "global Salafi jihad" as a revivalist movement "stretching from Morocco to the Philippines, eliminating present national boundaries." He characterizes Al Qaeda as the "vanguard" of the jihadi movement.[46]

The Meaning of Jihad

When Osama bin Laden and four other leaders of jihadi groups in Egypt, Pakistan, and Bangladesh issued a fatwa, or religious edict, in February 1998, it was titled "The World Islamic Front for *Jihad* Against the Jews and Crusaders." In the text, bin Laden explained that "religious scholars throughout Islamic history have agreed that *jihad* is an individual duty when an enemy attacks Muslim countries... After faith, there is no greater duty than fighting an enemy who is corrupting religion and the world."[47] Bin Laden, other Al Qaeda leaders, and their followers, supporters, and sympathizers around the globe use the term *jihad* frequently to describe their terrorist mission and deeds. Not surprisingly, the term has negative connotations in the West.

The literal meaning of *jihad* is striving or struggling in the path of God and the Prophet Muhammad. And there is a distinction between the *greater jihad*, as a personal spiritual and moral struggle, and the *lesser jihad*, as a violent struggle for the good of Islam. This distinction goes back to Muhammad, who reportedly said, "We return from the lesser jihad [warfare] to the greater jihad [the personal struggle to live a moral life]."[48] As for the more controversial of the two, Sageman explains,

> The lesser jihad is the violent struggle for Islam. Traditional Islamic jurisprudence saw jihad as an obligation in a world divided into the land of Islam (*dar al-Islam*) and the land of conflict (*dar al-harb*). The Muslim community, the umma, was required to engage in a jihad to expand dar al-Islam throughout the world so that all humankind could benefit from living within a just political social order. One school of interpretation diluted this belligerence by introducing the notion of land treaty (*dar al-suhl*), which had concluded a truce with dar al-Islam and was not subject to jihad.[49]

When it comes to the belligerent or lesser jihad, there is another distinction between defensive and offensive jihad—the first against intruders in Muslim territory, such as the mujahideens' fight against the Soviet invaders of Afghanistan or against American and other Western invaders of Iraq; the second to conquer non-Muslim land and convert infidels.

In another expert's view,

Osama bin Laden and Al-Qaeda symbolize a global jihad, a network of extremist groups threatening Muslim countries and the West, whose roots have proved deeper and more pervasive than most had anticipated. This new global threat, which emerged from the jihad against the Soviet Union's occupation of Afghanistan, has exploded across the Muslim world from Central, South, and Southeast Asia to Europe and America.[50]

In terms of personnel, organization, and tactics, the origins of the global jihadi movement can indeed be traced back to the Arab mujahideens' fight against Soviet invaders and against Afghan government troops in the 1980s, but the well-developed ideology of militant jihad that is at the core of the theoretical underpinnings, teachings, and actions of Al Qaeda and others in the contemporary jihadi movement has much deeper roots as more recently the endless stream of ISIS publications attest to.

Jihadi Ideology

Utilizing a "citation analysis" of texts available in print and on jihadi websites to identify the most influential theorists in the movement and differentiating between leading medieval and modern radical thinkers, two scholars found that in the first category, the works by Ibn Taymiyya are most popular among contemporary jihadis, whereas Sayyid Qutb is most influential among modern thinkers in this respect.[51]

The texts authored by Taymiyya, a jurist living in the thirteenth and fourteenth centuries, offer a universal rationale for fighting foreign invaders—at his time a call to fight against the Mongols or Tartars and today a perfect justification of violent jihad against Westerners that are present and/or have interests in the Muslim world. Taymiyya held that fighting invaders was not only the right but the duty of every devoted Muslim. He wrote furthermore that Mogul rulers who had converted to Islam were not real Muslims and that they and any other Muslim group not fully observing Islamic law must be defeated—a license to fight a holy war against Muslim rulers and regimes that violate the tenets of puritan Islam.

As for modern jihadi theorists calling for jihad against non-Muslims and the overthrow of local apostate regimes, the dominant ideologue remains to this day the late Egyptian Sayyid Qutb, perhaps the last of the influential laypersons in the jihadi movement as compared to trained Islamic and jihadi theological experts who are dominant today. The turning point in Qutb's life was his two-year stay in the United States in the late 1940s, during which he began his metamorphosis from an admirer of America and the West to jihadi revolutionary. Rejecting what he perceived as the moral decadence and materialism of Western societies, he joined the Muslim Brotherhood upon his return to Egypt, rose to be the organization's leading ideologue, and eventually clashed with the government. Allegedly involved in a plot to assassinate Egyptian president Gamal Abdel Nasser, Qutb was imprisoned and tortured but later allowed to write. In his most influential work, "Milestones," a manifesto of revolutionary religiopolitical Islam, Qutb declared that both Marxism and the West's model of democracy and capitalism had failed and that the world was harmed most of all by the loss of moral values. It was the responsibility of true Muslims to bring the world back onto the right path; this, however, was possible only after self-purification within the Muslim community. For Qutb, the world consisted of two camps: (1) Islam and (2) *jihiliyya*, the part characterized by barbarism, decadence, and unbelief—a state that existed in the world before the Prophet Muhammad delivered his divine message. According to Qutb, the choice is between those two camps—between the good and the evil, God and Satan. For him, far more people, Muslims included, are on the side of *jihiliyya* and therefore all Muslims have the duty to "take up arms in this fight. Any Muslim who rejects his ideas is just one more nonbeliever worthy of destruction."[52] Qutb wrote of the need "to initiate the movement of Islamic revival in some Muslim country" that would set "an example in order to fashion an example that will eventually lead Islam to its destiny of world domination."[53] For this to happen, he hoped for a vanguard that would translate his ideas into reality.

These ideas came to guide contemporary jihadi terrorists, especially the leading strata—Qutb's vanguard. Egyptian Ayman al-Zawahiri, who later rose to become Al Qaeda's second in command, was on the frontline in Qutb's vanguard in that "the same year [1966] that Sayyid Qutb went to the gallows, al-Zawahiri helped form an underground cell devoted to overthrow the government and establish an Islamic state. He was fifteen years old."[54] Osama bin Laden, too, came to embrace the tenets of Qutb's extremist teachings, as did other leaders and followers in the global jihadi network. Indeed, Qutb's younger brother and keeper of his legacy was reportedly one of bin Laden's advisors.[55]

Excerpts from Communications by Osama bin Laden and Ayman al-Zawahiri

From bin Laden's Post-9/11 Message, October 7, 2001

God has struck America at its Achilles heel and destroyed its greatest buildings, praise and blessings to Him. America has been filled with terror from north to south and from east to west, praise and blessings to God. What America is tasting today is but a fraction of what we have tasted for decades... So when God Almighty granted success to one of the vanguard groups of Islam, He opened the way for them to

(Continued)

(*Continued*)

destroy America utterly. I pray to God Almighty to lift them up to the highest Paradise.

From bin Laden's Remarks during Interview with Al-Jazeera, October 21, 2001

I say that the battle isn't between the al-Qaeda organization and the global Crusaders. Rather, the battle is between Muslims—the people of Islam—and the global Crusaders... These young men that have sacrificed themselves in New York and Washington, these are the ones that speak the truth about the conscience of our *umna*, they are its living conscience, which sees that it is imperative to take revenge against the evildoers and transgressors and criminals and terrorists, who terrorize the true believers. So, not all terrorism is restrained or ill-advised. There is terrorism that is ill-advised and there is terrorism that is a good act... So, America and Israel practice ill-advised terrorism, and we practice good terrorism because it deters those from killing our children in Palestine and other places.

From a Taped bin Laden Message, Addressed to the American People, Aired by Al-Jazeera, January 19, 2006

You have tried to prevent us from leading a dignified life, but you will not be able to prevent us from a dignified death. Failing to carry out jihad, which is called for in our religion, is a sin. The best death to us is under the shadows of swords. Don't let your strength and modern arms fool you. They win a few battles but lose the war. Patience and steadfastness are much better. We were patient in fighting the Soviet Union with simple weapons for ten years and we bled their economy and now they are nothing. In that, there is a lesson for you.

From an al-Zawahiri Videotape and Remarks Addressed to President-elect Barack Obama, November 19, 2008

As for the crimes of America which await you [President-elect Obama], it appears that you continue to be captive to the same criminal American mentality toward the world and toward the Muslims.

The Muslim Ummah received with extreme bitterness your hypo-critical statements to and stances toward Israel, which confirmed to the Ummah that you have chosen a stance of hostility to Islam and Muslims... you have climbed the rungs of the presidency to take over the leadership of the greatest criminal force in the history of mankind and the leadership of the most violent Crusade ever against the Muslims. And in you and in Colin Powell, [Condoleezza] Rice and your likes, the words of Malcolm X (may Allah have mercy on him) concerning "House Negroes" are confirmed.

You also must appreciate, as you take over the presidency of America during its Crusade against Islam and Muslims, that you are neither facing individuals nor organizations, but are facing a jihadi awakening and renaissance which is shaking the pillars of the entire Islamic world; and this is the fact which you and your government and country refuse to recognize and pretend not to see.[56]

From the 2014 Announcement of Declaring the Establishment of the ISIS Caliphate under the Leadership of Caliph Ibrahim (Abu Bakr al-Baghdadi)

So rush O Muslims and gather around your khalifah [caliphate], so that you may return as you once were for ages, kings of the earth and knights of war. Come so that you may be honored and esteemed, living as masters with dignity. Know that we fight over a religion that Allah promised to support. We fight for an ummah to which Allah has given honor, esteem, and leadership empowerment and strength on the earth. Come O Muslims to your honor, to your victory. By Allah, if you disbelieve in democracy, secularism, nationalism, as well as all the other garbage and ideas from the west, and rush to your religion and creed, then by Allah, you will own the earth, and the east and west will submit to you. This is the promise of Allah to you. This is the promise of Allah to you [...]

O soldiers of the Islamic State, Allah (the Exalted) ordered us with jihad and promised us with victory but He did not make us responsible for victory. Indeed, Allah (the Exalted) blessed you today with this victory, thus we announced the khilāfah in compliance with the order of Allah (the Exalted). We announced it because—by Allah's grace—we have its essentials.

(Continued)

(*Continued*)

By Allah's permission, we are capable of establishing the khilāfah. So we carry out the order of Allah (the Exalted) and we are justified—if Allah wills—and we do not care thereafter what happens, even if we only remain for one day or one hour, and to Allah belongs the matter before and after.[57]

Although there are dozens of modern and premodern theorists who have contributed or added to one or the other aspect of jihadi ideology, Qutb has remained for the time being the most influential one. Important here is that all influential theorists are hardliners and are in favor of violence. According to Sageman, "Salafi ideology determines its [the jihadi movement's] mission, sets its goals, and guides its tactics."[58] Even the training of self-described holy warriors and martyrs in the service of jihad is guided by this extreme ideology. After studying the doctrines for terrorist training as articulated by leading theorists, Brynjar Lia concluded,

> When preparing recruits for waging a terrorist campaign or participating in a protracted guerrilla war, the jihadi theorists unanimously agreed that ideological indoctrination and spiritual preparation should take precedence over physical and military training. In order to produce the kind of battle-hardened, martyrdom-seeking fighters that have filled the ranks of jihadi groups of the past, the jihadi theorists devote extraordinary attention to spiritual training.[59]

Not only recruits are the targets of the missionary fanaticism that permeates the jihadi movement. Wherever these extremists get a foothold, they force their convictions onto the population. Reporting from Iraq in the summer of 2008, Alissa J. Rubin wrote,

> Diyala residents and officials say [that] militants from Al Qaeda in Mesopotamia have worked to instill their radical Islamist vision in the population. Almost immediately after moving in four years ago, they began holding religion classes for men and women. "Even in Baquba, my niece went to some; she was shaken," said Shamaa Abad al-Kader, the headmistress of a school for girls in Muqdadiya who also serves on Diyala's provincial council. "They gathered people in the villages; they brought women into Baquba and gave them lectures on how to behave," Ms. Kader said. "These Al Qaeda men were going into the schools, into the mosques and they forced people to listen to them. My niece said the man who came to her school had a long beard and a sword with him."[60]

In Afghanistan, jihadis of the resurging Taliban used violence to force fellow Afghans to live according to their extremist Salafi convictions, as they had during their fundamentalist movement's five-year reign. During that period, girls were not allowed to get an education, but this changed after the Taliban was toppled in the wake of the post-9/11 invasion by a U.S.-led coalition force. When the Taliban regained strength in former strongholds like Kandahar, teachers and female students became the particular targets of brutal and often lethal attacks. In one incident, Taliban militants doused a group of school girls and their teachers with acid, several of whom were hospitalized with burnt faces. When arrested, the men confessed that "a high-ranking member of the Taliban had paid the militants 100,000 Pakistani rupees ($1,275) for each of the girls they managed to burn."[61] The Kabul government called the attack "un-Islamic," but for Taliban jihadis, this sort of terrorism was part of their holy fight to resurrect Afghanistan as a model of pure Salafi society.

To sum up, terrorism in the name of God has been practiced by the adherents of all major religions and by pseudoreligious sects. Today, however, jihadis commit far more and far more lethal terrorist attacks and pose by far the greatest threat inside and outside the Muslim world.

Homegrown Jihadis in the West—Including the United States

When tackling the threat of terrorism by homegrown or immigrated jihadis in the West in the post-9/11 years, terrorism experts pointed to the differences between the Muslim diaspora in Western Europe and American Muslims. The greater degree of radicalization of and violence by second- and third-generation Muslims in Europe in comparison to their American counterparts was not simply explained by pointing to greater vigilance on the part of American law enforcement. Rather, American Muslims' societal integration was seen as a protective wall against indoctrination and recruitment by jihadi propaganda and activities. "The nation as a melting pot, the American Dream, individualism, and grass-root voluntarism—these cultural values make American Muslims less likely than their European counterparts to accept the interpretation that there is a war against Islam," Marc Sageman wrote seven years after 9/11. "It seems easier to be anti-American from afar than from within."[62] In a 2007 report, Brian Jenkins noted that the

> absence of significant terrorist attacks or even advanced terrorist plots in the United States since 9/11 is good news that cannot entirely be explained by increased intelligence and heightened security. It suggests America's Muslim population may be less susceptible than Europe's Muslim population, if not entirely immune to jihadist ideology.

But he also cautioned that "it requires not majorities, but only handfuls to carry out terrorist attacks."[63]

This last point was driven home in 2009, when two lethal acts of terrorism and six foiled plots carried out or planned by American Muslims added up to the by far largest number of such cases in the United States in a single year. In the period from September 11, 2001, through December 31, 2008, there were a total of 12 cases in which American Muslims were charged with plotting terrorist strikes within the United States compared to six such cases in 2009 alone. None of these plotters was able to carry out their attacks. But in addition to the six foiled plots in 2009, terrorists succeeded in two cases: The most deadly of the two actual attacks occurred on November 5, when Army Major Nidal Hasan went on a shooting spree at the Army base at Fort Hood, Texas, killing 13 persons and injuring 28 others. Five months earlier, an American Muslim convert shot and killed a person and injured another at a military recruitment center in Little Rock, Arkansas. In between, a potentially most devastating attack on New York City's subway system was prevented, when Najibulla Zazi, a permanent resident of the United States, was arrested for trying to build and detonate a weapon of mass destruction. Two fellow American plotters, former high school classmates, were also charged as were several coconspirators abroad.

Shocking, too, was the failed bombing attempt at Times Square in the heart of Manhattan on May 1, 2010, a Saturday, when many New Yorkers and tourists populated the area. Around 6:30 p.m., an alert street vendor noticed smoke escaping from the inside of a sport utility vehicle (SUV) that was parked close by at 45th street. Then he heard the sound of what seemed like a firecracker. He alerted a mounted police officer. Within minutes, the police began to evacuate the area in and around Times Square. Luckily, the homemade bomb device inside the SUV did not explode as planned. Less than 54 hours later, Faisal Shahzad, the would-be bomber and recruit of the Pakistani Taliban, was arrested at Kennedy Airport before he could leave the United States for Pakistan.

Shahzad, a 30-year-old naturalized U.S. citizen, came from Pakistan as a 19-year-old, had studied, worked as a financial analyst, bought his own home, married, and became the father of two children. He did not come to the United States to escape poverty. As the son of a military officer, he had enjoyed a privileged upbringing in a rather liberal environment. When studying in the United States, he was interested in luxury cars, women, and drinking. By 2006, Shahzad had found religion and bought into the prevalent view on jihadi websites that he frequented, namely, "that the West is at war with Islam, and Muslims are suffering humiliation because they have strayed from their religious duty to fight back."[64]

As catastrophic terrorism hit Western Europe hard in the second decade of the twenty-first century the United States experienced the two most lethal terrorist attacks since 9/11 as well.

On December 2, 2015, Saed Rizwan Farook (age 29) and his wife Tashfeen Malik (also age 29) left their six-month-old daughter with his mother pretending to have a doctor's appointment. Instead, they drove from their home in the city of Redlands, California, to a training session and Christmas party at San Bernardino County's Health Department, where the husband worked as an inspector. After attending the event alone for a while Farook left abruptly. Sometime later the couple, wearing face masks and tactical gear and carrying semi-automatic pistols and rifles, returned to the festively decorated venue. In quick succession, they shot and killed 14 people and injured 22 before fleeing the scene. After a dramatic car chase, the couple was shot and killed by police. As it turned out, the attackers had left bags with explosives in the building before the shooting spree.

According to FBI investigators Farook, a native U.S. citizen of Pakistani descent, and his wife, born and raised in Pakistan, had communicated long before their engagement and marriage about the need for jihad and the glory of martyrdom. As FBI Director James Comey put it, the two perpetrators were "consuming poison on the Internet" and both had become radicalized "before they started courting or dating each other online" and "before the emergence of ISIL [ISIS]."[65] Nevertheless, before their attack Farook and Malik left Facebook messages pledging their allegiance to ISIS leader al-Baghdadi; ISIS in turn declared the couple "soldiers of the caliphate." The couple brought a baby into the world knowing all along that the little girl would grow up without her parents.

Even more deadly was the mass shooting in Orlando's Pulse Nightclub on June 12, 2016, where Omar Mateen (age 29), a U.S.-born citizen of Afghan descent, shot and killed 49 people and injured 53 more over a period of about three hours. Between his attacks, Mateen called and talked to 9-1-1 operators, personnel at a local TV station, and hostage negotiators of the Orlando police department. He swore allegiance to ISIS leader al-Baghdadi, claimed that his attack was in response to the recent killing of Abu Waheeb, a member of ISIS's leadership team, and, more generally, to American military intervention in the Middle East. At one point, he answered a text message from his second wife, who wondered where he was, by asking her whether she had watched television. Eventually, Mateen was killed by a controlled explosion set off by police.

Born on Long Island, New York, Mateen grew up in Florida, graduated from high school, and earned an associate college degree in criminal justice. Although born in the United States he seems not quite to fit in with his peers. Like the perpetrator of the truck-ramming attack in New York City, the Orlando mass shooter, a security guard well versed in handling guns, was described by his former and second wife as an abusive husband and by acquaintances and colleagues as a man with a volatile temper.

Not particularly religious during adolescence and young adulthood Mateen became a very devout Muslim after the divorce from his first wife, prayed regularly in his mosque, and went on a religious pilgrimage to Saudi Arabia. However, neither family members nor acquaintances remembered him expressing extremist views or mentioning ISIS.[66]

Contrary to the jihadis responsible for the deadly post-9/11 attacks listed in Table 5.1, plus many more unsuccessful plotters, most Muslims who were—and still are—fed up with U.S. military actions in Iraq, Afghanistan, Pakistan, Syria, and elsewhere do not become terrorists. How, then, can one explain the radicalization of the relatively few?

In a comprehensive study about homegrown jihadis in the United States, Canada, and Western Europe in the post-9/11 years, the NYPD identified the following four developmental stages in a distinct model of radicalization:

- *Pre-radicalization* refers to the life of individuals before they enter into the process of radicalization. As the case studies showed, most of the future terrorists lived ordinary lives, had ordinary private and professional aspirations, and had no histories of violence.
- *Self-identification* is the stage in which internal and external factors cause individuals to become interested in and adopt jihadi ideology as their own. In this phase, typically, they seek contacts with like-minded people.
- *Indoctrination* leads to the intensification of individuals' embrace of the justification for violent jihad. According to the NYPD report,

Table 5.1 Post-9/11 Deadly Terrorism inside the United States by Jihadists

Year	Incident	Number of Fatalities
2019	Pensacola Base Shooting	3
2017	New York Truck Ramming	8
2016	Orlando Nightclub Shooting	49
2015	Chattanooga Shooting	4
2015	San Bernardino Mass Shooting	14
2014	Washington and New Jersey Shooting	4
2014	Beheading in Oklahoma	1
2013	Boston Marathon Attack	4
2009	Little Rock Shooting	1
2009	Fort Hood Shooting	13
2006	Jewish Federation Attack in Seattle	1
2002	Los Angeles Airport	2

Source: Various open sources.

contrary to the self-identification stage, at this time "association with like-minded people is an important factor as the process deepens."

- *Jihadization*, unlike the previous stages, tends to be a short process. Here members of the cell accept the call of jihadi indoctrination, decide to become "holy warriors," and prepare to carry out terrorist acts.[67]

In the post-9/11 era, the Al Qaeda organization was the inspiration for most homegrown jihadi terrorism plots but was rarely, if at all, directly involved. However, the 2010 National Intelligence Estimate warned that "al-Qa'ida maintains its intent to attack the Homeland—preferably with a large-scale operation that would cause mass casualties, harm the US economy, or both" and "retains the capability to recruit, train, and deploy operatives to mount some kind of an attack against the Homeland."[68] If not the original Al Qaeda organization or Al Qaeda Central, the group's Taliban allies may have had their hands in two terror plots inside the United States in 2009 and 2010: The above-mentioned plotters of an attack on New York City's subway system and the would-be Times Square bomber trained in Taliban-controlled areas in Pakistan. In the case of the latter, the Pakistani Taliban actually claimed responsibility for his failed car bombing. While Al Qaeda Central and/or the Taliban may have continued to plot major attacks inside the United States, individuals and small cells posed a greater threat. One reason was and remained the association with like-minded people that NYPD researchers found to be an important factor in the radicalization process has shifted increasingly from the actual contact to virtual association via the Internet. As the NYPD analysis points out, "The Internet is a driver and enabler for the process of radicalization."[69] Similarly, the U.S. Senate Committee on Homeland Security and Governmental Affairs cautioned that "as the terrorists' Internet campaign bypasses America's physical borders and undermines cultural barriers that previously served as a bulwark against al-Qaeda's message of hate and violence, the threat of homegrown terrorist attacks in the United States increases."[70] The same was true, when ISIS became the biggest jihadist player in the second decade of the twenty-first century.

QAnon: A New Violent Extremist Religiopolitical Movement?

As noted in the previous chapter, the conspiracy theory QAnon, created by "Q" on social media and spread by his followers (Anons) online, grew into a fast-spreading movement. In their online posts, Anons endorsed and threatened violence against the Satanic enemies. And some of them carried out and plotted such attacks long before January 6, 2021, and during that fateful day's violent breach of the U.S. Capitol. Those who were charged with criminal offenses seemed to believe that they fought for the good of their country and the world against the destructive force of evil. They believed they were fighting a righteous religio political battle—not unlike jihadist groups, such as Al Qaeda and ISIS. They also believed that God had selected Donald Trump to defeat the evil-doers.

Exploring the reasons why so many people embraced QAnon, one expert noted that the "collective transition to a more dislocated 'second modernity' underlies the global spike in mass anxiety." Conspiracy theories, then, can serve as "simplifying devices that help individuals and communities to address this ontological anxiety, with anti-scientific discourses..."[71] QAnon offered and encouraged more than anti-scientific discourses, namely, an alternative religion.

In *Christianity Today*, Bonnie Kristian wrote, "Among QAnon's most troubling aspects are its use of the language and style of evangelical Christianity, its misuse of the Bible to disguise its deception, and its increasing function as a syncretic cult of semi-Christian heresy."[72] After examining the QAnon conspiracy theory and meeting true believers, Adrienne LaFrance concluded, "To look at QAnon is to see not just a conspiracy theory but the birth of a new religion."[73] She met a female QAnon believer who told her,

> I feel God led me to Q. I really feel like God pushed me in this direction. I feel like if it was deceitful, in my spirit, God would be telling me, 'Enough's enough.' But I don't feel that. I pray about it. I've said, 'Father, should I be wasting my time on this?' ... And I don't feel that feeling of *I should stop*.[74]

Some QAnon activists conducted online Sunday services that included "prayer, communion, and interpretation of the Bible in light of Q drops [Q's online messages] and vice versa."[75] The congregants were encouraged to establish their own congregations as a means to enlarge the movement.

Notes

1 Corey Kilgannon and Joseph Goldstein, "Sayfullo Saipov, the Suspect in the New York Terror Attack and His Past," *New York Times*, October 31, 2017, www.nytimes.com/2017/10/31/nyregion/sayfullo-saipov-manhattan-truck-attack.html, accessed December 1, 2018.
2 Mark Sedgwick, "Al-Qaeda and the Nature of Religious Terrorism," *Terrorism and Political Violence* 16 (4) (Winter 2004), p. 808.
3 Magnus Ranstorp, "Terrorism in the Name of Religion," working paper available from Columbia International Affairs Online, www.ciaonet.org.arugula.cc.columbia.edu:2048/wps/ram01/index.html.
4 "Anti-Abortion Killer Executed," *CBS News*, September 3, 2003, www.cbsnews.com/stories/2003/09/04/national/main571515.shtml.
5 Excerpts are from Paul Hill, "Defending the Defenseless," www.armyofgod.com/PHill_ShortShot.html.
6 "Anti-Abortion Killer Executed."

7 Ibid.
8 The transcript is available at www.independent.co.uk/news/world/europe/paris-attackers-gave-interview-to-french-tv-station-we-are-defenders-of-the-prophet-we-took-vengeance-said-cherif-kouachi-9969749.html, accessed June 15, 2015.
9 Ehud Sprinzak, "Extremism and Violence in Israel: The Crisis of Messianic Politics," *Annals of the American Academy of Political and Social Science 555* (January 1998), p. 123.
10 Ibid., 120.
11 Mark Juergensmeyer, *Terror in the Mind of God: The Global Rise of Religious Violence* (Berkeley: University of California Press, 2001), 57.
12 Ibid., 54.
13 Sprinzak, 123.
14 The quote is from a report by ABC News on *World News Sunday*, February 27, 1994.
15 Ibid.
16 Albert Bandura, "Mechanisms of Moral Disengagement," in Walter Reich, ed., *Origins of Terrorism: Psychologies, Ideologies, Theologies, States of Mind* (New York: Cambridge University Press, 1990), 164.
17 Ibid., 174–5.
18 These terms are used by Juergensmeyer, chs. 8 and 9.
19 Ibid., 182–3.
20 Jessica Stern, *Terror in the Name of God: Why Religious Militants Kill* (New York: HarperCollins, 2003), 167.
21 Ibid.
22 Audrey Kurth Cronin, "Behind the Curve: Globalization and International Terrorism," *International Security* 27 (3) (Winter 2002/03), p. 42.
23 Stern, xxv.
24 Ibid.
25 David C. Rapoport, "The Fourth Wave: September 11 in the History of Terrorism," *Current History* (December 2001).
26 Sedgwick, 797.
27 Ibid.
28 Ibid., 805.
29 Juergensmeyer, 221.
30 Stern, xix.
31 This is what Terry Noble, a leader in a Christian Identity organization, told Mark Juergensmeyer. See Juergensmeyer, 193.
32 Stern, xviii.
33 Ibid., 286.
34 Ibid., 285.
35 Juergensmeyer, 222.
36 Ranstorp, 8.
37 Colin Powell made this statement as guest of the NBC News program *Meet the Press* on October 19, 2008.
38 Mark Juergensmeyer, "Religion as a Cause of Terrorism," in Louise Richardson, ed., *The Roots of Terrorism* (New York: Routledge, 2006), 134.
39 Jeff Stein, "Can You Tell a Sunni from a Shiite?" *New York Times*, October 17, 2006; www.nytimes.com/2006/10/17/opinion/17stein.html, accessed December 6, 2008.
40 Vali Nasr, *The Shia Revival: How Conflicts within Islam Will Shape the Future* (New York: Norton, 2006), 34.
41 John L. Esposito, "Terrorism and the Rise of Political Islam," in Richardson, 146.

42 Ibid., 147.

43 *The 9/11 Commission Report* (New York: W.W. Norton, 2004), 466, footnote 11.

44 Ibid., 50.

45 "Al-Qa'ida's Foreign Fighters in Iraq," Harmony Project, Combating Terrorism Center at West Point; http://ctc.usma.edu/harmony/pdf/CTCForeign Fighter. 19.Dec07.pdf.

46 Marc Sageman, *Understanding Terror Networks* (Philadelphia: University of Pennsylvania Press, 2004), 1.

47 Bruce Lawrence, *Messages to the World: The Statements of Osama bin Laden* (London: Verso, 2005), 107, 115·

48 This quote is from Esposito, 149.

49 Sageman, 2.

50 Esposito, 145.

51 William McCants and Jarret Brachman, "Militant Ideology Atlas," Executive Report compiled and published by the Combating Terrorism Center at West Point.

52 *The 9/11 Commission Report*, 51.

53 Lawrence Wright, *The Looming Tower: Al Qaeda and the Road to 9/11* (New York: Knopf, 2006), 31.

54 Ibid., 37.

55 According to Youssef Aboul-Enein, "Sheik Abdel-Fatahl Al-Khalidi Revitalizes Sayid Qutb," West Point: The Combating Terrorism Center United States Military Academy.

56 Excerpts are from Lawrence, *Fox News*, www.foxnews.com/story/0,2933, 454624,00.html; and Information Clearing House, www.informationclearing house.info/article11615.htm, accessed December 5, 2008.

57 I copied the above paragraphs from the full text of the announcement linked to via the Long War Journal's website www.longwarjournal.org/archives/2014/06/ isis_announces_formation_of_ca.php. However, by early 2018, the text was no longer available.

58 Sageman, 1.

59 Brynjar Lia, "Doctrines for Jihadi Terrorist Training," *Terrorism and Political Violence* 20 (4) (October–December 2008), p. 537.

60 Alissa J. Rubin, "Despair Drives Suicide Attacks by Iraqi Women," *New York Times*, July 5, 2008, www.nytimes.com/2008/07/05/world/middleeast/05diyala. html?sq=despair%20drives%20suicide%20attacks%20by%20Iraqi%20 Women&st=cse&scp=1&pagewanted=print.

61 Abdul Waheed Waffa, "10 Arrested for Afghan Acid Attack," *New York Times*, November 25, 2008, www.nytimes.com/2008/11/26/world/asia/26afghan. html?scp=6&sq=taliban%20and%20school%20girls& amp;st=cse, accessed November 25, 2008.

62 Marc Sageman, *Leaderless Jihad* (Philadelphia: University of Pennsylvania Press, 2008), 98.

63 Brian M. Jenkins, "Outside Expert's View," in Mitchell D. Silber and Arvin Bhatt, eds., *Radicalization in the West: The Homegrown Threat* (New York City Police Department Report, 2007), 14.

64 Andrea Elliott, Sabrina Tavernise, and Anne Barnard, "For Times Sq. Suspect, Long Roots of Discontent," *New York Times*, May 15, 2010, www.nytimes. com/2010/05/16/nyregion/16suspect.html?sq=faisal%20shahzad%20 and%20times%20square&st=cse&scp=1&pagewanted=pr int, accessed June 8, 2010.

65 Al Baker and Marc Santora, "San Bernardino Attackers Discussed Jihad in Private Messages, F.B.I. Says," *The New York Times*, December 16, 2015.

66 There were claims by some sources that Mateen targeted the Pulse Nightclub because it catered to gays and that he actually was a closeted gay man himself.
67 Silber and Bhatt, 6–7.
68 For the 2010 "Annual Threat Assessment of the Intelligence Community," see http://isis-online.org/uploads/conferences/documents/2010_NIE.pdf, accessed June 10, 2010.
69 Silber and Bhatt, 8.
70 U.S. Senate Committee on Homeland Security and Governmental Affairs, "Violent Islamic Extremism, the Internet, and the Homegrown Terrorist Threat," May 8, 2008, 5.
71 James Fitzgerald, "Conspiracy, Anxiety, Ontology: Theorising QAnon," *First Monday*, 27 (5) (2022); https://journals.uic.edu/ojs/index.php/fm/article/view/12618/10639, accessed August 10, 2022.
72 Bonnie Kristian, "QAnon Is a Wolf in Wolf's Clothing," *Christianity Today*, August 26, 2020; https://www.christianitytoday.com/ct/2020/august-web-only/qanon-is-wolf-in-wolfs-clothing.html, accessed July 10, 2022.
73 Adrienne LaFrance, "The Prophecies of Q," *The Atlantic.com*, June 2020; https://www.theatlantic.com/magazine/archive/2020/06/qanon-nothing-can-stop-what-is-coming/610567/, accessed July 10, 2022.
74 Ibid.
75 Bonnie Kristian, "Is QAnon the Newest American Religion?," *The Week*, May 21, 2022; https://theweek.com/articles/915522/qanon-newest-american-religion, accessed July 10, 2022.

6   The Making of Terrorists
Causes, Conditions, Influences

During a United Nations (UN) conference on poverty in March 2002, President George W. Bush said that the United States was ready to challenge "the poverty and hopelessness and lack of education and failed governments that too often allow conditions that terrorists can seize and try to turn to their advantage."[1] A few months later, however, in an interview with Radio Free Europe/Radio Liberty, the president suggested otherwise when he stated that there was no direct link between poverty and terrorism: "Poverty is a tool for recruitment amongst these global terrorists," Bush said. "It's a way for them to recruit—perhaps. But poverty doesn't cause killers to exist, and it's an important distinction to make."[2] No doubt, the president had the kind of terrorism in mind that had led to the attacks on 9/11, but in expressing different assessments of the roots of terrorism, he reflected the different viewpoints in the long-running expert debate on this issue. There is no doubt that terrorism cannot be understood without exploring the real and perceived grievances of groups and individuals who resort to political violence. Grievances of this nature are of a domestic or international nature—or both. But although the same or similar conditions breed terrorists in some countries and not in others, scholars have put forth a multitude of explanations.

The idea that socioeconomic conditions, such as poverty, lack of education, and high unemployment, provide fertile ground for terrorism pre-dates the rise of international terrorism in the last 35 years or so and, more importantly, the recent focus on the roots of terrorism in Arab and Muslim countries. Based on his research examining the lynching of black Americans in the nineteenth and twentieth centuries by whites and the economic conditions over a long period of time, Arthur Raper concluded that the number of lynching attacks peaked in times of economic downturns and subsided in years of economic improvement.[3] But using more advanced economic indicators, other researchers did not find a relationship between the ups and downs in lynching incidents and economic conditions.[4] For example, there was no surge in these attacks during the Great Depression of the 1930s.

DOI: 10.4324/9781003289265-7

At first sight, the argument that poverty breeds terrorism also carries little weight with respect to experiences in the West from the late 1960s through the 1980s, when some of the world's richest countries (e.g., Germany, Italy, France, Belgium, and the United States) produced a relatively large number of very active terrorist groups of the left-wing variety. The founders, leaders, and rank-and-file members of the most prominent terrorist organizations during that period, from the Italian Red Brigades to the German Red Army Faction (RAF) and the French Direct Action, came typically from middle-class or upper-middle-class families and had studied at universities. The same was true for left-wing terrorists in the United States; many of them had finished college and earned professional degrees (medicine, law, teaching, social work, etc.). But, as Brent Smith and Kathryn Morgan found in their research, in the last decades of the twentieth century, right-wing terrorists in the United States had very different demographic characteristics than their left-wing counterparts: One-third of the right-wingers had not graduated from high school, only about 12 percent had a college degree, and a large number of them were "unemployed or impoverished self-employed workers."[5] In other words, the same society with the same macro-socioeconomic conditions produced one type of terrorist that came from the well-to-do segment of society and another type from the lower socioeconomic strata.

Regardless of such findings, the idea that terrorism is the result of "poverty, desperation, and resentment" in less developed countries around the globe has survived as a plausible explanation in the search for the causes of group-based political violence.[6] However, statistical evidence tells another story. As Walter Laqueur has pointed out, "In the forty-nine countries currently designated by the United Nations as the least developed, hardly any terrorist activity occurs."[7] Other recent studies have contradicted the economic deprivation thesis with respect to terrorism and terrorists in the Middle East. Claude Berrebi examined a wealth of data on individual terrorists in the West Bank and Gaza, on the general population in those areas, and on the economic conditions over time. He concluded,

> Both higher standards of living and higher levels of education are positively associated with participation in Hamas or PIJ [Palestinian Islamic Jihad]. With regard to the societal economic condition, I could not find a sustainable link between terrorism and poverty and education, and I interpret this to mean that there is either no link or a very weak indirect link.[8]

Research by Alan B. Krueger and Jitka Maleckova came to similar conclusions with respect to the Lebanese Hezbollah; their evidence suggests "that having a higher living standard above the poverty line or a secondary school or higher education is *positively* associated with participation in Hezbollah."[9] The same research also found "that Israeli Jewish settlers who attacked Palestinians in the West Bank in the early 1980s were overwhelmingly from high-paying occupations."[10] Like Berrebi, Krueger and Maleckova found no evidence for a direct causal relationship between poverty and education on the one hand and participation in or support of terrorism on the other.

Focusing on militants in the Lebanese Hezbollah organization who had already undertaken or were willing to carry out suicide missions, one researcher found that most of these terrorists or would-be terrorists "are from poor families" and "geoculturally immobile."[11] But in the absence of in-depth comparisons between the living standard of the population at large and actual or would-be suicide bombers, the meaning of "poor" in this context is not quite clear. Perhaps Berrebi's research explains the different findings: With respect to the Palestinian groups he studied, Berrebi found that suicide bombers came from higher economic circumstances and had a higher education than the population at large but came "from lower socio-economic groups when compared to other, non-suicidal, terrorists."[12] Based on his empirical data analysis, James A. Piazza did not find evidence for what he calls the "rooted-in-poverty thesis" at all.[13]

These findings have profound implications for policy-makers in their fight to attack the roots of terrorism. If indeed economic and educational conditions do not cause terrorism, efforts to improve economic conditions, especially individual incomes, living conditions, health care, and educational opportunities, would not decrease the number of terrorists and their supporters or do away with terrorism altogether. But so far, policies continue to be guided in many instances by the assumption that aid to improve the economic circumstances of countries or regions is part of prudent counterterrorism strategy. Thus, in the spring of 2009, when the Taliban ally of Al Qaeda gained territorial control in Pakistan and intensified its violence in both that country and Afghanistan, the Obama administration pushed for a massive U.S. aid package that in part aimed at financing school, hospital, and road projects in the Taliban stronghold of Swat Valley and similarly contested regions in Pakistan.

It has been argued that changes in the content of education would be a more promising way to go. In her examination of textbooks, teachers' guides, and other official material used in schools on the West Bank and in Gaza, Daphne Burdman found that

> Palestinian children are urged to violent actions against Israelis even when it is likely that they will be injured or die. They are encouraged to desire rather than fear the circumstances, because they will find a place in Paradise with Allah.[14]

Like Burdman, Berrebi has suggested that efforts to reduce terrorism should focus on changes in the curriculum for children on the West Bank and in Gaza. Similar issues have arisen with respect to other countries and regions. For example, in the aftermath of 9/11, there were reports about and criticism of schools and textbooks in Saudi Arabia that encouraged intolerance and hate against non-Muslims. Similar indoctrination of the young was reportedly practiced in Islamic schools in North America and other parts of the world that received financial support from Saudi Arabia. Students of an Islamic school in northern Virginia told a reporter that some of their teachers "teach students that whatever is kuffar [non-Muslim], it is okay to hurt or steal from that person."[15]

But while propaganda of hate might well condition its receivers to support and even commit political violence, it is far from clear, however, whether removing hateful texts and indoctrination from schools would reduce terrorism significantly or eradicate it. After all, terrorism has flourished in all kinds of environments—in democratic and non-democratic societies, in settings where young people were and were not indoctrinated into committing violence. Some scholars, among them Ted Gurr, consider liberal democracies less vulnerable to political violence than authoritarian systems because dissent and conflict can be brought into the legitimate political process. Indeed, Gurr's research indicates that repressive regimes have a higher incidence of political violence than liberal democratic settings.[16] But after analyzing global data on terrorist incidents from 1980 through 1987 with respect to the sites of terrorist strikes and the nationality of attackers and victims, William Eubank and Leonard Weinberg concluded that during the 1980s "terrorist violence was far more common in stable democracies than in autocratic settings" and that the perpetrators and the victims of terrorism were more likely to be the citizens of stable democracies than of less stable or partial democracies and of countries with limited authoritarianism or absolutism.[17]

How can one explain such contradictory findings? The most plausible explanations point to the fact that the two research projects covered different time periods and, more importantly, focused in the first case on domestic terrorism data and in the second case on international terrorism data. Both explanations seem reasonable. Citizens who live in countries with repressive regimes have more reasons to use violence against the ruling clique, but in the absence of civil liberties, it is likely that the authorities detect and crush opposition groups that have committed, or plan to commit, terrorism. If terrorist acts do occur in closed societies, the targeted governments have the means to prevent, curb, or spin the news coverage of such events. Democracies offer citizens opportunities to participate in the decision-making process, but when groups or individuals conclude that their grievances are not adequately addressed, they may be more inclined to resort to violence than their counterparts under authoritarian rule—if only because the free press will spread their "propaganda of the deed."

However, according to Piazza's research, there are also variables that transcend the peculiarities of political systems and serve as important predictors of terrorism, namely, "population [size, historical development], ethno-religious diversity, increased state repression and, most significantly, the structure of party politics."[18]

All of this leads to the conclusion that terrorists emerge in poor and in rich countries, in democratic and in authoritarian states, in stable and in nonstable countries, and in societies whose textbooks teach or do not teach hatred of other ideological, religious, or ethnic groups.

In the absence of a universal model that identifies the conditions that breed group-based political violence and terrorists, experts in the field have looked beyond the environmental conditions for other explanations. If some groups and movements remain nonviolent in spite of unaddressed political grievances and others decide to embrace violent tactics, then group dynamics, decision-making processes, and leader–follower relationships might explain the differences. Similarly, if some individuals under the same or similar conditions become terrorists while others do not, it is not far-fetched to suspect that an individual's traits and experiences affect, or even determine, whether he or she selects or rejects the terrorist path. Terrorism scholars are not of one mind in this respect, but have proposed different approaches and explanations, among them the following: (1) terrorists make rational choices, (2) terrorists are guided by personal traits and experiences, and (3) terrorists are the products of social interaction.

Terrorism as a Result of Rational Choice

Borrowing from the Prussian military theorist Carl von Clausewitz, who noted that war is the continuation of diplomacy, Gary Sick has suggested that terrorism "is the continuation of politics by other means."[19] While not discounting the possibility that persons with a predisposition to violence and fanatic beliefs are especially drawn to terrorism, Sick emphasizes that terrorism is the result of a deliberate choice made in particular political environments—at least in the early stage of a group's life span. "Their [group members'] choice of terrorism, as opposed to other possible forms of [political] behavior, is a function of the political environment," he writes. For Richard Shultz, too, terrorism "is calculated violence" that is "goal directed" and "employed in pursuit of political objectives."[20] In her exploration of terrorism as a logical choice, Martha Crenshaw concurs when she states that "Terrorism is likely to be a reasonably informed choice among available alternatives, some tried unsuccessfully."[21]

Thus, the Weathermen group in the United States was formed when its founders concluded that the anti-Vietnam War, anti-authority protests staged by the Students for a Democratic Society did not further their ideological goals. Similarly, the RAF in Germany emerged as the radical offspring of the Socialist Student Association. The Army of God, and other extreme antiabortion groups that resorted to terrorist methods, emerged and grew when its founders and recruits determined that the mainstream pro-life movement's attempts to work within the legitimate political process to outlaw legalized abortions were in vain.

Based on many years of research, Ehud Sprinzak rejected the notion of terrorists as psychologically challenged types or crazies and concluded, "Terrorism is not the product of mentally deranged persons. Terrorism, and ideological terrorism, in particular, is a political phenomenon par excellence and is therefore explicable in political terms."[22] On this count, Christopher Harmon agrees with Sprinzak and discards the notion of terrorist acts as mindless, stating,

> It is mostly on the surface that terrorism appears to be madness, or mindless. Behind the screaming and the blood there lies a controlling purpose, a motive, usually based in politics or something close to it, such as a drive for political or social change inspired by religion.
>
> The terrorist is not usually insane; he or she is more usually "crazy like a fox."[23]

If terrorism is not committed by crazies, is this sort of political violence the result of rational decisions that individuals and groups make? That begs the question of whether economic analysis and particularly rational choice theory are helpful in determining whether groups and individuals act rationally when they decide whether or not to engage in terrorist activity—and what kind of terrorism. Underscoring the relevance of the rational choice model in terrorism studies Bryan Caplan distinguishes between three types of individuals:

- Sympathizers who are not involved in violence;
- Active terrorists who belong to terrorist groups;
- Suicide terrorists who are willing to die.

He measures the rationality or irrationality of these three types by their "responsiveness to incentives, narrow-self-interest, and rational expectations."[24]

When calculating and assessing incentives to commit violence or not, all three types tend to make rational choices. Active terrorists and suicide bombers are guided by their commitment to their terrorist group. In the absence of nonviolent incentives, attacking the enemy is a rational choice; for the suicide bomber and his or her group this mode of attack is cost-effective and has a high rate of success as measured by the number of fatalities and inflicted damage (see also Chapter 8). If no risks were involved in carrying out violent attacks, terrorist sympathizers would become active terrorists as well.

The inactive sympathizer is most likely also guided by self-interest, is removed from group dynamics, and has rational expectations of the consequences of violence. Thus, for Caplan, the sympathizer "deviates only slightly from homo economicus."[25] In the same assessment, active terrorists come "probably close" to making rational choices in terms of narrow self-interest and rational expectations in their conviction that they will not die but succeed. In contrast, suicide bombers seem not rational on both narrow self-interest and rational expectations. How can it be in one's self-interest to die in order to kill others? And, since most suicide terrorists tend to be of the religious variety, how can it be a rational expectation to be rewarded in the after-life? Still, even suicide bombers fit one of Caplan's three rational choice criteria.

Recognizing that terrorists have "short-term organizational objectives and long-term political objectives," Louise Richardson characterized the more immediate or "secondary motives" as the "Three Rs" for "revenge, renown, and reaction."[26] No doubt, revenge for real or perceived injustice and humiliation, renown in the sense of obtaining publicity and glory, and the wish for reaction and overreaction on the part of their targets are common motives of all kinds of terrorist groups. In deciding to pursue the goals that Richardson calls the "Three Rs," terrorists presumably make some rational decisions.

The notion that terrorism is political in nature, goal oriented, and the result of rational or logical choices among several alternatives fits into the instrumental paradigm that recognizes terrorism as a means to specific political ends, such as removing foreign influence from a country or region, the removal of a regime, or national independence.[27]

Terrorism as a Result of Personal Traits and Experiences

Jerrold Post takes issue with the suggestion that terrorism is the result of rational choices made by the perpetrators of political violence. Instead, he argues that "political terrorists are driven to commit acts of violence as a consequence of psychological forces."[28] Based on his interviews with terrorists as well as memoirs and court records, Post suggests that "people with particular traits and tendencies are drawn disproportionately to terrorist careers."[29] A study of the background of 227 left-wing terrorists, most of them active in the Baader-Meinhof group or RAF, confirmed the idea that particular experiences and personality traits make some people more prone to become involved with terrorism than others. In the case of German left-wing terrorists, researchers found the following:

> No less than 69 percent of the men and 52 percent of the women reportedly had clashes with parents, schools, or employers—33 percent with their parents, 18 percent with employers—or prior records of criminal or juvenile offenses, many of them repeated entries.

Although there are no exact population averages or control groups with which to compare, the percentages are so large as to suggest in many cases a conflict-ridden youth aggravated by parental death, divorce, remarriage and other misfortunes of modern society.[30]

Konrad Kellen described this type of background using the example of Hans Joachim Klein, an eventual defector from the RAF. As a small boy and teenager, Klein was constantly mistreated and beaten by his father. According to Kellen,

> When Klein was in his teens, a girlfriend gave him a small chain to wear around his neck; the father ripped the chain off and beat him once again. Suddenly, however, young Klein rebelled and slapped his father's face, expecting to be killed a moment later for his transgression. But the old man treated his son with courtesy and respect from that moment on! The lesson for the younger Klein was probably that force and the infliction of pain can do the trick... Presumably Klein concluded, at some level, that if he could do this to his father, he could do it to the state as well.[31]

Despite the fact that many left-wing German terrorists had troubled backgrounds, Merkl has argued that "every German terrorist could just as well have turned away from terrorism, being a creature endowed with free will; and some did."[32] But what Jeffrey Ross has called individuals' "facilitating traits," such as alienation, depression, or antisocial behavior, may drive persons to join terrorist movements—especially when a particular group setting gives them for the first time in their lives the feeling that they belong, that they count.[33] Randy Borum takes a sensible in-between position by concluding that "certain life experiences tend to be commonly found among terrorists" and

> Histories of childhood abuse and trauma appear to be widespread... None of these contribute much to a causal explanation of terrorism, but may be seen as markers of vulnerability, as possible sources of motivation, or as mechanism for acquiring or hardening one's militant ideology.[34]

If one believes that terrorists are steered by their personal traits and a "special psycho-logic [that] is constructed to rationalize acts they are psychologically compelled to commit," as Post suggests, the instrumental paradigm falls on its face: Terrorism is not seen as the means to a particular political end, as a way to further one's political causes; rather, terrorism is the end itself, or, as Post puts it, "Individuals become terrorists in order to join terrorist groups and commit acts of terrorism."[35]

Risk Factors in the Making of Violent Extremists

Childhood trauma, adolescent behavior, and personal traits as risk factors in the making of violent extremists do not merely apply to left-extremists like members of the German RAF. A study based on extensive interviews with 44 former White Supremacists (38 males and 6 females from 15 U.S. states) revealed severe childhood trauma in that

- 43 percent experienced childhood physical abuse;
- 23 percent experienced adolescent sexual abuse;
- 41 percent experienced physical neglect;
- 36 percent experienced parental abandonment;
- 54 percent witnessed serious violence;
- 48 percent had mental health problems;
- 73 percent had abused alcohol and illegal drugs during adolescence.

As the researchers noted, these childhood experiences and adolescent behavioral problems by far exceeded those in the general population.[36]

Similarly, based on their in-depth case studies of 51 persons in the Netherlands who tried in vain or were successful in joining jihadist groups abroad between 2000 and 2013, three Dutch researchers found that 17 of the 51 had "a criminal history in petty theft, violence, burglary, and in some cases extortion and possession of child pornography."[37] This research revealed furthermore that psychological problems were far more prevalent among those trying to become jihadists in the years from 2011 to 2013 than in the preceding time period. Thus, 6 of 15 jihadists or would-be jihadists in those years had "mental issues according to health care professionals, varying from moderate mental instability to serious psychiatric disorders."[38] While this relatively small sample may not allow us to use these and other findings to generalize, it is nevertheless an interesting result.

Terrorism as a Result of Social Interaction

In her studies of members of the Italian Red Brigades, Donatella della Porta found that social interaction and social ties, not personal traits, explain why individuals join terrorist groups. Della Porta's research revealed that

In as many as 88 percent of the cases in which the nature of the tie with the recruiter is known, she or he is no stranger; in 44 percent, she or he is a personal friend; and in 20 percent, she or he is a relative.[39]

Similarly, a study of Lebanese Shi'ite terrorists established that they were "recruited by and from the concentric circles of kinship, friendship, or fellowship."[40] That is precisely what Marc Sageman found when he analyzed the personal background of 172 members of the global Salafi jihad movement, including Al Qaeda as its vanguard.[41] There was no evidence that these jihadis were brainwashed and enlisted by distinct recruiting efforts; rather, the key was, according to Sageman,

> Social affiliation through friendship, kinship, and discipleship; progressive intensification of beliefs and faith leading to the acceptance of the global Salafi jihad ideology; and formal acceptance to the jihad through the encounter of a link to the jihad.[42]

And then there are terrorist organizations that provide social services in communities that otherwise would not have health care, schools, or security forces. The Lebanese Hezbollah and the Palestinian Hamas are good examples of groups that consist of a community service arm, a political branch, and a terrorist corps. By coming to the aid of needy people in their communities, these organizations create large reservoirs for the recruitment of terrorists—especially in their religious schools. Potential recruits are often chosen at a very young age and well before they themselves have decided to become a terrorist. Instead, they are groomed for their future role.

According to Loretta Napoleoni, "People are not only carefully selected, their background is analyzed minutely, and every single detail is taken into consideration. If a candidate is judged to be suitable, he is indoctrinated, fed a special diet of religion, spiritualism and violence."[43] In the last several years, Western Europe has become an especially fertile breeding ground of new jihadis—young members of the Muslim diaspora who are disillusioned and alienated from the societies they live in.

Whether in London or Birmingham, Paris or Marseilles, Berlin or Cologne, and many other communities in the United Kingdom, France, Germany, and neighboring countries, some of these Muslim newcomers are likely to seek out and become part of social networks of fellow Muslims, where they join friends, relatives, or acquaintances. While pointing out that "the history of radical Islamism and the terrorist cells in Western Europe remains to be written," Walter Laqueur was nevertheless certain about one aspect: The idea that over time a European Islam would develop that was more liberal and open seemed to have been premature. In reality, a new generation grew up who were artificially

Hate and Violence as Addiction

Interestingly, when racial, ethnic, and/or religious supremacy percep-tions and intensive hate for the "other" inform an in-group's causes and its members' identities, group members might become consumed by hate and everything that magnifies related feelings. Ku Klux Klan or Neo-Nazi entities, for example, fit the profile of hate groups. Research suggests that hard-core White Supremacists become addicted to hate and the symbols and expressions of hate to such a degree that they remain vulnerable to relapse just like recovering alcoholics long after they have sworn off their hatefulness and left their groups. In extensive interviews with 89 former White Supremacists in the United States more than one-third of the interviewees described hate as a form of addiction; 62 percent revealed some kind of relapse after they had left groups.[45] One woman told researchers,

> Somebody needs to do a study... subject us to the [white power] music, to the literature, to the racial slurs and watch what fires in our brains. I guarantee you it's an addiction. I can listen to white power music and within a week be back to that mindset. I know it.[46]

It is entirely possible that this hate addiction is present in other extrem-ist and violent groups.

assimilated and in large part deeply disaffected. Among these alienated groups the preachers of jihad found their followers.[44]

But in his review of the relevant research, Malise Ruthven found evi-dence that neither alienation nor the embrace of religious and ideological extremism are the driving forces behind the establishment of terrorist jihadi cells. Instead, "the people who form terror groups have to know and trust one another. In most Muslim societies it is kinship, rather than shared ideological values, that generates relations of trust."[47]

Differences between Leaders and Followers

Today, when it comes to the making of terrorists, there may well be distinct differences between leaders and the second-tier activist strata on the one hand and rank-and-file followers and sympathizers on the other hand. It seems that those who decide in the first place to form a group in order to achieve their objectives by carrying out violence consider the

The Making of Terrorists: Causes, Conditions, Influences 151

alternatives, weigh their opportunities and challenges, and jump into action because of certain events or developments or opportunities. These are the people with strong ideological convictions regardless of whether these are of the secular or religious variety. Typically, the leadership cadre came together through personal contacts in the past, and it still does so in the age of digital communication. Here kinship and friendship are still the keys.

Those who eventually join may sympathize with and admire the group's leaders and actions, demands, and goals but may be far less informed about the ideological and operational underpinnings than the leadership and operator strata.

Take the example of the Islamic State. Its leaders, all Sunnis, discussed the blueprint for the organization at great length and detail while imprisoned in a U.S.-run detention facility in Iraq. Once free and upset about the mistreatment of Sunnis by the Shi'ite-controlled central government in Baghdad, these men built their organization according to plan with a priority given to the formation of a most brutal jihadi force and a mighty propaganda machine.

But even as the Islamic State's reach expanded and tens of thousands of men and women traveled to ISIS-controlled territory, most of these supporters had merely rudimentary knowledge of the group's religious orthodoxy and related political convictions.

After interviewing radicalized Muslim teenagers in the suburbs of Paris a French journalist concluded,

> They knew very little about religion. They had hardly read a book and they learnt jihad before religion. They'd tell me, 'You think with your head, we think with our hearts.' They had a romantic view of radicalism. I wondered how that happened.[48]

Social media posts revealed that young ISIS devotees have great admiration for the Islamic State and its jihadists, not unlike the sentiments displayed by fans of sports clubs and stars in the entertainment world. The Merriam-Webster online dictionary defines "fan" as "an enthusiastic devotee (as of a sport or a performing art) usually as a spectator" and "an ardent admirer or enthusiast (as of a celebrity or a pursuit)." When adding, according to the same dictionary source, that the term "fan" is probably a short form for "fanatic," it makes sense to consider these young Muslims in the West as part of a virtual fandom community similar to fanatic fan groups devoted to sports teams, pop bands, or Hollywood celebrities. Based on their analysis of Twitter data concerning the 2012 Eurovision Song Contest, Tim Highfield, Stephen Harrington, and Axel Bruns characterized "Twitter as an important new medium facilitating the connection and communion of fans."[49]

Cult Thinking in Terrorist Groups

Comparing terrorist groups with religious or religiopolitical cults may be another way to explain the power and obedience dynamics within terrorist groups. In his book "THEM and US: Cult Thinking and the Terrorist Threat" Arthur J. Deikman notes that people attracted to cults are not crazy but are guided by "two kinds of wishes: they want a meaningful life, to serve God or humanity; and they want to be taken care of, to feel protected and secure, to find a home."[50] While he deems the first motivation, namely, to do something good, as positive, he sees the second set of wishes, namely, to belong, find a home in a group of like-minded people, as "enabling cult leaders to elicit behavior directly opposite to the idealistic vision [of the first types of wishes]."[51] Deikman identifies four distinct behaviors by rank-and-file cult members: dependence on a leader, compliance with the group, devaluating the outsider, and avoiding dissent.

Applying his cult characteristics in a case study to Al Qaeda, Deikman found those traits in the "cult thinking" of Al Qaeda Central and suggested that the same dynamics are present in other types of violent extremist groups, including those in the West. It seems, though, that some terrorist groups are more akin to become cults than others, particularly those with narcissistic/charismatic leaders. The Japanese Aum Shinrikyo, best known for its 1995 lethal sarin attack in the Tokyo subway system, was a pseudo-religious cult created and ruled with an iron fist by Shoko Ashara. He forced his followers to sever all ties to their families and friends and dominated their lives and actions completely. Deikman, a psychiatrist, links the dependency on cult leaders and groups "to the longing for parents [that] persists into adulthood and results in cult behavior..."[52] The Liberation Tigers of Eelam in Sri Lanka, also called Tamil Tigers, fought for an independent Tamil state. Tamil Tigers, men, women, and children, were emotionally and financially dependent on Velupillai Prabhakaran, the charismatic leader of the group, and conformed completely to group-think in their particular fighting, supporting, or training sub-entities, including, committing suicide terrorism. Unlike the Aum's Ashara, Prabhakaran did not invent a religious tale to indoctrinate his followers.

Jerrold Post, a psychiatrist, examined the relationship between charismatic leaders and their followers in general and also in the context of terrorism. He found that childhood experiences result in "mirror-hungry" personalities of certain leaders and "idol-hungry" personalities of certain followers. According to Post, "The mirror-hungry charismatic and narcissistic leaders, rejected [as children] by cold and ungiving mothers, ...may be left emotionally hungry with an exaggerated need for love and admiration." The ideal-hungry followers "experience themselves as worthwhile only so long as they can relate to individuals whom they can admire for their prestige, power, beauty, intelligence, or moral stature."[53] Post recognized such leader-follower relationships between narcissistic political and religiopolitical leaders, such as "der Fuehrer" [the leader] Hitler in Germany and the Ayatollah Khomeini in Iran, and their most devoted followers but also in the relationships between terrorist leaders and rank-and-file terrorists in their groups.

The Lone Actor or Solo Terrorist

In Chapter 4, I addressed the solo or lone actor terrorist phenomenon in the context of contemporary White Supremacists. But there is lone actor terrorism—one individual, a pair, or even a small cell—in different types of terrorism: Far-Left, Far-Right, Religious, and Single- Issue Outliers. These terrorists do not have direct links to terrorist groups but know of and share the ideologies—grievances, justifications, demands, and targets—with specific groups or movements. In their minds, they may be part of "imagined communities" of which they know via media consumption: Books, political tracts, traditional news and entertainment media, and more recently the internet and social media. Once they feel part of such online communities some devoted "members" follow their community leaders' instructions. It is not unusual that an actual terrorist group claims responsibility for lone actor terrorism, if the perpetrator alleges to have acted on behalf of that group.

In September 1901, President William McKinley was assassinated by Leon Czolgosz, a self-described anarchist who was radicalized by anarchist newspapers and prominent anarchist individuals who in their writings and speeches called for violence against the powerful. Czolgosz acted alone. He was not a member of an extremist organization; he was an early lone actor terrorist. In April 1995, Timothy McVeigh detonated a powerful car bomb in front of the Alfred P. Murrah Federal Building in Oklahoma City killing 168 persons and injuring many, many more. He was radicalized by antigovernment and Neo-Nazi books and regular visits to gun shows. He acted alone, although he had an accomplice as he prepared his homemade killer bomb. McVeigh was not a member of an extremist organization; he was a lone actor or solo terrorist. In the more than nine decades between these incidents, there were many more solo attacks.

Yet, while lone actor terrorism is not a new phenomenon, there has been a dramatic increase in cases in which one individual or a pair carried out political violence against civilians or noncombatants. Jeffrey D. Simon points to "the key role that technology, particularly the Internet, is playing in the rise of the lone wolf" and the need "to revise our thinking about terrorism and shift away from an almost exclusive focus on terrorist groups and organizations toward a new appreciation for the importance of individual terrorists."[54]

Yes, indeed, the spread of hate, violent messages, and calls for individuals to carry out political violence via the Internet reach far more people in far more places around the globe than did terrorist propaganda before the digital age. Thus, we do have many more solo terrorists or small-cell terrorists than at any other time. As detailed in Chapter 15, social media in particular has been instrumental in radicalizing and recruiting individuals who may or may not team up with one, two, or three persons they are close to. Think of the Boston Marathon Bombing: Internet posts introduced Tamerlan Tsarnaev to the grievances of jihadists and their appeals to attack Westerners in their own environment. He downloaded detailed instructions for preparing pressure-cooker bombs from Al Qaeda in the Arabian Peninsula's online magazine *Inspire*. And, finally, he recruited his younger brother who joined him in their deadly attack in the heart of Boston.

Whether anarchist Czolgosz, antigovernment extremist McVeigh, the jihadist Tsarnaev brothers, or the right-extremist nativist Anders Breivik who, in 2011, killed 76 people in Norway in an unspeakable killing spree in the name of defending Christian Europe against Islamic invaders, they all were infected by viruses of hate spread by whatever was the latest communication technology of their times. While they were loners, they bought into extremist ideologies and acted according to the respective movements' propaganda—nowadays most prevalent on social media.

Terrorism expert Brian Jenkins made this very point. Noting before the rise of ISIS that "two-thirds of the homegrown al Qaeda-inspired terrorist plots in the United States since 9/11 have involved a single individual," he concluded,

> The term *lone wolf* would apply to only a few of these terrorist plotters. The behavior of many resembles more that of stray dogs. They sniffed at the edges of al Qaeda extremist ideology, participated vicariously in its online jihad, exhorting each other to action, carelessly throwing down threats, boasting of their prowess as warriors, of the heroic deeds they were ready to perform, barking, showing their teeth, hesitating, then darting forward until ensnared by the law.[55]

The Lack of a Universal Terrorist Profile

But when everything is said and done, it seems impossible to understand the roots of particular kinds of terrorism without considering the real or perceived political, socioeconomic, or religious grievances that feed into the formation of terrorist ideologies and serve as justifications for terrorist acts. "However impoverished and reduced it may be," Michel Wieviorka wrote, "there is always an ideology underlying a terrorist action."[56] This may be more the case for the founding fathers and mothers of terrorist groups than for the rank-and-file members. But in order to function and flourish, the founders and their heirs must translate real or perceived grievances into an ideological framework or mission statement. According to Jessica Stern,

> The most important aspect of organization is the mission. The mission is the story about Us versus Them. It distinguishes the pure from the impure and creates group identity. The organization's mission statement—the story about its raison d'être—is the glue that holds even the most tenuous organizations together.[57]

The Stages Leading to Terrorism

Terrorism is rarely, if ever, the result of a sudden impulse. People do not become terrorists on the spur of the moment. Groups and individuals resort to political violence when they make the move into the last stage of a process. By distinguishing between social movements, antimovements, and terrorism, Wieviorka recognized different types of opposition group-ings with different degrees of resistance to the existing power or powers and different courses of action coupled with their possible transitions from one type to another.[58] Similarly, Ehud Sprinzak identified three stages in liberal democracies—from strong opposition to intense opposi-tion (with protests and even small-scale violence) to outright terrorist activity: (1) crisis of confidence, (2) conflict of legitimization, and (3) cri-sis of legitimacy.[59] Once a group enters into the last stage, its grievances turn increasingly into intense hate of the enemy, who is dehumanized. "The regime and its accomplices are now portrayed as 'things,' 'dogs,' 'pigs,' 'Nazis,' or 'terrorists.' The portrayal is not accidental and occa-sional but repeated and systematic."[60] This pattern of dehumanizing the enemy applies to all types of terrorist groups—those on the extreme left and those on the extreme right; those who have extreme racist and reli-gious views. Because of his Vietnam policy, President Lyndon B. Johnson was called "baby killer" by the most extreme voices in the radical left of the 1960s; after the events at Waco, Texas, right-wing extremists called federal agents "baby killers" and Attorney General Janet Reno "butcher of Waco." Members of the German RAF also moved gradually into the last motivational stage. According to Merkl,

> Once an enemy had been declared and made into the absolute moral evil, the world became simple, and any means were justified for fight-ing this evil. Soon the 'struggle' itself became the goal, and this in turn could satisfy deep personal needs.[61]

A member of the Italian Red Brigades explained the terrorist mindset and motivation when in search of a victim this way:

Then you have singled out your victim; he is physically there; he is the one to be blamed for everything. In that moment there is already the logic of the trial in which you have already decided that he is guilty; you only have to decide about his punishment. So you have a very "emphatic" sense of justice; you punish him not only for what he has done but also for all the rest. Then, you don't care anymore which responsibilities that person has; you give him them all... he is only a small part of the machine that is going to destroy all of us.[62]

Expressing his hatred of Israelis, one Arab terrorist said, "You Israelis are Nazis in your souls and in your conduct... Given this kind of conduct, there is no choice but to strike at you without mercy in every possible way."[63] In defense of suicide missions, an Islamic terrorist said, "This is not suicide. Suicide is selfish, it is weak, it is mentally disturbed. This is *istishad* (martyrdom or self-sacrifice in the service of Allah)."[64]

First dehumanization, then the justification of killing as morally and religiously justified, are part of what Albert Bandura describes as a mechanism of moral disengagement on the part of groups that decide to commit terrorism:

One set of disengagement practices operates on the construal of the behavior itself. People do not ordinarily engage in reprehensible conduct until they have justified to themselves the morality of their actions. What is culpable can be made honorable through cognitive reconstrual. In this process, destructive conduct is made personally and socially acceptable by portraying it in the service of moral purposes. People then act on a moral imperative.[65]

Another way to trace the process of radicalization of terrorists is the one described in Chapter 5 developed especially to trace the making of jihadis who are born in or immigrated to Western countries. It is possible and indeed likely to fit the moral disengagement and dehumanization processes into the four stages of jihadi radicalization. And, vice versa, essential parts of those stages may be well suited to explain the radicalization stages of non-Muslims who turn into religious or secular terrorists.

In examining the causes of terrorism, Martha Crenshaw distinguishes between two major factors: (1) the preconditions that are at the heart of political, socioeconomic, or religious grievances felt by societal subgroups; and (2) the precipitants or specific events that trigger terrorist acts.[66] This twofold causation (see Table 6.1) can be traced with respect to most, if not all, groups or individuals who perpetrate terrorism. Although this chapter has discussed at some length the underlying political and personal circumstances as causes of terrorism, trigger events need further explanation. Typically, military or other violent government actions, often reactions to nonviolent or violent

Table 6.1 Causes of Terrorism/Formation of Terrorist Groups

Preconditions	Trigger Events
Grievances	Domestic, international, or both
Reactions:	*Reactions*:
Articulation of dissent and ideological differences	Most radical individuals split from larger opposition segment
Alienation from those in power	Core of leaders forms group for
Nonviolent protests	the purpose of more militant
Possibly some violence	action: terrorfare
Recruitment of members	Securing of resources (weapons, finances, hideouts, etc.)
Dehumanization of the enemy and moral disengagement	*Result*: Terrorist acts

Source: Author.

dissent, serve as catalysts for the formation of terrorist groups. Thus, brutal police actions against protesters during the Democratic Party's 1968 National Convention in Chicago triggered the formation of the Weathermen. One year earlier, the killing of a German student (Benno Ohnesorg) by the police during a demonstration in West Berlin against a visit of the Shah of Iran triggered massive student demonstrations as the prelude to the formation of the RAF. The defeat of the Arab states by Israel in the 1967 war became the precipitant for the formation of Palestinian terrorist groups, just as the first Persian Gulf War in 1991 and the use of Saudi Arabian bases by the U.S. military influenced the emergence of bin Laden's Al Qaeda terrorist organization. Even the terrorist actions of lone wolves can be associated with trigger events. For example, the 1993 inferno at Waco, Texas, hardened the antigovernment feeling of American right-wing groups and was the trigger event for Timothy McVeigh, who was responsible for the Oklahoma City bombing on the second anniversary of the events at Waco.

The would-be Times Square bomber was affected by such a particular event. In tracing Faisal Shahzad's road to terrorism, Andrea Elliott wrote,

As dawn broke on July 10, 2007, Pakistani commandos stormed the Red Mosque in Islamabad, ending a lengthy standoff with armed militants in a blaze of gunfire that left more than 100 dead. In Washington, officials applauded the siege as an important demonstration of Pakistan's willingness to confront Islamist militants.

Yet Faisal Shahzad, a Pakistani immigrant living in Connecticut, was outraged. He had prayed at the Red Mosque during visits home...

The episode was pivotal for Mr. Shahzad, setting him on a course to join a militant Pakistani group that would train him in explosives and bankroll his plot to strike at Times Square last month ... "That was the triggering event," said a person familiar with the case.[67]

The Roots of Terrorism: No Simple Answers

Recognizing a whole range of causes for the emergence of terrorism and the difficulty of identifying one or a few predominant ones, Jessica Stern wrote,

> I have come to see terrorism as a kind of virus, which spreads as a result of risk factors at various levels: global, interstate, national, and personal. But identifying these factors precisely is difficult. The same variables (political, religious, social, or all of the above) that seem to cause one person to become a terrorist might cause another to become a saint.[68]

Taken together, then, a variety of political, socioeconomic, and religious motives combined with personal conditions and trigger events provide merely clues for understanding the making of terrorists and the formation of terrorist groups, the motivations of individual recruits, and the decisions to commence violent campaigns. Also, there may be distinct differences between group founders and leaders on the one hand and rank-and-file members and lone like-minded autonomous cells and lone wolves on the other hand. In the absence of a predominant causal model, it is always difficult for target societies to comprehend fully the complex causes of a particular terrorist threat and more thorny yet to attack the roots of terrorism.

Notes

1 "Bush Ties Foreign Aid to Reform," *CBSNews.com*, March 22, 2002, www.cbsnews.com/stories/2002/03/21/politics/printable/504248.shtml, accessed June 30, 2003.
2 Jeffrey Donovan, "U.S.: Analysts See Weak Link between Poverty and Terrorism," www.rferl.org/nca/features/2002/11/27112002205339.asp, accessed June 29, 2003.
3 Arthur Raper, "The Tragedy of Lynching," Patterson Smith Reprint Series in Criminology, *Law Enforcement, and Social Problems*, Publication no. 25 (Montclair, NJ: Patterson Smith, 1969; originally published 1933).
4 Carl I. Hovland and Robert R. Sears, "Minor Studies of Aggression: Correlation of Lynchings with Economic Indices," *Journal of Psychology* 9 (1940), pp. 301–10.
5 Brent L. Smith and Kathryn D. Morgan, "Terrorists Right and Left: Empirical Issues in Profiling American Terrorists," *Studies in Conflict and Terrorism* 17 (1) (January–March 1994), p. 51.

6 See Allen Hammond, "Economic Distress Motivates Terrorists," in Laura K. Egendorf, ed., *Terrorism: Opposing Viewpoints* (San Diego, CA: Greenhaven Press, 2000), 77.

7 Walter Laqueur, *No End to War: Terrorism in the Twenty-First Century* (New York: Continuum, 2003), 15. The list of the world's least developed countries was based on several criteria: low per capita income, weak human resources, and low-level economic diversification.

8 Claude Berrebi, "Evidence about the Link between Education, Poverty, and Terrorism among Palestinians," unpublished paper, 2003, 1.

9 Alan B. Krueger and Jitka Maleckova, "Education, Poverty and Terrorism," unpublished paper, 2002, 1.

10 Ibid.

11 Ayla Schbley, "Defining Religious Terrorism: A Causal and Anthological Profile," *Studies in Conflict and Terrorism* 26 (2) (March–April 2003), p. 119.

12 Berrebi, 1.

13 James A. Piazza, "Rooted in Poverty? Terrorism, Poor Economic Development, and Social Cleavages," *Terrorism and Political Violence* 18 (1) (Spring 2006), p. 170.

14 Daphne Burdman, "Education, Indoctrination, and Incitement: Palestinian Children on Their Way to Martyrdom," *Terrorism and Political Violence* 15 (1) (Spring 2003), p. 97.

15 Valerie Strauss and Emily Wax, "Where Two Worlds Collide: Muslim Schools Face Tension of Islamic, U.S. Views," *Washington Post*, February 25, 2002, A1.

16 Ted Gurr, "Political Protest and Rebellion in the 1960s: The United States in World Perspectives," in Hugh Graham and Ted Gurr, eds., *Violence in America* (Beverly Hills, CA: Sage, 1979), 59–73.

17 William Eubank and Leonard Weinberg, "Terrorism and Democracy: Perpetrators and Victims," *Terrorism and Political Violence* 13 (1) (Spring 2001), pp. 160, 161.

18 Piazza, 159.

19 Gary G. Sick, "The Political Underpinnings of Terrorism," in Charles W. Kegley, Jr., ed., *International Terrorism: Characteristics, Causes, Controls* (New York: St. Martin's, 1990), 51.

20 Richard Shultz, "Conceptualizing Political Terrorism," in Kegley, 45.

21 Martha Crenshaw, "The Logic of Terrorism," in Walter Reich, ed., *Origins of Terrorism: Psychologies, Ideologies, States of Minds* (New York: Cambridge University Press, 1990), 10, 11.

22 Ehud Sprinzak, "Extreme Left Terrorism in a Democracy," in Reich, 78.

23 Christopher C. Harmon, *Terrorism Today* (London: Frank Cass, 2000), 201.

24 Bryan Caplan, "Terrorism: The Relevance of the Rational Choice Model," *Public Choice* 128 (1–2) (2006), p. 93.

25 Ibid.

26 Louise Richardson, *What Terrorists Want: Understanding the Enemy, Containing the Threat* (New York: Random House, 2006), ch. 4.

27 For more on the instrumental approach, see Martha Crenshaw, "Theories of Terrorism: Instrumental and Organizational Approaches," in David C. Rapoport, ed., *Inside Terrorist Organizations* (London: Frank Cass, 2001), 13–31.

28 Jerrold M. Post, "Terrorist Psycho-Logic: Terrorist Behavior as a Product of Psychological Forces," in Reich, 23.

29 Ibid., 25.

30 The results of a study of German terrorists are cited and commented on by Peter H. Merkl, "West German Left-Wing Terrorism," in Martha Crenshaw,

ed., *Terrorism in Context* (University Park: Pennsylvania State University Press, 1995), 203–4.

31 Konrad Kellen, "Ideology and Rebellion: Terrorism in West Germany," in Reich, 58.

32 Merkl, 204.

33 Jeffrey Ian Ross, "Beyond the Conceptualization of Terrorism: A Psychological-Structural Model of the Causes of This Activity," in Craig Summers and Eric Markusen, eds., *Collective Violence* (Lanham, MD: Rowman & Littlefield, 1999).

34 Randy Borum, *Psychology of Terrorism* (Tampa: University of South Florida, 2004).

35 Post, 25, 35.

36 Pete Simi et al., "Narratives of Childhood Adversity and Adolescent Misconduct as Precursors to Violent Extremism: A Life-Course Criminological Approach," *Journal of Research in Crime and Delinquency* 53 (4) (2016), pp. 536–63.

37 Jasper L. De Bie, Christianne J. de Poot, and Joanne P. van der Leun, "Shifting Modus Operandi of Jihadist Foreign Fighters from the Netherlands between 2000 and 2013: A Crime Script Analysis," *Terrorism and Political Violence* 27 (3) (2015), p. 426.

38 Ibid.

39 Donatella della Porta, "Left-Wing Terrorism in Italy," in Crenshaw, *Terrorism in Context*, 140.

40 Schbley, 119.

41 The global Salafi movement aims to restore authentic Islam and to establish one united Islamist state reaching from Morocco to the Philippines.

42 Marc Sageman, *Understanding Terror Networks* (Philadelphia: University of Pennsylvania Press, 2004), 135.

43 Loretta Napoleoni, *Modern Jihad: Tracing the Dollars behind the Terror Networks* (London: Pluto Press, 2003), 132.

44 Laqueur, 67, 68.

45 Pete Simi et al., "Addicted to Hate: Identity Residual among Former White Supremacists," *American Sociological Review* 82 (6) (2017), pp. 1167–87.

46 Ibid.

47 Malise Ruthven, "The Rise of the Muslim Terrorists," *New York Review of Books*, May 29, 2008, 33.

48 Margarette Driscoll, "My ISIS Boyfriend: A Reporter's Undercover Life with a Terrorist," *New York Post*, March 7, 2015.

49 Tim Highfield, Stephen Harrington, and Axel Bruns, "Twitter as a Technology for Audiencing and Fandom," *Information, Communication & Society* 16 (3) (2013), p. 315.

50 Arthur J. Deikman, *THEM against US: Cult Thinking and the Terrorist Threat* (Berkeley, CA: Bay Tree Publishing, 2003), 9.

51 Ibid.

52 Ibid., 3.

53 Jerrold Post, "Narcissism and the Charismatic Leader-Follower Relationship," *Political Psychology* 7 (4) (December 1986), pp. 678–9.

54 Jeffrey D. Simon, *Lone Wolf Terrorism: Understanding the Growing Threat* (Amherst, NY: Prometheus Books, 2013), 21.

55 Brian M. Jenkins, "Foreword," in Simon, *Lone Wolf Terrorism*, 7–11.

56 Michel Wieviorka, *The Making of Terrorism* (Chicago, IL: University of Chicago Press, 1993), 10.

57 Jessica Stern, *Terror in the Name of God: Why Religious Militants Kill* (New York: HarperCollins, 2003), 142.

58 Wieviorka, ch. 1.
59 Sprinzak, 64–85.
60 Ibid., 82.
61 Merkl, 206.
62 Della Porta, 150.
63 Quoted by Jerrold M. Post, Ehud Sprinzak, and Laurita M. Denny, "The Terrorists in Their Own Words: Interviews with 35 Incarcerated Middle Eastern Terrorists," *Terrorism and Political Violence* 15 (1) (Spring 2003), p. 178.
64 Ibid., 179.
65 Albert Bandura, "Mechanisms of Moral Disengagement," in Reich, 163.
66 Martha Crenshaw, "The Causes of Terrorism," *Comparative Politics* 13 (4) (1981), pp. 379–99.
67 Andrea Elliott, "A Militant's Path from Pakistan to Times Square," *New York Times*, June 22, 2010, www.nytimes.com/2010/06/23/world/23terror.html?hp, accessed July 9, 2010.
68 Stern, 283.

7 Women, Children, and Terrorism

After a female Palestinian teenager blew herself up in a supermarket in Jerusalem killing an Israeli girl in her teens and a security guard in 2002, President George W. Bush said, "When an 18-year-old Palestinian girl is induced to blow herself up and, in the process, kills a 17-year-old Israeli girl, the future is dying." The president expressed the shock that many people around the world felt when they learned of the suicide attack. The young age of both the attacker and the victim heightened the shock in this case.

Following the terrorist drama in a packed Moscow theater in the fall of 2002, one commentator asked,

> Who did not feel a deep unease at the sight of the female Chechen terrorists in the Moscow theater before it was stormed, with their eyes peering through the masks of their black burqas, with their Kalashnikovs, and their explosives strapped to their bodies?

Probably expressing the sentiments of many observers, the writer pointed out that terrorism is always disturbing, but that "there's an extra level of disquiet when the terrorists are female."[1]

The shock value of terrorism is far greater when perpetrated by women because in such cases a common assumption is that if "women decide to violate all established norms about the sanctity of life, they do so only as a last resort."[2] As a result, when female terrorists, especially suicide terrorists, strike, they get far more media attention than their male counterparts. Moreover, media professionals are far more inclined to explore the motives and the causes of female terrorists than their male counterparts.[3] This is, of course, precisely what terrorist groups want: mass-mediated debates about their causes and grievances.

So, whenever female terrorists strike, they receive far greater attention than male terrorists for the same type of actions. The reason is clear: In most, if not all, societies violence is associated with men—not women. That's even true for fictitious depictions of crime and terrorism. In October 2012, for example, NBC aired an episode of its long-running

DOI: 10.4324/9781003289265-8

series *Law and Order: SVU* titled "Acceptable Loss." What starts out as an investigation of a brutal prostitution ring, turns into the discovery of a terrorism plot and into the hunt for a terrorist believed to be ready to strike. Experienced police officers and a seasoned Homeland Security agent assume that the unknown terrorist is a male. In a shocking turn of events, they find that the terrorist is a beautiful young woman from South Asia. Once caught, Sophia gets the opportunity to tell her story and motive for turning to terrorism: An American drone strike in her village killed her father and set her on the path to take revenge in the United States. "Every terrorist has to tell a story," says one of the agents.

Well, yes, but it takes a *female* terrorist to tell a story that makes her a somewhat sympathetic figure.

When female terrorists plot or carry out attacks, popular culture considers them outliers, rare exceptions. But this is not reflected in the arrest records of law enforcement agencies nor in their lists of terrorist fugitives. In mid-2022, for example, the FBI listed 44 persons on its global list of "Most Wanted Terrorists," seven of which were females. Ahlama Mad al-Amimi, a Palestinian, was the only foreign national. The other six were American women who were involved in political violence in the last three decades of the twentieth century. Five of these women belonged to violent Far-Left groups, from the Black Liberation Army and Black Panthers to the 19th April Communist Cell. One of the females was sought for violence in the name of the Animal/Earth Liberation Front. The by far highest reward of $5 million was offered for information leading to the arrest or conviction of al-Amimi by the U.S. Department of State's Rewards for Justice Program. She was charged with participating in an August 9, 2001, suicide bomb attack at a pizza restaurant in Jerusalem that killed 15 people, including two U.S. nationals. The FBI offered a reward of up to $1 million for information directly leading to the apprehension of Joanne Chesimard who was charged with participating in the killing of one New Jersey State trooper and the wounding of one of his colleagues. For the others, the rewards were from $50,000 to $100,000. Interestingly, of the ten domestic terrorists that were most wanted by the FBI, five were females and five were males. Chesimard, perhaps because she was believed to have fled to Cuba, was not listed under domestic but global terrorism. Had she been listed on the domestic list of most wanted terrorists, where she belonged, females would have outnumbered males 6-5.

In a review of the representation of women in terrorist groups, Karla J. Cunningham noted,

> Not only have women historically been active in politically violent organizations, the regional and ideological scope of this activity has been equally broad. Women have been operational (e.g., regular) in virtually every region and there are clear trends toward

women becoming more fully incorporated into numerous terrorist organizations. Cases from Colombia, Italy, Sri Lanka, Pakistan, Turkey, Iran, Norway, and the United States suggest that women have not only functioned in support capacities, but have also been leaders in organizations, recruitment, and fund-raising, as well as tasked with carrying out the most deadly missions undertaken by terrorist organizations.[4]

While exact numbers are for obvious reasons not available, there is no doubt that the number of male members of violent extremist groups was in the past and remains today far higher than that of their female counterparts. Estimates range from 20 percent to 40 percent overall. But there are significant gender differences between terrorist entities with different ideologies, causes, and objectives in different societies in all kinds of countries, regions, and continents.

Typically, Far-Left terrorist groups have emphasized the recruitment of women, and Far-Right organization have been less interested in bringing women into their fold. As Christopher Harmon observed,

> If the presence of women helps to illuminate the recruitment patterns of successful leftist groups, a relative absence of women in the active hard core is a revealing indicator of different recruitment patterns among neo-Nazis and similar rightist militant groups. The latter generally do not seek out and promote women members.[5]

While it makes sense to use the differences between Far-Left and Far-Right terrorism to discuss the participation of females in those two types of political violence, the lines are less clear-cut in the recent past and present time. Also, certain religious, nationalist/separatist movements, utopian groups, and single-issue organizations do not fit into the ideological Far-Left versus Far-Right divide or are simply outliers from one or the other ideological extreme; they, too, need to be examined with respect to female participation—or exclusion.

Women and Violent Far-Left Extremism

There is a long tradition of female participation in Far-Left movements promoting and using violence to further their causes going back to the revolutionaries in Russia and the anarchists in Western Europe and the United States in the second half of the nineteenth and first two decades of the twentieth century. Emma Goldman, was among the influential anarchists and certainly the best-known female anarchist. Her speeches and written works influenced the anarchist ideology significantly and recruited especially workers into the anarchist cause. She was an early feminist and women's rights activist who promoted the equality of women as part of anarchist theory. While she herself did not participate in violent attacks, her partner Alexander Berkman tried unsuccessfully to assassinate the industrialist Henry Clay Flick; and she was blamed for having inspired McKinley assassin Leon Czolgosz.

While the early anarchist movement failed, female members in the terrorist groups emerging and growing in the 1970s and 1980s in the West followed Goldman's example in that they were guided like Goldman by feminist objectives and included them into their mission statements. Unlike Goldman who did not belong to an underground group, female members in the Red Army Faction in Germany, the Red Army Brigades in Italy, or the Weather Underground in the United States also fought for gender equality and for leadership roles within their respective groups, often against males who insisted on male dominance. A case in point was the Weather Underground. The group that was initially named "Weatherman" by male leaders changed the name under pressure from females in the group. Female members called themselves regularly Weatherwomen in their communication and formed at one point their own Women's Brigade. In early 1974, the Women's Brigade detonated an explosive device at the offices of the U.S. Department of Health, Education, and Welfare in San Francisco. In a message left at the site, the Women's Brigade wrote,

> This action is for all woman who:
>
> - wait in lines for too few food stamps and brave food distribution lines because our families have to eat;
> - worry through degrading forms and humiliating rule and regulations;
> - are kept out of paying jobs because there are no child-care programs;
> - struggle to raise our children while we're called 'pigs at the trough' and 'lazy parasites' by reactionary male politicians...[6]

While women played the second fiddle in the early phase of the group, they did not accept male dominance over time. Step by step they took over leadership roles and eventually outnumbered males. Bernardine Dohrn was among the founders of the group and became the most influential Weatherwoman, but others, such as Kathy Boudin, Diana Oughton, Naomi Jaffa, and several other females had influential roles as well. Just as important, women were well represented in the rank-and-file membership.

Unlike the well-known Weather Underground, the autonomous May 19th Communist Organization, a small autonomous cell of violent Far-Left extremists that carried out a multitude of armed robberies, attacks on police, and other deadly strikes during the late 1970s and early 1980s, was quickly forgotten by the news media and the general public. Perhaps, because the cell used different names. Thus, after detonating a bomb in the U.S. Capitol in November 1985, the terrorists called themselves "Armed Resistance Unit" when it sent message to a news organization claiming responsibility for targeting imperialists but also noting that nobody was hurt—this time. While there were female units or brigades within some groups, the May 19th Communist Organization was the only freestanding female terrorist organization. Obviously, the women founders of the group did not want to share control with males. They plant attacks, built explosive devices, and carried out their attacks. Hunted and in several cases arrested by law enforcement agencies, the cell was inactive by 1985. Two members of the group who were involved in attacks, Donna Joan Borup and Elizabeth Anna Duke were fugitives since 1982 and 1985 respectively. Both have been on the FBI's most-wanted terrorists list for several decades and remained there in the early 2020s.

The original Red Army Faction (RAF) had slightly more male than female members. The group was founded by two women, Ulrike Meinhof und Gudrun Ensslin, and two men, Andreas Baader und Horst Mahler. Eventually, the media came up with another name: the Baader-Meinhof Group. The two names were probably chosen because Baader was among the Far-Left extremists who carried out an arson attack on a Frankfurt department store two years before becoming a founding member of the RAF and Meinhof was a columnist of a socialist magazine with a respectable circulation. The second generation of RAF leaders who took over after the original leaders were arrested had more female than male leaders. Outside observers assumed that Mahler, a lawyer, was the ideological brain of the original RAF. Others assumed that Ensslin was both the chief ideologue and operational coordinator. She participated in a number of brutal attacks that resulted in multiple deaths. But one of Meinhof's twin daughters, a student of the RAF and a harsh critic of the terrorist group and her mother, insisted in a TV interview 50 years after the RAF founding that Meinhof was "the ideological head" of the group, that her mother, the journalist, wrote the most important RAF documents and communications.[7]

The Revolutionary Forces of Colombia (FARC) were among the largest revolutionary, left-extremist groups with a declared policy of gender equality. To a certain extent, this policy was implemented. Typically, women comprised between 20 percent and 40 percent of the total FARC force. Girls and women went through the same basic military training as boys and men did; they had to adhere to the same disciplinary rules; they had to accept the same hardships associated with life in an insurgent group that challenged the state's military forces. But that did not mean that with respect to gender the FARC was an equal opportunity organization. Indeed, some of the same gender problems that plagued women in civilian society (and in other terrorist organizations) were also prevalent in this insurgent group.[8]

Researchers who interviewed women and men who had left the FARC saw five reasons for the group's long practice of recruiting women:

1   The revolutionary ideology of the FARC insisted on gender equality and according to the organization that is precisely what is practiced within its ranks.
2   The inclusion of women increased the number and quality of the pool of potential recruits.
3   Female fighters had proven as tough as and even more goal oriented and brutal than their male counterparts—even if only because they had to prove their qualifications.
4   Women were exploited for FARC propaganda intended to soften the image of its fighters.
5   Women became sexual partners of males in the FARC and thereby were "essential for the morale and stability of the organization."[9]

While the FARC claimed that women joined because of their inequality and hardship in Colombia's civilian society, women who left the organization reported that there was no equality in the FARC either.

Women and Violent Far-Right Extremism

Unlike the violent Far-Left, in the past, the Far-Right variety of violent extremists did not even pretend that their groups granted equal rights for women or valued them as fighters for their causes. Still, there were in the more recent past a few cases in which females were enlisted as supporting cast in violent plots carried out by males:

- In 2002, Erica Chase (age 21) of Boston and her boyfriend Leo Felton planned to blow up Holocaust museums and targeted persons for violent attacks for their cause: Ridding the country of minorities— blacks, Latinos, Asians, and, most of all, Jews. Both were members of Neo-Nazi hate groups. Targets included the New England Holocaust Memorial, the U.S. Holocaust Museum in Washington, the Reverend Jesse Jackson, and other African American leaders.
- In 2003, Holly Dartez (age 28) was found guilty and sentenced to a year in prison for her participation in a Ku Klux Klan (KKK) cross-burning in Longville, Louisiana. She was the secretary of the local KKK chapter and drove four male Klansmen to the house of three African American men who had moved to Louisiana from Mississippi. All participants received prison sentences, but they achieved their goal of frightening their African American targets sufficiently that they did not move their families to Louisiana but instead returned to Mississippi.

In the Boston case, it seemed that Erica Chase came under the spell of 30-year-old Felton who had served 11 years in prison for attempting to kill a black taxi driver in New York City. In the Louisiana case, Holly Dartez drove the male Klansmen to the site of the cross-burning. In both cases, the males were the leaders, the females were convenient helpers as was typical for these sorts of organizations.

Since the Supreme Court's pro-choice *Roe v. Wade* decision in 1973 women were active in the violent antiabortion movement with groups, such as the Army of God, that embraced a reactionary agenda and attracted members with White nationalist views. Still active in the twenty-first century, these hard-core antiabortion warriors encourage and glorify violence against abortion providers. The "Army's" website displays a list of "Anti-Abortion Heroes of the Faith," among them women. The most prominent female "anti-abortion hero" is Shelley Shannon serving a 30-year prison sentence for the attempted murder of an abortion provider in Wichita, Kansas, and for carrying out two acid and several arson attacks against women's health centers. In one of her posts, Shannon writes:

> The accusation is made that it is not pro-life to close an abortion facility by destroying the building, and not pro-life to shoot an abortionist. I did a lot of blockades with Advocates For Life, Lambs of Christ, Operation Rescue, and other groups. I also did a lot of picketing and other pro-life activities. Sometimes I felt like a failure when I stood with a sign and didn't do everything I could to try to save babies lives. I let them kill the babies! I allowed it. When you stand and watch 20 or more babies being taken to their death, how is that more pro-life than making it so those babies cannot be killed?... Those who killed abortionists chose *life* for all the innocent babies he would have killed, and did our country a great service.[10]

But, again, by and large, in violent Far-Right groups only males were involved in militant activities; females were supposed to be caretakers, wives, and mothers supportive of their men and children.

January 6—A Turning Point for Women
in Violent Far-Right Extremism?

> I can't predict. I don't understand the resolve of the Deep State. Biden may still yet be our president. If he is, our way of life as we know it is over. Our Republic would be over. Then it is our duty to fight, kill and die for our rights.

This was the answer given by Jessica Watkins, the self-described commander of an Ohio militia affiliate of the Oath Keepers, when asked by one of her recruits after the 2020 presidential election what she predicted for the new year 2021.[11] She texted another recruit who trained with her, "If Biden gets the steal, none of us have a chance in my mind. We already have our necks in the noose. They just haven't kicked the chair yet." The recruit responded, "So I should get comfortable with the idea of death?" Watkins replied, "That's why I do what I do." The recruit assured her, "I hope the training will help me be ok with dying for country."

Following the violent assault on the U.S. Capitol on January 6, 2021, Watkins received a great deal of news coverage because of her prominent role in the preparation for and participation in the violent invasion. Along with eight others in her Oath Keepers' stack, she was indicted by a Grand Jury of the U.S. District Court for the District of Columbia with conspiracy to stop, delay, and hinder the congressional certification of the Electoral College vote and four other crimes. Later, she was 1 of 11 Oath Keepers, among them their founder and leader Stewart Rhodes, who were indicted for seditious conspiracy.

Lost in the "breaking news" barrage in the post-January 6th days and weeks was the starring role of a surprisingly large number of females among the first wave of violent intruders. Four of the nine members of the Watkins' stack were women—besides Army veteran Jessica Watkins who was 38 years old, the others were significantly older females: Laura Steele (52), Connie Meggs (59), and Sandra Parker (60). Two of women, Meggs and Parker, stormed side-by-side with their husbands into the Capitol.

More importantly, of 111 members of violent Far-Right extremist groups criminally indicted for their activities on January 6, 15 percent or 13.5 percent were females—a surprisingly large number for a reactionary movement that excluded women from participating in paramilitary training and employment.[12] The question was, whether the large number of females among the male-dominated White Supremacy/neo-Nazi groups signaled the arrival of something like women's liberation within this movement.

Dying for the Far-Right Cause

Other women involved in the January 6th insurrection, QAnon conspiracy theorists or members of the MAGA movement, were equally as brutal and willing to die for their cause as were Watkins and other female Oath Keepers. Thus, Lisa Eisenhart, a nurse, traveled from Tennessee to Washington, DC, to participate in the "Stop the Steal" rally. Along with her son, she was among the mob that invaded the U.S. Capitol. "This country was founded on revolution," she said afterward, "I'd rather die a 57-year-old woman than live under oppression. I'd rather die and would rather fight." Jennifer Leigh Ryan, a Texas

(Continued)

(Continued)

realtor, said during the assault on Capitol, "We are going to f—ing go in here. Life or death, it doesn't matter. Here we go." Rachel Powell, a 40-year-old mother of eight from western Pennsylvania, rammed a window with a pipe and made her way inside the Capitol Building. She urged others to follow her. Once inside, she gave "very detailed" instructions about the layout of the Capitol Building to other rioters and told them to coordinate, "if you are going to take the building."

To be sure, from the outset of White Supremacy, women were part of a very important supporting cast as the long history of the Ku Klux Klan attests. In the early 1900s, when the KKK experienced a revival and became active in electoral politics, women played important roles behind the scenes. Thus, as Seyward Darby, the author of *Sisters of Hate: American Women on the Front Lines of White Nationalism,* noted,

> By the mid-1920s, the W.K.K.K. [Women's KKK] was its own, very powerful entity headquartered in Arkansas with branches all over the country. They did a lot of recruiting, they registered voters, they'd watch one another's children so that they could cast ballots. But most important, they brought a sheen to this organization to make it look more dignified. The "we're just concerned citizens" card, if you will.[13]

More recent examples of women behind the scene of White Supremacy/neo-Nazi groups and activities are instructive as well: While women did not march along-side males in the confrontational "Unite the Right" march in Charlottesville, Virginia, in the summer of 2017, a woman, Erica Alduino, was reportedly instrumental in organizing the controversial event. "She was the one directing traffic on messaging apps and answering mundane but important questions like whether there would be shuttle buses to the rally. She didn't speak at the event."[14] It was just as interesting, when it was revealed in the aftermath of January 6th that a female lawyer, Kellye SoRelle, was the general counsel of the Oath Keepers and thus had a close working relationship with Stewart Rhodes, founder and leader of the group. SoRelle was present, when Rhodes met the leader of the Proud Boys, Enrique Tarrio, on the eve of January 6th in a garage in Washington, DC.[15]

Summing up, then, in the first decades of the twenty-first-century women were as important as earlier females in outwardly male White Supremacy/Neo-Nazi movements. But the events on January 6, 2021, revealed a significant change in the roles of women in some but not all violent Far-Right extremist groups. That is precisely what Seyward Darby, based on her contacts in the White Supremacy movement, concluded:

> The general thinking in this movement has always been that, in an ideal situation, women wouldn't have to be on the frontlines of anything. But because we're in this so-called apocalyptic state — if you are a person that believes the far-right ideology, everything is apocalyptic at all times, by the way — it's kind of like all hands-on deck: People need to take risks, women need to step up and be soldiers because so much is at stake.[16]

In other words, when the perceived show-down with the enemy is perceived as imminent, women are supposed to join the decisive battles. Both, the general perception of White Supremacist/neo-Nazi women as serving their men as wives and mothers and the turnaround in the face of an existential struggle to protect White America had a parallel in the Islamic State's principal rules on gender roles and changes when the so-called Caliphate lost ground in the defense of its territory.

ISIS Women before the Defeat of the Islamic State

At the height of ISIS's territorial gains, there were two all-women ISIS brigades, Al-Khansaa and Umn al-Rayan, but they were not fighting on the front lines. These armed brigades were functioning as religious police to enforce morality according to the Islamic State's interpretation of Sharia law. The Muslimas in these forces were as brutal as male jihadists fighting outside enemies. Thus, al-Khansaa policewomen allegedly disfigured the faces of women with acid for not wearing a niqab and tortured a mother for breastfeeding in public.[17]

In early 2015, the publicity arm of al-Khansaa posted the tract "Women of the Islamic State: A Manifesto on Women by the Al-Khansaa Brigade" on several social media sites.[18] According to the manifesto, "the fundamental function for women is in the house with her husband and children." As for the "ideal education, women were told only to learn the most rudimentary things, such as:

- From age seven to nine, there will be three lessons: *fiqh* [meaning Islamic jurisprudence and the understanding of the Sharia] and religion, Quranic Arabic (written and read) and science (accounting and natural sciences).
- From 10 to 12, there will be more religious studies, especially *fiqh*, focusing more on *fiqh* related to women and the rulings on marriage and divorce. This is in addition to the other two subjects. Skills like textiles and knitting, and basic cooking will also be taught.

- From 13 to 15, there will be more of a focus on Shariah, as well as more manual skills (especially those related to raising children) and less of the science, the basics of which will already have been taught. In addition, they will be taught about Islamic history, the life of the Prophet and his followers.[19]

In the most shocking passage, the guidelines stated that "it is considered legitimate for a girl to be married by the age of nine. Most pure girls will be married by sixteen or seventeen, while they are still young and active."

There were a few exceptions mentioned, namely, women were allowed to be outside their homes for:

- studying the science of religion;
- working as doctors or teachers according to Sharia law;
- participating in jihad in extraordinary emergencies, if the enemy is attacking her country and the men are not enough [sic] to protect it.

The last exception was of particular interest because by late 2017 an existential emergency existed, when ISIS had lost big chunks of its previously conquered territory and many male jihadists had been killed or forced to flee. In multiple appeals published in the organization's online magazine *Rumiyah*, its weekly newsletter Naba, and in social media, ISIS now called on females to join the battle. According to one call to arms in Naba,

> Today, in the context of this war against the Islamic state, and with all that is experienced of hardship and pain, it is mandatory for the Muslim women to fulfil their duty from all aspects in supporting the mujahideen in this battle, by preparing themselves as mujahidat in the cause of Allah, and readying to sacrifice themselves to defend the religion of Allah the Most High and Mighty.[20]

Soon thereafter, the Islamic State media center released several videos of female jihadists in action.

Female Terrorists: Stereotypes versus Reality

In the early 1980s, Martha Crenshaw noted,

> There has been considerable speculation about the prominent position of women in terrorist groups (not prominent in comparison to the number of women in the population at large but in proportion to the number of women active in politics or in leadership roles). It will be interesting to find out if female participation in violence will have an effect on general social roles or on the stereotyping of women.[21]

Whether the role of women in social, political, and professional settings has been affected by female roles in terrorist groups, if at all, is difficult to assess. But stereotypical images and prejudices have entered all along into discussions of the perennial question, why women become terrorists. Some answers put forth over the years reflect deep-seated gender stereotypes, some are based on facts, and still others are a mixture of both.

For the Sake of Love

What motivates women to become terrorists? When this question comes up, one common view is that females become terrorists to follow their lovers, husbands, or perhaps brothers or male friends into the organization. This gender stereotype relating to the power of love is rarely, if ever applied to male terrorists. As Robin Morgan suggests in her book The Demon Lover, women would have rather died than admit the fact that love motivated them to join terrorist groups.[22] For her, these women are merely "token" terrorists at "the intersection of violence, eroticism, and what is considered 'masculinity.'"[23] For Karla Cunningham, this perception "diminishes women's credibility and influence both within and outside organizations," although it is widely held.[24] While most female terrorists are driven by their ideological conviction, their grievances, and their goals as are their male comrades, romantic relationships are quite normal, especially in groups that operate in the underground. In some instances, couples were among the founders of terrorist groups. Romantic relationships between male and female terrorists have been the norm in Far-Left groups and to a lesser extent in reactionary, Far-Right, and religious entities that were male dominated.

Thus, two founders of the Red Army Faction in Germany, Gudrun Ensslin und Andreas Baader, became lovers several years before the establishment of the RAF. In the Weather Underground, there were several couples, such as Kathy Boudin and David Gilbert or Bernardine Dohrn and Bill Ayers, some of which had children during their underground activities. And then you had male terrorists who played the field. Ilich Ramirez Sanchez, known as Carlos the Jackal, who was the undisputed Don Juan of the terrorism scene in the latter part of the twentieth century. Although a Venezuelan, he joined the Popular Front for the Liberation of Palestine and worked closely with the German Red Army Faction and other revolutionary entities in Western Europe. He was involved in a multitude of terrorist attacks, the most sensational in 1975, when a team of terrorists raided the OPEC headquarters in Vienna, taking several dozen hostages and killing three persons. According to one account,

> One of Carlos's greatest joys was that he was able to claim an energetic sex life as a legitimate working expense, part of the important business of establishing cover and hide-outs...[at one point]

he had four regular girlfriends, two on either side of the [English] Channel, whose homes he sometimes used as safe-houses to hide arms, explosives, and false documents.[25]

In 1985, he married the German terrorist Magdalena Kopp, a member of the Frankfurt Revolutionary Cells and became father of their daughter one year later. After their divorce, the Jackal married a Palestinian woman, Lana Jarrar, who mysteriously disappeared. Imprisoned in France, where he serves a life sentence, Ramirez courted his defense lawyer Isabella Coutant-Peyre during his trial. The two married in 2001 and remained a couple past their 20th anniversary.

Female Terrorists Are Women's Libbers

In the 1970s, sociologists, psychologists, and political observers pointed to the feminist movement as the most likely explanation for the large number of women in left-wing terrorist groups. Criminologist Freda Adler explained female terrorist activity in an interview with the *New York Times* as a "deviant expression of feminism."[26] According to the *Times*, Adler said that the publicity surrounding terrorism gives female terrorists "a platform to say, 'I am liberated from past stereotypes, I am accepted in the ultimate masculine roles.'"[27] Earlier, in her book *Sisters in Crime*, Adler wrote, "Despite their broad political pronouncements, what the new revolutionaries [such as female members of the Weather Underground] wanted was not simply urban social gains, but sexual equality."[28]

In Europe, experts provided similar explanations for the large number of female members in terrorist organizations, such as the Red Brigades in Italy and the RAF in West Germany. According to one news account in 1977, "Italian and German sociologists and news commentators, all of them men, have suggested over the last few weeks that the significant female membership in radical and terrorist groups was an unwelcome consequence of the women's liberation movement."[29] Male sociologists and commentators in Europe were not the only ones to blame women's lib. A female German politician stated, "These women demonstratively negate everything that is part of the established feminine character."[30] A male professor in Munich wondered whether these female terrorists "see violence in society as [the] prerogative of males and ask, 'Why shouldn't we participate?'"[31] The former neighbor of the notorious female terrorist Susanne Albrecht complained, "She sang Communist songs all night and never cleaned the stairs."[32]

Female terrorists in traditionally male-dominated societies have also been hailed for furthering gender equality. Yassir Arafat, at the height of the second intifada, told thousands of women during a speech in Ramallah, "Women and men are equal. You are my army of roses that will crush Israeli tanks."[33] Soon thereafter, in early 2002 and following the first female suicide bombing in Israel proper, Abdel Hamuda, the editor of an Egyptian weekly, declared that this was a monumental event in that it "shattered a glass ceiling" and "elevated the value of Arab women and, in one moment, and with enviable courage, put an end to the unending debate about equality between men and women."[34] But it is far from clear that a larger segment of these women became terrorists in a quest for gender equality.

Take the example of female Palestinian suicide terrorists. Living in a milieu in which gender inequality is deeply rooted in religious and cultural traditions, young women with personal disappointments and emotional problems are particularly vulnerable to being recruited and trained as "martyrs." Indeed, after talking to the families and friends of four female suicide bombers and interviewing several women who had been recruited but did not finish their mission, Barbara Victor wrote,

> I discovered the hard reality that it was never another woman who recruited the suicide bombers. Without exception, these women had been trained by a trusted member of the family—a brother, an uncle—or an esteemed religious leader, teacher, or family friend, all of whom were men. What I also discovered was that all four who died, plus the others who had tried and failed to die a martyr's death, had personal problems that made their lives untenable within their own culture and society.[35]

These women's social environment made them vulnerable to male manipulation and exploitation. In Victor's judgment, "there were, in fact, very different motives and rewards for the men who died a martyr's death than for the women."[36] It seems that whereas men justified the rationale for "martyrdom" in political terms, women were told by their male handlers that their own or a family member's transgressions could only be redeemed by killing themselves to kill Israelis and enjoy happiness in paradise. These women were no women's libbers.

Women Commit Terrorism Because of Their Tactical Advantage

Although, as noted earlier, female terrorists are not rare, the conventional wisdom is that females are far less likely than males to commit political violence. As a result, women have far better chances of carrying out terrorist attacks without being intercepted than their male comrades. This has been long recognized by terrorists who oversee their groups' operations and are responsible for the success of attacks. Women are simply less likely to be suspects and therefore less likely to be denied access to potential targets and areas for attacks; they are less frequently selected for thorough security checks than males; and they can fake pregnancies for the sake of hiding weapons and explosives. As former German terrorist Bommi Bauman, member of a successor cell of the Baader-Meinhof group, observed,

> If a man in a high position, perhaps knowing that he may be a ztarget for terrorists, is approached by a woman, he may think, she is a prostitute. Women can go straight to the target's doorstep; sometimes they do it in pairs, two women, saying they are lost. If two men approached him, he would be suspicious.[37]

What Bauman described was precisely the script for several of the kidnappings and assassinations conducted by West German terrorists in which women exploited the fact that they were not as alarming as men—although it was well known that females were well represented in these groups. Terrorists elsewhere followed this blueprint as well. Before Dhanu, a female member of the Tamil Tigers, assassinated Rajiv Gandhi, she had "garlanded him, bowed at his feet, and then detonated a bomb that killed them both."[38] Playing the role of a female admirer of Gandhi, she did not have any problem with getting close to him. It is telling that one of the members of a two-person backup team was a young woman as well. The Kurdistan Workers Party, too, decided to use female members for suicide attacks because of their tactical advantages. But women were also more inclined to become human bombs because they wanted to prove themselves useful in a struggle in which they often could not match the physical strength of their male comrades. The wave of terrorist attacks against Russian targets by female suicide bombers was partially explained as Chechen groups taking advantage of the fact that Chechen females were able "to move more freely than Chechen men, who are routinely harassed by Russia's police and security services."[39] In early 2004, after Hamas claimed responsibility for dispatching the first female suicide bomber to kill Israelis, the group's spiritual leader, Sheik Ahmed Yassin, cited "purely tactical reasons" when asked why his organization had decided on selecting a woman, saying, "It could be that a man would not be able to reach the target, and that's why they had to use a woman."[40]

The authorities in some societies came to understand over time that female terrorists were just as likely as their male comrades to commit deadly acts of terrorism. When West Germany was faced with a wave of terror by the RAF and its successor groups, the country's counterterrorism units were allegedly ordered by their superiors to "shoot the women first."[41] In responding to the increased attacks by Chechen women, Russian authorities expanded their security checks to women with scarves and other clothing typical of Muslim women. In the long run, therefore, it is possible, if not likely, that the gender advantage will fade once it is clear that attacks by female terrorists are not exceptions, but common occurrences. For this to happen, however, it is not enough for top officials to understand that the female paradox is a myth in the realm of terrorism; rather, the men and women who implement anti- and counterterrorist policies day in and day out must have this understanding as well—and act accordingly. But this seems easier said than done. The U.S. Department of Homeland Security, for example, developed an official profile of a typical terrorist that focused on males only. Jessica Stern criticized this as "an important weakness in our counterterrorism strategy" and warned,

> Profiling men exclusively, and also focusing so tightly on countries known to harbor terrorists, are significant loopholes that have not been closed despite the FBI's recognition that al Qaeda has begun recruiting women, and despite the discovery last spring that an MIT-trained female scientist may have been providing logistical support to al Qaeda.[42]

Even in societies that have experienced repeated attacks by female terrorists, there is still a tendency to view and treat women differently. Israel is a perfect example here. In January 2004, when a 22-year-old Palestinian woman, pretending to be crippled, told Israelis at a Gaza checkpoint that she had metal plates in her leg that would sound the alarm, they allowed her to wait for a woman to search her in a special area. Moments later, the woman blew herself up and killed four Israelis. Lamenting the cynical exploitation of his soldiers' consideration for the dignity of women, the officer in charge said,

> We're doing our best to be humanitarian, to consider the problems associated with searching women. She said she had a medical problem, that's why the soldiers let her in, to check her in private because she is a woman. That's a very cruel, cynical use of the humanitarian considerations of our soldiers.[43]

While there are no profound gender differences with respect to terrorists' motives and actions, most societies continue to deem females less suspect and less dangerous than males. Indeed, indications are that more women will be recruited by terrorist groups in the future. After analyzing cross-national opinion surveys in 14 Muslim countries, two scholars concluded that female respondents were more likely to support terrorism in defense of Islam.[44] There is also evidence that female terrorists can be more committed to the terrorist cause and their comrades than their male counterparts. With respect to the Italian Red Brigades and similar groups, Luisella de Cataldo Neuberger and Tiziana Valentini found that a larger proportion of male members collaborated with law enforcement and distanced themselves from the activities and goals of their terrorist organizations, when imprisoned, than their female counterparts. Although not enough data are available for the first generation of RAF, women seemed less inclined than men to cooperate with the authorities once they were behind bars.[45]

Finally, while the tactical advantage of female terrorists is certainly a factor in their deployment in certain situations, this does not mean these women are not driven by strong convictions. This point was driven home in the 1966 documentary-style movie "The Battle of Algiers." The most compelling sequence depicts three Algerian women as bomb carriers for the Algerian National Liberation Front (NLF) during the liberation war against the French in the mid-1950s. Working with the NLF, the women changed from their traditional abayas into European clothing and used make-up and altered hairstyles to look like the hated French. With bombs in their handbags, they pass the French military's checkpoints, where soldiers flirt with them as they pass through. They seem completely calm and natural as they enter two crowded cafes and a busy Air France office leaving their bags unnoticed under tables and chairs. They take their time to survey the people marked to die or be maimed, among them a cute little boy. They leave safely before—on-after-the-other—the three targeted places explode into ruins. To be sure, male NFL leaders needed bomb carriers who were unlikely to be stopped and exposed as terrorists. But the three women depicted in the documentary-style movie were not exploited, not duped by male NFL fighters. The youngest of the women, Zohra Drif, for example, had attended a French high school and was a 20-year-old law student, when she contacted the NFL to become involved in the fight. Captured and sentenced to death by the French, she was eventually released without ever regretting her role as an NFL carrier of bombs and messages. She and her female partners believed that "God was on their side" and that killing to gain their country's independence was justified.[46] Yes, they exploited their female tactical advantage, but they believed in the cause of the National Liberation Front.

Suicide Terrorism as Family Project

Yusef (17) was a loving big brother who was happy when videotaping his younger brother Firman (15) and his sisters Fadhila (12) and Famela (8). Their dad, Dita Oepriarto, and mom, Puji Kuswati, were doting parents. The family lived in a multi-ethnic neighborhood of Indonesia's second largest city Surabaya and the children attended a private Muslim school that emphasized racial and religious harmony. The family had contact with Christian neighbors.

On May 13, 2018, the whole family carried out simultaneous suicide attacks against Christian churches. The father drove his explosive-laden truck into a church during Sunday service; his two sons blew themselves up on a motorcycle that they had driven to a second church; mother and daughters detonated their bombs near a third church. Twelve persons were killed and several dozens injured. It was one of Indonesia's most lethal terrorist attacks. Just as the close-knit family had lived, all its members died in a well-planned, three-pronged, suicide-homicide mission.

Hours later, a father of four accidentally detonated a bomb that he and his family planned to explode jointly near a Christian church. Instead, the bomb killed his wife and one of his daughters, landing him in prison.

The following day, five members of yet another family blew themselves up at a church, injuring ten bystanders and killing themselves, except for an eight-year-old girl that survived.

Even in the deadly annals of catastrophic terrorism, the joint suicide attacks of whole families opened a new, shocking, frightening chapter.

The three fathers met at a local Quranic studying group where their wives and children, too, were introduced to extremist propaganda. Dita Oepriarto, the mastermind of the attacks, turned out to be the leader of Jamaah Ansharut Daulah, an extremist Indonesian Muslim group affiliated with ISIS. Indeed, shortly after the attacks, ISIS claimed responsibility.

Outwardly, the suicide families were comfortable in their multi-ethnic, multi-religious settings. Neither the parents nor their children seemed particularly religious, the women and girls did not wear headscarves. It seems that precisely their apparent modern lifestyle was a clever camouflage of their extremist feelings, covert actions, and sinister plans.

They all seemed to have voluntarily embraced the plan to die themselves in order to kill others—Christians, infidels—and in the process go together to heaven.

The Making of Child Terrorists

"That's my boy," Khaled Sharrouf wrote on Twitter alongside a photo of his seven-year-old son using both hands to hold up a man's severed head. The photo, since removed from Twitter, was reportedly taken in

Raqqa, a Syrian city in the stranglehold of Islamic State militants, where the Australian father had taken his young family to join the fight.

The Islamic State is not the first terrorist organization to recruit and train young boys to commit unspeakable violence, but it is the first terrorist enterprise that documents and publicizes how it runs its training camps for young boys, many not older than nine or ten years and some significantly younger. Nor does ISIS make a secret of its objective to use its "Sharia camps" to produce a whole new generation of jihadists. Indeed, in one of these readily available online propaganda videos, one jihadist in an ISIS training camp for young boys declares proudly, "This generation of children is the generation of the Caliphate." Some fathers are complicit in transforming young children into eager killers. In one video, a man called Abdullah, the Belgian, is shown with his little son, perhaps five or six years old. The father prods the little boy again and again to say "The Islamic State." He asks questions like, "What have the infidels done?" The son finally answers, "They kill Muslims."[47]

One result of these indoctrination methods was shown in the most shocking online video in ISIS's long list of horror shows that depicted a young boy as executioner of two men who were allegedly Russian spies. In the video, the boy, holding a pistol, stands next to a grown-up jihadist who recites religious verses. The two condemned men are kneeling when the boy steps toward them firing several shots before and after the men collapse. The video ends with footage from an earlier production in which the same boy identified himself as Abdallah and said that he wanted to grow up to kill infidels.[48] There could not be a more troubling case of ruthless indoctrination, recruitment, and training with the sole purpose of producing killers and publicizing it all online.

When it comes to the indoctrination of children, both boys and girls, they tend to embrace whatever they are told by people closest to them, parents, siblings, teachers, group leaders, and so on. In Nazi Germany, boys and girls became members of the "Hitler Youth," where they wore uniforms and were socialized into the totalitarian regime's hateful propaganda.

Noting that of the many parties that recruit and use children, "the vast majority are non-state actors," the UN Special Representative of the Secretary General for Children and Armed Conflict, Radhika Coomaraswamy, told the General Assembly of several new developments:

> We are also discovering that more and more children are being used for military intelligence by different armed forces and groups around the world. . . We are increasingly concerned with the changing nature of warfare in different parts of the world and the difficult challenges it poses for child protection partners. In some wars we find children being used as suicide bombers—there were seven such cases in Afghanistan and several in Iraq in 2009.[49]

If anything, the misuse of children by terrorists, especially guerrilla-type organizations, has increased in the second decade of the twenty-first century. Earlier, the Afghan Taliban and Lashkar-e-Tayyiba and the Taliban in Pakistan began the practice of recruiting young boys from religious schools or madrassas as suicide bombers; Al Qaeda in Iraq, too, enlisted boys to attack U.S. troops and their allies. More recently, ISIS and its associate in Nigeria, Boko Haram, are the main offenders. ISIS's indoctrination and training camps are for boys only, whereas Boko Haram targets girls as well and kidnaps them typically from schools to drive home the point that females ought not to be educated. While some of the young girls are forced into marrying jihadists, others are forced or convinced to become suicide bombers.

What Happened to Our Children?

Beginning in 2016 ISIS tried to convince and prepare children in the West for attacks in their own neighborhoods—with stunning success in Germany, France, and elsewhere in Europe. In Germany alone, there were five ISIS-related attacks or foiled attacks involving teenagers:

- A 15-year-old girl of German-Moroccan origin who was in direct contact with an ISIS agent stabbed a German police officer in the neck with a kitchen knife in Hanover. He survived the attack after undergoing surgery.
- Three boys, all aged 16, built a homemade bomb and threw it at a Sikh temple, wounding three—one severely—and causing extensive damage. The leader of the group, who went by the name of The Emir, is a German-born son of ethnic Turks. After a court hearing, his distressed mother wondered, "What happened to our children?"
- A 17-year-old Afghan asylum seeker attacked passengers on a train traveling through southern Germany with a knife and ax, injuring four people, two seriously. He admitted later that he was "a soldier of ISIS."
- A 16-year-old Syrian asylum seeker was arrested in Cologne because he was in contact with an ISIS "official" who instructed him on how to build a bomb.
- A 12-year-old Iraqi-German boy, after contact with ISIS via the messenger service Telegram, left a homemade bomb near a

(Continued)

(Continued)

shopping mall in Ludwigshafen. The bomb failed to explode. The boy and his 17-year-old accomplice in Austria were arrested.

Intelligence services in France, too, foiled several plots by teenagers, among them one involving two girls and another planned by three boys.

All of these children and juveniles were radicalized and recruited by increasingly aggressive ISIS messaging, specifically tailored to boys and girls. As the so-called Islamic State lost ground on the Iraqi and Syrian battleground, its propaganda machine produced videos and computer games designed to hook children and teenagers. Once young targets of these propaganda tactics were captivated, personal contacts were sought and often established by actual ISIS operatives.

Commenting on the increased number of child terrorists in 2012 and thus before the establishment of ISIS, Mia Bloom warned that "the next generation of terrorists will not grow up to take up arms but will do so while still children."[50] Indeed, even groups that originally target boys only as cannon fodder enlist girls as less suspicious attackers. In early 2014, there was a most shocking news report from Afghanistan that an eight-year-old girl was prevented from carrying out a suicide attack against a police station in Khanshin. According to one dispatch, while Taliban commandos deployed female fighters before, this was the first known incident when a very young girl was sent on a suicide mission. It was reported furthermore that the child was the sister of a prominent Taliban commander. According to a spokesman for the Interior Ministry, "one of the Afghan soldiers spotted the girl wearing a suicide jacket. But she could not operate the button to detonate the suicide vest or she was arrested before she could carry out the attack."[51] As one would not expect otherwise, after the incident the little girl was reportedly "in a state of shock and confusion."[52]

In reality, the practice of deploying the very young, especially girls, was quite normal for a number of terrorist and insurgent groups. Thus, in December 2016, two 7-year-old girls blew themselves up and killed themselves in a market in Nigeria, killing another person and injuring 18 others. The authorities assumed that Boko Haram had kidnapped the girls and fitted them with suicide belts. One shocked eyewitness revealed later,

They got out of a rickshaw and walked right in front of me without showing the slightest sign of emotion. I tried to speak with one of them, in Hausa and in English, but she didn't answer. I thought they were looking for their mother. She headed toward the poultry sellers, and then detonated her explosives belt.[53]

Notes

1 Kevin Meyers, "The Terrible Sight of a Female Terrorist," www.telegraph. co.uk/opinion/main.jhtml?xml=/opinion/2002/10/27/do2707.xml, accessed July 20, 2003.

2 Alexis B. Delaney and Peter R. Neumann, "Another Failure of Imagination? The Spectacular Rise of the Female Terrorist," *International Herald Tribune*, September 6, 2004.

3 Ibid.

4 Karla J. Cunningham, "Cross-Regional Trends in Female Terrorism," *Studies in Conflict and Terrorism* 26 (3) (May–June 2003), p. 175.

5 Christopher Harmon, *Terrorism Today* (London: Frank Cass, 2000), 220.

6 Cited by Mona Cristina Rocha, "Militant Feminism and the Women of the Weather Underground Organization," Louisiana State University and Agricultural and Mechanical College, Doctoral Dissertation, 2014.

7 The interview was conducted in German and is available at https://www. youtube.com/watch?v=YT4ghCVsMYE, accessed July 19, 2022.

8 Keith Stanski, "Terrorism, Gender, and Ideology: A Case Study of Women who Join the Revolutionary Armed Forces of Columbia (FARC)," in James J. F. Forest, ed., *The Making of Terrorists, Volume I: Recruitment* (Westport, CT: Praeger Security International), 2006.

9 Natalia Herrera and Douglas Porch, "'Like Going to a Fiesta': The Role of Women in Columbia's FARC-EP," *Small Wars and Insurgencies* 19 (4) (2008), pp. 613–14.

10 www.armyofgod.com/ShelleyResponse.html, accessed September 30, 2014.

11 The information about and citations of Jessica Watkins and other women charged with criminal offenses on January 6, 2021, are taken documents made available by the Department of Justice documents at https://www.justice.gov/usao-dc/capitol-breach-cases and from news accounts.

12 While eventually more than 800 persons were charged, my data reflects the analysis of the first 659 charges as reflected in the data base of the Department of Justice available at https://www.justice.gov/usao-dc/capitol-breach-cases.

13 Alisha Haridasani, "For Far-Right Movements. Ashli Babbit Is Now a 'Rallying Cry'," *New York Times*, January 8, 2021, https://www.nytimes. com/2021/01/08/us/ashli-babbitt-capitol-president-trump.html, accessed July 20, 2022.

14 Anna North, "White Women's Role in White Supremacy Explained," *VOX. com*, January 15, 2021, https://www.vox.com/2021/1/15/22231079/capitol-riot-women-qanon-white-supremacy, accessed July 15, 2022.

15 Ryan J. Reilly, "Oath Keeper Lawyer Says Stewart Rhodes Wanted Her Trump Contacts Before Jan. 6 attack," *News.yahoo.com*, July 11, 2022, https://news. yahoo.com/oath-keepers-lawyer-says-stewart-153049983.html?fr=sycsrp_catchall, accessed July 19, 2022.

16 Haridasani.

17 Anita Peresin, "Fatal Attraction: Western Muslimas and ISIS," *Perspectives on Terrorism* 9 (3) (2015), p. 22, www.terrorismanalysts.com/pt/index.php/pot/article/view/427/0, accessed July 2, 2015.

18 The English version of the manifesto was published at www.quilliamfoundation. org/wp/wp-content/uploads/publications/free/women-of-the-islamic-state3. pdf, accessed July 14, 2015.

19 Ibid., 24.

20 Rita Katz, "How Do We Know ISIS Is Losing? Now It's Asking Women to Fight," *Washington Post*, November 2, 2017, www.washingtonpost.com/ news/posteverything/wp/2017/11/02/how-do-we-know-isis-is-losing-now-its-asking-women-to-fight-for-it/?utm_term=.9ae775dc8247, accessed May 21, 2018.

21 Martha Crenshaw, "Introduction: Reflection on the Effects of Terrorism," in Martha Crenshaw, ed., *Terrorism, Legitimacy and Power: The Consequences of Political Violence* (Middletown, CT: Wesleyan University Press, 1983), 24.

22 Robin Morgan, *The Demon Lover: The Roots of Terrorism* (New York: Washington Square Press, 2001), 204.

23 Ibid., xvi.

24 Cunningham, 171.

25 Morgan, 201.

26 Judy Klemesrud, "A Criminologist's View of Women Terrorists," *New York Times*, January 9, 1979, A24.

27 Ibid.

28 Freda Adler, *Sisters in Crime* (New York: Waveland Press, 1975), 20.

29 Paul Hofmann, "Women Active among Radicals in Western Europe," *New York Times*, August 14, 1977, 7.

30 Hanna-Renate Laurien, a conservative, was quoted by Kim Wilkinson, "The Hit Women," *Newsweek*, August 15, 1977, 30.

31 Michael Getler, "Women Play Growing Role in Slayings by West German Terrorist Groups," *Washington Post*, August 6, 1977.

32 Ibid.

33 Barbara Victor, *The Army of Roses: Inside the World of Palestinian Women Suicide Bombers* (New York: Rodale, 2003), 19.

34 James Bennett, "Arab Press Glorifies Bomber as Heroine," *New York Times*, February 11, 2002, 8.

35 Victor, 19.

36 Ibid.

37 Harmon, 219, 220.

38 Cunningham, 180.

39 Steven Lee Myers, "Female Suicide Bombers Unnerve Russians," *New York Times*, August 7, 2003, 1.

40 Hamas's first female suicide bomber was Reem al-Reyashi, a 22-year-old mother of two small children. Yassin was quoted in Greg Myre, "Gaza Mother, 22, Kills Four Israeli Soldiers," *New York Times*, January 15, 2004, A3.

41 *Shoot the Women First* was therefore chosen as the title of a book exploring the phenomenon of female terrorists. See Eileen MacDonald, *Shoot the Women First* (New York: Random House, 1992).

42 Jessica Stern, "When Bombers Are Women," *Washington Post*, December 18, 2003, A35.

43 Brigadier-General Gadi Shamni, the Gaza divisional commander, was quoted in Chris McGreal, "Human-Bomb Mother Kills Four Israelis at Gaza Checkpoint," *The Guardian*, January 15, 2004, 17.

44 C. Christine Fair and Bryan Shephard, "Who Supports Terrorism? Evidence from Fourteen Muslim Countries," *Studies in Conflict and Terrorism* 29 (2006), pp. 51–74.

45 Cataldo Neuberger and Valentini, especially ch. 1.
46 The reference to God is mentioned by Paul J. Magnarella, "Inside the Battle of Algiers: Memoir of a Woman Freedom Fighter," *Journal of Global South Studies* 38 (2) (Fall 2921), p. 429.
47 https://news.vice.com/video/the-islamic-state-part-2?utm_source=vicenews twitter, accessed December 20, 2014.
48 The video was released on January 13, 2015, but was soon removed from ISIS sites.
49 The text of the speech is available at www.un.org/children/conflict/english/16-jun-2010open-debate-security-council-statement.html, accessed July 10, 2010.
50 Mia Bloom, "Analysis: Women and Children Constitute the New Faces of Terrorism," *CNN.com*, August 6, 2012, http://security.blogs.cnn.com/2012/08/06/analysis-women-and-children-constitute-the-new-faces-of-terror/, accessed July 11, 2015.
51 "Afghanistan Girl Wearing Suicide Vest Detained," www.bbc.com/news/world-asia-25620543, accessed July 10, 2015.
52 Ibid.
53 Alex Matthews, "Two Girls of Just SEVEN Blow Themselves up in a Suicide Bomb Attack at a Market in Nigeria," *Daily Mail*, December 11, 2017, www.dailymail.co.uk/news/article-4022264/Girls-aged-7-8-stage-suicide-attack-Nigeria.html, accessed May 21, 2018.

8 Common Threads
Goals, Targets, and Tactics

Although some persons are psychologically more prone to become terrorists than others, it would be a mistake to dismiss terrorists and their deeds as crazy or capricious. Instead, as Bruce Hoffman has noted, a terrorist group's course of action—the selection of targets and tactics—is shaped by a variety of factors, among them the organization's ideology.[1] Indeed, there is little doubt that the ideology of a group, whether well or ill defined, determines the goals, the targets or victims, and, to some degree, the tactics or methods of terror as well. The size of a terrorist group matters, too. Comparing the small Al Qaeda Central group with organizations such as Hezbollah, Hamas, or ISIS in the context of social movement theory, it is obvious that the latter three are far stronger in terms of numbers and on that account get the greatest amount of attention and have the greatest impact on friends and foes as they display their repertoire of violent performances. But there are also exceptions to this rule, namely, when a relatively small terrorist group or cell—or even a single actor—manages to carry out acts of catastrophic terrorism.

As for the goals, terrorists tend to have two sets of political objectives, namely, short-term and long-term goals, and, typically, they have both sets in mind when they plan and execute an act of violence. In the case of Lebanese and Palestinian groups that were responsible for a series of hijackings and kidnappings in the 1970s and 1980s, the short-term objective most of the time was to win the release of imprisoned comrades. One shorter-term goal of Hezbollah was to force the pullback of American and French troops from Lebanon. Once these forces had been withdrawn following a horrific terror strike against their bases near Beirut in 1983, the group explained its ultimate long-term goal in an "Open Letter to Downtrodden in Lebanon and the World":

> As for Israel, we consider it the American spearhead in our Islamic world. It is the usurping enemy that must be fought until the usurped right is returned to its owners... This Islamic resistance must continue, grow, and escalate, with God's help, and must receive from all Muslims in all parts of the world utter support, aid, backing, and

DOI: 10.4324/9781003289265-9

participation so that we may be able to uproot this cancerous germ and obliterate it from existence.[2]

When the Weather Underground, the Symbionese Liberation Army, or the Baader-Meinhof Red Army Faction (RAF) pulled off bank robberies, their short-term goals were clear: They wanted money to support their lives in the underground. But they rationalized their crimes and their booty as means to further their ultimate or long-term goals—revolutionary systemic changes. In the case of the RAF, this meant nothing short of an international revolution. As one of the RAF's members described it,

> Even if the masses in the European metropolis don't put themselves on the side of the revolution—the working class among us is privileged and takes part in the exploitation of the Third World—the only possibility for those who build the Vanguard here, who take part in the struggle here, is to destroy the infra-structure of imperialism, destroy the apparatus.[3]

Do Terrorists Achieve Their Goals?

If one considers the philosophy and objectives of the Baader-Meinhof group and associated cells, it is crystal clear that they failed to achieve, or even further, their ultimate or strategic goals. However, they were quite successful in realizing their short-term or tactical objectives, such as the release of fellow terrorists. In this respect, the West German radical left was representative of other left-wing terrorists of this period in that these movements often did succeed in their short-term agendas. The same is true of other types of terrorists (right-wing, nationalist, single-issue, etc.) as well. Given this mixed bag of successes and failures, it has been argued that "the scorecard of struggle between nation-states and terrorists is not so clear."[4] While acknowledging terrorists' tactical successes, Robert A. Feary concluded in regard to their ultimate objectives that the result "is hardly a source of encouragement for terrorists."[5]

To be sure, the battlefield of terrorism is littered with utter failure in terms of long-term or ultimate strategic goals. But there were David-beats-Goliath results as well. One of the terrorist success stories was written by the Irgun Zvai Leumi, a Jewish militant group that operated in what was then the British mandate in Palestine, which committed terrorist acts against British targets. The most deadly and most notorious of these attacks targeted the British headquarters at the David Hotel in Jerusalem in 1946, resulting in the deaths of 91 persons. The terrorist campaign led to the withdrawal of the British from Palestine and the establishment of the state of Israel soon thereafter. According to David Fromkin,

Of course, Britain might have withdrawn anyway, at some other time or for some other reason. But that is really beside the point, for the Irgun wanted independence then and there, in order to open up the country for refugees from Hitler's Europe. They got what they wanted when they wanted it by doing it their own way.[6]

Similarly, the terrorist tactics of the National Liberation Front (FLN) forced France to withdraw from its North African colony of Algeria and open the way to Algeria's national independence.

So, does terrorism work? Sometimes it does, in that one "can find, well before Yassir Arafat's reception at the United Nations in 1974, historical illustrations of terrorism's efficacy."[7] However, citing the cases of Israel and Algeria, Fromkin has argued, "Terrorism wins only if you respond to it in the way that the terrorists want you to."[8] Philip Jenkins concluded that the case of the Algerian FLN demonstrated that terrorism and terrorists can realize their long-term goals. According to Jenkins,

> Several other movements have made the transition from loathed terrorists to respected politicians. At some stages of its history, the African National Congress used terrorist actions, but in 1994, the ANC became the governing party of South Africa, the most powerful state in black Africa. In Northern Ireland, the Irish Republican Army has often employed savage violence against civilians and noncombatants, of a sort that can only be described as terrorism. By the late 1990s, leading IRA supporter Gerry Adams was a prominent figure in Northern Irish politics and a member of the British Parliament. In Israel, too, the condemned Jewish terrorists of the 1940s had by the 1980s risen to the status of respected political leaders.[9]

All in all, then, the terrorist rate of success is pretty high when it comes to short-term goals but quite low when it comes to long-term objectives. Yet, the fact that some terrorist movements did accomplish their ultimate goals in the past continues to encourage contemporary terrorists' belief that they, too, may become exceptions to the rule.

The Selection of Targets

Once an ideological rationale has been embraced and the ultimate or long-term goal or goals have been established, the range of acceptable targets

> is determined by a number of factors, and the terrorists' ideology is central to this process, not only because it provides the initial dynamic for the terrorists' actions, but because it sets out the moral framework within which they operate.[10]

Ideology is more important than other factors because the doctrine "defines how the members of a group see the world around them."[11] More importantly, the terrorist doctrine identifies the pool of enemies from which the victims will be selected. The West German RAF, for example, considered the United States and NATO (including West Germany, a member state) as the core of the hated imperialist system. Thus, American citizens and NATO representatives and facilities were logical and legitimate targets. While the Italian Red Brigades (RB) shared the RAF's hatred of the global imperialist evil, in reality the movement's ultimate goal was the removal of the Italian regime. The result was, as C. J. M. Drake has pointed out, that the German left-wing terrorists' priority targets were the U.S. military and high-level German officials in politics and the corporate world. The RAF picked as victims individuals whom the group perceived as symbols of gross injustices and wrongdoing. Italian terrorists, on the other hand, attacked mostly low and middle-level targets—with a few exceptions, such as the kidnapping and killing of former Prime Minister Aldo Moro in 1978. Nearly all of the RB's targeted persons were Italians.[12]

The examples of the RAF and RB demonstrate that even when groups share the same ideological framework and the same enemies, they can differ in the selection of their victims. For the Italian terrorists, all police officers were legitimate and explicitly selected targets; for the West German terrorists, low-level police officers were never intentional targets—even though several were killed by accident during terrorist operations. Inside the West German terrorist movement, a marked change occurred after the founders of the RAF—Ulrike Meinhof, Horst Mahler, and Andreas Baader—had been arrested. On several occasions, their "heirs" targeted "innocent" people with no symbolic meaning. This was the case in several hijackings of airplanes. Reportedly, the RAF founders rejected these strikes against innocents as the "wilful dilution of the moral thrust of the first RAF by later recruits," and one of them, Klaus Juenschke, complained about "this degenerate crew that has the nerve... to boast of this cowardly murder and to present it as a new quality in the anti-imperialist struggle... in Western Europe."[13] By and large, however, even the new generation of German terrorists adhered to the careful selection of military, political, or corporate targets.

For many years, anti-American terrorism affected civilians who seemed to be randomly selected because they happened to be at the wrong place at the wrong time. However, often the victims were "not selected purely at random."[14] Instead, terrorists targeted U.S. citizens, persons carrying Israeli passports, members of a particular religious group (namely Jews), or simply those who visited a particular country. The Lebanese terrorists who hijacked a TWA airliner in 1985, for example, collected all passports and asked one of the flight attendants to sort out Israelis and passengers with Jewish-sounding names. After a terrorist assault on Lod

Airport in Israel in 1972, during which a number of foreign tourists were killed, one of the terrorists explained that "there are no innocent tourists in Israel."[15] The rationale was that if you are not for us, you are against us, or, as some terrorists have put it, "If you are not part of the solution, you are part of the problem."[16] Similarly, following the first World Trade Center bombing in 1993, the perpetrators of the first major international terrorist act on American soil stated,

> The American people are responsible for the actions of their government and they must question all of the crimes that their government is committing against other people. Or they—Americans—will be the targets of our operations that could diminish them.[17]

Osama bin Laden explained his jihad against all Americans in similar terms. He explicitly cited the will of God as the ultimate endorsement when he wrote, "All these crimes and sins committed by the Americans are a clear declaration of war on God, his messenger, and Muslims."[18]

In the conflict between Israelis and Palestinians, members of Palestinian terrorist groups, too, have rationalized the indiscriminate targeting of Israelis on the basis of what they consider the justice of their cause. This mindset is reflected in the remarks of Palestinian militants:

> The organization did not impose any limits with regards to damage or scope or nature of the armed attacks. The aim was to kill as many Jews as possible and there was no moral distinction between potential victims, whether soldiers, women or children.
>
> When it came to moral considerations, we believed in the justice of our cause... I don't recall ever being troubled by moral questions.[19]

Whereas Al Qaeda Central was all along a rather small group that often put years of planning into the preparation of spectacular attacks, the comparably large Islamic State's strike policy was more along the line of Palestinian groups and their goal to strike as often as possible killing one, two, or more persons at a time. Thus, ISIS's media center issued call after call for individuals to attack infidels wherever they are—with whatever means. The idea was that many small attacks would have similar or stronger effects than infrequent major strikes in that they most of all intimidated and frightened the enemy. While ISIS told followers repeatedly to target members of the military and police officers primarily, in other appeals the directive was to kill anyone, to kill indiscriminately. The mastermind and perpetrator of the Oklahoma City bombing in 1995, Timothy McVeigh, also justified the indiscriminate killing of innocents for his cause. After he had disclosed his plan to bomb the Alfred P. Murrah Federal Building to his friend Michael Fortier, he was asked about the fate of all the people in the building. McVeigh answered,

"Think about the people as if they were storm troopers in *Star Wars*. They may be individually innocent, but they are guilty because they work for the Evil Empire."[20]

In sum, then, the overall ideological framework and the associated assignment of blame for their grievances will guide some terrorists to select a limited number of target types and others to pinpoint huge groups of people, even a whole nation or several nations, as legitimate targets.

Terrorist Methods: From Primitive Bombs to WMD

As noted earlier, one can use social movement theory to study and understand terrorist movements. Whether a movement is nonviolent or violent, the goal is to stage public performances that draw the attention of the larger public and political leaders. While violence in public places always gets a great deal of attention, those actors with the most shocking repertoire of performances receive the greatest attention. Terrorists are well aware of this and justify violence as the only means of getting the attention they need and deserve. Describing the mindset of terrorists as they justify their violent means to achieve political ends, J. Bowyer Bell observed that for terrorists,

> the recourse to violence, often the last option, is a legitimate means to shape the future. The present is intolerable and violence the only way. As one Palestinian fedayi said, "We would throw roses if it would work." Since it does not, they throw bombs.[21]

The metaphor of the rose-throwing terrorist is, of course, in sharp contrast to the real-life damage that terrorists have caused for many years and to the fact that terrorists have used all kinds of violent methods— from stabbing or strangling their victims to dispersing nerve gas. The most obvious reason for changes in terrorist tactics over time was simply the availability of ever more convenient and potent means to attack and harm the targets of terrorism. Throughout the centuries, terrorists embraced each new technology for their purposes, from the revolver to sticks of dynamite, fertilizer bombs, rockets, and sarin gas. Advances in transportation technology, too, have affected the choice of terrorist methods as the derailment of trains, the hijacking of airplanes and ships, the suicide bombing of crowded buses, or the explosion of car or truck bombs have attested to—not to mention the attacks of 9/11, when terrorists turned airliners into devastating missiles.

The selection of one or more targets and the methods of attack go hand in hand. Both decisions are affected by the following factors:

- The degree of access to targets;
- The level of protection provided for targets;

- The general state of counterterrorist measures in the targeted society;
- The risks involved for the attacker(s);
- The probability of carrying out a successful mission.

For terrorists, nothing is more important than executing an act of terror successfully. As George Habash put it, "The main point is to select targets where success is 100% assured."[22] There are additional factors that figure into the selection of the particular terrorist method to be used in a given operation:

- The terrorists' level of training and skills;
- The availability of financial resources, mobility, and hideouts;
- The available weaponry;
- The decision either to limit a strike to the immediate victim(s) and spare innocent bystanders or to attack indiscriminately regardless of the number of innocent bystanders.

Modern terrorists have a broad range of choices when deciding on a particular mode of attack. Over 30 years ago, terrorism experts Robert Kupperman and Darrell Trent warned that terrorists were not only using "pistols, submachine guns, and bombs" but that they also had attempted to use "heat-seeking, surface-to-air rockets (SA-7s) and Soviet-made anti-tank weapons (RPG-7s) and that German terrorists had threatened to disperse mustard gas and nerve agents."[23] The more sophisticated among terrorist groups often write and distribute their own instruction manuals that describe the range of weapons recommended for terrorist strikes. Thus, the Provisional Irish Republican Army (IRA) issued a pamphlet describing various tactics, "including preparation and use of a variety of explosives, special culvert bombs for burial beneath roadways, and deployment of snipers. The text also mentioned submachine guns, pistols, grenades, rifles, automatic rifles, mortars, and rocket launchers." According to one expert, "All these [weapons] have been deployed in past strikes by the IRA, and all remain in regular service today. In that respect the IRA was very typical for contemporary terrorism."[24] This IRA list of suitable terrorist weapons shows that contemporary terrorist groups have access to a larger variety of weapons.

Most Common Methods of Terrorist Attacks

- Shootings;
- Bombings;
- Assassinations;
- Suicide attacks;
- Kidnapping/hostage-taking;
- Attacks on maritime targets;

- Missile attacks;
- Mass disruption/mass destruction.

For many years, the bombing of targets was by far the most often used terrorist method with the distinct type of suicide bombing included. But more recently shootings topped the list of terrorists' methods of attack followed by bombings and a multitude of other tactics.[25]

Terrorist actions result in either conclusive incidents or incidents of duration. Mass shootings, bombings, assassinations, and suicide missions are conclusive incidents because the actual acts occur in fractions of seconds—armed attacks can last longer but also end fairly quickly—whereas hijackings and kidnappings are incidents of duration because these terrorist events last for longer periods of time—hours, days, weeks, months, or even years. Although in a different league in terms of the likely damage, terrorism aimed at causing mass disruption and mass destruction also fits the category of conclusive incident as far as carrying out these tactics is concerned. The following sections summarize the characteristics of various terrorist methods or tactics.

Shooting

In the second decade of the twenty-first-century mass shootings by single actors or team of gunmen became the most used tactic used by terrorists. Typically, the perpetrators select populated sites for their armed attacks, such as schools, houses of worship, hotels, shopping centers, and similar public places. Indiscriminately shooting with high-powered assault weapons, they kill many people within a very short time. A gruesome example was the shooting spree by Brenton Tarrant in March 2019, when he shot to death 51 men, women, and children in two mosques in New Zealand. Terrorists use either fully automated firearms used by military forces around the world or semi-automatic firearms legally available in the United States but not in most other countries.

Bombing

For a long time, terrorists have preferred bombing to all other methods of attack because no other weapons are as readily available as incendiary or explosive devices. Just as important, this is an "easily learned technique that can be undertaken with minimal risk to the perpetrator" in that the "bomber operates with time and distance on his side."[26] Putting timers on devices allows perpetrators to detonate the explosives at the time of their choosing. Bombs come in many forms and "the possible operations for their use are almost infinite."[27] In most instances, terrorists' bombs are of the "do-it-yourself" variety because, as experts know, crude but potent bombs "can be fabricated from seemingly innocuous materials found in the open market."[28] Detailed instructions on the ingredients of bombs and how to mix or assemble them are readily and legally available in bookstores, in libraries, and on the Internet.

The website of the Animal Liberation Front (ALF), for example, has posted the "ALF Primer," which describes in detail how to build simple incendiary devices to commit arson, how best to place them in targeted facilities, and how to avoid being caught by the police. In the "Getting Started" section of the primer, the ALF details a "simple way to create an incendiary device" and a "different version of the same device" to be used by arsonists.[29] A variety of potent home-made explosives are described in easily available books, such as *The Anarchist Cookbook* or *Home Workshop Explosives*. In June 2003, one customer reviewer of *The Anarchist Cookbook* wrote the following on the Amazon.com website:

> Almost all (with the exception of a few) of the things in here are accurate in the sense that they show you BASICALLY how to do something, but also in the sense that the way it tells you how to do it is so dangerous that it will most likely fail... If you really want to know how to make homemade explosives try "Home Workshop Explosives" by Uncle Fester, now that book is a real deal. This book's techniques are taken from military handbooks that date back to about 30 years ago![30]

In October 2001, a Brazilian reader of Uncle Fester's *Home Workshop Explosives* wrote in a customer review on the Amazon.com site, "WOW! I just received the 2nd Revised Edition and Uncle Fester made a miracle: changed the best into something better... If you want the very best book on explosives manufacture [*sic*], this is the only one to have."[31]

But one does not even have to buy a book; instructions for putting together bombs were easy to come by in the past and still are today. Following the pipe bomb explosion in the Centennial Olympic Park in Atlanta in July 1996, the CNN.com website carried a story that detailed in its text and an accompanying illustration how such a device is put together. Readers learned the following:

> A pipe bomb is a fairly simple device—literally a length of a pipe capped at both ends and filled with an explosive. Often they are packed with nails and screws to heighten damage ... The pipes can be filled with low-order gunpowder or higher-order plastique. It can be rigged to go off instantly or with a timer.[32]

Seven years after the initial posting, the same story was still available on CNN's website. However, while the CNN story seemed to provide basic information about the nature of pipe bombs unwittingly, other websites carried explicit instructions on building explosives such as Molotov cocktails and bombs consisting of fertilizer and fuel.[33] The terrorist conspirators whose truck bomb nearly toppled one of the World Trade Center towers in 1993 did not encounter any problems when they bought the chemicals needed for putting together a powerful bomb. Simon Reeve describes how Ramzi Yousef, the mastermind of the first World Trade Center bombing, and his associates proceeded:

> Yousef, also using the name "Kamal Ibraham," one of his 11 aliases he used during his six months in the US, began ordering chemicals from a local firm called City Chemical, including 1,000 lbs (454 kg) of urea, 105 gallons of nitric acid, and 60 gallons of sulphuric acid. Yousef told City Chemical's salesman he knew exactly what he wanted: the nitrogen content of the urea crystals had to be 46.65 per cent and the sulphuric acid had to be 93 per cent pure.[34]

Timothy McVeigh and his accomplice, Terry Nichols, also purchased with ease the ingredients for the powerful truck bomb that completely destroyed the large Alfred P. Murrah Federal Building in Oklahoma City. According to Lou Michel and Dan Herbeck,

> On September 30 and October 18 [1994], Terry Nichols purchased a combined total of four thousand pounds of ammonium nitrate using the alias Mike Havens. McVeigh purchased smaller amounts. Whenever the opportunity presented itself, he pulled into the local feed and seed store of a small town and loaded up his car with fifty-pound bags of ammonium nitrate. He thought nothing of tossing ten bags into the backseat of the Road Warrior; he would have filled the trunk, too, if he weren't concerned about the unequal distribution in weight.
>
> Between McVeigh and Nichols, they made about eight purchases before they had the amount of ammonium nitrate they needed.[35]

Terrorists have also used plastic explosives with devastating results. The bombing of Pan Am Flight 103 in late 1988 was accomplished by the explosion of a small sheet of Semtex, a plastic explosive that was available at the time from the Czech Republic and Libya. The IRA "used it independently and liberally for bombs, such as those carried in a briefcase, or as a detonator for larger fertilizer bombs, just as non-Irish groups often do."[36]

Dynamite was the first explosive used by terrorists. The anarchists of the nineteenth century hailed Alfred Nobel's invention as the "tool for the destruction of society" in prose and even in poems.[37] Dynamite is still used by modern terrorists. Typically, they steal sticks of dynamite from military stockpiles, construction sites, or mines. More than 100 years

The Long History of Vehicle Bombs

On September 16, 1920, a horse-drawn wagon moved into the Wall Street area, stopping near the corner of 23rd Street across the head-quarters of J.P. Morgan and Company. The usual lunchtime crowd, mostly young employees, mingled around, paying no attention to a man who jumped out of the wagon and moved hastily away. A few seconds later a mighty bomb of dynamite and cast-iron weights exploded, tearing horse and wagon into pieces, killing a total of 38 people and injuring several hundred other persons. Flyers found near the Wall Street area demanded the release of political prisoners and were signed by "American Anarchist Fighters."

While anarchists and communists were immediately suspected, police investigations did not produce charges against individuals or groups. However, some historians believe that the bomber was Mario Buda, a member of an anarchist organization led by Italian immigrant Luigi Galleani and that Buda acted in revenge for the imprisonment of fellow Galleanists.

In the century since, terrorists selected cars and trucks far too often to carry and detonate bombs for the purpose of killing and maiming large numbers of people.

Nowhere were and still are mass car bombings more common than in the Middle East. Introduced first by the Stern Gang as a potent weapon against British and Palestinian foes, the tactic was later embraced by Palestinian groups and the Lebanese Hezbollah. The latter group was suspected of carrying out the 1983 truck bomb-ing outside Beirut that killed 241 U.S. Marines and 58 French military personnel.

Car and truck bombings have been utilized for decades by ter-rorists in other parts of the world as well. In Northern Ireland, both the IRA and Loyalist groups car-bombed for their causes as did the German Red Army Faction and the Basque separatist ETA.

Whether affiliated with organizations like Al Qaeda, ISIS, al-Shabaab, and Boko Haram or acting as lone wolves or autonomous cells, modern-day Jihadists, too, embraced the car-bombing tactic early on. Several of the more spectacular attacks of this sort were directed against Western targets. In 1993, an Al Qaeda-affiliated cell detonated an explosive-laden truck in the parking garage of the World Trade Center in New York City killing six people but failing to top-ple the building as intended. Far more deadly truck bombings were carried out by the same organization against the Khobar Towers, a housing facility for the U.S. military, in Dhahran, Saudi Arabia in 1998 and two years later against the U.S. embassies in Kenya and Tanzania with hundreds of fatalities. In 1995, Timothy McVeigh filled a Ryder truck with fertilizer and fuel oil and detonated a home-made super-bomb killing 168 persons, among them 19 children.

In the twenty-first century, truck and car bombs remain popular terrorist weapons.

ago, anarchist John Most tried to assemble an incendiary letter bomb, a device that modern-day terrorists have built and deployed as well—albeit in more sophisticated forms. The "Unabomber," Theodore Kaczynski, for example, killed and injured all of his victims by mailing them letter bombs.

Assassination

If they use bombs to assassinate their enemy, terrorists have a better chance of avoiding arrest than when using handguns. Depending on the circumstances, even the assassin who shoots his or her victim from close range may be able to flee the scene. In early 2002, for example, two assassins killed an Italian government consultant, Marco Biagi, in Bologna, by firing several shots as their victim entered his home. Both shooters sped away on a scooter. The Greek terrorists who in 2000 assassinated Stephen Saunders, a British military attaché in Athens, shot him with a.45-mm pistol and got away. But, by and large, shooting a target from close range is riskier than other tactics. Take the case of Yigal Amir, the young Israeli who killed Prime Minister Yitzhak Rabin in order to stop the Middle East peace process. Amir used a Beretta pistol to shoot Rabin and was immediately subdued and arrested by security forces.

Suicide Attack

When 19 members of the Al Qaeda organization flew hijacked airliners into buildings in New York and Washington, DC, on September 11, 2001, they introduced the United States to a terrorist tactic that until then had been widely used and feared in other parts of the world: suicide attacks. Immediately, the type of attack was compared to the practice of kamikaze during World War II, when some 4,600 Japanese nationals committed suicide by crashing their planes into enemy targets. But unlike the kamikaze flights that were undertaken as part of a country's war effort, the more recent suicide attacks were carried out by groups or individuals. As Adam Dolnik recalled before the 2003 defeat of Saddam Hussein's regime in Iraq,

> The modern practice of suicide bombings has its roots in Lebanon. The first major suicide attack by a non-state group occurred in December 1981, when 27 people died and more than 100 were wounded in the bombing of the Iraqi Embassy in Beirut. This attack was claimed by Al Dawa (The Call), the Iranian-backed Shia group that seeks to topple Saddam Hussein's regime in Iraq.[38]

For most Americans, however, the history of the modern suicide practice dates back to 1983, when a member of the Lebanese Hezbollah drove a truck laden with explosives into the American embassy in Beirut, killing himself and more than 60 other persons. Six months later, another member of the same organization ignited a truck bomb as he drove into the U.S. Marine barracks near Beirut airport, killing 241 Americans. Another lethal suicide attack against the French military stationed in Lebanon was carried out nearly simultaneously and resulted in the death of 58 French paratroopers. Indeed, more than 500 individuals died within a one-year period, from November 1982 to November 1983, as the result of five major suicide attacks in Lebanon. Lawrence Eagleburger, then undersecretary of state for political affairs in the Reagan administration, said at the time that it was nearly impossible to defend oneself if a driver is willing to kill himself.[39] American and French troops were withdrawn from Lebanon, and the Israeli Defense Forces retreated into the southern part of the country. The success of the suicide missions was undeniable.

From the perspective of terrorists, suicide terrorism has a number of advantages compared to other methods. According to Bruce Hoffman, "Suicide bombings are inexpensive and effective. They are less complicated and compromising than other kinds of terrorist operations. They guarantee media coverage. The suicide terrorist is the ultimate smart bomb."[40] The efficacy of the suicide tactic is best understood by terrorists themselves. After interviewing 250 of the most militant Palestinians in the 1990s, Nasra Hassan wrote,

> A Palestinian security official pointed out that, apart from a willing young man, all that is needed is such items as nails, gunpowder, a battery, a light switch, and a short cable, mercury (readily obtainable from thermometers), acetone, and the cost of tailoring a belt wide enough to hold six or eight pockets of explosives. The most expensive item is transportation to a distant Israeli town. The total cost of a typical [suicide] operation is about a hundred dollars.[41]

Furthermore, the planners of suicide missions do not have to make escape plans or fear the arrest of their operatives and the revelation of organizational secrets. More importantly, organizations that embrace suicide attacks as their tactic of choice appreciate that this terrorist method is more likely to succeed than most other means. According to Nasra Hassan,

> Military commanders of Hamas and Islamic Jihad remarked that the human bomb was one [of] the surest ways of hitting a target. A senior Hamas leader said, "The main thing is to guarantee that a large number of the enemy will be affected. With an explosive belt or bag, the bomber has control over vision, location, and timing."[42]

Suicide attacks are especially horrifying for targeting societies—for two reasons. First, as one expert concluded, this tactic is "reliably deadly" and "on average kills four times as many people as other terrorist acts."[43] Second, suicide attacks have lasting effects on the psyche of the target society because no one knows when, where, and how the next suicide attack will occur.

Because of their operational and psychological effectiveness, modern-day suicide attacks spread from Lebanon to an increasing number of other venues, among them Sri Lanka, Turkey, Chechnya, Argentina, and, of course, Israel. As Adam Dolnik has pointed out, religiously motivated terrorists are not the only ones who have embraced this tactic in the last three decades. To be sure, many of the suicide operations conducted by groups in the Middle East were and are carried out by devout Muslims. But secular groups have adopted the same tactic. In Lebanon, only about half of all suicide attacks recorded since the early 1980s were carried out by members of Hezbollah and Amal, both Shi'ite groups; several secular organizations were responsible for the rest. Similarly, although Hamas and the Palestinian Islamic Jihad, both religious Muslim groups, embraced suicide attacks as their most effective weapon against Israelis, the more secular Al-Aksa Martyrs Brigade followed suit, beginning in late 2001.[44]

But it was the Lebanese Hezbollah that created the mythos of the explosives-laden martyr in the Arab world and beyond—mostly because of the television images that were broadcast after such attacks. The result was what Christoph Reuter calls an extremely successful "martyr-marketing."[45] This marketing assures that there is never a shortage of individuals willing to die for a cause that they learn to perceive as far more important than their own lives. Nasra Hassan has described the post-incident glorification efforts after suicide attacks by Palestinian militants:

> The [suicide] operation doesn't end with the explosion and the many deaths. Hamas and Islamic Jihad distribute copies of the martyr's audiocassette or video to the media and to local organizations as a record of their success and encouragement to young men. His [the

suicide bomber's] act becomes the subject of sermons in mosques, and provides material for leaflets, posters, videos, demonstrations, and extensive coverage in the media. Graffiti on walls in the martyr's neighborhood praise his heroism. Aspiring martyrs perform mock reenactments of the operation, using models of exploding cars and busses.[46]

Religious terrorists undertake suicide missions in the belief that they will be rewarded with a privileged existence in paradise; secular suicide terrorists do not expect rewards from God. But the latter are also indoctrinated by sect-like groups that insist on absolute subordination to whatever their "higher cause" may be. This explains the suicide terrorism of the Liberation Tigers of Tamil Eelam (LTTE), commonly known as the Tamil Tigers, and the Kurdistan Workers Party (PKK). Although suicide bombings by Middle Eastern groups received far more publicity in the last 30 or so years, Sri Lanka (formerly Ceylon) experienced more such acts than any other country—an estimated 200 since the end of the 1980s. In their fight against the Sinhala-dominated central government, the LTTE's suicide corps, the Black Tigers, almost always targeted government officials and symbols of power as well as the country's infrastructure. In January 1996, for example, a group of suicide bombers attacked Sri Lanka's Central Bank, killing 86 persons and injuring more than 1,300. And in July 2001, an even larger contingent of suicide bombers attacked the International Airport in Colombo, destroying or damaging 13 military and civilian planes. Reuter described the indoctrination of designated LTTE suicide bombers as brainwashing.[47] Recruits learned that it was a disgrace to be caught alive by the enemy. For that reason, all members of the organization carried capsules of potassium cyanide, which they were required to bite into "when injured or when on the verge of capture."[48] The left-wing PKK conducted 15 suicide missions in southern Turkey during the late 1990s, targeting in all instances government representatives, members of the military, and military installations. The vast majority of the victims were policemen and soldiers, but a few civilians were killed and injured unwittingly. Like the Black Tigers in Sri Lanka, the PKK suicide bombers did not kill themselves in the name of God and on a fast track to eternal life in heaven, but rather to strengthen the group's political cause.

Following the first suicide bombings by militant Muslim groups in Lebanon, Shi'ite clerics were faced with the question of whether their religion condemned or allowed these acts. Sayyid Muhammad Husayn Fadlallah, for example, declared first that, based on his knowledge of Islamic law, he had reservations about using suicides for political ends. But, as Martin Kramer has pointed out, "Fadlallah eventually gave them [suicide attacks] the fullest possible endorsement short of an explicit *fatwa*."[49] This did not, however, resolve the issue for the Muslim clergy in Lebanon or elsewhere. To this day, some religious leaders, whether Shi'ites or Sunnis, sanction martyr missions against civilians if undertaken within a strategy of self-defense, while others speak out against this tactic.

Dolnik found that since the early 1980s, 18 terrorist organizations striking in 15 countries carried out more than 300 suicide missions. None of these attacks killed and injured as many individuals or caused as much damage as the multiple kamikaze flights into symbolic buildings in New York and Washington, DC, on September 11, 2001—not to mention the additional damage to the U.S. psyche. From the perspective of their masterminds, the suicide operations of 9/11 were successful; Osama bin Laden and his lieutenants expressed this much in their post-9/11 communications. As long as terrorists consider suicide attacks as the most effective of their tactics, they will continue to rely on human bombs and human missiles.

Robert A. Pape has rejected religious fanaticism as a plausible explanation for this phenomenon, arguing instead that "suicide terrorism follows a strategic logic, one specifically designed to coerce modern liberal democracies to make significant territorial concessions."[50] In other words, it is not whether a group is religious or secular, but whether its nationalist aspirations determine the tactical choice of suicide attacks. This conclusion fails to explain why some groups that fight for self-determination and statehood do practice suicide terrorism and why others with the same aspirations do not. Why did Palestinians embrace this method, but not ETA or the IRA? It seems that fanatical devotion to a religion and/or a charismatic leader of godlike stature is still the best explanation. In the case of the LTTE, its founder and leader, Velupillai Prabhakaran, "exercised godlike absolute control over the cadre and the organization seemed to resemble sects."[51] In this respect, the LTTE and the PKK were like twins, according to Reuter, in that, before his capture, Abdullah Ocalan's status in the PKK was the same as that of Prabhakaran in the LTTE: Ocalan was God or at least a saint, and the "PKK became a de facto sect."[52] Michael Radu, too, has characterized the Tamil Tigers and the Kurdish Workers Party as operating "more like religious sects under the absolute control of a charismatic leader."[53] After studying several nationalist groups, Aaron Horwitz identified a cultural tradition of glorifying suicide for the collective good as the one most powerful determinant: Where the tradition exists and is exploited by leaders, suicide terrorism has proven an attractive option; where no such tradition exists, suicide attacks have not been embraced as a terrorist tactic.[54]

Given the high publicity value of suicide terrorism, it is hardly surprising that the most lethal of such missions are sometimes claimed by two or more organizations that operate in the same environment. This underlines an observation by Mia Bloom, namely that "under conditions of group competition, there are incentives for further groups to jump on the 'suicide bandwagon' and ramp up the violence in order to distinguish themselves from the other organizations."[55] Whether such "outbidding" occurs depends also on the reaction of those in whose name terrorist groups and their members claim to act. According to Bloom, "If the domestic environment supports the use of suicide terror and an insurgent group does not use the tactic, they tend to lose market share and popularity."[56] In such a situation, a group may also try to regain support by launching suicide missions. Finally, competition between groups may also influence the selection of suicide terrorists that promise special attention of friends and foes—females rather than males, younger rather than older volunteers. In November 2006, for example, Hamas scored big in terms of news coverage and an outpouring of massive Palestinian support after the organization claimed sole responsibility for a suicide bombing carried out by the oldest suicide bomber by far on record: a 64-year-old mother of nine and grandmother of 36.

No other terrorist organizations carried out as many major suicide attacks as ISIS on military and civilian targets in Iraq, Syria, and more recently in Afghanistan. Add to this the fact that ISIS affiliates in Africa and Asia, too, rely mostly on suicide missions. In many of these attacks, several dozen and often more than a hundred persons die, with many more injured.

Kidnapping/Hostage-Taking

To kidnap one or more persons requires operational know-how and favorable conditions in order to succeed. To take hostages in a friendly environment or one in which the authorities are unable to provide for law and order is, of course, far less risky than finding hideouts in a hostile environment. The terrorists who held American hostages in Lebanon during most of the 1980s did not have to fear discovery and arrest because they were able to hide and operate in areas that they controlled or that were surrounded by sympathizers. In the past, hostage situations have often worked in favor of the captors in that the targeted governments or private corporations gave in to the demands in order to free the hostages. Terrorist groups in Colombia and elsewhere in Latin America, for example, have kidnapped foreigners on numerous occasions and released them when the hostages' employers in North America or Europe paid the ransom demanded.

Whatever the circumstances, a hostage-taking coup "requires intricate planning, split-second timing, a large support apparatus to sustain the group holding the victim, and the ability to remain secure while still communicating demands or negotiating with third parties."[57] Past hostage situations often ended with the eventual release of the captives, but there were other endings as well. In the 1980s, for example, Lebanese terrorists murdered two of their hostages, William Buckley and William Higgins.

But whereas terrorist kidnappers in the past used this tactic to pressure governments into giving in to their demands, the more recent kidnappings by Al Qaeda and affiliate cells had a different motive all along. They did not want to bargain, but preferred to kill their hostages in the most barbaric ways possible in order to send warnings to their target audiences by publicizing videotapes of their victims' gruesome ordeals and executions. This tactic was evident in early 2002, when kidnapped *Wall Street Journal* reporter Daniel Pearl was brutally murdered by terrorists in Pakistan. A year later, a young American contractor, Nicholas Berg, was beheaded by terrorists in Iraq, and an American engineer, Paul Johnson, Jr., suffered the same fate in Saudi Arabia.

But no other organization exploited its hostages as inhumanly as ISIS in an obvious and very successful effort to dominate the global news. Here is a summary of ISIS's killer propaganda:

- Tuesday, August 19, 2014. The media center of the Islamic State uploads its video "#NewMessagefromISIStoUS" to YouTube. The 4-minute, 40-second production shows the American journalist James Foley in an orange jumpsuit reminiscent of Arab prisoners held in the U.S. detention facility at Guantanamo Bay. Kneeling next to a black-clad, masked ISIS fighter, Foley delivers an extensive statement in which he calls on "his friends, family and loved ones... to rise up against my real killers—the U.S. government—for what will happen to me is only a result of their complacent criminality."
- After blaming strikes against the Islamic State for Foley's death the ISIS fighter pulls out a knife and decapitates his hostage. The camera then moves over to another kneeling captive, the American journalist Steven Joel Sotloff. According to the executioner, he will be the next victim.
- Less than two weeks later, an eerily similar 2-minute, 46-second video captures the beheading of Sotloff and ends with a death threat against British citizen David Haines who is already wearing an orange prison gown. This time, the video is posted on a file-sharing website.
- Ten days later, ISIS releases a 2-minute, 27-second video of Haines's beheading on Twitter. Shortly thereafter, there are more videos with the same images, the same threats.
- But nothing is more shocking than the 22-minute film that culminates in the burning of captured Jordanian pilot Moaz al-Kasasbeh alive. While the pilot was presumably executed weeks earlier, the video's release in early February 2015 indicates that ISIS's production staff needed time to present a "sophisticated" production worthy of Hollywood standards.

These atrocities were staged and marketed via social media with one goal: publicity. And, indeed, each of these cruel acts resulted in exceptional global media attention and in condemnations by President Obama and many other leaders of major powers after each of these incidents.

Beginning in the late 1960s, the hijacking of a commercial airliner was for a while the preferred terrorist tactic. Generally, these operations were carried out by at least two, but often more than two, terrorists who took control by threatening crew members and passengers with hand grenades and/or handguns. Whenever hijackers forced the pilots to land their planes in a country whose government was either sympathetic to them or too weak for a rescue attempt, they were able to negotiate for their immediate demands—typically, the release of fellow terrorists from prison or the payment of a ransom. When a hijacked plane touched down in an environment that was not hospitable to the terrorists aboard, the hijackers would threaten to harm hostages unless they were assured free passage out of the country. Whatever the particular circumstances, only sophisticated groups can pull off a skyjacking with the prospect of success because this tactic "demands patience on the part of the operatives and an ability to handle a 'duration operation.'"[58]

The risks that hijackers take in these operations depend in large part on the counterterrorist measures at the airports of departure and aboard the chosen planes. Good airport security can detect terrorists' weapons before they can be brought aboard a plane; armed sky marshals aboard an airliner can overpower terrorists and prevent them from taking control; and, finally, well-trained counterterrorist commandos can storm a hijacked plane on the ground. Indeed, once all of these counterterrorist means were in place in an increasing number of countries, the number of hijackings began to decrease in the 1980s.

Attacks on Maritime Targets

On April 2009, as the crew of the U.S. Navy destroyer USS *Bainbridge* looked on, four Somali pirates held the captain of the MV *Maersk Alabama*—a U.S.-flagged cargo ship carrying 17,000 metric tons of cargo—hostage in an unpowered lifeboat. After several other Navy ships arrived at the scene, the *Alabama* was escorted by military guards to its destination port in Kenya. In the meantime, negotiations to free the ship's captain failed. The drama off the Horn of Africa ended when a group of U.S. Navy SEALs, who had been flown to the site, killed three pirates in the lifeboat while one of their comrades was aboard the USS *Bainbridge* hoping to negotiate a substantial ransom. At the time of the incident, more than a dozen ships and more than 200 sailors were held by pirates who demanded many millions of dollars in ransom. But there were also credible reports that part of their ransom money was handed over to Al Shabaab—even before radical Islamists seized Xarardheere, one of the most notorious pirate coves along the Somali coast, in the spring of 2010.

Moreover, in interviews with news organizations, pirates justified their actions by claiming that European countries had dumped toxic waste into the ocean and destroyed their once-rich fishing grounds.

In the last three decades, only about 2 percent of all terrorist incidents qualified as maritime terrorism. The best remembered of these cases occurred in 1986, when Palestinian terrorists took over the Italian cruise ship *Achille Lauro* in the Mediterranean that had many American citizens aboard. They brutally killed a wheelchair-bound New Yorker, Leon Klinghoffer. The *Achille Lauro* terrorists did not succeed in getting comrades released from Israeli prisons, but because of the high success rate of African, Asian, and Latin American pirates in securing high ransom payments in the last several years and receiving enormous media attention around the globe, counterterrorism experts have voiced concern that more, and more spectacular, maritime terrorism could occur in the foreseeable future.

According to an expert assessment, the seven most likely scenarios for maritime terrorism are the following:

- Use of a commercial container ship to smuggle chemical, biological, or radiological (CBR) materials for an unconventional attack carried out on land or at a major commercial port such as Rotterdam, Singapore, Hong Kong, Dubai, New York, or Los Angeles.
- Use of a "trojan horse," such as a fishing trawler, resupply ship, tug, or similar innocuous-looking vessel, to transport weapons and other battle-related material.
- Hijacking of a vessel as a fundraising exercise to support a campaign of political violence directed toward ethnic, ideological, religious, or separatist designs.
- Scuttling of a ship in a narrow SLOC [sea-lane of communication] in order to block or disrupt maritime traffic.
- Hijacking of an LNG [liquefied natural gas] carrier that is then detonated as a floating bomb or used as a collision weapon.
- Use of a small, high-speed boat to attack an oil tanker or offshore energy platform to affect international petroleum prices or cause major pollution.
- Directly targeting a cruise liner or passenger ferry to cause mass casualties by contaminating the ship's food supply, detonating an onboard or submersible improvised explosive device (IED) or, again, by ramming the vessel with a fast-approach, small, attack craft.[59]

Missile Attacks on Fixed and Moving Targets

In November 2002, a surface-to-air missile was fired at an Israeli jetliner that was carrying a large group of tourists from the Kenyan resort of Mombasa back to Israel. Luckily, the rocket missed its target. There was no doubt that terrorists had launched the projectile at a time when a car bomb killed 14 persons in the lobby of an Israeli-owned hotel in the same resort. This was not the first time terrorists had used this tactic. In September 2000, for example, a rocket was fired from a handheld launcher at a distance of only a few hundred yards onto Great Britain's Intelligence Headquarters in the heart of London. Officials suspected that renegades of the IRA were responsible for the incident. Although the pictures taken after the audacious attack showed only minimal damage to the well-known MI6 building—once featured in a James Bond film (*The World Is Not Enough*)—these images heightened the fear of an escalation of terrorist violence in London and elsewhere in England. For years, the IRA used mortars and homemade launchers to attack military and civilian targets. According to Christopher Harmon,

> One of the most creative and ingenious use[s] of mortars was popularized by the IRA and by Japanese terrorists of the "Middle Core Faction" during the 1970s and 1980s. The groups place mortars in the back of an altered vehicle, creating a truly "mobile launcher" for urban terrorism. The method was used in 1991 in a bold attack on 10 Downing Street [the Prime Minister's residence]. It proved to be a psychological victory that could have had an even greater impact had one of the shells not struck a tree in the Prime Minister's garden rather than the residence itself.[60]

If they have the financial resources, today's terrorists do not have to rely on homemade mortars but can acquire sophisticated handheld missile launchers to project lethal rockets against fixed and moving targets. The facilitators of such sinister transactions are either some renegade countries or the striving black market that reaches into literally all continents.

Launching projectiles against enemy targets, even if done from some distance, comes with some risks. Unless terrorists operate in a friendly environment, operate within failed or failing states, or have secured getaway routes, there is always the risk of being caught.

Unconventional Tactics with Deadly Results

When the simultaneous hijacking of three commercial airliners allowed the 9/11 terrorists to use those planes as weapons of mass destruction, they resorted to an unconventional mode of attack. To be sure, this was not an unsophisticated mission. The attack was the result of long-term planning, and the hijackers had to learn to fly an airliner. Conversely, anyone with a car can ram his or her vehicle

Table 8.1 Period with Most Deadly Vehicle Ramming Attacks

Date	Place	Vehicle	Plus Knifing	Killed	Injured
July 2016	Nice	Truck	No	86	Hundreds
December 2016	Berlin	Truck	No	12	Dozens
January 2017	Jerusalem	Truck	No	4	10
March 2017	London	Car	Yes	5	10
April 2017	Stockholm	Truck	No	4	15
June 2017	London	Van	Yes	8	48
June 2017	London	Van	No	1	10
August 2017	Charlotte sville	Car	No	1	19
October 2017	Barcelona	Van	No	13	130
October 2017	Cambrils, Spain	Car	Yes	1	6
October 2017	New York	Truck	No	8	11

Source: Author, using open sources.

into a crowd of people causing harm. For that reason, this tactic—sometimes combined with knifing—has been promoted by some terrorist groups.

In 2010, Al Qaeda in the Arabian Peninsula recommended for the first time vehicle ramming in the group's online magazine *Inspire*. It was a call to followers in the West to attack infidels more often and use easily available weapons, such as a car or a truck. In the following years, there were several such attacks. ISIS made the same appeals on the heels of a horrific truck ramming in Nice in the summer of 2016 that killed 84 persons and injured hundreds of others. The years 2016 and 2017 witnessed a wave of car, van, and truck ramming attacks in Europe and North America. Table 8.1 lists those vehicle ramming incidents that resulted in deaths; there were others too, though without casualties, and some were stopped in time by police.

Mass Disruption and Mass Destruction

Without hurling bombs and missiles or assassinating individuals, without toppling skyscrapers, taking hostages, or releasing poison gas, terrorists can inflict great damage on any society they target. In early 1995, for example, "high-tech" terrorists cut the cables of Germany's public communication agency at three key underground crossroads in Frankfurt and disrupted all computer, telephone, and fax services in parts of the city—including the international airport, hospitals, and office buildings. Fortunately, the communications blackout did not cause planes to crash or patients to die. But the group that claimed responsibility, Keine Verbindung (No Connection), demonstrated the vulnerability of the communication system.

Terrorists who aim at seriously disrupting a country's or region's infrastructure could aim at hitting electric power grids and gas pipelines. A blackout of the New York Stock Exchange, the leading Wall Street firms, and the backup systems that were established in the wake of 9/11 would affect and perhaps paralyze the domestic and global financial markets. The accidental breakdown of the electric power supply structure in parts of the American Midwest and Northeast as well as in neighboring Canada on August 14, 2003, affected an estimated 50 million people, giving them a bitter taste of what would happen in the wake of massive terrorist attacks on power grids and other vital parts of the infrastructure. Such incidents do not simply disrupt the lives of people in the immediately affected areas but cause ripple effects that are felt throughout the country and abroad and that inflict high costs on individuals, the business community, and markets.

Even the mere threat of causing major disruption can have chaotic consequences, as happened in 1995, when a bomb threat was made against the air traffic control center responsible for directing traffic at two New York airports (John F. Kennedy and LaGuardia) and at Newark Airport in New Jersey. Although the bomb threat proved to be a hoax, landings and takeoffs at these three major airports were interrupted for hours; this, in turn, affected air traffic in the rest of the country as well. In the past, terrorist groups have repeatedly tried to damage electric power grids and pipelines in various parts of the world but have not caused a great deal of damage and disruption. But the potential for more sophisticated and more determined terrorists succeeding in such endeavors is high.

Security experts are especially worried about the prospect of devastating cyberterrorism. There is a reason for concern because, in 2002, the FBI made a shocking discovery as its agents investigated a mysterious pattern of surveillance of Silicon Valley computer systems:

> Working with experts at the Lawrence Livermore National Laboratories, the FBI traced trails of a broader reconnaissance. A forensic summary of the investigation, prepared for the Defense Department, said the bureau found "multiple casings of sites" nationwide. Routed through telecommunications switches in Saudi Arabia, Indonesia and Pakistan, the visitors studied emergency telephone

systems, electrical generation and transmission, water storage and distribution, nuclear power plants and gas facilities.

Some of the probes suggested planning for conventional attack, U.S. officials say. But others homed in on a class of digital devices that allow remote control of services such as fire dispatch and of equipment such as pipelines. More information about those devices—and how to program them—turned up on al Qaeda computers seized this year, according to law enforcement and national security officials.[61]

One of the nightmares that haunt security experts is a scenario in which terrorists launch a major physical attack in conjunction with a cyber-strike that prevents swift action by emergency response professionals. Imagine 9/11-like events and simultaneous cyber-attacks that knock out the 911 emergency systems and/or the electric power grid in the affected cities and regions. There are other dangers as well. For example, computers could be used to "remotely access cereal processing plants, change the levels of iron supplement, and sicken or kill the children of a nation as they eat their breakfast."[62] Or, terrorists could remotely alter the pressure in a gas line and cause a valve to fail so that "a block of a sleepy suburb detonates and burns."[63] No wonder that even before Al Qaeda became the most dangerous terrorist organization, experts warned,

> The danger today stems from induced disasters of vastly different magnitude. The vulnerability of society's life-supporting physical networks literally invites focus on sabotage and the low-intensity warfare of terrorist attacks. If successful, such assaults could exceed the self-healing limits of society.[64]

Seen this way, the step from terrorism of mass disruption to terrorism of mass destruction can be rather small or nonexistent. Pointing to new WMD, Robert Bunker wrote,

> While no such weapons have been utilized by terrorists to date, one troubling trend has developed recently involving laser strikes on commercial aviation and airborne law enforcement assets primarily in the Los Angeles metropolitan region since 1996. These include still unexplained incidents against Ontario, Pomona, and San Diego police helicopters. Lasers make ideal terrorist weapons and, in fact, possess a number of advantages over surface-to-air missiles (SAMs) in the areas of availability, functioning, and operational deployment. To further complicate matters, lasers, like computers, are drastically falling in price and their performance levels are greatly increasing.[65]

WMD poses the ultimate threat. But experts speak increasingly of CBRN (chemical, biological, radiological, and nuclear) weapons because

WMD can also stand for "weapons of mass disruption." Following the dismantling of the Eastern Bloc and the Soviet Union, stockpiles of nuclear weapons became accessible, and scientists and technicians who developed nuclear arms and chemical and biological agents in Russia and elsewhere in the East were for hire. Whether through official channels, the Russian mafia, or some unpaid scientists, some of these dangerous weapons and some of the human expertise found their way into countries with known ties to terrorist groups. The idea that terrorists might resort to WMD is a nightmare that was in the past merely the stuff of fiction. In his novel *The Turner Diaries*, right-wing leader William Pierce described how biological, chemical, and nuclear weapons were used for the Neo-Nazi conquest of North America and Europe. Now the threat of catastrophic terrorism is real. The most publicized case involved the Aum Shinrikyo cult in Japan and its repeated release of sarin nerve gas in 1995. But the Sri Lankan Tamil Tigers were the first terrorist group to resort to a chemical weapon when it launched a poison gas attack against a Sri Lankan military facility in 1990—half a decade before the sarin nerve gas attack in Japan shocked the world.[66]

In the United States, evidence has surfaced that "white supremacist, Christian Identity and elements of the militia movement have been experimenting with chemical and biological agents. However, these have been almost entirely low-grade incidents... [that] can hardly be described as the use of 'weapons of mass destruction.'"[67] The same can be said of an incident in 1984, when the Rajneesh cult poisoned salad bars in ten restaurants located in the Oregon community they lived in. The plan was to make enough citizens sick so that they were unable to vote against the sect's candidate in an upcoming local election. Yet the anthrax incident on the heels of the 9/11 attacks drove home the point that there is a clear and present danger of terrorists using biological or chemical agents such as WMD. This was indeed the judgment of a pair of experts in the field, who made the following assessment:

> Both chemical and biological agents can be obtained from government laboratories through the terrorist-organised crime nexus. By developing links with rogue scientists, terrorist groups can also purchase the equipment required to produce these agents in the open market. Although some biological agents are relatively difficult to produce, the process of production is within the reach of contemporary terrorist groups with access to university-qualified members, collaborators, supporters and sympathisers.[68]

So far, terrorist groups have not acquired nuclear arms. But Aum Shinrikyo and Al Qaeda tried to buy highly enriched plutonium from sources in Russia and other republics of the former Soviet Union in order to build their own nuclear weapons. It does not necessarily take the financial resources of a bin Laden to acquire potent weapons. Just as the U.S. Army is known to have lost track of large quantities of explosives stored in military facilities such as Fort Bragg, it is not impossible that groups or individuals could steal nuclear, biological, or chemical materials by breaking into some laboratory. And there is always the chance that a government that does not dare to fight openly against real or imagined enemies will supply terrorists with WMD—even of the nuclear kind.

Twenty years ago, a group of experts warned of a post-Cold War "nuclear anarchy" unless the United States and the international community prevented the worst-case scenario from unfolding. In case of inaction, they warned, "Terrorist groups would be able to shop at the Russian nuclear bazaar. Consider Hamas with nuclear weapons; the Red Brigade with nuclear weapons, the Chechens with nuclear weapons."[69] But Russia's stored nukes and their vulnerability to theft and sale to the highest bidders are not the only danger in this respect. In addition to Russia, seven other countries have nuclear weapons (China, France, India, Israel, Pakistan, the United States, and the United Kingdom), and by 2004, experts believed that North Korea had the material to build several nuclear weapons and that Iran was working toward the same goal. Whether provided by state sponsors or acquired on the nuclear black market, nukes in the hands of terrorists have become the ultimate terror threat. According to Rohan Gunaratna and Peter Chalk,

> With terrorist propensity to conduct mass casualty attacks, it is a question of time that Al-Qaeda or another terrorist group will acquire, develop and use a CBRN weapon in the foreseeable future. Unless a state sponsor provides a nuclear weapon to a terrorist group, it is highly unlikely that a terrorist group will be able to gain access to a nuclear weapon. However, it is likely that a terrorist group will acquire, develop or use a chemical, biological, or a radiological weapon.[70]

Today, no society can be confident that terrorists will continue to rely on "conventional" weapons and shy away from weapons of mass disturbance and mass destruction. In spite of this threat, Graham Allison, a leading expert on weapons and national security, suggests that the ultimate terrorist catastrophe is preventable by an urgent, aggressive, multifaceted effort of "denying terrorists access to nuclear weapons and weapons-grade material."[71]

In 2015, there were sporadic reports of chemical mortar shells filled with chlorine gas or the insecticide phosphine being launched by ISIS fighters against Kurdish militias. Reportedly, both chemical agents sickened the targeted fighters. The use of chemicals by ISIS was not exactly new but regional and international weapons experts were surprised and shocked that the chemical mortar shells were by all accounts fabricated in an ISIS facility. What was a top secret at the time, was finally revealed in 2022, namely, that the Islamic State was starting to build a dangerous WMD arsenal. In 2014, at the peak of ISIS's power in Iraq and Syria, the self-proclaimed Caliph of the Islamic State Caliphate, Abu Bakr al-Baghdadi, wanted to acquire weapons of mass destruction to use against western European cities and perhaps against the United States as well. To realize his plan, the ISIS leader hired Salih al-Sabawi who had been a key engineer in Saddam Hussein's WMD program that had manufactured an arsenal of deadly chemical and biological weapons. Within half-a-year, ISIS was able to produce mustard gas, a lethal chemical agent, and chlorine-filled rockets. Al-Sabawi and his staff were also interested in weaponizing botulinum toxin, ricin, and anthrax. When the United States and its allies learned about ISIS's WMD program and the formation and training of a team for the delivery of the deadly weapons, they marked al-Sabawi as a major target. He was killed by U.S. Special Forces in 2015 and laboratories and production facilities were destroyed sometime later. There is little doubt that ISIS leader al-Baghdadi was eager to deploy deadly chemical and biological weapons against western "evil doers" in their own territories.[72]

Most Likely CBRN Weapons in the Hands of Terrorists

States, terrorist groups, and individual terrorists could develop or acquire a multitude of CBRN materials in order to commit lethal and catastrophic political violence. Some groups inside and outside the United States have developed or acquired biological or chemical agents and tried to deploy them. Other terrorist organizations made similar efforts without succeeding. Some incidents receive far greater publicity than others. In 1995, after the Japanese Aum Shinrikyo cult attacked the Tokyo subway system with sarin, the incident was widely reported around the world. But evidence that extremists in the United States had managed to buy dangerous biological agents received little media attention. Jessica Stern found that in 1995 alone, there were three known cases that involved "survivalists" and "white supremacists" acquiring biological agents. According to Stern,

> In March [1995] two members of the Minnesota Patriots Council were arrested for producing ricin with which to assassinate a deputy U.S. marshal who had served papers on one of them for tax violations.
>
> In May, just six weeks after the Aum Shinrikyo incident, Larry Wayne Harris, a former member of neo-Nazi organizations, bought three vials of Yersinia pestis, the bacterium that causes bubonic plague, which killed nearly a quarter of Europe's population in the mid-fourteenth century.

In December a survivalist was arrested for trying to carry 130 grams of ricin across the border into Canada.[73]

Some of the most feared CBRN weapons that terrorists might use are considered in the following sections.

Chemical

Mustard gas is a chemical agent in gas or liquid form that in some states smells like mustard, but it has nothing to do with the mustard people eat with frankfurters and other foods. Mustard gas attacks the skin and causes severe blisters. When inhaled, it damages lungs, other organs, and even the cells' DNA, which can result in cancer and birth defects. Although not as lethal as some other chemical agents, when used as a weapon mustard gas is likely to inflict permanent injuries and suffering. There is no known case in which terrorists produced or acquired mustard gas.

Sarin, whether in the gas or liquid form, is among the most lethal of chemical weapons. It is far more deadly than cyanide and is able to kill victims within minutes. Whether inhaled or absorbed through the skin, this chemical material attacks the nervous system, muscles, and organs. The Japanese Aum Shinrikyo cult produced sarin in the 1990s in its own laboratories and used it as a terrorist weapon in its 1995 attack on the Tokyo subway system.

VX, a chemical agent, is considered the most lethal nerve gas known. When absorbed through the skin, VX attacks the nervous system and tends to kill victims within a very short time. It is believed that amateurs cannot produce this deadly material, but the scientists of the Aum Shinrikyo cult did produce traces of VX and used it in several assassination attempts, in which one victim was killed.

Biological

Anthrax is a type of bacteria that is well known in the United States as a biological weapon because a few weeks after the 9/11 attacks, a still-unknown person mailed letters with anthrax spores to a number of people in the media and in politics. Anthrax can enter the body through even the tiniest cut in the skin, through inhalation, and by ingestion with food. When anthrax spores are inhaled and enter the lungs, without treatment most victims die. The skin and stomach forms of anthrax are thought to be less lethal.

Smallpox is a virus that is easily spread from person to person and, in the past, it often killed millions of people during a single year. Declared eradicated more than 30 years ago, only the United States and Russia are known to have the smallpox virus stored—the United States in the Centers for Disease Control and Prevention and Russia in a repository that once fed the Soviet Union's biological weapons program. It seems unlikely that terrorists would use this virus because it is highly contagious. But there are concerns that a financially strong terrorist organization with scientists in its ranks could perhaps acquire smallpox through unemployed experts in the field who once worked in the Soviet Union's bioweapons program.

Botulinum toxin is the most poisonous biological agent known. According to one account, in its most concentrated form "one pound of it, if properly dispersed, could in theory kill a billion people."[74] The bacteria that produce the botulinum toxin are sometimes found in soil. When exposed to a potent form of this toxin, victims suffer muscle paralysis and die within a short time. It was reported that scientists in the Aum Shinrikyo cult "had tried to make germ weapons from anthrax and botulinum" and that they "had staged as many as a dozen unsuccessful germ attacks in Japan from 1990 to 1995."[75]

Ricin is a protein toxin that can be inhaled, ingested, or injected. Contained in castor beans, it can be extracted so that it is "two hundred times more potent than cyanide."[76] Since no antidote is known, victims will die. In early 2003, British police found a small quantity of ricin in a building on the outskirts of London and arrested seven Muslim extremists in connection with it.

Radiological

Dirty bombs are conventional explosive devices that also contain radioactive material. When a dirty bomb is set off, the dynamite (or whatever explosives are used) will spray the radioactive material and contaminate the targeted site. Depending on the radiation potency, weather conditions, and speed of emergency responders, the number of victims killed would vary. If, for example, a dirty bomb were to explode in New York's Times Square, this site and its environment would be uninhabitable for a long time. If terrorist groups were to get hold of radioactive material, it would be easy for them to construct a dirty bomb. There were reports that Al Qaeda had in fact built such a radiological weapon in Afghanistan before 9/11.

Nuclear Bombs

Documents found in Al Qaeda's former safe houses in Afghanistan revealed that bin Laden and his group were interested in learning as much as possible about nuclear weapons. Indeed, since the 1990s, bin Laden tried to acquire nuclear capabilities but there is no evidence that these efforts were successful. The Aum Shinrikyo cult, too, was interested in building nuclear weapons. Before he left office in early 2005, U.S. Attorney General John Ashcroft warned,

If you were to have nuclear proliferation find its way into the hands of terrorists, the entire world might be very seriously disrupted by a few individuals who thought to impose their will, their arcane philosophy, on the rest of mankind.[77]

Still, the nuclear nightmare scenario seems less likely than the threat of terrorists deploying chemical, biological, and even radiological weapons. Some experts reject the "alarmist scenarios" of catastrophic biological or chemical terrorism that are reinforced by certain government officials, sensational news reports, and Hollywood movies. But even the anti-alarmist school does not completely rule out such attacks.

Notes

1 Both of these points are articulated by Bruce Hoffman, *Inside Terrorism* (New York: Columbia University Press, 1998), 157.
2 "Open Letter to Downtrodden in Lebanon and the World," in Walter Laqueur and Yonah Alexander, eds., *The Terrorism Reader* (New York: Penguin, 1987), 318.
3 The West German terrorist Michael Bauman is quoted in David C. Rapoport, "The International World as Some Terrorists Have Seen It: A Look at a Century of Memoirs," in David C. Rapoport, ed., *Inside Terrorist Organizations* (London: Frank Cass, 2001), 44.
4 Robert Kupperman and Darrell Trent, *Terrorism: Threat, Reality, Response* (Stanford, CA: Hoover Institution, 1979), 7.
5 Robert A. Feary, "Introduction to International Terrorism," in Marius H. Livingston, ed., *International Terrorism in the Contemporary World* (Westport, CT: Greenwood Press, 1978), 31, 32.
6 David Fromkin, "Strategy of Terrorism," in Charles W. Kegley, Jr., ed., *International Terrorism: Characteristics, Causes, Controls* (New York: St. Martin's, 1990), 57.
7 Kupperman and Trent, 17.
8 Fromkin, 61.
9 Philip Jenkins, *Images of Terror: What We Can and Can't Know about Terrorism* (New York: Aldine de Gruyter, 2003), 81.
10 C. J. M. Drake, "The Role of Ideology in Terrorists' Target Selection," *Terrorism and Political Violence* 10 (2) (Summer 1998), p. 53.
11 Ibid., 56.
12 For an excellent account of the relationship between ideology and target selection and the differences between the RAF and RB, see Drake, 53–85.
13 Peter H. Merkl, "West German Left-Wing Terrorism," in Martha Crenshaw, ed., *Terrorism in Context* (University Park: Pennsylvania State University Press, 1995), 192.
14 Donna M. Schlagheck, *International Terrorism* (Lexington, MA: Lexington Books, 1988), 2.
15 Brian M. Jenkins, "Der internationale Terrorismus," *Aus Politik und Zeitgeschichte* B5 (1987): 25.
16 This slogan was popular among the radical left in the United States and was attributed to Huey Newton of the Black Panther Party. See Ibid., 25.
17 From a letter published in the *New York Times* on March 28, 1993, 35.

18 "Jihad against Jews and Crusaders, 23 February 1998," www.washingtonpost.com/wp-dyn?article&node=&contentId=A4993-2001Sep2.

19 Jerrold M. Post, Ehud Sprinzak, and Laurita M. Denny, "The Terrorists in Their Own Words: Interviews with 35 Incarcerated Middle Eastern Terrorists," *Terrorism and Political Violence* 15 (1) (Spring 2003), pp. 181, 183.

20 Lou Michel and Dan Herbeck, *American Terrorist: Timothy McVeigh and the Oklahoma City Bombing* (New York: Regan Books, 2001), 166.

21 J. Bowyer Bell, "Terror: An Overview," in Livingston, 38.

22 George Habash is quoted in Bowman H. Miller and Charles A. Russell, "The Evolution of Revolutionary Warfare: From Mao to Marighella to Meinhof," in Kupperman and Trent, 191.

23 Kupperman and Trent, 5.

24 Christopher C. Harmon, *Terrorism Today* (London: Frank Cass, 2000), 111.

25 According to the U.S. Department of State's Annual "Country's Report on Terrorism."

26 Miller and Russell, 193.

27 Ibid.

28 Kupperman and Trent, 52.

29 www.animalliberationfront.com, accessed July 21, 2003.

30 Amazon.com website, www.amazon.com, accessed July 21, 2003.

31 Ibid.

32 "Pipe Bombs: Low-Tech, Lethal Tools of Terror," www.cnn.com/US/9607/27/pipe.bomb.explain/.

33 One such site, Raisethefist.com, described how to build all kinds of bombs from crude pipe bombs to very potent explosives based on ammonium nitrate fertilizer mixed with gasoline. After the operator of the anarchist site and writer of the guide to explosives was arrested in early 2002, it was no longer accessible. A successor site did not carry the guide.

34 Simon Reeve, *The New Jackals: Ramzi Yousef, Osama bin Laden and the Future of Terrorism* (Boston, MA: Northeastern University Press, 1999), 146.

35 Michel and Herbeck, 164, 165.

36 Walter Laqueur, *A History of Terrorism* (New Brunswick, NJ: Transaction Publishers, 2002), 59.

37 Harmon, 113.

38 Adam Dolnik, "Die and Let Die: Exploring Links between Suicide Terrorism and Terrorist Use of Chemical, Biological, Radiological, and Nuclear Weapons," *Studies in Conflict and Terrorism* 26 (1) (January–February 2003), p. 25.

39 Eagleburger is quoted in Christoph Reuter, *Mein Leben ist eine Waffe* (Munich: Bertelsmann, 2002), 95.

40 Bruce Hoffman, "The Logic of Suicide Terrorism," *Atlantic Monthly*, June 2003, 40.

41 Nasra Hassan, "An Arsenal of Believers," *New Yorker*, November 19, 2001, 39.

42 Ibid.

43 Hoffman, "The Logic of Suicide Terrorism," 42.

44 See Dolnik, 22–27.

45 Reuter, 128.

46 Hassan, 41.

47 Reuter, 349.

48 Dolnik, 24.

49 Martin Kramer, "The Moral Logic of Hizballah," in Walter Reich, ed., *Origins of Terrorism* (New York: Cambridge University Press, 1990), 144.

50 Robert A. Pape, "The Strategic Logic of Suicide Terrorism," *American Political Science Review* 97 (3) (August 2003), p. 343.
51 Reuter, 344–45.
52 Ibid., 356, 358.
53 Michael Radu, "Radical Islam and Suicide Bombers," article distributed by the Foreign Policy Research Institute, October 21, 2003.
54 Aaron Baruch Horwitz, "Charisma, Repression, and Culture: The Making of a Suicide Terrorist," unpublished senior thesis, Department of Political Science, Columbia University.
55 Mia Bloom, *Dying to Kill: The Allure of Suicide Terror* (New York: Columbia University Press, 2005), 94.
56 Ibid., 95.
57 Ibid.
58 Miller and Russell, 195.
59 Michael D. Greenberg et al., *Maritime Terrorism: Risk and Liability* (Santa Monica, CA: Rand Corporation, 2006), 27.
60 Harmon, 113.
61 Barton Gellman, "The Cyber-Terror Threat," *Washington Post*, weekly edition, July 1–14, 2002, 6.
62 Robert J. Bunker, "Weapons of Mass Disruption and Terrorism," *Terrorism and Political Violence* 12 (1) (Spring 2000), p. 40.
63 Ibid.
64 Robert Kupperman and Jeff Kamen, *Final Warning: Averting Disaster in the New Age of Terrorism* (New York: Doubleday, 1989), 109.
65 Bunker, 35.
66 The Tamil Tigers' poison gas attack is mentioned by Bruce Hoffman, "A Nasty Business," *Atlantic Monthly*, January 2002 (retrieved from the ProQuest database on August 10, 2003).
67 David Claridge, "Exploding the Myth of Superterrorism," *Terrorism and Political Violence* 11 (4) (Winter 1999), p. 136.
68 Rohan Gunaratna and Peter Chalk, "Terrorist Training and Weaponry," in *Counter Terrorism*, 2nd ed., October 2002, Jane's, www.janes.com, accessed June 20, 2003·
69 Graham T. Allison et al., *Avoiding Nuclear Anarchy* (Cambridge, MA: MIT Press, 1996), 73.
70 Gunaratna and Chalk.
71 Graham T. Allison, "How to Stop Nuclear Terror," *Foreign Affairs* (January–February 2004), www.foreignaffairs.org, accessed October 4, 2004.
72 The existence of ISIS's WMD program was revealed by Joby Warrick, "ISIS planned chemical attack in Europe, new details on weapons program revealed." *Washington Post*, July 11, 2022, https://www.washingtonpost.com/national-security/2022/07/11/isis-chemical-biological-weapons/, accessed July 28, 2022.
73 Jessica Stern, *The Ultimate Terrorists* (Cambridge, MA: Harvard University Press, 1999), 7–8.
74 Judith Miller, Stephen Engelberg, and William Broad, *Germs: Biological Weapons and America's Secret War* (New York: Simon & Schuster, 2001), 39.
75 Ibid., 154.
76 Ibid., 215.
77 According to an Associated Press report. See "Ashcroft: Nuke Threat the Largest Danger," www.yahoo.com/news?tmpl=story&u=/ap/20050128/, accessed January 28, 2005.

9 Organizational Structures, State Sponsors, and the Financing of Terror

Traditionally, most terrorist movements have organized along the lines of the predominant hierarchical model of other organizations, whether they were of the legitimate kind, such as governments or corporations, or the illegitimate variety, such as crime syndicates. One leader or a group of leaders occupy the top of the organizational pyramid, while lieutenants and rank-and-file members populate the lower levels. The chain of command here is comparable to that in the military in that decisions are made at the top and communicated to and carried out by those below. The Provisional Irish Republican Army (IRA), for example, has been described as a "hierarchically-organized authoritarian structure ensuring both operational and non-operational efficiency."[1] Similarly, the Lebanese Hezbollah has been known to be governed "on the national and local level by the supreme political-religious leadership, composed of a small and select group of Lebanese *ulama* [community of learned men expressing the true content of Islam]."[2] The oldest among the Palestinian militant groups were perfect examples of hierarchical organizations built around forceful leaders—from Yassir Arafat's Palestinian Liberation Organization (PLO) and Al Fatah to the Abu Nidal Organization, George Habash's Popular Front for the Liberation of Palestine, and Abu Abbas's Palestine Liberation Front. The absolute commitment to the causes of their group displayed by the Black Tigers, the Liberation Tigers of Tamil Eelam's (LTTE) suicide brigade in Sri Lanka, and of all Tamil Tigers has been related to the strict hierarchical indoctrination and command system under the control of LTTE's charismatic founder Velupillai Prabhakaran. Similarly, under the leadership of Abdullah Ocalan, who was arrested in 1999 and put behind bars in Turkey, the Marxist Kurdistan Workers Party was commanded from the top.

However, many terrorist movements increasingly abandoned the hierarchical structure and adopted the "leaderless resistance" principle once practiced by the Communist Party. In a 1992 pamphlet, Louis Beam, a notorious American right-wing extremist, explained the advantages of dropping the hierarchical organization model as a means of preventing government agents from infiltrating and destroying the movement. Instead, the idea is to have all groups and individuals operate independently from one another and from a central command. According to Beam,

> At first glance, such a type of organization seems unrealistic, primarily because there appears [to be] no organization. The natural question thus arises as to how are the "Phantom cells" and individuals to cooperate with each other when there is no intercommunication or central direction? The answer to this question is that participants in a program of Leaderless Resistance through Phantom cells or individual action must know exactly what they are doing, and how to do it. It becomes the responsibility of the individual to acquire the necessary skills and information as to what is to be done. This is by no means as impractical as it appears, because it is certainly true that in any movement, all persons involved have the same general outlook, are acquainted with the same philosophy, and generally react to a given situation in similar ways.[3]

When he wrote the article, Beam had first-hand experience with the vulnerability of hierarchical organizations. He had been the Grand Dragon of the Texas Knights of the Ku Klux Klan and presided as the leader from the top of its organizational pyramid. For a long time, law enforcement agencies were very successful in penetrating the Klan organizations. Disillusioned with this sort of scrutiny, Beam joined the White Supremacy group Aryan Nations in order to promote and practice the leaderless cell concept. While acknowledging that independent cells or lone wolves needed to keep up with the "organs of information distribution such as newspapers, leaflets, computers, etc.," Beam failed to mention that it fell to leaders to provide such motivational and informational resources. But by emphasizing the responsibility of the individual in the leaderless resistance model, Beam recognized fully well that one person or a very small group is able to function as a "patriotic" resistance cell against "state tyranny."[4] The Oklahoma City bomber Timothy McVeigh was a perfect example of the functioning of an independent cell. He had a co-conspirator and friends who knew of the plot. There is no reason to believe that McVeigh received direct instructions, assistance, or financial resources from higher-ups in right-wing organizations. But he kept himself informed about the radical antigovernment sentiments in these circles and read fiction and nonfiction that detailed how to vanquish federal agents. Mir Aimal Kansi, a Pakistani who attacked and killed employees at the entrance to the CIA headquarters near Washington, DC, in 1993, acted as a one person or leaderless cell in a larger cause—the holy war declared by Islamic extremists against the United States.

Secular right-wing and left-wing organizations, single-issue groups, and religiously motivated movements embraced the concept of "leaderless cells" before and after Louis Beam discovered and promoted it. For example, when the founders of the Baader-Meinhof group and the Red Army Faction were in prison, their followers outside established "Revolutionary Cells" that continued to fight for the cause. Modern-day anarchists in the United States and elsewhere, particularly the Antifa (for antifascist) movement in Western Europe, rely on this organizational principle, as do the militia movements, the Animal Liberation Front, the Earth Liberation Front, and a host of other single-issue movements in the United States and Europe.

For many extremists, terrorism becomes "a career as much as a passion."[5] They become full-time or professional terrorists in contrast to others who are part-time or amateur terrorists. The members of the Marxist terror groups of the 1970s and 1980s became professional terrorists, if only because they had to operate underground; many committed adherents of the Far-Right antigovernment movements fall into the amateur category. As long as leaders (who tend to be full-timers) articulate the ideology of a particular movement, groups with predominantly professional members and those with overwhelmingly amateur adherents both prefer increasingly the leaderless resistance model.

Jihadis too, have bought into this principle. Thus, the so-called *Encyclopedia of Jihad*, at times available online, "provides instructions for creating 'clandestine activity cells,' with units for intelligence, supply, planning and preparation, and implementation."[6] Pointing out that this trend poses particular problems for law enforcement in the West, Jessica Stern has noted,

> In one article on the "culture of jihad" available on-line, a Saudi Islamist urges bin Laden sympathizers to take action without waiting for instructions. "I do not need to meet the Sheikh [Osama bin Laden] and ask his permission to carry out some operation," he writes, "the same as I do not need permission to pray, or to think about killing the Jews and the Crusaders that gather on our lands."[7]

But leaders remain crucial in one respect: Without leaders taking up a cause, formulating a philosophy, and convincing others to embrace what they preach, there will be neither hierarchical movements nor independently operating cells. Even when forceful individuals take the initiative, terrorist cells or larger organizations emerge only when actual or potential domestic and/or international factions are sympathetic to a particular cause. Only a few in such constituencies may favor a violent course of action and pursue it actively, but sympathizers are crucial in terms of hideouts, financial support, and reaction to counterterrorist measures.

The Internet that facilitates all kinds of social networks is also instrumental in connecting networks of dispersed cells devoted to political violence. In the process, new types of networks of groups, cells, or individuals, whether criminal or terrorist in nature, confront governments in a new type of conflict—what experts call "netwar."[8] The term *netwar* has a double meaning, indicating in the first place a cell-based organizational mode or network and, second, such networks' strong reliance on the Internet and other means of modern communication technology in order to communicate, coordinate, and indoctrinate. Or, to put it differently, the terrorists (or criminals) "depend on using network forms of organization, doctrine, strategy, and technology."[9] Recognizing that relatively new terrorist groups differ in their organizational philosophy and practice from older terrorist organizations, Michele Zanini observed,

> The rise of networked arrangements in terrorist organizations is part of a wider move away from formally organized state-sponsored groups to privately financed looser networks of individuals and subgroups that may have strategic guidance but enjoy tactical independence. Related to these shifts is the fact that terrorist groups are taking advantage of information technology to coordinate activities of dispersed members. Such technology may be deployed by terrorists not only to wage information warfare, but also to support their own networked organizations.[10]

Whether understood mostly as leaderless resistance cells that otherwise operate along traditional lines or as a trend toward the netwar principle that utilizes information technology, the basic idea of moving away from the strictly hierarchical organization was embraced by all kinds of domestic and transnational terrorist groups beginning in the 1980s. Two types of organizations in particular adopted the cell-based network mode early and wholeheartedly—the far right in the United States and Europe and extremist Islamic groups around the world. According to Michael Whine, "These types of organizations, comprised of geographically far-flung, radical, non-state components make them ideal users of networks and proponents of Netwar."[11] Well before the attacks of September 11, 2001, Zanini described a transnational Arab terrorism network that was different from traditional organizations of this kind in that it consisted of a variety of relatively autonomous groups. According to Zanini,

> The most notorious element of the network is Osama bin Laden, who uses his wealth and organizational skills to support and direct a multinational alliance of Islamic extremists. At the heart of this alliance is his own inner core group, known as Al-Qaeda ("The Base"), which sometimes conducts missions on its own, but more often in conjunction with other groups or elements in the alliance.[12]

What eventually became the most extensive terrorist network ever began as Al Qaeda's own move toward the cell model. Beginning in the mid-1990s, bin Laden sent trusted followers into many countries and regions to establish a global network of cells. In 1994, the first and perhaps most important of these cells was established in the United Kingdom.

The whole extent of the European cells became clear in the months and years after 9/11. During the trial of Al Qaeda operatives who had plotted to blow up a U.S. military base in Belgium, one of the prosecutors told the court that defendants had "established a 'spider's web' of Islamic radicals plotting attacks and recruiting fighters in Europe for al-Qaida and the now-deposed Taliban in Afghanistan."[13]

But the Al Qaeda network alone was not sufficient for bin Laden's grand design. In 1998, he convened a meeting in Afghanistan that was attended by the leaders of autonomous Islamic groups, among them the physician Ayman al-Zawahiri, the head of Egypt's Islamic Jihad, who soon thereafter became bin Laden's right-hand man. Also present were the leaders of Egypt's Gama'a al-Islamiyya, representatives of radical Pakistani groups, and the head of Bangladesh's Islamic Jihad. As a result of this meeting, the Al Qaeda leader established what he called the International Islamic Front (IIF) for Jihad against the Jews and Crusaders, a quickly growing international alliance of existing groups in exclusively or partially Muslim countries. Although up to then strictly reserved for Sunni Muslims, Al Qaeda also reached out to and cooperated with Shi'ite groups, in particular the Lebanese Hezbollah, or Party of God, one of the best-organized—albeit hierarchical—organizations. Hezbollah is known as a Lebanese organization with interests in neighboring countries, but the group has supporters, if not cells, in North and South America, Africa, and Europe as well. Last but not least, as a result of his growing fame as an anti-American and anti-Western mastermind of terror, bin Laden inspired the establishment of numerous new cells in many parts of the world.

Taken together, the Al Qaeda cells and the IIF's network of associated but independent organizations, many of which contain a multitude of nodes, formed an expansive terrorist network with a presence on most continents and in dozens and dozens of countries. The organizations that bin Laden put together corresponded in many respects to the archetypal netwar design as described by theorists:

> Ideally, there is no single, central leadership, command, or headquarters—no precise heart or head that can be targeted. The network as a whole (but not necessarily each node) has little to no hierarchy; there may be multiple leaders. Decision making and operations are decentralized, allowing for local initiative and autonomy.
>
> The capacity of this design for effective performance over time may depend on the existence of shared principles, interests, and goals—perhaps an overreaching ideology—which spans all nodes and to which the members subscribe in a deep way.[14]

To be sure, as the head and heart of Al Qaeda and the IIF network, bin Laden was something like a chairman of the board, with al-Zawahiri as the chief executive officer at his side. Trusted associates headed the following committees with responsibilities in specific areas:

- The Political Committee, or *Shura*: Responsible for issuing religious edicts or fatwa that justify and even order actions in the name of Islamic law—among them, terror against infidels.
- The Military Committee: Responsible for planning specific attacks and in charge of managing Al Qaeda's training camps.
- The Finance Committee: Responsible for the fundraising, budgeting, and financing of Al Qaeda's living and operational expenses.
- The Foreign Purchase Committee: Responsible for the acquisition of technical equipment (e.g., computers), weapons, and explosives.
- The Security Committee: Responsible for intelligence, counterintelligence, and the protection of Al Qaeda leaders and facilities.[15]

This elaborate organizational setup was first utilized during bin Laden's stay in the Sudan and later on in Afghanistan, where the Al Qaeda leader and his associates felt safe. An estimated 20,000 or so members of dozens of autonomous and affiliated groups and cells were trained by Al Qaeda operatives in camps in Afghanistan, the Philippines, Indonesia, Australia, Malaysia, and elsewhere. At the same time, Al Qaeda provided associated cells with financial resources, weapons, and logistics.[16]

After 9/11, when Al Qaeda's main hub in Afghanistan was lost, the network's secondary hubs (headquarters/camps of autonomous organizations) and nodes or cells became crucial to continuing the fight for the cause and to planning and carrying out terrorist activities. By 2003, terrorism expert Rohan Gunaratna explained,

> With the removal of its main Afghan base in October 2001, Al-Qaeda's leadership is now looking to associated groups to advance their territorial aims, as well as support Al-Qaeda's universal jihad. To this end, its organizers, trainers, financiers and human couriers have dispersed and are moving around the world to provide support to these groups.[17]

Although in hiding, bin Laden continued "to inspire many of the operatives he trained and dispersed, as well as smaller Islamic extremist groups and individual fighters who share his ideology."[18] But bin Laden was no longer involved in important decisions as he had been before when he personally "approved all al Qaeda operations, often selecting the targets and operatives."[19]

In the post-9/11 era, the following autonomous organizations were among the increasing number of groups that were part of the Al Qaeda/IIF network of terror:

- *Abu Sayyaf Group*, a small separatist group fighting for the establishment of an independent Muslim state in the southern Philippines. The group engaged in kidnappings for ransom, assassinations, and bombings and expanded its operations into Malaysia.
- *'Asbat al Ansar* (League of Followers), a Lebanese Sunni group that committed terrorism against domestic and international targets (among them, Americans).
- *Al-Gama'a al-Islamiyya* (Islamic Group, or IG), Egypt's largest militant organization, which conducted many terrorist attacks inside Egypt. Senior members of the group signed Osama bin Laden's 1998 fatwa that declared war against the United States.
- *Al-Jihad*, also called Egyptian Islamic Jihad, an extremist group founded in the 1970s, merged with Al Qaeda/IIF in 2001 but retained the ability to conduct independent operations.
- *Harakat ul-Mujahidin* (Movement of the Warriors, HUM), a radical Pakistani group that committed terrorist acts in Kashmir. Fazlur Rehman Khalil, the longtime leader of HUM, was among the cosponsors of Osama bin Laden's 1998 declaration of war against the United States.
- *Jemaah Islamiya* (JI), an extensive terrorism network in Southeast Asia with hubs and cells in Indonesia, Malaysia, southern Thailand, and the southern Philippines. The group cultivated strong ties to Al Qaeda. Many of JI's followers received training in bin Laden's training camps in Afghanistan as well as financial and logistical assistance. JI was responsible for the 2002 bombings of a Bali nightclub and the 2003 truck bombing of the Marriott Hotel in Indonesia's capital, Jakarta.
- *Lashkar-e-Tayyiba* (Army of the Righteous, LET), a radical Sunni group in Pakistan with ties to Al Qaeda. Abu Zubaydah, a close bin Laden associate, was arrested in early 2002 in a LET safe house in Faisalabad, Pakistan.

Al Qaeda's network structure proved crucial after the central leadership had fled Afghanistan and remained in hiding for many years. In some ways, Al Qaeda Central's expansion, especially after 9/11, resembled the organizational model of those multinational corporations that grow through mergers and acquisitions in different parts of the world and leave most, if not all, decision-making to the various national or regional affiliates. In the case of Al Qaeda, its "peripheral elements are minimally dependent on its core leadership."[20] But just as the headquarters of multinational corporations push for increased brand recognition and demand for their product, Al Qaeda uses virtual propaganda for the marketing of its brand of ideology. According to an early 2009 assessment,

Physical sanctuary in Pakistan has provided immense value to al-Qa'ida's efforts to regain control over the movement, and it has allowed the core group to better enable its affiliated organizations. The organization has expanded through selective mergers and affiliations in Somalia, Yemen, South Africa, West Africa, the Levant and Algeria. The al-Qa'ida affiliates that developed in these regions present a lesser, yet persistent threat strengthening the brand, further perpetuating the movement. Affiliate organizations offer greater opportunities for al-Qa'ida as well as increased risk due to loss of control of its message, brand and target selection. Despite the risks, al-Qa'ida has continued to expand.[21]

To be sure, just as corporate mergers are not without risks, the addition of cells and hubs to a virtual network may prove problematic if the individual parts move away from the objectives of the core. That happened as ISIS became the most prominent terrorist organization that attracted thousands of foreign fighters to establish, build, and defend the proclaimed caliphate. Since ISIS's leadership core had expertise in media and communication, computer technology, and guerrilla warfare, some terrorist groups switched their allegiance from Al Qaeda to ISIS. Such opportunistic moves benefitted new ISIS affiliates, for example, Al-Shabaab in Somalia that established its own media center with the assistance of ISIS experts. Others vacillated between their allegiance for one or the other group or split into pro-Al Qaeda and pro-ISIS factions.

ISIS: Organized Like a Police State

During the post-9/11 decade when bin Laden and Al Qaeda Central were widely accepted as leaders of the global jihadi movement, more spiritual than operational, though, a charismatic and ruthless jihadi rose in Iraq following the fall of Saddam Hussein as a result of the U.S. invasion and occupation of the country: The Jordanian-born Abu Musab al-Zarqawi who had spent time with Al Qaeda and the Taliban in Afghanistan before and after 9/11. Upon his return to Iraq, al-Zarqawi established Al Qaeda in Iraq, pledging his and his group's allegiance to Osama bin Laden. By 2005 he declared unilaterally a total war against Shi'ites in Iraq and launched many violent attacks. Al Qaeda Central protested when its Iraqi affiliate brutally executed Muslims and Westerners. But by that time al-Zarqawi was already the new star in the jihadi movement and on the FBI's list of most wanted terrorists with a $25 million reward for information leading to his capture, the same amount offered for such information about bin Laden.

After Al-Zarqawi was killed in 2006 during a U.S. airstrike, Al Qaeda in Iraq declined rapidly. This changed in 2010, when Abu Bakr al-Baghdadi became the leader of the group that by then had taken the name of Islamic State in Iraq (ISI). As most leaders of Al Qaeda Central were killed by drone strikes or arrested and the group weakened, the ISI leadership implemented step by step its well-laid plan to recruit and train a substantial number of fighters and thereafter conquer territory in Syria as a beachhead for an all-out assault on Iraq and eventually beyond. With a considerable footprint in Syria, the group called itself the Islamic State in Iraq and Syria (ISIS) or Islamic State in Iraq and the Levant (ISIL) before in 2014 declaring itself the Caliphate in charge of all Muslims.

In mid-2015, based on the reality of the jihadi movement, FBI Director James Comey said that ISIS was far more dangerous for the American homeland than Al Qaeda. He explained that

> the threat that ISIL presents to the United States is very different in kind, in type, in degree than Al Qaeda. ISIL is not your parent's Al Qaeda, it's a very different model. And by virtue of that model, it's currently the threat that we are worried about in the homeland most of all.[22]

Based on documents attributed to a killed ISIS leader with the code name Haji Bakr and investigative reports, the German news magazine *Der Spiegel* revealed in 2015 how ISIS planned in every detail the conquest of land and the domination of people. To begin with, followers were recruited for what they were told was the opening of a new missionary project. From the men attending instruction sessions, several were chosen and recruited to spy on the people of their villages. The plan was from the outset to establish a police state in which the group would have total control over the populace. To that end, spies were asked to do the following:

- List the powerful families;
- Name the powerful individuals in these families;
- Find out their sources of income;
- Name names and the sizes of (rebel) brigades in the village;
- Find out the names of their leaders, who control the brigades and their political orientation; Find out their illegal activities (according to Sharia law), which could be used to blackmail them if necessary.

Those selected as spies were told to note whether someone was a criminal or a homosexual, or was involved in a secret affair, so as to have ammunition for blackmailing later. Some were ordered to marry the daughters of influential families to gain influence in communities.[23] The blueprint also provided for the appointment of provincial commanders and councils with detailed prescriptions for the establishment and running of schools, daycare centers, a transportation system, and, most of all, a total surveillance system. As reported in *Der Spiegel*, "The nucleus of this godly state would be the demonic clockwork of a cell and commando structure designed to spread fear."[24]

With total control in the conquered territories, the Islamic State called on like-minded brothers, sisters, and whole families in the Muslim world and in the Western diaspora to immigrate to the Islamic State to strengthen the Caliphate and create a new generation of devoted Salafis and jihadis. As FBI Director Comey noted, "They [ISIS propagandists and recruiters] are preaching through social media to troubled souls, urging them to join their so-called caliphate in Syria and Iraq, or if you can't join, kill them [infidels] where you are."[25] The ISIS organizational and operational model was a far more ambitious design than that of Al Qaeda.

From Bureaucratic Pseudo-State to Online Caliphate

At its height, ISIS was the best organized terrorist organization with a state-like bureaucracy that drew heavily on the experiences of men who had been civil servants under previous Iraqi and Syrian administrations. Voluntarily or under duress these ISIS administrators implemented and recorded the enforcement by the letter of extreme moral codes and the detailed system of taxation. In 2018 when Rukmini Callimachi of the *New York Times* located stacks of ISIS documents in various parts of Iraq, the handwritten records showed that the "Caliphate" had collected taxes on literally all commercial transactions and private requirements—from the sale of farming products to birth and marriage licenses. By all reports, taxes, religious donations, and the sale of oil made ISIS the richest terrorist organization ever.[26] In return, though, even opponents of ISIS praised a better delivery of public services than they had ever experienced—from regular garbage removal to the building of roads.

After Iraqi and Kurdish forces, trained and assisted by U.S. Special Forces, pushed ISIS out of most of their territories in Iraq and Syria, the organization was reduced to a shadow of its short-lived glory. With its leadership strata and jihadi fighters either dead, arrested, or scattered, ISIS became more of a virtual than an actual factor in the region.

Yet, as the second decade of the twenty-first century neared its end, there was no reason to announce ISIS's demise. Similar to what happened after Al Qaeda's hasty exodus from Afghanistan in 2001, the Islamic State could count on a number of affiliates and, more importantly, safe havens with new opportunities. Afghanistan in particular became a new venue for ISIS violence. In 2017 and 2018,

(Continued)

(Continued)

a multitude of the most lethal terrorist attacks in the capital city of Kabul and around the country were carried out and claimed by ISIS. Moreover, the organization's propaganda machine continued to spit out its words and images of hate via social media, messaging services, and the dark web. If not originating with ISIS's media center, these communications came from the group's global network of "online jihadists."

How Terrorist Groups Decline or End

Several years after 9/11, Kurth Cronin published her book "How Terrorism Ends." It was a catchy title for a most interesting, scholarly study that was not about a utopian notion of the end of terrorism but rather about the various ways terrorist groups can and do decline and vanish. She listed and explored six major ways in which terrorist groups end, namely, by decapitation, negotiation, success, failure, oppression, and reorientation. Others selected different categories. I consider the following paths to the end of terrorist groups the most important ones:

- Decapitation/Removal of Leader(s);
- Defeat by Police or Military Force;
- Success, Group achieves ultimate goal(s);
- Transition to legitimate politics;
- Lack or loss of public support.

Decapitation. Once the American-led coalition invaded Afghanistan and began its hunt for Osama bin Laden and other Al Qaeda leaders, many observers wondered whether the arrest or death of bin Laden would also mean the end of Al Qaeda and even the IIF. While bin Laden remained on the run and in hiding, an estimated two-thirds of the Al Qaeda network's leaders were either arrested or killed.[27] This offered regional and local operatives opportunities to step into leadership roles; not only al-Zarqawi saw the opportunity. Al Qaeda in the Arabian Peninsula, al-Shabaab in Somalia, and Boko Haram in Nigeria became quasi-autonomous groups. It was telling that of the Al Qaeda network's first 14 attacks after 9/11, nine were independently planned, financed, and carried out by local cells.[28] Well before bin Laden's demise finally came on May 2, 2011, his actual influence had waned—although he was still respected as a spiritual leader in jihadi circles.

The case of Al Qaeda was not the first in which the removal or fugitive status of leaders led to greater decentralization. After the founders of Germany's Red Army Faction were arrested, they were not replaced by another set of similarly influential leaders. Instead, under the pressure of intensified police actions, the RAF operated along the line of the cell model. When Hamas's spiritual leader, Sheik Ahmed Yassin, was assassinated by Israel in early 2004, Dr. Abd-al-Azis al-Rantisi immediately succeeded him. But the subsequent assassination of al-Rantisi raised questions about the organization's future structure. Hamas's next overall leader Khaled Meshal continued to live in exile in Qatar which out of necessity left decision-making room for leaders in Gaza.

The death or arrest of a strong group leader can also result in internal fights for his or her succession and weaken or even break up a group. This happened in the American setting after William Pierce, the founder and leader of the right-wing National Alliance organization, died, and after Matthew Hale, the leader of the White Supremacy World Church of the Creator group, was arrested. In both cases, the man at the top had operated like an absolute ruler who did not allow strong associates with meaningful positions at his side. As a result, there were no designated successors with enough influence to carry on.

Defeat by Policy or Military Force. Typically, the defeat of terrorist organizations comes in the form of massive police and/or military campaigns that result in the death or arrest of many members. This was the fate of Italy's Red Brigades, Uruguay's Tupamaros, and many other leftist organizations. When followed up with amnesties for both prisoners and terrorists in hiding, governments seem especially effective in rooting out political violence. When Tupamaros founder Raul Sendic Antonaccio was pardoned, he asked his comrades to abandon terrorism in exchange for peaceful political participation. The adoption of so-called repentance laws in Italy convinced a number of Red Brigades' members to throw in the towel.

Complete military defeat of a terrorist organization with a sizeable military wing is the surest way to end terrorism albeit at the expense of international humanitarian law. This was the case when in 2009 the Sri Lankan military defeated the Tamil Tiger guerrillas decisively after more than 25 years of armed conflict. In the end, not only Tiger leaders and many fighters were killed but hundreds of civilians as well, among them children.

Success, Group achieves ultimate goal(s). Of course, the most obvious reason for ending terrorism is the realization of a terrorist organization's objectives. An example here is the terrorism committed by Irgun Zvai Leumi in the British mandate in Palestine that led to the desired withdrawal of the British and the establishment of the state of Israel.

Transition. After participating in negotiations with governments some terrorist groups abandon violence, lay down their weapons, and participate in the legitimate political process. That happened in Northern Ireland, after the 1998 peace agreement between the British government and the PIRA, brokered by former U.S. Senator George Mitchell. Nearly two decades later, negotiations led to the Colombian FARC's re-entry into electoral politics (see previous chapter's discussion on whether terrorist groups succeed).

Lack of loss of *public support.* When the RAF in Germany finally abandoned violence, they admitted that they failed to enlist public support. The beginning of ETA's end as a violent political group came when public support in the Basque country declined significantly. In Northern Ireland, peace negotiations were enhanced because both the general Catholic and Protestant publics were worn out and tired of the violent struggle. The RAF ceased to exist without any public support; the IRA worked in the legitimate political process.

Seth G. Jones and Martin C. Libicki examined the reason why 268 terrorist groups that went out of existence between 1968 and 2006 ended. As Figure 9.1 shows, they found that 43 percent gave up violence and chose instead to work within the political system; 40 percent ended by police actions, 10 percent realized their objectives and thus were successful, and merely 7 percent were defeated by military force. The research found, too, that the narrower terrorist groups' objectives are the more likely it is that they achieve them. Another interesting finding was that religiously motivated groups have significantly longer lives than secular ones. However, the best indicator of the longevity of terrorist groups seems to be their size. Jones and Libicki found that groups with 10,000 or more members have the longest and those with 100 and fewer members the shortest life spans.[29]

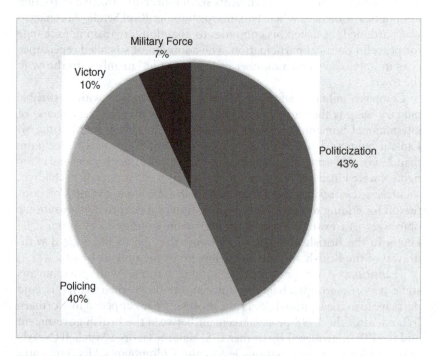

Figure 9.1 How Terrorist Groups End (1968–2006)
Source: Jones and Libicki, Rand Corporation

Terrorist Groups' Big Helpers: State Sponsors

Although terrorist organizations are nonstate actors by definition, some of them are generously sponsored or partially supported by the governments of nation-states. Decision-makers in target countries emphasize the complicity of governments because it is easier to threaten and punish state sponsors than terrorist organizations. Just as governments in the Eastern Bloc and Soviet client states elsewhere sponsored anti-Western terrorism during the Cold War, state support has remained an important factor in bolstering terrorists and their deeds.

According to three laws (section 6(j) of the Export Administration Act, section 40 of the Arms Export Control Act, and section 620A of the Foreign Assistance Act), U.S. secretaries of state are required to designate states as sponsors of terrorism if they determine that they have "repeatedly provided support for acts of international terrorism."[30] This designation triggers the following sanctions against state sponsors of terrorism:

1   A ban on arms-related exports and sales.
2   Controls over exports of dual-use items, requiring 30-day Congressional notification for goods or services that could significantly enhance the terrorist-list country's military capability or ability to support terrorism.
3   Prohibitions on economic assistance.
4   Imposition of miscellaneous financial and other restrictions, including:

- Requiring the United States to oppose loans by the World Bank and other international financial institutions;
- Exception from the jurisdictional immunity in U.S. courts of state-sponsor countries, and all former state-sponsor countries (with the exception of Iraq), with respect to claims for money damages for personal injury or death caused by certain acts of terrorism, torture, or extrajudicial killing, or the provision of material support or resources for such acts;
- Denying companies and individuals tax credits for income earned in terrorist-list countries;
- Denial of duty-free treatment of goods exported to the United States;
- Authority to prohibit any U.S. citizen from engaging in a financial transaction with a terrorist-list government without a Treasury Department license;
- Prohibition of Defense Department contracts above $100,000 with companies in which a state sponsor government owns or controls a significant interest.[31]

After Cuba was taken off the U.S. Department of State's country list of state sponsors of terrorism, only three such countries remained: Iran,

Syria, and the Democratic People's Republic of Korea (North Korea). The following excerpts from the 2020 State Department's "Country Reports on Terrorism" summarize U.S. charges against the three countries.

IRAN: Designated as a State Sponsor of Terrorism in 1984, Iran continued its terrorist-related activity in 2016, including support for Hizballah, Palestinian terrorist groups in Gaza, and various groups in Syria, Iraq, and throughout the Middle East. In 2016, Iran supported various Iraqi Shia terrorist groups, including Kata'ib Hizballah, as part of an effort to fight ISIS in Iraq and bolster the Assad regime in Syria. Iran views the Assad regime in Syria as a crucial ally and Syria and Iraq as crucial routes to supply weapons to Hizballah, Iran's primary terrorist partner. Iran has facilitated and coerced, through financial or residency enticements, primarily Shia fighters from Afghanistan and Pakistan to participate in the Assad regime's brutal crackdown in Syria. Iranian-supported Shia militias in Iraq have committed serious human rights abuses against primarily Sunni civilians and Iranian forces have directly backed militia operations in Syria with armored vehicles, artillery, and drones.

Since the end of the 2006 Israeli-Hizballah conflict, Iran has supplied Hizballah with thousands of rockets, missiles, and small arms, in direct violation of UN Security Council resolution (UNSCR) 1701. Iran provides the majority of financial support for Hizballah in Lebanon and has trained thousands of its fighters at camps in Iran.

Iran has historically provided weapons, training, and funding to Hamas and other Palestinian terrorist groups, including Palestine Islamic Jihad and the Popular Front for the Liberation of Palestine-General Command. These Palestinian terrorist groups have been behind a number of deadly attacks originating in Gaza and the West Bank, including attacks against Israeli civilians and Egyptian security forces in the Sinai Peninsula.

Iran has provided weapons, funding, and training to Bahraini militant Shia groups that have conducted attacks on the Bahraini security forces. On January 6, 2016, Bahraini security officials dismantled a terrorist cell, linked to IRGC-QF, planning to carry out a series of bombings throughout the country.

SYRIA: Designated in 1979 as a State Sponsor of Terrorism, the Assad regime continued its political and military support to a variety of terrorist groups affecting the stability of the region as the Syrian conflict entered its sixth year. The regime continued to provide political and weapons support to Hizballah and continued to allow Iran to rearm the terrorist organization. The Assad regime's relationship with Hizballah and Iran grew stronger in 2016 as the regime became more reliant on external actors to militarily fight the Syrian opposition. These groups played a critical role in the regime's seizure of eastern Aleppo in December. President Bashar al-Assad remained a staunch defender of Iran's policies, while Iran exhibited equally energetic support for the Syrian regime. Statements supporting terrorist groups, particularly Hizballah, were often in Syrian government speeches and press statements.

Over the past decade, the Syrian government has played an important role in the growth of terrorist networks in Syria through the Assad regime's permissive attitude towards al-Qa'ida and other terrorist groups' foreign terrorist fighter facilitation efforts during the Iraq conflict. Syria served for years as a hub for foreign terrorist fighters, and the Syrian government's awareness and encouragement for many years of violent extremists' transit through Syria to enter Iraq for the purpose of fighting Coalition troops, is well documented. Those very networks were among the violent extremist elements which terrorized the Syrian and Iraqi populations in 2016.

DEMOCRATIC PEOPLE'S REPUBLIC OF KOREA (North Korea). Designated in 2017 because DPRK government repeatedly provided support for acts of international terrorism, as North Korea was implicated in assassinations on foreign soil. The DPRK was previously designated as a State Sponsor of Terrorism in 1988 primarily because of its involvement in the 1987 bombing of a Korean Airlines passenger flight. The DPRK's designation was rescinded in 2008 after a thorough review found the DPRK met the statutory criteria for rescission. In 2017 the Secretary of State determined the DPRK had repeatedly provided support for acts of international terrorism since its State Sponsor of Terrorism designation was rescinded in 2008. The DPRK also has failed to take action to address historical support for acts of international terrorism. Four Japanese Red Army members wanted by the Japanese government for participating in a 1970 Japan Airlines hijacking continue to shelter in the DPRK. The Japanese government also continues to seek a full accounting of the fate of numerous Japanese nationals believed to have been abducted by DPRK state entities in the 1970s and 1980s; only five such abductees have been repatriated to Japan since 2002.

As Table 9.1 shows, North Korea appeared on the list of state sponsors of terrorism in late 2017—actually for the second time. It was first put on the U.S. State Department's list of terrorist state sponsors in 1988, the year after agents of the Pyongyang regime planted a bomb on a South Korean airliner causing it to crash. All 110 passengers and crew members were killed. Twenty years later, in 2008, North Korea was taken off the list, when the George W. Bush administration believed that it would help to negotiate an anti-nuclear deal. Even though these hopes never materialized, the country remained off the list until November 2017, when President Donald Trump put it back on. This step was, according to the president, taken in order to "increas[e] pressure on the rogue nation to abandon its pursuit of nuclear weapons."[32] It seemed that in this case the

list of state sponsors of terrorism was used for political expediency unre-
lated to a government's support of nonstate terrorism.

States that sponsor international terrorism over longer periods of
time share several characteristics: repressive governments, ambitious
political and/or religious goals that transcend their own borders, and a
tendency to blame an outside enemy (or enemies) for their own domestic
or regional problems. Governments and terrorists cooperate when both
sides determine that they benefit from such a relationship (see Table 9.2).

Table 9.1 U.S. State Department: List of State Sponsors of Terrorism
(June 2022)

Country	Designation Date
Democratic People's Republic of Korea (North Korea)	November 20, 2017
Iran	January 19, 1984
Syria	December 29, 1979

Source: U.S. Department of State.

Table 9.2 Needs of Terrorists and Motives of State Sponsors

What Terrorists Need	Why States Sponsor Terrorism	State Sponsors Listed by the U.S. Government in 2018
Bases of operation	Shared goals and grievances	Iran
Training facilities	Same enemy(ies)	Sudan
Financial support Weapons	Want terrorists to carry out violent acts	Syria
Intelligence/logistic support	Ability to deny involvement in terrorism	North Korea
Opportunities for recruitment	Avoidance of counterterrorist strikes	
Safe havens	Divert domestic radicals' frustrations to outside target(s)	

Source: Author.

Typically, state sponsors provide support in the form of training camps, safe havens, financial resources, logistical expertise, weapons, and so on. In return, terrorist groups carry out terror strikes against targets that sponsor states cannot attack without risking retaliation. For more than two decades, Iran has systematically and generously provided organizations abroad with all kinds of support that terrorists need.

The Case of Saudi Arabia

Martha Crenshaw wrote, shortly after the attacks of 9/11, that for 30 years most acts of international terrorism against the United States were committed "because of United States support for unpopular local governments or regional enemies."[33] Add to this the fact that oppressive regimes in the region were not unhappy when their most militant critics directed their fury and terror against others, namely the United States and Israel. Indeed, for the sake of protecting their own back, these regimes channeled the hatred of these groups to outside targets. To that end, some of the regimes also provided financial support to terrorists or allowed individuals and organizations within their countries to do so as long as the militants did not strike inside their borders.

While other countries in the region, especially those on the oil-rich Arabian Peninsula, supported and/or tolerated terrorism that targeted Israel, Saudi Arabia's role in financing a global network of terrorist breeding grounds was unique. According to a staff report for the National Commission on Terrorism Attacks Upon the United States,

> Saudi Arabia is a key part of our international efforts to fight terrorist financing. The intelligence community identified it as the primary source of money for al Qaeda both before and after the September 11 attacks. Fund-raisers and facilitators throughout Saudi Arabia and the Gulf raised money for al Qaeda from witting and unwitting donors and divert funds from Islamic charities and mosques. The Commission staff found no evidence that the Saudi government as an institution or as individual senior officials knowingly support or supported al Qaeda; however, a lack of awareness of the problem and a failure to conduct oversight over institutions created an environment in which such activity has flourished.[34]

But whether the Saudi government, some of the princes of the House of Saud, or their wives transferred funds directly to Al Qaeda or related cells and individuals was of less concern than the well-known practice of Saudi Arabia's rulers of indirectly facilitating preachers of hate and terror abroad. Loretta Napoleoni describes an extensive "mosque network," sponsored by Saudi Arabian funds, as "the ideological partner of the terror financial network; it complements it and is as complex and comprehensive a web as its monetary counterpart."[35]

This global mosque network is the result of a symbiotic relationship between the guardians of Wahhabism, the most fundamentalist version of Islam, and the ruling House of Saud. In return for the religious leadership's support of Saudi Arabia's rulers, the government has traditionally supported the strict implementation of Wahhabi teaching and Wahhabism's missionary zeal. Because Muslims are required to make charitable donations (known as *zakat*), a great deal of money flows into the coffers of charitable organizations in the oil-rich countries around the Persian Gulf. For many years, most of the generous giving by wealthy Saudis went to "government-linked charities with the dual mission of doing good works and propagating the country's strict Wahabbi Islam."[36] In order to divert growing opposition to their own regime, the Saudi rulers encouraged the Wahhabi colonization drive "as a release valve for the most extreme religious strains inside Saudi Arabia."[37] This was especially the case after the end of the first Persian Gulf War. According to Dan Murphy,

> In the 1990s, many of the kingdom's most militant and committed preachers and young men were sent overseas to work and preach. They were given tacit approval for militant activities abroad so long as the same methods were not brought to bear against the monarchy, which men like Osama bin Laden consider to be corrupt and illegitimate.[38]

By establishing mosques, financed by Saudi charities, Wahhabi mullahs found first of all fertile ground in those parts of the world where Muslims had not enjoyed religious freedom for a long time, namely in several of the newly independent former Soviet republics. Mosques and religious schools were also established in Africa, South and Southeast Asia, and elsewhere in the developing world. While aggressive in those regions, the approach was more discreet in the West. But the result was the same, as Napoleoni observed:

> In the West, the Mosque Network's main operations have been recruiting and fundraising. So successful have they been in performing these tasks that several mosques have now become hotbeds of potential terror fighters, who have been fed an explosive mixture of religion and political ideology.[39]

Contrary to the Saudi rulers' intention to export the domestic discontent, Osama bin Laden and his followers did not lose sight of their number-one target. Beginning in 2003 and intensifying in 2004, Al Qaeda cells mounted a deadly terrorist offensive inside Saudi Arabia. Starting in May 2003 with the truck bombing of a Riyadh housing compound for Westerners that killed 35 persons and injured more than 200, there was a multitude of bold attacks on foreigners, including one on the U.S. consulate in Jeddah in late 2004, as well as kidnappings and executions. The immediate victims of these acts of terrorism were mostly Americans and other foreigners, but the House of Saud was a target as well. Bin Laden and his followers wanted to drive foreigners, including those working in the oil industry and U.S. military personnel, out of the country and thereby weaken Saudi Arabia's economy and defense. The offensive was at least partially successful in that some foreign companies reduced their presence in Saudi Arabia. More recently, ISIS has attacked the kingdom relentlessly and made great efforts to expand its influence in the country with the goal of removing the House of Saud.

Even as the Saudi government officially fought terrorist elements within and without, wealthy individuals and groups in the country still made sizeable donations to terrorist groups in the region.

Failed and Failing States and "Brown Areas"

The typical state sponsor of terrorism displays a strong central government firmly in control of its territory, but weak states present problems with respect to terrorism as well. In the absence of a strong central government, terrorists have free reign in the territory of these countries, or parts thereof. Colombia is a good example in that the central government manages to exert its authority over some parts of the country but not in others. As a result, a number of domestic terrorist and paramilitary groups control chunks of the country and, at times, fight each other for what they perceive as valuable pieces of real estate—especially those where farmers grow coca plants, the prime ingredient in cocaine. Yemen is an example of a failed state in which effective governmental authority has not been exercised for a long time, leaving room for Al Qaeda and more recently ISIS groups.

And then there are states with functioning central governments that nevertheless contain geographical areas in which the government cannot or does not try to exert its authority and control. The territory of the Philippines, for example, contains what have been defined as "brown areas"—geographical enclaves where the government has no or little control. As a result, terrorist groups like the Abu Sayyaf group, an Al Qaeda affiliate, operate in the southern Philippines in spite of repeated efforts by government troops to destroy the terror organization once and for all.

From the American perspective, one of the most explosive "brown areas" is the so-called tri-border area (TBA), where Argentina, Brazil, and Paraguay meet. According to Benedetta Berti,

> The Triple Frontera is one of the most important commercial centers of South America, with approximately 20 thousand people transiting on a daily basis from the neighboring states to the free-trade area of Ciudad del Este in Paraguay. The intense volume of people and goods entering the TBA, together with its porous borders, are

two important factors that originally attracted criminal and armed groups to this area. Additionally, the relative ease with which money is locally laundered and transferred to and from regions overseas constitutes a very powerful incentive to maintain a base of operations in the TBA.[40]

No wonder that terrorist organizations with very different agendas and ideologies have found a haven to exchange operational expertise and financial resources. Hezbollah in particular has for decades had a strong presence here. Al Qaeda leaders obviously recognized the opportunities offered by the triple frontier region because a map of the area was found in an Al Qaeda safe house in Afghanistan. While there is no conclusive evidence that Al Qaeda Central was ever active in the TBA, jihadis have reportedly established training facilities in this brown area and are using the region as a launching pad to recruit all over Latin America. According to terrorism expert Walter Purdy, this "region is one of the world's emerging threat areas that terrorists could use to stage attacks."[41]

Had the Assad regime in Syria controlled all of the country, ISIS, al-Nusra, and other jihadist groups would not have been able to move in, conquer, and occupy chunks of territory from which to launch attacks against the central government and in the case of ISIS against neighboring Iraq. When Muammar Gaddafi ruled Libya, his regime oppressed all dissidents whether violent or nonviolent. However, after his demise the struggle for power among a multitude of factions allowed organized terrorist groups, most of all ISIS, to establish affiliates in the country.

Involuntary Host Countries

When governments invite or allow terrorists to operate, train, or hide within their borders, their countries are what one may call "voluntary hosts" of terrorist organizations and/or individual members. Sudan allowed bin Laden and a group of fellow Al Qaeda operators to live in the country. Under Gaddafi, Libya was a safe haven for various terrorists as were Cuba and other countries.

Ironically, there are far more nation-states that have become involuntary hosts of either domestic or international terrorists than there are state sponsors or voluntary hosts. As discussed earlier, because failing or failed states are unable to defeat terrorists, they often become involuntary hosts of terrorist groups. But liberal democracies are just as vulnerable to becoming involuntary host countries and hideouts for terrorists—albeit for very different reasons.

Democratic countries and their peoples provide an environment conducive to breeding their own terrorism and attract terrorists from abroad because of their commitment to freedom and civil liberties.

Political and religious tolerance, open borders, freedom of movement, increased diversity of the populace because of immigration, and political asylum opportunities are among the reasons why terrorists seek out democratic states. Terrorists know that it is much easier to operate in free societies than under repressive regimes—unless they are allied with those regimes. If there was any question about the abundance of terrorist cells in democratic states that do not share the characteristics of failing and failed states, the post-9/11 years removed such doubts. After all, investigations uncovered that Al Qaeda operatives and like-minded cells existed and operated in the United States, Canada, the United Kingdom, France, Germany, Italy, Spain, Belgium, and the Netherlands, as well as in other democracies in Europe and elsewhere. As terrorist attacks in Europe, North America, and Australia demonstrated in the second decade of the twenty-first century, ISIS adherents plotted strikes in their homelands.

Financing Terrorism

After 9/11, U.S. President George W. Bush and his secretary of state, Colin Powell, stated that money is the oxygen or lifeblood of terrorism and that the administration was therefore intensifying efforts to dry up terrorist organizations' financial resources. To follow the money trail is a solid counterterrorist tactic in that the flow of money can help to identify donors, middlepersons, and even recipient cells and their members, but there is no evidence that lack of money puts terrorist groups out of business. For sure, in order to support themselves, operate training facilities, acquire weapons, and travel, professional terrorists need substantial (and amateur terrorists need some) financial resources. And there are known cases in which terrorists had to scale down their plans because they lacked the necessary funds. Nimrod Raphaeli cites the first World Trade Center bombing in 1993 as one such incident in that "due to the lack of funds, the terrorists were unable to build as large a bomb as they had intended."[42] But by and large, terrorists have been very resourceful in financing their violence.

For a long time, Western observers assumed that Osama bin Laden's inherited fortune allowed him to support the terrorist operations in Afghanistan and around the world. But the National Commission on Terrorism Attacks Upon the United States found that bin Laden's personal wealth was far more modest than was widely assumed. According to the commission,

> Bin Laden never received a $300 million inheritance. From about 1970 until approximately 1994, he received about $1 million per year—a significant sum, but hardly a $300 million fortune that could be used to finance a global jihad.[43]

The truth is probably somewhere in between the "huge fortune" and hard-pressed-for-money versions. If there was ever any shortage of money, Peter Bergen points out that "lack of money was no impediment to al Qaeda's almost simultaneous bombings of the American embassies in Kenya and Tanzania on 7 August 1998."[44] When governments deprive terrorists of their financial resources, they hope to prevent further acts of terror. But terror organizations have proven resourceful in finding new sources to finance their operations. After the U.S. government announced that it would aggressively go after terrorist funds, bin Laden declared such measures ineffective. "By the grace of Allah," he said, "Al-Qaeda has more than three different alternative financial networks."[45]

Martin S. Navias has identified three sources of funding that are unique to terrorist organizations and difficult to cut off.[46] But there is at least one additional (and not at all unique) way to finance terrorism. These are the four most common funding sources:

- *State sponsors provide financial support.* Such support can be indirect in that the sponsoring government provides living quarters, training camps, weapons, and so on free of charge; and it can be direct in that the terrorist group receives cash payments or can draw from legally established and funded bank accounts. There are many examples of this kind of support, for example, Iran's sponsorship of Hezbollah, Libya's past sponsorship of secular Palestinian groups, Saudi Arabia's monetary support of charitable front organizations for terrorists, or Saddam Hussein's generous payments to the families of Palestinian suicide bombers. Apart from confiscating funds in banks within their borders and putting pressure on state supporters, governments that are the targets of sponsored terrorist groups have difficulties in stopping this sort of support.

- *Private organizations/individuals provide donations.* The stronger the sentiments in favor of a terrorist group's motives and goals, the greater is the likelihood of organizations collecting a large number of small donations for, and wealthy individuals donating significant sums to, terrorist groups. As Navias points out, "Significantly, such funds may be generated in terrorist host states or in states that are the target of the terrorist group's activities or are at least hostile to them."[47] This financing scheme is particularly crafty when the recipients of donations are involved not only in terrorism but in social services and legitimate political activities as well. The Palestinian Hamas, for example, provides educational opportunities, health care, and other social services while its military branch commits acts of terrorism. The Lebanese Hezbollah has carried out terrorist acts while participating in the legitimate political process.

- *Terrorists use their own legitimate businesses to fund violent acts.* This is by far the least likely way to finance terrorism, and the most obvious example is Al Qaeda. The organization was originally funded by Osama bin Laden's inheritance and by the profits of the commercial enterprises he established in the Sudan.[48] Of course, many hate groups that overtly or covertly encourage political violence rake in profits by selling books, T-shirts, posters, CDs, and other items—most often via their online stores.
- *Terrorists get involved in criminal activities to finance their operations.* The first three funding sources are significant, but many, if not most, terrorist groups are also involved in criminal activities in order to finance their operations. Typically, past and contemporary terrorists have committed bank robberies, pulled off kidnappings to extort ransom money, and engaged in profitable drug trafficking. Smuggling drugs has been a particularly popular source of funding for terrorist groups in the Middle East, in South Asia, in Southeast Asia, and in Latin America. Focusing particularly on terrorism financing in Southeast Asia, Aurel Croissant and Daniel Barlow concluded,

> Stripping away ideological goals, most terrorist organizations in the region have a strong tradition utilizing the same techniques as organized crime. Southeast Asia has long been a center for laundering and generating illegitimate funds from criminal activities such as illicit drug production and the small arms trade; decade old insurgent groups, ethnic armies, and organized crime have long used the region to acquire and channel funds to accomplish their purposes.[49]

When part of a loosely linked terrorist network, groups may transfer money to affiliates via front firms or charities. In the case of Al Qaeda and local affiliates, for example,

> Funds flow into and out of Southeast Asia to support both Al Qaeda and local organizations. Once transnational terrorist organizations have generated funds from local activities or received funds from foreign sponsors, the money is distributed to allied front organizations or individuals.[50]

South America's TBA where the borders of Argentina, Brazil, and Paraguay converge is also notorious as a source of terrorism financing. A significant part of the money that is raised by terrorist groups here or transferred to them by their supporters stems from criminal activities, such as drug trafficking and counterfeiting of goods. Affiliates and supporters of Hamas, Hezbollah, and Al Qaeda along with Latin American groups raise a great deal of money here through criminal activities. Tracing these funds is difficult because "money transfers in this area is done through informal value transfer systems, such as the hawala system" or, in other words, outside conventional banks.[51]

To get their hands on money, terrorists use different illegal methods in different parts of the world. In the West, for example, they are likely to commit credit card fraud, sell forged passports, violate intellectual property rights, and smuggle persons illegally into countries.[52] But although essential for the operation of terror organizations and their violent activities, the lack of financial resources is unlikely to reduce terrorism significantly—if at all.

The Ten Richest Terrorist Groups in the World

Running potent terrorist groups requires financial resources. To begin with, the living costs for full-time terrorists and their dependents need to be covered in addition to weapons, training camps, operational planning, off- and online propaganda, and other activities. Some organizations, such as Hamas and Hezbollah have political, military, and social service arms requiring substantial operation budgets. The financial positions of these groups over time reveal their strengths and weaknesses, the ups and downs in comparison to other terrorist organizations. Thus, Forbes' occasional lists of the ten terrorist organization in the world with the most robust financial resources provides welcome information.

Nine of the ten terrorist groups on the 2022 Forbes list were also represented in the previous, 2018 line-up. The Pakistani Lashkar-e-Taiba entity was no longer on the list and the Houthi movement in Yemen was the only newcomer. Indeed, the probably greatest surprise of the latest rankings was that the Houthis were in second place with an estimated annual income of $2 billion right behind the Taliban with $2.5 billion in the first place. At the time of the ranking, the Taliban controlled the Afghan government but not all factions of its organization. And the Iran-supported Houthis were in control of some Yemini territory and some local governance. Hezbollah, also on the receiving end of financial support from Iraq, held third place with an annual income of about $1.2 billion, most of it from the illegal activities of the group. Surprisingly, Al Qaeda and its affiliates followed with

$600 million in the fourth place followed by Hamas with $500 million and the Kurdish Workers Party (PKK) with $250 million. ISIS, once believed to be the richest terrorist group, moved with an estimated yearly income of 150 million two places down from the fifth place in 2018 to the seventh rank in the 2022 list. The Real IRA, a militant off-shoot of the Provisional Irish Republic that does not recognize the peace agreement, was with $70 million in place eight, followed by Kara'ib Hizbollah in Iraq with $50 million and the Palestinian Islamic Jihad with $35 million. Interestingly, nine of the listed entities were Muslim groups and only one, the Real IRA was non-Muslim but a secular group in Christian Northern Ireland and the Republic of Ireland.

Completely absent from the list were the many violent Far-Right extremist groups operating mostly in Europe, North America, and Australia, although some of them, too, had significant financial resources that were perhaps more difficult to estimate.

Narco-Terrorism or Narco-Funded Terrorism?

Although drug smuggling is a major source of income for many terrorist organizations, it is far more precise to speak of *narco-funded terrorism* than to use the more common term *narco-terrorism*, which blurs the differences between groups involved in political violence and those engaged in crime. For this very reason, Abraham H. Miller and Nicholas A. Damask rejected the "narco-terrorism" characterization as a "myth" exploited since the 1980s by policymakers interested in linking drug traffickers and terrorists. While not denying that cooperative ties between terrorist organizations and drug cartels exist, Miller and Damask mentioned the turf battles and often deadly clashes between the two sets of groups. They use the Latin American example to pinpoint the fundamental differences between the goals of terrorist organizations and those of drug cartels:

> Left-wing insurgents seek to create economic structures where the government controls economic enterprises. Drug traffickers desire governments where intervention in the economy is at a minimum, where ideology is of minimal concern, and where bribery is easily accepted.
>
> What brings traffickers and insurgents together are not common goals but a common enemy—the government.

The narco-terrorism idea is, consequently, based on simplistic stereotypes which emphasize the few similarities between terrorists and traffickers and ignore the many differences.[53]

A case in point is Colombia where the FARC and the smaller M19 (Movement 19 April) struggled for years with financial difficulties that weakened their recruitment and operational abilities. This changed in the early 1980s, when the left-wing revolutionary terrorists and the drug cartel found common ground: In exchange for protecting the members of the cartel from the military, the FARC was allowed to levy "a 10 percent protection tax on all coca growers in areas under its control."[54] Both sides profited greatly from the deal because their alliance led to a vast expansion of the narco-business. Nevertheless, the fundamental difference between the drug mafia and its terrorist partners remained, in that for the former the lucrative criminal activity was the ultimate objective, whereas for the FARC and M19 involvement in and financial riches from the drug business was a means to their political ends, namely to further and one day realize their ideological agendas.

Notes

1 John Horgan and Max Taylor, "The Provisional Irish Republican Army: Command and Functional Structure," *Terrorism and Political Violence* 9 (3) (Autumn 1997), p. 3.
2 Magnus Ranstorp, "Hizbollah's Command Leadership: Its Structure, Decision Making and Relationship with Iranian Clergy and Institutions," *Terrorism and Political Violence* 6 (3) (Autumn 1994), p. 304.
3 Louis Beam, "Leaderless Resistance," *Seditionist* 12 (February 1992). The pamphlet is available on several websites.
4 Ibid.
5 Jessica Stern, "The Protean Enemy," *Foreign Affairs* (July–August 2003), 28.
6 Ibid., 34.
7 Ibid., 34, 35.
8 See, for example, John Arquilla and David Ronfeldt, "The Advent of Netwar: Analytical Background," *Studies in Conflict and Terrorism* 22 (3) (July–September 1999), pp. 193–206.
9 Ibid., 193.
10 Michele Zanini, "Middle Eastern Terrorism and Netwar," *Studies in Conflict and Terrorism* 22 (3) (July–September 1999), p. 247.
11 Michael Whine, "Cyberspace—A New Medium for Communication, Command, and Control by Extremists," *Studies in Conflict and Terrorism* 22 (3) (July–September 1999), p. 232.
12 Zanini, 250.
13 Constant Brand, "Suspect Convicted in Belgian Terror Trial," *Associated Press*, September 30, 2003 (retrieved from Yahoo! News on October 1, 2003).
14 Arquilla and Ronfeldt, 197.
15 This organizational structure was described in the National Commission on Terrorism Attacks Upon the United States, "Overview of the Enemy," Staff Statement no. 15, 2–3.

16 For more on this, see Rohan Gunaratna, "Al-Qaeda's Operational Ties with Allied Groups," *Jane's Intelligence Review*, February 1, 2003.

17 Ibid.

18 "Overview of the Enemy," 12.

19 Ibid., 11.

20 The Combating Terrorism Center, "Al-Qa'ida's Five Aspects of Power," *CTC Sentinel* 2 (1) (January 2009), p. 4.

21 Ibid.

22 Comey made the remark during an appearance at the Aspen Institute, www.aspeninstitute.org/about/blog/fbi-director-isil-not-your-parents-al-qaeda, accessed July 24, 2015.

23 Christoph Reuter, "The Terror Strategist: Secret Files Reveal the Structure of the Islamic State," *Der Spiegel*, April 18, 2015, www.spiegel.de/international/world/islamic-state-files-show-structure-of-islamist-terror-group-a-1029274.html, accessed June 30, 2015.

24 Ibid.

25 Comey at the Aspen Institute.

26 For a detailed analysis of the first stack of ISIS files, see Rukmini Callimachi, "The ISIS Files," *New York Times*, April 4, 2018, www.nytimes.com/interactive/2018/04/04/world/middleeast/isis-documents-mosul-iraq.html, accessed May 22, 2018.

27 According to Marc Sageman, who compiled a biographical database of the Al Qaeda network's operatives. See Terence Henry, "Al-Qaeda's Resurgence," *Atlantic Monthly*, June 2004, 54.

28 Ibid.

29 Seth G. Jones and Martin C. Libicki, *How Terrorist Groups End* (Santa Monica, CA: Rand Corporation, 2008).

30 U.S. Department of State, "Country Reports on Terrorism," April 2008; www.state.gov/s/ct/rls/crt/2007/103711.htm, accessed January 13, 2009.

31 Ibid.

32 Michael D. Shear and David E. Sanger, "Trump Returns North Korea to List of State Sponsors of Terrorism," *New York Times*, November 20, 2017, www.nytimes.com/2017/11/20/us/politics/north-korea-trump-terror.html, accessed May 24, 2018.

33 Martha Crenshaw, "Why America? The Globalization of Civil War," *Current History* (December 2001), p. 425.

34 National Commission on Terrorist Attacks Upon the United States, "Staff Monographs," http://govinfo.library.unt.edu/911/staff_statements/index.htm, accessed July 20, 2015.

35 Loretta Napoleoni, *Modern Jihad: Tracing Dollars behind the Terror Networks* (London: Pluto Press, 2003), 128.

36 Dan Murphy, "Saudi Crackdown on Charities Seen as Incomplete," *Christian Science Monitor*, June 9, 2004, www.csmonitor.com/2004/0609/p07p02-wome.html, accessed January 31, 2004.

37 Ibid.

38 Ibid.

39 Napoleoni, 131.

40 Benedetta Berti, "Reassessing the Transnational Terrorism–Criminal Link in South America's Tri-Border-Area," *Terrorism Monitor* 6 (18) (September 22, 2008).

41 Mentioned in A. Brownfeld, "Terrorists in the Triple Frontier," *Jane's Terrorism and Security Monitor*, February 12, 2003.

42 Nimrod Raphaeli, "Financing of Terrorism: Sources, Methods, and Channels," *Terrorism and Political Violence* 15 (4) (Winter 2003), p. 60.

43 "Overview of the Enemy," 4.

44 Peter Bergen, "The Bin Laden Trial: What Did We Learn?," *Studies in Conflict and Terrorism* 24 (6) (November–December 2001), p. 430.

45 Bin Laden is cited by Raphaeli, 61.

46 Martin S. Navias, "Finance Warfare as a Response to International Terrorism," in Lawrence Freedman, ed., *Superterrorism: Policy Responses* (Malden, MA: Blackwell Publishing, 2002), 68, 69.

47 Ibid., 68.

48 Simon Reeve, *The New Jackals* (Boston: Northeastern University Press, 1999), ch. 9.

49 Aurel Croissant and Daniel Barlow, "Following the Money Trail: Terrorist Financing and Government Responses in Southeast Asia," *Studies in Conflict & Terrorism* 30 (February 2007), p. 135.

50 Ibid.

51 Berti. For more on the TBA's importance as a source for terrorist financing, see Matthew Levitt, *Hamas: Politics, Charity, and Terrorism in the Service of Jihad* (New Haven, CT: Yale University Press, 2006), 71–72.

52 Raphaeli, 61.

53 Abraham H. Miller and Nicholas A. Damask, "The Dual Myths of 'Narco-Terrorism': How Myths Drive Policy," *Terrorism and Political Violence* 8 (1) (Spring 1996), p. 124.

54 Napoleoni, 40.

Part II
Counterterrorism

10 Terrorism and American-Led Post-9/11 National Security Strategies

August 30, 2021. At the end of a tumultuous exit from Afghanistan by U.S. and allied forces the final U.S. military aircraft takes off from Hamid Karzai International Airport in Kabul. After the C-17 is in the air, Taliban fighters fire their guns into the air in celebration of the completed withdrawal of foreign forces from Afghanistan. The 20-year long war on terrorism in Afghanistan, America's longest war, has ended in this South Asian country, where the Taliban have taken over the Kabul government. In a press briefing at the Pentagon, General Kenneth F. McKenzie, the head of U.S. Central Command, notes that the mission had brought Osama bin Laden to justice along with many other Al-Qaeda co-conspirators but that it had not been a cheap mission. "The cost, in American lives, was 2,461 U.S. service members killed and more than 20,000 wounded," he says.

The costs of the total war on terrorism that the United States fought along with allies on many fronts in the 20 years after 9/11 were significantly higher. More than 900,000 persons died on all sides due to hostilities in Afghanistan, Iraq, Syria, Libya, Pakistan, Somalia, and elsewhere, among them more than 7,000 members of the U.S. military with many more injured. The total costs for the United States' treasury added up to about $8 trillion, not including "future interest costs on borrowing for the wars."[1] Yet, while the war in Afghanistan and earlier the war in Iraq ended, America's fight against jihadists abroad continued. According to Brown University's "Cost of War Project," in 2022 American soldiers were involved in counterterrorism activities in 85 countries around the globe.[2]

From the outset of the Afghanistan war, U.S. forces were supported by the International Security Assistance Forces (ISAF), established by a UN resolution and eventually commanded by NATO. At its peak, 42 countries contributed troops to ISAF. When the ISAF mission ended in 2014, it was replaced by the NATO-led Resolute Support Mission (RSM), a multinational non-combat force that was authorized by the UN through 2024. The peace agreement between the Trump administration

DOI: 10.4324/9781003289265-12

and the Taliban led to the 2021 withdrawal of U.S. forces and their RSM allies with the latter also caught and unhappy about the chaotic end of their mission.

Since American allies, especially fellow-NATO members, were affected by and heavily involved in the U.S.-led post-9/11 war on terrorism, this chapter reviews the relevant national security strategies during the presidencies of George W. Bush, Barack Obama, Donald Trump, and Joe Biden. While the focus of his three predecessors' counterterrorism strategies was on international or transnational terrorism, Biden was the first U.S. president to issue a National Strategy for Countering Domestic Terrorism besides recognizing the continuing threat of international terrorism in his National Security Strategy.

The Unexpected 9/11 Catastrophe

On September 11, 2001, at 8:30 p.m. EDT, a grave President George W. Bush addressed a shocked nation from the Oval Office. At first, he called that day's devastating attacks on American soil by transnational terrorists "acts of mass murder." But toward the end of his short speech, he declared, "America and our friends and allies join with all those who want peace and security in the world, and we stand together to win the war against terrorism."[3] Contrary to the reference to crime at the outset, the war analogy was not meant as a rhetorical exclamation mark. Not law enforcement, but the use of military force became the centerpiece of Washington's post-9/11 response to transnational terrorism and threats that the administration linked to this kind of political violence. Simon Dalby observed that after 9/11 there was "the immediate assumption that the struggle against terror was a matter best prosecuted as a matter of warfare rather than by diplomacy and police action."[4]

Although the most deadly strikes in the history of modern terrorism, the destruction of the World Trade Center and the partial demolition of the Pentagon, symbols of America's economic might and military superiority, were not the first anti-American operations masterminded by Osama bin Laden and carried out by Al Qaeda or like-minded groups or cells. But the first World Trade Center bombing of 1993, the truck bombings of U.S. embassies in Kenya and Tanzania in 1998, the strike against the USS *Cole* in 2000, and violence against Americans in Saudi Arabia and elsewhere did not register as manifestations of a major national security threat. Instead, as Ian Lesser concluded in 1999 and thus before 9/11, "most contemporary analyses of terrorism focus on terrorist political violence as a stand-alone phenomenon, without reference to its geopolitical and strategic context."[5] This was hardly surprising because the realist conceptualization of geopolitics with its focus on the nation-state and the assumption that every state tries to maximize its national interest was the guidepost of American security and foreign policy. In this understanding, threats in the international context emanate from states—especially, from powerful states. Threats from nonstate actors do not fit the realist paradigm. As a result, international relations scholars ignored terrorism as well. Martha Crenshaw observed,

> [Before 9/11] the security studies and international relations fields were not especially hospitable to scholars interested in terrorism precisely because it was not considered an important problem for the discipline or for the development of grand strategy. As an intellectual approach, it did not lend itself to abstract theory or modeling. The study of terrorism was too policy-oriented to be of serious academic significance.[6]

When experts warned of terrorism as a serious threat to America's national security and suggested that it needed to be integrated into the national security strategy, they almost always thought of nightmare scenarios: Weapons of mass destruction (WMD) in the hands of terrorists. Identifying the preoccupation with body counts as the root of a limited perception of the transnational terrorist threat, Paul Pillar concluded,

> The underlying paradigm—that terrorism is to be measured in the numbers of dead Americans, and that counterterrorism is thus largely a matter of preparing for attacks (particularly CBRN attacks) that could cause many such deaths—is shared by people with widely different appraisals of the terrorist threat and of the priority and resources that should be devoted to countering it.[7]

While the bipartisan U.S. Commission on National Security/21st Century highlighted the danger of WMD in the hands of terrorists, it also pressed for a national security strategy and policies that included threats from nonstate actors. In its "Phase I Report on the Emerging Global Security Environment for the First Quarter of the 21st Century" that was released in September 1999, the commission made the following, utterly alarming and—as 9/11 would show—prophetic assessment:

> While conventional conflicts will still be possible, the most serious threat to our security may consist of unannounced attacks on American cities by sub-national groups using genetically engineered pathogens. Another may be a well-planned cyber-attack on the air traffic control system on the East Coast of the United States, as some 200 commercial aircraft are trying to land safely in a morning's rain and fog.[8]

The commission concluded that

> Taken together, the evidence suggests that threats to American secu-
> rity will be more diffuse, harder to anticipate, and more difficult to
> neutralize than ever before. Deterrence will not work as it once did;
> in many cases it may not work at all.[9]

Although the co-chairs of the panel, former Senators Gary Hart, a
Democrat, and Warren Rudman, a Republican, as well as former U.S.
Representative Newt Gingrich, a commission member, testified before
several congressional committees, their alarming predictions received
"scant attention" as the *Financial Times* noted—belatedly—one day
after 9/11.[10] Because almost all news organizations ignored the report
completely, the public was not informed about the commission's dire
conclusions.

The National Commission on Terrorism did not fare better when
it released its report three months before the kamikaze attacks on the
World Trade Center and the Pentagon. The political class and the news
media were simply not interested. In their executive summary, the commissioners warned of dangerous groups operating inside the United
States and abroad and that their objectives were more deadly than those
of previously active terrorists.[11] The *Omaha World-Herald*, one of the
few news organizations that took notice of the report, editorialized that
the commission "envisioned a level of evil more pervasive than common
sense and experience suggest actually exists."[12] All of this changed on
September 11, 2001. Since then, as one observer noted, "American concern for national security has been almost totally focused on, some might
argue transfixed by, the problem of international terrorism and its likely
reoccurrence on American soil."[13] And Crenshaw stated,

> The attacks of September 11 propelled terrorism from obscurity to
> prominence in the wider field of international relations and foreign
> and security policy. It now took center stage in the grand strat-
> egy debate. Scholars who had previously ignored terrorism now
> acknowledged it was a major national security concern; in fact, some
> saw the threat of terrorism as an occasion for a complete reorienta-
> tion of post–cold war foreign policy.[14]

President Bush and his closest advisors did not wait for the foreign
policy establishment and international relations scholars to fit what was
widely perceived as a novel type of catastrophic terrorism into a post-
9/11 national security strategy and the nation's foreign policy priorities.
Instead, the president's remarks on September 11, 2001, and his subsequent speeches signaled the end of piecemeal, case-by-case responses
to terrorist incidents and the beginning of a newly emerging national

security strategy built around the so-called war against terrorism, or what the administration eventually came to call "global war on terrorism" and still later "the long war." This war was to be fought against terrorist organizations, groups, cells, and individuals but also—and indeed most of all—against state sponsors of terrorism. The goal was not simply to defeat the perpetrators of terrorism and their state supporters but at the same time to replace authoritarian and repressive regimes by democratic ones and thereby rid the world of terrorism or at least reduce this threat.

Seven days after 9/11, the U.S. Congress authorized President Bush

> to use all necessary and appropriate force against those nations, organizations, or persons he determines planned, authorized, committed, or aided the terrorist attacks that occurred on September 11, 2001, or harbored such organizations or persons, in order to prevent any future acts of international terrorism against the United States by such nations, organizations or persons.[15]

Two days later, in his live televised address to a joint session of Congress and the American people, the president equated conventional warfare and the terrorist attack on the World Trade Center and Pentagon when he said,

> On September the 11th, enemies of freedom committed an act of war against our country. Americans have known wars—but for the past 136 years, they have been wars on foreign soil, except for one Sunday in 1941. Americans have known the casualties of war—but not at the center of a great city on a peaceful morning. Americans have known surprise attacks—but never before on thousands of civilians. All of this was brought upon us in a single day—and night fell on a different world, a world where freedom itself is under attack.[16]

It is noteworthy that both the congressional war authorization and the presidential address mentioned not only terrorist organizations and individuals but also "nations" as targets for military action in the nation's new war against terrorism. "Every nation, in every region, now has a decision to make. Either you are with us, or you are with the terrorists," the president said. "From this day forward, any nation that continues to harbor or support terrorism will be regarded by the United States as a hostile regime."[17] Although the 9/11 attacks were masterminded by Al Qaeda's leadership and carried out by 19 of its followers, decision-makers clung to the state-centric assessments and response options of the past that were better suited for fighting against nation-states rather than nonstate actors like Al Qaeda and the terrorist organization's affiliates.

Neoconservative ideologues inside and outside the Bush administration recognized immediately that the war against terrorism offered an ideal pretext to further their agenda, which listed the toppling of Iraqi President Saddam Hussein as a priority. In the earliest months of the Bush presidency, the neocons had gained considerable influence in the White House and the Department of Defense. As deputy secretary of defense, Paul Wolfowitz in particular had pushed relentlessly for the removal of Iraq's president and the Baathist regime. According to Bob Woodward's account,

> Wolfowitz had edgy, hawkish views. The reasons for getting rid of Saddam were: It was necessary and it would be relatively easy. Wolfowitz believed it was possible to send in the military to overrun and seize Iraq's southern oil fields—1,000 wells, which had about two-thirds of Iraq's oil production—and establish a foothold. . . From the enclave, support would be given to the anti-Saddam opposition, which would rally the rest of the country and overthrow the dictator.[18]

Wolfowitz advocated an immediate attack against Iraq. He

> Argued that if there were even a 10 percent chance that Saddam Hussein had been behind the 9/11 attacks, maximum priority should be placed on eliminating that threat. He also argued that the odds in fact were far greater than one in ten.[19]

Wolfowitz and his boss, Secretary of Defense Donald Rumsfeld, failed to convince the president and other national security advisors to go to war against Saddam Hussein in Iraq or simultaneously against Al Qaeda and the Taliban in Afghanistan, but at the direction of the president, the Pentagon continued to plan for the invasion of Iraq. Just a few days after 9/11,

> Bush told [Secretary of State] Rice that the first target of the war on terrorism was going to be Afghanistan. 'We won't do Iraq now,' the president said, 'we're putting Iraq off. But eventually we'll have to return to that question.'[20]

The neocons were instrumental in shaping the Bush Doctrine and its codification in the 2002 "National Security Strategy of the United States of America," but their core ideas had been developed and expressed since the end of the Cold War.[21] In an assessment of the post-9/11 national security strategy, Simon Dalby wrote,

> Little of this geopolitical thinking is very new, although some innovations were obviously needed in a hurry in September 2001 given the novelty of Osama Bin Laden's tactics. The key themes of

American supremacy, the willingness to maintain overwhelming military supremacy over potential rivals and the proffered option of preventive war to stop potential threats from even emerging, were all sketched out in the first Bush presidency at the end of the cold war in the period following the war with Iraq in 1991 when Dick Cheney was Defense Secretary and Colin Powell and Paul Wolfowitz were at the heart of Washington's defense bureaucracy. The related key assumption that America has the right to assert its power to reshape the rest of the world to its liking also carries over from the early 1990s.[22]

The neocons' American exceptionalism trumped the tenets of realists and liberal internationalists so that the "neoconservative vision of American foreign policy provided the theoretical and policy content of the Bush doctrine which in turn underpinned the justification to invade Iraq in 2003 and depose the leadership of Saddam Hussein."[23] One expert noted that "9–11 gave the neo-cons the pretext on which to make their strategy of military primacy the operational code for the American state."[24] While a U.S.-led military coalition drove Al Qaeda and the Taliban out of Afghanistan and into Pakistan, administration officials were already planning the Iraq invasion and preparing the nation for the next front in the war against terrorism. The news media not only reported but in fact embraced the administration's arguments in favor of both military moves. Based on his content analysis of editorials and op-ed articles in elite newspapers, one scholar concluded that the Bush administration gained support for both the Afghanistan and Iraq wars "by linking security and moral indignation."[25] Presumably, the American public's strong support for both wars was influenced by media opinion-makers who bought into the administration's post-9/11 foreign policy and its "heavy dose of moralist opinion that condemned evil enemies and touted American virtues."[26]

President Bush's Strategy to Counter International Terrorism

George W. Bush's State of the Union address on January 29, 2002, his graduation speech at West Point four months later, additional statements by the president and other high administration officials, and the 2002 "National Security Strategy" contained the basic elements of America's new national security strategy, or what has been called the Bush Doctrine. As far as national security strategy and foreign policy were concerned, nothing changed in the following years. The principles enunciated in the 2002 document were also the most important components of the 2006 "National Security Strategy of the United States of America."[27] After studying the 2006 document, one foreign policy expert concluded that "one would be hard pressed to find much evidence that the president has backed away from what has become known as the Bush doctrine."[28] The following sections summarize the three most important components of the Bush Doctrine that relate to terrorism and counterterrorism according to the national security strategy.

Making the World Safer and Better

According to the preamble of the 2002 "National Security Strategy" that the president signed, "The great struggles of the twentieth century between liberty and totalitarianism ended with the decisive victory for the forces of freedom—and the single sustainable model for national success: freedom, democracy, and free enterprise."[29] The United States will use its military, political, and economic might in the service of international peace and the spread of freedom, democracy, and economic progress; 9/11 is seen as a wake-up call and an opportunity to reshape the world in the American image. For this reason, the overriding premise and rationale of the Bush Doctrine were articulated in distinctly upbeat passages, as the following excerpt attests:

> The United States will use this moment of opportunity to extend the benefits of freedom across the globe. We will actively work to bring the hope of democracy, development, free markets, and free trade to every corner of the world. The events of September 11, 2001, taught us that weak states like Afghanistan can pose as great a danger to our national interests as strong states. Poverty does not make poor people into terrorists and murderers. Yet poverty, weak institutions, and corruption can make weak states vulnerable to terrorist networks and drug cartels within their borders.[30]

The Bush administration stated explicitly that "the aim of this strategy is to help make the world not just safer but better."[31] It was left to others to speculate how the president's faith as a born-again Christian figured into his post-9/11 foreign policy mission. One international relations expert wrote that

> There is reason to believe that just as his [George W. Bush's] coming to Christ gave meaning to his previously aimless and dissolute personal life, so the war on terrorism has become, not only the defining characteristic of his foreign policy, but also his sacred mission.[32]

Preemption before Threats Become Imminent

According to the Bush Doctrine, the United States and other democracies were seriously threatened by terrorist organizations and rogue states that sponsor political violence and could supply terrorists with WMD.

Acknowledging the dangers of asymmetrical warfare, the president said at West Point,

> Enemies in the past needed great armies and great industrial capabilities to endanger the American people and our nation. The attacks of September the 11th required a few hundred thousand dollars in the hands of a few dozen evil and deluded men.[33]

In the new geopolitical setting, deterrence along the lines of the Cold War's mutual assured destruction (MAD) assumptions was thought to be obsolete and in need of being replaced by military preemption, if necessary. In President Bush's words:

> For much of the last century, America's defense relied on the Cold War doctrines of deterrence and containment. In some cases, those strategies still apply. But new threats also require new thinking. Deterrence—the promise of massive retaliation against nations— means nothing against shadowy terrorist networks with no nation or citizens to defend. Containment is not possible when unbalanced dictators with weapons of mass destruction can deliver those weapons on missiles or secretly provide them to terrorist allies. We cannot defend America and our friends by hoping for the best. We cannot put our faith in the word of tyrants, who solemnly sign nonproliferation treaties, and then systemically break them. If we wait for threats to fully materialize, we will have waited too long. Our security will require all Americans to be forward-looking and resolute, to be ready for preemptive action when necessary to defend our liberty and to defend our lives.[34]

In the Bush Doctrine, then, threats were to be dealt with before they became imminent. The 2006 "National Security Strategy" cited the Iraq Survey Group's finding that Saddam Hussein "continued to see the utility of WMD" and could have reactivated his WMD program; the document left no doubt that the invasion of Iraq and the removal of Saddam Hussein was justified according to the preemption provision of the Bush Doctrine.

Unilateral Use of Force

As the 2002 "National Security Strategy" put it, "While the United States will constantly strive to enlist the support of the international community, we will not hesitate to act alone, if necessary, to exercise our right of self-defense."[35] This position was hardly surprising because a "commitment to the maintenance of a unipolar international system and to the doctrine of preemption is unilateralist to the core."[36] In the months and years after 9/11, when Americans feared additional terror strikes, the notion of going it alone against terrorists and their state sponsors, if needed, was an easy sell for the administration.

However, unilateralism was not only part of the grand strategy that the neoconservatives pushed in the 1990s but also George W. Bush's preference before and after he became president. Once in the White House,

> Bush displayed little willingness to cater to world public opinion or to heed the cries of outrage from European countries as the United States interpreted its interest and the interests of the world in its own way. Thus, the Bush administration walked away from the Kyoto treaty, the International Criminal Court, and the protocol implementing the ban on biological weapons.[37]

In sum, then, the 9/11 attacks, the threat of further strikes, and the war against terrorism were seized by the Bush administration as an opportunity to enshrine the principle of unilateralism along with the right to preemptive action and the use of U.S. superiority to reshape the world according to American values as the core components of America's national security strategy.

Concluding that "in its trial run, the Bush Doctrine has been found wanting," Andrew Bacevich suggested that there was an urgent need for Congress "to abrogate that doctrine" and thereby reduce "the likelihood that we will see more Iraqs in the future."[38]

President Obama's Strategy to Counter International Terrorism

In early April 2009, Michael Leiter, director of the National Counterterrorism Center, signaled a more holistic approach to America's national security strategy that differed from the centrality of the war on terrorism in the Bush Doctrine, when he said,

> Counterterrorism is part of larger U.S. policy. Counterterrorism rarely, if ever, should be the lead in that policy. The challenges we face—the terrorism challenges we face are different in different regions of the world and are interconnected to broader U.S. policy interests. Counterterrorism should be, in most cases, the tail, and we should not wag the broader policy dog. I think it is important for me to say that because I want to make clear that the counterterrorism community understands its role. We should be influencing a lot of policy, we should be informing a lot of policy, but ultimately there are broader issues here. Whether or not it's in Pakistan and Afghanistan or Somalia, counterterrorism is not the only interest the U.S. government has.[39]

A few weeks later, in his commencement address at the U.S. Military Academy at West Point, President Obama outlined a new security doctrine that differed from the Bush Doctrine in two main points. First, Obama did not mention at all the need and right for preemptive strikes before threats become imminent that his predecessor had declared and acted upon in the case of Iraq. This shift was hardly surprising since Obama had repeatedly characterized the Iraq intervention "a war of choice" in contrast to what he called "a war of necessity" in Afghanistan against Al Qaeda and Taliban insurgents. Second, without mentioning his name or referring to his doctrine, Obama repudiated his predecessor's go-it-alone strategy by emphasizing the need for multilateral cooperation and alliances. At West Point, he said pointedly,

> The burdens of this century cannot fall on our soldiers alone. It also cannot fall on American shoulders alone. Our adversaries would like to see America sap its strength by overextending our power. And in the past, we've always had the foresight to avoid acting alone. We were part of the most powerful wartime coalition in human history through World War II. We stitched together a community of free nations and institutions to endure and ultimately prevail during a Cold War. Yes, we are clear-eyed about the shortfalls of our international system. But America has not succeeded by stepping out of the currents of cooperation—we have succeeded by steering those currents in the direction of liberty and justice, so nations thrive by meeting their responsibilities and face consequences when they don't.[40]

Obama's positions were detailed in the May 2010 "National Security Strategy." This document elaborated on the aforementioned remark from Michael Leiter, namely that counterterrorism should mostly be the tail on the whole national security policy dog. After a reference to the wars in Iraq and Afghanistan, the following paragraph put the fight against terrorism into the larger perspective of global threats:

> Yet these wars—and our global efforts to successfully counter violent extremism—are only one element of our strategic environment and cannot define America's engagement with the world. Terrorism is one of many threats that are more consequential in a global age. The gravest danger to the American people and global security continues to come from weapons of mass destruction, particularly nuclear weapons. The space and cyberspace capabilities that power our daily lives and military operations are vulnerable to disruption and attack. Dependence upon fossil fuels constrains our options and pollutes our environment. Climate change and pandemic disease threaten the security of regions and the health and safety of the American people. Failing states breed conflict and endanger regional and global

security. Global criminal networks foment insecurity abroad and bring people and goods across our own borders that threaten our people.[41]

According to the Obama administration, a strong national security posture begins at home and includes a strong and competitive economy and educational system, and a move toward energy independence. While not surrendering the right to act unilaterally in defense of the nation and its interests, the Obama Doctrine embraced international organizations and actions within multilateral alliances. This remained President Obama's position. In his 2015 "National Security Strategy" document, he reiterated that sometimes military force is needed and that in such cases the United States will resort to military deployment, if needed unilaterally even though the preference is to act in concert with allies.

   Although there was a notable rhetorical shift from the Bush Doctrine to Obama's national security strategy concerning unilateral and multilateral actions, American forces outnumbered by far the combined coalition troops in Iraq and Afghanistan in both administrations. And while the troop level in Iraq decreased steadily after a strong and successful deployment surge in 2007, President Obama kept his campaign promise to refocus the war in Afghanistan and bolster American troop strength there significantly. A few weeks into his presidency, he summarized the objectives in Afghanistan and neighboring Pakistan when he said,

> I want the American people to understand that we have a clear and focused goal: to disrupt, dismantle and defeat al Qaeda in Pakistan and Afghanistan, and to prevent their return to either country in the future. That's the goal that must be achieved. That is a cause that could not be more just.[42]

President Trump's Strategy to Counter International Terrorism

In the introduction of his administration's first "National Security Strategy" document of December 2017,[43] President Donald Trump reiterated his campaign promises, namely, to "Make America Great Again" and to enact "America First" policies. In particular, he wrote,

> The American people elected me to make America great again. I promised that my Administration would put the safety, interests, and well-being of our citizens first. I pledged that we would revitalize the American economy, rebuild our military, defend our borders, protect our sovereignty, and advance our values. During my first year in office, you have witnessed my America First foreign policy in action.

We are prioritizing the interests of our citizens and protecting our sovereign rights as a nation. America is leading again on the world stage [. . .]

When I came into office, rogue regimes were developing nuclear weapons and missiles to threaten the entire planet. Radical Islamist terror groups were flourishing. Terrorists had taken control of vast swaths of the Middle East. Rival powers were aggressively undermining American interests around the globe. At home, porous borders and unenforced immigration laws had created a host of vulnerabilities. Criminal cartels were bringing drugs and danger into our communities. Unfair trade practices had weakened our economy and exported our jobs overseas. Unfair burden-sharing with our allies and inadequate investment in our own defense had invited danger from those who wish us harm. Too many Americans had lost trust in our government, faith in our future, and confidence in our values.

Nearly one year later, although serious challenges remain, we are charting a new and very different course [emphasis added].

Although President Trump claimed that he and his administration had embarked on a completely new foreign and security policy, this was hardly the case with respect to actual actions taken in the name of counterterrorism. Although President Trump renounced President Obama's counterterrorist policies, neither his administration's declared security strategy nor actual actions of the U.S. military in Afghanistan, Iraq, Syria, Yemen, and several African countries signaled fundamentally different approaches. Indeed, Trump like Obama before him sent more troops to Afghanistan, more into the fight against ISIS, and kept U.S. Special Forces engaged in Yemen, African countries, and even more so in the fight against ISIS in Iraq and Syria. The difference was mostly rhetorical in that Trump's language was far harsher and far more aggressive than Obama's measured words.

While by and large quite similar to the policies of his two predecessors, President Trump's 2018 "National Strategy for Counterterrorism of the United States of America" made a few notable points. To begin with, obviously in a rejection of President Obama's terms "violent extremism" and "violent extremists," the Trump administration's document used the phrases "radical Islamist terrorists" and "radical Islamic terrorism."[44]

While there was no mentioning of banning Muslims from the United States or building a wall along the South-West border, President Trump's controversial promises and actions seemed implicit in the following bullet point: "This strategy places America first and emphasizes protection of the homeland—building strong borders, strengthening security at all ports of entrance into the United States."

Finally, the counterterrorism strategy set a goal that its authors must have known to be unachievable: the elimination of the terrorist threat to the United States.

President Biden's Strategy to Counter International and Domestic Terrorism

Twenty years after 9/11, in his administration's "Interim National Security Strategic Guidance," President Joe Biden made a sharp turn away from the "war on terrorism" that George W. Bush had declared immediately after those horrific attacks. Thus, the new national security strategy, issued merely weeks after the change of guards in Washington, was guided by the following principle:

> The United States should not, and will not, engage in 'forever wars' that have cost thousands of lives and trillions of dollars. We will work to responsibly end America's longest war in Afghanistan while ensuring that Afghanistan does not again become a safe haven for terrorist attacks against the United States.[45]

Biden and his national security advisers did not ignore the continued threat of international terrorism. They promised to "maintain the proficiency of special operations forces to focus on crisis response and priority counterterrorism and unconventional warfare missions" and emphasized the need for cooperation with allies abroad.

But the Biden administration's national security strategy, which was devoted to foreign policy and international relations, reflected also the president's main concern with domestic terrorism, when it stated,

> Despite significant successes against international terrorism, a diffuse and dispersed threat to Americans remains. Domestic violent extremism challenges core principles of our democracy and demands policies that protect public safety while promoting our values and respecting our laws. We must adapt our approach to counterterrorism, including by aligning our resources to evolving threats. We will work as a coordinated, unified federal government to use the full array of tools at our disposal in concert with state, local, tribal, private sector, and foreign counterparts.[46]

By mentioning "foreign counterparts" as partners of U.S. stakeholders in the fight against domestic terrorism in America, the Biden administration signaled its understanding of the dangerous international alliances between violent extremist groups within a multitude of Western countries described in Chapter 4.

The Biden administration's urgency in dealing with the domestic terrorism threat was based on the growing number of lethal attacks by violent Far-Right extremists in the preceding years—and perhaps even more so by the events of January 6, 2021, in which organized violent extremists played starring roles. On his first full day as president, Joe

Biden requested from the intelligence community (IC) a full assessment of domestic terrorist threats. In its analysis, the IC concluded with respect to domestic violent extremism (DVE) that "racially or ethnically motivated violent extremists (RMVEs) and militia violent extremists (MVE) present the most lethal DVE threats, with RMVEs most likely to conduct mass-casualty attacks against civilians and MVEs typically targeting law enforcement and government personnel and facilities..."[47] With this threat assessment in hand, Biden's national security team formulated the National Strategy for Countering Domestic Terrorism that contained four short- and long-term strategic categories:

- Efforts to understand and share information regarding the full range of domestic terrorism threats.
- Efforts to prevent domestic terrorists from successfully recruiting, inciting, and mobilizing Americans to violence.
- Efforts to deter and disrupt domestic terrorist activity before it yields violence.
- Efforts to address the long-term issues that contribute to domestic terrorism in our country to ensure that this threat diminishes over generations to come.[48]

The authors of this first domestic counterterrorism strategy tried to take partisan politics out of the discussion and handling of this growing problem in stating,

> It is critical that we condemn and confront domestic terrorism regardless of the particular ideology that motivates individuals to violence. The definition of "domestic terrorism" in our law makes no distinction based on political views left, right, or center - and neither should we. . . . In a democracy, there is no justification for resorting to violence to resolve political differences.[49]

Interestingly, two European counterterrorism experts examined the U.S. strategy on countering domestic terrorism as a blueprint for the European Union to approve its own counterterrorism model. Perhaps a hopeful sign of increased U.S.-European cooperation in the struggle against domestic terrorism.[50]

America's Controversial "Drone War"

As President Obama noted in early 2015,

> we have moved beyond the large ground wars in Iraq and Afghanistan that defined so much of American foreign policy over the past decade. Compared to the nearly 180,000 troops we had in Iraq and

Afghanistan when I took office, we now have fewer than 15,000 deployed in those countries.[51]

Just as the troop withdrawal from Iraq had earlier, the drastic reduction of U.S. troops in Afghanistan drew criticism, especially among Republicans.

At the time, the actual "war against terrorism" was mostly fought via drones or Predators or what within the intelligence and military community were benignly called UAVs for unmanned aerial vehicles. It was during George W. Bush's presidency that drones were first deployed against terrorists, but there were far more such UAV strikes during the Obama administration.

During the George W. Bush administration, the CIA and U.S. military launched a total of 51 drone strikes, most of them in Pakistan. There was a dramatic increase during the Obama years, when a total of 586 drone-launched missiles were carried out in Pakistan, Yemen, and Somalia. In the four years of the Trump presidency, there were a total of 403 such attacks in Yemen, Somalia, and Pakistan. In the first 18 months of Joe Biden's presidency, merely nine drone attacks occurred. As Table 10.1 shows, in Yemen the number of U.S.-launched drones went from merely one during the Bush years to 185 under President Obama and 188 during the Trump presidency. There were only two drone attacks in Yemen in the first 18 months of Biden's presidency. In Pakistan, most drone strikes were carried out on Obama's watch, while most drone attacks occurred in Somalia during the one-term Trump presidency.

Statistics about the targeted strikes via drone-delivered missiles are difficult to come by because administrations tend to lack transparency in this respect. Thus, the available numbers reflect in large part open sources and the reports of human rights organizations. Furthermore, not included in the statistical data are the many drone attacks during the fight against ISIS in Iraq and Syria. This much is known: Since the war on terrorism began during the Bush presidency, thousands of terrorists were killed but hundreds of civilians as well.

Table 10.1 U.S. Counterterrorism Drone Strikes

	Pakistan	Somalia	Yemen
Pres. G.W. Bush (8 years)	48 strikes	12 strikes	1 strike
Pres. B. Obama (8 years)	353	48	185
Pres. D. Trump (4 years)	13	202	188
Pres. J. Biden (18 months)	0	7	2

Source: New America Foundation.

The issue with unmanned Predators was and is precisely that often not merely terrorists and their supporters are killed and injured but also innocent bystanders, including children. President Obama addressed this problem in a speech at the National Defense University, noting that the commando operation in Pakistan that led to the capture and death of Osama bin Laden cannot be the norm because of the tremendous risks involved—including the unintended killing of innocent civilians. He did not deny that drone strikes, like other weapons of war, cause the death of civilians and that he and others involved in these decisions were "haunted by the civilian casualties." But he also justified the continuation of drone warfare with the following argument:

> As Commander-in-Chief, I must weigh these heartbreaking tragedies against the alternatives. To do nothing in the face of terrorist networks would invite far more civilian casualties—not just in our cities at home and our facilities abroad, but also in the very places like Sana'a and Kabul and Mogadishu where terrorists seek a foothold. Remember that the terrorists we are after target civilians, and the death toll from their acts of terrorism against Muslims dwarfs any estimate of civilian casualties from drone strikes. So doing nothing is not an option.
>
> Where foreign governments cannot or will not effectively stop terrorism in their territory, the primary alternative to targeted lethal action would be the use of conventional military options. As I've already said, even small special operations carry enormous risks. Conventional airpower or missiles are far less precise than drones, and are likely to cause more civilian casualties and more local outrage. And invasions of these territories lead us to be viewed as occupying armies, unleash a torrent of unintended consequences, are difficult to contain, result in large numbers of civilian casualties and ultimately empower those who thrive on violent conflict.[52]

The efficacy of drone warfare in the fight against terrorists was demonstrated in July 2015, when a missile fired from a UAV killed a prominent Al Qaeda leader, Muhsin al-Fadhli, near Sarmada in Syria. Although not as widely known and feared as ISIS, the small but very potent Al Qaeda cell named Khorasan was considered the one terrorist group most capable of striking the United States and other Western countries. Reportedly, Al Qaeda leader Ayman al-Zawahiri ordered al-Fadhli to form this cell in Syria with a small number of men with American or European passports free to travel without problems into Western countries. According to counterterrorism experts inside and outside the U.S. government, the death of the Khorasan leader was a major blow for what was left of Al Qaeda Central. But such successes cannot argue away the dark side of the drone war. According to David Cole,

> Drones are controversial for many reasons. They inflict intense anxiety on those who live under their shadow, the vast majority of whom are innocent civilians, and therefore they inspire deep resentment. They are the ultimate imperialist weapon, projecting force in other countries without risking vulnerability.[53]

While President Obama said publicly that he was troubled by civilian deaths and injuries, his successor Donald Trump was not concerned about killing civilians as collateral damage in attacks against terrorists. On his first full day in office, during a visit to the CIA's headquarters, he urged the agency to get more drones ready to be deployed in the fight against ISIS in Iraq and Syria. According to one account,

> When the agency's [CIA's] head of drone operations explained that the CIA had developed special munitions to limit civilian casualties, the president seemed unimpressed. Watching a previously recorded strike in which the agency held off on firing until the target had wandered away from a house with his family inside, Trump asked, "Why did you wait?" one participant in the meeting recalled. On the campaign trail, Trump often said he would "take out" the families of terrorists.[54]

In this respect, it seems that President Trump meant what he said during the campaign. See Chapter 12 for a discussion of the killing and maiming of civilians in drone attacks as human rights violations. During the first 18 months of the Biden Administration, there were very few drone strikes.

Notes

1 According to the Brown University's "Cost of War" Project, https://watson.brown.edu/costsofwar/papers/summary, accessed April 20, 2022.
2 Ibid.
3 www.whitehouse.gov/news/releases/2001/09/20010911-16.html.
4 Simon Dalby, "Geopolitics, Grand Strategy and the Bush Doctrine," IDSS discussion paper, October 2005, 12.
5 Ian O. Lesser, "Countering the New Terrorism: Implications for Strategy," in Ian O. Lesser et al., eds., *Countering the New Terrorism* (Santa Monica, CA: Rand, 1999), 140.
6 Martha Crenshaw, "Terrorism, Strategies, and Grand Strategies," in Audrey Kurth Cronin and James M. Ludes, eds., *Attacking Terrorism: Elements of a Grand Strategy* (Washington, DC: Georgetown University Press, 2004), 77. Crenshaw's analysis distinguishes between strategy that "typically refers to military operations" and "is concerned with the relationship between means and ends"; grand strategy, which "represents a more inclusive conception that explains how a state's full range of resources can be adapted to achieve national security"; and "foreign policy defines the goals of strategy and 'grand' or high strategy" and "is a statement of purpose" (75, 76).

7 Paul R. Pillar, *Terrorism and U.S. Foreign Policy* (Washington, DC: Brookings Institution Press, 2001), 5.
8 http://govinfo.library.unt.edu/nssg/Reports/NWC.pdf, accessed October 1, 2008.
9 Ibid.
10 Edward Alden, "Report Warned of Attack on American Soil," *Financial Times*, September 12, 2001, 5.
11 Report of the National Commission on Terrorism, "Countering the Changing Threat of Terrorism," Pursuant to Public Law 277, 105th Congress, 49.
12 "Secure, Yes, But Also Free," *Omaha World-Herald*, June 12, 2000, 6.
13 Donald M. Snow, *National Security for a New Era* (New York: Pearson Longman, 2007), 1.
14 Crenshaw, 82.
15 Authorization for Use of Military Force, September 18, 2001, Public Law 107-40 SJ Res. 23, 107th Congress, http://news.findlaw.com/wp/docs/ terrorism/ sjres23.es.html, accessed September 30, 2008.
16 www.whitehouse.gov/news/releases/2001/09/print/20010920-8.html, accessed September 29, 2008.
17 Ibid.
18 Bob Woodward, *Plan of Attack* (New York: Simon & Schuster, 2004), 22.
19 Louise Richardson, *What Terrorists Want: Understanding the Enemy, Containing the Threat* (New York: Random House, 2006), 189.
20 Ibid., 26.
21 "The National Security Strategy of the United States of America," September 2002, www.whitehouse.gov/nsc/nss.pdf, accessed October 10, 2008.
22 Dalby, 3.
23 Brian C. Schmidt and Michael C. Williams, "The Bush Doctrine and the Iraq War: Neoconservatives vs. Realists," paper presented at the Annual Conference of the British International Studies Association, Cambridge, UK, December 17–19, 2007, 5.
24 Dalby, 15.
25 Andrew Rojecki, "Rhetorical Alchemy: American Exceptionalism and the War on Terror," *Political Communication* 25 (1) (January–March 2008), p. 81.
26 Ibid.
27 The National Security Strategy of the United States of America," March 2006, www.whitehouse.gov/nsc/nss/2006/, accessed October 10, 2008.
28 Philip H. Gordon, "The End of the Bush Revolution," *Foreign Affairs* (July/ August 2006), www.foreignaffairs.org/20060701faessay85406/philip-h-gordon/the-end-of-the-bushrevolution.html?mode=print, accessed October 11, 2008.
29 "The National Security Strategy of the United States of America," 2002.
30 Ibid.
31 Ibid., 1.
32 Robert Jervis, "Understanding the Bush Doctrine," *Political Science Quarterly* 118 (3) (2003), p. 379.
33 www.whitehouse.gov/news/releases/2002/06/20020601-3.html, accessed September 1, 2008.
34 Ibid.
35 Ibid., 6.
36 Schmidt and Williams, 9.
37 Robert Jervis, "Understanding the Bush Doctrine," *Political Science Quarterly* 118 (3) (2003), p. 366.
38 Andrew J. Bacevich, "Rescinding the Bush Doctrine," *Boston Globe*, March 1, 2007, www.boston.com/news/globe/editorial_opinion/oped/articles/2007/03/01/rescinding_the_bush_doctrine/, accessed October 11, 2008.

39 From a speech delivered at the Aspen Institute in Washington, DC, April 9, 2009. The transcript is available at www.nctc.gov/press_room/speeches/2009-04-09_aspen-inst-speech.pdf, accessed May 12, 2009.

40 The full speech is available at www.whitehouse.gov/the-press-office/remarks-president-united-states-military-academy-west-point-commencement, accessed June 22, 2010.

41 The full document is available at www.whitehouse.gov/sites/default/files/rss_viewer/national_security_strategy.pdf, 8, accessed June 24, 2010.

42 The full speech is available at www.whitehouse.gov/the_press_office/Remarks-by-the-President-on-a-New-Strategy-for-Afghanistan-and-Pakistan/, accessed June 25, 2010.

43 The White House, "A New National Security Strategy for a New Era," December 2017, www.whitehouse.gov/articles/new-national-security-strategy-new-era/, accessed January 14, 2018.

44 The text of the 2018 National counterterrorism strategy is available at https://www.dni.gov/index.php/features/national-strategy-for-counterterrorism, accessed September 22, 2022.

45 The document is available at https://www.whitehouse.gov/wp-content/uploads/2021/03/NSC-1v2.pdf, accessed January 1, 2022.

46 Ibid.

47 The document is available at https://www.dhs.gov/sites/default/files/publications/21_0301_odni_unclass-summary-of-dve-assessment-17_march-final_508.pdf, accessed August 1, 2022.

48 The document is available at https://www.whitehouse.gov/wp-content/uploads/2021/06/National-Strategy-for-Countering-Domestic-Terrorism.pdf, accessed August 1, 2022.

49 Ibid.

50 Eviane Leidig and Charlie van Mieghem, "The US National Strategy on Combating Domestic Terrorism as a model for the EU," International Centre for Counter-Terrorism, September 2021; https://kbb9z40cmb2ap-wafcho9v3j-wpengine.netdna-ssl.com/wp-content/uploads/2021/09/the-us-national-strategy-on-countering-domestic-terrorism-as-a-model-for-the-eu-1-1.pdf, accessed July 2, 2022.

51 From the 2015 National Security Strategy, www.whitehouse.gov/sites/default/files/docs/2015_national_security_strategy.pdf, accessed July 26, 2015.

52 The transcript of the speech was published by the *New York Times*, www.nytimes.com/2013/05/24/us/politics/transcript-of-obamas-speech-on-drone-policy.html, accessed July 20, 2015.

53 David Cole, "The New America: Little Privacy, Big Terror," *New York Review of Books*, August 13, 2015, 20.

54 Greg Jaffe, "For Trump and his Generals, 'Victory' Has Different Meanings," *Washington Post*, April 5, 2018, www.washingtonpost.com/world/national-security/for-trump-and-his-generals-victory-has-different-meanings/2018/04/05/8d74eab0–381d-11e8–9c0a-85d477d9a226_story.html?utm_term=.4a8c299d6592, accessed May 24, 2018.

11 The Utility of Hard and Soft Power in Counterterrorism

Who won the war on terrorism? That was a momentous question as America commemorated the twentieth anniversary of the most devastating terrorist strikes on September 11, 2001, a difficult question to answer. Some national security experts and terrorism scholars reviewed and critiqued the two decades of U.S.-led counterterrorism strategy directed against Al Qaeda, the group responsible for the attacks, its affiliates around the world, host entities, such as the Taliban in Afghanistan, and successor groups, such as ISIS and its web of franchises outside of Iraq and Syria. In short, the 20-year-long post-9/11 counterterrorism campaigns by the United States and its allies were strictly carried out against foreign terrorists and their supporters—mostly abroad with the exception of those jihadists who perpetrated violence in the name of those groups in North America and Europe. So, it was timely to discuss 20 years after the outbreak of the war on terrorism and the withdrawal of American and NATO troops from Afghanistan a few months earlier, whether the American superpower or Al Qaeda, ISIS, and an assortment of their affiliates had won the war. In his essay "The Good Enough Doctrine: Learning to Live with Terrorism," Daniel Byman explained,

> Instead of a decisive victory, the United States appears to have settled for something less ambitious: good enough. It recognizes that although jihadi terrorism may be impossible to fully and permanently eradicate—or the costs of trying to do so are simply too high—the threat can be reduced to the point where it kills relatively few Americans and no longer shapes daily life in the United States...
>
> To a remarkable degree, the United States itself has been insulated from the threat. Jihadism remains alive and well abroad and is not going away anytime soon, but the current U.S. doctrine is a politically feasible and comparatively effective way of managing the issue. Good enough, it turns out, is good enough.[1]

DOI: 10.4324/9781003289265-13

Ben Rhodes, a member of President Obama's national security team, was far more critical of the 20-year-old war on terrorism claiming that America's enemies hijacked its foreign policy. According to Rhodes,

> By any measure, the 'war on terrorism' was the biggest project of the period of American hegemony that began when the Cold War ended—a period that now reached its dusk. For 20 years, counterterrorism has been the overarching priority of U.S. national security policy.[2]

To be sure, this overblown focus on the war on terrorism came at the expense of many equally or more important conflicts and problems, such as the rise of China's power and influence and the catastrophic consequences of global warming. "To replace the war on terror with a better generational project," Rhodes wrote at the end of his analysis, "Americans have to be driven by what they are for, not what they are against."[3]

Examining bin Laden's utopian worldview and his expectation that the 9/11 attacks would be a "decisive blow" against the American superpower, Nelly Lahoud used the Al Qaeda leader's communications to show that he "never anticipated that the United States would go to war in response to the assault." Since the invasion of Afghanistan by American and allied forces came as a complete surprise, "bin Laden had no plan to secure his organization's survival."[4] Yet, because Al Qaeda Central's leaders were forced to hideout in the mountainous areas of Pakistan near the Afghan border, their international affiliates worked on in the Middle East, Africa, and elsewhere, Lahoud concluded at the twentieth anniversary of 9/11.

Washington cannot quite claim victory against al Qaeda and its ilk, which retain the ability to inspire deadly, if small-scale attacks. The past two decades, however, have made clear just how little jihadist groups can hope to accomplish. They stand a far better chance of achieving eternal life in paradise than of bringing the United States to its knees.[5]

Since the war on terrorism did not eradicate or defeat terrorism, as presidents George W. Bush, Barack Obama, and Donald Trump promised, and jihadist violent extremism was alive and well in many parts of the world as the twentieth anniversary of 9/11 was commemorated, neither America and its allies nor Al Qaeda and like-minded groups could claim victory. However, the U.S.-led coalition fared better, if only because Al Qaeda and ISIS were not able to launch another 9/11-like attack in the United States or elsewhere in the West. However, while the withdrawal of all U.S. and NATO troops from Afghanistan in 2021 marked the end of the war declared after the 9/11 attacks, the fight against jihadist groups abroad continued. U.S. and some allied Special Forces were deployed in many places where Al Qaeda and ISIS affiliates were active. Indeed, when Al Qaeda leader Ayman al-Zawahiri was assassinated in 2022–21 years after 9/11, the terrorist organization he left behind was alive and well. According to one report,

Al Qaeda is in more countries and has more total fighters than it did on September 11, 2001, when it attacked the United States. Some of its franchises that have sprung up since then, particularly in Somalia and the Sahel region of West Africa, are ascendant, seizing swaths of territory from weak governments and spending millions of dollars on new weapons, despite a decade's effort to weaken and contain them.[6]

At the same time, remnants of ISIS fighters who had survived and avoided capture when they lost the territory of their so-called Caliphate, reverted to a guerrilla war in the region.

In the following section, I discuss at length the options of states in their responses to hostilities by foreign and domestic terrorists. The chapter ends with a discussion of how to respond to the increased threat of domestic terrorism in the West in the third decade of the twenty-first century.

Hard and Soft Power in Counterterrorism

Immediately after the kamikaze strikes on the territory of the world's most powerful (and, indeed, only) superpower, 9/11 was compared to the attack on Pearl Harbor. But by pointing to the similarity of the two sneak attacks, most commentators failed to mention the most obvious difference: In the case of Pearl Harbor, a government ordered the aggression and targeted members of the military, but in the case of New York and Washington, members of an international terrorist network planned and carried out the attacks on defenseless civilians. By equating the two events, it seemed logical to invoke the war metaphor. What political leaders and the media dubbed immediately as an "Attack on America," an act of war, called for a likewise rhetorical response—the "war against terrorism" or the "war on terror" that President George W. Bush promptly declared. Noting that, in the context of terrorism, the noun *war* is more likely to be followed by *on* rather than *against*, Geoffrey Nunberg explained,

The "war on" pattern dates from the turn of the century, when people adapted epidemiological metaphors like "the war on typhus" to describe campaigns against social evils like alcohol, crime and poverty—endemic conditions that could be mitigated but not eradicated. Society may declare a war on drugs or drunken driving, but no one expects total victory. "The war on terror," too, suggests a campaign aimed not at human adversaries but at a pervasive social plague.[7]

That was the way John Kerry understood the meaning of the "war on terrorism." During the 2004 presidential campaign, he said that "the only realistic goal was to contain the problem, to reduce it to the status of nuisance rather than a central, encompassing fixation; he drew an analogy with containing prostitution and gambling."[8] But George W. Bush was reelected and continued to fight conventional wars against terrorism in Afghanistan and Iraq. Neither his campaign opponent Kerry nor national security/foreign policy experts convinced him that a "central lesson of counterterrorism is that terrorism cannot be 'defeated'—only reduced, attenuated, and to some degree controlled."[9]

Before Barack Obama took the oath of office in January 2009, Joseph Nye criticized the Bush Doctrine (discussed in Chapter 10) as "based on a flawed analysis of power in today's world." Looking ahead to a different foreign policy approach by the incoming administration, Nye wrote, "Obama's election itself has done a great deal to restore American soft power, but he will need to follow up with policies that combine hard and soft power into a smart strategy of the sort that won the Cold War."[10] Nye recommended a mix of hard and soft power as the basis for America's grand strategy in the post-Cold War era well before 9/11. During her testimony as secretary of state designee before the Senate Foreign Relations Committee's confirmation hearing, Hillary Clinton spoke of the need for "smart power" as a mix of hard and soft power.

> The president-elect and I believe that foreign policy must be based on a marriage of principles and pragmatism, not rigid ideology. On facts and evidence, not emotion or prejudice. Our security, our vitality, and our ability to lead in today's world oblige us to recognize the overwhelming fact of our interdependence. We must use what has been called "smart power," the full range of tools at our disposal— diplomatic, economic, military, political, legal, and cultural—picking the right tool, or combination of tools, for each situation. With smart power, diplomacy will be the vanguard of foreign policy.[11]

By that time, the experiences in Afghanistan and Iraq had shown that overwhelming power might prevail in conventional but not asymmetric warfare. As one expert put it, such conflicts "require the application of all elements of national power. Success will be less a matter of imposing one's will and more a function of shaping behavior—of friends, adversaries, and most importantly, the people in between."[12] Others expressed the same ideas more bluntly. Andrew Bacevich, for example, suggested that the "war in Afghanistan (like the Iraq war) won't be won militarily. It can be settled—if imperfectly—only through politics."[13]

Defining Power—Hard and Soft

The German sociologist Max Weber defined politics as "striving for a share of power or for influence in the distribution of power, whether between states or between groups of people contained within one single state." For Weber,

Anyone engaged in politics is striving for power, either power as a means to attain other goals (which may be ideal or selfish), or power 'for its own sake,' which is to say, in order to enjoy the feeling of prestige created by power.[14]

Military power and economic muscle are, as Joseph Nye put it, "examples of hard command power that can be used to induce others to change their positions. Hard power Hard power can rest on inducements (carrots) or threats (sticks)."[15] Whereas hard power is unequivocal, soft power is subtle. For Nye, soft power "co-opts people rather than coerces them. Soft power rests on the ability to set the political agenda in a way that shapes the preferences of others."[16]

Even leaders deeply involved in defense, national security, and military affairs can appreciate the utility of smart power, namely, using both the hard and soft varieties. Thus, in the fall of 2007, at the height of the war on terrorism, U.S. Secretary of Defense Robert Gates called on his own government to invest more in the resurrection of America's 'soft power' capacity. He criticized the post-Cold War

gutting of America's ability to engage, assist, and communicate with other parts of the world—the 'soft power,' which had been so important throughout the Cold War. The State Department froze the hiring of new Foreign Service officers for a period of time. The United States Agency for International Development saw deep staff cuts—its permanent staff dropping from a high of 15,000 during Vietnam to about 3,000 in the 1990s. And the U.S. Information Agency was abolished as an independent entity, split into pieces, and many of its capabilities folded into a small corner of the State Department.[17]

Lost in the process of war America's expertise in public diplomacy—communications by the government to the publics in foreign countries. During the Cold War era, information about the United States, its values, and its citizens' way of life was beamed into the communist world. There were cultural and educational exchanges that established people-to-people meetings and often lasting and connections.

Today's global information and communication networks, especially the Internet, offer new opportunities for innovative soft power approaches, including a new public diplomacy that counters the propaganda of terrorist movements.

Military Hard Power

Conventional Warfare: It is clear, then, that conventional warfare against relatively small and widely dispersed terrorist groups does not work in most cases. As noted in Chapter 8, a study of all terrorist groups that were active around the world from 1968 through 2006 found that merely 7 percent ended because they were militarily defeated. When a nation-state is challenged by large, well-armed, and well-trained guerrilla-like groups that use terrorist tactics, its military forces prevailed in a few cases. For example, the Peruvian military defeated the insurgent Shining Path; the Sri Lankan armed forces were victorious against the Tamil Tigers. Israeli Defense Forces defeated the Lebanese Hezbollah's military wing decisively. In these and other cases, the terrorist entities were controlling territories within a country (Peru, Sri Lanka) or in a neighboring state Lebanon).

Commando Raids: Short of going to war against state sponsors or conducting air strikes against terrorist sponsor states and terrorist groups, commando attacks on terrorist homes and training grounds, the use of commandos to hunt down terrorists, and the utilization of surrogates to attack terrorists are options chosen by various target countries. Using commandos increases the accuracy of attacks and minimizes the risk of harming innocents. But sending special forces teams into a hostile environment entails also the risk of members being captured, injured, and killed. Using surrogates, on the one hand, eliminates the risk of a country's own personnel being harmed and allows officials to deny responsibility if an attack fails or results in collateral damage. On the other hand, however, the sponsoring government may lose control over proxies. This was the case in 1985 when a car bomb exploded in Beirut and killed innocent Lebanese bystanders. Allegedly, the Central Intelligence Agency (CIA) had hired indigenous operatives for the attack but lost control over their operation. More recently, during the post-9/11 invasion of Afghanistan, members of U.S. Special Forces paid Afghan tribesmen to assist in the hunt for bin Laden, Al Qaeda members, and Taliban leaders. But the Afghans were reportedly also taking bribes from the other sides and warned them of impending actions by the U.S.-led coalition. Before the highly skilled SEAL commando of the U.S. Special Forces succeeded in neutralizing bin Laden in 2011, decision-makers in Washington were well aware of the high-risk nature of the mission. This assessment did not change after the operation. As President Obama said after the success,

> Our operation in Pakistan against Osama bin Laden cannot be the norm. The risks in that case were immense. The likelihood of capture, although that was our preference, was remote given the certainty that our folks would confront resistance. The fact that we did

not find ourselves confronted with civilian casualties, or embroiled in an extended firefight, was a testament to the meticulous planning and professionalism of our Special Forces, but it also depended on some luck.[18]

Yet, in certain predicaments, some experts recommend fighting ruthless terrorists with equally ruthless campaigns that "must be highly selective, fought in secret, targeting only those responsible and never acknowledging guilt."[19]

The model for commando campaigns with a multitude of raids remains Israel's response to a deadly attack on the country's athletes at the 1972 Olympic Games in Munich. Prodded by then Prime Minister Golda Meir, the best and brightest of Israel's military and intelligence elite formed a commando unit with the code name "Mivtzan Elohim," meaning "Wrath of God." Members were charged with hunting down every member of Black September, the group responsible for the Munich operation. For years, Wrath of God commandos tracked down leaders and followers of Black September in the Middle East and Europe, killing them one by one until the job was done in 1979. Along the way, mistakes were made—for example, when an Arab in Scandinavia was falsely identified as the Palestinian leader of the Munich attack and killed. But, as one observer wrote approvingly, "Despite some spectacular foul-ups... Mossad [Israel's intelligence agency] has racked up a deadly record of hits on Palestinian terrorists without ever bragging about it. The terrorists know who did it, and that's enough for the Israelis."[20]

Others recommended that the United States should establish a counterterrorist commando unit along the lines of the Wrath of God model as one more aggressive option in its counterterrorism posture.

Assassinations: "Wrath of God" was an assassination campaign. Governments typically do not speak about, or deny, their involvement in the assassination of terrorists. But in some situations, officials admit to such targeted killings as preventive and retaliatory actions, if only to satisfy a fearful populace's demand for more protection. Thus, in the fall of 2000, Israeli officials acknowledged publicly that their military was targeting and killing individual Palestinians accused of actual attacks on Israeli citizens or of planning such deeds. While Palestinians spoke of "state terrorism" and "assassinations," a highly placed government official in Israel explained these acts as countermeasures and said that the "most effective and just way to deal with terror is the elimination or incarceration of the people who lead these organizations."[21] After Israeli forces targeted an alleged mastermind of a Palestinian terror attack but killed several civilians in the process, Israeli Foreign Minister Shimon Perez reacted angrily when an interviewer used the term *assassination* to characterize the action. "Suicide bombers cannot be threatened by

Targeted Assassinations of Top Al Qaeda and ISIS Leaders

The U.S. Military and CIA targeted and assassinated a large number of high-ranking jihadists during the long post-9/11 fight against terrorism, among them the following top leaders of Al Qaeda and ISIS:

June 2006: Abu Musab al-Zarqawi, the leader of Al Qaeda in Iraq, was killed in an airstrike on a safe house near Baghdad. Six other persons were also killed in this strike. The Iraqi affiliate of Al Qaeda became eventually the Islamic State of Iraq and Syria—ISIS.

May 2011: Osama bin Laden, founder and leader of Al Qaeda, was killed during an ambitious and risky raid by a team of U.S. Navy SEALs who flew from Afghanistan to Abbottabad, Pakistan, where bin Laden was hiding in a compound. The hunt for bin Laden was dramatized in the 2012 film "Zero Dark Thirty."

September 2011: Anwar al-Awlaki, a Yemini-American Imam, had a huge number of internet followers, when he was killed by a missile fired from a U.S. drone. A leader of Al Qaeda in the Arabian Peninsula, he was the first U.S. citizen killed by a drone strike. Two weeks later, his 16-year-old son Abdulrahman al-Awlaki, too, died in a drone strike.

September 2019: Hamza bin Laden, one of Osama bin Laden's sons, was killed by U.S. Special forces in a counterterrorism raid in the border area between Afghanistan and Pakistan. The young bin Laden had ambitions to become his father's successor.

October 2019: Abu Bakr al-Baghdadi, ISIS's leader and self-proclaimed Caliph of the so-called Islamic State Caliphate, killed himself and three members of his family by detonating a bomb as U.S. Special Forces launched an assault on his hide-away compound in Syria's Idlib province.

February 2022: Abu Ibrahim al-Hashimi al-Qurayshi, leader of ISIS and successor of Abu Bakr al-Baghdadi, died during a raid on a house in Syria's rebel-held Idlib province by U.S. Special Forces. Al-Qurayshi killed himself and members of his family by detonating a bomb.

July 2022: Maher al-Agal, a key Islamic State leader who built and was liaison to the network of ISIS affiliates outside of Iraq and Syria, was killed in a U.S. drone strike in northwest Syria.

July 2022: Ayman al-Zawahiri, leader of Al Qaeda Central since the Osama bin Laden was "neutralized" by U.S. Navy Seals, was killed by a CIA drone strike as he stood on the balcony of a private residence in Kabul, Afghanistan. He was the only one killed.

death," he argued. "The only way to stop them is to intercept those who sent them."[22] And Prime Minister Ariel Sharon made clear that "actions to prevent the killing of Jews" would continue.[23] Indeed, Israel intensified its campaign to kill the leaders of terrorist groups. But whether taking out Hamas leader Sheik Yassin, his successors, and a host of others in the higher circles of Palestinian terror groups reduced violence against Israel in the long run was far from sure. Even more than terrorist foot soldiers, their leaders become martyrs in death and attract new recruits.

After 9/11, there was a debate in the mass media in the United States on the best outcome of the ongoing hunt for Osama bin Laden. To arrest or to "neutralize" (i.e., assassinate) the Al Qaeda leader was the question. There was fear of a wave of terror attacks inside the United States if bin Laden was arrested and tried by the American judiciary. There was also concern that the United States could lose influence over the procedures if bin Laden was caught and brought before an international tribunal. As for neutralizing the Al Qaeda boss, assassinations were outlawed by the United States following the disclosure that the CIA was involved in assassination plots against foreign leaders during the 1960s and 1970s. To be sure, bin Laden was not a head of state or leader in a nation-state. Nevertheless, after 9/11, the issue was whether the president and Congress should lift the ban on assassination when known terrorists were the targets. Michael Ignatieff proposed three conditions for targeted assassination in the fight against terrorism: "Only as a last resort, only when capture is impossible without undue risk to American lives and only where death and damage to innocent civilians can be avoided."[24] President Bush did not repeal the executive order banning assassinations, nor did Congress introduce legislation to allow targeted assassinations of terrorists. But after 9/11, President Bush issued a finding that authorized the CIA to kill or capture terrorist leaders.[25] Indeed, in the fall of 2002, a pilotless Predator plane operated by the CIA fired a Hellfire antitank missile at a car in Yemen and killed a key Al Qaeda leader and five others. This operation was, no doubt, a targeted assassination coup and confirmed that the assassination of terrorists was part of the American arsenal in the fight against terrorism and was part and parcel of what I described in the previous chapter as drone war.

Even a U.S. citizen turned terrorist was put on the CIA's assassination list in the spring of 2010 after the National Security Council approved the targeted killing of American-born cleric Anwar al-Awlaki who was hiding in Yemen. Al-Awlaki, a charismatic preacher, called for violence against Americans and recruited jihadis for attacks in the United States. Nidal Hasan, the perpetrator of the Fort Hood massacre in the fall of 2009, and Umar Farouk Abdulmutallab, the would-be Christmas Day (2009) bomber, were disciples of al-Awlaki as were several other known terrorists. When asked by Jake Tapper of ABC News whether al-Awlaki was on the CIA's assassination list, CIA director Leon Panetta answered,

> Awlaki is a terrorist and yes, he's a US citizen, but he is first and foremost a terrorist and we're going to treat him like a terrorist. We don't have an assassination list, but I can tell you this. We have a terrorist list and he's on it.[26]

Al-Awlaki was killed in 2011 by a missile fired from an unmanned drone in Yemen. Two weeks later al-Awlaki's 16-year-old son Abdulrahman al-Awlaki, also a U.S. citizen, was killed in another drone strike.

Hostage Rescue Missions: In the late 1960s and early 1970s, when hostage-taking was the most popular terrorist tactic, military and police experts began to discuss suitable rescue methods. But, as Pillar has recalled, it was the "unsuccessful German attempt to rescue the Israeli athletes kidnapped at the Olympic Games in Munich in 1972 [that actually] led major European governments to develop highly skilled commando units with this mission."[27] Germany, for example, established a counterterrorist commando called Grenzschutzgruppe 9 (GSG-9) within its border patrol, and the United Kingdom designated the special commandos of the Special Air Service (SAS) as a counterterrorist force. Israeli commandos were the first to stage a spectacular rescue mission in 1976 after terrorists hijacked an Air France airliner en route from Tel Aviv to Paris and forced the pilot to land at Entebbe, Uganda. Although the Ugandan authorities supported the hijackers, who threatened to kill their Israeli hostages, an Israeli C-130 plane with 86 highly trained commandos aboard landed at the airport. Within a few minutes, the paratroopers struck down the terrorists and rescued 95 passengers. Although two passengers were killed in the crossfire and the leader of the rescue commandos, Jonathan Netanyahu, died in the exchange, the raid on Entebbe became "a worldwide sensation—a clearcut victory against terrorism."[28]

Delta Force, perceived as counterterrorist commandos, was already in the planning stage when officially established as a counterterrorism unit in November 1977 during the Carter presidency. In the previous months, commandos of Germany's GSG-9 had stormed a hijacked Lufthansa plane at the airport of Mogadishu, Somalia, rescuing all 86 passengers. Delta Force, under the command of Colonel Charles Beckwith, became a formidable counterterrorist asset—especially after becoming part of the so-called SOF that combined special units from each of the military services after the failure of the rescue mission during the Iran hostage crisis, which had been partially blamed on poor coordination between the various military services. (However, unlike Mogadishu, where the government of Somalia had welcomed the rescue raid by German commandos, the American rescue force flew into an extremely hostile environment in Iran. To be sure, Israeli commandos faced hostility at Entebbe as well—and succeeded—but without taking away from the brilliant execution of their coup, they had the benefit of surprise on their side because this was the first rescue of its kind.)

In recent times, foreigners have been typically taken hostage one at a time or in small groups and held in hideouts in Iraq, Pakistan, Afghanistan, Saudi Arabia, and elsewhere by transnational terrorists, which has made rescue attempts highly unlikely or impossible.

Although domestic rescue operations tend to be less problematic, they are not unlike efforts to free hostages held abroad when the captors control territory within a state. Colombia is an instructive example. For years, the FARC kidnapped and held hundreds of hostages, many of them for long periods of time and in spite of many attempts by Colombian security forces to free them. But the combined efforts of military intelligence and commandos eventually pulled off one of the most stunning, nonviolent hostage rescue coups on July 2, 2008, when they freed 15 hostages from a FARC jungle camp—among them former Colombian presidential candidate Ingrid Betancourt and three Americans. After they had infiltrated the terrorist/guerrilla organization for months, the rescuers posed as FARC fighters and convinced guards that they had come with an order to gather the hostages from three different locations and march them to a centrally located place from where they would fly to a meeting with an international delegation. Camouflaged rescuers, real FARC fighters, and the hostages marched 90 miles through the jungle. When a helicopter landed, Colombian security forces disguised as FARC operatives got off, handcuffed the hostages, and ordered them aboard, along with two of the FARC guards. As the latter were overpowered soon after lift-off, the hostages learned that they were finally free. Betancourt had spent more than six years, and the three American defense contractors more than five years, in captivity.

The high risks involved in rescue missions were demonstrated in a tragic way in 2014, when U.S. Special Forces made two failed attempts to rescue American photo-journalist Luke Sommers who was held hostage and whose life was threatened by Al Qaeda in the Arabian Peninsula. After the failure of the first attempt in November, there was a second try one month later. This time, American commandos reached the terrorist compound, but while they were involved in a fierce firefight, terrorists managed to kill Sommers and South African hostage Pierre Korkie.

Non-Military Hard Power

Economic Sanctions: Like military actions, economic sanctions are imposed by governments in order to affect the behavior of the targets of such measures. Trade and foreign aid sanctions are meant to change the behavior of governments, whereas financial sanctions can be imposed against both states and nonstate actors. Trade sanctions prohibit the exporting and importing of goods to and from target countries; foreign aid sanctions stop financial and other assistance, such as loans, to targeted governments; financial sanctions concentrate typically on the freezing of financial assets of foreign governments or organizations so that they cannot be moved from the frozen bank accounts. All of these economic sanctions have been imposed as counterterrorist measures by the U.S. government.

Indeed, when the U.S. Department of State identifies states as sponsors of terrorism, this designation triggers automatically a multitude of U.S.-imposed sanctions that include the prohibition of certain exports and access to a variety of foreign assistance programs. In addition, specific sanctions tend to be legislated against sponsor states. But sanctions require careful consideration. While they inflict costs on the targeted states and in some cases on organizations, they also result in losses to the businesses and workers of exporting sectors in the country that imposes sanctions. Moreover, unless other countries decide in favor of sanctions, unilaterally imposed measures of this kind tend to be less harmful than intended. In the past, even the United States' allies in Europe were not at all eager or willing to join the former in a multilateral sanction regime. This was true with respect to Iran, Syria, and Cuba.

Whatever the reason for sanctions, the "scholarly literature on economic statecraft is generally sceptical, portraying the use of economic sanctions and other strategies as ineffective or even counterproductive."[29] Robert Pape, for example, concluded that based on the evidence "economic sanctions are not likely to achieve foreign policy objectives."[30] However, Pillar points to Libya as probably the "best case of sanctions helping to shape a state sponsor's behavior on terrorism-related matters."[31] In the Libyan case, as a study by Stephen D. Collins revealed, unilateral economic sanctions by the United States (and the bombing of Libyan cities) did not discourage the Gaddafi government from sponsoring terrorism, but UN-backed multilateral economic sanctions did reduce Libyan-supported terrorist attacks markedly.[32] The multilateral sanctions imposed by the UN Security Council were particularly intended to press Libya to surrender the suspects in the terrorist attack on Pan Am Flight 103. Thus, "the evidence clearly demonstrates that following the application of multilateral sanctions Libyan support for terrorism declined precipitously."[33] Similarly, when Muammar Gaddafi signaled in late 2003 his willingness to dismantle WMD, this decision seemed influenced by his desire to end all sanctions in order to improve his country's economy.

Drying Up Financial Resources: Money has been identified as the most important fuel of terrorism. President George W. Bush and U.S. Secretary of State Colin Powell called money the oxygen and lifeblood of terrorism as they ordered measures to dry up the financial resources of Al Qaeda and other terrorist groups in the wake of 9/11. To be sure, terrorists need money to support themselves, their training facilities, their weaponry, and the planning and execution of their terrorist actions. But Pillar has correctly pointed out that efforts to defeat terrorism by imposing financial controls encounter two major problems in that (1) terrorism in terms of killing innocents is cheap and (2) "the money that does flow in the terrorist world is extremely difficult to track."[34] Tracking terrorists' financial resources is severely hampered by several factors, among them their habit of using false names and their preference for using unorthodox financial transactions—among them money laundering—and getting involved in criminal activities, such as drug trafficking. Moreover, actual terrorist attacks are rather cheap. Although prepared for many months in advance and involving dozens of people besides the actual suicide bombers, the whole 9/11 plot did not cost more than $400,000. The Madrid train bombings that required two years of preparations were staged for an estimated $10,000. And even the most devastating explosive belts for single suicide bombers can be assembled for around $100. Following the money trail may be more successful in identifying the members of terrorist cells and thereby increasing law enforcement officials' chances of hunting down and arresting terrorists, and less successful at putting terror organizations once and for all out of business.

Soft Power and Counterterrorism

Besides hard power, namely military and economic measures, there are also less drastic options available in response to specific terrorist incidents and terrorism threats in general. In assessing the utility of soft power, one needs to distinguish between state sponsors and terrorist groups or networks.

Deterrence: Like many other leading international relations scholars and policy-makers, Robert Jervis believes that contemporary terrorist threats "cannot be contained by deterrence" because "terrorists are fanatics, and there is nothing that they value that we can hold at risk; rogues like Iraq [under Saddam Hussein] are risk-acceptant and accident prone. The heightened sense of vulnerability increases the dissatisfaction with deterrence."[35] Thus his conclusion that concludes that deterrence has a "limited efficacy" for countering today's major terrorist threats.[36] But Robert F. Trager and Dessislava P. Zagorcheva argue that "the claim that deterrence is ineffective against terrorists is wrong." According to these two political scientists,

> Even seemingly fanatical terrorists, intensely motivated by religious beliefs, are not irrational in a sense that makes them impossible to deter.
>
> Some essential elements of terrorist support systems are likely to be less motivated and therefore vulnerable to traditional forms of deterrence, particularly at early decision nodes in the lengthy process of preparation required for major attacks.
>
> Even the most highly motivated terrorists, however, can be deterred from certain courses of action by holding at risk their political goals, rather than life and liberty.

For Trager and Zagorcheva, "the ability to hold political ends [of terrorist groups] at risk... stands by far the best chance of fracturing the global terrorist network, one of the most important objectives of counterterrorism policy."[37]

Diplomacy: The prospect for deterrence is different with respect to state sponsors of terrorism. But without diplomatic contacts, without talking to the sponsors of terrorism it is impossible to figure out whether there are prospects for deterrence or not.

For over four decades, the United States like other states insisted that they will not negotiate with terrorists and will not give in to terrorists' demands. In the United States, this policy was put in place during the Nixon administration and officially embraced by all administrations thereafter. Yet, diplomacy represents a useful instrument in efforts to solve specific terrorist situations, to convince other governments to join counterterrorist measures, and to suspend their support of terrorists. Diplomatic efforts tend to be especially urgent during hostage situations, when the wellbeing and even the lives of victims are at stake. During the Iranian hostage crisis, there were many attempts to find diplomatic solutions to the deadlock—even though the United States and Iran had broken off their diplomatic ties. In this case, members of the Swiss embassy in Tehran and officials of the United Nations were among the third parties that negotiated on behalf of the United States, and, eventually, Algerian officials were instrumental in brokering the agreement that led to the end of the crisis. Diplomacy had a chance because Iranian authorities had great influence over the hostage-holders.

During the TWA hijacking crisis in 1985, there was also a great deal of media diplomacy that involved Washington officials and Lebanese individuals explaining their positions and responding to each other's suggestions and demands on television. More importantly, contacts between Washington officials and the Israeli government and the role of the Red Cross were crucial in negotiating the release of Arab prisoners by Israel and the freeing of the hostages by their Hezbollah captors.

Going the diplomatic route does not guarantee satisfactory solutions. Although the United States and the Taliban did not have diplomatic relations, the military actions against both Al Qaeda and Taliban facilities in Afghanistan were preceded by indirect diplomatic exchanges facilitated by third parties, especially Pakistan. But failed efforts in some instances should not discourage diplomatic initiatives in other cases. In the words of the National Commission on Terrorism,

> Diplomacy is an important instrument, both in gaining the assistance of other nations in particular cases and convincing the international community to condemn and outlaw egregious terrorist practices... The United States should strengthen its efforts to discourage the broad range of assistance that states provide to international terrorists. A key focus of this initiative must be to reduce terrorists' freedom of movement by encouraging countries to stop admitting and tolerating the presence of terrorists within their borders.[38]

Finally, diplomacy is "linked with all the [other] elements of counterterrorism," as Paul Pillar observed, whether one thinks of military measures, international cooperation in the areas of intelligence and law enforcement, efforts to dry up terrorists' financial resources, or economic sanctions.[39]

Severing diplomatic relations with terrorist sponsors, an option repeatedly chosen by the United States, demonstrates a targeted country's determination to punish state sponsors of terrorism. But this option eliminates direct diplomacy as a counterterrorist instrument aiming at the exploration of incentives that could weaken a government's willingness to support terrorism.

Of course, even without formal diplomatic ties, direct government-to-government contacts are not out of the question and can be one factor in paving the way for policy changes on the part of a state sponsor of terrorism. Again, Libya is the most obvious case in point. In 2003, the country was taken off the U.S. State Department's list of state sponsors of terrorism after American–Libyan contacts resulted in Muammar Gaddafi's decision to discontinue his WMD program and any involvement in terrorism; he furthermore agreed to compensate the families of victims that perished in Libyan-sponsored terrorist incidents. By the end of 2008, 28 years after diplomatic ties were broken off between Washington and Tripoli, the two countries were ready to restore full relations. As mentioned before, Gaddafi's desire to end his country's economic and political isolation influenced his decision greatly, but diplomacy was instrumental in sealing the ultimate outcome.

Whether the U.S. president should directly negotiate with Iranian leaders or not was a major bone of contention during the 2008 presidential campaign, with Barack Obama agreeing to talk to America's adversaries, including Iran, without prior conditions, and John McCain rejecting direct and highest-level diplomacy. At the same time, the Bush administration sent contradictory signals. In May 2008, President Bush said in a speech before the Knesset and immediately after mentioning Iran's President Mahmoud Ahmadinejad,

> Some seem to believe that we should negotiate with the terrorists and radicals, as if some ingenious argument will persuade them they have been wrong all along. We have heard this foolish delusion before. As Nazi tanks crossed into Poland in 1939, an American senator declared: "Lord, if I could only have talked to Hitler, all this might have been avoided." We have an obligation to call this what it is— the false comfort of appeasement, which has been repeatedly discredited by history.[40]

Two months after the president categorically rejected a dialogue with Iranian leaders and attacked those who recommended direct talks, the U.S. State Department's third-ranking official, William J. Burns, traveled to Geneva to participate in talks, along with representatives of the European Union, with Iran's nuclear negotiator Saeed Jalili. During the Obama presidency, the long negotiation about Iran's nuclear program in Vienna between the United States, the United Kingdom, France, Germany, the European Union, Russia, and China on the one hand and Iran on the other hand were all along strictly about the most pressing problem, namely the threat of the latter possessing nuclear weapons. Iran's support of Hezbollah, Hamas, and other terrorist groups were not part of these negotiations. In the spring of 2018, President Donald Trump announced the United States' withdrawal from the nuclear agreement. Nevertheless, however imperfect the agreement was, the Vienna negotiations demonstrated that when nation-states are involved, diplomacy has a chance.

Negotiation with Terrorists: Whether to talk to and negotiate with terrorist groups depends first of all on the particular circumstances. Hostage situations are the most likely cases when governments are willing to deal directly or indirectly with terrorists in order to save the lives of fellow citizens. In the Iran hostage crisis, in the arms-for-hostages deals between Washington and Tehran for the sake of Americans held hostage by Hezbollah in Lebanon, and in many other less prominent cases, governments and corporations have negotiated and struck deals with terrorists, without admitting it, to free hostages. This practice continues to this day.

Giving in to the demands of terrorists in order to free hostages is problematic because such bargains might encourage further hostage-takings by the same groups or by other organizations.

It is very difficult but not impossible to negotiate the abandonment of terrorism and bringing groups into the legitimate political process. Northern Ireland serves as an excellent example. After decades of bloody violence and a long, protracted peace process, Northern Ireland finally turned the corner in early 2007, when Sinn Fein, the political wing of the Irish Republican Army (IRA), and the Democratic Unionist Party, representing the Protestant majority, formed a government in which Ian Paisley, the long-time Protestant opponent of any meaningful political role for the Catholic minority, became the first minister (or prime minister) and Martin McGuinness, a former IRA commander, the deputy first minister. As the case of Northern Ireland demonstrates, negotiated peace agreements rarely hold after the first try; instead, it is far more likely that the road to peace is paved with broken accords and renewed outbreaks of violence. Cease-fire agreements between the Sri Lankan government and the Tamil Tigers, between Spain's government and the Basque ETA, and between the Israeli government and Hamas were repeatedly negotiated and broken. Yet, given the poor track record of military actions in ending terrorism, the negotiation route may well be the most promising option in certain cases. In the rare Sri Lankan case, however, the Tigers were defeated totally by the overwhelming force of the military after peace negotiations failed repeatedly.

One needs to recognize that the goals and ideologies of organizations determine whether there are opportunities for common ground and compromises. Separatist groups may be inclined to settle for a significant degree of political, economic, and social autonomy short of full independence, if only because they risk otherwise the support of their constituencies. Organizations with uncompromising objectives, on the other hand, will not move from their ultimate goals. While it was possible to negotiate with Marxist militants, such as the Baader-Meinhof terrorists in Germany, about the release of their hostages in return for freeing some of their imprisoned comrades, it did not make sense to talk about the group's categorical stand on its final objective: The destruction of capitalism and democracy in the Federal Republic of Germany and elsewhere in the West. Religious terrorists, too, tend to have absolute demands and goals that defy compromise. A comparison between the secular Palestinian al-Fatah, a terrorist organization before—at least officially—it abandoned terrorism, and the religious Palestinian Hamas is instructive. While al-Fatah seemed open to settling for a compromise two-state solution with Israel, Hamas did not retreat from its ultimate objective—the removal of Israel from the map of the Middle East.

Aware that suggestions to actually talk to Al Qaeda might be considered "tantamount to treason," Louise Richardson seems to reject the profound difference between "traditional" terrorists with more realistic goals and utopian terrorists with apocalyptic objectives, when she suggests,

> If anything, we appear to know less about the nature of our adversaries in the war on terrorism than we did when we began. We take as a

given that their demands are so extreme as to be non-negotiable, but it would be worth finding out if that is, in fact, the case...

Ayman al-Zawahiri has clearly emerged as the chief spokesman and strategist of the al-Qaeda leadership, and while it is far from clear that he has the authority to carry his followers with him, the opportunity to engage him is one that should not be missed, no matter how much opprobrium we hold for him.[41]

For those who rejected talks with al-Zawahiri, bin Laden's successor, or ISIS leader al-Baghdadi, such negotiations would elevate Al Qaeda, ISIS, and their affiliated groups and like-minded, unorganized followers to legitimate political actors without any incentive to abandon violence. As for Al Qaeda, one expert noted,

There is no sign that al Qaeda has changed its thinking on the utility of violence. And it is hard to conceive of a viable process of primary negotiations in which Al Qaeda could be included. Al Qaeda has global aspirations and no firm territorial base, and there is no clearly defined territory in which its aims could be satisfied through constitutional means. Under these conditions, opening negotiations would be a counterproductive move: it would provide al Qaeda with political legitimacy.[42]

Scott Atran and Robert Axelrod, too, examined the utility of negotiating with terrorist groups on the State Department's list of terrorist groups and concluded that "there are groups, like Al Qaeda, that will probably have to be fought to the end."[43] But they also made the following argument that was similar to Richardson's suggestions:

It's an uncomfortable truth, but direct interaction with terrorist groups is sometimes indispensable. And even if it turns out that negotiation gets us nowhere with a particular group, talking and listening can help us to better understand why the group wants to fight us, so that we may better fight it.[44]

In June 2010 the Supreme Court ruled in *Holder v. Humanitarian Law Project* that even expert contacts with terrorist groups constitute "material support," lend "legitimacy" to an organization, and were therefore illegal.[45]

The Taliban, too, was for a long time considered by Washington and its allies as an entity not trustworthy for serious negotiations. Yet, the Trump administration by-passed the Kabul government that the United States had helped to install and signed in February 2020 the so-called Doha Agreement with the Taliban. While the United States promised the withdrawal of all U.S. and allied forces within 14 months, the

Taliban merely pledged to prevent Al Qaeda to operate in territories they controlled. Even before the troop withdrawal was fully completed, the Taliban defeated Afghan's Security Forces and prepared their forceful take-over of the Kabul government. Reportedly, President Trump's National Security Advisor John Bolton "recognized the dangers of signing a bad deal with the Taliban and sought to convince the president to back away from what was shaping up to be less of a "peace" agreement and more of a poorly masked surrender agreement.

When Al-Qaeda leader al-Zawahiri was assassinated in July 2022 as he stood on the balcony of his hideaway house in the middle of Kabul, it was obvious that the Taliban had not adhered to their promise. As one national security expert wrote,

After countless hours of negotiations, the most the U.S. negotiator could extract from the Taliban was a flimsy pledge to "not allow" Al Qaeda to "use the soil of Afghanistan to threaten the security of the United States and its allies." The language is weak and meaningless.[46]

The Doha Agreement might well become the best model for (1) rejecting negotiations with the most notorious terrorists or their supporters, and (2) if negotiations take place, the agreed-upon obligations must be carefully worded and enforceable with the latter condition next to impossible in international settings.

Public Diplomacy. Unlike traditional, government-to-government diplomacy, public diplomacy is conducted by one government and aimed at foreign publics. So far, the record of American post-9/11 public diplomacy in the Arab and Muslim world has been a fiasco and thus a far cry from the success story during the Cold War. The three pillars of American public diplomacy of the Cold War era—the spread of information via foreign language broadcasts into the communist world, cultural exchanges, and educational exchanges—need to be adapted to the global realities of the twenty-first century.[47] In the age of information, when a multitude of global television and radio networks and the Internet provide instant news, information, and communication, the successful broadcast strategies of the past will no longer work. There are more vehicles and opportunities to reach and engage larger audiences overseas than ever before—but only with innovative programs conceived, produced, and presented by professionals who speak the languages and know the cultures of the target audiences and, of course, the public relations goals of the United States.

Although well financed in the years after 9/11, the U.S. government's Arab-language television network al-Hurra and radio station al-Sawa, for example, neither displayed the excellence of their Cold War predecessors, such as "Voice of America" or "Radio Free Europe," nor founded promising new approaches for a completely different media and communication environment. As for the Internet, Secretary of Defense Robert Gates was right on target when he said the following:

Public relations was invented in the United States, yet we are miserable at communicating to the rest of the world what we are about as a society and a culture, about freedom and democracy, about our policies and our goals. It is just plain embarrassing that al-Qaeda is better at communicating its message on the internet than America. As one foreign diplomat asked a couple of years ago, "How has one man in a cave managed to out-communicate the world's greatest communication society?" Speed, agility, and cultural relevance are not terms that come readily to mind when discussing U.S. strategic communications.[48]

While a modernized public diplomacy model must focus on the Internet's ample opportunities for virtual cultural and educational exchanges, it should never do so at the expense of direct exchanges since surveys reveal that many Arabs and Muslims are in favor of such interactions. However, while far from satisfactory during the Bush administration and making strides during the Obama presidency, the Department of State's public diplomacy section took a hit in terms of qualified personnel and financial resources as the Trump White House shrank severely the government's diplomatic arm. More harmful was that the U.S. Agency for Global Media (USAGM) with the onetime crown jewels of America's public diplomacy— Radio Free Europe/Radio Liberty, Radio Free Asia, the Middle East Broadcasting Networks and Radio Martí—was politicized during the Trump years. While the Biden administration restored budgetary resources for the Department of State's public diplomacy efforts, the rehiring of highly qualified professionals in the field and the reestablishment of non-partisan credibility of the USAGM news outlets took time.

Of course, public diplomacy should recognize the importance of moderate opinion-makers in targeted countries, such as academics, clerics, and media personnel, particularly news analysts, editorial writers, and columnists encouraging them to speak out against terrorism in their own countries and regions. In the wake of the 2004 terrorist attack by Chechen separatists on a Russian school in Beslan, a number of Muslim clerics condemned the attacks—but such condemnations were often not categorical but permitted explicitly or implicitly such lethal strikes against Israelis and other infidels who had not, like Russia, supported the Palestinian cause. Other Muslim leaders have pointed out that most of the deadly and gruesome terrorist attacks at the dawn of the twenty-first century have been perpetrated by Muslims. At the height of the violent uproar over the Danish cartoons that depicted the Prophet Muhammad, for example, some Arab opinion-makers questioned the Muslim world's violent mass protests against drawings and its collective silence about jihadis who beheaded their Western hostages and posted the videotapes of these executions on the Internet. After a Jordanian military pilot was cruelly burned to death by ISIS executioners in 2015, many Muslims around the world condemned the group. Grand Imam Ahmed al-Tayeb of Cairo's Al-Azhar Mosque said the militants "deserve the Quranic punishment of death, crucifixion or the chopping off of their arms for being enemies of God and the Prophet Muhammad."[49] Since such voices are the best hope for promoting nonviolence and for condemning violence in their own communities, countries, and regions, they should be highlighted in public diplomacy efforts.

Conciliation and Peace: One option—the effort on the part of stable democratic governments to offer conciliation, compromise, and peace to individuals or organizations instead of fighting and repressing them—is frequently omitted from responses to terrorism. As Peter C. Sederberg has pointed out,

> We tend to underestimate the possibility that the democratic principles themselves may suggest effective response. Negotiations, compromise, and conciliation rest at the heart of democratic processes, but commentators usually dismiss them as irrelevant or even dangerously ineffective.[50]

A chance for conciliation and compromise may exist if individual terrorists recognize the hopelessness of their struggle and if organizations are not dead set on totally destroying the state they fight. Italy's "repentance" law of 1980, for example, was an effort to lure individual terrorists away from the Red Brigades, win their collaboration, and thereby weaken and defeat the terror organization. To be sure, the time was right, in that the growing brutality of the Red Brigades' terror strikes horrified an increasing number of its members, some of whom no longer believed that their armed struggle could succeed. But while some terrorists took the opportunity, many others did not. Identifying "group dynamics" as keeping terrorists in the fold, Donatella della Porta found,

> Many of the militants who were in the process of quitting terrorism were in fact compelled to react to the "betrayal" of some of their fellow comrades by confirming their loyalty to the organization. Solidarity toward comrades also influenced the process of quitting underground organizations. Interviews expressed such sentiments as "You do not give up on the basis of an individual decision."[51]

In June 2004, after a series of deadly terror attacks in Saudi Arabia, King Fahd called on militant followers of Al Qaeda to turn themselves into the law enforcement authorities within a one-month period in which "the door of forgiveness" would be open. This limited amnesty was offered with the warning that unless militants surrendered, they would face the full might of state wrath. Shortly after the amnesty was announced, two of Saudi Arabia's most wanted terrorists surrendered. But a Saudi group linked to Osama bin Laden predicted in an online news release that the initiative would end in "utter failure... to stop the jihad."[52] There was no threat in this particular case, but would-be defectors might not have left their groups for fear of being punished. The limited amnesty was not successful at all.

Just like conciliation efforts directed at individuals, peace initiatives aimed at bringing governments and organizations together and finding nonviolent compromises have had mixed results in the past. In South Africa, a long process of peace involving the minority government and the African National Congress (ANC) was successful in that it led to the establishment of a democratic government in 1994. After the "getting-to-know-each-other" phase, the parties set a negotiation agenda and agreed on visible compromises: The government released ANC prisoners, and the ANC terminated its armed struggle. This was followed by actual negotiations, the implementation of the negotiated agreement, and, finally, a process of "truth and conciliation."[53] The willingness of all parties to participate in negotiations to resolve the century-old conflict in Northern Ireland in the 1990s peacefully moved them toward a lasting, nonviolent, political solution. In the Middle East, a negotiated solution to the Israeli–Palestinian conflict seemed repeatedly on track in the last decades, but opponents of compromise on both sides derailed the peace process at crucial junctures. Although negotiations between the Spanish government and the Basque separatist group ETA resulted in a cease-fire agreement in the 1990s, in the long run the terrorists rejected a compromise solution and resumed their campaign of terror.

It seems that conflicts between states and domestic groups that commit terrorism are more susceptible to conciliation and compromise than are clashes between a nation-state on the one hand and foreign terrorist groups or an international terrorism network on the other. Secular groups may be more willing than religious organizations to partake in negotiations. Individual followers of charismatic leaders may be lured away from their terrorist activities by amnesty offers, but it is unlikely that the leaders of global terrorist networks like those established by Al Qaeda and ISIS and their principal foe—the United States—would travel the road of reconciliation and compromise. And yet, conciliation should never be discounted as one of many options for responding to terrorism. Indeed, governments can use a stick and carrot at the same time or, as Sederberg suggested, "combine conciliatory and repressive elements."[54]

How to Counter Contemporary Domestic Terrorism

In an analysis titled "From 9/11 to 1/6," terrorism expert Cynthia Miller-Idriss points to an unintended consequence of Western countries' post-9/11 preoccupation with defeating jihadist terrorism. Recognizing direct links between the attacks of 9/11 and the war against jihadist terrorism on the one hand and the rise of violent Far-Right extremism in America and Europe on the other hand, she writes,

> In the wake of the 9/11 attacks, the rise of violent jihadism reshaped American politics in ways that created fertile ground for right-wing extremism. The attacks were a gift to peddlers of xenophobia, white supremacism, and Christian nationalism: as dark-skinned Muslim foreigners bent on murdering Americans, al Qaeda terrorists and their ilk seemed to have stepped out of a far-right fever dream.

The U.S.-led war on terrorism, which involved the near-complete pivoting of intelligence, security, and law enforcement attention to the Islamist threat, leaving Far-Right extremism to grow unfettered. In recent years, right-wing radicals in the United States and Europe have made clear that they are willing and able to embrace the tactics of terrorism; they have become, in some ways, a mirror image of the jihadis whom they despise.[55]

It may well be that members of the violent Far-Right movement in the West learned from their jihadist counterparts and copycatted their tactics. But does this also mean that the major counterterrorism components designed to fight jihadist terrorists abroad and at home should be used to deal with domestic terrorists of the Far-Right and also the Far-Left variety?

A number of hard and soft powers described above in the context of international terrorism could be utilized in responses to violent domestic extremists in the United States and other Western countries—at considerable risk. Take the deployment of military units or counterterrorism commandos at home. In the United States, for example, the Posse Comitatus Act (PCA) prohibits the domestic deployment of active-duty military. But there are exceptions as cited in the Insurrection Act that allow Federal forces to quell civil disturbances and restore law and order. In the past, the military has been repeatedly deployed as the following examples show:

- 1957–58 School Desegregation in Little Rock. President Dwight Eisenhower issued an executive order to send the Army's 101st Airborne Division to Arkansas to maintain law and order during the integration of Central High School in Little Rock.
- 1963 Integration of the University of Alabama: After a court ordered the University of Alabama to admit two Black students, the state's governor, George Wallace, personally prevented the two students to enter the University building. President John F. Kennedy federalized the Alabama National Guard to enforce the order of a federal district court in Alabama. Federalized National Guard troops were also deployed to prevent attacks on civil rights marchers in the South in the early 1960s.

- 1968, Riots in response to Dr. Martin Luther King's Assassination: 13,600 troops occupied Washington, the largest number to be deployed in a U.S. city since the Civil War. Thousands of National Guard and U.S. Army troops were deployed in Baltimore and Chicago respectively to restore law and order.

Yet, to use troops to fight domestic terrorists in the United States or elsewhere in the West would deepen the already significant ideological and partisan differences. This, then, could potentially result in civil war-like conflicts that some of the most extremist elements among contemporary violent extremists planned and hoped more recently.

In almost all cases, decision-makers would be best advised to reject military hard power as counterterrorist option in domestic settings. The case of Northern Ireland serves as example for the failure of military force to defeat militants during a conflict that lasted several decades.

The violent breach of the U.S. Capitol in January 2021, in which well-organized groups played leading roles, raised the question of whether violent domestic groups should be treated like international terrorist organizations. Answering this question in the affirmative would mean that the United States and other countries would designate violent extremist domestic entities as terrorist organizations and thereby adopt new restrictive laws or apply existing legislation and measures to domestic terrorism. Indeed, in the wake of the events of January 6, 2021, some politicians, among them President Biden, underlined the need for new legislation. But Brian Jenkins, a terrorism and counterterrorism expert, urged caution:

> The campaign against homegrown jihadists is not the model for dealing with domestic violent extremists. Prevention may be more difficult to achieve for a variety of reasons...Unlike the jihadists, domestic political extremists have a potential constituency. Jihadist ideology never gained traction in America's Muslim communities. Jihadists were isolated. In contrast, the beliefs motivating America's domestic extremists, especially those on the far right, run deep in American society. Reflecting antipathy toward what some see as a tyrannical federal government, fewer tips from the community can be expected. Informants may be harder to recruit.[56]

And if informants are recruited and deliver intelligence, indicted domestic terrorists may not be found guilty by juries of their peers. A case in point was the planned kidnapping of Michigan Governor Gretchen Whitmer who was the target of Far-Right militants she had angered by issuing strict Covid-19 mandates at the height of the pandemic in

2020. When a group of male extremists planned Whitmer's kidnapping, an FBI informer taped their conversations that detailed their plan to try and execute Whitmer after abducting her from her summer home. Six participants in the foiled plot were indicted, two pleaded guilty and became witnesses against the four others. The jurors acquitted two of the four defendants and did not agree on verdicts for the other two members of the group. The jury had reservations about the informant and the FBI. Just as important, the defendants were native American Christians with names like Adam and Barry—and not Muslims with names like Ahmed or Muhammad. When retried several months later, the two defendants whose first trial ended with a hung jury, were found guilty of plotting the kidnapping of Governor Whitmer.

Like Jenkins aware of the different perceptions of domestic and international terrorists, Daniel Byman took a middle ground, when he suggested that

> treating domestic extremism just like foreign terrorism would be a mistake, but moving a bit in that direction would be desirable. Federal law enforcement in the United States should have the legal authority to take on more responsibility for addressing domestic terrorism. However, given the power of many terrorism-related laws and the political connotations, the terrorism label should be used sparingly, and the new authorities should be tightly defined and monitored.[57]

Jenkins placed domestic terrorism into "an arena fraught with danger to the country, for the perceived foe is us."[58] His perception of domestic terrorists as "us" compared to foreign terrorists as "them" was not far-fetched. In one of my terrorism/counterterrorism seminars, we simulated responses to two similar terrorist situations, one abroad and involving jihadists, and one domestic, involving violent Far-Right extremists. In each case, we knew about intelligence revealing that several terrorists were hiding in buildings after killing several victims. In the case abroad, several students who spoke up, supported a counterterrorism strike to neutralize the jihadists; in the domestic case, the first student taking a position recommended waiting the domestic terrorists out and not killing the perpetrators. "After all, they are Americans—like us," the student said.

Although there was no doubt that domestic terrorism was not treated like international terrorism in Western democracies, in reaction to increased violent domestic extremism law enforcement and intelligence communities in the United States and other Western countries began to pay more attention to counter political violence at home than in the previous decades.

Notes

1 Daniel Byman, "The Good Enough Doctrine," *Foreign Affairs*, September/October 2021, 32 (32–43).
2 Ben Rhodes, "Them and US: How America Lets Its Enemies Hijack Its Foreign Policy," *Foreign Affairs*, September/October 2021, 22.
3 Ibid., 31.
4 Nelly Lahoud, "Bin Laden's Catastrophic Success," *Foreign Affairs*, September/October 2021, 13.
5 Ibid., 21.
6 Eric Schmitt and Helene Cooper, "Al-Zawahiri's Death Puts the Focus Back on Al Qaeda," *New York Times*, August 12, 2022, https://www.nytimes.com/2022/08/02/us/politics/al-qaeda-terrorism-isis.html, accessed August 10, 2022.
7 Geoffrey Nunberg, "How Much Wallop Can a Simple Word Pack?," *New York Times*, July 11, 2002, sec. 4, 7.
8 Donald M. Snow, *National Security for a New Era* (New York: Pearson Longman, 2007), 299.
9 Paul Pillar, *Terrorism and U.S. Foreign Policy* (Washington, DC: Brookings Institution Press, 2001), 218.
10 Joseph S. Nye, Jr., "Obama's Foreign Policy Must Combine Hard and Soft Power," *Huffington Post*, December 3, 2008, www.huffingtonpost.com/joseph-nye/obamas-foreign-policiesm_b_147108.html?view=print, accessed December 11, 2008.
11 Secretary of State Hillary Clinton made these remarks during her testimony as secretary of state designee before the U.S. Senate Foreign Relations Committee's confirmation hearing on January 13, 2009. For the transcript, see www.npr.org/templates/story/story.php?storyId=99290981, accessed January 14, 2009.
12 Defense Secretary Robert Gates made these remarks in his Landon Lecture at Kansas State University, November 26, 2007.
13 Andrew J. Bacevich, "Think Again: What's Our Definition of Victory?" *Newsweek*, December 8, 2008, 38.
14 The quotes are from Max Weber's lecture "The Profession and Vocation of Politics," www.as.ysu.edu/~polisci/syllabi/weber.htm, accessed December 11, 2008.
15 Joseph S. Nye, Jr., *The Paradox of American Power* (New York: Oxford University Press, 2002), 8.
16 Ibid., 9.
17 Defense Secretary Robert Gates made these remarks in his Landon Lecture at Kansas State University, November 26, 2007. The text of the lecture is available at www.defenselink.mil/speeches/speech.aspx?speechid=1199, accessed December 1, 2008.
18 www.nytimes.com/2013/05/24/us/politics/transcript-of-obamas-speech-on-drone-policy.html, accessed July 20, 2015.
19 Holger Jensen, "The United States Should Retaliate against Terrorist Groups," in Laura K. Egendorf, ed., *Terrorism: Opposing Viewpoints* (San Diego, CA: Greenhaven Press, 2000), 164.
20 Ibid.
21 Deborah Sontag, "Israel Acknowledges Hunting Down Arab Militants," *New York Times*, December 22, 2000, A12.
22 Perez was quoted in Clyde Haberman, "In the Mid-East This Year, Even Words Shoot to Kill," *New York Times*, August 5, 2001, sec. 4, 3.
23 Ibid.

24 Michael Ignatieff, "Lesser Evils," *New York Times Sunday Magazine*, May 2, 2004, www.nytimes.com/2004/05/02/magazine/lesser-evils.html?scp= 1&sq=michael%20ignatieff,%20lesser%20evils&st=cse, accessed May 20, 2009.
25 For more on the CIA authority, see James Risen and David Johnson, "Threats and Responses: Hunt for Al Qaeda; Bush Has Widened Authority of CIA to Kill Terrorists," *New York Times*, December 15, 2002, 1.
26 Panetta made this remark during his appearance on the ABC News program *This Week*, June 27, 2010.
27 Pillar, 98.
28 David C. Martin and John Walcott, *Best Laid Plans: The Inside Story of America's War against Terrorism* (New York: Harper & Row, 1988), 35.
29 Stephen D. Collins, "Dissuading State Support of Terrorism: Strikes or Sanctions?," *Studies in Conflict & Terrorism* 27 (1) (January/February 2004), p. 3.
30 Robert Pape, "Why Economic Sanctions Do Not Work," *International Security* 22 (Fall 1997), p. 110.
31 Pillar, 167.
32 Collins.
33 Ibid., 15.
34 Pillar, 94, 95.
35 Jervis, 7.
36 Richard Betts, "The Soft Underbelly of American Primacy," in Demetrious James Caraley, ed., *September 11, Terrorist Attacks, and U.S. Foreign Policy* (New York: Academy of Political Science, 2002), 46.
37 Robert F. Trager and Dessislava P. Zagorcheva, "Deterring Terrorism: It Can Be Done," *International Security* 30 (3) (Winter 2005/2006), pp. 88–89.
38 Countering the Changing Threat of International Terrorism: Report of the National Commission on Terrorism, Pursuant to Public Law 277, 105th Congress, 17, 18.
39 Pillar, 73.
40 The transcript of President George W. Bush's speech on May 15, 2008, is available at www.whitehouse.gov/news/releases/2008/05/20080515-1.html.
41 Louise Richardson, *What Terrorists Want: Understanding the Enemy, Containing the Threat* (New York: Random House, 2006), 212.
42 Peter R. Neumann, "Negotiating with Terrorists," *Foreign Affairs* 86 (1) (January/February 2007), p. 136.
43 Scott Atran and Robert Axelrod, "Why We Talk to Terrorists," *New York Times*, June 29, 2010.
44 Ibid.
45 The *Holder v. Humanitarian Law Project* ruling is available at www.supremecourt.gov/opinions/09pdf/08–1498.pdf, accessed July 1, 2010.
46 Lisa Curtis, "How the Doha Agreement Guaranteed US Failure in Afghanistan," *Hoover Institution*, November 2, 2021, https://www.hoover.org/research/how-doha-agreement-guaranteed-us-failure-afghanistan, accessed August 2, 2022.
47 For public diplomacy in the information age, see Geoffrey Cohen and Amelia Arsenault, "Moving from Monologue to Dialogue to Collaboration: The Three Layers of Public Diplomacy," in Geoffrey Cohen and Nicholas J. Cull, eds., *Public Diplomacy in a Changing World*, Annals of the American Academy of Political and Social Science Series, Vol. 616 (Philadelphia, PA: Sage, March 2008), 46–52.
48 The remarks were made during the Landon Lecture at Kansas State University, November 26, 2007.

49 Reported by the Associated Press, http://news.yahoo.com/leader-egypt-religious-institution-enraged-killing-090829436.html;_ylt=A0LEVzu WmrZVCg 8AOh1XNyoA;_ylu=X3oDMTEzb2k0bmQ5BGNvbG8DYmYxBHBvcwM3B HZ0aWQDVklQNDQyXzEEc2VjA3Ny#, accessed July 27, 2015.
50 Peter C. Sederberg, "Conciliation as Counter-Terrorist Strategy," *Journal of Peace Research* 32 (3) (1995), p. 298.
51 Donatella della Porta, "Left-Wing Terrorism in Italy," in Martha Crenshaw, ed., *Terrorism in Context* (University Park: Pennsylvania State University, 1995), 153.
52 Reuters, "Qaeda Says Saudi Militant Amnesty Will Fail," *Yahoo! News*, June 30, 2004, www.yahoo.com, accessed July 6, 2004.
53 For more, see "Reconciliation and Community: The Future of Peace in Northern Ireland," Conference Report, Project on Justice in Times of Transition, June 6–8, 1995, Belfast, Northern Ireland.
54 Sederberg, 299.
55 Cynthia Miller-Idriss, "From 9/11 to 1/6: The War on Terror Supercharged the Far Right," *Foreign Affairs* September/October 2021, 56.
56 Brian Jenkins, "Countering Domestic Terrorism May Require Rethinking of Intelligence Strategy," *The Rand Blog*, October 5, 2021, https://www.rand.org/blog/2021/10/countering-domestic-terrorism-may-require-rethinking.html, accessed July 20, 2022.
57 Daniel Byman, "Should We Treat Domestic Terrorists Like We Treat ISIS?," *Foreign Affairs*, October 3, 2017, https://www.foreignaffairs.com/articles/united-states/2017-10-03/should-we-treat-domestic-terrorists-way-we-treat-isis, accessed August 21, 2022.
58 Jenkins.

12 Preventing Terrorism
The Crucial Role of Good Intelligence

The previous chapter discussed hard and soft power responses to terrorism from hard military actions to soft public diplomacy approaches that overwhelmingly can be and have been utilized mostly against international terrorism abroad and in certain cases against domestic terrorists as well. The most important takeaway from the discussion of military power as a means to counter terrorism is clear: With few exceptions, military might does not work because it does not defeat the extreme ideas that motivate leaders and followers of nonstate terrorist entities. Preventing terrorism within the territory of a state by home-grown violent extremists or those acting on behalf of foreign terrorist entities resembles in many respects the efforts to prevent organized crime. In the United States and other Western countries, law enforcement and intelligence agencies have decades of institutional experience in fighting violent political extremism, mostly from the Far-Left, starting in the late 1960s. By the late 1980s and early 1990s, Marxist terrorists from the American Weather Underground to the Italian Red Brigades and the German Red Army Faction were dead, behind bars, or had surrendered. These groups were not defeated by military hard power but rather by policing models used in fighting crime and good intelligence. Yet, in spite of dealing with homegrown terrorists for many years, American and other Western intelligence and law enforcement agencies were not able to prevent deadly jihadist attacks in their homelands—most of all the catastrophe of 9/11 and more recently violence carried out by homegrown extremists.

Were the 9/11 Attacks Preventable?

At the time of the 9/11 attacks, there were 16 separate federal agencies charged wholly or partially with collecting and analyzing intelligence to protect the country's national security. While there was a certain degree of interagency cooperation pre-9/11, the system still worked largely along the design prescribed by the 1947 National Security Act. That act, signed into law by President Harry Truman after World War II and during the

DOI: 10.4324/9781003289265-14

early stages of the Cold War, focused almost exclusively on intelligence concerning foreign foes.

As one expert noted, the National Security Act of 1947 assigned four responsibilities to the intelligence community, namely,

> supporting the president, engaging in clandestine activities abroad in support of national policy goals, protecting the United States against Soviet penetration, and supporting strategic military operations. The director of central intelligence and the Central Intelligence Agency (CIA) are given responsibility over the first two, the Federal Bureau of Investigation (FBI) over the third, and military intelligence units over the fourth.[1]

In the post-Cold War years, the act was no longer in tune with the geopolitical realities but remained the legal underpinning of a system with a clear distinction between foreign and domestic intelligence. Most importantly, while there were vertical reporting requirements, there were none prescribing horizontal interagency intelligence sharing. Indeed, as one expert noted,

> At the time of the act's passing, little thought was given to the need for a national-level intelligence apparatus in Washington that could synthesize information from across the government to inform policymakers and help support real-time tactical decisions. That reality, coupled with practices that led to a "stovepiping" of intelligence, arrested the growth of information sharing, collaboration, and integration.[2]

The lack of vertical and horizontal intelligence sharing among agencies impeded opportunities to thwart the 9/11 plot. Investigations found afterward that various agencies possessed bits of intelligence that perhaps could have led to the discovery of the hijacking plot and its terrible consequences. As Philip Heymann pointed out,

> The FBI and the CIA were unwilling or unable to exchange information quickly and effectively; this applied even more to furnishing information to the Immigration and Naturalization Service [INS]. The INS did not learn from the CIA what identified terrorists were entering the United States and where they were.[3]

The FBI seemed slow in tracking suspects inside the country when the CIA provided intelligence about their identity.

Perhaps more shocking was the disclosure that higher-ups at the FBI headquarters in Washington ignored the leads and thwarted the investigations of FBI agents in field offices that should have led to the arrests of the 9/11 plotters before they could strike. Agents in the field reported to their Washington superiors that foreign flight school students insisted on learning how to pilot commercial jetliners but were not at all interested in take-offs and landing procedures. Coleen Rowley, an agent and lawyer in the Minneapolis field office of the FBI, testified before the Senate Judiciary Committee that she and her colleagues were frustrated because FBI headquarters had obstructed their efforts to investigate Zacarias Moussaoui, allegedly the designated twentieth hijacker in the 9/11 plot and one of the suspicious flight school students.

According to one account, Rowley was particularly incensed because FBI headquarters rejected a warrant request to examine Moussaoui's computer. It was only after 9/11 that the FBI got the warrant and reportedly found information related to commercial planes and crop dusters on the computer's hard drive. The government grounded crop-dusting planes temporarily because of what it found.[4] Some observers concluded that the Minneapolis investigation, if not hampered by FBI higher-ups, could have produced evidence about the identity of foreigners and their suspicious interest in piloting commercial jets in flight. The likelihood of discovering the plot before it was too late should have been enhanced by an alert agent in the FBI's Phoenix field office whose memo informed superiors in Washington about several Arabs who were training in a flight school in Arizona. But again, officials at the FBI headquarters showed no particular interest.

Besides serious problems in the culture of individual agencies and turf battles between different agencies, a multitude of other deficiencies had been identified well before 9/11. In a June 2000 report to President Clinton titled "Countering the Changing Threat of International Terrorism," the National Commission on Terrorism warned that its members had "identified significant obstacles to the collection and distribution of reliable information on terrorism to analysts and policymakers" and that "these obstacles must be removed."[5] Among the identified problems before and after 9/11 were the following:

- *Lack of information sharing.* The most glaring problem was the failure of the various members of the intelligence community to share information.

  Law enforcement agencies are traditionally reluctant to share information outside of their circles so as not to jeopardize any potential prosecution. The FBI does promptly share information warning about specific threats with the CIA and other agencies. But the FBI is far less likely to disseminate terrorist information that may not relate to an immediate threat even though this could be of immense long-term or cumulative value to the intelligence community... The problem is particularly pronounced with respect to information in the FBI's field offices in the United States, most of which never reaches the FBI headquarters, let alone other U.S. government agencies or departments.[6]

• An investigation by the staff of the 9/11 Commission came to the same conclusion: "The [intelligence] Community lacked a common information architecture that would help to ensure the integration of counterterrorism data across CIA, NSA, DIA, the FBI, and other agencies."[7]

• *Insufficient human intelligence.* The National Commission on Terrorism stated,

> Inside information is the key to preventing attacks by terrorists. The CIA must aggressively recruit informants with unique access to terrorist plans. That sometimes requires recruiting those who have committed terrorist acts or related crimes, just as domestic law enforcement agencies routinely recruit criminal informants in order to pursue major criminal figures.[8]

• Therefore, the Commission recommended, the CIA must act on the recognition that "the aggressive recruitment of human intelligence sources on terrorism is one of the intelligence community's highest priorities."[9]

• *Lack of state-of-the-art information technology.* One reason why the FBI and other intelligence agencies failed in the past to connect the dots of the available intelligence to pinpoint the connections between suspected terrorists and the targets of terrorist plots was the lack of state-of-the-art information technology—although, as the National Commission on Terrorism concluded well before 9/11, "The ability to exploit information collected—process it into understandable information and prioritize it—is essential to an effective global counterterrorism program."[10] The lack of sufficient financial resources delayed the modernization of information technology in all intelligence agencies. As far as the FBI was concerned, its "ability to exploit the increasing volume of terrorism information has been hampered by aging technology."[11] At the CIA, the Counterterrorism Center in particular was "suffering from inadequate resources" and therefore "had to cut back or eliminate plans for an increased operational tempo to meet the globalization of terrorism and for development and acquisition of technology designed to assist in combating terrorists."[12] With respect to the NSA, the National Commission on Terrorism concluded that the NSA, because of its inability to "keep pace with the information revolution... is losing its capability to target and exploit the modern communication systems used by terrorists, seriously weakening the NSA's ability to warn of possible attacks."[13]

- *Shortage of linguists.* The NSA in particular, but the rest of the intelligence community as well, "face a drastic shortage of linguists to translate raw data into useful information."[14] At a time when the global network of terrorists presided over or inspired by bin Laden represents the most serious terrorism threat to the United States, the NSA collects vast amounts of raw data in a multitude of languages and even unique dialects. Without qualified linguists translating this material into English, intelligence of this kind is not at all useful for analysts and policy-makers. But since the translation of highly sensitive intelligence information can only be entrusted to persons eligible for the highest level of security clearance, the hiring of additional linguists has been slow—even after 9/11.

These problems were not aggressively attacked before 9/11 because, as Heymann pointed out, terrorism "posed a minimal risk at home."[15] The result was complacency. "We were focused on attacks on Americans abroad, although we should have been able to imagine terrible attacks at home, even of the sort that took place [on 9/11]."[16]

The Boston Marathon Attacks and the Fort Hood Shootings

In March 2011, Russia's Federal Security Service informed the FBI that Tamerlan Tsarnaev of Boston was a follower of radical Islam and might join underground groups in Dagestan. FBI agents investigated and interviewed the young man and his family without finding evidence of terrorist links. Tamerlan's name was nevertheless put into a customs and border protection watch list so that authorities would be alerted if he crossed U.S. borders. In September 2011, Russia's Federal Security Service alerted the CIA with the same information emphasizing Tsarnaev's intention to travel overseas. These tips were not shared within or between the agencies. The Boston police department was not informed. When Tsarnaev flew to Dagestan in early 2012 and returned within six months, no FBI agent was notified. Tsarnaev's misspelled name and an erroneous date of birth on some documents prevented his name from coming up on the watch list. It was only after he and his younger brother carried out the deadly Boston bombings in April 2013 that FBI and CIA agents looked again into the Russian alerts.

Afterward, critics blamed the FBI, CIA, and other agencies for not preventing the devastating attack. Senator Susan Collins (R-ME), a senior member of the Senate's Intelligence Committee complained,

There still seem to be serious problems with sharing information, including critical investigative information. That is troubling to me, that this many years after the attacks on our country in 2001 that we still seem to have stovepipes that prevent information from being shared effectively, not only among agencies but also within the same agency in one case.[17]

The House Committee on Homeland Security wrote in its report on the Boston bombings that the committee was "concerned that officials are asserting that this attack could not have been prevented, without compelling evidence to confirm that is the case."[18]

An earlier, lethal attack raised also questions about the ability of government agencies to recognize and act on warning signals for likely terrorist threats against the U.S. homeland. Thus, before he killed 13 persons and injured another 28 at the Fort Hood Army base in late 2009, U.S. Army Major Nidal Malik Hasan had openly expressed his growing opposition to the wars in Iraq and Afghanistan on religious grounds. Although email exchanges between Hasan and Anwar al-Awlaki, an extremist imam in Yemen who preached jihad against Americans, were intercepted before the Fort Hood incident, "a Defense Department analyst examined them and decided the queries were part of Major Hasan's research and warranted no further investigation."[19] Addressing the findings of a Pentagon report on the Fort Hood shooting spree, Defense Secretary Robert Gates noted that

as a department, we have not done enough to adapt to the evolving domestic internal security threat to American troops and military facilities that has emerged over the past decade. In this area, as in so many others, this department is burdened by 20th-century processes and attitudes mostly rooted in the cold war.[20]

January 6, 2021: An Intelligence Failure?

Whatever one calls the violent breach of the U.S. Capitol on January 6, 2021 (1/6)—an insurrection, a coup attempt, or domestic terrorism, the agencies charged with protecting Americans from violence failed to warn law enforcement agencies of the serious threat of violence. Thus, the officers of the Capitol Police were outnumbered by the angry crowd of Trump supporters who managed to violently invade the halls of Congress. The question was whether this was the result of poor intelligence collection, a breakdown in analyzing raw intelligence and connecting the dots, or a failure to issue threat alerts. According to one expert analysis,

Intelligence collection did not fail. In fact, it was robust. Rather, the failure was in the analysis of intelligence and the failure of senior government officials to issue warnings based on that intelligence.[21]

Post-January 6 investigations showed that the FBI and the Department of Homeland Security (DHS) received human intelligence (HUMINT) and signal intelligence (SIGINT) from a multitude of sources, among them regional fusion centers in various states, the New York City Police Department's excellent counterterrorism division, and their own intelligence units. They also should have been well aware of the threats issued in the context of the 1/6 protests in Washington, DC, on Parler, Telegram, Twitter, and other social media platforms.

When everything was said and done, there were troubling reports by career bureaucrats about the politicization of executive agencies that were top-heavy with political appointees that ignored or watered down intelligence alerts about the plans of militant White Supremacists and anti-government extremists for that fateful day.

Post-9/11 Successes in Preventing Terrorism

The Boston Marathon Attacks in 2013 and the Breach of the U.S. Capitol in 2021 were high-profile cases, in which the post-9/11 intelligence community did not perform adequately. But those and several other failures should not overshadow the many instances in which intelligence and law enforcement agencies stopped serious terrorist plots.[22] One of those cases involved a plot that targeted highly populated places in New York City. The three plotters communicated through internet messaging applications. Their conversations revealed, according to the U.S. Department of Justice, that they planned to carry out bombings and shootings in heavily populated areas of New York City during the Islamic holy month of Ramadan in 2016, all in the name of ISIS. One of the three, Abdulrahman El Bahnasawy, a Canadian, traveled to New Jersey to scout targets; a second man, Talha Haroon, was in Pakistan planning to travel to New York in time for the attack; the third plotter, a medical doctor, was in the Philippines sending money to Bahnasawy for the purchase of firearms and material for suicide belts. Unbeknown to the plotters, a fourth man who had joined in their conversations was an FBI agent, not the fellow jihadist he pretended to be. The plot was foiled when the FBI arrested the 18-year-old Canadian in May 2016; soon thereafter his would-be accomplices were taken into custody by police in their respective countries.[23]

Contrary to actual terrorist attacks that always receive a great deal of media, elite, and public attention, failed and foiled attacks are not at all or not prominently covered by the news media. In many cases, law enforcement and intelligence agencies do not reveal busted plots because they do not want to give away their counterterrorism tactics; in other cases, they do not want to warn plotters still at large.

In the past, a few foiled attacks were heavily publicized because they involved dramatic actions by attentive civilians. Thus, in December 2001, the would-be shoe bomber Richard Reid was prevented from igniting the explosives hidden in his shoes by fellow passengers on an American Airlines flight from Paris to Miami. Similarly, on Christmas Day 2009, one passenger on a Northwest Airlines flight from Amsterdam to Detroit jumped the young Nigerian Umar Farouk Abdulmutallab before he could set off the explosives hidden in his underpants. Such spectacular prevention efforts remain rare.

Intelligence Agencies' Division of Labor

Two basic ways to collect information about governments and nonstate actors, groups, or individuals, perceived to threaten a nation state's national security, namely, human intelligence (HUMINT) and signal intelligence (SIGINT), namely, electronic interceptions of communication, eavesdropping devices, surveillance from the air by planes and drones. In many countries, such as the United States and the United Kingdom, there is a division of intelligence gathering between the domestic and global realm. Thus, in the United States, the CIA and military intelligence agencies focus on global intelligence, whereas the FBI is the lead agency for domestic intelligence. In the United Kingdom, MI6 (MI stands for military intelligence) gathers foreign intelligence and reports to the Foreign Office; MI5, similar to the FBI, is charged with domestic counterintelligence and reports to the Home Office.

In some countries, the intelligence agencies are allowed to act on the information they gather, in other countries they are prohibited from doing so. For example, the two spy agencies in the United Kingdom, MI6 and MI5, are limited to the collection of intelligence, while the police or military are charged with acting on the information they receive. The two corresponding agencies in the United States, CIA and FBI, on the other hand, act on the information they gather, such as arresting a person inside the country or tracing and attacking targets militarily abroad. While differences exist, most democratic countries have intelligence systems similar to the American and British models.

Since most foiled plots do not receive publicity, most people are not aware of how many of them were thwarted. Nor do most people know that the prevention rate increased significantly after the 9/11 attacks compared to the pre-9/11 years. Researchers at the Rand Homeland Security and Defense Center examined a total of 150 successfully executed and foiled terrorist plots against U.S. targets by secular homegrown terrorists and jihadists. When they compared the data for the seven years before

9/11 with that of the seven post-9/11 years, they found that "from 1995–2001, only 31.9% of plots were foiled. Following the 9/11 attacks, from 2002 through 2012, 80.6% of plots were thwarted prior to reaching execution."[24] This was a rather stunning increase in the success rate concerning halted plots that were predominantly planned against domestic targets and in fewer cases directed at American facilities or places with a significant number of U.S. citizens.

Of all 150 cases, federal, state, and local law enforcement, including informants of those agencies, foiled more than one-third (36 percent) of all those terrorist plots. Intelligence agencies were responsible for thwarting 10 percent of the plots. This means that nearly half (46 percent) of the plots were stopped by law enforcement and intelligence communities. Community policing aimed at improving relations between officers and people in communities they serve and perhaps the enduring post-9/11 public service announcements, "If you see something, say something!" may have contributed to the fact that nearly one-fifth (19 percent) of all plots were foiled based on information coming from the public.[25]

Erik J. Dahl's more recent research revealed that in the nearly 20 years after the attacks of 9/11, "there have been many more attempted and plotted attacks prevented in the U.S. than there have been deadly attacks successfully completed."[26] Indeed, whereas there were 81 terrorist attacks that killed one or more victims in the United States during that period, 230 plots were foiled by the counterterrorism community during the same time frame. According to Dahl, "most of these attempted plots were prevented by law enforcement, especially at the state and local levels, using the traditional tools of police."[27]

All these data suggest that in the post-9/11 years, the U.S. counterterrorism community has been quite successful in preventing terrorist attack in the homeland!

To be sure, law enforcement and intelligence agencies have very difficult tasks. Whereas terrorists need to be successful only once to pull off a catastrophic attack, the intelligence and law enforcement agencies are expected to be successful in preventing terrorist attacks all the time—although common sense tells us that this will not be the case. The following sections discuss America's post-9/11 intelligence community that is similarly organized in comparable Western democracies, reform efforts to improve collaboration within and between intelligence and law enforcement agencies, the importance of international cooperation, and preparedness for man-made and natural disasters.

Post-9/11 Organizational and Functional Changes

In the wake of 9/11, the Bush administration and Congress decided that changes in gathering, coordinating, and analyzing intelligence were needed. Following the adoption of the Intelligence Reform and

Terrorism Prevention Act of 2004 (Public Law 108-458), the most drastic reorganization of the intelligence community since the adoption and implementation of the National Security Act of 1947 was undertaken. Most importantly, the act created the new position of Director of National Intelligence (DNI) as the head of the intelligence community. The primary task of the DNI is to enforce collaboration between the 16 existing intelligence agencies and, most importantly, to improve cooperation between those concentrating on foreign intelligence on the one hand and domestic intelligence on the other.

When President George W. Bush nominated John Negroponte as the first DNI, he characterized the new office and its occupant's role this way:

> John will lead a unified intelligence community, and will serve as the principle [*sic*] advisor to the President on intelligence matters. He will have the authority to order the collection of new intelligence, to ensure the sharing of information among agencies, and to establish common standards for the intelligence community's personnel. It will be John's responsibility to determine the annual budgets of all national intelligence agencies and offices and direct how these funds are spent. Vesting these authorities in a single official who reports directly to me will make our intelligence efforts better coordinated, more efficient, and more effective.[28]

In addition to ordering the creation of the DNI, the law prescribed the establishment of a National Counter Terrorism Center (NCTC). Staffed by analysts from all intelligence agencies, the NCTC is part of the Office of the Director of National Intelligence and, according to its website, has the mission to "lead and integrate the national counterterrorism (CT) effort by fusing foreign and domestic CT information, providing terrorism analysis, sharing information with partners across the CT enterprise, and driving whole-of-government action to secure our national CT objectives."[29]

Given the perennial turf battles among various agencies and departments, however, it proved difficult for the DNI and the NCTC to discharge their awesome responsibilities. It was probably no coincidence that President Bush selected a longtime diplomat, John Negroponte, as the first DNI, and a career Air Force intelligence officer and director of the NSA, Lt. Gen. Michael Hayden, as deputy DNI. Their most crucial task was clear—to unify the intelligence community and keep it unified. The Department of Defense in particular resented a strong DNI who would be able to meddle in its several intelligence agencies. This reaction was hardly surprising. The Pentagon, after all, receives about 80 percent of the total funds allotted to the intelligence community. When the new position was created, it was far from certain what authorities the DNI would really have. Although the president said that the DNI would have centralized intelligence-gathering and budgetary authorities, he seemed to assure others in the intelligence community, especially the civilian and military leadership in the Department of Defense, that there would be continuity rather than change when he said,

> The law establishing John's [Negroponte's] position preserves the existing chain of command and leaves all our intelligence agencies, organizations, and offices in their current departments. Our military commanders will continue to have quick access to the intelligence they need to achieve victory on the battlefield.[30]

Negroponte, a career diplomat with no previous experience in any of the intelligence agencies, left his cabinet-level post in early 2007 after only 19 months to become Deputy Secretary of State. At the time, observers in Washington wondered, "whether Mr. Negroponte was there long enough to lay the foundation of real change and whether his transfer suggested that the Bush administration was less committed than it claimed to be to an intelligence overhaul that President Bush had billed as the most significant restructuring of American spy agencies in half a century."[31]

President Bush nominated an experienced intelligence specialist to succeed Negroponte as DNI: Retired Admiral Mike McConnell, a former director of the NSA. One of the challenges of his new job was, as he wrote, that the DNI

> needs to transform the culture of the intelligence community, which is presently characterized by a professional but narrow focus on individual agency missions. Each of the sixteen organizations within the intelligence community has unique mandates and competencies. They also have their own cultures and mythologies, but no one agency can be effective on its own. To capture the benefits of collaboration, a new culture must be created for the entire intelligence community without destroying unique perspectives and capabilities.[32]

President Obama followed his predecessor's lead in that he appointed men with stellar careers in the military and the intelligence community: First, Dennis C. Blair, a retired U.S. Navy admiral, and, upon his resignation in the wake of the Christmas Day would-be underwear bombing, Air Force Lt. Gen. James Clapper. President Donald Trump appointed Daniel Coats, U.S. Senator from Indiana and former Ambassador to Germany, to be the fifth Director of National Intelligence. As U.S. Senator, Coats had served on the Senate Select Committee on Intelligence. He resigned in July 2019 after repeatedly clashing with Donald Trump over the President's Russia and North Korea policy. In the remaining 18 months of the Trump administration, the position was filled by the sixth DNI

John Radcliff followed by three acting DNIs, John Maguire, Richard Grenell, and Lora Shiao. President Biden appointed Avril Haines as seventh and first female Director of Intelligence. An expert on national security, she served during the Obama years as Assistant to the President and Principal Deputy National Security Advisor. Previously, she was the Deputy Director of the Central Intelligence Agency.

Although perceived as a coordinating entity, the Office of the DNI has become a new, large intelligence bureaucracy with the National Counter Terrorism Center, the Cyber Threat Intelligence Integration Center, the National Counterproliferation Center, and the National Counterintelligence and Security Center under its roof. As Table 12.1 shows, of the 16 members of the national intelligence community, the Department of Defense has by far the largest number of intelligence agencies under its umbrella: The DIA, the NSA, the National Reconnaissance Office, the National Geospatial Intelligence Agency, and the intelligence arms of each of the four military branches. In other words, 8 of the 17 members are parts of the Department of Defense that also is part of the IC community.

Most of the intelligence agencies, the intelligence arms of the military services, and intelligence sections of departments listed in Table 12.1 are solely or mostly involved in foreign intelligence. But in post-9/11 America the domestic intelligence apparatus grew enormously, especially with respect to the FBI and the newly established Department of Homeland Security.

The FBI is at the core of U.S. domestic intelligence. Established in 1908 as the Bureau of Investigation, largely in response to anarchist terrorism, the FBI (thus renamed in 1935) grew steadily during World War II and the Cold War. The agency, part of the U.S. Department of Justice, was

Table 12.1 Members of the U.S. Intelligence Community

Member Agencies or Intelligence Arms of Member Departments	
Air Force Intelligence	Coast Guard Intelligence
Army Intelligence	Central Intelligence Agency
Defense Intelligence Agency	Department of Energy
Marine Corps Intelligence	Department of Homeland Security
National Geospatial Intelligence Agency	Department of State
National Reconnaissance Office	Department of the Treasury
National Security Agency	Drug Enforcement Administration
Navy Intelligence	Federal Bureau of Investigation

Source: U.S. Intelligence Community (https://www.intelligence.gov/).

through the decades involved in investigating domestic cases of terrorism. Its involvement in anti-American transnational terrorism began in the 1980s during the Reagan administration. Following a wave of deadly terrorist attacks on U.S. military and diplomatic targets in the Middle East, Congress expanded the FBI's investigative authority and the right to make arrest to foreign venues in cases that involved American victims of terrorism. But most of all the FBI was a law enforcement agency.

The widely perceived failures in the pre-9/11 period led to post-9/11 calls for the establishment of a new domestic intelligence agency that was not part of any department but was a freestanding creature like the CIA, the major foreign intelligence agency. The most often mentioned model abroad was that of the United Kingdom with MI5 or the Security Service responsible for domestic intelligence but without police and arrest powers, and MI6 or the Secret Intelligence Service responsible for foreign intelligence. A host of other countries, most of them unitary countries with centralized governmental powers, have similar models. Germany, like the United States, a federal republic with 16 states, also has two central intelligence agencies, the Federal Office for the Protection of the Constitution (Amt fuer Verfassungschutz) for domestic intelligence, with offices in each of the states, and the Federal Intelligence Service (Bundesnachrichtendienst) for foreign intelligence. But unlike the FBI, Germany's domestic spy agency has no federal policing power that is reserved for the Federal Police (Bundespolizei). Reorganized in 2005, the Federal Police is responsible for border-, railway-, and aviation-security. It also houses the elite counterterrorism commando GSG-9 and assists the police of individual states, if so asked.

In the United States, the idea of a new, freestanding domestic spy agency was rejected. Yet, even without it, there was a robust growth of domestic or homeland security intelligence. Most of all, the FBI morphed into a major domestic intelligence agency, so that today, according to the agency,

> the mission of the FBI is to protect and defend the U.S. against terrorism and foreign intelligence threats, to uphold and enforce the criminal laws of the U.S., and to provide leadership and criminal justice services to federal, state, municipal, and international agencies and partners.[33]

In other words, preventing terrorism became the FBI's priority. In the process, the bureau's personnel grew by roughly 10,000 and hundreds of agents were switched from criminal investigation to counterterrorist intelligence. At its headquarters, the agency established in 2005 a "National Security Service" that united its intelligence, counterintelligence, and counterterrorism divisions. Finally, the agency established throughout the country more than 100 Joint Terrorism Task Forces plus

Field Intelligence Groups located within the 56 FBI field offices in all parts of the United States.

In early 2022, the Department of Justice (DOJ) launched a unit dedicated specifically to domestic terrorism. The DOJ had already a team devoted to the handling of both international and domestic cases, but that section was mostly focused on international terrorists. The establishment of the new unit signaled a refocusing of the DOJ's attention on the growing threat of violent domestic extremism.

The establishment of the Department of Homeland Security (DHS) was a direct result of 9/11. The new department brought together, under one umbrella, 22 entities that had been either independent or part of larger departments and agencies (see Figure 12.1). Along with the creation of the DNI and ODNI the establishment of the DHS was the major initiative in the post-9/11 reforms.

By 2022, the DHS had about 240,000 employees and was the third largest department behind the Department of Defense (DOD) and the Department of Veteran Affairs. Its budget for the fiscal year 2022 came to $52.81 billion. An essential part of DHS resources is devoted to intelligence. As Erik J. Dahl revealed,

> Within the Department of Homeland Security there are at least nine separate intelligence elements, including the Office of Intelligence and Analysis and intelligence organizations of six separate DHS components: Customs and Border Protection, Immigration and Customs Enforcement, Citizenship and Immigration Services, Transportation Security Administration, the Coast Guard, and the Secret Service.[34]

In addition, the DHS established 79 so-called "fusion centers" around the country which were in 2011 praised by then DHS Secretary Janet Napolitano

> as focal points where information about threats can be gathered, analyzed, and shared among federal, state, local, tribal, territorial, and private sector partners. Fusion centers also support and interact regularly with FBI-led Joint Terrorism Task Forces (JTTF), which coordinate resources and expertise from across the federal government to investigate terrorism cases.[35]

A year later, however, the U.S. Senate Homeland Security and Governmental Affairs Committee's Permanent Subcommittee on Investigations issued a critical report that revealed that "despite reviewing 13 months' worth of reporting originating from fusion centers" investigators could not "identify a contribution... to disrupt an active terrorist plot."[36] Instead, the investigation found a multitude of problems, among them that

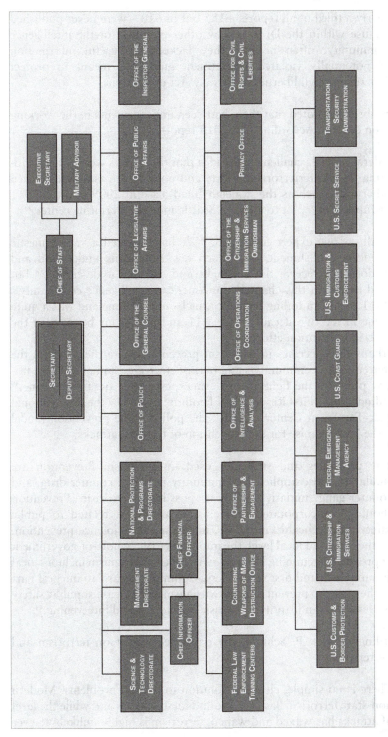

Figure 12.1 Organization of the Department of Homeland Security

Source: Department of Homeland Security

nearly a third of all reports – 188 out of 610 – were never published for use within the DHS and by other members of the intelligence community, often because they lacked any useful information or potentially violated Department guidelines meant to protect Americans' civil liberties or Privacy Act protections.[37]

Other observers noted that there had been improvements in the working of fusion centers. According to a 2015 report,

> federal officials challenged the idea that the centers were not contributing to counterterrorism efforts and pointed to cases that showed otherwise—such as the 'Raleigh Jihad' case in 2009 and the 2011 disruption of a plot to attack a Seattle military recruiting center.[38]

All in all, as one expert concluded, "We have created a vast domestic intelligence establishment, one which few Americans understand and which does not receive the oversight and scrutiny it deserves."[39] But as noted earlier in this chapter, the American intelligence community's post-9/11 record in foiling terrorist attacks in the homeland was a quite good one in the two decades after 9/11 and in fact far better than the pre-post-11 prevention efforts.

Perhaps the successes in terrorism prevention were the result of the counterterrorism community's embrace of strategies similar to those utilized by police in the fight against crimes, especially organized crime.[40] According to the "First Responder's Toolbox" issued by the U.S. National Counter Terrorism Center in 2017, the police crime prevention model holds the best promise for the prevention of terrorist attacks:

> The principles and strategies used in Terrorism Prevention are similar to those applied to community policing, counter-drug, and counter-gang initiatives. Where possible, Terrorism Prevention should be incorporated into existing programs related to public safety, public health, resilience, inclusion, and violence prevention. At the state and local level, the importance of a whole-of-government approach to stemming Homegrown Violent Extremism includes local communities and first responders. Communities are an integral part of the effort to prevent violent extremism and can assist public safety professionals in identifying at-risk individuals and intervening.[41]

According to Alex P. Schmid, the renowned expert on terrorism and counterterrorism,

> There is no simple, clear-cut solution to wicked problems. Modern non-state terrorism has been around for 150 years and while the level of attacks has waxed and waned, terrorism is highly unlikely to ever

go away. Complete prevention is impossible short of closing down open societies and sealing borders but preventive measures can have measurable effects *over time* – there are no quick fixes.[42]

Lack of Congressional Oversight

Resistance to change did not come only from intelligence agencies and their parent organizations in the executive branch; the hardest nut to crack according to the 9/11 Commission was Congress. Pointing out that 88 congressional committees and subcommittees were involved in overseeing one or another aspect of homeland security, the Commission recommended the drastic streamlining of oversight in the areas of intelligence and counterterrorism within Congress. In the 9/11 Commission's words,

> Congressional oversight for intelligence—and counterterrorism—is now dysfunctional. Congress should address this problem. We have considered various alternatives: A joint committee on the old model of the Joint Commission on Atomic Energy is one. A single committee in each house of Congress, combining authorizing and appropriation authorities, is another.[43]

If enacted, this recommendation would result in Congress's ability to discharge effectively its oversight responsibilities and free homeland security and intelligence personnel from testifying in front of several dozen committees. But while the U.S. House of Representatives and the U.S. Senate legislated reforms in the executive branch, there were no signs that an equally important reform along the lines of the 9/11 Commission's recommendation of a joint committee or single committee in each chamber was seriously considered. At best, there was some tinkering with the existing structures. Republicans and Democrats alike were not willing to make such drastic changes.

By late 2008, nothing had changed. As the Commission on the Prevention of Weapons of Mass Destruction, Proliferation, and Terrorism wrote, "That Congress has yet to adequately organize itself to cope with the nuclear age, much less the post-9/11 era, is deeply troubling and demands action."[44] The commissioners noted that, in the House, 16 committees and 40 subcommittees still had jurisdiction over the DHS, and that, in the Senate, 14 full committees and 18 subcommittees shared oversight responsibilities. A decade after 9/11, the intelligence/homeland security sector had a workforce of 854,000 with top security clearance. According to one account,

> At least 20 percent of the government organizations that exist to fend off terrorist threats were established or refashioned in the

wake of 9/11. Many that existed before the attacks grew to historic proportions as the Bush administration and Congress gave agencies more money than they were capable of responsibly spending.[45]

Neither the White House nor congressional committees were able to oversee effectively the massive intelligence–homeland security complex. There were calls for a bipartisan commission to investigate, review, and make suggestions for a drastic reorganization of a bureaucracy consisting of "some 1,271 government organizations and 1,931 private companies [that] work on programs related to counterterrorism, homeland security and intelligence in about 10,000 locations across the United States."[46] Following a two-year investigation of the U.S. intelligence apparatus *Washington Post* reporters Dana Priest and William M. Arkin concluded,

> The top-secret world the government created in response to the terrorist attacks of Sept. 11, 2001, has become so large, so unwieldy and so secretive that no one knows how much money it costs, how many people it employs, how many programs exist within it or exactly how many agencies do the same work.[47]

Given the growing partisan and ideological polarization in the Congress, nothing changed for the better in this respect during the Obama and Trump presidencies and the first part of the Joe Biden's term.

Transnational Cooperation

Intelligence is essential not only in the prevention of terrorism but also in law enforcement agencies' efforts to hunt down the perpetrators of terrorism, the architects of terrorism, and the supporters of terrorist groups. While one objective here is to bring terrorists to justice, an even more urgent goal is to get arrested terrorists to reveal information about planned terror plots, accomplices, financial resources, and weapon suppliers. In cases of transnational terrorism, successful investigations require close and continued international cooperation between intelligence and law enforcement agencies. After 9/11, most Americans associated efforts to prevent further terror strikes with the military actions abroad, from Afghanistan to Iraq to Yemen, Syria, the Philippines, and Africa. But the work of the domestic intelligence and law enforcement agencies and extraordinary international cooperation were equally—or more—important.

Two years after 9/11, more than 3,000 terrorism suspects had been arrested. Although hundreds were captured during the Afghanistan war, most of the leading figures of Al Qaeda and their followers were caught as a result of cooperation between American police and intelligence agencies and their counterparts abroad. This resulted in many arrests in Pakistan and other countries in the region. But, as the Department of State's report on "Patterns of Global Terrorism" for 2002 detailed, success stories were also reported from other parts of the world, especially Western Europe, because of bilateral and multilateral cooperation efforts.[48] These trends continued during the following years. Moreover, the 9/11 strike and subsequent terrorist attacks shocked international and regional organizations into focusing more on their antiterrorism capabilities and expanding them:

- The United Nations (UN) adopted resolutions that obligate member states to take specific actions to combat terrorism, especially in the area of interrupting the financing of terrorism. The UN established the Counterterrorism Committee and a mechanism to oversee the implementation of the agreed-upon measures.
- INTERPOL, the International Police Organization (with 181 member countries), strengthened its efforts in information sharing and law enforcement with respect to anti- and counterterrorism significantly. In particular, the Fusion Task Force, established in 2002, can assist member countries in their terrorism investigations. "Project Tent," part of the Fusion Task Force, collects information on individuals known to have attended terrorist training camps.
- Europol, the European version of INTERPOL, and Eurojust, a transnational investigative body within the European Union, established policies and mechanisms to ensure increased information sharing and cross-border law enforcement in order to combat terrorism.
- The Southeast European Cooperative Initiative (SECI), with a SECI Center in Bucharest; the Southern African Development Community (SADC); and the Southern Africa Regional Policy Cooperative Organization (SARPCO) are efforts to function in their respective regions along the Europol and Eurojust models.
- Project Pacific, the result of an Asian regional conference in Sri Lanka, aims at increasing member states' proactive and operational cooperation in order to combat terrorism.

Given that Western democracies were and continue to be the special targets of Al Qaeda, ISIS, and like-minded organizations, cells, and lone wolves, cooperation between the United States and European countries was and remains of great importance. In a policy paper on post-9/11 transatlantic cooperation, a group of distinguished experts wrote that despite fundamental differences in counterterrorism approaches,

> The United States and the European Union have shared a commitment to making their evolving collaboration against terrorism a success. During the past three years, they have reached agreement on many new arrangements, such as the Container Security Initiative

and Passenger Name Records (PNR), but also on terrorist financing, sharing of evidentiary information, extradition of suspected terrorists, and many others. They have built close ties between parts of their bureaucracies that had rarely been in contact before, and involving officials from working level to Cabinet secretary and European commissioner.

The question now before the United States and the EU is whether and how to build on the cooperation achieved thus far and ensure that this post–9/11 partnership continues into the future. This will not be easy. Legislation and other agreements must be implemented and enforced. Existing areas of cooperation must be extended, and collaboration in new areas must be explored and developed. The good news is that the United States and the European Union have established basic mechanisms for building cooperation through regular consultations and have successfully concluded some basic agreements.[49]

The threat of transnational terrorism will not be contained unilaterally but must be faced by bilateral and multilateral cooperation. One issue between Washington and the European Union arose over the transfer of data from Europe's Swift money-transfer system to American counterterrorism investigators who tried to identify terrorist organizations, individual terrorists, and their supporters by following the money-transfer orders among more than 9,000 banks and other financial institutions in some 200 countries. European politicians were concerned about the violation of privacy rights and, in early 2010, voted against an agreement on data access. By mid-2010, though, the United States and the European Union agreed on additional safeguards in the data-transfer process by putting Europol in charge of screening American requests.

While transnational information sharing on the jihadist terrorist threat worked quite well in the post-9/11 years, the same was not the case in more recent times with respect to violent Far-Right extremism in Western countries. The problem was that Western security agencies did not recognize this as a serious threat—or simply ignored it. But as one terrorism expert wrote several months after the events of January 6, 2021, the rise in Far-Right violence got belatedly the attention of international organizations and individual governments:

> From the UN Security Council to national parliaments to militaries and security agencies, there are currently dozens of commissions, special task forces, and investigations taking place across the globe to explore ways to counter the new threat.[50]

As the Biden administration released in 2021 the first ever "National Strategy for Countering Domestic Terrorism" with a detailed plan of action, other Western governments, too, adopted new legislation and measures not merely to respond to homegrown terrorist threats but to prevent radicalization in the first place. President Biden noted in his foreword to the domestic counterterrorism strategy the need to work "with our allies and foreign partners." And there were signs that friendly governments, from the United Kingdom to New Zealand, and multinational organizations from the United Nations to the European Union were ready for closer cooperation in this area as well.

Preparedness for Man-Made and Natural Disasters

Recognizing that even the most elaborate and skillful preventive measures would not eliminate terrorist acts altogether, the federal government, states, and local communities in the United States—and the comparable authorities in many other countries around the world—intensified their efforts to improve the preparedness for emergency responses after 9/11. Here, preparations for man-made and natural disasters are very similar or even the same. When Hurricane Katrina devastated New Orleans and other areas along the Gulf coast in late August 2005 and caused many deaths and human tragedies, it became obvious that neither the federal government nor state and local emergency responders were adequately prepared to deal effectively with such a catastrophe. As U.S. Senator Joseph Lieberman of Connecticut pointed out in a stinging criticism of federal preparedness, Katrina should have been "a lesser challenge to the nation's emergency-management apparatus than the 9/11 attacks: It [the hurricane] was preceded by 72 hours of increasingly dire predictions."[51] Indeed, while the stunningly flawed or nonexistent preparedness measures before Katrina struck and the botched emergency response afterward laid bare the soft underbelly of America's preparedness for predictable disasters, they did far more so with respect to unpredictable terrorist events. After all, terrorists do not give warnings as do weather forecasters.

The failure to prepare for and respond to natural and man-made disasters was shocking to Americans and people around the globe. After all, homeland security had become the single most important objective in American domestic and foreign policy after 9/11.

Assessments were even more negative when it came to the public's knowledge of preparedness in the case of terrorist attacks. Although government officials mentioned and the news media reported frequently on the seriousness of the terrorist threat in the post-9/11 years, this did not result in markedly improved preparedness knowledge among ordinary citizens and did not remedy major problems within and among emergency response agencies. Public opinion survey data revealed "a national state of unpreparedness for emergency events" in the post-9/11 years.[52] And the assessment of professional responders was just as grim, summed up in the conclusion that "overall, the existing government response system is more accurately described as disarrayed, disconnected, uncoordinated, underfunded, and discredited."[53]

Other countries were plagued by similar preparedness and response problems. This became painfully clear after four suicide bombers struck London's transit system in July 2005. In a comprehensive report that was released nearly a year after the deadly terrorist attacks, a review committee listed a multitude of shortcomings in the response system, among them failures of communication between the emergency services, since police, fire, and emergency medical services used different radio systems. Also, there was "a lack of planning to care for survivors" and "of basic equipment, including stretchers and triage cards, and too few essential supplies such as fluids at the affected sites."[54]

Following those flaws, there were indications that preparedness for both man-made and natural catastrophes improved in the following years. When there were unspeakable failures, such as the lack of response to Hurricane Maria's devastation of Puerto Rico and the death of more than 4,600 persons, these were not caused by a lack of preparedness and response capabilities but rather by wrong decisions taken at the highest levels of the federal government.

Notes

1 Mike McConnell, "Overhauling Intelligence," *Foreign Affairs* 86 (4) (July–August 2007), p. 51.
2 Ibid., 50.
3 Philip B. Heymann, *Terrorism, Freedom and Security: Winning without War* (Cambridge, MA: MIT Press, 2003), 64.
4 "Whistle-Blower Testifies," www.ABCNews.com, accessed October 21, 2003.
5 Report from the National Commission on Terrorism, "Countering the Changing Threat of International Terrorism," June 2000, 7.
6 Ibid., 15, 16.
7 9/11 Commission, "The Performance of the Intelligence Community," Staff Statement no. 11, 12.
8 Report from the National Commission on Terrorism, 8.
9 Ibid.
10 Ibid., 13.
11 Ibid., 14.
12 Ibid.
13 Ibid.
14 Ibid.
15 Heymann, 4.
16 Ibid., 64.
17 Ed O'Keefe, "Senators: Boston Bombings Exposed Possible Counter-terrorism 'Stovepipes'," *Washington Post*, April 23, 2013, www.washingtonpost.com/blogs/post-politics/wp/2013/04/23/senators-boston-bombings-exposed-possible-counter-terrorism-stovepipes/.
18 The full text of the report is available at http://homeland.house.gov/sites/homeland.house.gov/files/documents/Boston-Bombings-Report.pdf, accessed July 30, 2015.

19 Elisabeth Bumiller and Scott Shane, "Pentagon Report on Fort Hood Details Failures," *New York Times*, January 15, 2010, www.nytimes.com/2010/01/16/ us/politics/16hasan.html?ref=nidal_malik_hasan, accessed July 5, 2010.

20 Ibid.

21 Mitchell D. Silber, "Domestic Violent Extremism and the Intelligence Challenge," *Atlantic Council*, May 21, 2021, https://www.atlanticcouncil.org/ in-depth-research-reports/domestic-violent-extremism-and-the-intelligence-challenge/, accessed August 15, 2022.

22 For an intelligent discussion of thwarted plots and those that otherwise failed, see Erik J. Dahl, "The Plots that Failed: Intelligence Lessons Learned from Unsuccessful Terrorist Attacks Against the United States," *Studies in Conflict & Terrorism* 34 (8) (2011), pp. 621–48.

23 The charges against the three men were unsealed by the U.S. Department of Justice on October 6, 2016. The document is available at www.justice. gov/opa/pr/charges-unsealed-against-three-men-plotting-carry-out-terrorist-attacks-new-york-city-isis, accessed February 15, 2018.

24 Kevin J. Strom, John S. Hollywood, and Mark Pope, "Terrorist Plots against the United States: What We Have Really Faced, and How We Might Best Defend against It," Rand Homeland Security and Defense Center, September 2015.

25 Ibid.

26 Erik J. Dahl, "Assessing the Effectiveness of the Department of Homeland Security 20 years after 9/11." Watson Institute at Brown University, November 7, 2021, 5.

27 Ibid., 7.

28 President Bush's remarks were made during a White House press conference on February 17, 2005.

29 www.dni.gov/index.php/nctc-home.

30 Ibid.

31 Mark Mazzetti and David Sanger, "Spy Chief's Choice to Step Back Feeds Speculation," *New York Times*, January 5, 2007, www.nytimes.com/2007/ 01/05/washington/05intel.html?_r=1&oref=slogin.

32 McConnell.

33 "Organization, Mission and Functions Manual: Federal Bureau of Investigation," available at www.justice.gov/jmd/organization-mission-and-functions-manual- federal-bureau-investigation, accessed December 3, 2018.

34 Erik J. Dahl, "Domestic Intelligence Today: More Security but Less Liberty?" *Homeland Security Affairs* 7 (September 2011).

35 Janet Napolitano, "Progress toward a More Secure and Resilient Nation," *Homeland Security Affairs* 7 (September 2011).

36 www.hsgac.senate.gov/imo/media/doc/10-3-2012%20PSI%20STAFF%20 REPORT%20re%20FUSION%20CENTERS.2.pdfn, accessed June 3, 2018.

37 Ibid.

38 Jason Barnosky, "Fusion Centers: What's Working and What Isn't?," *Brookings*, March 2015, www.brookings.edu/blog/fixgov/2015/03/17/fusion-centers-whats-working-and-what-isnt/, accessed May 30, 2018.

39 Dahl.

40 For an excellent analysis of the utilization of a predominant police model in preventing crime in the prevention of terrorism, see Kelly A. Berkell, "A Criminological Approach to Preventing Terrorism: Situational Crime Prevention and the Crime Prevention Literature," in Alex P. Schmid, *Handbook of Terrorism Prevention and Preparedness* (The Hague: ICCT Press Publication, 2021). The book is available online, https://icct.nl/app/ uploads/2021/10/V10.4-Handbook-ONLINE.pdf, accessed August 20, 2022.

41 The text of the National Counter Terrorism Center's "First Responder's Tool Box" is available at https://www.dni.gov/files/NCTC/documents/jcat/firstresponderstoolbox/First-Responders-Toolbox—Terrorism-PreventionA-Form-of-Violence-Reduction.pdf, accessed August 19, 2022.

42 Alex P. Schmid, *Handbook of Terrorism Prevention and Preparedness* (The Hague: ICCT Press Publication, 2021). The book is available online, https://icct.nl/app/uploads/2021/10/V10.4-Handbook-ONLINE.pdf, accessed August 20, 2022.

43 *The 9/11 Commission Report* (New York: W.W. Norton, 2004), 420.

44 Commission on the Prevention of Weapons of Mass Destruction, Proliferation, and Terrorism, *World at Risk* (New York: Vintage Books, 2008), 89.

45 Priest and Arkin.

46 Ibid.

47 Ibid.

48 U.S. Department of State, "Patterns of Global Terrorism 2002," www.state.gov/s/ct/rls/pgtrpt/2002/html.

49 David L. Aaron et al., "The Post 9/11 Partnership: Transatlantic Cooperation against Terrorism," Policy Paper, The Atlantic Council of the United States, December 2004, http://se2.isn.ch/serviceengine/FileContent? serviceID=PublishingHouse&fileid=314CA3A0-B359-B009-DA3B-9D9FA889FBEE&lng=en.

50 Miller-Idriss, 62.

51 www.nola.com/katrina/pdf/hs_katrinarpt_lieberman.pdf.

52 Irwin Redlener and David A. Berman, "National Preparedness Planning: The Historical Context and Current State of the U.S. Public's Readiness, 1940–2005," *Journal of International Affairs* 59 (2) (Spring/Summer 2006), p. 87.

53 Sang Ok Choi, "Emergency Management: Implications from a Strategic Management Perspective," *Journal of Homeland Security and Emergency Management* 5 (1) (2008), Article 1, 7.

54 BBC News, "London Assembly Report on 7/7," June 5, 2006, http://news.bbc.co.uk/2/hi/uk_news/england/london/5048806.stm.

13 Balancing Security, Civil Liberties, and Human Rights

A government's first duty is to protect the lives and property of its citizens. Therefore, political leaders tend to take extraordinary measures during times of crisis in the name of providing security. But after devastating terrorist strikes, democratic governments must resist the temptation to go too far—otherwise, they play into the hands of the very same terrorists they set out to defeat. Terrorists want to change the behavior of the societies they attack. When they strike democracies, they want to scare their targets into weakening or abandoning their most esteemed values: their respect for civil liberties and human rights. This was precisely what bin Laden wanted to accomplish with the attacks of 9/11, and he believed in fact that he succeeded. In an interview with Al Jazeera, bin Laden said,

> The values of this Western civilization under the leadership of America have been destroyed. Those awesome symbolic towers that speak of liberty, human rights, and humanity have been destroyed. They have gone up in smoke.
> The proof came, when the U.S. government pressured the media not to run our statements that are not longer than a few minutes. They felt that the truth started to reach the American people, the truth that we are not terrorists as they understand it but because we are being attacked in Palestine, Iraq, Lebanon, Sudan, Somalia, Kashmir, the Philippines, and everywhere else.[1]

While he overstated by far what was happening in the United States and elsewhere in the West, bin Laden left no doubt that he was delighted about his enemies' reactions. Earlier terrorists anticipated also that governments would overreact and, as a result, frustrate and infuriate their own citizens. Well before 9/11, Paul Wilkinson warned against "overreaction" and repressive measures that "could destroy democracy far more rapidly and effectively than any campaign by a terrorist group." But he also cautioned against "underreaction" in the face of terrorist threats.[2] In other words, governments must strive for a balance between providing security on the one hand and respecting civil liberties and human rights

DOI: 10.4324/9781003289265-15

on the other, between effective anti- and counterterrorist measures on one side and highly esteemed societal values on the other.

What is the distinction between anti- and counterterrorism? In the 1980s, Marc A. Celmer wrote that "antiterrorist actions are designed as defensive measures to prevent the occurrence of terrorism as opposed to counterterrorist measures, which are offensive in nature and are designed to respond to a terrorist act."[3] While antiterrorism is still understood as defensive in nature, the common meaning of counterterrorism transcends offensive measures. When threatened by terrorism, governments adopt and implement a whole range of policies and measures in order to prevent further terrorist strikes. Hunting down terrorists, punishing supporters of terrorist activities, launching retaliatory strikes, tightening security measures, and strengthening preparedness programs are all parts of an overall counterterrorism strategy. Typically, a host of governmental institutions and actors as well as the private sector get involved in counterterrorist measures. Counterterrorism, then, encompasses strategies and tactics adopted in response to terrorism. According to one encyclopedia entry,

> Counter-terrorism is not specific to any one field or organization, it involves entities from all levels of society. For instance, businesses have security plans and sometimes share commercial data with government. Local police, fire fighters, and emergency personnel (often called "first responders") have plans for dealing with terrorist attacks. Armies conduct combat operations against terrorists, often using special forces.[4]

Antiterrorist policies and actions, then, are part of the overall counterterrorist approaches that a country adopts in response to terrorism and the threat thereof.

Years before the U.S. government adopted its first comprehensive anti- and counterterrorism laws, European democracies, such as Germany, Greece, and the United Kingdom, enacted many measures in response to frequent terrorist strikes within their borders. Between 1970 and 1989, the Federal Republic of Germany adopted ten amendments to its criminal code that provided the judiciary and police with more justifications for investigating and arresting suspects. After 9/11, "Rasterfahndung," a combination of profiling and data mining that had been used in the Federal Republic's struggle against the Red Army Faction and its successor groups, was revived. Describing the earlier practice, Peter Katzenstein wrote,

> A newly developed "computer matching" (*Rasterfahndung*), tailored to the fight against terrorism, scans large data sets to identify overlapping clusters of what are regarded as suspicious traits, in the hope of

targeting police work more efficiently and effectively. For example, in the 1970s the police got access to the files of the West German utility companies and identified those customers who paid their bills in cash or through third parties. This group of potential suspects was narrowed down further through checks with data on residence registration, which is compulsory in West Germany, automobile registration, receipt of social security or child care payments as well as other data sources. What remained was a list of names of potential terrorist suspects: those who did not receive pensions or child allowances, who were not registered, had no automobiles and who paid their utility bills in cash or through third parties. Traditional police investigation, including surveillance and house searches, was concentrated on this list of potential suspects.[5]

The post-9/11 Rasterfahndung concentrated on Muslims and Arabs in their twenties and thirties and data assembled by travel agencies, telecommunication companies, universities, and other public and private institutions. In early 2006, Germany's Constitutional Court (*Bundesverfassungsgericht*) ruled in the case of a Moroccan plaintiff that Rasterfahndung is legal only in the face of a "real threat" to the security of the country or the life of a citizen.

Within months after 9/11, Germany enacted two comprehensive antiterror laws with many far-reaching provisions that, for example, expanded jurisdiction of law enforcement agencies beyond German borders, allowed authorities to ban religious groups if they promoted violence, and expanded the power of border patrol agents to screen and search persons and their belongings. In 2006, following the botched plot to bomb two German trains by Lebanese students, Chancellor Angela Merkel and her government pushed for expanded closed-circuit camera systems in train stations and other public places. A camera at the Cologne main terminal had provided the grainy images of two young men boarding a train and led to the quick arrest of one of the would-be bombers.

Beginning with the Northern Ireland Act of 1973 that toughened emergency provisions to deal with terrorism in Northern Ireland, the United Kingdom enacted several antiterrorism laws, like Germany, in reaction to 9/11 and the multiple suicide attacks on London's transit system in July 2005: The Crime and Security Act of 2001, the Prevention of Terrorism Act of 2005, and the Terrorism Act of 2006. Even before the events of 2001, when British authorities were mostly concerned about terrorism in the context of the conflict in Northern Ireland, British intelligence and law enforcement agencies were authorized by the Regulation of Investigatory Powers Act of 2000 and the 2001 Crime and Security Act "to evaluate communications data for patterns suggestive of terrorist activities."[6] Moreover, to monitor communications data, a law enforcement or intelligence agency need only to complete a written application, which is considered by a designated individual within the body or agency.[7] As John Yoo testified before a U.S. Senate Committee,

> The British have greater power [than American law enforcement] to detain a terrorist without criminal charge. Section 23 of the Terrorism Act of 2006 sets forth a procedure under which a suspect may be detained for up to 28 days before he must be charged with a crime or released. After 48 hours, judicial approval is required, and is required a second time if the authorities wish to detain the suspect beyond 7 days. The judge does not need to find probable cause, but must be satisfied that "there are reasonable grounds for believing that the further detention of the person to whom the application relates is necessary to obtain relevant evidence whether by questioning him or otherwise or to preserve relevant evidence," and "the investigation in connection with which the person is detained is being conducted diligently and expeditiously." The suspect has access to counsel and may make written or oral communications before the judge; however, the suspect and his counsel may also be excluded from portions of the hearing. The British government has already invoked this power to detain the individuals arrested in conjunction with the August, 2006 plot to blow up airliners departing Britain. This allowed the plot to be halted, but also allows more evidence to be gathered prior to formally charging the suspects with crimes.[8]

Coming on the heels of successful and failed suicide bombings in London, the Antiterrorism Act of 2006 made it a crime to glorify or encourage political violence. But just like earlier German and Greek laws that prohibited the glorification of terrorism in news reports or the publication of communications by terrorists during a terrorist incident, this particular provision was too broad to be effective.

More recently, in reaction to several terrorist shootings on Parliament Hill in Ottawa, the Canadian government proposed and adopted the 2015 Anti-Terrorism Act to strengthen the ability of the Canadian Intelligence Service to counter terrorism within and prevent Canadian nationals from joining terrorist groups abroad. After terrorists stormed into the offices of the satirical weekly *Charlie Hebdo* in early 2015 killing 11 persons, the French government reacted immediately by writing broader new laws on phone-tapping, planning to hire 3,000 new employees for the surveillance of persons with suspected ties to jihadists, and ordering prosecutors to crack down on hate speech and "glorifying terrorism." Since the terrorist duo that carried out the massacre claimed that they were killed because *Charlie Hebdo* was guilty of blasphemy in depicting the Prophet Muhammad, several European countries reconsidered their blasphemy laws. In the case of Germany, for example, there were loud voices demanding the strengthening of the anti-blasphemy law;

others opposed such changes as curbing freedom of expression. Although introduced in Parliament in the fall of 2014, the United Kingdom's 2015 Counterterrorism and Security Act gained momentum in the wake of the *Charlie Hebdo* shooting and was adopted within weeks. The new law expanded the authority of border personnel and police in the investigation of terrorist suspects and placed responsibility on the educational, penal, and health sector as well as on localities to "have due regard to the need to prevent people from being drawn into terrorism" when exercising their functions.

U.S. Anti- and Counterterrorism Laws

Just as foreign governments reacted to particular terrorist incidents and threats in the past, so did U.S. presidents and members of the U.S. Congress. Beginning in the 1980s, the United States responded with legislative and executive initiatives to each major anti-American act of terrorism. But until 1996, when Congress and President Bill Clinton reacted to the Oklahoma City bombing, antiterrorism laws did not intrude markedly on the civil liberties of individuals. During the 1980s, when Americans abroad as well as diplomatic and private American facilities in foreign countries were frequently the targets of terrorism, presidents and both houses of Congress were eager to demonstrate that they were doing something. Typically, presidents established commissions and asked them for recommendations and congressional committees held hearings. Administration officials and members of Congress, regardless of whether they were Democrats or Republicans, were eager to claim that they had initiated or sponsored legislation to tighten security in the air, on water, and on foreign soil. During this period, the Omnibus Diplomatic Security Act of 1986 became the most comprehensive package of new or revised security laws. For example, this act directed the State Department to establish a Diplomatic Security Service, intensify the protection of U.S. embassies and other governmental facilities abroad, and expand a facility construction program to harden diplomatic missions overseas. The act (Public Law 99-399) also established a reward program for the capture of terrorists, a program to provide for greater security at U.S. military bases abroad, measures for seaport and shipboard security, initiatives to combat nuclear terrorism, and a framework for the compensation of terrorism victims.

Strongly affected by the first World Trade Center bombing in 1993 and introduced in Congress two months before the Oklahoma City bombing, the Antiterrorism and Effective Death Penalty Act of 1996 (Public Law 104-132) was in some respects a softened version of what President Clinton had asked for. For example, a provision that would have given police more authority in the surveillance of suspected terrorists was scratched. Still, opponents rejected the measure as containing "some of the worst assaults on civil liberties in decades."[9] The law made it a crime for individuals or groups, whether citizens or noncitizens, to provide money or material support to groups designated by the Secretary of State as foreign terrorist organizations; another section provided for the establishment of a special court to handle the deportation of aliens suspected of terrorist activities while protecting classified information. The Antiterrorism Act required for the first time that plastic explosives must contain chemical "taggents" that allow law enforcement to track their sources. Acknowledging the pleas of victims of terrorism and their families, this law allowed U.S. citizens to bring civil actions against the governments of countries that the Secretary of State had designated as state sponsors of terrorism.

None of the previously adopted laws, executive orders, and other government initiatives came close to the burst of post-9/11 measures taken by the White House, the Congress, the Department of Justice, and other parts of the U.S. government. According to Laura Donohue, in the eight weeks following the events of 9/11,

> the President issued dozens of Proclamations and Executive Orders and the Executive Branch engaged in a widespread antiterrorist campaign. Congress introduced 323 bills and resolutions and adopted 21 laws and resolutions relating to the attacks and the war against terrorism.[10]

Within days of the terror attacks on New York and Washington, DC, the Bush administration presented Congress with proposals to expand police and prosecutorial powers to enhance the fight against terrorism. Some six weeks later, both houses of Congress voted in overwhelming majorities for the Uniting and Strengthening America by Providing Appropriate Tools Required to Intercept and Obstruct Terrorism Act, which is better known by its catchy name: The USA PATRIOT Act of 2001 (Public Law 107-56). Few lawmakers, if any, were familiar with the details of the hastily written provisions of the bill when they cast their votes. In the absence of news reports that described and scrutinized the most important provisions of either the legislative proposals or the final version of the bill that the president signed into law, the public remained clueless as to the content of the new law.

The USA PATRIOT Act vastly increased the authority of government agents to track and gather information by conducting "sneak and peek searches" in homes, offices, or other private places without informing the targets of such searches in advance. The government's wiretap authority was expanded, as was information sharing among various federal agencies. By simply certifying a need for the material sought in an investigation of international terrorism, government agents got the authority to subpoena any individual's records at places such as libraries, bookstores, telephone companies, Internet providers, and universities. The act directed the U.S. Attorney General to hold foreigners who were suspected terrorists for up to seven days before charging them with a crime or beginning deportation procedures. As Laura Donohue put it,

> The USA PATRIOT Act not just allowed but required the detention of anyone the AG [Attorney General] had reasonable grounds to believe was connected to terrorism or was a threat to national security. The statute did not specify a time period. Detention without trial could continue until the suspect was either deported or determined no longer a threat.[11]

Furthermore, the law stipulated the establishment of a system to fingerprint and photograph foreigners at their entrance point into the United States, a controversial measure that was in place by the beginning of 2004.

Supporters of the act emphasized that many of its most controversial provisions would expire in 2005 unless renewed by congressional and presidential actions. But this did not pacify conservative and liberal critics, who—as they became aware of the details in the USA PATRIOT Act—rejected a number of provisions as assaults on constitutionally guaranteed civil liberties. Pointing to the vastly different reactions to the massive antiterrorism law, Charles Doyle of the Congressional Research Service wrote, "Although it is not without safeguards, critics contend some of its provisions go too far. Although it grants many of the enhancements sought by the Department of Justice, others are concerned that it does not go far enough."[12]

David Cole and James Dempsey concluded that "the PATRIOT Act radically transformed the landscape of government power, and did so in ways that virtually guaranteed repetition of some of law enforcement's worst abuses of the past."[13] Such fears were justified. The inspector general of the U.S. Department of Justice found dozens of cases in which the civil liberties and civil rights of detained terrorism suspects were violated in the enforcement of the PATRIOT Act. One of the cases described in the inspector general's report concerned "allegations that during a physical examination a Bureau of Prisons physician told the inmate, 'If I was in charge, I would execute every one of you, because of the crimes you all did.'"[14] The same physician was accused of treating other inmates "in a cruel and unprofessional manner."[15] After a Bureau of Prisons investigation substantiated the allegations, the physician was reprimanded—not fired. Far more troubling than this mistreatment of individuals was the inspector general's conclusion that many of the foreign detainees "languished in unduly harsh conditions for months, and that the department had made little effort to distinguish legitimate terrorist suspects from others picked up in roundups of illegal immigrants."[16] Most of these detainees in detention centers in the United States were held for immigration violations—in many cases for many months without an opportunity to have their cases reviewed by an independent judiciary authority.

In April 2005, the U.S. Senate and House of Representatives held the first in a series of oversight hearings in a prolonged debate on whether to renew the 16 provisions of the USA PATRIOT Act set to expire at the end of the year. There was wide agreement that most parts of the comprehensive law were uncontroversial tools for law enforcement agencies in their efforts to prevent terrorism. But loud voices on the left and right of the political spectrum demanded the removal or modification of those parts of the act that went too far in allowing the FBI and other agencies to curb political dissent and spy on Americans. Particularly controversial were those sections allowing the government to get access to medical, library, and other personal records and to search a person's home—in both cases without notifying individuals of such actions.

While the original USA PATRIOT Act of 2001 was passed by huge majorities in both houses of Congress (98–1 in the Senate and 356–56 in the House), there was more opposition four years later, when the Senate voted 89–11 and the House 280–138 for the USA PATRIOT Improvement and Reauthorization Act of 2005 and the USA PATRIOT Additional Reauthorization Amendments Act of 2006. Still, overwhelming majorities of both parties cast their votes in favor of these bills—perhaps because they strengthened congressional and judicial oversight in several areas, especially with respect to wiretapping, access to personal records, and "sneak and peek" search warrants. But when President Bush signed both acts into laws (Public Law 109–177 and Public Law 109–178) in March 2006, his signing statement made clear that he reserved the right to ignore such oversight provisions.

President's Statement on H.R. 3199, the "USA PATRIOT Improvement and Reauthorization Act of 2005"

Today, I have signed into law H.R. 3199, the "USA PATRIOT Improvement and Reauthorization Act of 2005," and then S. 2271, the "USA PATRIOT Act Additional Reauthorizing Amendments Act of 2006." The bills will help us continue to fight terrorism effectively and to combat the use of the illegal drug methamphetamine that is ruining too many lives.

The executive branch shall construe the provisions of H.R. 3199 that call for furnishing information to entities outside the executive branch, such as sections 106A and 119, in a manner consistent with the President's constitutional authority to supervise the unitary executive branch and to withhold information the disclosure of which could impair foreign relations, national security, the deliberative processes of the Executive, or the performance of the Executive's constitutional duties.

The executive branch shall construe section 756(e)(2) of H.R. 3199, which calls for an executive branch official to submit to the Congress recommendations for legislative action, in a manner consistent with the President's constitutional authority to supervise the unitary executive branch and to recommend for the consideration of the Congress such measures as he judges necessary and expedient.

George W. Bush
The White House, March 9, 2006.

Several months before the second version of the USA PATRIOT Act became the law of the land, President Bush confirmed news reports that the National Security Agency (NSA) was eavesdropping without warrants on international telephone and email communications of American citizens and noncitizens in this country who were suspected of being in contact with terrorists. This NSA practice violated the Foreign Intelligence Surveillance Act (FISA) of 1978 that excluded U.S. citizens and resident aliens from electronic surveillance and requires authorization by a special Foreign Intelligence Surveillance Court for such surveillance of suspected foreign intelligence agents inside the United States. Shortly after 9/11, President Bush authorized the NSA to wiretap U.S. citizens and foreign nationals without warrants issued by the FISA court. When the warrantless wiretap practice was revealed, some of President Bush's harshest critics suggested that he had broken the law and should be impeached. But, as Eric Lichtblau reported, nothing really changed in the year following the eavesdropping revelations: "For all the sound and fury in the last year, the National Security Agency's wiretapping program continues uninterrupted with no definitive action by either Congress or the courts on what, if anything, to do about it."[17]

President Bush, however, pushed for and won the legalization of greater spying powers in the last year of his second term. On July 2008, he signed the FISA Amendment Act (FAA) of 2008 into law after enough Democrats (including then Senator Barack Obama) and Republicans in both congressional chambers voted in favor of significantly "updating" the original FISA law. In the first place, the new FISA version expanded (1) the administration's power for up to seven days to undertake emergency wiretapping of foreigners without court warrants in "exigent" national security circumstances and (2) the emergency wiretapping of citizens to seven days without court warrants as long as the Attorney General certifies the wiretap target's connection to terrorism. Moreover, the new law provided legal immunity to telecommunication companies that carried out illegal wiretaps for the Bush administration in the post-9/11 years.

Less than 24 hours after the FAA of 2008 was signed into law, the American Civil Liberties Union filed a lawsuit on behalf of a number of plaintiffs who challenged the constitutionality of the new law.

It was once again left to the courts to decide whether the constitution was on the side of proponents or opponents of the FAA provisions. Just like the Bush administration, the Obama administration tried to fend off legal actions against warrantless wiretaps by invoking the "state secrets" doctrine. But the U.S. Court of Appeals for the Ninth Circuit in California rejected the government's appeal to dismiss a suit by the al-Haramain Islamic Foundation that alleged that the organization had been the target of illegal wiretaps by the NSA. The three-judge panel did not embrace the Justice Department's argument that the proceedings would reveal state secrets but gave green light to the plaintiffs' legal proceedings. In the second case, the Obama administration repeated the "state secrets" claim of the Bush administration in a suit filed by AT&T customers against the telecommunication company for cooperating with the NSA's wiretap program. This was one of about 40 suits against telecoms filed around the country after President Bush acknowledged in 2005 that he had allowed the NSA to monitor communications between U.S. residents and suspected terrorists abroad without warrants. In short, then, in the first weeks and months of the Obama administration, there were more similarities than differences in the positions taken on these wiretapping cases.

Edward Snowden: Hero or Villain?

In early June 2013, after Edward Snowden spilled the beans about the NSA's massive post-9/11 eavesdropping program, Daniel Ellsberg, the leaker of the Pentagon Papers, called Snowden a hero and wrote,

> In my estimation, there has not been in American history a more important leak than Edward Snowden's release of NSA material... Snowden's whistleblowing gives us the possibility to roll back a key part of what has amounted to an "executive coup" against the US constitution. Since 9/11, there has been, at first secretly but increasingly openly, a revocation of the bill of rights for which this country fought over 200 years ago... That is what Snowden has exposed, with official, secret documents. The NSA, FBI, and CIA have, with

the new digital technology, surveillance powers over our own citizens that the Stasi—the secret police in the former "democratic republic" of East Germany—could scarcely have dreamed of. Snowden reveals that the so-called intelligence community has become the United Stasi of America.[18]

Jay Rosen defined what he called "the Snowden effect" as "direct and indirect gains in public knowledge from the cascade of events and further reporting that followed Edward Snowden's leaks of classified information about the surveillance state in the U.S." Media critic Rosen pointed to "journalists who were not a party to the transaction with Snowden" but who were now beginning to report on these matters.[19]

Snowden was considered a hero by some and a traitor by others. But there was no denying that he had laid bare U.S. intelligence agencies' widespread eavesdropping programs which violated basic civil liberties. According to the leaked information the NSA broke into communications links of major data centers around the globe enabling the agency to spy on hundreds of millions of American and foreign user accounts. What agents learned from intercepted conversations resulted in certain instances of charges of assisting terrorist organizations, plotting terrorist acts, or planning other terrorist-related wrongdoings and thus threatening America's national security. But in the vast majority of cases, innocent citizens were spied upon.

As noted above, during his first term in office and beyond President Obama followed the footsteps of his predecessor concerning the surveillance activities of the NSA and his administration's positions when legal challenge against the surveillance regime arose. In May 2011, Obama praised the Congress for reauthorizing three strong provisions for three years, namely,

1 Section 206 which provides authority for roving surveillance of targets who take steps that may thwart Foreign Intelligence Surveillance Act (FISA) surveillance;
2 Section 215 which provides authority to compel production of business records and other tangible things with the approval of the FISA court;
3 Section 6001 of the Intelligence Reform and Terrorism Prevention Act, which provides authority under FISA to target non-U.S. persons who engage in international terrorism or activities in preparation therefore, but are not necessarily associated with an identified terrorist group (the so-called "lone wolf" provision).

The shocker of Snowden's leak revelations, however, ignited a lively debate on the right balance between legitimate security arrangements on the one side and the protection of civil liberties on the other side. More importantly, less than three months after the Snowden leaks, President Obama charged an expert panel to make recommendations

> designed to protect our national security and advance our foreign policy while also respecting our longstanding commitment to privacy and civil liberties, recognizing our need to maintain the public trust (including the trust of our friends and allies abroad), and reducing the risk of unauthorized disclosures.[20]

Released in December 2013, the 308-page report and its 46 specific recommendations were intended to rein in what critics called the National Security State.

The USA Freedom Act: From President Barack Obama's "Weekly Address," May 30, 2015

As President and Commander in Chief, my greatest responsibility is the safety of the American people. And in our fight against terrorists, we need to use every effective tool at our disposal—both to defend our security and to protect the freedoms and civil liberties enshrined in our Constitution.

Today, when investigating terrorist networks, our national security professionals can seek a court order to obtain certain business records. Our law enforcement professionals can seek a roving wiretap to keep up with terrorists when they switch cell phones. We can seek a wiretap on so-called lone wolves—suspected terrorists who may not be directly tied to a terrorist group. These tools are not controversial. Since 9/11, they have been renewed numerous times. FBI Director James Comey says they are "essential" and that losing them would "severely" impact terrorism investigations. But if Congress doesn't act by tomorrow at midnight, these tools go away as well.

The USA Freedom Act also accomplishes something I called for a year and a half ago: it ends the bulk metadata program—the bulk collection of phone records—as it currently exists and puts in place new reforms. The government will no longer hold these records; telephone providers will. The Act also includes other changes to our surveillance laws—including more transparency—to help build confidence among the American people that your privacy and civil liberties are being protected. But if Congress doesn't act by midnight tomorrow, these reforms will be in jeopardy, too.

It doesn't have to be this way. The USA Freedom Act reflects ideas from privacy advocates, our private sector partners, and our national security experts. It already passed the House of Representatives with overwhelming bipartisan support—Republicans and Democrats. A majority of the Senate—Republicans and Democrats—have voted to move it forward.

So what's the problem? A small group of senators is standing in the way. And, unfortunately, some folks are trying to use this debate to score political points. But this shouldn't and can't be about politics. This is a matter of national security. Terrorists like al Qaeda and ISIL aren't suddenly going to stop plotting against us at midnight tomorrow. And we shouldn't surrender the tools that help keep us safe. It would be irresponsible. It would be reckless. And we shouldn't allow it to happen.[21]

Note: Three days later and the same day the U.S. Senate had passed the bill following the example of the U.S. House of Representatives President Obama signed the 2015 USA Freedom Act into law.

Because of the inter- and intra-party conflicts in both chambers of Congress, where some conservative members insisted on retaining strong surveillance measures and libertarians and liberals insisted on meaningful changes, it took a year and a half for the 2015 USA Freedom Act finally to be adopted by both houses of Congress and signed into law by President Obama. It was, as one observer noted,

the first legislative overhaul passed in response to the 2013 disclosures of former National Security Agency contractor Edward Snowden, who revealed the NSA's bulk collection of telephone "metadata" and the legal rationale for it—the little-noticed Section 215 of the USA Patriot Act, passed in the months after the Sept. 11, 2001, attacks.[22]

Most importantly, the 2015 law bans the bulk collection of data of Americans' telephone records and Internet metadata. It limits the government's data collection to the "greatest extent reasonably practical," meaning security agencies cannot collect all the data from a particular service provider or broad geographic region, says a local jurisdiction or area code. Instead of bulk data collection, the government is authorized to collect from phone companies up to "two hops" of call records related to a suspect, if there is "reasonable" suspicion that someone is linked to a terrorist organization. Also, three Patriot Act provisions reauthorized in 2011 allowing roving wiretaps and the surveillance of so-called lone wolves were extended through 2019.

The USA PATRIOT Act was not reauthorized by Congress in 2020 and thus expired. But a number of the intrusive Act's provisions were made permanent in 2005 and, along with other laws, continued to allow the authorities to surveil citizens and non-citizens.

The Rights of "Enemy Combatants"

Controversies arose also over the legal rights of so-called enemy combatants, who were held in Guantanamo Bay, the U.S. military base in Cuba, and over the torture and abusive treatment of foreign nationals held in American-controlled detention facilities in Afghanistan, Iraq, Guantanamo, and elsewhere. By characterizing hundreds of foreigners and a few American citizens as enemy combatants—not prisoners of war or criminals—President Bush and his administration denied these men the protections afforded to prisoners of war under the Geneva Convention and the civil liberties that the U.S. Constitution extends to accused criminals. To be sure, post-9/11 terrorism did not fit the familiar threats associated with war and crime. But, as Ronald Dworkin pointed out,

> The fact that terrorism presents new challenges and dangers does not mean that the basic moral principles and human rights that the criminal law and the laws of war try to protect have been repealed or become moot. We must instead ask what different scheme—what third model—is appropriate to respect those principles while still effectively defending ourselves.[23]

The more than 600 foreign nationals held for years in Guantanamo Bay were either captured in Afghanistan as Al Qaeda or Taliban fighters or turned over to American authorities by foreign governments. Yet, according to international agreements, it was not up to the American side to decide unilaterally their legal status by declaring them "enemy combatants" or "unlawful combatants." Instead, as Anthony Lewis explained,

> The Third Geneva Convention, which the United States has signed and ratified, says that when there is doubt about a prisoner's status, the question is to be determined by a 'competent tribunal.' That means an independent one. The Bush Administration has refused to comply with the Geneva Convention.[24]

For other observers, the issue was not as clear-cut. Assuming that the terrorist threat against the United States was, is, and will remain terribly serious, Michael Ignatieff outlined a "necessity of lesser evils" position in the fight against terrorism and suggested that

> to defeat evil, we may have to traffic in evils: indefinite detention of suspects, coercive interrogations, targeted assassinations, even pre-emptive war. These are evils because each strays from national and international law and because they kill people or deprive them of freedom without due process. They can be justified only if they prevent the greater evil.[25]

But the outcome of this approach requires, too, that the formal and informal democratic institutions discharge their responsibilities and control the "lesser evils." As Ignatieff put it,

> Only if our institutions work properly—if Congress reviews legislation in detail and tosses out measures that jeopardize liberty at no gain to security, if the courts keep executive power under constitutional control and if the press refuses to allow itself to become "embedded" with the government—can the moral and constitutional hazards of lesser evils be managed.[26]

During major crises, especially when national security is at stake, U.S. presidents tend to claim extraordinary powers. Past presidents were rarely checked by other actors and institutions inside and outside of government when they suspended fundamental civil liberties. For nearly three years that seemed the case after 9/11. While perhaps expected from Congress, where the president's party controlled both houses, that still left the judiciary. However, as Lewis remarked,

> The Supreme Court has usually been reluctant to intervene. When the Japanese relocation program [that removed 120,000 Americans of Japanese descent from their homes and confined them to camps on President Franklin D. Roosevelt's order] reached the Court, a majority declined to look past the military judgment that Japanese-Americans might be disloyal, though events had proved them false.[27]

However, with respect to the post-9/11 enemy combatants, the U.S. Supreme Court did rein in the president and the executive branch in several cases. First, a 6–3 majority ruled that foreign detainees in Guantanamo Bay had the right to apply for a writ of habeas corpus, the ancient right of prisoners to challenge the lawfulness of their detention.[28] Second, the Court decided that a U.S. citizen—although declared an enemy combatant by the executive branch—was entitled to his or her constitutional right of due process and that even the president did not have the power to deprive U.S. citizens of their Fifth Amendment rights to "life, liberty, or property, without due process of law." In a rare occurrence, the probably most liberal justice (John Paul Stevens) and the perhaps most conservative member of the Supreme Court (Antonin Scalia) were in the 7–1 Court majority in the case of Yaser Esam Hamdi, a U.S. citizen who was captured during hostilities in Afghanistan. In the prevailing opinion, Justice Sandra Day O'Connor wrote,

> Striking the proper constitutional balance here is of great importance to the nation during this period of on-going combat. But it is equally vital that our calculus not give short shrift to the values that this country holds dear or to the privilege that is American citizenship. It is during our most challenging and uncertain moments that our nation's commitment to due process is most severely tested; and we must preserve our commitment at home to the principles for which we fight abroad.[29]

Taken together, these decisions made clear that, as Justice O'Connor put it, "a state of war is not a blank check for the president."[30] Rather than allow Hamdi's lawyers to challenge his detention in court, the U.S. Departments of Justice and Defense decided in a complete turnaround that the suspected terrorist Hamdi was not a threat at all. After he renounced his U.S. citizenship as a condition of his release, Hamdi was flown to Saudi Arabia and became a free man.[31]

As the administration pondered how to translate the Supreme Court's decisions into practice with respect to the Guantanamo prisoners, any satisfactory solution would still leave in limbo an unknown number of foreign nationals who were held, as human rights organizations charged, in secret U.S. detention facilities abroad. According to Human Rights First (formerly the Lawyers Committee on Human Rights), nearly three years after 9/11 the U.S. government was "holding prisoners in a secret system of off-shore prisons beyond the reach of adequate supervision, accountability, or law."[32] These detainees were being held for extended periods of time without access to legal counsel, without a right to have their imprisonment reviewed by an independent authority, and without visits by the International Red Cross, Human Rights Watch, or other organizations. This policy was and is indefensible. Even though he endorsed "lesser evils" against the terrorist threat, Ignatieff also insisted that

> no detainee of the United States should be permanently deprived of access to counsel and judicial process, whether it be civilian federal court or military tribunal. Torture will thrive wherever detainees are held in secret. Conduct disgracing the United States is inevitable if suspects are detained beyond the reach of the law.[33]

The issue of how to try "enemy combatants" seemed finally decided in June 2006, when the U.S. Supreme Court ruled in *Hamdan v. Rumsfeld* that military commissions set up by the Bush administration violated the Geneva Conventions and the Uniform Code of Military Justice. Thus, the 5–3 decision in favor of Salim Ahmed Hamdan, who had worked in Afghanistan as Osama bin Laden's driver and bodyguard, held that "enemy combatants" are protected by the Geneva Conventions and, additionally, that the congressional Authorization for Use of Military Force against Terrorists of September 2001 did not grant President Bush the authority to create new tribunals without congressional mandate.[34] Within a few months, the Congress adopted and President Bush signed into law the Military Commissions Act of 2006 (Public Law 1009-366), which contained provisions that reestablished the very military tribunals that the Supreme Court ruled unconstitutional in *Hamdan v. Rumsfeld* and denies aliens detained by the U.S. government and determined to be enemy combatants the right of habeas corpus.

On December 14, 2006, Judge James Robertson of the U.S. District Court for the District of Columbia ruled that the Military Commissions Act did not allow Hamdan to contest his detention before a federal court. A year earlier, the same judge had granted Salim Ahmed Hamdan's habeas petition and thereby stopped his war crime trial at Guantanamo. But according to Judge Robertson, the Military Commissions Act "was unambiguous in denying Guantanamo detainees the use of a habeas corpus statute."[35]

Hamdan challenged the constitutionality of the congressional statute, but in October 2007 the U.S. Supreme Court refused to review his case. Charged with conspiracy and providing material support for terrorism, Hamdan's military commission trial took place in the summer of 2008 at Guantanamo. The six-member commission acquitted him of the more serious charge (conspiracy) and found him guilty of the lesser charge (providing material support). The prosecution asked for a 30-year prison term to life imprisonment but the commission opted for a 66-month prison term—61 months of which had been served already. In November 2008, Hamdan was sent to Yemen, where he was to serve the last month of his sentence.

At the time of Hamdan's release, about 250 "unlawful enemy combatants" remained in the Guantanamo facility—about 100 of them citizens of Yemen. It was left to the Obama administration to decide what to do with those detainees and the Guantanamo prison. During his presidential campaign, Obama said that Guantanamo was a sad chapter in American history and promised "we're going to close Guantanamo. And we're going to restore habeas corpus... We're going to lead by example—by not just word but by deed. That's our vision for the future."[36] Two days after his inauguration, President Obama issued an executive order for the prompt closing of the facility after an immediate review of all detainees' records.[37] But in the face of relentless attacks by critics in Congress and elsewhere, the White House retreated from its promise to close the prison, transfer the remaining detainees to prisons in the United States, and try them in the regular court system. In the eyes of the president's detractors, bringing terrorists or suspected terrorists into the United States, even if in maximum security facilities, endangered homeland security. There was a massive and sustained protest, when the Justice Department announced that 9/11 mastermind Khalid Sheik Mohammed would be tried in a Federal Court in downtown Manhattan. Again, the administration retreated and searched for alternative venues.

> A day before he left office President Obama informed the U.S. Congress that, of the once close to 800 detainees in the U.S. facility at Guantanamo Bay, forty-one remained. During the eight years of his presidency Obama had failed to get congressional approval to close the prison. In his letter he stated with regret, For 15 years, the United States has detained hundreds of people at the detention facility at Guantánamo Bay, a facility that never should have been opened in the first place. Terrorists use it for propaganda, its operations drain our military resources during a time of budget cuts, and it harms our partnerships with allies and countries whose cooperation we need against today's evolving terrorist threat."[38]

At the end of July 2022, 21 years after 9/11, 36 detainees remained imprisoned in the Guantanamo detention facilities, 20 of which recommended for transfers to other countries if certain security arrangements could be made.

Torture: Leaders and Followers

At Abu Ghraib prison, outside of Baghdad, an Iraqi prisoner... Manadel al-Jamadi, died during an interrogation. His head had been covered with a plastic bag, and he was shackled in a crucifixion-like pose that inhibited his ability to breathe; according to forensic pathologists who have examined the case, he asphyxiated.[39]

In the fall of 2007, during his confirmation hearing before the U.S. Senate's Judiciary Committee, Attorney General designate Michael Mukasey claimed to be clueless as to the nature of waterboarding. He said that he did not know whether this interrogation technique constituted torture. In a letter to the committee, he seemed to side with the administration's position that CIA interrogations of terrorists or suspected terrorists are exempt from antitorture laws that the military and others must follow.[40] He was confirmed as the highest U.S. official to enforce the laws of the land. Once in office, Mukasey did not change his position. Instead, during an appearance before the Senate Judiciary Committee, he said that he would not rule out the use of torture in the future.[41]

Waterboarding has been used as a method of torture for hundreds of years. In more recent times, it has been practiced by state and nonstate human rights violators. According to one account, "in some versions of the technique, prisoners are strapped to a board, their faces covered with cloth or cellophane, and water is poured over their mouths to simulate drowning; in others, they are dunked headfirst into water."[42] In the past, U.S. authorities considered this particularly gruesome interrogation method to be torture and punishable as a war crime. Thus, following World War II, "U.S. military commissions successfully prosecuted as war criminals several Japanese soldiers who subjected American prisoners to waterboarding. A U.S. army officer was court-marshaled in 1968 for helping to waterboard a prisoner in Vietnam."[43]

But that changed after 9/11. Waterboarding and other torture techniques were no longer off-limits in the "war on terror." A few reports about "aggressive interrogation" methods of so-called enemy combatants in U.S.-run prisons abroad had been published earlier, but most Americans learned about such gross human rights violations in the spring of 2004, when CBS News on *60 Minutes* and Seymour Hersh in the *New Yorker* revealed the torturous treatment of detainees at Abu Ghraib. Administration officials blamed the isolated incidents on rogue soldiers, but eventually, evidence showed that "harsh" interrogation practices—indeed, torture—were backed by opinions written and approved by legal experts in the White House and the Departments of Justice and Defense in express violation of the United Nations Convention against Torture, the U.S. Constitution, and the Uniform Code of Military Justice.[44]

Referring to what administration critics called "Torture Memos," Donald P. Gregg, national security advisor from 1982 to 1988 to then Vice President George H. W. Bush, wrote in 2004:

> Recent reports indicate that Bush administration lawyers, in their struggles to deal with terrorism, wrote memos in 2003 pushing aside longstanding prohibitions on the use of torture by Americans. These memos cleared the way for the horrors that have been revealed in Iraq, Afghanistan and Guantánamo and make a mockery of administration assertions that a few misguided enlisted personnel perpetrated the vile abuse of prisoners.
>
> I can think of nothing that can more devastatingly undercut America's standing in the world or, more important, our view of ourselves, than these decisions. Sanctioned abuse is deeply corrosive—just ask the French, who are still seeking to eradicate the stain on their honor that resulted from the deliberate use of torture in Algeria.[45]

But in spite of evidence to the contrary, the administration denied that detainees were being or had been tortured. After the U.S. Congress adopted and the president signed a bill with antitorture provisions in October 2006, President George W. Bush insisted in his signing statement that the new law "will allow the Central Intelligence Agency to continue its program for questioning key terrorist leaders and operatives."[46] He claimed that it was the president's prerogative to decide what methods CIA interrogators were allowed to use. But in the same breath, he continued to tell Americans and the rest of the world, "The United States does not torture. It's against our laws and it's against our values. I have not authorized it."[47] Similarly, right after Vice President Richard Cheney stated in a radio interview the "dunk in water" (meaning waterboarding) in the interrogation of detainees was a "no-brainer," he added, "We don't torture. That's not what we're involved in."[48]

The White House clung to the "we-do-not-torture" line even after CIA director Michael V. Hayden admitted in early 2008 that waterboarding had been used during the interrogations of three leading Al Qaeda figures: Abu Zabaydah, Abd al-Rahim al-Nashiri, and Khalid Sheik Mohammed.[49] In reaction, a White House spokesperson said that President Bush would "authorize waterboarding future terrorism suspects if certain criteria are met."[50] And Vice President Cheney "vigorously defended the use of harsh interrogation techniques on a few suspected terrorists, saying that the methods made up 'a tougher program, for tougher customers.'"[51] Neither the president nor the vice president considered waterboarding or "harsh interrogation techniques" to be torture. Not surprisingly, on March 8, 2008, President Bush announced during his regular Saturday morning radio address that he had vetoed legislation that would have prohibited the CIA from using waterboarding and other harsh interrogation tactics. He justified his veto by stating that the prohibitions "would take away one of the most valuable tools on the war on terror." And he added that "this is no time for Congress to abandon practices that have a proven track record of keeping America safe."[52] In other words, torturing terrorists and suspected terrorists remained part of Bush's "war on terrorism." Besides prohibiting torture altogether, the vetoed bill would have banned the following:

- Forcing a prisoner to be naked, perform sexual acts or pose in a sexual manner;
- Placing hoods or sacks over the head of a prisoner, and using duct tape over the eyes;
- Waterboarding;
- Using military working dogs;
- Inducing hypothermia or heat injury;
- Depriving a prisoner of necessary food, water, or medical care.

On December 11, 2008, the Senate Armed Services Committee released the executive summary of its 18-month inquiry into the treatment of detainees held in U.S.-run prison facilities abroad. The committee found "that the authorization of aggressive interrogation techniques by senior officials was both a direct cause of detainee abuse and conveyed the message that it was okay to mistreat and degrade detainees in U.S. custody."[53] The detailed conclusions of the document attributed responsibility for the mistreating and, yes, torturing of detainees to President Bush, members of his cabinet (in particular Defense Secretary Donald Rumsfeld), the National Security Council, and military leaders. Addressing Abu Ghraib in particular, the Senate committee concluded that the abuse there was not just a case of "a few soldiers acting on their own" but rather the result of policies approved by "senior military and civilian officials."[54] Nevertheless, only a handful of the lowest-level soldiers were convicted for the mistreatment of detainees, while the only officer charged, a lieutenant colonel in command of the interrogations at the Abu Ghraib prison, was acquitted by a military court.

If there were any heroes in this dark chapter, they were the lawyers in the military services who questioned proposed "aggressive interrogation" policy and defended and judged Guantanamo prisoners in a professional fashion. As David Cole noted,

> Documents disclosed in the course of the [Senate] hearings now show that when the coercive measures were under consideration, top lawyers for every branch of the military—Army, Navy, Air Force, and Marine Corps—objected that the tactics might be illegal.[55]

But when the legal counsel to General Richard Myers, chairman of the Joint Chiefs of Staff, began to review the legal questions involved here, the general "ordered that the legal inquiry be quashed" at the request of the Defense Department's general counsel.[56]

Human Rights Violation in the Name of Counterterrorism

The United Nations Convention against Torture that prohibits along with torture other "cruel, inhuman, or degrading treatment" was adopted in 1984 and four years later ratified by the United States. The following is a summary of humanitarian laws against torture by the International Committee of the Red Cross:

(Continued)

(Continued)

> There is an absolute ban on torture and other cruel, inhuman or degrading treatment and outrages upon personal dignity under international humanitarian law (IHL) and international human rights law (IHRL). The prohibition of torture and other forms of ill-treatment derives from the Geneva Conventions of 1949, their Additional Protocols of 1977, the Convention against Torture and Other Cruel, Inhuman or Degrading Treatment or Punishment of 1984, and other international instruments. Both IHL and IHRL converge and complement each other in establishing a comprehensive legal framework for the prevention and punishment of acts of torture and other forms of ill-treatment.[57]

Accordingly, the gross mistreatment of prisoners, whether one calls it torture, abuse, humiliation, or cruel treatment, is prohibited and punishable according to international human rights laws. In the post-9/11 years, the Bush administration refuted claims of torture or in the benign language of officialdom "enhanced interrogation" techniques in U.S.-run detention centers abroad—even in the face of unspeakable images of mistreated detainees at Abu Ghraib prison in Iraq.

In an interview shortly after the Abu Ghraib revelations, William F. Schulz, Executive Director of Amnesty International, warned that in their fight against terrorism governments "have resorted to many of the same tactics [as terrorists]" and that "by violating human rights themselves, those governments lend a degree of credibility to the use of those kinds of tactics in the first place."[58]

Obama on Torture and Rendition

Two days after his inauguration, President Obama issued an executive order that:

1   Reversed the torture policies of the previous administration and banned the inhumane and degrading treatment of detainees by requiring the use of the U.S. Army Field Manuals as a guide for terror interrogations;
2   Ordered the closing of secret CIA prisons;
3   Provided the International Committee of the Red Cross access to all U.S.-held detainees;
4   Established an interagency task force to conduct a review of detention policies and procedures.[59]

But although the president banned torture, his administration supported what came down to the outsourcing of it during the Bush administration and did not ban rendition altogether. The Obama administration's position in the case of Maher Arar was particularly troubling. Arar, a Syrian-born Canadian, was wrongly suspected of being a terrorist, arrested in 2002 by U.S. authorities during a stopover in New York, and sent by the CIA in another "extraordinary rendition" procedure to Syria, where he was tortured for about a year during interrogation. After a Federal District Judge dismissed Arar's suit designed to hold officials responsible for his torment accountable, the Second Circuit Court of Appeals upheld the Federal District Court's dismissal. Subsequently, the Supreme Court refused to consider the case and thereby shut the door on an innocent victim of the U.S. government's post-9/11 practice of outsourcing torture. Like the Bush administration earlier, the Obama administration asked the court not to accept the case for national security considerations and the protection of diplomatic relations (presumably with Syria and other countries at the receiving end of extraordinary rendition practices). Moreover, the Obama administration warned that the case could question "the motives and sincerity of the United States officials who concluded that petitioner could be removed to Syria."[60]

The Obama administration did not ban the CIA from continuing rendition practices but promised to put better safeguards in place to prevent torture. But if the humane treatment of rendered terrorists or alleged terrorists was indeed a concern, why move these interrogations to tough foreign government agents in the first place?

As for President Trump, during a Republican primary debate, he said, "Can you imagine these animals, over in the Middle East that chop off heads, sitting around and seeing that we're having a hard problem with waterboarding? We should go for waterboarding and we should go tougher than waterboarding."[61] Shortly after he moved into the White House, Trump said in an interview that "waterboarding is a viable interrogation technique" and added hesitantly that he would defer to members of his cabinet who opposed torture.[62]

The Drone War and Human Rights Violations

As described in Chapter 10, the number of drone-launched missiles increased drastically during the Obama presidency. Human rights and civil liberties organizations at home and abroad expressed their concern over civilian victims of drone strikes frequently. Thus, in 2015, ten NGOs stated the following in a letter to President Obama:

> Based on a review of a wide range of civilian casualty estimates, we are especially concerned that the administration may be consistently undercounting and overlooking civilian casualties. Moreover,

the administration may be employing an overbroad definition of "combatant" or "militant" that would lead it to undercount civilian casualties. These concerns heighten the need to ensure there are effective mechanisms to track and respond to civilian harm. Moreover, in the context of armed conflict, a track record of undercounting civilian casualties may cause the United States to make an inaccurate assessment of the proportionality element of lethal action—itself a violation of the laws of war.[63]

The customary rules of International Humanitarian Law prescribe that there must be always a distinction between civilians and combatants in armed conflicts and that civilians must not be attacked.[64] Substantial and perhaps undercounted numbers of civilian victims can and do raise doubts about the observation of human rights in the deployment of drones. Most of all, the drone war turned people in the targeted countries against the United States as the following excerpts from a news report aired on the CBS Evening News on May 23, 2013, attest to:

SCOTT PELLEY: Most drone deaths are happening in Pakistan, the figures can't be completely reliable but it is estimated that since 2004 as many as twenty-seven hundred militants have died in drone strikes. Estimates of civilian deaths range from two hundred and fifty to eight hundred. Elizabeth Palmer looked at all of this for us in Islamabad. (Begin VD)

ELIZABETH PALMER: A vast majority of Pakistanis resent American drone strikes. Shazad Ackbar, a former prosecutor turned human rights lawyer, has collected hard evidence of civilian casualties from drone strikes.

ELIZABETH PALMER: These are what's left of the missile that's fired from the drone?

SHAZAD ACKBAR: Yeah, yeah.

ELIZABETH PALMER:... Ackbar told us the drone strikes have killed more than a thousands [sic] of civilians—a figure the U.S. disputes.

SHAZAD ACKBAR: This is a Pakistani child. He was sleeping in the courtyard. So — a shrapnel hit him, so he died.

ELIZABETH PALMER: At a funeral for two of Ackbar's clients, a policeman and a pharmacist, killed in a strike near the Afghan border, the crowd chanted "any friend of America is a traitor." (Crowd protesting)

ELIZABETH PALMER: Critics have long argued that drones make more enemies for the U.S. than they kill.

The last sentence was then and remains the most important one: Human rights violations in drone warfare (as in torture) may not reduce the terrorist threat at all but create more enemies and possibly more supporters of terrorism and recruits.

Notes

1 "Transcript of bin Laden's October Interview," with Al Jazeera correspondent Tayseer Alouni, www.cnn.com/2002/world/asiapcf/south/02/05/binladen. transcript/index.html.

2 Paul Wilkinson, *Terrorism versus Democracy: The Liberal State Response* (London: Frank Cass, 2001), 94, 95.

3 Marc A. Celmer, *Terrorism, U.S. Strategy, and Reagan Policies* (New York: Greenwood Press, 1987), 13.

4 www.wikipedia.org/wiki/counter-terrorism, accessed January 30, 2005.

5 Peter J. Katzenstein, "West Germany's Internal Security Policy: State and Violence in the 1970s and 1980s," Occasional Paper number 28, published by the Center for International Studies, Cornell University, 1990.

6 John Yoo in his testimony before the Subcommittee on Homeland Security (Senate Appropriation Committee), September 18, 2006, 4, www.freerepublic. com/focus/f-news/1705339/posts.

7 Ibid.

8 Ibid., 2.

9 David Cole and James X. Dempsey, *Terrorism and the Constitution* (New York: New Press, 2002), 117.

10 Laura K. Donohue, "Fear Itself: Counter-Terrorism, Individual Rights, and U.S. Foreign Relations Post 9/11," paper presented at the Annual Meeting of the International Studies Association, March 24–27, 2002, New Orleans.

11 Ibid.

12 Charles Doyle, "The USA PATRIOT ACT: A Sketch," Congressional Research Service, April 18, 2002.

13 Cole and Dempsey, 167.

14 Kevin Bohn, "Patriot Act Report Documents Civil Rights Complaints," CNN. com/Law Center, July 31, 2003.

15 Ibid.

16 Philip Shenon, "Report on USA PATRIOT Act Alleges Civil Rights Violations," *New York Times*, July 21, 2003, 1.

17 Eric Lichtblau, "Despite a Year of Ire and Angst, Little Has Changed on Wiretaps," *New York Times*, November 25, 2006; http://select.nytimes.com/ search/restricted/article?res=FA0A10F9385A0C768EDDA8099.

18 Daniel Ellsberg, "Edward Snowden: Saving Us from the United Stasi of America," *Huffington Post*, June 10, 2013. The post is available at www. theguardian.com/commentisfree/2013/jun/10/edward-snowden-united-stasi-america, accessed March 20, 2015. For the "hero" remark, see www.huffingtonpost.com/2013/06/10/edward-snowden-daniel-ellsberg-whistleblower-history_n_3413545.html, accessed March 20, 2015.

19 Jay Rosen, "The Snowden Effect: Definition and Examples," *PressThink*, July 5, 2013; http://pressthink.org/2013/07/the-snowden-effect-definition-and-examples/, accessed March 17, 2015.

20 "Liberty and Security in a Changing World: Report and Recommendations of the President's Review Group on Intelligence and Communication Technology," December 12, 2013; https://s3.amazonaws.com/s3.documentcloud.org/ documents/930353/2013-12-12-rg-final-report.pdf, accessed July 29, 2015.

21 www.whitehouse.gov/the-press-office/2015/05/30/weekly-address-pass-usa-freedom-act, accessed July 25, 2015.

22 Mike DeBonis, "Congress Turns Away from Post-9/11 Law, Retooling U.S. Surveillance Powers," *Washington Post*, June 2, 2015, www.washingtonpost. com/politics/senate-moves-ahead-with-retooling-of-us-surveillance-powers

/2015/06/02/28f5e1ce-092d-11e5-a7ad-b430fc1d3f5c_story.html, accessed July 28, 2015.

23 Ronald Dworkin, "Terror and the Attack on Civil Liberties," *New York Review of Books*, November 6, 2003.

24 Anthony Lewis, "The Justices Take on the President," *New York Times*, January 16, 2004, A21.

25 Michael Ignatieff, "Lesser Evils," *New York Times Sunday Magazine*, May 2, 2003, www.nytimes.com/2004/07/25/books/review/25STEELL.html?scp=1&sq=Ignatieff%20the%20lesser%20evil&st=cse, accessed May 20, 2009.

26 Ibid.

27 Lewis.

28 See *Rasul v. Bush*, No. 03-334. The 6–3 decision was announced on June 29, 2004.

29 See *Hamdi v. Rumsfeld*, No. 03-6696.

30 Ibid.

31 Since the Supreme Court handed down a rather narrow decision with respect to the foreign detainees at Guantanamo, cases on behalf of these "enemy combatants" continued to be heard.

32 Human Rights First, press release of June 17, 2004.

33 Ignatieff.

34 Chief Justice John Roberts, who had ruled against Hamdan while serving on the D.C. Circuit Court of Appeals, recused himself from the Supreme Court case.

35 Neil A. Lewis, "Judge Sets Back Guantanamo Detainees," *New York Times*, December 14, 2006, 32.

36 Elizabeth White, "Obama Says Gitmo Facility Should Close," *Washington Post*, June 24, 2007, www.washingtonpost.com/wp-dyn/content/article/2007/06/24/AR2007062401046.html, accessed December 30, 2008.

37 For the text of the Executive Order, see www.whitehouse.gov/the_press_office/ClosureOfGuantanamoDetentionFacilities/, accessed May 14, 2009.

38 The text of the letter is available at www.documentcloud.org/documents/3382071-Obama-White-House-report-to-Congress.html, accessed May 30, 2018.

39 Jane Mayer, "A Deadly Interrogation," *New Yorker*, November 14, 2005, www.newyorker.com/archive/2005/11/14/051114fa_fact, accessed May 20, 2009.

40 www.talkingpointsmemo.com/docs/mukasey-dems/?resultpage=1&amp.

41 Philip Shenon, "Mukasey Will Not Rule Out Waterboarding," *New York Times*, January 31, 2008; www.nytimes.com/2008/01/31/washington/ 31justice.html, accessed February 2, 2008.

42 http://hrw.org/english/docs/2006/10/26/usdom14465.htm.

43 Ibid.

44 The Eighth Amendment of the U.S. Constitution forbids the use of "cruel and unusual punishments," which is widely interpreted as a prohibition of the use of torture. The Uniform Code of Military Justice forbids torture outside the United States.

45 Donald P. Gregg, "After Abu Ghraib; Fight Fire with Compassion," *New York Times*, June 10, 2004.

46 www.whitehouse.gov/news/releases/2006/10/20061017-1.html.

47 www.whitehouse.gov/news/releases/2006/09/20060906-3.html.

48 www.whitehouse.gov/news/releases/2006/10/20061024-7.html.

49 www.nytimes.com/2008/02/06/washington/06intel.html?scp=11&sq=waterboarding&st=nyt.

50 Dan Fromkin, "We Tortured and We'd Do It Again," *Washingtonpost.com*, February 6, 2008; www.washingtonpost.com/wp-dyn/content/blog/2008/02/06/BL2008020602244_pf.html, accessed February 11, 2008.
51 David Stout and Scott Shane, "Cheney Defends the Use of Harsh Interrogation," *New York Times*, February 7, 2008, www.nytimes.com/2008/02/07/washington/07cnd-intel.html?hp.
52 Presidential radio address on March 8, 2008, www.whitehouse.gov/news/releases/2008/03/20080308.html, accessed March 9, 2008.
53 From U.S. Senator Carl Levin's news release, http://levin.senate.gov/newsroom/release.cfm?id=305735, accessed December 28, 2008.
54 From the summary of the "Senate Armed Services Committee Inquiry into the Treatment of Detainees in U.S. Custody," http://armed-services.senate.gov/Publications/EXEC%20SUMMARYCONCLUSIONS_For%20Release_12%20December%202008.pdf, accessed December 30, 2008.
55 David Cole, "What to Do about the Torturers?," *New York Review of Books*, January 15, 2009, 22.
56 Ibid.
57 The International Committee of the Red Cross's document is available at https://r.search.yahoo.com/_ylt=AwrBT7hnegdZO5MAzypXNyoA;_ylu=X3oDMTByOHZyb21tBGNvbG8DYmYxBHBvcwMxBHZ0aWQDBHNlYwNzcg--/RV=2/RE=1493691111/RO=10/RU=https%3a%2f%2fwww.icrc.org%2fen%2fdownload%2ffile%2f1025%2fprohibition-and-punishment-of-torture-icrc-eng.pdf/RK=0/RS=w6iJXgP7xpemQcQGrwNb7eWuN8k-, accessed May 1, 2017.
58 Newsweek Staff, "The War on Terror Is Not Working," *Newsweek.com*, www.newsweek.com/war-terror-not-working-128307, accessed May 29, 2018.
59 For the full text of the executive order, see www.whitehouse.gov/the-press-office/background-president-obama-signs-executive-orders-detention-and-interrogation-polic, accessed July 12, 2010.
60 "No Price to Pay for Torture," *New York Times*, June 15, 2010.
61 Tessa Berenson, "Donald Trump Defends Torture at Republican Debate," *Time*, March 3, 2017; http://time.com/4247397/donald-trump-waterboarding-torture/, accessed May 20, 2018.
62 Reena Flores, "Trump Says Intelligence Officials Tell Him Torture Works," *CBS News*, January 25, 2017; www.cbsnews.com/news/trump-says-intelligence-officials-tell-him-torture-works/, accessed April 15, 2018.
63 The letter is available on the website of the Human Rights Institute of Columbia University at https://web.law.columbia.edu/sites/default/files/microsites/human-rights-institute/files/Letter%20to%20President%20and%20Statement%20on%20Targeted%20Killings.pdf, accessed May 1, 2017.
64 For The Laws of War, see https://humanrightsinvestigations.org/the-laws-of-war/, accessed May 2, 2017.

Part III
Terrorism in the News Media and on the Internet

14 Terrorist Propaganda and the Mainstream Media

This chapter and the following one are devoted to the centrality of communication, publicity, and propaganda in the terrorist calculus. Although these chapters comprise the last part of the book, they are as important, and perhaps more so, than the previous text. However, the centrality of media of communication in political violence carried out by nonstate actors is best understood in the overall contexts of terrorism and counterterrorism, the topics of the two previous parts of this textbook. Indeed, it has been suggested that without any publicity, there would not be any terrorism. The idea is similar to the notion of the tree that falls in the forest—an event that is not reported in the press so that it is as if the tree did not fall. This and the idea of vanishing terrorism without publicity are exaggerations. But there is evidence that terrorists often plan their attacks in order to get the greatest amount of media attention as described in this and the next chapter.

Figure 14.1 depicts what I call the triangle of political communication and how it is utilized by terrorists who aim to influence general publics, friends and foes and governments and all kinds of political actors as shown in the two lower corner boxes of the triangle. In order to reach those target audiences, terrorists need forms of communication that disperse their explicit and implicit messages. As the box on top of the triangle shows, there are three types of communication:

- Interpersonal, communication between two persons or groups of people;
- Mass Communication, the traditional media—off- and online print, radio, television; and
- Mass Self-Communication via internet sites and, most of all social media platforms that reach large audiences.

In this chapter, I focus on off- and online mainstream media controlled by gatekeepers that determine what news is reported and how it is reported. While social media allowing terrorist mass self-communication receives rightly a great deal of attention in our times, my position is that mass

DOI: 10.4324/9781003289265-17

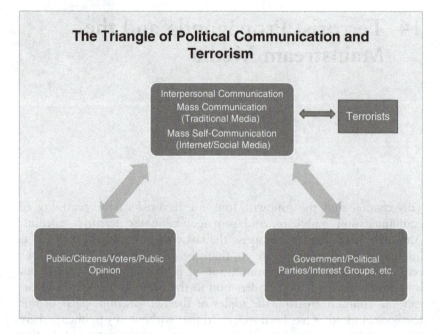

Figure 14.1 Terrorism and the Triangle of Political Communication
Source: Author

communication via mainstream media remains thus far the most important news source. In Chapter 15, I concentrate on online communication whose content terrorists control themselves.

Terrorist Propaganda and the News Media

In mid-August 2014, the Islamic State (also called ISIS for the Islamic State of Iraq and Syria, or ISIL for the Islamic State in Iraq and the Levant) shocked the world with a close to five-minute video uploaded on YouTube. The involuntary star of the production was the American journalist James Foley wearing an orange jumpsuit and kneeling next to a masked ISIS fighter. Under duress, the hostage called the U.S. government his real killer and exclaimed that he wished he wasn't an American. But condemning the Washington government did not save Foley's life. The ISIS fighter pulled out a knife and beheaded his hostage while the camera captured every second of this most brutal execution.

One day later, President Barack Obama appeared in front of cameras and microphones and declared, "The entire world is appalled by the brutal murder of Jim Foley by the terrorist group, ISIL." He promised that

> the United States of America will continue to do what we must do to protect our people. We will be vigilant and we will be relentless.

When people harm Americans, anywhere, we do what's necessary to see that justice is done. And we act against ISIL, standing alongside others.[1]

Most Americans did not see the video. On YouTube, the clip was quickly blocked. Although available on some sites, most people either did not want to see the horror or could not find the full clip. But everyone who watched television, listened to radio, visited the Internet, or looked at the front page of a newspaper was aware of the execution. The already heavy coverage of ISIS before Foley's execution increased significantly after the release of the video. As Table 14.1 shows, in leading print and TV media the number of articles about or mentioning ISIS, ISIL, or the Islamic State tripled in the month following the release of the decapitation video compared to the month before the posting of the ISIS video. Similarly, as seen in Table 14.2, articles with ISIS, ISIL, or Islamic State in the headlines increased dramatically after the beheading video was

Table 14.1 Mainstream Media Reporting on ISIS before and after Foley Beheading: Articles about or Mentioning ISIS

	Month Prior to Beheading (July 18– August 18, 2014)	Month Following Beheading (August 19– September 19, 2014)
New York Times	124	375
Newsweek	3	15
CNN.com	45	296

Source: Marissa Young (2015).

Table 14.2 Mainstream Media Reporting on ISIS before and after Foley Beheading: Number of Articles with Islamic State, ISIS, or ISIL in Headline

	Month Prior to Beheading (July 18– August 18, 2014)	Month Following Beheading (August 19– September 19, 2014)
New York Times	3	99
Newsweek	1	5
CNN.com	31	95

Source: Marissa Young (2015).

released from merely three in the month before to 99 in the *New York Times*, from one to five in *Newsweek*, and from 31 to 95 on CNN.com. The coverage patterns were not different in the rest of the news media.

After he beheaded several other hostages according to ISIS videos, the executioner, who reportedly grew up in England, became known as "Jihadi John" around the world. In mid-2015, a Google search of the term "Jihadi John" produced 6,280,000 results; a search in the archive of the *New York Times* brought up 266 stories; there were 78 such articles in the *Washington Post* and 229 at CNN.com.

Those who run the Islamic State's media center are public information and propaganda specialists. Abu Muhammad al-Adnani al-Shami who is in charge of ISIS's public information operations could be compared to Joseph Goebbels who ran the ministry of propaganda in Nazi Germany.

Mainstream media, including their online content, continue to be the most important news sources. Terrorist propagandists know this well. As someone with rare insider information of the working of ISIS's propaganda machine put it,

> Crucifixions, beheadings, the hearts of rape victims cut out and placed upon their chests, mass executions, homosexuals being pushed from high buildings, severed heads impaled on railings or brandished by grinning "jihadist" children—who have latterly taken to shooting prisoners in the head themselves—these gruesome images of brutal violence are carefully packaged and distributed via Islamic State's media department. *As each new atrocity outdoes the last, front-page headlines across the world's media are guaranteed.*[2]

In July 2010, some ten weeks after the failed attempt to detonate a bomb in New York City's busy Times Square area, an Arab TV network aired a video in which the would-be bomber Faisal Shahzad justified his plan to harm Americans as revenge for "oppressed Muslims" and "for all the *mujahedeen*." Obviously produced well before the Times Square incident, the videotape contained passages in which Shahzad read from religious texts and used them as launching pads for threats against America. "Eight years have passed by in Afghanistan and you'll see that the Muslim war has just started, and we will tell you how until Islam is spread on the whole world," he said at one point. Dressed in traditional Pakistani garb, the naturalized U.S. citizen held an assault rifle in his hand—an obvious effort to evoke the image of a fierce jihadist. That was in line with what he had called himself as he pleaded guilty in the federal court in Manhattan: A Muslim soldier.

Besides being aired first in newscasts by al Arabiya television and thereafter by TV networks and stations around the world, aired excerpts of the 40-minute video were available on the al Arabiya website and YouTube. Just as important, other media—radio, print, and blogs—reported the release of the video and its content.

While the Times Square attempt failed, the event itself and the would-be bomber's subsequent threats, explanations, and justifications received an enormous amount of media attention. This was hardly surprising because not only major terrorist attacks but, in fact, even minor strikes and sometimes failed or foiled acts of terrorism are reported and often overreported. This is precisely what terrorists want.

Following the attacks of September 11, 2001, Osama bin Laden gloated that "these young men [the hijackers] said in deeds, in New York and Washington, speeches that overshadowed other speeches made everywhere else in the world. The speeches are understood by both Arabs and non-Arabs—even Chinese."[3] Bin Laden expressed what terrorists at all times believed and acted upon, namely, that terrorism is "propaganda by the deed" or "propaganda of the deed" as nineteenth-century anarchists put it. After comparing the publicity success of Black September's attack on Israeli athletes during the 1972 Olympic Games in Munich, Abu Ubeid al-Qurashi, a leading Al Qaeda operative, boasted that "September 11 was an even greater propaganda coup. It may be said that it broke a record in propaganda dissemination."[4]

Students of terrorist violence and communication are well aware that for terrorists "the immediate victim is merely instrumental, the skin of a drum beaten to achieve a calculated impact on a wider audience."[5] Regardless of their grievances, goals, size, and secular or religious convictions, all terrorist groups strive to maximize their media impact. As Osama bin Laden wrote in a letter to Taliban leader Mullah Muhammed Omar, "It is obvious that the media war in this century is one of the strongest methods; in fact, its ratio may reach 90% of the total preparation for the battles."[6] To be sure, some terrorist groups are more media savvy than others. The Palestinian Hamas is among those with sophisticated press and publicity operations, as the following case demonstrates:

> It is August 19, 2003. In Jerusalem, a city bus packed with families returning from Judaism's holiest site, the Western Wall, is ripped to pieces by a powerful explosion. It is an unspeakable scene of carnage. Twenty people, among them six children, are killed. More than a hundred are injured. Traumatized survivors and witnesses. Disheartened rescuers. Shortly after the blast and well before the dead and critically injured men, women, and children are identified, a cell of the Palestinian Hamas group releases a written press statement claiming responsibility for the attack and a pretaped video of the "martyr" explaining his deed. The videotape shows twenty-nine-year-old Raed Abdul Hamid Misk holding a rifle in one hand and a Qu'ran in the other. The father of two young children with a pregnant wife, and the imam of a Hebron mosque, justifies his attack on innocents partially in Arabic and partially in English. His wife does not seem surprised when she says, "All his life he was saying, 'Oh God, I wish to be a martyr.'"[7]

By making the videotape available to the media nearly simultaneously with the explosion, the terrorists calculated correctly that the news media would pay a great deal of attention to Misk. He did not fit the profile of Palestinian suicide bombers—not in terms of his profession, age, or family status. This assured him and his act special media attention around the world when details about his victims were not yet available. During the following days, the media's interest in this unlikely terrorist remained high. Five days after the attack, for example, the *New York Times* illustrated a general story on suicide attacks with a huge color photograph of Misk; taken three days before he killed himself in order to kill others, the photograph showed the smiling father with his three-year-old son and two-year-old daughter in his arms. Here was a compelling image that made people wonder what conditions could drive such a man to become a human bomb. This was precisely the effect that terrorists hope for. In this particular case, the news added up to an utterly successful publicity campaign that could not have been better orchestrated by the best experts on Madison Avenue.

The same was true for an earlier case that unfolded in Russia's capital. Soon after heavily armed Chechen separatists seized a theater in Moscow on October 21, 2002, their accomplices delivered videotapes to the Moscow bureau of the Arab satellite news network Al Jazeera. They explained that they had chosen to die on "the path of struggling for the freedom of the Chechen."[8] The videotape was played by TV networks and stations around the world. As many of the hundreds of hostages inside used their cellphones to communicate with families and friends, some of them conveyed the chilling messages of their captors to the Russian public and especially to Russian President Vladimir V. Putin. The hostage-holders left no doubt that they would blow up the building and kill hundreds of innocent people unless the Putin government ordered the withdrawal of Russian troops from Chechnya. At the height of the siege, one of the captors grabbed the cellphone from a hostage who was speaking to a local radio station and delivered a tirade against Russia's war against the Chechen people.

Although local politicians noted how media savvy these hostage-takers were, the Chechens did not break new ground. During the Iranian hostage crisis of 1979–81 and subsequent hostage situations in and around Beirut throughout the 1980s, the captors repeatedly produced videotapes that depicted the plight of their American hostages. Such tapes were made available to Western news organizations—in some instances with the mutual understanding that the material would be aired unedited. Similarly, terrorists have used cellphones for as long as they have been available to communicate their demands and grievances to their target audiences. Thus, the Abu Sayyaf, Muslim separatists in the southern Philippines, utilized cellphones to contact radio stations and communicate their demands for the release of their Western and Asian hostages.

Former British Prime Minister Margaret Thatcher was right when she said that publicity is the oxygen of terrorism. Terrorists at all times understand this and act accordingly. Some 2000 years ago, the Zealots, an extreme religious sect, attacked Roman occupiers in Palestine in crowded places, often on the most holy days. Eye-witnesses would tell family members, neighbors, friends what they had seen and heard. This interpersonal communication assured Zealots that the horror of their attacks was spread throughout the communities they wanted to reach.

The anarchists of the nineteenth century explained their political violence as "propaganda of the deed" and thereby indicated that their terror strikes were designed to get their messages across to their targets: the governments they opposed and the publics they wanted to shock and turn against the existing regimes.

Whenever possible, terrorists do not depend on the media's gatekeepers to facilitate their desire for publicity, but rather try to convey their messages directly. This was also true for earlier terrorists. Thus, using his anarchist newspaper *Freiheit* as a platform, John Most urged his comrades to prepare posters in advance of their terrorist actions in order to explain their motives rather than depend on hostile newspapers to carry their message. More recent terrorists have utilized copying machines, mobile radio transmitters, their own television stations, cellphones, audiotapes, videotapes, and, most of all, the Internet. But the traditional mass media—namely newspapers, newsmagazines, radio, and television—remain the most important targets in the terrorist publicity scheme because they are still the predominant sources of information. Even when terrorists post their own video productions on their own websites, most people learn of new releases from reports in the traditional media.

Because they guarantee freedom of expression and press freedom, liberal democracies have been especially susceptible to terrorist messages; the fundamental civil liberties in democracies play into the terrorists' appetite for publicity. But the proliferation of global television networks has increased terrorists' opportunities to address audiences additionally in those parts of the world where governments curb the domestic press.

Publicity: The Universal Terrorist Goal

Although publicity is what one may call a universal goal of terrorists, it is never their only and ultimate objective. As described in Chapter 8, terrorists have short-term and long-term political ambitions and goals. But they are well aware that publicity is the absolutely necessary means to their ultimate political ends. In their writings and in interviews, terrorists have revealed that they understand the importance of publicity in their scheme. Take the case of Leila Khaled, who, as a member of the Popular Front for the Liberation of Palestine (PFLP), participated in hijacking operations. In 2000, 30 years after a quadruple hijacking coup that made her famous, she revealed in an interview that she had to be pushed by the PFLP leadership to meet with media representatives and explain the group's causes. She said that she told Dr. George Habash, the PFLP's leader, that she was afraid of talking to reporters. Habash thought it strange that this woman was not afraid to hijack airplanes but balked at meeting the press. He told her that she had participated in the hijacking to tell the whole world about the Palestinian cause and that she had to speak for her comrades who were in jail. And Khaled obeyed and faced the press.

Terrorists have demonstrated time and again that they understand the importance of the mass media by the way they have acted during and after terrorist incidents. Reporting from Tehran during the Iran hostage crisis in 1979, CBS correspondent Tom Fenton recognized that the captors, who claimed to be students but may have been part of the Revolutionary Guards, were very resourceful in getting the press to report their side of the story. According to Fenton,

> It did not take them long to realize that this is a media event. The students have even attempted to buy off television networks by offering an unpublished American embassy secret document in return for five minutes unedited air time.[9]

The Red Army Faction (RAF) in West Germany and its successor cells timed their terrorist attacks so that the news coverage would be particularly generous: They struck on days when the news holes in newspapers were larger than on other days. Reporters who covered the TWA hijacking ordeal in 1985 noted that the hijackers and their Hezbollah supporters in Beirut were well aware of the geographic reach of the American media, the audience size of different media types, the working of press pools, and the advantages of scheduling live interviews during TV networks' popular morning and early evening news broadcasts. According to some reports, graduates of media studies and communications programs at American universities acted as advisors to the hijackers and those who negotiated on the terrorists' behalf. Following these experts' advice, the militants granted television reporters preferential treatment for the sake of reaching the largest audiences. But there was another reason for favoring television over print: Terrorists were aware that visual images affect audiences far more deeply and for longer periods of time than the spoken or written word. In other words, terrorists knew in the past, as they know today, that one picture is worth a thousand words—and probably more.

In a real sense, then, the immediate victims of bombings, hijackings, kidnappings, and other terrorist acts are simply pawns in the plays that terrorists stage in order to engage their domestic and international audiences. But unlike the producers who stage a drama on Broadway or in theaters elsewhere, terrorists cannot reach their intended audiences unless they generate a great deal of news coverage.

An Alternative View: Contemporary Terrorists Do Not Need Publicity

When terrorists struck in the 1970s and 1980s, they typically claimed responsibility for their deeds and communicated their motives. But more recently, the perpetrators of major terrorist attacks have often failed to claim responsibility in an explicit and timely fashion. Some experts in the field concluded, therefore, that a new "terrorism of expression" or "expressive terrorism" had emerged. Typically committed by religious or pseudoreligious fanatics, the new "faceless" superterrorism is said to have no publicity goals. According to Avishai Margalit, these terrorists "lack clearly defined political ends" but give vent to "rage against state power and to feelings of revenge." They want to inflict the greatest amount of pain on their targets.[10] But this argument has weaknesses. Proponents of the expressive terrorism theory point to the first World Trade Center bombing in 1993 as a milestone. But this case was in reality one in which the perpetrators did claim responsibility and explained their grievances against the United States in a typewritten letter mailed to the *New York Times*. The FBI determined that the letter was authentic and found the typewriter on which it had been written in the possession of a man who turned out to belong to the group that had plotted the bombing.

In other instances, terrorists left important clues that revealed their motives. Timothy McVeigh and his accomplice Terry Nichols did not contact news organizations to claim responsibility for the Oklahoma City bombing. However, by detonating their destructive bomb on the second anniversary of the FBI's and other federal agents' ill-fated actions against a heavily armed group of religious extremists, the Branch Davidians, in Waco, Texas, the duo ensured that the media would figure out their motive—revenge for Waco. McVeigh wanted the greatest amount of news coverage for his act of terrorism. Before he was executed in June 2001, he said in an interview, "I don't think there is any doubt the Oklahoma City blast was heard around the world." McVeigh said furthermore that he had attacked the Alfred P. Murrah Federal Building in Oklahoma City because it had "plenty of open space around it, to allow for the best possible news photos and television footage." He left no doubt that he wanted to "make the loudest statement... and create a stark, horrifying image that would make everyone who saw it stop and take notice." Anticipating that he might be killed or arrested after fleeing the bombing site, McVeigh left an envelope filled with newspaper articles and documents in his getaway car to make sure that the world would be informed of his motives.[11]

Following the simultaneous bombings of the U.S. embassies in Kenya and Tanzania in August 1998, Osama bin Laden was covered as the likely architect of these terrorist strikes—although there was no immediate claim of responsibility. But two months earlier, the Saudi exile had told journalists that Americans were "easy targets" and that this would be obvious "in a very short time."[12] Michel Wieviorka has pointed out that some terrorists do not seek media attention. But he neverthe-less recognizes that the perpetrators of political violence will get news coverage—regardless of whether they seek it or not.[13]

It is likely that terrorists who make no claims would be pleased when their deeds are highlighted in the news. For this reason, Dale Van Atta has rejected the notion of the media's diminished role in the terrorist calculus, arguing that the

> Very act of intending to kill hundreds in airplane and building explo-sions means they [terrorists] seek sensational coverage for their deeds... Like it or not, the media is still an integral part of achieving the terrorist's aim—and therefore must be as judicious and responsi-ble as possible in its reportage.[14]

Thomas Friedman, the Pulitzer Prize-winning *New York Times* column-ist, has suggested that bin Laden transcends the scope of a mere terrorist because of his geopolitical aspirations and that the Al Qaeda leader employs "violence not to grab headlines but to kill as many Americans as possible to drive them out of the Islamic world and weaken their soci-ety."[15] But bin Laden and his associates contradict this conclusion. Thus, an Al Qaeda training manual advised recruits to target "sentimental land-marks" such as the Statue of Liberty in New York, Big Ben in London, and the Eiffel Tower in Paris because their destruction would "generate intense publicity."[16] In the Al Qaeda training camps in Afghanistan, a video production crew produced propaganda material that was peddled to the Arab TV network Al Jazeera. Even when Al Qaeda's leaders were on the run, they were, thanks to Arab TV networks, frequently making the news.

But no other terrorist organization built a more sophisticated media and propaganda center than the Islamic State. While part of the propa-ganda was designed to control people in those Syrian and Iraqi regions that the organization controlled, another part targeted Muslims and non-Muslims in the rest of the world, not merely through Arabic language communication but also through media in English, French, German, and other languages.

Media-Related Terrorist Goals

Although the history of terrorism is littered with failures as far as the ultimate or long-term objectives of terror movements are concerned, terrorists are stunningly successful in spreading their "propaganda by the deed," and they harm their target societies in many different ways.

As a general rule, terrorist incidents further the perpetrators' universal or media-related goals—regardless of whether they also advance their short-term or long-term political objectives. There are three goals in particular that terrorists tie to news coverage and other forms of communication: (1) they want attention; (2) they want their grievances, demands, and objectives recognized; and (3) they want to win respect and even gain legitimacy in some circles, countries, or regions. The obvious question is, of course, to what extent do media organizations facilitate these objectives?

The Attention-Getting Goal

The most fundamental role of a free press is to inform the public fully. Thus, the issue here is not whether the media should cover terrorist events, but rather how much and what kind of coverage should be devoted to terrorist incidents. Violence has always been an attractive topic for the press, regardless of whether it is criminal or political in nature. News organizations tend to over-cover terrorist strikes when they are especially dramatic and shocking and offer plenty of human interest. The 444 days of the Iran hostage crisis were a case in point in that during November and December 1979 the three television networks—ABC News, CBS News, and NBC News—respectively devoted 54, 50, and 48 percent of their evening news broadcasts to the incident. Although the volume decreased in the following 12 months, the hostage situation remained the number-one news story throughout its duration—even though not a single hostage was killed. During the two weeks of the TWA hijacking crisis in 1985, about two-thirds of the networks' evening news broadcasts were filled with reports on the drama in Lebanon and its effects elsewhere. Media expert Benjamin Bagdikian called the coverage of the TWA incident "excessive for strictly self-serving, competitive reasons" and complained that, as a result, other important news had been obliterated.[17] Although the print press has escaped similar criticism, newspapers and newsmagazines displayed the same appetite for terrorist dramas as the television networks. During the 1985 TWA hijacking situation, for example, the *New York Times* devoted an average of 19 percent, the *Washington Post* 18 percent, and the *Los Angeles Times* 15 percent of their total national/international news coverage to this incident. However, unlike the television networks with their limited airtime for newscasts, newspapers tend to have enough space to report on other news developments as well.[18] And while the broadcast networks and the print media overemphasize reporting on terrorism, their coverage pales in comparison to that of the all-news cable and satellite networks.

There was, however, one shocking incident in the early 1970s that received at the time an unprecedented amount of news coverage: the assault on members of Israel's national team during the 1972 Olympic Games in Munich by the Palestinian Black September group. The architects of the assault had chosen this site to take advantage of the international media present in Germany to report on the sports competition. It was estimated at the time that between 600 and 800 million people around the globe watched the deadly drama in Munich. Nearly three decades after the Munich ordeal, cable and satellite television and a multitude of specialty channels have joined the broadcast networks. CNN and other truly global networks are watched around the world. As a result, one can assume that far more people saw the horrific images of 9/11 than those of the events in Munich. In the United States, television and radio reported virtually nothing else in the days and nights following the 9/11 attacks. Not even commercials were aired. Most sports and entertainment channels switched to crisis news, many of them carrying the coverage of one of the networks; others suspended their programming altogether and simply showed the American flag on the screen. Newspapers and magazines devoted all or most of their news to the crisis. The media abroad, too, dedicated an extraordinary amount of time and space to the terrorist strikes in the United States.

All Americans were aware of the 9/11 attacks. Opinion polls showed that 99 percent of the American public followed the news of the terrorist attacks by watching television or listening to the radio. Most adults identified television and radio as their primary sources for crisis information, but nearly two-thirds also mentioned the Internet as one of their information sources.[19] This initial universal interest in terrorism news did not weaken quickly. Probably affected by the news of anthrax attacks along the U.S. east coast, more than 90 percent of the public kept on watching the news about terrorism "very closely" or "closely" nearly six weeks after the events of 9/11.[20] For the architects of the 9/11 terror, this was a perfect score with respect to their desire to get attention. Moreover, foreign audiences were just as aware of the horrible events in the United States as were Americans.

By getting the attention of their target audience, terrorists achieve another objective: they intimidate their target society and spread fear and anxiety in the population. After all, terrorism is psychological warfare. The perpetrators of this sort of violence want to get to the psyche of the society they target. Public opinion surveys taken in the weeks after 9/11 revealed that many Americans were traumatized and feared that they or their loved ones could become the victims of future terrorism. Many suffered from depression and were unable to sleep. In some other countries, especially in Europe, the public expressed similar fears and anxieties. These feelings did not evaporate in the following months and even years—especially not in the United States. As one would expect, the public's concerns reflected the volume of the news devoted to terrorism and the events of 9/11 in particular. In the months preceding 9/11, when Americans were asked about the most important problem their country faced, terrorism was not mentioned at all. As Figure 14.2 shows, after the strikes in New York and Washington, terrorism ranked high in the

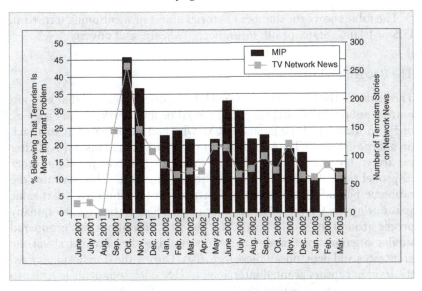

Figure 14.2 Post-9/11 News on Terrorist Threat and Public Opinion

Source: Pippa Norris, Montague Kern, and Marion Just, *Framing Terrorism: The News Media, the Government, and the Public* (New York: Routledge, 2003)

Table 14.3 News Coverage of Major Issues January 1, 2014–December 31, 2014

	New York Times	*Washington Post*
Terrorism	3,040	2,292
ISIS or Islamic State	1,676	3,516
Health Insurance	1,293	3,567
Medicare	617	1,362
Poverty	1,905	2,808

Source: Compiled by author from the Lexis/Nexis and *Washington Post* archive.

public's perception of what was the most important problem (MIP) for the United States. As the volume of terrorism news declined somewhat during the following months, the public's ranking of the terrorism threat subsided similarly.

Nothing changed as far as the mainstream media's appetite for terrorism-related news was concerned. As Table 14.3 shows, in the two leading American newspapers the coverage of terrorism and in particular of ISIS by far dwarfed the news about equally or perhaps more important public affairs issues, such as poverty, health insurance, and Medicare.

The table shows the number of stories about or mentioning terrorism, ISIS or Islamic State, health insurance, Medicare, and poverty.

The Recognition Goal

The leader of the PFLP, Dr. George Habash, once explained that by committing political violence, his group forced people to ask, "What is going on?"[21] A member of the Japanese RAF who had participated in an attack on a large crowd at Tel Aviv airport in 1972 explained his motives after his arrest: He and his comrades had killed 28 innocent people in order to propel the Palestinian cause onto the world stage. This was also the rationale behind Black September's attack on Israeli athletes that same year during the Olympic Games. During this hair-raising incident, many people around the world learned for the first time about this group and similar organizations, and—more importantly—they learned about the grievances and demands of these terrorists. During the Iran hostage crisis, the Iranian captors granted interviews to U.S. correspondents in order to air their grievances against the United States. CBS News correspondent Tom Fenton reported about a meeting with the young hostage-holders:

> They spoke bitterly about corruption and murder under the deposed Shah's regime, America's role in supporting him, their deep resentment when he was allowed to enter the United States, and their fear that the American government is trying to topple the new Iranian regime.[22]

Terrorists also get hostages to speak out in support of their causes, grievances, and demands—sometimes by force, sometimes by persuasion, and sometimes by exposing their captives to situations in which the so-called Stockholm syndrome, the tendency of some hostages to identify with their captors, kicks in. During the 1985 TWA hijacking crisis, one of the hostages said during a news conference his captors had staged, "We understand that Israel is holding as hostage [sic] a number of Lebanese people who undoubtedly have as equal a right and as strong a desire to go home as we do." He called on the governments and people involved in the negotiations to free him and the other American hostages to "allow justice and compassion to guide their way."[23]

Government officials are critical of the media's willingness, if not eagerness, to give terrorists a public platform to articulate their motives. Former National Security Advisor Zbigniew Brzezinski, for example, criticized television news in particular for permitting terrorists to appeal directly to the American public.[24] But journalists and others in the news media consider it part of their responsibility to present all important views and put the news about terrorist incidents into a larger political context. Tom Brokaw once said,

Terrorism often does have political roots and we have to deal with these political roots. It is not always, although it appears that way, a mindless act of sheer terrorism for the sake of terrorism. There is generally some political context as well and I think we have to work harder at putting it into some kind of political context, however strong or weak that context might be.[25]

A content analysis of news reports on terrorism aired by the three TV networks (as mentioned, ABC News, CBS News, and NBC News) from 1981 through 1986 found that 74 percent were predominantly "episodic" (focusing on individual acts of terrorism and their effects) and 26 percent "thematic" (framing terrorism in the larger context of a political problem). This means that a surprisingly large proportion of the news on terrorism—more than a quarter of the total reporting—described, articulated, or commented on the root causes of terrorist violence. In contrast, this same study found that only 11 percent of all domestic crime stories during this six-year period were "thematic" in nature.[26]

Before the 9/11 terror attacks, the vast majority of American news organizations reported far less from abroad than their European counterparts. Moreover, foreign news reporting was predominantly episodic and concentrated on a particular case at hand, rather than thematic and focusing on underlying conditions, developments, and attitudes. After 9/11, there was far more thematic or contextual coverage of Arab and Muslim countries than before the attacks. By striking hard at the United States, the terrorists enticed the media to explore their grievances in ways that transcended by far the quantity and quality of the pre-crisis coverage. This had an impact on the public in the United States and elsewhere in the West. Suddenly, people wanted to know why people in faraway countries wanted to kill Americans. Nobody seemed more aware of these attitudinal changes than Osama bin Laden. According to a videotaped conversation, he told his associates,

> In Holland, at one of the centers, the number of people who accepted Islam during the days that followed the operations [of 9/11] were more than the people who accepted Islam in the last eleven years.
>
> I heard someone on Islamic radio who owns a school in America say: "We don't have time to keep up with the demands of those who are asking about Islamic books to learn more about Islam." This event made people think, which benefited Islam greatly.[27]

There are no data on conversions to Islam in the West on the heels of the 9/11 attacks, but universities and adult education programs added courses on Islam and the Middle East because of the increased demand. News coverage helped kindle this sudden interest. One comprehensive content analysis of religious news in ten American daily newspapers, nine newsmagazines, and one wire service (the Associated Press) found that stories on Islam and Muslims dominated this coverage in the weeks following the events of 9/11. Indeed, 70 percent of the stories fully devoted to religion concerned Islam and Muslims, and the remaining 30 percent dealt with Christianity and Christians, multi-faith issues, Judaism and Jews, nondenominational issues, and Buddhism and Buddhists.[28]

It is certainly understandable that after 9/11 the media devoted an extraordinary amount of column inches and airtime to Muslims, Arabs, and the religion of Islam at home and abroad. But one would have wished that the press had paid more attention to the sentiments among Arabs and Muslims in the years and decades before 9/11—not as a direct result of an act of terrorism. If one accepts the notion that terrorists strike in order to publicize their grievances, bin Laden and Al Qaeda were extraordinarily successful in realizing this objective. And again, more than a decade later, nothing changed except that other organizations, such as ISIS, al-Shabaab, Boko Haram, and Al Qaeda in the Arabian Peninsula were covered along the same lines.

The Respectability/Legitimacy Goal

On September 26, 1990, during the build-up to the first Persian Gulf War in 1991, Dr. George Habash of the PFLP was interviewed by Ted Koppel on the ABC News *Nightline* program. Habash threatened a wave of terrorism against American targets if the United States made a military move against Iraq. Saudi Arabia's ambassador to the United States, Prince Bandar bin Sultan, was another guest on the program. Koppel made no distinction between his two guests. Thus, it is not unreasonable to conclude that an appearance by an acknowledged terrorist side by side with an accredited diplomat bolstered the status of Habash. Or take the case of antiabortion terrorist Paul Jennings Hill, who was executed in Florida in September 2003—nine years after he had killed a physician and his security guard outside an abortion clinic in Pensacola. Before he targeted Dr. John Britton in 1994, Hill had promoted the killing of abortion providers by comparing them to Adolf Hitler; he condemned women who had abortions as "accessories to murder." The news media gave Hill, a former Presbyterian minister, plenty of opportunities to promote his crusade. According to the *New York Times*,

> Even before his crimes, Mr. Hill was known for advocating violence against abortion providers and his extreme views had won him a high profile. With a serene voice and smile, he became a spokesman for the cause after another doctor, David Gunn, was shot to death by Michael Griffin at Pensacola's other clinic in 1993... In the months following Dr. Gunn's murder, Mr. Hill appeared on television shows like "Nightline" and "Donahue," where he drew parallels between

killing an abortion doctor and killing Hitler. Mr. Hill insisted that murdering abortion providers was "justifiable homicide," a defense he attempted to use in his trial but that the judge would not allow.[29]

John O'Sullivan has correctly argued that the media, and especially television, bestow respectability and perhaps even legitimacy upon terrorists—simply by interviewing them the same way legitimate political actors are interviewed.[30] The same can be said about reporters who attend the news conferences staged by terrorist groups or about reports that refer to the "spokespersons" of terrorist organizations and the "communiqués" they release. Osama bin Laden and his associates did not give interviews and did not hold news conferences after 9/11, but they communicated via fax messages, audiotapes, and videotapes. In the months following the attacks of 9/11, TV audiences found it impossible to miss the image of Osama bin Laden when channel surfing. This prominence in the news made bin Laden a household name around the world. To be sure, in the United States and many other countries, the Al Qaeda leader did not win the hearts and minds of the people. Instead, he became the evildoer-in-chief. But this played into his hands as well. After all, terrorists do not want to be loved by their targets; they want to be feared. This is especially true when they strike on the territory of a foreign enemy. The much publicized events of 9/11 in particular made bin Laden and Al Qaeda household words and earned them admiration in those communities for which they claim to wage jihad. While survey and news organizations reported declining support for bin Laden beginning in 2005 compared to his high approvals in the immediate post-9/11 years, poll data revealed, in fact, continued solid approval of the Al Qaeda leader and his organization in the following years. In Muslim countries, vast majorities were well aware of the grievances articulated by bin Laden and other Al Qaeda leaders and, most importantly, agreed consistently "with nearly all of al Qaeda's goals to change US behavior in the Muslim world, to promote Islamist governance, and to preserve and affirm Islamic identity."[31]

In 2014 and 2015, when President Obama, British Prime Minister Cameron, and many other heads of governments made mass-mediated statements condemning ISIS atrocities, this was seen by the organization's leadership and their propagandists as signs of their growing importance, as being a factor in politics and policy considerations of powerful nation-states.

Bedfellows in a Marriage of Convenience

All in all, then, terrorists are very successful in realizing their three media-dependent objectives in that they receive news coverage that assures them a great deal of public and elite attention, spells out their causes and grievances, and earns them respect and even legitimacy in some circles.

This is not to say that the media in countries plagued by domestic and/ or foreign terrorism are wittingly supporting groups and individuals that perpetrate political violence. Take the case of the United States. The American media and terrorists are not accomplices. However, they are involved in a symbiotic relationship in that they feed off each other: The media want dramatic, shocking, disconcerting news that keeps readers, listeners, and viewers captivated and that bolsters the circulation of the print press and the ratings of the electronic media. Terrorists need to spread their propaganda to further their ultimate political objectives. To put it differently, the news media and terrorists are not involved in a love story; they are strange bedfellows in a marriage of convenience.

Following the Iran hostage crisis, Gary Sick observed that the situation "was the longest running human interest story in the history of television, in living colors from the other side of the world. Commercially it was a stunning success." Furthermore, he wrote, "It may never be known how many pairs of pantyhose and how many tubes of toothpaste were sold to this captive audience as a direct result of the hostage crisis, but the numbers are substantial."[32] Much has changed in the media landscape since the Iran hostage crisis ended in early 1981. Financial considerations became far more pressing in news organizations because of increasingly fierce competition caused by the proliferation of television channels, the emergence of the Internet as an increasingly attractive news source, and the creation of mega-media corporations with more commitment to profits than to serious news.

Under these circumstances, it is unrealistic to expect the media to curb their appetite for the news that terrorists provide. One wonders whether there could be an altogether different approach to prevent terrorism in the first place—with the assistance of media organizations. If terrorists strike primarily in order to force the media to publicize their deeds and their motives, why not cover the grievances of groups and individuals before they resort to terrorism? As desirable as the solution seems at first sight, it may be unrealistic to believe that the news media could grant terrorists a degree of access and coverage that would satisfy their appetite for front-page news.

Years ago, the widely respected journalist David Broder suggested that

> the essential ingredient of any effective antiterrorist policy must be the denial to the terrorist of access to mass media outlets. The way by which this denial is achieved—whether by voluntary means of those of us in press and television, self-restraint, or by government control—is a crucial question for journalists and for all other citizens who share our beliefs in civil liberties.[33]

While many in the American media would agree that the fourth estate, as the press is sometimes called, would be well advised to exercise self-restraint with respect to terrorism coverage, few would wish for government-imposed restrictions. In the past, some liberal democracies—for example, the United Kingdom, Germany, and Greece—adopted press laws that restricted news coverage during terrorist incidents and especially during hostage situations. These laws were enacted in response to domestic terrorism. But given the strong commitment to the First Amendment's constitutional guarantee of a free press, government censorship is less likely in the United States and is certainly not a desirable solution. The late publisher of the *Washington Post*, Katharine Graham, once said,

> Publicity may be the oxygen of terrorists. But I say this: News is the lifeblood of liberty. If the terrorists succeed in depriving us of freedom, their victory will be far greater than they ever hoped and far worse than we ever feared. Let it never come to pass.[34]

And she was right, of course.

Media and Terrorist Contagion

On July 14, 2016, Mohamed Lahouaiej-Bouhlel (age 31) drives a 20-ton truck into a huge crowd watching Bastille Day fireworks in Nice, France, killing 86 and injuring several hundred persons. The perpetrator is shot; ISIS claims responsibility. The shocking incident receives prominent and extensive global news coverage.

Six months later, when a terrorist truck rammed at a Christmas market in Berlin and killed 12 persons and injured dozens more, people around the world learned about the horror story in "breaking news" reports. Throughout 2017, there were nine more truck or car-ramming incidents in which pedestrians were killed plus several more without lethal consequences—all covered prominently.

It is not hard to imagine that lone actors were inspired by news coverage that showed how easily available cars or trucks had been used as deadly weapons against unsuspecting pedestrians in crowded places. Thus, this simple terrorist tactic spread across country borders like an epidemic virus (see also Chapter 8).

The argument that media content can be a factor in motivating copycat violence is not new. Based on their analysis of terrorist incidents in the 1960s and 1970s around the globe, researchers concluded that some terrorist methods of attacks (hijackings, kidnappings, and bombings) were more contagious than others (assassinations, raids). These scholars found that publicity provided by the news media was a factor in the decision of terrorists to imitate terror methods they deemed effective. As they put it, "Visible and unusual violence is in essence newsworthy and attracts international publicity necessary for cross-regional and cross-cultural spread."[35]

The breaking-news-all-the-time coverage of ISIS atrocities was not lost on disgruntled ISIS devotees. A few weeks after the gruesome decapitation of James Foley in 2014, 30-year-old Alton Nolen attacked former colleagues at a food plant in Moore, Oklahoma, beheading Colleen Hufford and seriously wounding a second woman. Nolen was a convert to Islam who had tried to convert his colleagues—without success. A month later, when Zale Thompson, 32, and another convert to Islam, attacked a group of New York police officers with a hatchet, the conclusion was that he had planned to behead his targets. Similar incidents took place in Europe, Australia, and elsewhere. There is little doubt that these successful and failed decapitations were examples of copycat attacks.

However, the adoption of effective terrorist tactics does not cause terrorism since those tactics tend to be imitated or adapted by groups, cells, and individuals that have already embraced the terrorist cause. Inspirational contagion is more alarming for the targets of terrorism because this is the stuff that actually makes terrorists. One of the founders of the RAF, Horst Mahler, revealed "how television newscasts had triggered the 'shock... [which led to] self-liberation... [and] the basis for RAF ideology.'"[36] In other words, television's terrorism news played a crucial role in formulating his group's ideology of terrorist action and thus the RAF's raison d'être. This account did not surprise researchers whose data revealed that terrorist ideology spread from the Third World, particularly from Latin American and Palestinian terrorist leaders and groups, to Western Europe in the early 1970s. Noting that radicals in Germany and elsewhere in Western Europe received this sort of inspirational information from the mass media, the three scholars figured that "physical contacts [for example, between RAF and Palestinian groups] followed rather than preceded the decision to adopt terrorism."[37]

Writing more than a quarter-century later, Mark Sedgwick suggested that

> contagion is possible at two levels, and can happen in two ways. On one level a group might copy a particular terrorist technique, and on another level a group might copy a general terrorist strategy. Either of these might happen directly or indirectly. All these forms of contagion take place. The primary form, however, is the adoption of a general terrorist strategy without direct contact. All other forms of contagion are secondary to this.[38]

It is hardly surprising that contagion effect tends to be far stronger among those individuals and groups that share the cultural and religious background of organizations and leaders with inspirational ideologies. Whereas kinship and friendship brought the members of the Al Qaeda

Central organization together, the mighty "Afghan wave" that reached literally all continents in the post-9/11 years was mostly driven by mass-mediated inspirational contagion.[39] As Marc Sageman noted at the time,

> The present threat has evolved from a structured group of al Qaeda masterminds, controlling vast resources and issuing commands, to a multitude of informal local groups trying to emulate their predecessors by conceiving and executing operations from the bottom up.[40]

Without the global media and communication environment, the inspirational diffusion of terrorist ideology would not be as strong as it is in the previous centuries.

Defending the Media

Those who defend the media in this context point to terrorist situations in which reporters withheld sensitive information for fear that the news could harm American citizens. For example, a number of reporters learned that several Americans had escaped from the U.S. embassy in Tehran when it was taken over by militants in late 1979 and that these people had taken refuge in the Canadian embassy. Not one word was publicized until the Americans had left Iran. Other observers mention prudent intraorganizational guidelines that specify how to report and how not to report terrorist incidents, especially hostage situations. Indeed, most news organizations have adopted such guidelines. The problem is that these guidelines are not adhered to in the face of actual terrorist incidents.

The best case in defense of the media is based on their public-service role during terrorist situations. News organizations, especially radio and television networks and stations, are as essential for the management of a terrorist attack as they are during and after devastating earthquakes, floods, hurricanes, riots, or other natural and human-made disasters. This is particularly true of local and regional media outlets. In the case of the Oklahoma City bombing, for example,

> The local broadcast and cable stations functioned as conduits of communication between public officials and citizens in the affected city and region. For example, by disseminating officials' appeals to donate blood for the injured victims at specific locations, not to enter the immediate disaster area, or to contribute warm clothing for rescue workers, the media provided an excellent public service. Since many officials, who were involved in managing the crisis, followed

the news about the disaster, the stations facilitated also the difficult task of coordinating emergency services that involved a great number of organizations and individuals.[41]

The media performed in an equally exemplary way in the hours and days following the terrorist attacks of 9/11 in New York, Washington, and Pennsylvania. According to one account,

> For crisis managers, the mass media offered the only effective means to tell the public about the immediate consequences of the crisis— what to do (donate blood of certain types, where to donate and when) and what not to do (initially, for example, not trying to drive into Manhattan because all access bridges and tunnels were closed). In this respect, the media served the public interest in the best tradition of disaster coverage.[42]

When people are directly or indirectly affected by an emergency, they immediately turn to the news media for information. If there is no electric power, battery-powered radios may be available. At no other times are radio and television audiences larger than during and after major disasters. According to one media scholar, the reasons for this demand are obvious:

> Information about [a] crisis, even if it is bad news, relieves disquieting uncertainties and calms people. This mere activity of watching or listening to familiar reporters and commentators reassures people and keeps them occupied. It gives them a sense of vicarious participation, of "doing something."
>
> News stories [also] serve to reassure people that their grief and fear are shared.[43]

Television and radio offer crisis managers the opportunity to address the public directly whenever they desire. About two hours after the first plane had hit one of the World Trade Center towers, Mayor Rudy Giuliani was in the studio of New York 1, an all-news cable channel in New York City, to urge New Yorkers to remain calm and to evacuate lower Manhattan. But while the mayor was collected, decisive, and cool, he did not minimize what had happened but spoke of "a horrible, horrible situation."[44] By providing a public meeting place literally around the clock, whether via broadcasting, cable, or print, news organizations served the public's interest well in the hours and days after the terrorists struck New York and Washington. Perhaps that was the most important reason why the American public looked far more favorably upon the news media in the weeks after 9/11 than before the shocking events. However, these newly found public sympathies for the media were short-lived and soon replaced by far more critical public attitudes toward the press.

Treason or Public Service?

In mid-2006, when the *New York Times* revealed that the Bush administration monitored the flow of money through banking systems, including Swift, the Belgian-based banking consortium, in order to discover money trails to terrorist groups, administration officials and others condemned the paper for obstructing counterterrorist efforts and thereby helping terrorists. President Bush said,

> We're at war with a bunch of people who want to hurt the United States of America, and for people to leak that program, and for a newspaper to publish it, does great harm to the United States of America.[45]

There were similar condemnations, even charges of treason, after media organizations published reports on illegal electronic surveillance by the National Security Agency, the existence of secret CIA prisons for terrorist suspects abroad, and the CIA's practice of rendering alleged terrorists captured by American agents abroad to "third countries, countries with notorious reputations for political prisoners, such as Egypt, Syria, Morocco, and Uzbekistan."[46] Even local revelations resulted in controversies about the limits of press freedom. In December 2006, for example, the *New York Times* published a prominently placed report revealing that "the PATH train tunnels under the Hudson River are far more vulnerable to a bomb attack than previously thought, and that a relatively small amount of high explosives could cause significant flooding of the train system within hours."[47] In all of these cases—and many other stories about vulnerable and ill-protected possible terrorist targets—the crucial question is always whether such revelations harm American national security or actually help to alleviate wrongs and shortcomings in counterterrorism and homeland security efforts.

It is far from easy to decide whether to publicize or withhold sensitive material. With respect to the PATH tunnels' vulnerability to even a small bomb blast, one wonders whether the *New York Times'* public revelation, followed by similar stories in the *Los Angeles Times* and the *Wall Street Journal*, was the only and the best choice. The motive of the person who leaked the information to the news media was to force the responsible higher-ups in the Port Authority of New York and New Jersey to address the problems. It is entirely possible that an editor could have alerted the governors of New York and New Jersey to the Hudson tunnels' vulnerability and thereby assured action—without publicizing the material. Although it is well known that terrorists are well informed about the vulnerabilities of all kinds of sites in all kinds of target countries, why point them to particularly problematic venues?

In short, the still influential gatekeepers of the mainstream media must always be aware of and evaluate whether and how to report terrorism-related information that might benefit violent extremists.

Notes

1 White House, "President Obama Delivers a Statement on the Murder of James Foley," text of statement is available at www.whitehouse.gov/ photos-and-video/video/2014/08/20/president-obama-delivers-statement-murder-james-foley, accessed October 1, 2014.

2 Malise Ruthven, "Inside the Islamic State," *New York Review of Books*, July 9, 2015, citing Abdel Bari Atwan, *Islamic State: The Digital Caliphate* (London: Saqi, 2015); emphasis added.

3 Brigitte L. Nacos, *Mass-Mediated Terrorism: The Central Role of the Media in Terrorism and Counterterrorism* (Lanham, MD: Rowman & Littlefield, 2002), 49.

4 Barry Rubin and Judith Colp Rubin, *Anti-American Terrorism and the Middle East* (New York: Oxford, 2002), 274.

5 Alex P. Schmid and Jenny de Graaf, *Violence as Communication: Insurgent Terrorism and the Western News Media* (London: Sage, 1982), 14.

6 The quote is contained in Combating Terrorism Center: Document #AFGP-2002–6000321.

7 These quotes were published in many reports in both the print and the broadcast media.

8 Michael Wines, "Hostage Drama in Moscow: The Moscow Front; Chechens Kill Hostage in Siege at Russian Hall," *New York Times*, October 25, 2002, A1.

9 Fenton reported this on the CBS *Evening News* on December 6, 1979. Similar observations were made by other broadcast and print correspondents during the long hostage crisis.

10 Avishai Margalit, "The Terror Master," *New York Review of Books*, October 5, 1995, 19.

11 McVeigh revealed a great deal about his right-wing ideology, his motives, and his desire for publicity in interviews with a reporter from the *Buffalo News*. Interview with Lou Michel, April 2001. See also Lou Michel and Dan Herbeck, *American Terrorist: Timothy McVeigh and the Oklahoma City Bombing* (New York: Regan Books, 2001), esp. 168, 169, 227, 245, 382.

12 Based on what bin Laden said in this particular news conference, as well as in other communications, it was not difficult to pinpoint him as the driving force behind the bombings in East Africa. The quotes from his news conference in Khost, Afghanistan, are from Dale Van Atta, "Carbombs and Cameras: The Need for Responsible Media Coverage," *Harvard International Review* (Fall 1998), p. 66.

13 Michel Wieviorka, *The Making of Terrorism* (Chicago, IL: University of Chicago Press, 1993), 46, 47.

14 Van Atta, 68.

15 Thomas L. Friedman, "No Mere Terrorist," *New York Times*, March 24, 2002, sec. 4, 15.

16 Hamza Hendawi, "Terror Manual Advises on Targets," http://story.news. yahoo.com/, accessed February 11, 2002.
17 Bagdikian's testimony before a congressional committee was mentioned in "Closer Look at Network Coverage of TWA flight 847," *Broadcasting*, August 5, 1985.
18 For more on the coverage of terrorist incidents in the 1980s and early 1990s, see Brigitte L. Nacos, *Terrorism and the Media* (New York: Columbia University Press, 1994).
19 According to a *Los Angeles Times* telephone poll on September 13–14, 2001, 83 percent of the respondents said they watched the news "very closely," 15 percent "closely," and 2 percent "not too closely." Nobody chose the response option "not closely at all." The Gallup Organization found in a survey conducted on September 14–15, 2001, that 77 percent of the public followed the news "very closely," 20 percent "somewhat closely," 2 percent "not too closely," and 1 percent "not at all." An ABC/*Washington Post* poll on September 11, 2001, found that 99 percent of the public followed the news on television and radio. Polling adults online on September 11 and 12, 2001, Harris Interactive found that 93 percent identified television and radio as their primary news source, and 64 percent mentioned the Internet as one of their primary sources.
20 According to a survey conducted by the Pew Research Center for the People and the Press on October 17–21, 2001, 78 percent of the respondents said they watched terrorism news "very closely," 22 percent watched "closely," 5 percent "not closely," and 1 percent gave no answer. This was about the same level of interest as in mid-September (13–17), when 74 percent of survey respondents revealed that they watched terrorism news "very closely" and 22 percent "closely." In fact, more Americans watched this kind of news "very closely" in the second half of October than in mid-September.
21 Habash is quoted in Martha Crenshaw, "The Logic of Terrorism," in Walter Reich, ed., *Origins of Terrorism* (New York: Cambridge University Press, 1990), 18.
22 Nacos, *Terrorism and the Media*, 61.
23 Ibid., 62.
24 Neil Hickey, "The Impact of Negotiations: What the Experts Say," *TV Guide*, September 21, 1985.
25 Brokaw made his remarks during a seminar on "The Media and Terrorism," organized by the Center for Communications, Inc., October 23, 1985.
26 Shanto Iyengar, *Is Anyone Responsible? How Television Frames Political Issues* (Chicago, IL: University of Chicago Press, 1991), ch. 4.
27 From a bin Laden videotape presumably made in mid-November 2001.
28 "A Spiritual Awakening: Religion in the Media, December 2000–November 2001," study prepared by Douglas Gould & Co. for the Ford Foundation.
29 Abby Goodnough, "Florida Executes Killer of an Abortion Provider," *New York Times*, September 4, 2003, A16.
30 John O'Sullivan, "Media Publicity Causes Terrorism," in Bonnie Szumski, ed., *Terrorism: Opposing Viewpoints* (St. Paul, MN: Greenhaven, 1986), 73.
31 Steven Kull et al., "Public Opinion in the Islamic World on Terrorism, al Qaeda, and US Policies," The Program on International Policy Attitudes at the University of Maryland, 20.
32 Gary Sick, *All Fall Down: America's Tragic Encounter with Iran* (New York: Penguin, 1986), 258–9.
33 Broder made his remarks during a seminar on "The Media and Terrorism," organized by the Center for Communication, Inc., October 23, 1985.

34 Katharine Graham, "The Media Must Report Terrorism," in Szumski, 81.
35 Manus I. Midlarsky, Martha Crenshaw, and Fumihiko Yoshida, "Why Violence Spreads: The Contagion of International Terrorism," *International Studies Quarterly* 24 (1980), p. 279.
36 Gabriel Weimann and Conard Winn, *The Theater of Terror: Mass Media and International Terrorism* (New York: Longman, 1994), 217.
37 Midlarsky et al., 282.
38 Mark Sedgwick, "Inspiration and the Origins of Global Waves of Terrorism," *Studies in Conflict & Terrorism* 30 (2007), p. 102.
39 Ibid., 106–7.
40 Marc Sageman, *Leaderless Jihad* (Philadelphia: University of Pennsylvania Press, 2008), vii.
41 Brigitte Nacos, *Terrorism and the Media: From the Iran Hostage Crisis to the Oklahoma City Bombing* (New York: Columbia University Press, 1996), xiii, xiv.
42 Nacos, *Mass-Mediated Terrorism*, 51.
43 Doris Graber, *Mass Media and American Politics* (Washington, DC: Congressional Quarterly Press, 1997), 143.
44 For more on the media and crisis management, see Nacos, *Mass-Mediated Terrorism*, ch. 6.
45 Sheryl Gay Stolberg, "Bush Condemns Report on Sifting of Bank Records," *New York Times*, June 27, 2006, http://select.nytimes.com/search/restricted/article?res=F50610FB3C540C748EDDAF0894DE404482.
46 Raymond Bonner, "The CIA's Secret Torture," *New York Review of Books*, January 11, 2007, 28.
47 William K. Rashbaum and William Neuman, "Path Tunnels Seen as Fragile in Bomb Attack," *New York Times*, December 22, 2006, http://select.nytimes.com/search/restricted/article?res=F2071EFC3A550C718EDDAB0994DE404482.

15 Terror and Hate in Cyberspace

Reviewing the futuristic projections of terrifying scenarios by a pair of authors, legal scholar David Cole wrote,

> They breathlessly imagine a world in which "technologies of mass empowerment" give everyone the capacity to inflict serious harm on everyone else, from anywhere. They envision a day in which a malevolent person can from the comfort of his living room, direct a tiny "spider drone" into the home of his enemy, where it will kill the victim in his shower, after first extracting a DNA sample and checking it against a worldwide database to ensure that it's got the right victim.[1]

Actually, there was no need for futuristic horror scenarios. Present-day reality was disconcerting enough. A comprehensive Cyberspace Policy Review requested by President Obama stated,

> Threats to cyberspace pose one of the most serious economic and national security challenges of the 21st Century for the United States and our allies. A growing array of state and non-state actors such as terrorists and international criminal groups are targeting U.S. citizens, commerce, critical infrastructure, and government. These actors have the ability to compromise, steal, change, or completely destroy information.[2]

This assessment was more of an understatement than hype. As the former White House Coordinator for Security, Infrastructure Protection, and Counterterrorism Richard A. Clarke warned around the same time: "Cyber war is real. Cyber war happens in the speed of light. Cyber war is global. Cyber war skips the battle field. Cyber war has begun."[3]

Moreover, the top CIA cyberspecialist Tom Donahue shocked international security experts from governments and electric, water, oil, and gas companies with the disclosure that unknown attackers had hacked the computer systems of utility companies in several regions outside the

DOI: 10.4324/9781003289265-18

United States and in at least one case caused power outage that affected several cities. "We do not know who executed these attacks or why, but all involved intrusions through the Internet," he said.[4] Even more disconcerting were revelations that hackers had intruded into the U.S. Air Force's air traffic control system and managed to embed software in the nation's critical power grid and the telecommunication and financial services computer systems. While no damage was detected, the hackers may have planned to utilize their access at a later date, perhaps during a crisis—including a terrorist attack.

Contrary to other experts, Richard Clarke worried only about cyberwar—not cyberterrorism. Thus, he argued,

> Unfortunately, one thing that is too often believed is that there is a threat of "cyber terrorism." Cyber terrorism is largely a red herring and, in general, the two words "cyber" and "terrorism" should not be used in conjunction because they conjure up images of bin Laden waging cyber war from his cave. He probably can't, at least not yet.[5]

But Clarke also recognized that a "well-funded terrorist group might find a highly skilled hacker club that would do a cyber attack in return for a lot of money, but that has not happened to date."[6] Here Clarke discounted the ability of terrorist organizations to recruit experts with advanced degrees in many areas, including high technology. But just as the prospect of cyberwar threatens states' national security, so does the possibility of cyberterrorism.

Thus, in February 2017, the Department of Defense Science Board's Task Force on Cyber Deterrence issued a report that included non-state actors as likely perpetrators of cyber-attacks and mentioned ISIS in particular. "Non-state actors, though generally less capable than nation-states, also have conducted cyber attacks," the Science Board reported. "A recent example is the October 2016 distributed denial of service attacks on the internet domain name system (DNS) provider Dyn, for which the hacker groups Anonymous and New World Hackers claimed responsibility."[7] A few months later, in May 2017, the so-called WannaCry ransomware cyber-attack affected more than 200,000 computers across 150 countries, caused damages estimated from hundreds of millions to billions of U.S. dollars, and extorted high sums in the bitcoin cryptocurrency from targeted institutions and corporations. Citing the incident, two experts warned,

> There is reason to believe that terrorist groups such as al Qaeda and ISIS could copy the tactic. In doing so, they would cause as much damage (loss of data and equipment) and chaos (in hospitals and other public utilities) as possible, comparable to the chaos and panic that could be caused by a chemical or biological attack.[8]

There is evidence that terrorists and their sympathizers are aware of the potential for cyberterrorism. Indeed, there have been specific calls for virtual jihad for years. For example, a poster on the pro-Al Qaeda site Azzam.com recommended the hacking of computers and specified important targets:

> Among the targets of hacking should be military installations, intelligence departments such as NSA, CIA, FBI, MI5, Mossad, NASA, civilian police forces and national guards, so called "united nations peace keeping troops" which are none other than the army of democracy and America and any and every disbelieving organization responsible for military and economic support against the muslims.[9]

Following a massive power failure in the American Northeast in the summer of 2003, a poster on a pro-Al Qaeda site claimed, wrongly, that supporters of bin Laden were responsible for the blackout. According to the poster,

> In compliance with the order of the Commander of the Mujahids, Usamah bin Ladin (may God preserve him), to strike America's economic links, the Abu al-Misri Brigades struck at two important electricity generating targets in the region of the American East, including the most important cities of America and of Canada.
>
> The soldiers of God cut off the power to the above named cities, plunging the lives of Americans into darkness, just as the criminals had plunged the lives of the Muslim peoples of Iraq, Afghanistan, and Palestine into darkness.
>
> We say to the Muslims that this is not the strike that has been expected. This is something called a war of skirmishes (to wear down the enemy).
>
> We say to the people of Afghanistan and Kashmir that the gift of the Shaykh of the Mujahids, Usamah bin Ladin, is on its way to the White House.[10]

All kinds of hackers have attacked "enemy" computers and taken down websites in the context of terrorism and counterterrorism. In 2000, for example, Israeli hackers and their supporters abroad launched electronic attacks against Islamic militants' websites, while Palestinians and their supporters in the Middle East, the United States, and elsewhere targeted sites in Israel and the United States. At one point, a picture of the Israeli flag occupied the website of Hezbollah's television station, Al-Manar, for 12 hours and Israel's national anthem was heard whenever someone accessed Hezbollah's site. While this seemed like a coup in the struggle for propaganda supremacy, an attack on the site of the American Israeli Public Affairs Committee, a lobbying organization based in the United

States, had far more serious consequences: Besides plastering the site with anti-Israeli slogans, a Pakistani hacker accessed thousands of email addresses and credit card numbers stored in the organization's computers, sent anti-Israeli messages to these addresses, and published the stolen credit card data on the Internet.

It was never learned whether Israeli or Arab individuals threw the first cyberbomb in this electronic tit-for-tat exchange: Both sides invaded hostile websites and/or swamped them with so many emails that they became hopelessly overloaded and completely incapacitated. Israeli hackers put the sites of the Palestinian National Authority, Hezbollah, and Hamas temporarily out of commission; Arab militants and Muslim sympathizers elsewhere hit Israeli sites just as hard by taking down those of the foreign ministry, the Israeli Defense Forces, the prime minister, the Knesset (Parliament), the Bank of Israel, and the Tel Aviv Stock Exchange. Appeals on both sides drew a large number of supporters who participated in the campaigns. By simply clicking their mouses, visitors to the respective sites triggered automated email systems that sent out messages on their behalf. Hezbollah attributed the crashing of its site, which normally got between 100,000 and 300,000 hits a day, to "nine million hits per day, mainly from Israel, the United States, and to a lesser degree from Canada and South Africa."[11]

What the Palestinians came to call "Internet intifada" and Islamic extremists termed an "e-jihad" bolstered their hope that the Internet offered them a level playing field. Hezbollah's webmaster, Ali Ayoub, quoted the late Ayatollah Ruhollah Khomeini of Iran, who once hypothesized that if every Arab threw a bucket of water on Israel, the Jewish state would drown. According to Ayoub, "This is exactly what happened, supporters of the resistance from all over the world, both Arabs and foreigners, are contributing."[12]

These cyber-attacks changed nothing in the actual Middle East conflict, but they did reward both sides with attention in the conventional news media. In this sense, the electronic attacks and counterattacks represented another dimension of terrorism—with a comforting twist: No human life was lost, no human being was injured, and the material and psychological damages were minor in comparison to real terror strikes. In the real world, only a limited number of extremists commit and actively promote mass-mediated political violence; in cyberspace, far more sympathizers are willing to click the mouse and participate in cyber-attacks. The prospect of devastating cyberterrorism was more disconcerting. Several years ago, *New York Times* columnist Thomas Friedman outlined the following horror scenario:

> In five years, with the Internet being used to run more and more systems, if someone is able to knock out the handful of key Internet switching and addressing centers in the U.S. (until recently, a quarter

of all Internet traffic passed through one building in Tyson's Corner, Va., next to Morton's steak house), here's what happens: many trains will stop running, much air traffic will grind to a halt, power supplies will not be able to be shifted from one region to another, there will be no e-mail, your doctor's CAT scanner, which is now monitored over the Internet by its manufacturer, won't work if it breaks.[13]

But this would not be the worst-case scenario that security experts inside and outside the U.S. government have come to fear. American analysts have seen enough evidence on Al Qaeda's computers to conclude that

> Terrorists are at the threshold of using the Internet as a direct instrument of bloodshed. The new threat bears little resemblance to familiar financial disruptions by hackers responsible for viruses and worms. It comes instead at the meeting point of computers and the physical structures they control.[14]

No evidence exists for the above-mentioned claim that the power blackout in the American Northeast in August 2003 was the result of cyberterrorism. But attacks on power grids are among real threats that counterterrorism experts have warned of. During a 2002 conference for security experts, the participating experts admitted "that they had no idea how the [American electrical] power grid would respond to a cyber attack."[15] Worse yet, security experts foresee any number of horror scenarios that are likely to kill many people. Among the potential acts of cyberterrorism that Barry C. Collins has described are the following:

> A CyberTerrorist will remotely access the processing control systems of a cereal manufacturer, change the levels of iron supplement, and sicken and kill the children of a nation enjoying their food. That CyberTerrorist will then perform similar remote alterations at a processor of infant formula. The key: the CyberTerrorist does not have to be at the factory to execute these acts.
>
> A CyberTerrorist will place a number of computerized bombs around a city, all simultaneously transmitting unique numeric patterns, each bomb receiving each other's pattern. If bomb one stops transmitting, all the bombs detonate simultaneously. The keys: 1) the CyberTerrorist does not have to be strapped to any of these bombs; 2) no large truck is required; 3) the number of bombs and urban dispersion are extensive; 4) the encrypted patterns cannot be predicted and matched through alternate transmission; and 5) the number of bombs prevents disarming them all simultaneously. The bombs will detonate.
>
> A CyberTerrorist will remotely alter the formulas of medication at pharmaceutical manufacturers. The potential loss of life is unfathomable.

The CyberTerrorist may then decide to remotely change the pressure in the gas lines, causing a valve failure, and a block of a sleepy suburb detonates and burns. Likewise, the electrical grid is becoming steadily more vulnerable.[16]

Suggesting that cyberterrorism can prevent a nation from eating, drinking, moving, and living, Collins emphasized that he did not describe scenarios that were borrowed from the realm of science fiction, but that all of these catastrophes could be triggered today—in the real world.

And then there are terrorist hackers using their skills for psychological warfare in cyberspace. Thus, in early January 2015, hackers claiming to work for ISIS hacked the social media sites of the U.S. Military's Central Command, occupying both the Twitter and Facebook sites with their pro-ISIS propaganda. Calling themselves the Cyber Caliphate, the online jihadists placed their name on top of the pages with the sub-header "I love you isis." A reference to the U.S. military's involvement in fighting ISIS in Iraq and Syria from the air was followed by the threat message, "We broke into your networks and personal devices and know everything about you. You'll see no mercy infidels. ISIS is already here, we are in your PCs, in each military base. US soldiers! We're watching you!" One of the posts left on the sites was a 52-page spreadsheet titled "Retired Army General Officer Roster" that included the addresses, emails, and retirement dates of many former generals. The Pentagon was alarmed enough to call the named officers and inform them of the list that some observers deemed a "hit list."[17]

This reaction in the Pentagon was not far-fetched since Al Qaeda in the Arabian Peninsula (AQAP) had repeatedly pinpointed people in the West as their targets, among them Stéphane Charbonnier, the editor of *Charlie Hebdo*, and one of the satirical magazine's staffers killed during the terrorist attack on the publication's headquarters. For years, the publication of most wanted individuals or hit lists was the domain of AQAP. It is well known that competition between groups results in outbidding, and ISIS's posting of a list of retired generals on the Central Command's virtual bases was likely an outbidding coup in the eyes of ISIS supporters.

In March 2015, an ISIS cyber unit that called itself "Islamic State Hacking Division" posted a list of 100 wanted members of the American military with names, photographs, and addresses on its website: "With the huge amount of data we have from various different servers and databases, we have decided to leak 100 addresses so that our brothers in America can deal with you," the post warned. This was followed by the following appeal to ISIS followers in the United States: "Now we have made it easy for you by giving you addresses, all you need to do is take the final step, so what are you waiting for?" In other words, this was a hit list. It did not matter whether the data were the result of another hacking incident on the part of ISIS or whether it was gathered from open sources as Defense Department officials claimed. The threat was once again a blow landed by the jihadists in their psychological warfare and was serious enough for the Pentagon to warn every one of the listed persons.[18]

Cyberattack to Poison a Florida Town's Water Supply

On February 5, 2021, an unknown hacker—or hackers—launched a cyberattack on a water treatment plant in Oldsmar, a small town of about 15,000 people, in Florida. Obviously, the goal was to poison the town's water supply. The ransomware intrusion raised the level of sodium hydroxide or lye in the water to 100 times its normal level.

Luckily, a plant employee noticed that the cursor moved across his screen without him using his mouse accessing functions in control of water treatments. Once the hacker had exited the system, the plant employee reset the normal sodium hydroxide level, before alarming his supervisor.

The identity of the hacker(s) was not established. Therefore, it is not known whether this was a case of cybercrime or cyberterrorism. But without the timely intervention by the plant worker, there could have been dire consequences. As one expert revealed,

> If the system's changes went unnoticed and increased the amounts of sodium hydroxide, the water supplied by the Oldsmar water plant would be unsafe for human consumption. The effects of increased sodium hydroxide in the water could have caused severe burns to the skin, irritation of the eyes, nausea, induced vomiting, severe chest and stomach pains, and damage to the mouth, throat, and digestive system.[19]

Add to this a completely different case of actual cyberterrorism in which an innocent teenager simply because of his religion and nationality was lured into a prearranged ambush under the pretense of a passionate romance (see box "Internet 'Love Story' as Terrorist Trap"). But while the fate of Ofir Rahum is a unique case—for the time being, that is—the use of the Internet by terrorists and their sympathizers for a variety of purposes is very common.

Internet "Love Story" as Terrorist Trap

In at least one case, the Internet was used to lure an unsuspecting teenager into a terrorist trap. Ofir Rahum, a 16-year-old Israeli living with his parents in Ashkelon, was in love. He met his 25-year-

(Continued)

(*Continued*)

old girlfriend, Sali, in an Internet chat room. She had told him she was an Israeli of Moroccan descent living in Jerusalem. Ofir and Sali corresponded non-stop via email. "You don't know how much I am waiting for Wednesday," Ofir wrote Sali in the middle of January 2001. Wednesday was the day they would finally have a personal meeting. Sali had asked Ofir to meet her in Jerusalem for a romantic encounter in her girlfriend's apartment. She had urged him not to inform his parents of his plans, and he had promised to keep their secret. On the morning of January 18, 2001, instead of going to school, Ofir traveled by bus to Jerusalem, where Sali met him at the central bus terminal. They took a taxi to her car that she had parked north of the city. Together they drove toward Ramallah—although Ofir was probably unaware of their destination. After Sali stopped her car rather suddenly, a man with a Kalashnikov appeared from nowhere, ordering Ofir out of the car. When the teenager refused, the man shot him. The killer drove off with the body. Sali left the scene to meet a girlfriend for lunch.

Three days later, Sali was arrested by Israeli police officers, who began to shed light on what turned out to be a terrorist kidnapping via the Internet. Sali turned out to be Amana Mona, a Palestinian woman from Bir Naballah who worked as a journalist and was a member of the Al Fatah organization. She explained that she decided to strike after covering the funerals of many Palestinians who were killed in the conflict with Israel, and that she wanted to inflict pain on an Israeli family. According to her mother, "Seeing mothers crying all the time gave her the idea."[20] After her arrest and first appearance in a Jerusalem court, *Newsweek* wrote that this young woman from a middle-class family in the West Bank "hardly fits the profile of a terrorist."[21] But whether she fit the stereotype of a Palestinian terrorist or not, Amana Mona did not have any regrets. She told journalists that she was proud of her actions and that she had acted for the Palestinian people.

Mona was sentenced to life in prison. According to Israeli sources, she led a revolt by two dozen female Palestinian inmates in Israel's Neve Tirza prison in July 2002. According to *Yediot Aharonot*, an Israeli newspaper,

> Mona had her own "personal army" in the Neve Tirza prison, and had controlled activities of the Palestinian women, as well

as those of the Israeli Arab women serving time there. During morning breaks outdoors, Mona would organize the women in marching drills, the singing of nationalist songs and paramilitary exercises.[22]

But eventually, when the female Israeli Arab inmates refused to obey Mona's orders, the two groups attacked each other and had to be separated by prison officials. Mona was transferred to another prison.

Social Media as an Ideal Alternative to Mainstream Media

In 1853, when Karl Heinzen, an early theorist of anarchist ideology and fierce advocate of terrorist strikes, self-published his pamphlet titled "Murder and Liberty," he mocked the mainstream media of his time, daily and weekly newspapers, as mouthpieces of the ruling class and asked fellow radicals to distribute his brochure in all places, in letters, packages, wherever. After 160 years, in 2013, when Al Qaeda in the Arabian Peninsula posted the first issue of its magazine *Azan* online, its editors complained about the vicious propaganda disseminated by the "satanic" international media. Their publication, they explained, was controlled by those committed to the truth.

As this comparison shows, terrorists have always tried to find alternative media they could control. For example, the Brazilian Marxist revolutionary Carlos Marighella, who became the idol of many left-wing terrorists far beyond Latin America, recommended in the post-World War II period the use of copying machines to produce large numbers of propaganda pamphlets and manifestos. As broadcasting transmitters became lighter and easy to transport, groups with direct or indirect involvement in terrorism established their own radio and television facilities. In the early 1990s, the Lebanon-based Hezbollah organization started its own television station, Al-Manar. Soon thereafter, Al-Manar's satellite channels became popular in Palestinian homes on the West Bank and Gaza and in several Arab countries. Eventually, Al-Manar could be seen around the globe except for those countries that blocked its channels. In Colombia, left and right-wing terror groups utilized mobile radio transmitters. The Revolutionary Armed Forces of Colombia (FARC) broadcast over an increasingly large number of channels. Disc jockeys tend to play popular songs, such as "Guerrilla Girls" or "Ambush Rap," with lyrics adapted to the FARC cause. This light diet is always served with frequent doses of direct propaganda. As one disc jockey explained, "We're doing the shooting from the radio."[23]

Today all other means of communication, print and broadcasting included, pale in comparison to the opportunities that the Internet offers terrorists and hatemongers. To begin with, hate groups and terrorist organizations utilize online media for the same objectives that they hope to further through the traditional media's coverage: They disseminate propaganda material to get the attention of friend and foe, to intimidate the enemy, and to impress potential sympathizers and supporters; they explain their grievances and demands, justify violence, and portray themselves as legitimate political and/or religious actors. In addition, computer-based communications seem ideal to further several other important objectives, namely: (1) radicalization, recruitment, and incitement; (2) self-reporting of violence; (3) planning and executing terrorist operations; (4) retrieving valuable information; and (5) raising funds.

Radicalization, Recruitment, and Incitement

Among the terrorism-related cases, the FBI announced in the first half of 2015 were several that provided some clues about online radicalization and recruitment. Here are excerpts from two FBI news releases:

Case 1: Shannon Conley, 19, of Arvada, Colorado, was sentenced today (January 23, 2015) by U.S. District Court Judge Raymond P. Moore to serve 48 months in federal prison, followed by three years on supervised release, for conspiracy to provide material support to a designated foreign terrorist organization. Conley met the co- conspirator on the Internet. During their communications, they shared their view of Islam as requiring participation in violent jihad. The co-conspirator communicated to Conley that he was an active member of a group fighting in Syria known as ISIS. The two became engaged and worked together to have Conley travel to Syria to join her new fiancé. Conley also intended to fight if it became necessary to do so. In furtherance of the conspiracy, Conley joined the U.S. Army Explorers (USAE) to be trained in U.S. military tactics and in firearms. She traveled to Texas and attended the USAE training. She also obtained first aid/nursing certification and National Rifle Association certification. On March 29, 2014, the co-conspirator, together with others, arranged for an airline ticket for Conley to travel to Turkey. On April 8, 2014, Conley traveled to Denver International Airport and attempted to board the flight to Turkey. She was then arrested by FBI agents.[24]

Case 2: Asher Abid Khan, 20, was taken into custody this morning [May 26, 2015] without incident. The criminal complaint alleges Khan and a friend devised a plan to travel to Turkey and on to Syria for the purpose of joining and waging jihad on behalf of ISIL. Khan had allegedly asked a Turkish-based foreign terrorist fighter facilitator that "I wana join ISIS can you help?" He also told someone else that "I wana die as a Shaheed [martyr]," according to the allegations.

Khan's friend allegedly made it to Syria and ISIL with the assistance of Khan and the foreign terrorist fighter facilitator. Khan had been living in Australia with a relative and made it to Istanbul, Turkey, where he was to meet up with his friend in their quest to join ISIL, according to the complaint. However, Khan's family sent him false information regarding his mother's health and he was deceived into returning home to Texas.[25]

In both cases, social media were instrumental in guiding the would-be jihadis to make their way to the Islamic State's caliphate. While the FBI releases do not reveal whether social media were also instrumental in the radicalization of Shannon Conley and Asher Abid Khan, there are plenty of examples of young Westerners who were radicalized through social media propaganda. In both cases, though, the would-be jihadis were in close contact with ISIS handlers—in the case of Conley the online handler became her virtual fiancé; in the case of Khan the ISIS handler assisted with flight and meet-up arrangements typical once radicalized Westerners were ready to join ISIS in Syria or Iraq.

Six decades ago Donald Horton and R. Richard Wohl coined the term "para-social interaction" based on their observations about the relationship between mass media personalities and their audiences. They noted, "One of the most striking characteristics of the new mass media—radio, television, and the movies—is that they give an illusion of face-to-face relationship with the performer."[26] While for most people para-social interactions take place side by side with actual social relationships, for some persons they become their sole social life. As the authors explain, for socially inept or isolated persons the media persona "is readily available as an object of love—especially when he succeeds in cultivating the recommended quality of 'heart.'"[27] Admiring audience members "play a psychologically active role which, under some conditions, but by no means invariably passes over into the more formal, overt, and expressive activism of *fan behavior.*"[28]

In the Internet age, social media platforms offer groups, movements, and individuals ample opportunities for mass self-communication and for the establishment and cultivation of para-social relationships with audiences and particularly susceptible individuals. The fans that today's originators of para-social interactions win over are no longer mere spectators but participants in virtual interactions, tying them even closer to their idols and whole fan communities.

A case in point were a few ISIS women who established social media accounts on platforms like Flickr, Tumbler, Instagram, or Telegram in order to radicalize and recruit impressionable young girls in Muslim majority countries and in the West. I followed the account of one of these "online sisters" who used the name Um Umbaydah and took on the role of a sympathetic advisor to young women and teenage girls. Many of those asking for advice told Um that they wanted to join ISIS. She seemed happy to answer all questions posted by her growing girl fan community. One of the most asked questions concerned the girls' parents who did not want their daughters to leave their families. In each case, Um advised the girls to disobey their parents and leave their homes. She told them that this was what Allah wanted them to do. For me, the most striking in these exchanges was that the girls were in so many ways like average teenagers. Thus, they wondered whether there were hair dryers, beauty care products, or certain foods available in the Islamic State community.

Preaching Hate and Violence

Extreme hate of other ideological, ethnic, racial, or religious groups can lead to violence against "the other" and can be carried out by state and nonstate actors. As mentioned earlier, Nazi Germany's propaganda preached an extreme hatred of Jews before and during the unspeakable genocide of Jews in Germany and in conquered countries. Unlike organizations such as ISIS, Al Qaeda, and like-minded groups, many domestic hate groups in the United States and other Western democracies do not openly recommend violence but have been known to incite fellow posters and commenters on their online discussion boards where they preach hate and glorify the founding fathers and ideologies of their movements. Thus, in early 2015, when most of the world mourned the lethal attack on members of the satirical weekly *Charlie Hebdo* and honored the victims' stand for press freedom with the slogan "Je suis Charlie," a post on Vanguard News Network Forum, a most vicious Neo-Nazi site, showed Adolf Hitler's picture and proclaimed, "Je suis Hitler!" The attached video starred the uniformed Nazi leader in one of his many ugly anti-Semitic speeches that blamed Jews for all evils in the world. For these kinds of hate sites, white Caucasians are the superior race whose purity and dominance are threatened by Jews, Blacks, Hispanics, Asians, and Muslims. Thus, it was not surprising that immediately after the attack on the French magazine *Charlie Hebdo* conspiracy theories were forwarded in one discussion thread at Vanguard News Network.

One poster wrote,

> Something to keep in mind: These murderers claim to be "al-Qaeda in Yemen." Hmmmm! Yemen is predominately Shia, as is Syria and Iran. Now who really hates, and I mean really hates Shia (Syria and Iran?). Who is always screaming that the US should attack Syria and Iran? I'm guessing that if these murderers are not caught, or are killed before they can be interrogated, then plain-and-simple. . . this was an Israeli operation.

Another conspiracy theorist calling himself AntiZOG (in Neo-Nazi circles, ZOG stands for Zionist Occupied Government) was sure that

Mossad had a hand in this, the motivation could be to take some of the pressure off jews [*sic*] in France, and further vilify, and point the spotlight on, Islamists—not that they aren't dangerous scum—but. . . net result: this works out for jews, in that outrage is directed away from jews, and quite likely, no jews were killed—only a dozen sacrificial goyim, most of whom were left-wing pets, who would not dare write such cartoons against the self-chosen or criticize the Holohoax.

Yet another contributor wrote,

Folks, this [*Charlie Hebdo*] is precisely and exactly the sort of publication that National Socialist would have thrown on a pyre, along with all the other dirty Jew books that they burned, porn etc. In 2014, we have white people rushing to the defence of the sort of filth that Hitler would have ordered to be destroyed. Ironically, while we do that, the only people that appear to have retained the spirit of Hitler are. . . Muslims.[29]

How does hate speech relate to terrorist violence? In April 2014, after Neo-Nazi Frazier Glenn Cross stormed onto the grounds of two Jewish institutions in Kansas and allegedly shot three strangers to death, one research report found,

In the last five years alone—since the election of the nation's first black president—registered members of Stormfront (an incredible 286,000 people, though many are inactive) have been responsible for the murders of close to 100 people. The killers had certain commonalities. They were frustrated, unemployed white men living with their mothers or an estranged spouse or girlfriend. And they typically posted for years before beginning to kill, drawing sustenance and support from their fellow racists and anti-Semites. Cross, too, was nurtured by the Internet—in his case, by a rival neo-Nazi Web forum known as Vanguard News Network. In recent years, the former North Carolina Klan leader posted there more than 12,000 times.[30]

Stormfront's appeal transcended U.S. borders. Members and frequent or occasional visitors reside in many countries, especially Europe and Australia. Anders Behring Breivik, who bombed a government building in Norway, killing eight people and then massacred 69 people at a youth summer camp in 2011, was a Stormfront online user.

Stormfront remained active in the 2020s but its discussion boards were nearly tame in comparison to technologically far more sophisticated and far more extreme sites, such as Daily Stormer, National Vanguard, National Alliance, and many, many others. Following dehumanizing attacks on Blacks and Jews, a comment to a racist article posted on the National Vanguard site in the summer of 2022 ended with these words:

"Any White person who can see the threat to the future of the White race today and who refuses, whether from cowardice or selfishness, to stand up for his/her people does not deserve to be counted among them."[31]

Left-extremist groups that implicitly and in some cases explicitly call for violence against public and private capitalist institutions have been active in several European countries, among them Germany and Greece. As noted in Chapter 13, in those countries, free speech rights are not extended to "hate speech" and the "glorification of terrorism." Thus, there are no websites like stormfront.org and similar ones. In Germany, the left-extremist group with the generic name "linksunten" was seemingly part of the Antifa (for antifascist) movement and used Indymedia. org for its postings and actual calls for violence. Thus, in December 2014, there was a call for action in the city of Leipzig that did not preclude violence. The online appeal listed the names and addresses of 50 public agencies and private companies to be targeted. Soon thereafter, hundreds of masked activists took over the city's streets, attacked police officers, threw stones into windows, destroyed cars, and sprayed graffiti all over buildings and streets.

Self-Reporting of Violence

Just looking at the headlines and pictures in any issue of ISIS's slick online magazines *Dabiq* and more recently its replacement *Rumiyah* will show you that the group documents all its violence meticulously. Whether the beheadings of Western hostages, the burning of a Jordanian captive, or the execution of infidels in the conquered territories, you see it all in the pages of the online magazines as you do in the videos posted on YouTube or other social media sites. According to Natascha Bhuiyan, "ISIS presents not only scenes of crucified, stoned, or beheaded victims, but also the dead bodies of innocent, bleeding Iraqi children, the victim's intestines packed up in boxes or heads hanging on spikes."[32] Indeed, no other terrorist group has publicized its unspeakably brutal violence as detailed and widely as ISIS.

Contemporary terrorists can and do utilize the Internet to go public even in the midst of staging horrific terrorist strikes. Particularly shocking were the communication tactics of the Somalian terrorist organization al-Shabaab during its attacks inside the upscale Westgate Mall in Nairobi, Kenya, when 67 persons were killed and many more injured. Christopher Anzalone's research revealed that the group's media department used its Twitter account to tweet "a continuous stream of 'updates' and commentary throughout the assault."[33] The terrorists inside the mall, too, tweeted "updates" of their own horrible killing spree. Intelligence experts suspected that the terrorists themselves had set up a mobile command center before they launched their attack and used it to communicate with al-Shabaab headquarters and via tweets with friendly and hostile publics. Most of all, al-Shabaab's press office HSM (Harakat al-Shabaab al-Mujahidin) used Twitter to attract the greatest possible attention. According to one account,

> The HSM Press account purportedly posted "updates" on the ongoing siege at a time when conflicting reports abounded. These included tweets announcing the attack on the "Kenyan Kuffar [unbelievers] inside their own turf," denying the cessation of fighting between "the mujahidin" and the Kenyan military and police, alleging that the Kenyan government was "pleading" with the attackers inside the mall to negotiate, and reports of the calmness of the attackers despite being under siege by Kenyan security forces. Al-Shabab also claimed via Twitter that it had "singled out" only "unbelievers" in the attack and had "escorted out" Muslims before the attack began, announcing that the defense of Muslim lands "is one of the foremost obligations after faith & defending against the aggressive enemy is our right as Muslims."[34]

Planning and Executing Terrorist Operations

Terrorists utilize computer technology and the Internet to plan and coordinate their violent actions. Former FBI Director Louis J. Freeh told the Citizens Crime Commission of New York,

> When Ramzi Yousef [the mastermind of the World Trade Center bombing] was being tracked in the Philippines, he left behind a laptop computer that itemized plans to blow up [eleven] U.S. airliners in the Western Pacific on a particular day. All of the details and planning were set forth in that laptop computer.[35]

Part of the information was encrypted and difficult to decode, but it revealed for the first time how sophisticated terrorists utilized computers for planning their operations. Even before the 9/11 attacks, U.S. intelligence agencies knew that Al Qaeda operatives used the Internet to communicate with each other. According to one account,

> Hidden in the X-rated pictures of several pornographic Websites and the posted comments on sports chat rooms may lie the encrypted blueprints of the next terrorist attack against the United States or its allies. It sounds farfetched, but U.S. officials and experts say it's the latest method of communication being used by Osama bin Laden and his associates to outfox law enforcement.[36]

U.S. officials disclosed that bin Laden and others were "hiding maps and photographs of terrorist activities on sports sites, chat rooms, pornographic bulletin boards and other websites."³⁷ It has become increasingly difficult to unlock the encrypted messages and images, and it is even harder finding them in the first place among the many millions of sites, boards, and chat rooms on the World Wide Web.

According to Timothy L. Thomas, "The Internet is being used as a 'cyberplanning' tool for terrorists. It provides terrorists with anonymity, command and control resources, and a host of other measures to coordinate and integrate attack options."³⁸ American law enforcement specialists found evidence that the 9/11 terrorists used the Internet to coordinate their operation. Their email messages contained code words and never mentioned what they were really up to in plain language. According to one terrorism expert, "They knew exactly what to do. I mean, they went to Internet cafes and libraries, they erased the hard drives."³⁹ Al Qaeda's chief of operations, Abu Zubayda, used the Internet to keep in touch with the men who actually carried out the mission. The extent of Al Qaeda's dependence on cyberspace communication was discovered when several of the group's computers were found in Afghanistan and after Zubayda was arrested in Pakistan in early 2002. Effective command and control would be far more difficult to establish and maintain for Al Qaeda's terrorism network without the advantages of the Internet. As Thomas has noted, "The Internet's potential for command and control can vastly improve an organization's effectiveness, if it does not have a dedicated command and control establishment, especially in the propaganda and internal coordination areas." Noting that Internet chat rooms are one vehicle for command and control, the same expert explained that one particular website, "alneda.com, has supported al Qaeda's efforts to disperse forces and enable them to operate independently, providing leadership via strategic guidance, theological arguments, and moral inspiration."⁴⁰

The team that attacked ten sites in Mumbai, India, in November 2008 held hostages in several locations, caused the death of 173 and injured several hundred persons, utilized an unprecedented range of digital-age information and communication technology. They carried BlackBerrys and cellphones with exchangeable SIM cards that made it difficult to track them; they navigated from Karachi to Mumbai with the guidance of a Global Positioning System, and they carried CDs with high-resolution satellite images of their target sites. They communicated with their operation bosses and with each other via email and satellite telephone, and they followed live TV coverage as security forces tried to respond to the hostage situations in several locations. (See box "Excerpts from Conversations.")

Talking about the lessons learned from the Mumbai attacks before the U.S. Senate Committee on Homeland Security & Governmental Affairs, New York's Police Commissioner Raymond Kelly said that the handlers of the Mumbai terrorists directed the operations from outside the attack zone using cellphones and other portable communication devices. As Kelly said,

> This phenomenon is not new. In the past, police were able to defeat any advantage it might give hostage takers by cutting off power to the location they were in. However, the proliferation of handheld devices would appear to trump that solution.[41]

Excerpts from Conversations between Mumbai Terrorists and Operation Leaders during the Hostage Situation in November 2008

Hotel Taj Mahal, November 27, 2008: 03:10 hrs

RECEIVER: Greetings!

CALLER: Greetings! There are three Ministers and one Secretary of the Cabinet in your hotel. We don't know in which room.

RECEIVER: Oh! That's good news! It is the icing on the cake.

CALLER: Do one thing. Throw one or two grenades on the Navy and police teams, which are outside.

RECEIVER: Sorry, I simply can't make out where they are.

Nariman House, November 27, 2008: 22:26 hrs

CALLER: Brother, you have to fight. This is a matter of prestige of Islam. Fight so that your fight becomes a shining example. Be strong in the name of Allah. You may feel tired or sleepy but the Commandos of Islam have left everything. Their mothers, their fathers. Their homes. Brother, you have to fight for the victory of Islam. Be strong.

RECEIVER: Amen!

Oberoi Hotel, November 27, 2008: 03:53 hrs

CALLER: Brother, Abdul. The media is comparing your action to 9/11. One senior police officer has been killed.

ABDUL REHMAN: We are on the 10th and 11th floor. We have five hostages.

CALLER 2: Everything is being recorded by the media. Inflict the maximum damage. Keep fighting. Don't be taken alive.

CALLER: Kill all hostages, except the two Muslims. Keep your phone switched on so that we can hear the gunfire.

(Continued)

(*Continued*)

FAHADULLAH: We have three foreigners including women. From Singapore and China.

CALLER: Kill them. (Voices of Fahadullah and Abdul Rehman directing hostages to stand in a line, and telling Muslims to stand aside. Sounds of gunfire. Cheering voices in background, Kafka hands telephone to Zarar.)

ZARAR: Fahad, find the way to go downstairs.

Nariman House, November 27, 2008: 19:45 hrs

WASSI: Keep in mind that the hostages are of use only as long as you do not come under fire because of their safety. If you are still threatened, then don't saddle yourself with the burden of the hostages, immediately kill them.

RECEIVER: Yes, we shall do accordingly, God willing.

WASSI: The Army claims to have done the work without any hostages being harmed. Another thing: Israel has made a request through diplomatic channels to save the hostages. If the hostages are killed, it will spoil relations between India and Israel.

RECEIVER: So be it, God willing.

WASSI: Stay alert.

Source: New York Times [42]

Following the breach of the U.S. Capitol on January 21, 2021, thousands of U.S. Department of Justice's documents that charged and indicted members of organized groups revealed how their members utilized social media and other advanced communication technologies to communicate with each other. The indictments of Stewart Rhodes and ten other Oath Keepers charged, for example, that the defendants "were using websites, social media, text messaging, and encrypted messaging applications to communicate with co-conspirators."[43] In this particular indictment as in almost all 1/6 cases against members of organized Far Right Groups, there were many pages filled with the transcripts of written and spoken communications between group members as well as descriptions of streamed videos that captured and often celebrated their violence near and in the Capitol.

Retrieving Valuable Information

Even the most sophisticated terror organizations know that they can find a great deal of useful information on the Internet. In a training manual that Al Qaeda left behind in Afghanistan, recruits were instructed to use open sources (libraries, journals, government documents, Internet sites, etc.) because, as the text revealed, 80 percent of the information about the vulnerabilities of the enemy are publicly available. The group's leaders were also aware that the bulk of this information could be accessed on the Internet. On the hard drive of an Al Qaeda computer, also found in Afghanistan, U.S. experts discovered that it had been used to access a French site that posts a "Sabotage Handbook" with "sections on tools of the trade, planning a hit, switch gear and instrumentation, anti-surveillance methods and advanced techniques."[44] In the past, chat room participants discussed potential targets for cyberterrorism attacks. According to one account, "Targets that terrorists have discussed include the Centers for Disease Control and Prevention in Atlanta; FedWire, the money-moving clearing system maintained by the Federal Reserve Board; and facilities controlling the flow of information over the Internet."[45]

Before the overabundance of information available on the Internet, it took far more time, money, and effort for terrorists to find what they perceived as ideal targets. Timothy McVeigh's selection of the Alfred P. Murrah Federal Building in Oklahoma City for the April 1995 catastrophic bombing of the building was a case in point. He checked telephone books for the pages listing federal government agencies to find their locations in various states. He looked for a building that housed at least two of three federal agencies that were involved in the 1993 lethal conflict between the Branch Davidian sect and federal law enforcement. He and his accomplices Terry Nichols and Michael Fortier visited federal buildings in several states, among them Texas, Arizona, Arkansas, and Missouri, before McVeigh settled on Oklahoma City. McVeigh had been a computer whiz kid in high school, but when he planned his horrific attack, information that was easily accessible on the Internet a decade or so later was not yet available then.

Raising Funds

Most terrorist and hate groups use the Internet to raise money for their activities. Even the well-funded Al Qaeda network utilizes websites to solicit contributions. For this purpose, some websites have publicized account numbers at particular banks specifically set up for fundraising. Jessica Stern found that the Lasch-I-Taiba, or Army of God, in Pakistan utilized the World Wide Web to raise funds for its radical activities. Indeed, "Laschkar and its parent organization, Markaz ad-Da'wa

Irshad (Center for Islamic Invitation and Guidance) have raised so much money, mostly from sympathetic Wahhabis in Saudi Arabia, that they are reportedly planning to open their own bank."[46] If they do not dare to direct their own fundraising operations or aim at targeting larger audiences to solicit contributions, terrorist groups are content to have front organizations collect donations via the Internet. Terrorists have also resorted to criminal activities in cyberspace to finance their activities, with credit card fraud first on the list of their offenses. According to a leading French antiterrorism investigator, "Many Islamist terror plots in Europe and North America were financed through such criminal activity."[47]

Whatever their causes, international and domestic terrorist and hate groups try to raise funds online. In most instances, these appeals target people of modest means in the hope that they will sacrifice for the cause. The now defunct American anti-abortion underground group "Army of God" had a permanent post on its website that asked with great urgency for donations. "By now, you've probably heard about the massive effort launched by the baby butchers and their evil lackeys to destroy the Christian gallery websites," site visitors read. "Every month that passes our expenses grow in direct proportion to the number of people we impact with this website. . . That's why we need your donations every month."

Nobody, however, has been as sophisticated as jihadis and their supporters who are known to have discussed in various social media the advantages of Bitcoin as an ideal currency for raising donations and purchasing weaponry. As one researcher found several years ago,

> Although some websites affiliated with terrorist organizations have begun collecting Bitcoin donations, this practice appears to be relatively limited. One example would be http://kavkazcenter.com. It is possible that as the technical capacity of these organizations increases, their use of digital currencies will also increase. This increase is likely to be small however, in relation to overall terror financing through other channels such as hawala, kidnapping, front companies, narcotics sales, oil sales, and many more.[48]

In the 2020s, when Bitcoin had competition from Ethereum, Monero, Litecoin, and others, these cryptocurrencies were rapidly embraced by criminals, especially drug dealers and ransom-seekers. But hate groups that preached violent extremism followed suit. The National Alliance asked supporters to donate via Bitcoin and advised them to scan the QR code or copy and paste the bitcoin wallet address. The National Vanguard gave donors the choice to pay via its Bitcoin, Litecoin, and Monero wallets. Even the less sophisticated Stormfront asked supporters to submit donations via Bitcoin, Ethereum, or Litecoin.

Yet, domestic groups in the West were late-comers compared to jihadist organizations, such as Al Qaeda and ISIS. Some unknown jihadist or a sympathizer wrote years an instructional text titled "Bitcoin wa Sadaqat al Jihad" that explained the transfer of the then sole cryptocurrency from Western countries into the accounts of jihadist organizations. Still, based on their research, Shacheng Wang and XIxi Zhu wrote in 2021, "The current evidence shows that the dependence of terrorist organizations on cryptocurrency is not significant, and the use of cryptocurrency for terrorist financing is still in its early stages, as it is not a mature method of terrorist financing." But they recognized the potential for becoming "convenient for terrorist organizations to raise funds"—especially with an improvement of anonymous transactions.[49]

All told, the Internet, like many other technological advances, can be used in positive and negative ways. Terrorists and hate groups have seized cyberspace rather quickly for their sinister purposes. But the other side of the coin is this: counterterrorism communities tend to get many valuable leads about terrorist plots by monitoring these actors' online activities.

Notes

1 David Cole, "The New America: Little Privacy, Big Terror," *New York Review of Books*, August 13, 2015, 20.
2 The full text of the Cyberspace Policy Review is available at www.whitehouse. gov/assets/documents/Cyberspace_Policy_Review_final.pdf, accessed July 8, 2010.
3 Richard A. Clarke and Robert K. Knake, *Cyber War: The Next Threat to National Security and What to Do about It* (New York: HarperCollins, 2010), 30–31.
4 Ellen Nakashima and Steven Mufson, "Hackers Have Attacked Foreign Utilities, CIA Analyst Says," *Washington Post*, January 19, 2008; Jeannie Larson, "The Federal Government Role in Cyber Security," presentation, October 29, 2009; www.issa-oc.org/html/Jeanie_Larson_Presentation.pdf, accessed July 6, 2010.
5 Clarke and Knake, 135.
6 Ibid., 136.
7 www.acq.osd.mil/dsb/reports/2010s/DSB-cyberDeterrenceReport_02-28-17_ Final.pdf, accessed June 6, 2018.
8 Amrit P. Acharya and Arabinda Acharya, "Cyberterrorism and Biotechnology," *Foreign Affairs*, June 1, 2017; www.foreignaffairs.com/articles/world/2017-06-01/cyberterrorism-and-biotechnology, accessed June 6, 2018.
9 Posted in the "jihad" category of the discussion section of IslamicAwakening. com, www.as-sawah.com/discus/, accessed September 12, 2003.
10 Ibid.
11 This is a quote from a Reuter dispatch of October 20, 2000, "Hizbollah Says Pro-Israelis Damaged Its Website," www.dailynews.yahoo.com/h/ nm/20001020/wr/mideast_hizbollah_d_l.html.
12 Ayoub was quoted in Ranwa Yehia, "Hizbollah: Arabs Have 'Tremendous Power to Fight' on New Cyber Front," (*Beirut*) *Daily Star On Line*, www. dailystar.com.lb/30_10_00/art2.htm, accessed October 30, 2000.

13 Thomas Friedman, "Digital Defense," *New York Times*, July 27, 2001, A19.
14 Barton Gellman, "Cyber-Attacks by Al Qaeda Feared: Terrorist at Threshold of Using Internet as Tool of Bloodshed," *Washington Post*, June 27, 2002, A1.
15 Ibid.
16 Barry C. Collins, "The Future of Cyber Terrorism: Where the Physical and Virtual Worlds Converge," speech delivered at the 11th Annual International Symposium on Criminal Justice Issues, http://afgen.com/terrorism1.html, accessed September 17, 2003.
17 This account is from various stories publicized in the news media.
18 Michael S. Schmidt and Helene Cooper, "ISIS Urges Sympathizers to Kill U.S. Service Members It Identifies on Website," *New York Times*, March 21, 2015, www.nytimes.com/2015/03/22/world/middleeast/isis-urges-sympathizers-to-kill-us-service-members-it-identifies-on-website.html, accessed March 23, 2015. See also, http://securityaffairs.co/wordpress/35203/hacking/isis-cell-calls-on-supporters-to-kill-100-us-military-personnel.html, accessed March 23, 2015.
19 Edgar Namoca, "Oldsmar Water Treatment Facility Attack," Posted at University of Hawaii, March 4, 2021, https://westoahu.hawaii.edu/cyber/ics-cybersecurity/ics-weekly-summaries/oldsmar-water-treatment-facility-attack/, accessed August 30, 2022.
20 The quote is from Dan Ephron and Joanna Chen, "Ofir's Fatal Attraction," *Newsweek*, April 2, 2001, 39.
21 Ibid. For my account of this case of terrorism, I drew from many media accounts, among them the mentioned story in *Newsweek* and Deborah Sontag, "Israelis Grieve as Youth Who Was Lured to His Death on the Internet Is Buried," *New York Times*, January 20, 2001, www.nytimes.com/2001/01/20/technology/20MIDE.html?pagewanted=all.
22 http://webisraelinsider.com/Articles/Security/1295.htm, accessed April 14, 2005.
23 Karl Prenhaul, "Colombia's Rebels Hit the Airwaves," *Newsday*, December 24, 2000, A20.
24 The full FBI report is available at www.fbi.gov/denver/press-releases/2015/arvada-woman-sentenced-for-conspiracy-to-provide-material-support-to-a-designated-foreign-terrorist-organization.
25 For the full FBI release, see www.fbi.gov/houston/press-releases/2015/texas-resident-charged-withconspiracy-to-provide-material-support-to-isil, accessed August 4, 2015.
26 Donald Horton and R. Richard Wohl, "Mass Communication and Para-Social Interaction: Observations on Intimacy at a Distance," *Psychiatry* 19 (3) (1956), p. 215.
27 Ibid., 223.
28 Ibid., 228; emphasis added.
29 http://vnnforum.com/showthread.php?t=232708, accessed January 15, 2015.
30 According to the Southern Poverty Law Center, www.splcenter.org/news/2014/04/17/splc-report-users-leading-white-supremacist-web-forum-responsible-many-deadly-hate-crimes, accessed August 4, 2015.
31 National Vanguard, "Comments Archive," https://nationalvanguard.org/comments-archive/, accessed August 12, 2022.
32 Natascha Bhuiyan, "ISIS: The Propaganda Jihad," unpublished research paper, 2014, 12.
33 Christopher Anzalone, "The Nairobi Attack and Al-Shabab's Media Strategy," *CTC Sentinel* 6 (10) (2013), p. 3, www.ctc.usma.edu/posts/the-nairobi-attack-and-al-shababs-media-strategy, accessed January 12, 2015.
34 Ibid., 3–4.

35 Freeh's speech was published in *Vital Speeches of the Day* on October 1, 1999. The transcript contained a typing error that Freeh referred to as a plan to attack "1 U.S. airliners" simultaneously; the correct number was 11 airliners. See also Simon Reeve, *The New Jackals* (Boston: Northeastern University Press, 1999), ch. 4, for details about this foiled plan.

36 Jack Kelley, "Terror Groups Hide Behind Web Encryption," *USA Today*, February 6, 2001, 7A.

37 Ibid.

38 Timothy L. Thomas, "Al Qaeda and the Internet: The Danger of 'Cyberplanning,'" *Parameters* (Spring 2003), pp. 112–23, http://carlisle-www.army.mil/usawc/Parameters/03spring/thomas.htm.

39 Steve Emerson made this remark during a conversation with Chris Matthews on CNBC's *Hardball with Chris Matthews*, March 2, 2002.

40 Thomas.

41 http://hsgac.senate.gov/public/_files/010809Kelly.pdf.

42 The document is available at http://graphics8.nytimes.com/packages/pdf/nyregion/city_room/20090109_mumbaitranscripts.pdf, accessed January 14, 2009.

43 The indictment is available at https://www.justice.gov/opa/press-release/file/1462481/download, accessed August 30, 2022.

44 Gellman.

45 Thomas, 118.

46 Jessica Stern, "Pakistan's Jihad Culture," *Foreign Affairs* (November–December 2000), p. 120.

47 Timothy L. Thomas identified Jean-François Richard as the French investigator he quoted.

48 Aaron Brantly, "Funding Terrorism Bit by Bit," *CTC Sentinel* 7 (10) (2014), p. 4, www.ctc.usma.edu/v2/wp-content/uploads/2014/10/CTCSentinel-Vol7Iss 101.pdf, accessed January 23, 2015.

49 Shacheng Wang and Xixi Zhu, "Evaluation of Potential Cryptocurrency Development in Terrorist Financing." *Policing* 15 (4) (September 2021), p. 2337.

16 Conclusion
Living with Terrorist Threats

There is a great deal of disagreement about the causes of terrorism and the most effective ways to respond to this sort of political violence. But there is agreement on one crucial point: Terrorism will not disappear as the weapon of choice in the hands of domestic and international groups and individuals who cannot fight their declared enemies in legitimate political arenas or in traditional wars. According to Walter Laqueur, "Even in the unlikely case that all global conflicts will be resolved—that all the political, social, and economic tensions of this world will vanish—this will not necessarily be the end of terrorism."[1] It is equally unlikely that terrorism that is rooted in the Arab and Muslim world would end if Israel were to disappear from the map of the Middle East because a variety of other domestic and international conditions breed discontent and fuel terrorist ideas and deeds in the region. The same is true for other parts of the world and other countries. Moreover, there can be no doubt that the United States will remain a major target of international terrorism for the foreseeable future, because, as Paul Pillar concluded, "U.S. policies and the U.S. presence overseas can vary, but the United States' place as sole superpower, leader of the West, and principal exporter of modern culture do not seem likely to change."[2]

Although terrorist organizations come and go, those who represented in the last several decades the greatest danger seemed more impervious than most previous movements. The Muslim extremists, who were energized by Osama bin Laden's declaration of war against "Crusaders and Zionists" and by Al Qaeda's attacks against the United States, bought into bin Laden's strategy to further long-term goals. Patience informed not only these terrorists' long-term strategy but also their modes of operation. Al Qaeda and like-minded groups did not hastily plot their terror strikes, but prepared and rehearsed for years. Their ideological fervor and their justification of unlimited violence were unequivocal. Omar Bakri Muhammad, the head of a radical Islamic group in London and a suspected follower of bin Laden, told an interviewer, "Terror is the language of the twenty-first century. If I want something, I terrorize you to achieve it."[3] This statement went to the heart of this terrorist calculus

DOI: 10.4324/9781003289265-19

and its assumption that terrorism triggers fear in target audiences that goes far beyond the damage inflicted. If you are patient enough, Omar Bakri Muhammad and like-minded people believe, violence will terrorize your targets sufficiently that you eventually get what you want. According to Muhammad, bin Laden and Al Qaeda had immediate and long-term goals: "They are engaged in a defensive jihad against those who attacked Islam. In the long run, they want to re-establish the Islamic state, the Caliphate. And to convert the whole world."[4] However preposterous such objectives seemed at the time, they motivated rank-and-file terrorists and produced a brand of terrorism that killed indiscriminately in order to inflict the greatest psychological damage on their target audiences. A good example of this mindset was the would-be Times Square bomber: Before he attempted to detonate a car bomb in the heart of Manhattan on May 1, 2010, the Pakistani-born, naturalized U.S. citizen Faisal Shahzad justified his motives in a "martyr video" that was later aired by the Arab TV network Al Arabiya. Shahzad, who called himself "a Muslim soldier" as he pleaded guilty in a federal district court in New York, warned on the video that the "Muslim war" would not end "until Islam is spread on the whole world."[5]

Nearly a decade after 9/11, two leading terrorism scholars, Leonard Weinberg and William Eubank, suggested that based on their research "some evidence indicates [that the current] Fourth Wave of modern [religious] terrorism may be on a downward trajectory."[6] That optimistic view was proven wrong by the rise of ISIS and its reign of terror inside and outside its conquered territory in Syria and Iraq. More importantly, in the early 2020s, there were signs that Al Qaeda and ISIS were far from defeated and instead expanded their presence not only in Afghanistan under the rule of the Taliban but also in Africa and South and East Asia. Besides, given the instability in Syria and Iraq, fighters of both groups conducted selected strikes and waited for opportunities to resurface from their hiding places. At times, the loss of leaders through targeted killings or arrests can be the beginning of a terrorist group's end. This did not happen to Al Qaeda after first Osama bin Laden and then Ayman al-Zawahiri were assassinated. And it did not happen to ISIS after first Abu Bakr Baghdadi and then two of his successors were killed.

The Taliban's return to power in 2021 made Afghanistan once again a venue for jihadists to strengthen their ranks and expand their operations into neighboring countries, including former republics of the Soviet Union. Some observers warned that Afghanistan could become a staging ground for major terrorist strikes in the West. The seemingly carefree presence of Ayman al-Zawahiri in Kabul in the summer of 2022 demonstrated that the Al Qaeda leader and his associates had returned to their former safe haven with unlimited freedom to directly communicate with associates around the globe. On the other hand, the ISIS-Khorasan fighters who operated in Afghanistan were not welcome by Afghan leaders, but they were strong and ruthless enough to launch devastating terror attacks in Kabul and elsewhere in the country. With the relationship between the Taliban and the United States at the lowest point, there was little hope for the American-Afghan counterterrorist alliance envisioned in the Doha Agreement between those two sides.

Whatever the durability of the Fourth Wave of religious terrorism may be, for the time being, the webs of Al Qaeda and ISIS groups remain a threat. And while the potential for devastating domestic terrorism in the United States and other Western countries is a real threat today, this possibility has existed for decades as the following foiled plots in the post 9/11 era attested to:

- In December 2008, according to an FBI report, a cache of radioactive materials suitable for building "dirty bombs" was found in the house of James Cummings in Belfast, Maine, along with literature on how to build such bombs. Cummings, who was killed by his wife in what seemed an act of self-defense, was known as a fan of Adolf Hitler and had ties to White Supremacy groups. Reportedly upset about Barack Obama's victory in the November 2008 presidential election, he had told his wife and ten-year-old daughter how he planned to set off his bombs and kill his family during an attack in Washington, DC, at the inauguration of the president.
- In August 2004, 66-year-old Gale William Nettles was charged with plotting to blow up a federal building in downtown Chicago with a truck bomb similar to the one used by Oklahoma City bomber Timothy McVeigh. Nettles, a convicted felon, had bought 500 pounds of what he thought was explosive fertilizer from an undercover agent and rented a locker to store the bomb-making material. The would-be bomber had first told fellow inmates at a Mississippi prison that he was planning violent revenge against the federal government for convicting and imprisoning him for his counterfeiting activities. In this case, thanks to the involvement of undercover agents, the bomb-making fertilizer was in fact benign material.
- Even more alarming was the accidental disruption of a terrorist plot in early 2003, when FBI agents were directed to a weapons arsenal in the Texas countryside that contained a large number of guns, pipe bombs, and a cyanide bomb "big enough to kill everyone in a 30,000-square-foot building."

It took the starring roles of violent Far-Right extremist groups, such as the Oath Keepers and Proud Boys, during the breach of the U.S. Capitol on January 6, 2021, that finally got the attention of the political class, the news media, and the general public. But whereas jihadist terrorism in the late twentieth and early twenty-first century was universally condemned in the targeted West, violent homegrown Far-Right and Far-

Left extremism was seen and judged through ideological and partisan lenses. In other words, while a very limited number of Westerners embraced jihadist causes, far larger numbers of people in Western countries agreed with and actually joined violent extremist groups in more recent times. In several European countries and in the United States, the appeal of White Supremacy and neo-Nazism has been particularly strong in the military and law enforcement circles. This was hardly surprising because violent extremist groups are particularly interested to indoctrinate and recruit persons who are well trained in the handling of weapons and explosives.

A 2022 analysis of the leaked membership roster of the Oath Keepers, the by far largest violent extremist organization in the United States, was a shocking eye-opener: While current and former members of the military, law enforcement, and first responders were dominant among the more than 38,000 due paying members, there were "also elected officials, government employees, teachers, religious figures, and businessmen, among others."[7] Members pledged allegiance to the Oath Keepers' mission and many promised to indoctrinate and recruit others. Here are just a few examples of these kinds of pledges:

- A town justice in New York state wrote, "I am currently traveling our nation…educating people on the constitution and our founding fathers' idea of gov. We meet a lot of vets and police who feel the way we do. I'll pass the word [sic]."
- Another member pledged "As a [sic] Active Duty Marine I could spread the word of the Oath Keepers to Many [sic] places as a [sic] move from station to station. I would love to attend any event that is close to my current location."
- A former Chief Master Sergeant in the Air Force wrote, "I am a true patriot and have many connections to spread the Oath keeper [sic] mission."
- A physician mentioned in his pledge, "Many of my patients are police officers, troopers, FBI agents, CIA and in the military. I have the ability to spread the world of this organization to my patients. I showed 2 troopers this week the web link."
- A self-described minister and educator located in North Carolina offered his skill sets including "Public speaking, membership drives, have current access and interaction with many current and retired servicemembers through church and my current work as quality control director for a [sic] assault weapons manufacturer."[8]

Besides the heavy representation of former and present members of the uniformed services among Oath Keepers, the analysis of the leaked membership rolls revealed also that there were several hundred present and former appointed and elected public officials and many members from literally all walks of life. In other Western countries, most of all Germany, violent Far Right extremists were also discovered among the military and in law enforcement. In the summer of 2020, Germany's Minister of Defense Annegret Kramp-Karrenbauer dissolved the second company of the Bundeswehr's Elite Special Forces KSK (Kommando Spezialkraefte) for "far-right extremism within its ranks." The minister characterized the unit as having a "toxic leadership."[9]

Comparing the fight against terrorism with public health experts' struggle against communicable diseases, Paul Pillar concluded,

> Some of the threats are waxing; some are waning. Some are old; others are new. Much of the challenge and the frustration comes from the fact that just as things are going well on one front—and occasionally even so well that a problem is eradicated altogether (small pox, the Red Army Faction)—a different and perhaps even more threatening problem emerges (AIDS, al-Qaida). Attention and resources get shifted around as threats evolve, but the effort as a whole can never stop.[10]

Such an analogy is helpful in understanding the perennial nature of the terrorist threats in both the domestic and the international arenas.

In this book, I set out to explain the calculus of terrorism and trace its influence on the utility of political violence by weak nonstate actors, the making of terrorists and terrorist organizations, and their strategies, tactics, and organizational structures. The idea furthermore was to describe and assess how targeted governments respond, how the media report, and how the public is targeted by both terrorist and counterterrorist propaganda. Most importantly, the question was and is whether and to what degree terrorist assumptions are borne out by the results of their violent deeds. The conclusion is unequivocal: Even small groups and lone actors can become political factors in strong nation-states, and at times in the international political arena as well, when they commit political violence—especially when their terror is of the spectacular kind. Terrorists force nation-states to react, and often they get their target societies to overreact at the expense of violating their most fundamental values.

The question, then, is how societies can cope with serious terrorist threats without being overwhelmed by the psychological warfare that terrorists wage. There are no silver bullets for this predicament. But the more people know about the dangers they face, the greater is the chance that they will not be consumed by fear before actual terrorist attacks occur and that they will not panic once terrorist strikes are carried out. Public officials must provide and citizens must insist on realistic threat assessments that neither minimize nor maximize the dangers based on the best intelligence available.

Politicians must accept that partisan expedience should never enter counterterrorist discussions, measures, and policies. Terrorists aim at influencing politics and policies in their target countries. But neither politicians nor the public should play into their hands. If the architects of the train bombings in Madrid on March 11, 2004, struck in order to influence the outcome of Spain's national elections three days later, they were successful: Prime Minister José María Aznar and the Popular Party, supporters of the American invasion and occupation in Iraq, were defeated, and José Luis Rodríguez Zapatero and the Socialist Party, opponents of the Iraq war, won the election. Yet, it was far from clear that the Spanish electorate voted out Aznar because of the massive terror attack. Instead, observers believed that Spaniards punished Aznar because his government immediately blamed the bombings on Basque separatists and discounted Muslim extremists as possible perpetrators in spite of evidence to the contrary.

Regardless of the true reason for Aznar's defeat, administration officials in Washington warned in the summer of 2004 that Al Qaeda was likely to strike the United States again in order to influence the presidential election. In early 2005, similar claims were made in the United Kingdom with respect to upcoming elections. There was no doubt in both cases that terrorists could strike again at any time before or after the election. But to associate threat alerts with the upcoming elections validated bin Laden and his followers as powerful players for partisan politics' sake. Indeed, in early August 2004, after Secretary of Homeland Security Tom Ridge went public with a warning ahead of the November elections, 28 percent of Americans believed that this particular alert was "politically motivated," 50 percent thought it was based on "real intelligence," and 12 percent thought it was based on "some of both" factors.[11] Residents of New York City were even more skeptical in their assessment of the administration's motives, in that 46 percent believed "strongly" and 17 percent believed "somewhat" that this particular terrorism alert, supposed to last through Election Day, had political purposes.[12]

Since then, using the threat of terrorism to gain partisan advantage became common. During the 2016 presidential race, Hillary Clinton called Donald Trump a "recruiting sergeant for the terrorists" and "offered herself as a seasoned warrior against terrorism."[13] Mr. Trump returned fire hours later, blaming Mrs. Clinton and President Obama's handling of immigration and the Iraq war for bringing terrorism to American shores.[14] Following the Orlando nightclub shooting, then candidate Trump "suggested the sitting commander-in-chief is aiding and abetting terrorism."[15] This was hardly surprising since Trump was the most prominent promoter of the birther conspiracy theory which claimed that Obama was not born in the United States and might be a Muslim.

President Trump continued to question leading Democrats' toughness vis-à-vis terrorists. After Democratic Senators criticized his nominee for CIA Director, Gina Haspel, President Trump tweeted,

> My highly respected nominee for CIA Director, Gina Haspel, has come under fire because she was too tough on Terrorists. Think of that, in these very dangerous times, we have the most qualified person, a woman, who Democrats want OUT because she is too tough on terror. Win Gina!

In the 2020 election campaign, the incumbent President Trump and his challenger, former Vice-President Joe Biden accused each other to support or condone violent extremists. Trump claimed that Biden to be soft on "Black Lives Matter" and Antifa violence, while Biden blamed Trump for his refusal to condemn White Supremacists and neo-Nazis.

Even without good intelligence in hand, government officials warn too quickly of likely terrorist strikes—typically before high holiday and major sports events. If public officials make threat alerts in the absence of specific evidence, the news media must not scare the public by reporting prominently and frequently on vague information. Terror alerts play into the hands of terrorists because the mere threat of terrorism affects target audiences nearly as much as real strikes.

Public officials, experts, educators, and the news media have an obligation to educate and inform the public about the calculus of terrorism so that citizens understand the scheme of political violence in which the psychological impact on target societies surpasses the number of people killed and injured. Every person who is killed in a terrorist event means a tragic, utterly unnecessary loss. But we must also keep in mind that many more people die each year because of traffic accidents, crimes, cancer, heart attacks, and suicides than in terrorist incidents. Well over one million persons died in the United States as result of the Covid pandemic. In the fall of 2022, when mask- and other Covid health restrictions were no longer in place, around between 400 and 500 Covid-infected Americans still died each day. That was no longer "breaking news."

Societies must become aware of these facts and realize that the psychological impact of terrorism is disproportionate to the likelihood that an individual will become a victim of terror strikes. Therefore, just as terrorists exploit the triangle of communication for their propaganda scheme (see Chapter 14), knowledgeable public and private sources must use the same communication vehicles to disseminate reliable and useful information that counters the fear tactics of terrorist foes. The public has a right to know—even if the truth means learning about the likelihood that terrorists, sooner or later, will acquire and use weapons of mass destruction. But for the authorities to discuss possible horror scenarios makes sense only if they inform the public at the same time on the state of emergency preparedness in their communities. It is equally important that the public and private sectors tell the public what to do and what not to do in case of catastrophic terrorism.

A well-informed and well-prepared society is less likely to panic in the face of a terrorist crisis and more likely to opt for proportional counterterrorist responses at home and abroad than a clueless audience. It is necessary to act decisively in the area of prevention and preparedness, on efforts to apprehend terrorists and to disrupt terrorist operations, recruiting, training, indoctrination, and financing schemes.

However, the establishment of an overblown intelligence/homeland security complex in the post-9/11 years attests to overreaction on the part of the U.S. government and powerful interests. According to a two-year investigation by *Washington Post* reporters Dana Priest and William M. Arkin,

- Some 1,271 government organizations and 1,931 private companies work on programs related to counterterrorism, homeland security, and intelligence in about 10,000 locations across the United States.
- An estimated 854,000 people, nearly 1.5 times as many people living in Washington, DC, hold top-secret security clearances.
- Many security and intelligence agencies do the same work, creating redundancy and waste. For example, 51 federal organizations and military commands, operating in 15 U.S. cities, track the flow of money to and from terrorist networks.
- Analysts who make sense of documents and conversations obtained by foreign and domestic spying share their judgment by publishing 50,000 intelligence reports each year—a volume so large that many are routinely ignored.[16]

This did not change since that study was published a dozen years ago. Instead, the budgets of the all agencies involved in counterterrorism increased significantly.

In the fight against jihadist terrorism, the U.S. State Department's public diplomacy efforts to win the hearts and minds of Muslims around the world were not successful (see Chapter 11). But this should not prevent the search for new approaches to counter violent political extremism at the home front. The Biden administration's 2021 "National Strategy for Countering Domestic Terrorism" mentions the need for confronting the long-term contributors to domestic terrorism. This would certainly mean new approaches to terrorism prevention. Since it is very difficult to de-radicalize hard-core violent extremists, there must be robust effort to find and try out new methods to prevent indoctrination and radicalization in the first place. Biden's strategy envisions reducing racism and polarization and reduced access to firearms. Those are ambitious, long-term objectives. In the meantime, there should be great efforts to working with local leaders and communities who are best situated to identify and work with persons most vulnerable to radicalization, and move against social media platforms with the most violent accounts along the latest EU model.

Based on his fine analysis of the at least partially violent QAnon online community, James Fitzgerald issued

> a call to explore more empathetic engagement with conspiracy adherents, arguing that until we (re)discover a more inclusive, agonistic politics, QAnon and other fantastical conspiracy movements will continue to arise and some may metastasize into violent action. New forms of resilience to (online) polarization can be built on this principle.[17]

Indeed, in the face of ever more people in Western democracies embracing violent ideas and violent extremist groups, there must be increased efforts to understand the roots of their anger and alienation as part of countering these dangerous trends. This cannot be done by terrorism and counterterrorism experts alone. It needs cooperation across multiple fields, including political psychologists, psychiatrists, social work, and others. As neighbors, friends, colleagues, acquaintances, or even family members become infected by the virus of hate and violence, experts must intensify the search for effective remedies.

Notes

1 Walter Laqueur, *No End to War: Terrorism in the Twenty-First Century* (New York: Continuum, 2003), 231.
2 Paul R. Pillar, *Terrorism and Foreign Policy* (Washington, DC: Brookings Institution Press, 2001), 233.
3 From an interview conducted by the Portuguese reporter Paulo Moura, *Harper's Magazine*, July 2004, 23.
4 Ibid., 25.
5 John Rikey, "Arab Television Airs Faisal Shahzad Terror Video," *Newsday*, July 14, 2010.
6 Leonard Weinberg and William Eubank, "An End to the Fourth Wave of Terrorism?" *Studies in Conflict & Terrorism* 33 (7) (2010), p. 600.
7 ADL Center on Extremism, "The Oath Keepers Data Leak: Unmasking Extremism in Political Life," September 6, 2022, https://www.adl.org/resources/report/oath-keepers-data-leak-unmasking-extremism-public-life, accessed September 9, 2022.
8 Ibid.
9 "German Commando Company Is Dismantled Due to Far-Right Culture," *The Guardian*, July 1, 2020. https://www.theguardian.com/world/2020/jul/01/german-commando-company-disbanded-after-extremist-rightwing-culture-discovered, accessed September 8, 2022.
10 Pillar, 218.
11 According to a Fox News survey that was conducted on August 3–4, 2004.
12 According to a Pace University survey of August 12–31, 2004.

13 Alexander Burns and Nicholas Confessore, "After Bombing, Hillary Clinton and Donald Trump Clash over Terrorism," *New York Times*, September 19, 2016, www.nytimes.com/2016/09/20/us/politics/donald-trump-hillary-clinton.html, accessed June 6, 2018.

14 Ibid.

15 Tina Nguyen, "Trump Suggests Obama Has Secret Pro-Terrorist Agenda," *Vanity Fair*, June 13, 2016, www.vanityfair.com/news/2016/06/donald-trump-obama-muslim, accessed June 7, 2018.

16 Dana Priest and William M. Arkin, "A Hidden World, Growing beyond Control," *Washington Post*, July 19, 2010, http://projects.washingtonpost.com/top-secret-america/articles/a-hidden-worldgrowing-beyond-control/print/, accessed July 19, 2010.

17 James Fitzgerald, "Conspiracy, Anxiety, Ontology: Theorising QAnon," *First Monday* 27 (5) (2022), https://journals.uic.edu/ojs/index.php/fm/article/view/12618/10639, accessed September 20, 2022.

Appendix
Major Terrorist Incidents since the Late 1970s

Incidents That Deliberately Targeted Americans and/or American Interests

The Iranian Hostage Crisis (1979–81)

On November 4, 1979, several hundred young Islamic militants, all self-proclaimed students and followers of Iran's supreme ruler, Ayatollah Ruhollah Khomeini, seized the American embassy in Tehran, burned the compound's U.S. flag, and took 62 Americans hostage. Initially, U.S. officials in Washington and in Tehran viewed the takeover as yet another annoying but manageable incident in the midst of the fundamental political and societal changes that followed the fall of the Shah Mohammed Reza Pahlavi regime, the triumph of the Islamic revolution, and the return of the Ayatollah Khomeini from exile in Paris. After all, a similar takeover of the embassy nine months earlier had ended quickly, after pro-Khomeini revolutionary guards had freed the American hostages and removed the militants from the embassy. But in this case, the three American officials who happened to be in Iran's foreign ministry at the time of the seizure pleaded in vain for the Iranian authorities to free once again the embassy staff.

The anti-American sentiment in Iran, especially among the supporters of the Islamic revolution and the establishment of an Islamic state, had markedly increased because the Carter administration had allowed the ailing shah to enter the United States to seek medical treatment a few days before the embassy seizure. What the White House considered a humanitarian gesture was seen by many Iranians as yet another sign of American support for the man who during his reign had brutally oppressed dissent. In this anti-American hysteria among militant Islamic elements, it did not matter that President Jimmy Carter, a strong advocate of human rights, had pressed the shah for reforms. The Ayatollah Khomeini recognized immediately the usefulness of the hostage crisis for his domestic purposes. The idea was to unite against a powerful and "evil" enemy, the United States, which he came to call "the Great Satan." Thus, one day after the successful takeover, Khomeini and several of his highly placed supporters sided publicly with the hostage-holders; they supported their demands, primarily the return of the shah and his assets to Iran. Just like the militants who were in control of the U.S. embassy, the Ayatollah justified the predicament of the Americans by characterizing them as "spies" and the embassy as a "spy nest" (only a group of 13 embassy staffers, predominantly women and African Americans, were not deemed spies and were released a few weeks after the takeover). Khomeini moved swiftly against possible opponents.

In Iran, the Ayatollah Khomeini was able to exploit the hostage standoff to consolidate his power; in the United States, President Carter, after receiving an initial burst of public support, was increasingly blamed for allowing a gang of terrorists and a comparably weak country to hold the United States hostage—blamed by his political opponents in the Republican Party, by fellow Democrats, and by an increasing share of the American public. As criticism of Carter's "do-nothing" approach grew, the president ordered a highly complex and risky rescue mission by members of the counterterrorism unit Delta Force, who had trained for such an operation since shortly after the embassy takeover. Delta Force commandos were flown to a rendezvous place in the Iranian desert dubbed "Desert One," from where they were to fly aboard helicopters into the area of Tehran to stage a complicated attempt to rescue the hostages. But only five of the six helicopters needed for the operation (out of a total of eight) landed at Desert One in operational condition. Charles Beckwith, the mission commander, had no choice but to abort the rescue attempt. Tragically, during the refueling operations before takeoff, eight soldiers were killed when a transport plane and a helicopter collided. The failure of the mission and, even more so, the deadly disaster at Desert One weakened Carter's support further. While the president overcame challenges in his own party and again became the Democrats' candidate, Republican Ronald Reagan won the presidential election in November 1980.

With the shah dead (he had succumbed to his illness during the summer in a Cairo hospital), Carter defeated, and the victory of the Islamic revolution sealed, the hostages in Iran had outlived their usefulness for Khomeini and his supporters. After negotiating the transfer of close to $8 billion of the shah's assets to Iran, the Iranian authorities released the hostages on January 20, 1981—only minutes after Jimmy Carter's presidency had ended and Ronald Reagan had been sworn in as president. For 444 days, as the media reminded the U.S. public day in and day out, the United States had been held hostage.

Two Catastrophic Bombings in Beirut (1983)

On April 18, 1983, a delivery truck loaded with 400 pounds of explosives sped past the guards in front of the U.S. embassy in Beirut and, as it reached the front portico of the building, blew up in a powerful explosion that destroyed the central part of the building. Sixty-three people, among them 17 Americans, were killed, and 120 others were injured. General John Vessey, the chairman of the Joint Chiefs of Staff, called the most lethal attack on an American diplomatic facility "an inexplicable aberration."[1] As it turned out, the first anti-American suicide bombing was only the beginning of a sustained terror campaign against Americans by fundamental Lebanese Shi'ite groups, namely the Hezbollah (Party of God) and the Lebanese Islamic Jihad, who were inspired by the Iranian revolution and actively supported by the Iranian Revolutionary Guards and thus by the Iranian leadership. What these circles resented most of all was the presence of U.S. Marines and other foreign forces on Lebanese territory even though the troops, together with their French and Italian counterparts, had come to restore law and order after Israel had invaded in the hunt for members of the Palestinian Liberation Organization (PLO) and had carried out the evacuation of PLO leader Yassir Arafat and his followers from Lebanon.

Far more devastating blows followed six months later, on October 23, 1983, when suicide bombers drove their explosive-laden trucks simultaneously into the U.S. Marine Corps' and the French forces' compounds outside Beirut. Two hundred and forty-one American Marines and 58 French servicemen were killed. President Reagan called the terrorist attacks "despicable" and expressed his "outrage." But while immediately after he learned of the carnage the president emphasized his determination to keep a force in Lebanon, four months later his administration decided to withdraw all the Marines. The terrorists had achieved their goal.

TWA Hijacking and Hostage Situation (1985)

Nothing seemed out of the ordinary for the eight crew members and the 145 passengers when TWA Flight 847 took off on June 6, 1985, from the airport in Athens, Greece. But once in the air, two heavily armed members of the Lebanese Hezbollah hijacked the Boeing 727, forcing the pilot to fly to Beirut and not, as scheduled, to Rome, Italy. En route, the hijackers brutally beat a young Navy diver, Robert Stethem, and searched for passengers with Israeli passports or Jewish names. After refueling in Beirut, the terrorists ordered the pilot to fly to Algiers, where some women and children were released, then return to Beirut airport, where they killed Stethem and dumped his body on the tarmac before ordering yet another stop in Algiers and a third flight to Beirut. Eventually, Nabih Berri, a lawyer, negotiated on behalf of the hijackers, who demanded the release of hundreds of Shi'ites from Israeli prisons. Seventeen days after the ordeal began and after intensive negotiations involving Berri, the United States, the Israeli government, the Red Cross, and, of course, the terrorists, the hostages were released—with the understanding that Israel would free the prisoners. Behind the scenes, the Reagan administration had pressed Israel to agree to this solution and violate its declared policy of making no concessions to terrorists.

The Achille Lauro Seizure (1985)

In April 2003, following the defeat of Saddam Hussein's Iraqi regime, members of the U.S. Special Operations Forces captured Muhammad Abbas—better known by his *nom de guerre* Abu Abbas, one of the more notorious terrorist leaders of the 1970s and 1980s—outside of Baghdad. Nearly 18 years earlier, Abbas had masterminded, and four members of the Palestine Liberation Front (PLF) had carried out, one of the most brutal acts of terrorism. The ordeal began on October 7, 1985, when four heavily armed Palestinian men, seemingly passengers, seized the Italian cruise ship *Achille Lauro* off the Egyptian coast.[2] They demanded the release of 50 of their comrades from Israeli prisons. Because some 750 travelers had gone ashore at Alexandria for an excursion earlier in the day, less than 100 passengers and 344 crew members were aboard at the time. Singling out Americans and Jews, the Palestinians terrorized their hostages relentlessly. In an unspeakably cruel act, one of the terrorists killed 69-year-old Leon Klinghoffer, a New Yorker, who was partially paralyzed and confined to a wheelchair. After one of the terrorists shot Klinghoffer in the head and chest, he forced members of the crew to throw the body overboard. Soon thereafter, Egyptian officials convinced the terrorists to surrender by promising them free passage to a destination of their choice.

However, U.S. fighter planes intercepted the Egyptian airliner that carried Abu Abbas, one of his aides, and the four *Achille Lauro* hijackers, forcing the intercepted plane to land at a NATO base in Sigonella, Italy. There, Italian troops prevented U.S. Special Operation Forces from apprehending the Palestinians. Instead, the Italians took the four *Achille Lauro* terrorists into custody and allowed Abbas and his aide to leave the country. Pressured by the Reagan administration, Italy tried Abbas in 1986 *in absentia* and sentenced him to life in prison.

The Lebanon Hostages (1982–91)

Foreigners were kidnapped in and around Beirut throughout the 1980s by members of radical Shi'ite groups that had close ties to Iran. Various groups claimed responsibility, but it was widely assumed that Hezbollah was behind most of these hostage-takings. Starting with the kidnapping of David Dodge, acting president of the American University of Beirut, a total of 17 American men were held hostage by these circles. Of these hostages, three were killed brutally: William Buckley, the CIA station chief in Beirut; Peter Kilburn, a librarian at the American University of Beirut;

and Marine Lieutenant Colonel William Higgins. One of the hostages was able to escape; the others were held under gruesome conditions for various lengths of time. When one or another captive was released, others were grabbed. Terry Anderson, an Associated Press correspondent, was by far the longest held of the "Lebanon hostages," spending 2,454 days (or close to seven years) in captivity.

The motives were not always clear. For example, at times the captors demanded the release of prisoners from Kuwait, Israel, and Germany; on other occasions, they seemed driven by the desire to gain publicity and attention at home and abroad. As the result of an arms-for-hostages deal between the Reagan administration and the Iranian government, several of the long-term U.S. hostages were released, but they were quickly replaced by others. The secret transactions between the White House and Iranian officials were a blatant violation of the official policy that President Reagan and his administration claimed to support, namely, not to give in to the demands of terrorists and not to make deals with terrorists.

The captives, among them Anderson, were finally freed in late 1991 after lengthy negotiations involving Iranian, Israeli, American, and United Nations officials. Although no side admitted to a quid pro quo, the Iranian authorities reportedly paid the hostage-holders between $1 and $2 million for each of the Western hostages released after July 1991.

The Bombing of Pan Am Flight 103 (1988)

On December 21, 1988, Pan Am Flight 103, which had originated in Frankfurt, Germany, was en route to New York after a stopover at Heathrow Airport when it was blown out of the sky over Lockerbie, Scotland. All 259 persons aboard, among them 35 undergraduate students at Syracuse University, and 11 persons on the ground were killed. Had it not been for a delay at Heathrow, the explosion would have occurred over the Atlantic and its cause never been resolved. But with evidence on the ground in hand, the British authorities established that a small sheet of plastic explosives had been hidden in a radio cassette player inside a suitcase. Early on, there was the suspicion that the bombing was meant to avenge the accidental destruction of an Iranian civil airliner over the Persian Gulf by the USS *Vincennes* and that the Iranians had contracted with terrorists to do their dirty work. Bombing devices similar to the one used to destroy the Pan Am airliner were found in the possession of members of the Popular Front for the Liberation of Palestine–General Command (PFLP–GC) in Germany, but two Libyan agents were eventually identified as the perpetrators. This led to the suspicion that the downing of Pan Am Flight 103 was Libya's belated revenge for the 1986 bombing of Tripoli and Benghazi by the United

States. It took years of sanctions by the United States and the United Nations and sustained pressure by the families of the Pan Am 103 victims before Libya's ruler, Muammar Gaddafi, handed over the two agents, Abdelbaset al-Megrahi and Al Amin Fhima, to the Netherlands in 1999, where they were tried by a Scottish court. In early 2001, al-Megrahi was found guilty and sentenced to a minimum of 20 years in prison, and Fhima was found not guilty and released.

The First World Trade Center Bombing (1993)

The first bombing of the World Trade Center (WTC) in New York on February 26, 1993, marked the beginning of a new chapter in the history of anti-American terrorism. While the destruction of Pan Am Flight 103 in 1988 could be understood as a precursor to the catastrophic terrorism of the 1990s and thereafter, the 1993 bombing of the building in downtown Manhattan was the first major act of international terrorism inside the United States. Although the blast of more than 1,000 pounds of explosives in the parking garage beneath the Wall Street area's signature building did not, as the perpetrators had planned, topple at least one of the 110-story twin towers, its effects were far-reaching and transcended the immediate costs—six persons killed, more than 1,000 injured, and massive damage to the WTC. The most severe consequences were to the American psyche, in that the "explosion in the bowels of the World Trade Center's twin towers dispelled for ever the myth that terrorists are simply not able to stage their violent spectaculars inside the United States."[3] The "Liberation Army Fifth Battalion" claimed responsibility for the bombing and warned that more targets inside the United States, among them nuclear facilities, would be attacked. Demanding that the United States sever its diplomatic ties to Israel and change its Middle East policy, the terrorists justified their deed in writing: "The American people must know that their civilians who got killed [in the WTC blast] are not better than those who are getting killed by American weapons and support."[4]

Several of the conspirators involved in the elaborate planning and execution of the WTC bombing were non-Afghan veterans of the fight against the Soviet invaders in Afghanistan, and in that role had received significant American support. But after the Soviet military was out of Afghanistan and no more assistance was forthcoming from the United States, these displaced mujahideen (holy warriors) had turned against their onetime American benefactor. Those who had settled in the New York and New Jersey area were followers of Sheik Omar Abdel-Rahman, an anti-Western, anti-American, Muslim preacher. Before coming to the United States in the beginning of the 1990s, Sheik Abdel-Rahman was the leader of the extremist Islamic Group in Egypt and was allegedly involved in the assassination of Anwar Sadat, Egypt's president. Sheik Abdel-Rahman and four other men were accused of having plotted the WTC bombing in 1993, found guilty, and sentenced to lifelong prison terms.

The mastermind of this bombing, Ramzi Ahmed Yousef, was arrested in Pakistan and extradited to the United States in 1995. FBI investigators traced an early, if indirect, link between Yousef and Osama bin Laden. In 1997, Yousef was found guilty by a jury in New York and sentenced to 240 years in prison.

The Oklahoma City Bombing (1995)

Shortly after 9:00 a.m. on April 19, 1995, a powerful truck bomb explosion destroyed the Alfred P. Murrah Federal Building in downtown Oklahoma City. One hundred and sixty-eight persons, among them 19 children who had attended a daycare center in the office building, were killed, and hundreds were injured. As the architect of the devastating terror who had personally ignited the bomb, Timothy McVeigh, a veteran of the Persian Gulf War, was eventually tried, convicted, and sentenced to death. His accomplice, Terry Nichols, was also brought to justice. By striking on the second anniversary of the FBI's ill-fated raid on the Branch Davidian sect's compound in Waco, Texas, during which sect leader David Koresh and 80 of his followers died, the perpetrators revealed their roots in the radical-right milieu whose hatred of the federal government had been fueled by deadly encounters between, on the one hand, federal law enforcement agents and, on the other, individuals such as survivalist and White Supremacist Randy Weaver and groups such as the Branch Davidian sect.

As soon as McVeigh was identified as a suspect, the media reported on his links to the extreme right, his visit to the site of the Branch Davidians' compound in Waco, and how this experience had magnified his hate of the federal government. The news revisited another incident that had intensified the antigovernment sentiments in the militia, patriot, and White Supremacist movements: The deadly encounter between Randy Weaver and federal agents at Ruby Ridge, Idaho, in 1992, during which Weaver's wife and son and a deputy U.S. marshal were killed. Both incidents were on McVeigh's mind when he planned his act of terrorism.

McVeigh died with the conviction that the "statement" he had made by bombing the federal building in Oklahoma City was not simply heard around the world but was also heard by the federal government and federal law enforcement agencies in particular. He believed that the FBI and other agencies altered their rules of engagement during standoff situations similar to those at Waco and Ruby Ridge and, more importantly, that these changes were the direct result of his terrorist act.[5]

The Khobar Towers Attacks (1996)

On June 25, 1996, a potent truck bomb was exploded outside the U.S. military's Khobar Towers housing area in Dhahran, Saudi Arabia, killing 19 Americans and injuring 515 other persons, among them 240 U.S. citizens. The Dhahran facility housed at the time more than 3,000 members of the military involved in enforcing the no-fly zone over Iraq. Several groups claimed responsibility for the attack, but U.S. authorities were convinced that Iran had sponsored the perpetrators. It took five years before the United States indicted 13 Saudis and one Lebanese for the bombing.

The Bombings of U.S. Embassies in Kenya and Tanzania (1998)

On August 7, 1998, two suicide bombers drove their explosive-laden cars close to the U.S. embassies in Nairobi, Kenya, and Dar es Salaam, Tanzania, before igniting their powerful bombs. The explosions killed 291 persons and injured more than 5,000 in Nairobi; an additional ten persons were killed and 77 wounded in Dar es Salaam. The attacks were directed against U.S. facilities, but most of the casualties were Kenyans and Tanzanians. A group calling itself the Islamic Army for the Liberation of Holy Places claimed responsibility for the near-simultaneous blasts, but U.S. investigators suspected immediately that bin Laden's Al Qaeda organization was responsible. In response, President Bill Clinton ordered missile strikes against Al Qaeda training camps in Afghanistan and a pharmaceutical plant in Sudan that the U.S. administration described as a chemical weapons-related facility. Bin Laden and his associates had lived in Sudan before they moved on to Afghanistan.

Within the next few months, the U.S. District Court for the Southern District of New York indicted a dozen individuals, among them Osama bin Laden, his chief of military operations, Muhammad Atef, and several members of Al Qaeda in the two east African bombings. According to the Department of State, "At the end of 2000, one suspect had pled guilty to conspiring in the attacks, five were in custody in New York awaiting trial, three were in the United Kingdom pending extradition to the United States, and 13 were fugitives, including Usama Bin Laden."[6]

The Bombing of the USS Cole (2000)

On October 12, 2000, the crew of the USS *Cole* readied the mighty U.S. Navy destroyer to be docked and refueled in the Yemeni port of Aden, when a small boat with two men aboard moved straight toward the *Cole*'s hull and exploded in a powerful blast. Seventeen sailors were killed, 39 others were injured, and the ship was severely damaged.

The suicide bombing was a stunning terrorist act and a success, in that a small fiberglass boat with some hundred pounds of explosives had taken on the most powerful of the United States' warships outfitted with an arsenal of guided missiles and a sophisticated radar system. The pictures of the massive hole in the *Cole*'s hull and of the crew's desperate and ultimately successful fight to prevent their ship from sinking "added up to a stunning David and Goliath metaphor: A powerful symbol of the world's most formidable military superpower was incapacitated by members and/or agents of a comparatively weak group unable to fight the mighty United States in open warfare."[7]

Because of the boldness of the attack and bin Laden's family roots in Yemen, law enforcement authorities in Yemen and in the United States suspected immediately that Al Qaeda was behind the attack. Two suspects with alleged ties to the terrorist organization were arrested and jailed in Yemen, but more than two years after the attack the two men and eight other suspected followers of bin Laden managed to escape from prison. The following month, federal prosecutors in the United States indicted Jamal Ahmed al-Badawi and Fahd al-Quso for planning the terrorist strike against the *Cole*. According to the indictment, the men had been recruited by Al Qaeda, had attended training camps in Afghanistan, and had planned an earlier attack on another Navy destroyer, the *Sullivan*, that "was called off when their boat sank under the weight of its own explosives."[8]

The Attacks of 9/11 (2001)

On September 11, 2001, after a long period of elaborate preparations abroad and inside the United States, 19 male members of the Al Qaeda network set in motion what up to then seemed an unthinkable terrorist attack inside the United States. Hijacking nearly simultaneously four airliners shortly after takeoff from airports on the east coast by attacking crew members and passengers with box cutters and knives, the terrorists took command of the planes in order to fly them into predetermined buildings. The chain of events unfolded as follows:

1   Five of the terrorists hijacked American Airlines Flight 11 that departed Boston at 7:45 a.m. for a flight to Los Angeles. One hour later, the terrorists piloted the machine into the North Tower of the WTC in New York.

2   Five of the terrorists hijacked United Airlines Flight 175, also taking off from Boston and bound for Los Angeles, at 7:58 a.m. An hour and seven minutes later, the aircraft was flown deliberately into the South Tower of the WTC. When the two buildings collapsed soon thereafter, more than 2,800 persons, among them hundreds of

firefighters and police officers, were killed, and many others were injured.[9]

3   Four terrorists took control of United Airlines Flight 93 after it left Newark at 8:01 a.m. on its scheduled trip to San Francisco. When passengers learned from cellular phone conversations with members of their families that two hijacked planes had been flown into the WTC towers, they decided to fight the hijackers. Two hours after takeoff, Flight 93 crashed in Pennsylvania's Stony Creek Township. It is believed that the terrorists intended to fly the plane into a building in Washington, DC, most likely the Capitol, and that the courageous action by passengers foiled this plan.

4   Five terrorists took control of American Airlines Flight 77 after it had departed Dulles Airport, Washington, DC, at 8:10 a.m. en route to San Francisco. Twenty-nine minutes later, the aircraft was crashed into the Pentagon in Arlington, Virginia, just outside of the U.S. capital, killing 189 persons, injuring others, and destroying part of the building.[10]

International terrorism against Americans had frequently shocked and intimidated the U.S. public and preoccupied several U.S. presidents during the closing decades of the twentieth century. But the events of 9/11 convinced American leaders and the American public that international terrorism represented the number-one threat to their national security and national interest. Based on his pre- and post-9/11 communications, this was precisely the reaction that Osama bin Laden and his brain trust had intended and anticipated. The Al Qaeda leader hoped to shock the United States into a state of mind that would assure that its decision-makers would overreact in both domestic and foreign policies.

Fort Hood Massacre (2009)

On November 5, 2009, U.S. Army Major Nidal Hasan carried out a mass shooting at Fort Hood, Texas, killing thirteen and wounding 28 others. Hasan, a Muslim, was to be deployed in Afghanistan later that month. He had been in contact with Anwar al-Awlaki, a Yemeni-American imam who encouraged his followers to kill American soldiers and civilians.

Wisconsin Sikh Temple Shooting (2012)

On August 5, 2012, six persons were killed and three others injured at a Sikh temple in Oak Creek, Wisconsin, by 40-year-old Wade Michael Page, a White Supremacist, who wrongly assumed that Sikhs were Muslims. After being shot by police, Page killed himself.

Boston Marathon Bombings (2013)

On April 15, 2013, three persons were killed and close to 200 injured, when two homemade pressure cooker bombs were detonated within seconds of each other near the finish line of the Boston Marathon. As they fled the scene with the plan to drive to New York for additional attacks, the brothers Tamerlan and Dzhokhar Tsarnaev killed a police officer on the MIT campus and injured a Boston transit police officer critically. While Tamerlan was killed in a shoot-out with police, his younger brother was captured, tried, and sentenced to death.

Charleston Church Shooting (2015)

On June 17, 2015, nine persons were killed and another one seriously injured by 21-year-old White Supremacist Dylann Roof at the end of a Bible study gathering at the Emanuel African Methodist Episcopalian Church in Charleston, South Carolina. Roof, who confessed to the shooting, had posted a manifesto online that revealed his racist attitudes toward African Americans.

Chattanooga Attack on Military Targets (2015)

On July 16, 2015, 25-year-old Muhammad Youssef Abdulazeez opened fire first on a military recruiting center and then on a Naval Reserve training center. Five Marines were killed and a local police officer seriously injured. The perpetrator was also killed during a gunfight with police. Reportedly, hours before his shooting spree, Abdulazeez texted the following Islamic verse to a friend: "Whosoever shows enmity to a friend of mine, then I have declared war against him."

Deadly Attack against Planned Parenthood Clinic (2015)

On November 27, 2015, Robert Lewis Dear, Jr., an antiabortion extremist who called himself "a warrior for the babies" shot his way into a Planned Parenthood facility in Colorado Springs killing three persons and five police officers and four civilians. After a five-hour stand-off, police smashed an armored car into the building, forcing the shooter to surrender.

San Bernardino Mass Shooting (2015)

On December 2, 2015, a married couple targeted an early Christmas party of San Bernardino County's Department of Health employees for a deadly mass shooting that killed 14 persons and injured seriously

22 others. Syed Rizwan Farook and Tashfeen Malik fled the scene in their SUV but were eventually intercepted by police and killed during a shoot-out. FBI investigators found evidence that the shooters had embraced violent extremism and what they perceived as martyrdom via jihad.

Orlando Nightclub Shooting: Most Lethal Attack since 9/11 (2016)

On June 12, 2016, Omar Mateen, a 29-year-old security guard, entered a gay nightclub in Orlando and in the following three hours carried out the most lethal terrorist attack since 9/11, shooting to death 49 persons and injuring 43 other club patrons. Since the "Pulse" nightclub staged a "Latin Night" on that date, most of the victims were Latinos from the greater Orlando area. Mateen was eventually shot by officers of the Orlando Police Department. During the ordeal, Mateen dialed the 9-1-1 police emergency number to explain his motives. According to the police, the shooter identified as a follower of ISIS leader Abu Bakr al-Baghdadi, explained his violence as a response to U.S. actions in Iraq and Syria, and demanded an end to U.S. military actions in those countries.

Vehicular Terrorism on Halloween (2017)

On October 31, Halloween Day, 29-year-old Sayfullo Saipov, an immigrant from Uzbekistan, drove a rented truck into runners and cyclists in Hudson River Park in Lower Manhattan killing eight persons and injuring eleven more. After the truck collided with a school bus Saipov left the vehicle wielding guns toward one policeman who shot and arrested him. As it turned out, the weapons were a paintball and a pellet gun. The Islamic State flag found in the truck along with documents revealed the attacker's allegiance to ISIS.

Mass Shooting in Pittsburgh Synagogue (2018)

On October 27, 2018, White Nationalist Robert Bowers (46) entered the Pittsburgh Tree of Life synagogue with an assault rifle and three handguns. He immediately began shooting parishioners who had gathered for Saturday morning service. Eleven people were killed and six were injured. The sole suspect was arrested and charged with 29 federal crimes and 36 state crimes. He had a history of posting hateful anti-Semitic and anti-immigrant messages on social media frequented by White Nationalists. As he received medical treatment Bowers told a SWAT officer that "all these Jews have to die."

Shoppers Gunned Down in El Paso

August 3, 2019: A 21-year-old man entered a Walmart supermarket in El Paso, Texas, and shot into a crowd of mostly Latino shoppers. When Patrick Crusius left the store, 23 of his victims were dead and another 23 were injured. In his so-called manifest, Crusius claimed that he was inspired by the White Supremacist who killed 51 Muslim worshippers in the Christchurch, New Zealand, four months earlier.

Deadly Shooting at Pensacola Air Station (2019)

December 6, 2019. On a seemingly quiet Friday, a 21-year-old Saudi Air Force Second Lieutenant opened fire on U.S. Navy sailors in a classroom building at the Pensacola Air Station in Florida. Mohammed Saeed Alshamrani killed three and injured eight U.S. servicemen with whom he had trained. During the attack, Alshamrani expressed opposition to American military actions abroad. Al-Qaeda in the Arabian Peninsula claimed responsibility for the attack.

White Supremacist Targeted Black Shoppers

May 14, 2022: 18-year-old Payton Gendon targeted Black shoppers in a supermarket in the East Side neighborhood of Buffalo, N.Y., killing ten and injuring three more. The recent high school graduate posted a "manifesto" online in which he identified himself as a "white nationalist" and avenger of "white genocide." Like the El Paso terrorist, Gendon mentioned White Supremacism's "great replacement" theory

A Few Notable Incidents Abroad

March 20, 1995: Twelve persons were killed and 5,700 were injured as a result of a sarin nerve gas attack in a crowded subway station in the heart of Tokyo, Japan. Nearly simultaneously, a similar release of nerve gas occurred in the subway system of Yokohama. The Aum Shinrikyo sect was blamed for the attack and its leader brought to justice. The same cult was responsible for another nerve gas attack in the Japanese city of Matsumoto the previous June. In this case, seven persons died and 150 fell sick. The lethal incident in Tokyo's subway alarmed people around the world and magnified the fear that terrorists would increasingly resort to biological, chemical, and even nuclear weapons of mass destruction.

October 12, 2002: A mighty truck bomb exploded in a popular section of Bali, Indonesia, in the midst of popular nightclubs, cafes, and bars that were mostly frequented by foreign tourists. Two hundred persons from more than 20 countries were killed, most of them Australians. Seven Americans died in the blast, which was perpetrated by terrorists with ties to the extremist Jemaah Islamic group and to Al Qaeda. Terrorism experts suspected that the perpetrators intended to harm Westerners and particularly Americans.

March 11, 2004: Within 15 minutes and at the height of the morning rush hour, a total of at least eight backpack bombs exploded first on a commuter train inside Madrid's Atocha station, then on a crowded commuter train entering the station, and finally on a third train entering the Santa Eugenia station about nine miles from Atocha. One hundred and ninety-one persons were killed and 1,500 were injured. Although the unknown Al-Quds al-Arabia group claimed responsibility for the attacks as punishment for Spain's participation in the "crusade alliance" in Iraq, Spanish officials were quick to name the Basque separatist group ETA as the primary suspect. Three days after the carnage in Madrid, José Luis Rodríguez Zapatero and his Socialist Party defeated Prime Minister José María Aznar and his conservative Popular Party. Aznar, a staunch supporter of the U.S.-led war against Iraq, had contributed 1,300 Spanish troops to the invasion forces.

September 1–3, 2004: A large group of heavily armed Chechen extremists took over a school in Beslan in south Russia and held more than 1,200 children, parents, and teachers hostage. On day three of the incident, the captors detonated explosives that they had rigged around the interior of the school—especially the gym, where many of the hostages were held. At least 330 hostages, about half of them children, were killed, and many more were injured.

July 7, 2005: Four nearly simultaneous suicide attacks on the London transit system killed 56 victims and injured over 700. Three of the bombs exploded in underground trains and the fourth in a double-decker bus. Two weeks later, another quadruple attack on a bus and three underground trains was unsuccessful when the bombs failed to detonate. In both cases, Muslims who were British citizens or residents were identified as the terrorists or would-be terrorists.

July 23, 2005: Several car bombs exploded at tourist hotels in Sharm el-Sheikh in Egypt, killing 88 and wounding more than 100 persons.

November 9, 2005: Three explosions in three hotels in Amman, Jordan, killed 60 persons and injured more than 100. Within days, Jordanian authorities identified the three suicide bombers and connected them to an Al Qaeda-affiliated group led by Abu Musab al-Zarqawi who was also responsible for many terrorist attacks in post-invasion Iraq.

November 26–29, 2008: Ten heavily armed terrorists opened fire on civilians in ten different sites in Mumbai, India, and eventually held hostages in two hotels and one Jewish community center. When Indian security forces gained control, 173 persons were dead, five Americans among them, and hundreds were injured. All but one of the terrorists were killed in the incident that according to Indian authorities was planned, directed, and carried out by members of the Pakistani terrorist

424 *Appendix: Major Terrorist Incidents since the Late 1970s*

organization Lashkar-e-Taiba.

July 22, 2011: Thirty-two-year-old Anders Behring Breivik, an extreme Euro-nativist, set off a car bomb near government buildings in Oslo, Norway, killing eight people. He then made his way to the island of Utoya, where he shot and killed 69 young persons who were participating in a youth camp organized by the Workers' Youth League. Before he perpetrated his terrorist deeds, he posted a manifesto online that explained his Euro-centrist, anti-Muslim ideas.

January 7, 2015: Said and Chérif Kouachi, two brothers, shot their way into the offices of the French satirical weekly *Charlie Hebdo* in Paris, France, killing eleven staffers and injuring eleven others. As they fled the scene, they killed a police officer. Before they died in a shoot-out with police, they revealed that they acted on behalf of Al Qaeda in the Arabian Peninsula in revenge for the magazine's publishing of cartoons depicting the Prophet Muhammad.

October 31, 2015: A Russian charter flight carrying 217 passengers and seven crew members from the Red Sea resort of Sharm el-Sheikh, Egypt, to St. Petersburg crashed shortly after taking off, killing everyone on board. Shortly after the incident, ISIS's Sinai branch claimed responsibility for what Russian and Egyptian authorities eventually identified as an explosion caused by a potent explosive device smuggled onto the plane.

November 13, 2015: In a horrific six-stop killing spree in Paris a team of ISIS-affiliated jihadis took the lives of 130 civilians and injured hundreds more. It was the most deadly terrorist attack in French history. Among the locations targeted were a music hall, a sports stadium and several bar and restaurant terraces. Ninety persons were shot to death during a siege at an "Eagles of Death Metal" concert inside the Bataclan. Police actions prevented follow-up strikes plotted for the following days.

July 14, 2016: As a jolly crowd celebrated Bastille Day on the Promenade de Anglais in Nice, France, Mohamed Lahouaiej-Bouhlel drove his truck deliberately into the people killing 86 and injuring several hundred more. According to an ISIS statement the Tunisian perpetrator, who was shot and killed by police, acted on behalf of the organization.

May 22, 2017: As thousands of fans were leaving Manchester Arena after a concert with U.S. pop star Ariana Grande, 22-year-old suicide bomber Salman Abedi detonated his homemade explosive device killing 22 persons and injuring more than 50. While ISIS claimed responsibility for the attack there was no evidence of direct ties between Abedi and the terrorist organization.

June 3, 2017: After driving their van intentionally into pedestrians on London Bridge the three occupants ran to the Borough Market area stabbing people inside and outside restaurants and bars. Eight persons were killed and 48 injured. The three jihadis were eventually shot dead by police.

August 17, 2017: In a seemingly lone wolf attack 22-year-old Younes Abouyaaqoub drove a van into pedestrians in a popular tourist area of Barcelona, Spain. Thirteen persons were killed and more than a hundred injured. As the attacker fled on foot he killed another person in order to get control over the victim's car. Several hours later, five men drove a car into pedestrians in the town of Cambrils causing the death of one person and injuring six others. The six perpetrators were eventually killed in shoot-outs with police as were two additional members of what police said was a 12-man Jihadi terrorist cell; the other four members were arrested.

March 15, 2019: A lone gunman entered two mosques in Christchurch, New Zealand, gunning down worshipping men, women, and children. Brenton Tarrant killed 51 and injured another 40 peaceful worshippers because of their religious beliefs and race. The White Supremacist revealed his motives in a manifesto titled "The Great Replacement" that became a blueprint for subsequent violence carried out by White Supremacists in Europe and the United States.

April, 21, 2019. On Easter Sunday, eight suicide bombers detonated explosives in three churches during Easter services and three luxury hotels full of tourists in a coordinated terrorist attack. In total, 269 persons were killed and about 500 injured. The attack was allegedly in retaliation for the Christchurch killings of Muslim worshippers. The eight perpetrators were killed. ISIS claimed responsibility for the attack but it was not confirmed that the Sri Lankan jihadis were ISIS fighters as the leader of the Islamic State, Abu Bakr al-Baghdadi claimed.

August 26, 2021. During the chaotic mass evacuation from Afghanistan, a suicide terrorist detonated his explosive belt in a crowd of people gathered at Hamid Karzai International Airport. Immediately thereafter several ISIS-Khorasan Province fighters opened fire into the crowd; U.S. troops responded by trying to shoot the gunmen. A total of 183 persons were killed, most of them Afghans but among the fatalities were also 13 U.S. military members. The U.S. military did not deny that some people may have been accidentally killed by U.S. troops responding to the terrorist attack.

The "Forgotten" Most Lethal Terrorist Attacks Abroad

On October 14, 2017, a truck bombing killed 512 and injured more than 300 additional persons in Somalia's capital Mogadishu. The potent bomb was detonated when the truck was stopped at a checkpoint.

(Continued)

(Continued)

According to the authorities, the real target of the attack directed by the terrorist group Al-Shabaab was a compound that houses international peacekeepers and agencies.

On November 24, 2017, several dozen men, some of them carrying an Islamic State flag, detonated a massive bomb in a mosque in North Sinai, Egypt, and gunned down fleeing worshipers; 311 persons were killed and more than 100 injured. According to some reports the attack was in response to mosque leaders' cooperation with Egyptian security forces involved in fighting ISIS's affiliate in the Sinai.

While these two incidents were the most lethal of 2017, hundreds of other terrorist attacks in Africa, the Middle East, South Asia, and other regions with Muslim majorities or sizable Muslim minorities killed and maimed tens of thousands in 2017 alone. To list all of these cases for the last several decades would fill a book.

I decided to focus in this appendix on summarizing major incidents directed against Americans at home or abroad and notable attacks overseas mostly against Westerners because these receive the greatest attention from the media, the public, and governments and thus figure most prominently in counterterrorist reactions and policies.

Notes

1 David C. Martin and John Walcott, *Best Laid Plans: The Inside Story of America's War on Terrorism* (New York: Harper & Row, 1988), 105.
2 Originally, the quartet planned to take hostages once the ship reached one of the ports-of-call—Ashodod, Israel. But when a member of the crew happened upon the Palestinians as they cleaned their weapons in their cabin, they changed their plan and acted immediately.
3 Brigitte L. Nacos, *Terrorism and the Media: From the Iran Hostage Crisis to the Oklahoma City Bombing* (New York: Columbia University Press, 1996), 2.
4 Alison Mitchell, "Letter Explained Motive in Bombing, Officials Now Say," *New York Times*, March 28, 1993, 1.
5 Lou Michel and Dan Herbeck, *American Terrorist: Timothy McVeigh & the Oklahoma City Bombing* (New York: Regan Books, 2001), 378–9.
6 U.S. Department of State, "Patterns of Global Terrorism 2000," Released April 30, 2001, www.state.gov/j/ct/rls/crt/2000/, accessed December 5, 2018.
7 Brigitte L. Nacos, *Mass-Mediated Terrorism: The Central Role of the Media in Terrorism and Counterterrorism* (Lanham, MD: Rowman & Littlefield, 2002), 7.
8 Eric Lichtblau, "Aftereffects: The Cole Bombing; U.S. Indicts 2 Men for Attack on American Ship in Yemen," *New York Times*, May 16, 2003, A17.

9 Nearly a year after 9/11, the official number of victims killed in the WTC stood at 8,823. As of August 2002, 2,726 death certificates related to the WTC attack had been filed, according to the Centers for Disease Control and Prevention and "Mortality Weekly Report," September 11, 2002, no. 51 (special issue), 16–18, www.cdc.gov/mmwr/preview/mmwrhtml/mm51SPa6. htm.
10 The timeline of the events on 9/11 is described in "September 11 and Review of Terrorism 2001," in U.S. Department of State, "Patterns of Global Terrorism, 2001," 1. See also Nacos, *Mass-Mediated Terrorism*, ch. 2.

Bibliography

Abrahams, Max. "Why Terrorism Does Not Work." *International Security* 31:2 (Fall 2006): 42–78.

Acharya, Amrit P., and Arabinda Acharya. "Cyberterrorism and Biotechnology." *Foreign Affairs*, June 1, 2017; https://www.foreignaffairs.com/articles/world/2017-06-01/cyberterrorism-and-biotechnology, accessed June 6, 2018.

Adams, James. "Virtual Defense." *Foreign Affairs* 80:3 (May–June 2001): 98–112.

Adams, William C., ed. *Television Coverage of the Middle East*. Norwood, NJ: Ablex, 1981.

Adler, Freda. *Sisters in Crime*. New York: Waveland Press, 1975.

Alali, A. Odasuo, and Kenoye Kelvin Eke, eds. *Media Coverage of Terrorism: Methods of Diffusion*. Newbury Park, CA: Sage, 1991.

Allison, Graham T., Owen R. Coté, Steven E. Miller, and Richard A. Falkenrath. *Avoiding Nuclear Anarchy*. Cambridge, MA: MIT Press, 1996.

Altheide, David L. "Three-in-One News: Network Coverage of Iran." *Journalism Quarterly* 59 (1982): 482–6.

Altheide, David L. "Format and Symbols in TV Coverage of Terrorism in the United States and Great Britain." *International Studies Quarterly* 31 (1987): 161–76.

Arquilla, John, and Theodore Karasik. "Chechnya: A Glimpse of Future Conflict?" *Studies in Conflict and Terrorism* 22 (1999): 207–29.

Arquilla, John, and David Ronfeldt. "The Advent of Netwar: Analytical Background." *Studies in Conflict and Terrorism* 22 (1999): 193–206.

Ash, Timothy Garton. "Is There a Good Terrorist?" *New York Review of Books*, November 29, 2001; www.nybooks.com/articles/14860, accessed April 2, 2002.

Atta, Dale Van. "Carbombs and Cameras: The Need for Responsible Media Coverage of Terrorism." *Harvard International Review* (Fall 1998): 66–70.

Avrich, Paul. *Sacco and Vanzetti: The Anarchist Background*. Princeton, NJ: Princeton University Press, 1991

Bach Jensen, Richard. "The United States, International Policing and the War against Anarchist Terrorism, 1900–1914." *Terrorism and Political Violence* 13:1 (Spring 2001): 15–46.

Bacevich, Andrew J. "Rescinding the Bush Doctrine." *Boston Globe*, March 1, 2007.

Bagdikian, Benjamin. *The Media Monopoly*, 6th ed. Boston: Beacon Press, 2000.

Barber, Benjamin R. *Jihad vs. McWorld*. New York: Ballantine Books, 1996.

Barnosky, Jason. "Fusion Centers: What's Working and What Isn't?" *Brookings*, March 2015; www.brookings.edu/blog/fixgov/2015/03/17/fusion-centers-whats-working-and-what-isnt/, accessed May 30, 2018.

Baudrillard, Jean. *The Transparency of Evil*. London: Verso, 1993.

Beirich, Heidi, "Midwifing the Militias." *Southern Poverty Law Center's Intelligence Report*, Spring 2010; https://www.splcenter.org/fighting-hate/intelligence-report/2010/midwifing-militias, accessed June 1, 2010.

Bennett, Lance W. *News: The Politics of Illusion*. New York: Longman, 2001.

Bennett, Lance W., and David L. Paletz, eds. *Taken by Storm: The Media, Public Opinion, and U.S. Foreign Policy in the Gulf War*. Chicago, IL: University of Chicago Press, 1994.

Bergen, Peter. "The Bin Laden Trial: What Did We Learn?" *Studies in Conflict and Terrorism* 24:6 (2001): 429–34.

Berkel, Kelly A., "A Criminological Approach to Preventing Terrorism: Situational Crime Prevention and the Crime Prevention Literature," in Alex P. Schmid, ed., *Handbook of Terrorism Prevention and Preparedness*. The Hague: ICCT Press Publication, 2021. https://icct.nl/app/uploads/2021/10/V10.4-Handbook-ONLINE.pdf, accessed August 20, 2022.

Berman, Mark. "Was the Charlottesville Car Attack Domestic Terrorism, a Hate Crime or Both?" *Washington Post*, August 14, 2017; https://search.yahoo.com/search?p=stabbing+attack+New+York+city&fr=yfp-t&fp=1&toggle=1&cop=mss&ei=UTF-8, accessed January 15, 2018.

Betts, Richard K. "The Soft Underbelly of American Primacy: Tactical Advantages of Terror," in Demetrios James Caraley, ed., *September 11, Terrorist Attacks, and U.S. Foreign Policy*. New York: Academy of Political Science, 2002.

Bhuiyan, Natascha. "ISIS: The Propaganda Jihad." Unpublished research paper, Columbia University, 2014.

Biddle, Stephen D. "American Grand Strategy After 9/11: An Assessment." https://press.armywarcollege.edu/monographs/752/, 2005.

Bloom, Mia. *Dying to Kill: The Allure of Suicide Terror*. New York: Columbia University Press, 2005.

Bok, Sissela. *Mayhem: Violence as Public Entertainment*. Reading, MA: Perseus Books, 1998.

Borradori, Giovanna. *Philosophy in a Time of Terror: Dialogues with Jürgen Habermas and Jacques Derrida*. Chicago, IL: University of Chicago Press, 2003.

Borum, Randy. *Psychology of Terrorism*. Tampa: University of South Florida, 2004.

Bray, Mark. *ANTIFA: The Anti-Fascist Handbook*. Brooklyn, NY: Melville House, 2017.

Bryant, Jennings, and Dolf Zillmann, eds. *Perspectives on Media Effects*. Hillsdale, NJ: Lawrence Erlbaum, 1986.

Brzezinski, Zbigniew. *Power and Principle*. New York: Farrar, Straus and Giroux, 1983.

Bunker, Robert J. "Weapons of Mass Disruption and Terrorism." *Terrorism and Political Violence* 12:1 (Spring 2000): 37–46.

Burdman, Daphne. "Education, Indoctrination, and Incitement: Palestinian Children on Their Way to Martyrdom." *Terrorism and Political Violence* 15:1 (2003): 96–123.

Burrough, Bryan. "The Bombings of America that We Forgot." *Time*, September 20, 2016.

Brutus. *Foreign Conspiracy against the Liberties of the United States.*" New York: H.A. Chapin & Co, 1841.

Byman, Daniel. *Deadly Connections: States That Sponsor Terrorism.* New York: Cambridge University Press, 2005.

Byman, Daniel. "The Decision to Begin Talks with Terrorists: Lessons for Policymakers." *Studies in Conflict and Terrorism 29:5* (2006): 403–14.

Byman, Daniel. "The Good Enough Doctrine: Learning to Live with Terrorism." *Foreign Affairs 29:5* (September/October 2021): 32–52.

Byman, Daniel. "Should We Treat Domestic Terrorists Like We Treat ISIS?" *Foreign Affairs*, October 3, 2017; https://www.foreignaffairs.com/articles/united-states/2017-10-03/should-we-treat-domestic-terrorists-way-we-treat-isis, accessed August 21, 2022.

Caplan, Bryan. "Terrorism: The Relevance of the Rational Choice Model." *Public Choice 128:1–2* (2006): 91–107.

Catton, William R., Jr. "Militants and the Media: Partners in Terrorism?" *Indiana Law Journal 53* (1978): 703–15.

Celmer, Marc A. *Terrorism, U.S. Strategy, and Reagan Policies.* New York: Greenwood Press, 1987.

Chase, Alston. "Harvard and the Unabomber." *Atlantic Monthly 285:6* (June 2000): 41–65.

Choi, Sang Ok. "Emergency Management: Implications from a Strategic Management Perspective." *Journal of Homeland Security and Emergency Management 5:1* (2008): Article 1, 7.

Chomsky, Noam. *The Culture of Terrorism.* Boston, MA: South End Press, 1988.

Claridge, David. "Exploding the Myth of Superterrorism." *Terrorism and Political Violence 11:4* (Winter 1999): 133–58.

Clarke, Richard A., and Robert K. Knake. *Cyber War: The Next Threat to National Security and What to Do about It.* New York: HarperCollins, 2010.

Cohen, Geoffrey, and Amelia Arsenault. "Moving from Monologue to Dialogue to Collaboration: The Three Layers of Public Diplomacy," in Geoffrey Cohen and Nicholas J. Cull, eds., *Public Diplomacy in a Changing World, Annals of the American Academy of Political and Social Science Series*, Vol. 616. Philadelphia, PA: Sage, March 2008.

Cole, David. "The New America: Little Privacy, Big Terror." *New York Review of Books*, August 13, 2015.

Cole, David, and James X. Dempsey. *Terrorism and the Constitution: Sacrificing Civil Liberties in the Name of National Security.* New York: New Press, 2002.

Collins, Stephen D. "Dissuading State Support of Terrorism: Strikes or Sanctions?" *Studies in Conflict & Terrorism 27:1* (January/February 2004): 1–18.

Cook, Timothy E. "Domesticating a Crisis: Washington Newsbeats and Network News after the Iraqi Invasion of Kuwait," in W. Lance Bennett and David L. Paletz, eds., *Taken by Storm: The Media, Public Opinion, and U.S. Foreign Policy in the Gulf War.* Chicago, IL: University of Chicago Press, 1994.

Cotter, John M. "Sounds of Hate: White Power, Rock and Roll and the Neo-Nazi Skinhead Subculture." *Terrorism and Political Violence 11:2* (1999): 111–40.

Crelinsten, Ronald D. "Television and Terrorism: Implications for Crisis Management and Policy-Making." *Terrorism and Political Violence* 9:4 (1997): 8–32.

Crenshaw, Martha. "The Causes of Terrorism." *Comparative Politics* 13:4 (1981): 379–99.

Crenshaw, Martha, ed. *Terrorism, Legitimacy, and Power: The Consequences of Political Violence*. Middletown, CT: Wesleyan University Press, 1983.

Crenshaw, Martha, ed. *Terrorism in Context*. University Park: Pennsylvania State University Press, 1995.

Crenshaw, Martha. "Why America? The Globalization of Civil War." *Current History 100:650* (December 2001): 425–32.

Crenshaw, Martha. "Terrorism, Strategies, and Grand Strategies," in Audrey Kurth Cronin and James M. Ludes, eds., *Attacking Terrorism: Elements of a Grand Strategy*. Washington, DC: Georgetown University Press, 2004.

Crenshaw, Martha, and John Pimlott, eds. *Encyclopedia of World Terrorism*. Armonk, NY: M. E. Sharpe, 1997.

Croissant, Aurel, and Daniel Barlow. "Following the Money Trail: Terrorist Financing and Government Responses in Southeast Asia." *Studies in Conflict & Terrorism 30* (February 2007): 131–56.

Cunningham, Karla J. "Cross-Regional Trends in Female Terrorism." *Studies in Conflict and Terrorism 26:3* (May–June 2003): 171–95.

Cusick, Suzanne G. "Music Torture/Music as Weapon." *Trans*, 2006, www.sibetrans.com/trans/articulo/152/music-as-torture-, accessed January 18, 2018.

Cutlip, Scott M. "Public Relations and the American Revolution." *Public Relations Review 2:4* (Winter 1976): 11–24.

Czernicki, Candance A. "The Catholic Press Response to Nativism in the 1850s and 1920s." M.A. thesis, Marquette University, 1999, 20–21.

Dahl, Erik J. "Domestic Intelligence Today: More Security but Less Liberty?" *Homeland Security Affairs* 7 (September 2011).

Dahl, Erik J. "The Plots that Failed: Intelligence Lessons Learned from Unsuccessful Terrorist Attacks Against the United States." *Studies in Conflict & Terrorism 34:8* (2011): 621–48.

Dahl, Erik J. "Assessing the Effectiveness of the Department of Homeland Security 20 years after 9/11." Watson Institute at Brown University, November 7, 2021

Dalby, Simon. "Geopolitics, Grand Strategy and the Bush Doctrine." IDSS Discussion Paper, October 2005.

Danitz, Tiffany, and Warren P. Strobel. "The Internet's Impact on Activism: The Case of Burma." *Studies in Conflict and Terrorism* 22 (1999): 257–69.

De Bie, Jasper L., Christianne J. de Poot, and Joanne P. van der Leun. "Shifting Modus Operandi of Jihadist Foreign Fighters from the Netherlands between 2000 and 2013: A Crime Script Analysis." *Terrorism and Political Violence* 27:3 (2015): 416–40.

De Cataldo Neuberger, Luisella, and Tiziana Valentini. *Women and Terrorism*. New York: St. Martin's, 1996.

Deikman, Arthur J. *THEM against US: Cult Thinking and the Terrorist Threat*. Berkeley, CA: Bay Tree Publishing, 2003.

Della Porta, Donatella. *Clandestine Political Violence*. New York: Cambridge University Press, 2013.

Delli Carpini, Michael X., and Bruce A. Williams. "Television and Terrorism: Patterns of Presentation and Occurrence, 1969 to 1980." *Western Political Quarterly 40:1* (1987): 45–64.

Dempsey, James X. "Counterterrorism and the Constitution." *Current History* (April 2000): 164–68.

Dershowitz, Alan M. *Why Terrorism Works: Understanding the Threat, Responding to the Challenge.* New Haven, CT: Yale University Press, 2002.

Dolnik, Adam. "Die and Let Die: Exploring Links between Suicide Terrorism and Terrorist Use of Chemical, Biological, Radiological, and Nuclear Weapons." *Studies in Conflict and Terrorism 26:1* (January–February 2003): 17–35.

Drake, C. J. M. "The Role of Ideology in Terrorists' Target Selection." *Terrorism and Political Violence 10:2* (1998): 53–85.

Durham, Martin. "The American Far Right and 9/11." *Terrorism and Political Violence 15:2* (Summer 2003): 96–111.

Edelman, Murray. *Political Language: Words That Succeed and Policies That Fail.* New York: Academic Press, 1977.

Edelman, Murray. *Constructing the Political Spectacle.* Chicago, IL: University of Chicago Press, 1988.

Egendorf, Laura K., ed. *Terrorism: Opposing Viewpoints.* San Diego, CA: Greenhaven Press, 2000.

Esch, Joanne. "Legitimizing the War on Terror: Political Myth in Official-Level Rhetoric." *Political Psychology 31:3* (2010): 357–91.

Esposito, John L. "Terrorism and the Rise of Political Islam," in Louise Richardson, ed., *The Roots of Terrorism.* New York: Routledge, 2006.

Eubank, William, and Leonard Weinberg. "Terrorism and Democracy: Perpetrators and Victims." *Terrorism and Political Violence 13:1* (2001): 155–64.

Fair, Christine, and Bryan Shephard, "Who Supports Terrorism? Evidence from Fourteen Muslim Countries." *Studies in Conflict and Terrorism 29* (2006): 51–79.

Fanon, Frantz. *The Wretched of the Earth.* New York: Grove Weidenfeld, 1963.

Feaver, Peter D., and Hal Brands. "Trump and Terrorism: U.S. Strategy after ISIS." *Foreign Affairs,* March/April 2017, https://www.foreignaffairs.com/articles/2017-02-13/trump-and-terrorism, accessed May 29, 2018.

Fidas, George C. "The Terrorist Threat: Existential or Exaggerated? A 'Red Cell' Perspective." *International Journal of Intelligence and Counter Intelligence 21* (2008): 519–29.

Finkel, Michael. "The Child Martyrs of Karni Crossing." *New York Times Magazine,* December 24, 2000.

Fitzgerald, James. "Conspiracy, Anxiety, Ontology: Theorising QAnon." *First Monday 27:5* (2022), https://journals.uic.edu/ojs/index.php/fm/article/view/12618/10639, accessed August 10, 2022.

Forest, James J. F. "Criminals and Terrorists: An Introduction to the Special Issue." *Terrorism and Political Violence 24:2* (2012): 171–9.

Forster, Arnold. "Violence on the Fanatical Left and Right." *The ANNALS of the Academy of Political and Social Science 364:1* (2016): 141–8.

Freedman, Lawrence, ed. *Superterrorism: Policy Responses.* Malden, MA: Blackwell Publishing, 2002.

Frenkel, Sheera. "Proud Boys Regroup, Focusing on School Boards and Town Councils." *New York Times*, December 14, 2021, https://www.nytimes.com/2021/12/14/us/proud-boys-local-issues.html, accessed July 4, 2022.

Gaddis, John Lewis. "And Now This: Lessons from the Old Era for the New One," in Strobe Talbot and Nayan Chanda, eds., *The Age of Terror*. New York: Basic Books, 2001.

Gerbner, George, and L. Gross. "Living with Television: The Violence Profile." *Journal of Communication* 26:2 (1976): 173–99.

Gerbner, George et al. "The 'Mainstreaming' of America: Violence Profile No. 11." *Journal of Communication* 30:3 (Summer 1980): 10–29.

Gilboa, Eytan. *Media and Conflict: Framing Issues, Making Policy, Shaping Opinions*. Ardsley Park, NY: Transnational Publishers, 2002.

Gordon, Avishag. "Terrorism on the Internet: Discovering the Unsought." *Terrorism and Political Violence* 9:4 (1997): 159–65.

Gordon, Philip H. "The End of the Bush Revolution." *Foreign Affairs*, July/August 2006.

Graber, Doris. *Mass Media and American Politics*. Washington, DC: Congressional Quarterly Press, 1997.

Graham, Hugh, and Ted Gurr, eds. *Violence in America*. Beverly Hills, CA: Sage, 1979.

Greenberg, Michael D., Peter Chalk, Henry H. Willis, Ivan Khilko, and David S. Ortiz. *Maritime Terrorism: Risk and Liability*. Santa Monica, CA: Rand Corporation, 2006.

Guelke, Adrian. "Wars of Fear: Coming to Grips with Terrorism." *Harvard International Review* 20:4 (Fall 1998): 44–47.

Gunaratna, Rohan. "Central Asian Republics," in Frank Shanty and Raymond Picquet, eds., *Encyclopedia of World Terrorism, 1996–2002*. Armonk, NY: M. E. Sharpe, 2003, 357–61.

Hallin, Daniel L. *The "Uncensored War": The Media and Vietnam*. New York: Oxford University Press, 1986.

Haridasani, Alisha, "For Far-Right Movements. Ashli Babbit Is Now a 'Rallying Cry.'" *New York Times*, January 8, 2021, https://www.nytimes.com/2021/01/08/us/ashli-babbitt-capitol-president-trump.html, accessed July 20, 2022.

Harmon, Christopher C. *Terrorism Today*. London: Frank Cass, 2000.

Herman, Edward, and Gerry O'Sullivan. *The Terrorism Industry: The Experts and Institutions That Shape Our View of Terror*. New York: Pantheon Books, 1989.

Herrera, Natalia, and Douglas Porch. "'Like Going to a Fiesta': The Role of Women in Columbia's FARC-EP." *Small Wars and Insurgencies* 19:4 (2008): 613–14.

Hershberg, Eric, and Kevin W. Moore, eds. *Critical Views of September 11: Analyses from around the World*. New York: New Press, 2002.

Hewitt, Christopher. "The Political Context of Terrorism in America: Ignoring Extremists or Pandering to Them?" *Terrorism and Political Violence* 12:3–4 (2000): 323–44.

Heymann, Philip B. *Terrorism, Freedom, and Security: Winning without War*. Cambridge, MA: MIT Press, 2003.

Hickey, Neil. "Money Lust: How Pressure for Profit Is Perverting Journalism." *Columbia Journalism Review* 37:2 (July–August 1998): 28–36.

Highfield, Tim, Stephen Harrington, and Axel Bruns. "Twitter as a Technology for Audiencing and Fandom." *Information, Communication & Society* 16:3 (2013): 315–31.

Hinckley, Ronald H. *People, Polls, and Policy Makers: American Public Opinion and National Security.* New York: Lexington Books, 1992.

Hoffman, Bruce. "'Holy Terror': The Implications of Terrorism Motivated by a Religious Imperative." *Studies in Conflict and Terrorism* 18:4 (1995): 271–84.

Hoffman, Bruce. "Why Terrorists Don't Claim Credit." *Terrorism and Political Violence* 9:1 (1997): 1–6.

Hoffman, Bruce. *Inside Terrorism.* New York: Columbia University Press, 1998.

Hollihan, Thomas A. *Uncivil Wars: Political Campaigns in the Mega Age.* Boston, MA: Bedford/St. Martin's, 2001.

Holmes, Robert L. *Nonviolence in Theory and Practice.* Belmont, CA: Wadsworth, 1990.

Honderich, Ted. "After the Terror: A Book and Further Thoughts." *Journal of Ethics* 7 (2003): 161–81.

Honig, Sidney B. "The Sicarii in Masada: Glory or Infamy?" *Tradition: A Journal of Orthodox Jewish Thought* 11:1 (Spring 1972): 5–30.

Horgan, John, and Max Taylor. "The Provisional Irish Republican Army: Command and Functional Structure." *Terrorism and Political Violence* 9:3 (Autumn 1997): 1–32.

Horton, Donald, and R. Richard Wohl. "Mass Communication and Para-Social Interaction: Observations on Intimacy at a Distance." *Psychiatry* 19:3 (1956): 215–29.

Houen, Alex. *Terrorism and Modern Literature: From Joseph Conrad to Ciaran Carson.* New York: Oxford, 2002.

Huntington, Samuel P. *The Clash of Civilizations and the Remaking of World Order* New York: Simon & Schuster, 1996.

Israeli, Raphael. "A Manual of Islamic Fundamentalist Terrorism." *Terrorism and Political Violence* 14:4 (2002): 23–40.

Iyengar, Shanto. *Is Anyone Responsible? How Television Frames Political Issues.* Chicago, IL: University of Chicago Press, 1991.

Iyengar, Shanto, and Donald R. Kinder. *News That Matters.* Chicago, IL: University of Chicago Press, 1987.

Jackson, Mary R. "Violence in Social Life." *Annual Review of Sociology* 28 (2002): 387–415.

Jacobs, Lawrence R., and Robert Y. Shapiro. *Politicians Don't Pander: Political Manipulation and the Loss of Democratic Responsiveness.* Chicago, IL: University of Chicago Press, 2000.

Jenkins, Brian M. *International Terrorism: A New Kind of Warfare.* Santa Monica, CA: Rand Corporation, 1974.

Jenkins, Brian M. "Der internationale Terrorismus." *Aus Politik und Zeitgeschichte B5* (1987): 17–27.

Jenkins, Brian M. "Countering Domestic Terrorism May Require Rethinking of Intelligence Strategy." *The Rand Blog,* October 5, 2021, https://www.rand.org/blog/2021/10/countering-domestic-terrorism-may-require-rethinking.html, accessed July 20, 2022.

Jenkins, Philip. *Images of Terror: What We Can and Can't Know about Terrorism*. New York: Aldine de Gruyter, 2003.

Jensen, Richard Bach. "The United States, International Policing and the War against Anarchist Terrorism, 1900–1914." *Terrorism and Political Violence* 13:1 (2001): 15–46.

Jervis, Robert. "Understanding the Bush Doctrine," in Demetrios James Caraley, ed., *American Hegemony: Preventive War, Iraq, and Imposing Democracy*. New York: Academy of Political Science, 2004.

Johnson, Bridget. "ISIS Claims Escalating Use of Wildfire Arson as Terror Tactic." *Homeland Security TODAY*, May 28, 2019, https://www.hstoday.us/subject-matter-areas/counterterrorism/isis-claims-escalating-use-of-wildfire-arson-as-terror-tactic/, accessed July 6, 2022.

Jones, Seth. "Who Are Antifa, and Are they a Threat?" *Center for Strategic & International Studies*, June 4, 2020, https://www.csis.org/analysis/who-are-antifa-and-are-they-threat, accessed June 23, 2022.

Jones, Seth G., and Martin C. Libicki. *How Terrorist Groups End: Lessons for Countering al Qa'ida*. Santa Monica, CA: Rand Corporation, 2008.

Juergensmeyer, Mark. *Terror in the Mind of God: The Global Rise of Religious Violence*. Berkeley: University of California Press, 2000.

Juergensmeyer, Mark. "Religion as a Cause of Terrorism," in Louise Richardson, ed., *The Roots of Terrorism*. New York: Routledge, 2006.

Kaplan, Jeffrey. "Right Wing Violence in North America." *Terrorism and Political Violence* 7:1 (1995): 44–95.

Katz, Daniel. *Public Opinion and Propaganda*. New York: Dryden Press, 1954.

Katz, Rita. "How Do We Know ISIS Is Losing? Now It's Asking Women to Fight." *Washington Post*, November 2, 2017.

Kayyem, Juliett. "There Are no Lone Wolves." *Washington Post*, August 4, 2019, https://www.washingtonpost.com/opinions/2019/08/04/there-are-no-lone-wolves/#:~:text=There%20are%20no%20lone%20wolves.%20A%20mass%20shooting,need%20to%20fight%20the%20%E2%80%9CHispanic%20invasion%20of%20Texas.%E2%80%9D, accessed June 24, 2022.

Kegley, Charles, Jr., ed. *International Terrorism: Characteristics, Causes, Controls*. New York: St. Martin's, 1990.

Keohane, Robert O., and Joseph S. Nye, Jr. "Power and Interdependence in the Information Age." *Foreign Affairs* 77:5 (September–October 1998): 81–94.

Kernell, Samuel. *Going Public: New Strategies of Presidential Leadership*, 3rd ed. Washington, DC: Congressional Quarterly Press, 1997.

Korte, Laura. "The Southwest Is Bone Dry. Now, a Key Water Source Is at Risk." *Politico*, July 6, 2022, https://www.politico.com/news/2022/07/06/colorado-river-drought-california-arizona-00044121, accessed July 6, 2022.

Kristian, Bonnie. "QAnon Is a Wolf in Wolf's Clothing." *Christianity Today*, August 26, 2020, https://www.christianitytoday.com/ct/2020/august-web-only/qanon-is-wolf-in-wolfs-clothing.html, accessed July 10, 2022.

Kristian, Bonnie. "Is QAnon the Newest American Religion?" *The Week*, May 21, 2022, https://theweek.com/articles/915522/qanon-newest-american-religion, accessed July 10, 2022.

Kupperman, Robert, and Jeff Kamen. *Final Warning: Averting Disaster in the New Age of Terrorism*. New York: Doubleday, 1989.

Kupperman, Robert, and Darrell Trent. *Terrorism: Threat, Reality, Response.* Stanford, CA: Hoover Institution, 1979.

Kurth Cronin, Audrey. "Behind the Curve: Globalization and International Terrorism." *International Security* 27:3 (Winter 2002/3): 87–89.

Kurth Cronin, Audrey. "How al-Qaida Ends." *International Security* 31:1 (Summer 2006): 7–48.

Kurth Cronin, Audrey. "ISIS Is Not a Terrorist Group." *Foreign Affairs* 94:2 (March/April 2015).

Kurth Cronin, Audrey, and James M. Ludes, eds. *Attacking Terrorism: Elements of a Grand Strategy.* Washington, DC: Georgetown University Press, 2004.

Kurzman, Charles, and David Schanzer. "The Growing Right-Wing Terror Threat." *New York Times*, June 16, 2015.

Kuzma, Lynn M. "Trends: Terrorism in the United States." *Public Opinion Quarterly 64:1* (Spring 2000): 90–105.

LaFrance, Adrienne, "The Prophecies of Q." *The Atlantic.com*, June 2020, https://www.theatlantic.com/magazine/archive/2020/06/qanon-nothing-can-stop-what-is-coming/610567/, accessed July 10, 2022.

Lahoud, Nelly, "Bin Laden's Catastrophic Success." *Foreign Affairs*, September/October 2021, 10–21.

Laqueur, Walter. *The Age of Terrorism.* Boston: Little, Brown, 1987.

Laqueur, Walter. *The New Terrorism: Fanaticism and the Arms of Mass Destruction.* New York: Oxford University Press, 1999.

Laqueur, Walter. *A History of Terrorism.* New Brunswick, NJ: Transaction Publishers, 2002.

Laqueur, Walter. *No End to War: Terrorism in the Twenty-First Century.* New York: Continuum, 2003.

Laqueur, Walter, and Yonah Alexander, eds. *The Terrorism Reader.* New York: Penguin, 1987.

Lawrence, Bruce. *Messages to the World: The Statements of Osama bin Laden.* London: Verso, 2005.

Leidig, Eviane, and Charlie van Mieghem. "The US National Strategy on Combating Domestic Terrorism as a model for the EU." *International Centre for Counter-Terrorism*, September 2021, https://icct.nl/publication/us-national-strategy-countering-domestic-terrorism-model-eu/, accessed August 5, 2022.

Lesser, Ian O. "Countering the New Terrorism: Implications for Strategy," in Ian O. Lesser, John Arquilla, Bruce Hoffman, David F. Ronfeldt, and Michele Zanini, eds., *Countering the New Terrorism.* Santa Monica, CA: Rand, 1999.

Levitt, Matthew. *Hamas: Politics, Charity, and Terrorism in the Service of Jihad.* New Haven, CT: Yale University Press, 2006.

Lia, Brynjar. "Doctrines for Jihadi Terrorist Training." *Terrorism and Political Violence 20:4* (October–December 2008): 518–42.

Lippmann, Walter. *Public Opinion.* New York: Free Press, 1949.

Livingston, Maurius H., ed. *International Terrorism in the Contemporary World.* Westport, CT: Greenwood Press, 1978.

Livingston, Stephen. *The Terrorism Spectacle.* Boulder, CO: Westview Press, 1994.

MacArthur, John R. *Second Front: Censorship and Propaganda in the Gulf War.* Berkeley: University of California Press, 1993.

McCants, William, and Jarret Brachman. "Militant Ideology Atlas." Executive Report compiled and published by the Combating Terrorism Center at West Point.

McConnell, Mike. "Overhauling Intelligence." *Foreign Affairs 86:4* (July–August 2007): 49–58.

Macdonald, Andrew. *The Turner Diaries*, 2nd ed. New York: Barricade Books, 1996.

MacDonald, Eileen. *Shoot the Women First.* New York: Random House, 1992.

McMullan, Ronald K. "Ethnic Conflict in Russia: Implications for the United States." *Studies in Conflict and Terrorism 16:3* (1993): 201–18.

Magnarella, Paul J. "Inside the Battle of Algiers: Memoir of a Woman Freedom Fighter." *Journal of Global South Studies 38:2* (Fall 2021): 428–31.

Marighella, Carlos. "Handbook of Urban Guerrilla Warfare," in Walter Laqueur and Yonah Alexander, eds., *The Terrorism Reader.* New York: Penguin, 1987.

Martin, David C., and John Walcott. *Best Laid Plans: The Inside Story of America's War on Terrorism.* New York: Harper & Row, 1988.

Matsuda, Mari J. "Public Response to Racist Speech: Considering the Victim's Story." *Michigan Law Review 87* (1989): 2320–36.

Matthews, Alex. "Two Girls of Just SEVEN Blow Themselves up in a Suicide Attack at a Market in Nigeria." *Daily Mail*, December 11, 2017.

Michel, Lou, and Dan Herbeck. *American Terrorist: Timothy McVeigh and the Oklahoma City Bombing.* New York: Regan Books, 2001.

Midlarsky, Manus I., Martha Crenshaw, and Fumihiko Yoshida. "Why Violence Spreads: The Contagion of International Terrorism." *International Studies Quarterly 24* (1980): 262–98.

Miller, Abraham H. and Nicholas A. Damask. "The Dual Myths of 'Narco-Terrorism': How Myths Drive Policy." *Terrorism and Political Violence 8:1* (Spring 1996): 114–31.

Miller, Judith, Stephen Engelberg, and William Broad. *Germs: Biological Weapons and America's Secret War.* New York: Simon & Schuster, 2001, 315–6.

Miller-Idriss, Cynthia. "From 9/11 to 1/6: The War on Terror Supercharged the Far Right." *Foreign Affairs*, September/October 2021, 54–64.

Morgan, Robin. *The Demon Lover: The Roots of Terrorism.* New York: Washington Square Press, 2001.

Most, John, and Emma Goldman. "Anarchy Defended by Anarchists." *Metropolitan Magazine 4:3* (October 1896).

Nacos, Brigitte L. "Presidential Leadership during the Persian Gulf War." *Presidential Studies Quarterly 24:3* (Summer 1994): 563–75.

Nacos, Brigitte L. *Terrorism and the Media: From the Iran Hostage Crisis to the World Trade Center Bombing.* New York: Columbia University Press, 1994.

Nacos, Brigitte L. "After the Cold War: Terrorism Looms Larger as a Weapon of Dissent and Warfare." *Current World Leaders 39:4* (August 1996): 11–26.

Nacos, Brigitte L. *Terrorism and the Media: From the Iran Hostage Crisis to the Oklahoma City Bombing*, rev. ed. New York: Columbia University Press, 1996.

Nacos, Brigitte L. "Accomplice or Witness? The Mass Media's Role in Terrorism." *Current History* 99 (April 2000): 174–78.

Nacos, Brigitte L. *Mass-Mediated Terrorism: The Centrality of the Media in Terrorism and Counterterrorism*. Lanham, MD: Rowman & Littlefield, 2002.

Nacos, Brigitte L., Robert Y. Shapiro, and Pierangelo Isernia, eds. *Decision-making in a Glass House: Mass Media, Public Opinion, and American and European Foreign Policy in the 21st Century*. Lanham, MD: Rowman & Littlefield, 2000.

Namoca, Edgar. "Oldsmar Water Treatment Facility Attack." *Posted at University of Hawaii*, March 4, 2021, https://westoahu.hawaii.edu/cyber/ics-cybersecurity/ics-weekly-summaries/oldsmar-water-treatment-facility-attack/, accessed August 30, 2022.

Napoleoni, Loretta. *Modern Jihad: Tracing Dollars behind the Terror Networks*. London: Pluto Press, 2003.

Napolitano, Janet. "Progress toward a More Secure and Resilient Nation." *Homeland Security Affairs* 7 (September 2011).

Nasr, Vali. *The Shia Revival: How Conflict within Islam Will Shape the Future.* New York: Norton, 2006.

Ness, Cindy D. "In the Name of the Cause: Women's Work in Secular and Religious Terrorism." *Studies in Conflict and Terrorism* 28:5 (September–October 2005): 353–73.

Neumann, Peter R. "Negotiating with Terrorists." *Foreign Affairs* 86:1 (January/February 2007): 128–39.

Nimmo, Dan, and James E. Combs. *Nightly Horrors: Crisis Coverage in Television Network News*. Knoxville: University of Tennessee Press, 1985.

Norris, Pippa. *Montague Kern, and Marion Just, Framing Terrorism: The News Media, the Government, and the Public*. New York: Routledge, 2003.

North, Anna. "White Women's Role in White Supremacy Explained." *VOX.com*, January 15, 2021, https://www.vox.com/2021/1/15/22231079/capitol-riot-women-qanon-white-supremacy, accessed July 15, 2022.

Nye, Joseph S., Jr. *The Paradox of American Power*. New York: Oxford University Press, 2002.

Nye, Joseph S., Jr., and William A. Owens. "America's Information Edge." *Foreign Affairs* 75:2 (March–April 1996): 20–36.

O'Sullivan, John. "Media Publicity Causes Terrorism," in Bonnie Szumski, ed., *Terrorism: Opposing Viewpoints*. St. Paul, MN: Greenhaven, 1986.

Page, Benjamin I., and Robert Y. Shapiro. *The Rational Public*. Chicago, IL: University of Chicago Press, 1992.

Paletz, David L., and Alex P. Schmid. *Terrorism and the Media*. Newbury Park, CA: Sage, 1992.

Pape, Robert A. "Why Economic Sanctions Do Not Work." *International Security* 22 (Fall 1997): 90–136.

Pape, Robert A. "The Strategic Logic of Suicide Terrorism." *American Political Science Review* 97:3 (August 2003): 343–61.

Parker, Tom, and Nick Sitter. "The Four Horsemen of Terrorism: It's Not Waves, It's Strains." *Terrorism and Political Violence* 28:2 (2016): 197–216.

Piazza, James A. "Rooted in Poverty? Terrorism, Poor Economic Development, and Social Cleavages." *Terrorism and Political Violence 18:1* (2006): 159–77.

Picard, Robert G. "News Coverage as the Contagion," in A. Odasuo Alali and Kenoye Kelvin Eke, eds., *Media Coverage of Terrorism*. Newbury Park, CA: Sage, 1991.

Pillar, Paul R. *Terrorism and U.S. Foreign Policy*. Washington, DC: Brookings Institution Press, 2001.

Pluchinsky, Dennis A. "Germany's Red Army Faction: An Obituary." *Studies in Conflict and Terrorism 16:2* (1993): 135–57.

Pluchinsky, Dennis A. "The Terrorism Puzzle: Missing Pieces and No Boxcover." *Terrorism and Political Violence 9:1* (1997): 7–10.

Posen, Barry R. "The Struggle against Terrorism: Grand Strategy, Strategy, and Tactics." *International Security 26:3* (Winter 2001–2002): 39–55.

Post, Jerrold M. "Narcissism and the Charismatic Leader-Follower Relationship." *Political Psychology 7:4* (December 1986): 675–88.

Post, Jerrold M., Ehud Sprinzak, and Laurita M. Denny. "The Terrorists in Their Own Words: Interviews with 35 Incarcerated Middle Eastern Terrorists." *Terrorism and Political Violence 15:1* (2003): 171–84.

Ranstorp, Magnus. "Hizbollah's Command Leadership: Its Structure, Decision Making and Relationship with Iranian Clergy and Institutions." *Terrorism and Political Violence 6:3* (Autumn 1994): 303–39.

Ranstorp, Magnus, and Gus Xhudo. "A Threat to Europe? Middle East Ties with the Balkans and Their Impact upon Terrorist Activity throughout the Region." *Terrorism and Political Violence 6:2* (1994): 196–223.

Raphaeli, Nimrod. "Financing of Terrorism: Sources, Methods, and Channels." *Terrorism and Political Violence 15:4* (Winter 2003): 59–82.

Rapoport, David C. "Fear and Trembling: Terrorism in Three Religious Traditions." *American Political Science Report 78:3* (September 1984): 658–77.

Rapoport, David C. "To Claim or Not to Claim; That Is the Question—Always!" *Terrorism and Political Violence 9:1* (1997): 11–17.

Rapoport, David C. "The Fourth Wave: September 11 in the History of Terrorism." *Current History 100:650* (December 2001): 419–24.

Rapoport, David C., ed. *Inside Terrorist Organizations*. London: Frank Cass, 2001.

Rapoport, David C. "The Four Waves of Rebel Terror and September 11." *Anthropoetics 8:1* (2002): 1–14.

Raufer, Xavier. "The Red Brigades: Farewell to Arms." *Studies in Conflict and Terrorism 16:4* (1993): 315–25.

Redlener, Irwin and David A. Berman. "National Preparedness Planning: The Historical Context and Current State of the U.S. Public's Readiness, 1940–2005." *Journal of International Affairs 59:2* (Spring/Summer 2006): 87–103.

Reeve, Simon. *The New Jackals: Ramzi Yousef, Osama bin Laden and the Future of Terrorism*. Boston, MA: Northeastern University Press, 1999.

Reich, Walter, ed. *Origins of Terrorism: Psychologies, Ideologies, Theologies, States of Mind*. New York: Cambridge University Press, 1990.

Reilly, Ryan J. "Oath Keeper Lawyer Says Stewart Rhodes Wanted Her Trump Contacts Before Jan. 6 Attack." *News.yahoo.com*, July 11, 2022, https://news.yahoo.com/oath-keepers-lawyer-says-stewart-153049983.html?fr=sycsrp_catchall, accessed July 19, 2022.

Reuter, Christoph. *Mein Leben ist eine Waffe*. Munich: Bertelsmann, 2002.

Rhodes, Ben. "Them and US: How America Lets Its Enemies Hijack Its Foreign Policy." *Foreign Affairs* 100:5 (September/October 2021): 22–31.

Ridgeway, James. *Blood in the Face: The Ku Klux Klan, Aryan Nation, Nazi Skin Heads, and the Rise of a New White Culture*. New York: Thunder Mouth Press, 1995, 68.

Richardson, Louise. "Terrorists as Transnational Actors." *Terrorism and Political Violence* 11:4 (1999): 209–19.

Richardson, Louise, ed. *The Roots of Terrorism*. New York: Routledge, 2006.

Richardson, Louise. *What Terrorists Want: Understanding the Enemy, Containing the Threat*. New York: Random House, 2006.

Rojecki, Andrew. "Rhetorical Alchemy: American Exceptionalism and the War on Terror." *Political Communication* 25:1 (January–March 2008): 67–88.

Ronfeldt, David. "Netwar across the Spectrum of Conflict: An Introductory Comment." *Studies in Conflict and Terrorism* 22 (1999): 189–92.

Rotella, Sebastian. "Global Right-Wing Extremism Networks are Growing." *ProPublica,* January 22, 2021, https://www.propublica.org/article/global-right-wing-extremism-networks-are-growing-the-u-s-is-just-now-catching-up, accessed June 23, 2022.

Rubenstein, Richard E. *Alchemists of Revolution: Terrorism in the Modern World*. New York: Basic Books, 1987.

Rubin, Barry, and Judith Colp Rubin. *Anti-American Terrorism and the Middle East*. New York: Oxford, 2002.

Rubin, Bernard. *When Information Counts: Grading the Media*. Lexington, MA: Lexington Books, 1985.

Sageman, Marc. *Understanding Terror Networks*. Philadelphia: University of Pennsylvania Press, 2004.

Sageman, Marc. *Leaderless Jihad*. Philadelphia: University of Pennsylvania Press, 2008.

Said, Edward W. *Covering Islam: How the Media and the Experts Determine How We See the Rest of the World*. New York: Pantheon, 1981.

Sedgwick, Mark. "Inspiration and the Origins of Global Waves of Terrorism," *Studies in Conflict & Terrorism* 30 (2007): 97–112.

Schbley, Ayla. "Defining Religious Terrorism: A Causal and Anthological Profile." *Studies in Conflict and Terrorism* 26:2 (2003): 105–34.

Scheuer, Jeffrey. *The Sound Bite Society: Television and the American Mind*. New York: Four Walls Eight Windows, 1999.

Schlagheck, Donna M. *International Terrorism*. Lexington, MA: Lexington Books, 1988.

Schlesinger, Philip, Graham Murdock, and Philip Elliott. *Televising "Terrorism": Political Violence in Popular Culture*. London: Comedia, 1983.

Schmid, Alex P. *Handbook of Terrorism Prevention and Preparedness*. The Hague: ICCT Press Publication, 2021. The book is available online, https://icct.nl/app/uploads/2021/10/V10.4-Handbook-ONLINE.pdf, accessed August 20, 2022.

Schmid, Alex P., and Jenny de Graaf. *Violence as Communication: Insurgent Terrorism and the Western News Media*. Beverly Hills, CA: Sage, 1982.

Schmidt, Brian C., and Michael C. Williams. "The Bush Doctrine and the Iraq War: Neoconservatives vs. Realists." Paper presented at the Annual Conference of the British International Studies Association, Cambridge, UK, December 17–19, 2007.

Schmitt, Eric, and Helene Cooper. "Al-Zawahiri's Death Puts the Focus Back on Al Qaeda." *New York Times*, August 12, 2022, https://www.nytimes.com/2022/08/02/us/politics/al-qaeda-terrorism-isis.html, accessed August 10, 2022.

Sederberg, Peter C. "Conciliation as Counter-Terrorist Strategy," *Journal of Peace Research 32*:3 (1995): 295–312.

Sedgwick, Mark. "Al-Qaeda and the Nature of Religious Terrorism." *Terrorism and Political Violence 16*:4 (Winter 2004): 795–814.

Seib, Philip. *Going Live: Getting the News Right in a Real-Time, Online World.* Lanham, MD: Rowman & Littlefield, 2001.

Shanahan, James, and Michael Morgan. *Television and Its Viewers: Cultivation Theory and Research.* New York: Cambridge University Press, 1999.

Sick, Gary. *All Fall Down: America's Tragic Encounter with Iran.* New York: Penguin, 1986.

Silber, Mitchell D. "Domestic Violent Extremism and the Intelligence Challenge." *Atlantic Council*, May 21, 2021, https://www.atlanticcouncil.org/in-depth-research-reports/domestic-violent-extremism-and-the-intelligence-challenge/, accessed August 15, 2022.

Simi, Pete, et al. "Narratives of Childhood Adversity and Adolescent Misconduct as Precursors to Violent Extremism: A Life-Course Criminological Approach." *Journal of Research in Crime and Delinquency 53*:4 (2016): 536–63.

Simi, Pete, et al. "Addicted to Hate: Identity Residual among Former White Supremacists." *American Sociological Review 82*:6 (2017): 1167–87.

Simon, Jeffrey D. *The Terrorist Trap: America's Experience with Terrorism.* Bloomington: Indiana University Press, 1994.

Simon, Jeffrey D. *Lone Wolf Terrorism: Understanding the Growing Threat.* Amherst, NY: Prometheus Books, 2013.

Smith, Brent L., and Kathryn D. Morgan. "Terrorists Right and Left: Empirical Issues in Profiling American Terrorists." *Studies in Conflict and Terrorism 17*:1 (1994): 39–57.

Snow, Donald M. *National Security for a New Era: Globalization and Geopolitics.* New York: Pearson Longman, 2007.

Soufan, Ali. "Hamza bin Laden: From Steadfast Son to Al-Qa'ida's Leader in Waiting." *CTC Sentinel 10*:8 (September 2017), https://ctc.usma.edu/hamza-bin-ladin-from-steadfast-son-to-al-qaidas-leader-in-waiting/, accessed June 7, 2018.

Soufan Center. "IntelBrief: White Supremacy Extends Reach from Ukraine to US Military." September 30, 2019, https://thesoufancenter.org/intelbrief-white-supremacy-extremists-extend-reach-from-ukraine-to-u-s-military/, accessed June 22, 2022.

Soufan Center. "The Atomwaffen Division: The Evolution of the White Supremacy Threat." August 2020, https://thesoufancenter.org/wp-content/uploads/2020/08/The-Atomwaffen-Division-The-Evolution-of-the-White-Supremacy-Threat-August-2020-.pdf, accessed June 20, 2022.

Soufan Center. "IntelBrief: The Islamic State is Not Finished in Iraq and Syria." November 1, 2021, https://thesoufancenter.org/intelbrief-2021-november-1/, accessed June 28, 2022.

Spadaro, Paola Andrea. "Climate Change and Global Security." *Journal of Strategic Security 13:4* (2020): 58–80.

Sprinzak, Ehud. "Extremism and Violence in Israel: The Crisis of Messianic Politics." *Annals of the American Academy of Political Science 555* (January 1998): 114–26.

Stanski, Keith. "Terrorism, Gender, and Ideology: A Case Study of Women who Join the Revolutionary Armed Forces of Columbia (FARC)," in James J. F. Forest, ed., *The Making of Terrorists, Volume I: Recruitment.* Westport, CT: Praeger Security International, 2006.

Sterling, Claire. *The Terror Network.* New York: Berkeley, 1982.

Stern, Jessica. *The Ultimate Terrorists.* Cambridge, MA: Harvard University Press, 1999.

Stern, Jessica. *Terror in the Name of God: Why Religious Militants Kill.* New York: HarperCollins, 2003.

Stern, Jessica. "The Protean Enemy." *Foreign Affairs* (July–August 2003): 27–40.

Stern, Kenneth S. *A Force upon the Plain: The American Militia Movement and the Politics of Hate.* New York: Simon & Schuster, 1996.

Stern, William J. "What Gangs of New York Misses." *City Journal*, January 14, 2003, https://www.city-journal.org/html/what-gangs-new-york-misses-9983. html, accessed June 2, 2022.

Stohl, Michael. "Characteristics of Contemporary International Terrorism," in Charles W. Kegley, Jr., ed., *International Terrorism: Characteristics, Causes, Controls.* New York: St. Martin's, 1990.

Strom, Kevin, John S. Hollywood, and Mark Pope. "Terrorist Plots against the United States: What We Have Really Faced, and How We Might Best Defend against It." Rand Homeland Security and Defense Center, September 2015.

Summers, Craig, and Erik Markusen. *Collective Violence.* Lanham, MD: Rowman & Littlefield, 1999.

Tarrow, Sidney G. *Power in Movement: Social Movements and Contentious Politics.* New York: Cambridge University Press, 2011.

Tilly, Charles, and Sidney Tarrow. *Contentious Politics.* New York: Oxford University Press, 2007.

Tilly, Charles, and Lesley J. Wood. *Social Movements*, 2nd ed. Boulder, CO: Paradigm, 2009.

Trager, Robert F., and Dessislava P. Zagorcheva. "Deterring Terrorism: It Can Be Done." *International Security 30:3* (Winter 2005): 87–123.

Tulis, Jeffrey K. *The Rhetorical Presidency.* Princeton, NJ: Princeton University Press, 1987.

Walzer, Michael. *Arguing About War.* New Haven, CT: Yale University Press, 2004.

Wang, Shacheng, and Xixi Zhu. "Evaluation of Potential Cryptocurrency Development in Terrorist Financing." *Policing 15:4* (September 2021): 2337.

Ward, Colin. *Anarchism: A Very Short Introduction.* New York: Oxford University Press, 2004

Weimann, Gabriel, and Conrad Winn. *The Theater of Terror: Mass Media and International Terrorism.* New York: Longman, 1994.

Weinberg, Leonard, and William Eubank. "An End to the Fourth Wave of Terrorism?" *Studies in Conflict & Terrorism 33:7* (2010): 594–602.

Whine, Michael. "Cyberspace: A New Medium for Communication, Command, and Control by Extremists." *Studies in Conflict and Terrorism 22* (1999): 231–45.

Whine, Michael. "Islamist Organizations on the Internet." *Terrorism and Political Violence 11:1* (1999): 123–32.

Wieviorka, Michel. *The Making of Terrorism.* Chicago, IL: University of Chicago Press, 1993.

Wilkinson, Paul. "The Media and Terror: A Reassessment." *Terrorism and Political Violence 9* (1997): 132–34.

Wilkinson, Paul. *Terrorism versus Democracy: The Liberal State Response.* London: Frank Cass, 2001.

Wolfsfeld, Gadi. "The News Media and the Second Intifada." *Harvard International Journal of Press/Politics 6:4* (2001): 113–18.

Woodward, Bob. *Plan of Attack.* New York: Simon & Schuster, 2004.

Wright, Lawrence. *The Looming Tower: Al Qaeda and the Road to 9/11.* New York: Knopf, 2006, 31.

Victor, Barbara. *The Army of Roses: Inside the World of Palestinian Women Suicide Bombers* (New York: Rodale, 2003).

Yankelovich, Daniel. *Coming to Public Judgment.* Syracuse, NY: Syracuse University Press, 1991.

Young, Marissa. "Inside ISIS: How the Islamic State Is Using Media to Capture World Attention." Unpublished seminar paper, Columbia University, 2015.

Zanini, Michele. "Middle Eastern Terrorism and Netwar." *Studies in Conflict and Terrorism 22* (1999): 247–56.

Index